D0349800

Jerome Kern

Jerome D. Kern
(Theatre and Music Collection, Museum of the City of New York)

Jerome Kern
His Life and Music

Gerald Bordman

New York   Oxford
OXFORD UNIVERSITY PRESS
1980

Copyright © 1980 by Oxford University Press, Inc.

Library of Congress Cataloging in Publication Data

Bordman, Gerald Martin.
 Jerome Kern: his life and music.

 Includes index.
 1. Kern, Jerome, 1885–1945. 2. Composers—
United States—Biography.
ML410.K385B7   782.8′1′0924 [B]   79-13826
ISBN 0-19-502649-7

Printed in the United States of America

ML
410
K385
B7

Preface

For many lovers of our lyric stage Jerome Kern remains, more than a third of a century after his death, our finest composer. But even among those who might prefer one or two of our other melodic masters, there is hardly a dissenting voice in granting Kern primacy as the most significant composer in the history of the American musical theatre. By virtually universal consent, Kern's 1914 classic "They Didn't Believe Me" established a basic pattern for all modern show songs; the Princess Theatre musicals, on which he collaborated with Guy Bolton and P. G. Wodehouse, brought musical comedy into the twentieth century; and his work with Oscar Hammerstein II on *Show Boat* pointed the way to contemporary "musical plays."

Had Kern lived he would now be in his mid-nineties, so, inevitably, most of his associates and acquaintances are gone too. Happily, those who have survived, with few exceptions, were delighted to share their recollections and souvenirs.

Kern's daughter, Mrs. Betty Kern Miller, not only gave me hours of her time but allowed me to study all the manuscript material she retains. When my manuscript was finished she read it carefully to catch any errors that might have crept in.

Alfred Simon and Dr. Norman Josephs spent days at my farm playing all of Kern's extant music. Much of the penetrating musical analysis in this book is really theirs, not mine.

Ron Lowden, who had once contemplated a Kern biography, selflessly gave me all of his voluminous notes. They proved invaluable.

Brief, but equally grateful, acknowledgment must be made to Louis Aborn, the late Milton Ager, Fred Astaire, Louise Bale, Mrs. Morag E. Barton, Bob Baumgart, Robert Russell Bennett, Pandro Berman, the late Mr. and Mrs. Guy Bolton, Jill Bomser, Hal Borne, Donald Bowman, Esq., Eric Braun, James Burke, Saul Chaplin, Matilda ("Goldie") Clough,

Richard Coe, Charles Collins, Stuart Cooke, Mrs. J. W. Cooper, Jack Cummings, Gladys Dale, the late Alice Delysia, Adolph Deutch, Dorothy Dickson, Dan Dietz, Howard and Lucinda Ballard Dietz, Adele Dixon, Lady Frances Donaldson, Alfred Drake, Mrs. Marion Dudek, Mrs. Vernon Duke, Irene Dunne, Mrs. A. Einzig, Mary Ellis, Mrs. Leonard Epstein, Peggy Fears, Hugh Fordin, Michael Freedland, Arnold F. Gates, Mrs. Ira Gershwin, Julie Goldsmith Gilbert, Ruth Goetz, Herbert G. Goldman, the late Max Gordon, John Green, Stanley Green, Sylvan Greene, Robert Grimes, Binnie Hale, Mrs. Oscar Hammerstein II, William Hammerstein, William Harbach, Alan Hewitt, Hayes Hibbard, Emily Higgins, Stanley Holloway, Edward ("Teddy") Holmes, Mrs. Simon Hornby, P. A. Howgill, Dr. Harold Hyman, David A. Jasen, Dean Kay, Mannie Kean, Gene Kelly, Jacques Kelly, Robert Kimball, Ted Klein, Joanna Kleiner, Esmond Knight, Alfred Knopf, Mr. and Mrs. Edwin Knopf, Eleanor Knowles, Rabbi Bertram W. Korn, Miles Kreuger, Mr. and Mrs. A. C. Lampke, Evelyn Laye, William T. Leonard, Edwin Lester, Joshua Logan, Louis A. Lotito, Frank Mallalieu, Matty Malnick, Rouben Mamoulian, Raymond Mander and Joe Mitchenson, Jessie Matthews, Terry L. Mayer, Duff Merrick, Joanne E. Miller, Vincente Minnelli, Mrs. Nathan Newman, Frederick Nolan, Dennis Norden, Reuel Olin, Hermes Pan, Abraham J. Peck, Harriet Pilpel, David Poland, John Pyle, Louis Rachow, Ralph Reader, Pat Restaino, Leo Robin, Richard Rodgers, Berthe Schuchat, Arthur Schwartz, Vivienne Segal, Frank Sleep, the late Queenie Smith, Rabbi B. Sobel, Dr. Orin Suthern, Norma Terris, Mrs. J. Graham Tewksbury, Heather Thatcher, Richard Wall, Harry Warren, James O. Young, Sr., and Mr. and Mrs. Davis Zimmerman.

Among the libraries and other institutions consulted, special thanks must go to Hobart Berolzheimer, Geri Duclow, Elaine Ebo, and Laura Sims of the theatre collection at the Free Library of Philadelphia; to Paul Myers and his superb staff at the Theatre Collection, Library and Museum of the Performing Arts at Lincoln Center (a division of the New York Public Library), and the excellent staff of the music department at the Library of Congress. The library staffs at Lincoln University and Millersville State Teachers College were particularly accommodating. Thanks, too, to Anthony Slide of the Academy of Motion Picture Arts and Sciences, Dian J. Spitler of the Atlantic City Free Public Library, Ellen M. Oldham of the Boston Public Library, Barbara M. Soper of the Buffalo and Erie County Public Library, David Cernak of the Chicago Public Library, J. Richard Abell of the Public Library of Cincinnati and Hamilton County, Elizabeth M. Stewart of the Hartford (Conn.) Public Library, Dr. Weisert of the Universitatarchiv Heidelberg, Joan Gilmore of the Los Angeles Civic Light Opera Company, Edith M. Prise of the Museum and Library of Maryland History, Charles F. Cummings of the Newark (N.J.) Public Library, Virginia Bulow of the Onondaga County (N.Y.) Public Library, Barbara Mahon at the St. Louis Municipal Opera, Timothy McGowan and Dorothy C. Neff at the Schenectady County (N.Y.) Public Library, W. H. Crain of the University of Texas, Larry L. Manuel of the Wilmington (Del.) Public Library, Julie D'Acci, Alice Siemering, and Christine Rongone at the Wisconsin Center for Film and Theater Research (U. of Wisc.), Nancy E. Gaudette at the Worcester (Mass.) Public Library, and Mary Ellen Moore at the Yale University Library.

I owe profuse thanks to Joellyn Ausanka, my editor's secretary, who retyped my seemingly illegible final draft; to Oxford's fine manuscript editors, Leona Capeless and Caroline Taylor; and to my editor, Sheldon Meyer.

Gerald Bordman

Yellow Wood Farm
Kirk's Mills, Pa.
October 1979

NOTE

A few apparent inconsistencies need to be explained, especially the wording and spelling of certain song titles. The rule we have applied is that, wherever possible, programs and quotations have been reproduced as we found them. Thus, "Ka-lu-a" is spelled "Kailua" in *Good Morning, Dearie*'s program, while the original *Show Boat*'s playbill included "Old Man River" in the first act and "Ol' Man River" in the second. Sometimes a song was given one title in the program and a totally different one in its sheet music. When we could, we have identified these in discussion of the music. With one or two exceptions, notably "Long Ago And Far Away," the exact published title is used in the text itself. But inconsistencies were not confined to song titles. For example, *Roberta*'s program seemingly used the terms "Scene" and "Scena" indiscriminately, and this, too, has been followed.

Jerome Kern

In analyzing Kern's songs we have tried to steer a middle course, trusting that the reader has some basic knowledge of musical theory but not imposing the burden of more learned terminology such as, say, enharmonic modulation—though, alas, enharmonic modulation was a favorite device of Kern's. Instead, in such cases, we have written of an apparent key change. Such an expression may not be totally accurate, but it should convey some idea of the practice employed.

G. B.

Contents

Prologue 3

1   From Bohemia 6
2   Juvenilia 18
3   The West End and the Great White Way 30
4   Family Matters and a Continuing Apprenticeship 52
5   Whole Scores and a Scorching 74
6   Turning Points 92
7   The Princess Theatre 106
8   An Intermission and the Beginning of the
    Annus Mirabilis 125
9   A Perfect Little Show and the Conclusion of the
    Annus Mirabilis 143
10 A New Home, New Hits, and an Interesting Failure 162
11 Delights and Disappointments 186
12 The Great Glorifier 202
13 Transatlantic Shuttle 215
14 Two Fascinating Failures 244
15 A Circus Queen, a City Chap, and Christopher Cross 261
16 *Show Boat* 275
17 London and Literature; Boats and Broadway 293
18 The "Talkies," and New Producers 311
19 A Near Miss and a Sad Failure 334
20 Hollywood, for Good! 350
21 Broadway, Briefly—and New Horizons 377
    Index 409

Jerome Kern

Prologue

The list of mourners was long and awesome, like the catalogues of ships and gods and heroes ancient Greek bards loved to intone. Only now it was the giants of the American musical theatre assembling—assembling in the chapel of the Ferncliff Crematory at Hartsdale to pay homage to its greatest composer, Jerome Kern. Virtually every major figure from the musical stage was present, a veritable cast of surviving characters from the composer's life. The New York *Times* list of those paying their final respects occupied two full paragraphs and included Max Gordon, Irving Berlin, Otto Harbach, Richard Rodgers, Edna Ferber, Dorothy and Herbert Fields, Deems Taylor, Mary Martin, Cole Porter, Sigmund Romberg, Dr. Harold Hyman, Louis Dreyfus, Dr. Oliver Austin, Lily Pons, and André Kostelanetz. The list was far from complete.

A man who was both a lawyer and friend to Kern, Mark Holstein, read the Twenty-third and Ninetieth Psalms, then Oscar Hammerstein II, with whom Kern had collaborated so often and so happily, stepped forward to deliver a prepared eulogy. He never quite finished it. Unable to keep the promise of his opening sentence, he gave way to emotions that overwhelmed him. On the paper he held before him was this brief, touching tribute.

> I have promised myself not to play upon your emotions—or on mine.
>
> We, in this chapel, are Jerry's "family." We all knew him very well. Each of us knows what the other has lost.
>
> I think he would have liked me to say a few simple words about him. I think he would not have liked me to offer you feeble bromides of consolation—butterfly wings of trite condolence against the solid wall of our grief. He would have known our grief was real, and must be faced.
>
> On the other hand, I think Jerry would have liked me to remind you that today's mourning and last week's vigil will soon

recede from our memories, in favor of the bright recollections of him that belong to us.

At the moment, Jerry is playing "out of character." The masque of tragedy was never intended for him. His death yesterday and this reluctant epilogue will soon be refocused into their properly remote place in the picture. This episode will soon seem to us to be nothing more than a fantastic and dream-like intrusion on the gay reality that was Jerry's life.

His gaiety was what we will remember most—the times he made us laugh. It's a strange adjective to apply to a man, but you'll understand what I mean: Jerry was "cute." He was alert and alive. He "bounced." He stimulated everyone. He annoyed some. He never bored anyone at any time. There was a sharp edge to everything he thought or said.

We all know in our hearts that these few minutes we devote to him now are small drops in the ocean of our affections. Our real tribute will be paid over many years of remembering, of telling good stories about him, and thinking about him when we are by ourselves.

We, in this chapel, will cherish our special knowledge of this world figure. We will remember a jaunty, happy man whose sixty years were crowded with success and fun and love. Let us thank whatever God we believe in that we shared some part of the good, bright life Jerry led on this earth. . . .

Robert Russell Bennett, Kern's orchestrator for the last half of the composer's career, was one of many mourners the *Times* overlooked. Although Bennett and Kern had developed a warm professional friendship, their closeness rarely extended to socializing after work. Bennett was known to have expressed his superiority to the tinkly Broadway music his orchestrations enriched, and Kern had been perceptive enough to understand that Bennett's disdain, however qualified in his own case, precluded the easy give and take of an enduring, private friendship. Yet out of respect and duty Bennett came to Hartsdale to join his theatrical associates, many of whom, he concluded, were far more personally attached and would be far more moved than he could be. Only when it was too late did he realize his true feelings for the composer. Leaving the service, he turned to his wife in self-amazement and said, "Look at me. I'm crying."

Jerry's "family" was not alone in its grief. Harry Truman, who just seven months earlier had been elevated to the presidency, spoke for the nation when he wired:

> I am among the grateful millions who have played and listened to the music of Jerome Kern, and I wish to be among those of his fellow Americans who pay him tribute today. His melodies will live in our voices and warm our hearts for many years to come, for they are the kind of simple, honest songs that belong to no time or fashion. The man who gave them to us earned a lasting place in his nation's memory.

Around the country newspapers devoted long editorials to him. Washington's *Evening Star* hailed him as "one of the greatest melodists who ever lived." But the New York *Times* said what had to be said most succinctly, with its editorial banner: "HIS MUSIC WILL NOT DIE."

Hammerstein's eulogy only hinted at the complex, often contradictory man who could elicit so strong and surprising a reaction as Bennett's tears. Two words that recurred in interview after interview, "impish" and "pixyish," were counterbalanced by more hesitant confessions that Kern was also "dogmatic," "authoritarian," "stubborn," or "difficult." On one matter there was almost no dissent or conflict. From the first towering master of our musical stage, Victor Herbert, who early on predicted Jerome Kern would inherit his mantle, to Kern's heir, the greatest of our contemporary composers, Richard Rodgers, there has been virtually universal agreement that Jerome Kern was not only our greatest melodist but that he was the most significant figure in the history of our musical stage.

Yet Kern and his genius did not arise suddenly out of nowhere. The distant, obscure figures that first moulded his character were, as far as we can know them, themselves endearing and fascinating.

1

From Bohemia

On Wednesday, September 20, 1820, in the village of Lieben, near Prague, Emanuel and Henrietta Kakeles welcomed to their family a son they named Seligman. Most likely the baby was only one of many children in the household, for families were customarily large in a time when infant mortality was high and when many hands were required to scrape out a living. Just what sort of livelihood Emanuel eked out is unrecorded. We know of him and his wife only because they are named on Seligman's death certificate. We can only surmise that their lives were as circumscribed as the lives of other poor Jews in mid-nineteenth-century Bohemia.

In the early 1840s Seligman married Bertha Amselberg (or Anselberg), daughter of Isaac and Rosa Amselberg. As the young Kakeles family began to grow, Seligman became painfully aware that his prospects were no better than those of his parents. He chose a course many of his compatriots chose: emigration. And he elected to employ the hard but practical method many young married men used, leaving behind his wife and two daughters until he could find himself a trade and a secure home. Seligman sailed for New York in 1846, but when he brought his family over two years later and settled them in a small apartment at 108 Delancey Street, there is good reason to believe he had still not found a comfortable home or good job. Loneliness rather than success seems to have made him summon his family.

Yet even the solace they afforded could not overcome the uncertainties of poverty. By 1850 Seligman was corresponding with the celebrated abolitionist and philanthropist, Gerrit Smith, pouring out his heart in letters at once pathetically naïve and noble, all couched in uncertain English. Calling himself a "runaway white slave," Seligman recounted the agony of being abruptly dismissed from his job by his insensitive employer, a Mr. Canse:

> I was panic struck and remonstrated to him if he had no employment at all for me as the winter is there, no means to live an[d] I would be ruined with my little family[.] [H]e listened indifferently and proposed me to go to Brooklyn to his factory and see if I could do there all kinds of work—I had to consent and so improved my condition; have to work very hard and 37½ cents expenses ferry money every week from my <u>means of grace</u> $5 per week.

Seligman's income was so small and precarious that he could not send his young daughters to school because he had no warm winter clothing for them. Worse, his employer's behavior became intolerable, forcing him to quit. Other than his family's love he had little but his deep religious convictions to sustain him. Somehow he perceived his devotion to Judaism and his admiration of his co-religionists as a justification for his plea for aid from Smith:

> I am most sure and convinced that you love the Jews and you have good reasons for it too, to love an industrious, temperant and religious nation[.] You will seldom find murder, intemperance and infidelity among the Jews, and intemperance is the most cause which compels me to abandon my employer to which he indulges very freely. I would have done so long ago but I cannot give away the dirty water before I have the clean one.

In return for Smith's encouraging words, if not for any real financial aid, the Kakeleses named their first boy after both Seligman's father and Smith, Emanuel Gerrit Kakeles. Smith sent a gift in the baby's honor.

In his last known letter to Smith, after the landlord had raised his rent to a burdensome $8.30 a month, Kakeles wrote that he would like to purchase four lots on 89th Street. He had a friend who would buy two of them from him. On the remaining pair he hoped to "erect a little cottage . . . and establish there my future home and so avoid the crowd and enjoy the pure fresh airs in the suburbs of the city." He asked Smith for a loan of $450,

an apartment in an old brick row house at 146 East 49th Street, two short blocks from Henry's stables at 130 East 51st Street. Although the Kerns remained on 49th Street for the next ten years, Henry's place of business changed often. Henry's business moves were more than matched by the frequency with which Fannie presented him with new Kerns to feed. The first, Joseph, was born on April 8, 1875. He was to be one of seven babies—all boys—that Fannie would have, four of whom would die in infancy or early childhood. Edwin followed two years after Joseph, and then came three sons—Milton, Charles, Irving—none of whom lived beyond his sixth year. With Irving's arrival on January 25, 1883, the need for larger quarters grew pressing. In the spring of 1884, Henry and Fannie took a more spacious apartment in an old brick house at 411 East 56th Street. By the time they moved in three-year-old Charles was dead. Milton had died much earlier, leaving the Kerns a family of five.

Half a century later 411 East 56th Street would be an especially chic address, situated a stone's throw from Sutton Place and Beekman Place. But in 1884 the area was stolidly middle class and still home to a number of large breweries and industrial plants. If the great chateaux and palaces of Fifth Avenue and Madison Avenue were only a five-minute walk away, that walk was a trip to another world. Almost all row houses on the block had been converted into apartments, and most on the north side of the street—405 to 421—were owned by one Terence Farley. The houses were relatively unimposing, even though appraised in 1884 at an impressive $5500. Whether out of necessity or preference, the Kern apartment seems to have been unusually large. An 1890 police census shows only three other tenants sharing the building, compared with three or four families who divided most of the block's other houses. Growing up next door at 409 was a future Broadway composer, Louis A. Hirsch.

The Kerns' sixth boy was born two years and two days after their fifth and, for what it is worth, exactly 129 years after Wolfgang Amadeus Mozart. Legend records that Fannie was riding home from Jerome Park when she first felt the pangs that told her the baby's birth was imminent. As the story goes, she accordingly named the new boy after the park. The story is highly doubtful. Jewish custom, admittedly not always practiced, dictated that children were named after respected, deceased relatives or friends. In any case, the baby delivered to the Kerns on January 27, 1885, was named Jerome David Kern. The original birth certificate is lost, and lost with it is the time of day the baby arrived. Indeed, the extant certificate is unusual to say the least, for it is signed Jerome D. Kern. Why Kern chose to fill out a new one in August of 1942 is unknown. But it does afford an example of that combination of integrity and wit Kern often displayed. Normally, certificates were signed by either a doctor or midwife, who would then cross out the inapplicable term after swearing to the statement, "I hereby certify that I attended professionally at the birth of this child, who was born alive at the hour and on the date stated above, and that all the facts in this certificate and report of birth are true to the best of my knowledge, information and belief." Before signing, Kern drew a heavy line through the word "professionally." Kern listed his mother's age at time of birth as thirty-three (she was actually thirty-two) and failed to list any age for his father. He listed his father's trade as "Merchant," although Henry did not give up stabling until young Jerry was six years old.

A year after Jerry's birth Henry Kern moved his stables again. In June of 1889 Irving died; the Kerns were once again a family of five. About the same time Henry may have briefly become a street-sprinkling contractor.*

The brief switch in occupations may have hinted at some problem behind the scenes, for Henry retained his stables for only two more years and then set up as a merchant at 86 Broad Street. What sort of merchandise Henry offered remains another of the many facts lost in his history. The 1895–96 Directory lists the merchandise as "waste," but whether this is a clue or an error is uncertain. Again, to the extent that street sprinkling was connected to street cleaning and street cleaning in turn removed the most undesirable wastes, there may indeed have been some relationship.

Henry's change of trade must have coincided with young Jerry starting school. Unfortunately, all of Kern's schooling is something of a closed book. For the most part we cannot say with certainty even what schools he at-

---

* Several biographies and sketches of Kern's life state that his father had street-sprinkling concessions, and some go so far as to suggest his father was the head of the street sprinklers' association. But only once, in the City Directory for 1889–90, did Henry ever list his trade as sprinkler. Of course, sprinklers in the nineteenth century required stables for their horses and equipment, so the change is not far-fetched. However, no extant New York City records show Henry's name anywhere in the city's dealings with sprinkling contractors, nor do the few surviving contracts carry Henry's signature. Jerry did tell his daughter, now Mrs. Betty Kern Miller, that his father long held some private sprinkling contracts. He recalled his father saying that they would only clean those properties that paid a fee. Sprinklers were turned off as non-paying addresses were passed. In any event, by the very next year the City Directory once more listed Henry's occupation as stabler.

tended, and in those few instances where names are known, records that might have fleshed out our skeletal knowledge are lacking. All through his later life, although he gave scores of interviews, Kern never seems to have been asked nor to have wanted to reveal much about his earliest school days. No interview remains in which Kern harks back beyond his high school career. Nor is help forthcoming from New York City authorities, who cannot determine what school a youngster living at 411 East 56th Street would have been required to attend. One puzzling recollection, recorded long after Kern's death, suggests that in our ignorance we may not have been pointing our search in the right direction. In an NBC memorial, broadcast on November 29, 1955, shortly after the tenth anniversary of Kern's death, Joseph Miron, son of J. C. Miron, a turn-of-the-century actor, claimed to have been young Jerry's schoolmate. He remembered Jerry as a "wistful, sensitive kid, whose only interest seemed to be music." He was, Miron recalled sadly, "a very, very nervous type and very retiring, and in the schoolyard he was always in a lot of trouble because of a lot of antagonistic boys who made fun of a little fellow like that. The kids at school used to gang up on him." Miron professed to have bribed off the bullies with candy.

Regrettably, this rare, vivid glimpse of Jerry's school days is suspect. Miron set the scene in 1897 at Elmhurst, Long Island, although by that year twelve-year-old Jerry was to leave New York City to move even farther away from Long Island. Parenthetically, the recollections of many other figures in that 1955 program are filled with such obvious howlers that Miron's story must be doubted.

That even at an early age young Jerry's "only interest seemed to be music" is highly probable. If Kern the man spoke meagerly of his school days, it was with even greater reticence that he spoke of his childhood home life. About the only vignette he offered was his recollection of eight-handed concerts he, his mother, and two surviving brothers gave for their father. Since his brothers were so much older than he, and Edwin, at least, seems to have left the household by the time Jerry was ten or eleven, the composer-to-be must have come to the piano at an extremely early age to be capable of collaborating with such advanced pianists.

Kern never mentioned the precise moment when he determined to become a composer. Probably he himself soon forgot it. In so musical a household a decision of this sort may have come naturally and without fanfare. Conceivably, Jerry's earliest ambitions may have been to write so-called classical music. His earliest musical training and his earliest musical experiences undoubtedly were with the standards of this branch of music—the songs fledgling pianists play even today. But more than likely his mother's tenth birthday present to him determined his direction and permanently changed his life, for her gift was a visit to his first Broadway musical. Sadly, Kern never specified what the musical was, although an educated guess can be hazarded.

Since Jerry's tenth birthday fell a day away from the popular Saturday matinee, we can reasonably assume that the occasion took place on January 26, 1895. No real matter if it were a week or two on either side. In that era, before technological entertainments flooded the scene, Manhattan, like almost every large American city, was dotted with neighborhood theatres, called "combination houses," which offered their stages to touring companies of recent Broadway successes or of shows designed especially for the road. Yet, given the importance of the occasion to Master Jerome and his parents, the Kerns may well have chosen to attend one of the Rialto's major playhouses, just a short, convenient ride away. Before examining the musical that probably served as Jerry's introduction to his future world, it may be wise to take a broader look at the musical theatre of the time.

If musical plays had sung and danced their way across American stages since colonial days, a rage for lyric theatre had not truly exploded until the runaway success of *The Black Crook* in 1866, a mere twenty-nine years before. But even the haphazardly assembled spectacles that followed *The Black Crook* failed to ignite the interest that blazed up thirteen years later when Gilbert and Sullivan's *H.M.S. Pinafore* arrived on our shores. Its success was phenomenal by any criteria, but, more importantly, it demonstrated to American writers and managers (as producers were then called) the artistic and commercial possibilities of artfully conceived, coherent musical plays. For the short run, it also implanted in the minds of these producers and of theatregoers the notion that only the English were gifted with sufficient genius to assemble worthwhile lyric works. Not merely authors, but designers, directors, and, often, stars were more readily welcomed if they spoke with a British accent. When the miraculous well which had supplied inspiration for Gilbert and Sullivan's brilliant, preposterous satires ran dry, John Hollinshead was on hand to give first London, then New York, his Gaiety Theatre burlesques. In a sense, these shows reflected more accurately the true nature of the era's theatre, a theatre still casting its limelight on traditions evolved in a more roistering epoch, when playhouses were held at arm's length, markedly outside the mainstream of everyday life, and when the theatre, in its turn, bowed to this segregation by flaunting its artificiality and absurdity, as well as by its restrained defiance of convention. Perhaps nowhere was all of this better evidenced than in the "trouser role." At a time when well-bred young ladies were covered from neck to toe, shapely actresses exposed their attractive legs by assuming men's parts and dressing in tights. Again and again, especially in musicals, the "hero" was portrayed by a reigning female star. Similarly, comic harridans were played by men. In a time of cheap labor producers were able to fill their stages more with people than with scenery, and casts of sixty, a hundred, and even a hundred and fifty or two hundred were commonplace.

Just three years before Jerry Kern attended his first musical, George Edwardes, who had succeeded Hollinshead at London's Gaiety, mounted the earliest of what became known as the modern Gaiety musical comedies, *In Town.* The show and its successors revolutionized the popular lyric stage. Plots became less outlandish, characters in these plays less unworldly or less regal. Chorus girls, shop girls, dashing young officers, and men-about-town began to supplant the kings, queens, pirates, and fairies of the older shows. Of course, these shop girls often made marriages that in true Cinderella fashion assured them places in the pages of Debrett's *Peerage.* Careful attention was given to scenery and to fashionable costumes. Gaiety musical comedies regularly initiated fads among fashion-conscious ladies. The first of these shows to arrive in New York, *A Gaiety Girl,* appeared in the very season that the Kerns introduced their son to musical theatre.

All this while, Americans were developing their own art, even though for the most part they labored in Gilbert and Sullivan's well-trodden path, without either Gilbert's scintillatingly literate wit or Sullivan's enchanting melodies. The best were Harry B. Smith and Reginald DeKoven, who had first braved Broadway together in 1887 with *The Begum* and who had triumphed in 1891 with *Robin Hood,* a comic opera that promised to be America's first enduring achievement. On November 20, 1894, a name that was to outshine both Smith and DeKoven appeared on the scene, that of Victor Herbert. But Herbert's premiere effort, *Prince Ananias,* was a failure, closing three weeks before Jerry's birthday. At the end of the previous season Broadway was beguiled by the first modern revue, *The Passing Show.* Clearly, it was a musical theatre in flux.

If our surmise about the date of Kern's visit is correct, then seven choices confronted his parents. But five of these—*A Milk White Flag, Rob Roy,*

Notoriety, Off the Earth, and *The 20th Century Girl*—can be more or less readily rejected. Quite possibly Fannie and Henry selected a show created for children, *The Brownies.* This musical took audiences to a never-land where the Brownies thwart the villainous Dragonfels's attempts to prevent the marriage of Prince Florimel to Princess Titania. But the show was at the end of its run at the Fourteenth Street Theatre, a house at the southern extreme of the theatre district. The logical selection would seem to have been the season's biggest musical hit, *Little Christopher Columbus,* or, as its title was abbreviated to by January, *Little Christopher.* In any case, it is typical enough of the era's musicals to serve as a model for the earliest shows young Jerry must have seen.

The show was a London hit that had been imported the preceding fall. George R. Sims and Cecil Raleigh had written the libretto, while Belgian-born Ivan Caryll had composed the music. In typical period fashion the material was heavily revised for American audiences, and the musical's conductor, German-born Gustave Kerker, was enlisted to create additional songs. The producer and director was Edward E. Rice, a now forgotten but once supremely important figure in the American musical theatre. Since Rice plays a momentous role in Kern's career, he will be discussed later. Programs of the period customarily gave a synopsis of the plot, and the playbill of the Garden Theatre where *Little Christopher* was berthed was no exception, obligingly offering a detailed preview of developments. It disclosed that the hero is a cabin boy on an American liner and is in love with Guinevere, daughter of the Second Mrs. Tanqueray Block, the widow of a wealthy pork-packer. Mrs. Block, in the fashion of the nouveau riche of her day, is determined to marry her daughter to a title. To this end she hires a bogus detective to investigate her daughter's suitors. Comic complications land all the principals in jail, where Christopher is forced to dress as a famous lady dancer. Further adventures take them from Spain to the court of the Bey of Barataria and then to the Midway Plaisance of the Chicago World's Fair. In the end Christopher is discovered to be the last lineal descendant of his namesake. The "Argument" concluded: "From the slender, but definite parent stalk of plot, there shoot out in every direction little tendrils of affection which curl about the hearts of the personages involved. And the latter, like the prince and princess of fairy tales, live happily ever after."

Playgoers in 1895, even if they dismissed the story as implausible and puerile, could appreciate nuances lost on most modern readers. Many of the principal characters were named for characters in current or recently popular plays—the Second Mrs. Tanqueray Block being only the most obvious. And expected character types appeared as certainly as the expected odd names. Disguise-loving detectives, rich widows, and tramps were stock characters in musical after musical. One amusing touch was the omission of the pork- or sausage-packer (a character dear to the heart of every German dialect comedian then flourishing on the musical stage), but, as the playbill revealed, even he was given a quiet nod.

A further glance at the program assured playgoers other commonplaces of the time would be observed. Little Christopher was a trouser role, and Mrs. Block was played by a man.

The plot was, however, never sacrosanct. Again in the fashion of the day, specialty acts were brought in on the slightest excuse (and sometimes inexcusably) and were often changed, as the program twice promised, "from week to week." Specialties included eccentric dancers and trained animals.

Once the curtain rose, playgoers were subjected to the most banal dialogue and to music that was little better. Only a highly discerning listener could probably separate Caryll's contributions from Kerker's without referring to the program. The songs, while pleasant, were elementary—critics waved them aside as "tinkly." And the music received the lyrics it deserved. A typical lyric began: "Rumpty tumpty, rumpty tumpty, That's the song I sing." Repetition and child-like expressions, often coupled with fustian involutions, comprised the words of almost every song.

There was obviously no high art in *Little Christopher*, although for its day it may have offered some highly professional mounting. If, as we assume, this was Jerome Kern's first show, we wonder if he recalled the scene on the Midway Plaisance of the Chicago Fair thirty-two years later, when he himself had to write music for a similar setting, the opening of the second act of *Show Boat*.

Apart from brief, passing mentions of his tenth-birthday present, Kern never seems to have spoken publicly or privately about his earliest playgoing. Looking back years after Kern's death, some of his schoolmates recalled Jerry's delight at seeing Victor Herbert's first hit, *The Wizard of the Nile*. They remember how quickly and adroitly he played songs from the show. But *The Wizard of the Nile* did not open until November 1895, and so was probably not the first show he saw. Still, the fact that his boyhood friends recall his playing this music and not *Little Christopher*'s or that from some lesser score suggests how even at this early date Kern's good taste allowed him to separate dross from gold. No doubt young Jerry's playgoing continued, although a major event may have made Manhattan's theatres slightly less accessible to him. In early 1897 Henry and Fannie bought a house in Newark, New Jersey, the only home they ever owned. The building, appraised for tax purposes at $5800, was a three-story brick structure with a wooden dependency in the rear and was located at 39 Nelson Place, an area of homes occupied largely by German and German-Jewish families. These two groups accounted for many of the leading shopkeepers of the time, and the area was just a few minutes walk from Newark's principal shopping district. Henry's interest was a new enterprise for him, D. Wolff and Co. at 125 Market Street. Henry's initial relationship to the firm is unknown—that is, whether he came into it merely as an employee or as a part owner. His rise was swift, though. At the time of his earliest association, directories listed Wolff as a clothier, but the listing soon changed as the store embarked on an expansion. There is good cause to suspect that Henry was the driving force behind the change. In leaving New York, the Kerns left behind one final, sad memory—the loss of their youngest son, Bertram, who had joined Milton, Charles, and Irving in their tiny graves at Salem Fields.

2

Juvenilia

Newark in the Gay Nineties was not the dispiriting city it has become today. In the few years before the Kerns had moved across the river the city had flexed its muscles and displayed itself in all its youthful vigor. It had grown large almost overnight—doubling and tripling its population. It quickly became self-sufficient and self-confident. True, New York was conveniently, or threateningly, close at hand, but in the 1890s it was no rapid train ride away. Slow-moving ferries at Hoboken and elsewhere still provided the principal links. As a result Newark developed its own restaurants, art colonies, social clubs, and theatres. For a while it even became a tryout town, and several of Kern's later shows were to try their wings there.

Young Jerry was enrolled at the Thirteenth Avenue School, and on graduation entered Newark High School in the fall of 1899. Jerry's academic gifts were unexceptional, but his exuberant charm and his notable pianistic abilities quickly earned him special attention. Before long he was frequently called upon to play the piano and even the school organ at assemblies. His fledgling attempts at song-writing also delighted his fellow students. In early 1901 the senior class asked Jerry, then still a junior, to assist them in creating a class show. Since he was the only student outside the graduating class so honored his talents must have been singular even at that early date. Unfortunately no programs of the March 8, 1901, performance survive—if any, indeed, were issued—and a description of the entertainment in the school magazine, *The Acropolis,* may not disclose all of Jerry's contributions. The entertainment was a minstrel show, called *The Melodious Menu,* and featured all the expected minstrel turns. Among songs the youngsters sang were "I Ain't Agoin' To Weep No More," "Miss Phoebe," and "Ma Butterfly." Whether these were old blackface favorites or original pieces is unrecorded. But another song received prominent mention, even if the magazine was not certain of its exact title. The article noted, " 'Ma Angelina' [called "My Angeline" elsewhere in the same article] was composed by Mr. J. D. Kern particularly for the occasion and was rendered, for the first time, by Mr. [Robert L.] Davis. Mr. Kern's superior ability as a pianist is too well known among the scholars of the high school to require further comment. . . ." Those in the audience unaware of Jerry's excellent playing were soon enlightened, for the bill included "selections by J. D. Kern, as 'Mr. Weary Willie,' upon the piano." According to the Newark *Evening News,* young Jerry made his entrance on a velocipede, before slipping into his ragtime medley. So captivating was the turn that "Mr. Kern responded with several hearty encores." Jerry and Davis doubled in brass, serving as stage managers for the event. The affair was successful enough to call for the scheduling of two additional performances later in the year.

Whatever Jerry's feelings at hearing his fellow students applaud his songs, he must have been even more eager to hear the public at large react. Late in 1901 he was approached by the Newark Yacht Club to write a score for a musical satire it wanted to mount. Despite its name, so suggestive of a leisure class, the club was not especially exclusive; it was not even devoted largely to sailing and racing. Primarily a gathering of fun-lovers, it cut democratically across class lines. Its members congregated more frequently in the back room of the Neil and Tompson Cafe at 181 Market Street, just down the block from Wolff's, than they did at their clubhouse on the Hackensack River. The Neil of Neil and Tompson was Robert Neil, a sometime actor who had received his training with the Columbia Theatre Stock Company when that long-gone troupe also had included a youngster named Victor Moore. Neil's partner, Rosewell G. Tompson, had written a spoof of *Uncle Tom's Cabin,* and Neil agreed to stage it. If contemporary newspapers got their facts correct, the partners did not have to look far for a composer and lyricist, for the papers called Jerry a member of the club, even though he was only sixteen. Willing performers were everywhere.

Charles P. Gillen, a young real estate salesman who had a small office above a paint store next door to the cafe, was quickly assigned a minor role. Gus Troxler, a local "physical culture" teacher, was awarded the part of Simon Legree, called Svengali Legree in Tompson's text. Tompson himself took on the part of Little Eva. In fact, all the principal female roles were assumed by men, one Nicholas J. Tynan becoming Topsy Wheat Cake and a Daniel Blakeman becoming Aunt Ophelia Sophedelia Obedelia Prim. Ladies did appear, but only as a chorus of "Pickaninnies." Exactly who played Uncle Tom is uncertain. No program seems to have survived, and local papers give two different names for performers in the role. An ensemble listed merely as "Gluckman's orchestra" provided musical accompaniment.

The club booked the Kreuger Auditorium for its offering. The auditorium was an imposing house, built by a local beer baron in an attempt to outshine the rival Ballantine wealth. Although the show was slated for only one performance, Newark papers helped it along with little items now and then. Despite Newark's recent surge into big-city status, something of a small-town flavor pervaded these publicity items. Rehearsals, papers advised, were to begin in mid-December, adjourning for the Christmas season. A week before the performance, papers informed their readers that tickets were available not only at the Auditorium but at Holzhauer's drug store as well. Additionally, they disclosed that as an inducement to attend the production colorful souvenir programs would be distributed, a red-bordered blue club button pinned to each program. The pins could be removed and worn.

Loss of the program for the January 27, 1902, performance prevents a precise recounting of the musical's scenes and songs. The *Daily Advertiser*, however, did give one fascinating hint about the sets when it mentioned that the first act occurred on a Mississippi River steamboat, the *Siren*. More importantly, the paper printed a reasonably detailed, if slightly confused, musical program, best reconstructed as follows:

Uncle Tom's Cabin

ACT I

1. Overture, Medley, "Uncle Tom's Cabin" ...... *Jerome Kern*
   [Did this mean that the composer conducted the overture?]

2. Opening Chorus, "Yo! Ho! When You're In the Chorus" ..
                                             Company
3. Song, "I Never Do A Thing Like That" .. *Marks and Speech*
4. Song, "The Mighty Svengali Legree" .... *Legree and Chorus*
5. Song, "Song Of The Sheriffs" .... *Bing and Sheriffs*
6. Conversation Song, "When Rogers Come To Town" ......
                              Ophelia, Topsy and Eva

ACT II

7. Opening Chorus .... *Company*
8. Song, "Ma Blossom" .... *Ophelia and Chorus*
9. Topical Song, "Things Have Changed From Then To Now"
                                 Eva and Company
10. Song, "Marcella" .... *Topsy and Miss Irene Hedden*
11. Grand Finale .... *Entire Company*

In reviews following the performance no one received more attention than Kern. The Newark *Evening News* wrote:

> Mr. Kern's music was made the basis of many congratulatory speeches to the young composer last night. It is lively and tuneful and is well suited to amateur performance by reason of its simplicity and plainly marked rhythm. Two negro songs led in the affections of the audience last night. One called "Ma Blossom" was sung by Daniel Blakeman, as Aunt Ophelia, and a chorus armed with Japanese lanterns, and the other, "Marcella," rendered by Nicholas J. Tynan as Topsy, assisted by little Miss Irene Hedden. The latter was admirably done, both by the comedian and his small companion, and was executed until both were out of breath. "The Mighty Svengali Legree," in march time, sung by Gustave Troxler and the chorus, had a fine swing, and "When Rogers Come to Town," in which reminiscences of the Reuben and the Maid series [a series presented in annual productions starring two "Dutch" comedians, Gus and Max Rogers] were interspersed in an original air, showed cleverness in both music and verses.

Later in his review the critic also singled out two topical songs, "Things Have Changed From Then To Now" and "I Never Do A Thing Like That." The *Daily Advertiser* waxed equally enthusiastic, exclaiming early in its review: ". . . the music, the result of Mr. Kern's effort, was catchy and up to date. In fact it was much better than some of the music heard in many of the comic operas on the stage to-day. . . . Mr. Kern has showed great ability as a composer." However, later in the notice the critic revealed that some of the audience's enthusiasm may have been carefully programmed: "In the second act Mr. Kern takes advantage of an intentional break on Mr. Tompson's part to step upon the stage and correct him. Of course that is a cue for the audience to recognize the talented young musician, and they certainly pay him a glowing tribute. He and Mr. Tompson stood side by side and both kept receiving bouquets."

The business of young Jerry dashing on stage to make a correction is intriguing. In later years he would cause associates to quake with fear when his critical eye or ear caught an imperfection, and he would stop rehearsals to rush forward and adjust matters. If this sort of behavior came naturally and early to him, if even in his teens he was the demanding perfectionist of his later years, then quite possibly the scene was added as an amused, tolerant response to his behavior at rehearsals.

None of the music was published and none survives, unless perhaps Jerry quietly reused some of the melodies later. Were the songs as good as critics suggested, there is no reason to think Jerry did not re-employ them. All through his career he would carefully save better tunes that for one reason or another initially failed to find wide favor, and would seek out more hopeful niches for them. In any case, the applause his songs earned was undoubtedly his happiest birthday present. Jerry had turned seventeen on opening night.

Although these early songs may now be irretrievably lost, we know that at least one must have been truly memorable. Thirty years later, Charles Gillen, by 1932 Newark's Director of Parks and Public Property, could still sing "Things Have Changed From Then To Now" with all its verses. In fact, a reporter for the *Sunday Call,* sent to interview Gillen on other matters, was so taken by the fact that Gillen's staff was forever whistling a catchy tune he had never heard before that he devoted a long article to Gillen's recollections of *Uncle Tom's Cabin* instead of the matter he was sent to write about.

Sometime after the yacht club show, Jerry left high school without bothering to be graduated. If such a decision sounds shocking today, at least for someone of Jerry's background, it was neither uncommon nor unreasonable at the turn of the century. For the most part, high school then was an essential stepping stone only for youngsters contemplating an academic career. Writing songs for the masses required at most a limited, specialized study of music—and such figures as Irving Berlin would soon show that even such study was not an absolute necessity. Jerry apparently decided to take this specialized schooling in Germany, although he may have had to broach the matter differently to his father.

It must be remembered that, before the rise of Nazism, German-American Jews were devoutly loyal to their fatherland. If they could afford it, they paid return visits regularly, sailing faithfully on German ships. Henry may have encouraged Jerry to make just such a trip, and Jerry would have quickly accepted as an opportunity for musical schooling. Biographies and articles on Kern, including many published in his lifetime, have stated that young Jerry studied at Heidelberg, implying some formalized curriculum at the great university. But a check of Heidelberg's records for the period shows that Kern was never enrolled at the school and, more importantly, when Kern was carefully quoted he told a different story. For example, in a 1918 interview he recalled, "I had some European training in a small town outside of Heidelberg." Unfortunately he never specified where or with whom. One of the indications he gave of when this training occurred was in a 1932 Philadelphia interview, where he placed it before his association with The Lyceum Publishing Company. Since, as we shall see, his connection with Lyceum began in the summer of 1902, Kern must have sailed shortly after the Newark show and returned within four or five months. His German schooling can have been neither prolonged nor probing. Nevertheless he must have reaped minor advantages from it, and it may well have been valuable and idyllic enough to confirm him in his ambition to pursue his labors.

In deciding to embrace composing as a profession young Jerry almost unquestionably received his mother's affectionate encouragement. His father had other ideas and plainly no intention of letting a wife and son combine to sway him. By 1902 Henry had risen to become Wolff's executive vice president. He had assisted in the store's expansion from a modest clothier to a miniature department store. With prospects for further growth so obvious in Henry's eye, he saw an opportunity to help his youngest son establish a foothold in the business world. After all, Joseph was already in trade and Edwin was carving a place for himself in the legal world. Furthermore, Henry was no doubt aware of the slight off-color image that still clung to artists and theatre folk. In Henry's society, a society that had more often than not elevated itself by its own bootstraps, the thought of willingly embracing a somewhat disreputable calling was anathema. Whether by threats or cajoling, or merely by exerting his position as head of the household, Henry won. But his victory was short-lived and Pyrrhic, resulting in one of the most celebrated stories about Jerome Kern.

Henry was undoubtedly a loving father. Having gained his point, he probably was anxious to make Jerry's first experiences as easy and pleasant as possible. Luckily, Wolff's had opened not only a house-furnishings department but even a small area in which it sold pianos. The store needed to buy two more pianos, so Henry hit on the notion of letting Jerry go to the Bronx, to the Italian manufacturer with whom Wolff traded, and select the two best instruments. Jerry dutifully went. He was greeted by the head of the family that owned the factory and, guilefully or not, was invited to lunch. At lunch the food and wine were generous, especially the wine. Before Jerry left he signed a purchase order for two hundred pianos. The story, which has a ring of medieval hyperbole, is nevertheless true. Jerry's daughter Betty recalls how often he loved to tell it and how consistent his figures were. "You can't imagine," he would say to her, "what it looks like for two hundred pianos to come off vans." Henry was exasperated! Recountings of the story often add that the elder Kern was forced to rent additional space. More to the point, Henry agreed that Jerry did not belong in the business world. Young Jerry was allowed to venture out into the superficially glamorous, but actually hard-nosed arena of music.

His first encounters quickly tarnished the sheen. Although he may well have carried reviews of *Uncle Tom's Cabin* in his portfolio alongside his songs, his reception was discouraging. Jerry's luck changed only when a family friend turned out to be a niece of the music publisher Edward B. Marks. Marks was respected in the trade both for his acuity and his warmth. Since Marks was summering with his family in Arverne, Long Island, his niece, Stella, agreed to accompany Jerry to his home. Marks was immediately struck by the "little fellow with tight green pants" whom Stella introduced to him as "Romie Kern, from Newark." (Thirty-four years later Kern told columnist Sidney Skolsky his favorite color was still green—"even for trousers.") Coming at once to the business at hand, she advised her uncle that the boy wanted to be a songwriter. Marks invited Jerry to the piano and was impressed by the obvious talent his pieces disclosed. Regrettably, Marks had no openings at the moment—at least not in the composing department. But he urged Jerry to accept a position at his jobbing plant making "bills and invoices." Eager now for any entry, Jerry took the post. With the cockiness of youth, coupled with a deep-seated conviction of his appreciable merits, Jerry may well have figured that Marks's firm, Lyceum, would be issuing his songs soon enough. Marks even may have offered to publish one of Jerry's samples as an inducement.

The first published song to carry the name Jerome D. Kern came from Lyceum's presses almost at once. Lyceum copyrighted it that very summer, on September 5, 1902. "At The Casino," subtitled "A Reverie," was a short piano piece of no special distinction. That the song was not a show-type number is surprising, but Kern probably found it easier to get this little exercise in print than buck the fearsome competition of Tin Pan Alley tunesmiths and Broadway interpolators. The title was pointless, and vague enough to have allowed the composer to consider it a discreet obeisance to New York's leading musical comedy house, the Casino, at 39th and Broadway.

Several months later Lyceum published a similar piece, "In A Shady Bungalow." This time Jerry established more secure connections with the theatre world by subtitling the work "An Entr-Acte." Artistically the piece represented a great stride forward, a marked advance melodically and harmonically from the earlier, shorter piece. If some of its themes sounded like the pseudo-Orientalia so popular at the time, they were nonetheless pleasant, attractively varied, and never cloying. A copyright date of May 5, 1903, indicates some time elapsed between the two songs, a time Kern put to profitable use, as evidenced in his growing artistry. What Kern did in this time, besides drudging at Lyceum, was to resume his schooling, enrolling at the New York College of Music, then at 128 East 58th Street.

Although the school has long since been absorbed by New York University, it remained for many years the city's oldest independent music school, having been chartered in 1878. Alexander Lambert became its director in 1889 and was nearing the end of his tenure when Kern matriculated. Under Lambert's aegis the school attracted some of the finest musical pedagogues of the day: Paolo Gallico, Albert von Doenhoff, Austin Pierce, and Lambert himself. Jerry took counterpoint with Pierce, studied piano with the martinetish Doenhoff, and apparently, although not certainly, took harmony and composition with Gallico and Lambert. The school's records no longer go back to Kern's day, but Kern himself recalled he had been a good if unexceptional student.

Perhaps even more important to his career than this final schooling was his move to another publisher, T. B. Harms, a move he made in the summer or fall of 1903. Marks remembered the move and told of it when he published his life story. Writing his autobiography at the end of his life, his recollections were sometimes fuzzy, so he occasionally smudged the facts. His statement that young Jerry worked for Lyceum "for three years" is patently in error. But his version of how Jerry's departure took place seems to be correct: "Several years later he inherited a piece of money. He came to us and offered to invest in the firm if we could make him a junior partner, but we had no need of more capital." Kern himself in later years allowed that he had purchased his initial interest in Harms with money from an inheritance. Since the only conceivable inheritance would have come from moneys left him by his grandfather, who died at the end of November 1903, it seems remarkable that the will could have been probated, the money in hand, and a copyright arranged all within one month. Of course, the association with Harms may not have begun with the partnership. The head of the company, Max Dreyfus,* in his shrewdness, may have been able to put Kern off for several months while he further assessed his young composer's abilities. Time sequences make this likely.

How Kern came to select Harms is interesting. Someone at Lyceum was quick to appreciate that a billing office was no place for so talented and ambitious a youngster. Jerry's salary was raised to $7.00 a week, and he was assigned to Wanamaker's Department Store as a song-plugger. The young composer found his allotted time fell between slots awarded to two more famous songwriters from more prestigious houses: Jean Schwartz and Ernest Ball. Because they were better known and busier, Schwartz and Ball were sometimes forced to cut short their stints, and occasionally the press of other business kept them away entirely. Kern quickly determined it was to his advantage to arrive early and be prepared to remain late. Yet in his youthful generosity he did not confine himself to plugging just Lyceum's songs. Ball arrived late one day to hear Jerry playing one of Ball's own pieces. He made a point of talking to the youngster and found out that Jerry was eager to move to another house. Matching Jerry's generosity with his own, Ball suggested he try not Witmark, Ball's publisher, but Harms. Ball's reasoning was simple. At that moment Witmark was in its glittering heyday. Its roster included Victor Herbert, Julian Edwards, Gustav Luders, and a host of once shining, now obscure names. Virtually every major

---

* It is important to note that Dreyfus controlled two houses, Harms and T. B. Harms. Although Kern's connection was solely with T. B. Harms, for the sake of brevity T. B. Harms will often be referred to here simply as Harms.

Broadway score of the era carried Witmark's imprimatur. Harms, on the other hand, was struggling to get out from under the atrophying effects of its founders' policies; under Dreyfus's aegis it was prepared to make whatever gambles might ensure success. Whereas at Witmark an unknown composer would be shoved aside, at Harms he would be given a respectful hearing.

T. B. Harms had been founded in 1880 by Tom and Alex (or Alec) Harms. They were bright, good-natured men—"too good," as their competitor Isidore Witmark noted, "for their own benefit." Alex soon dropped out. And when the tooth-and-nail battle for composers and distribution grew too intense for Tom, he sold a majority interest to his onetime song-plugger, Dreyfus. Max Dreyfus was of medium height and very thin, and his balding head accented his slightly Semitic features. He was always neatly groomed and markedly reserved. Every bit as intelligent as Tom Harms, he was far better suited to the hard nature of the music business. Most of all, he was blessed with an exceptional ear for up-and-coming talents.

One look at the offices told Kern just how shaky Harms had become. The offices, situated on East 22nd Street, were in a depressingly dilapidated building. Ushered into Dreyfus's private suite, Kern was startled to see a Prince Albert coat folded neatly across a piano, a silk hat resting beside the coat. Dreyfus was wearing a morning suit. The coat and hat deeply impressed Kern, since he was, by his own admission, "a first-class snob." Happily, Kern in turn impressed Dreyfus. When he informed Dreyfus he was earning seven dollars a week, Dreyfus mistakenly thought he had said eleven and offered to better it by one dollar. In effect, Jerry had garnered a five-dollar raise, nearly doubling his previous salary. That Jerry began as a meagerly salaried employee reinforces the supposition that he did not become a partner at once. But if Max Dreyfus's first favorable impressions of Jerry were never called into question, Jerry's first impressions of Max's sartorial splendors were. Jerry soon learned that the hat and suit had been rented for a funeral.

While Jerry was not immediately made a partner in Harms, Dreyfus nevertheless quickly went to work to place some of Jerry's tunes and just as quickly succeeded. Broadway heard its first Kern melodies a week short of two years after Newark had applauded his work.

Seymour Hicks and Walter Slaughter's *An English Daisy* was a British failure that two astute American showmen, Joe Weber and Lew Fields, nevertheless felt might appeal to Broadway's still staunchly Anglophile theatregoers. In a procedure common at the time, they jettisoned much of the original composer's score in favor of domestic interpolations. Except for a few great artists such as Victor Herbert and John Philip Sousa, who regularly inserted restrictive clauses in their contracts, most composers were neither talented enough nor strong enough to prevent performers and producers from adding any extraneous song they believed would make a stir. In a practical sense these performers and producers were often justified. Many a show's success in this period came not from its basic score but from an added number by another hand. Furthermore, the practice served not only to enliven often stodgy scores, but to afford unknown composers opportunities for a hearing. Even so, sensitive writers and critics bewailed the jolting hodgepodge of style and tone that usually resulted. In joining the ranks of hopeful interpolators, Kern embarked on a policy that soon made his name well known in the trade and to a much lesser extent to the public.

An English Daisy began its American career on December 1, 1903, with a rousingly successful seven-week tryout in Boston. Kern's emotions must have gone on a roller-coaster ride when he read the judiciously considered review in the staid *Evening Transcript*. If his eye did not jump up and down the column searching out a reference to his songs, then he first came upon the unnamed critic's rejection of "musical numbers ad libitum by diverse composers of so-called music." Only further on could he have spotted one of his two songs singled out for special attention, when the critic noted that "Truly Shattuck . . . has one chance, in the second act, with 'Wine, Wine,' a spirited number, which she gives in splendid fashion." *An English Daisy* opened a shorter, less profitable New York stand at the Casino on January 18, 1904. Manhattan's critics were not as entertained as Boston's had been, and not one of the six leading dailies mentioned Kern's contributions.

Both Kern songs had lyrics by Edgar Smith, a Weber and Fields loyalist, who had been charged with adapting the musical to American tastes. "Wine, Wine! (Champagne Song)" is a cheerful drinking song in 6/8 time which demonstrates a surprising debt to Victor Herbert's school of writing both in its softly syncopated tempos (gently flowing alternations of eighth and quarter notes in its verse) and in its harmonies (the first part of the chorus moves from its basic F to end with an underchording of A-minor followed by E-natural seventh and back to A-minor). The song's range is over an octave, demanding a good, well-trained voice to project it properly. Kern dedicated the song to Miss Ethel Prince, a lady who remains unidentifiable.

Regrettably, Kern never published his other song, "To The End Of The World Together."

At the same time Dreyfus began arranging for Jerry's songs to be interpolated into Broadway musicals, he provided two methods for supplementing the composer's income. For the next ten years Jerry often served as rehearsal pianist for shows in which his songs were added. This practice allowed him to be on hand if a further number were needed. Jerry could dash off a melody then and there. Less frequently, Jerry went on tour as accompanist to Broadway and vaudeville favorites such as Marie Dressler and Edna Wallace Hopper. Here again he might have an opportunity of adding an occasional number.

With no immediate prospects of interpolating his songs in other shows, Kern, conceivably at Dreyfus's instigation, may have set sail to spend the remainder of the season in London. The trip was to prove the beginning of a life-long romance with England and the English.

3

The West End and the Great White Way

Of all the commonplaces and delights of 1903 London none meant more to young Kern than the theatrical hubbub in the West End. It was a theatrical district in the throes of a major facelifting, although a nineteen-year-old American might not have appreciated the full extent of the change. On July 4, 1903, the old Gaiety on the Strand raised its curtain for one final performance. Down the street a new Gaiety was being erected as part of the Aldwych-Kingsway scheme, and would open on October 26, 1903. Shaftesbury Avenue, in time London's brightest theatrical thoroughfare, had been cut through only seventeen years earlier, in 1886. By the date of Kern's visit it boasted the London Pavilion at its Piccadilly Circus end—the street's oldest house, built in 1885—and the Palace at Cambridge Circus. In between stood the Shaftesbury, the Lyric, and the new Apollo. Apart from the Gaiety the most desirable house for musicals was probably Daly's, a little jewel of an auditorium situated not far from Shaftesbury Avenue on the edge of Leicester Square.

The lyric stage was given over almost wholly to George Edwardes's school of musical comedy. Londoners could applaud such musicals as *The School Girl, A Country Girl, The Earl and the Girl, The Girl from Kay's, The Duchess of Dantzig,* and the show awarded the honor of opening the new Gaiety, *The Orchid.* Half of these shows ran over a year; none less than seven months. London hits of the period regularly ran far longer than hits of the same era in New York. A small, tightly knit group of writers and producers was responsible for the steady parade of musical offerings. Paul Rubens, Howard Talbot, Sidney Jones, and Lionel Monckton customarily provided music, to texts by Owen Hall, Adrian Ross, or Percy Greenbank. George Edwardes remained the most celebrated impresario, although he worked increasingly with Charles Frohman, an American whose London schedule was almost as hectic as his Broadway program. Indeed, connections with the New York stage were growing and in some quarters were viewed not as mutually advantageous but merely as alarming entanglements. Edwardes himself, on the occasion of the old Gaiety's closing, remarked that the dollar's growing strength, America's higher ticket prices, and her higher professional fees were causing many young English talents to rush overseas, and he looked with a certain concern on the future of native English musical comedy. He seemed to take no cognizance of currents moving in precisely the opposite direction which would ultimately affect the London stage far more than the momentary exodus. Of course there was no need for him to be aware of an American teenager peddling songs in London theatrical circles, but he might have mentioned that an American musical was one of the hits of the London season.

The musical, at the Shaftesbury, was *In Dahomey*. On Broadway this first black musical ever to play a major New York auditorium had been greeted in 1902 by critics with a markedly nervous approval and had been more or less ignored by most white theatregoers. Its New York run was a mere fifty-three performances. Because London had far fewer blacks and its relationship with them was quite different, the West End could wave aside Broadway's fear and prejudices and succumb wholeheartedly to the infectious black cake-walking and to the great comedy of Bert Williams and George Walker. It did just that. *In Dahomey* chalked up an exhilarating 251 performances. More so than occasional ragtime numbers sung in music halls, it firmly introduced Britain to black rhythms and styles that were to shape the American musical scene and the American musical theatre for the rest of the century and were to play no small part in the triumph of that same lyric stage.

For all practical purposes, films, radio, television—the technological entertainments of future generations—did not exist, apart from a few primitive exceptions to be noted shortly. Yet competition and a healthy theatrical economics allowed musicals to be lavishly mounted. As was the case in America, sets for a single show were customarily created by several designers, each a specialist at his particular type of decor. At this time London was probably a bit ahead of New York in the imaginativeness and excellence of its sets. Although painted flats were still often employed to depict scenes later re-created in more three-dimensional terms, architecturally conceived sets were utilized whenever they would prove effective. Few librettists could resist a scene that allowed, say, a spectacular staircase to be dramatically introduced. Furthermore, as in America, relatively cheap labor costs permitted musicals to fill the stage with casts of forty, fifty, even sixty performers, the women almost invariably dressed in the drapey luxury of the day. Curtains rose time and again on stage pictures of studied elegance. To some extent the elaborateness of sets and costumes was necessary to soften the rather harsh effects of turn-of-the-century lighting. Gas and calcium lights were fast giving way to electricity, but dimmers were extremely primitive and within reach of only the best houses. Nor could filters be changed with ease. Except for one or two spotlights controlled from a booth in the furthest heights of a house, all lighting came directly from the stage, especially from footlights, which lit the stage and performers from underneath and at close range. The subtleties of modern lighting were at best far-fetched dreams. Partly as a result of these lighting problems and partly as a carryover from days of even less workable lighting and larger theatres, make-up could often be grotesquely artificial, not merely for patently grotesque comedians but even for young leading men and ingenues. Juveniles made up with what was called "five and nine," a pale yellow base topped with a nutty brown. The mouth was customarily outlined in black and the eyes with blue, dotted with red. Ingenues "hot-blacked" their eyelashes, utilizing a wax-like mascara that was melted in a spoon over a candle flame. The wax, applied with a hairpin, extended the lashes preposterously.

Like everything else about Kern's 1903–4 London stay, no records exist to disclose the extent of his theatregoing. But his love of the theatre and the fact that he was by no means poor suggest he may have gone frequently to see entertainments. Even so, at nineteen Kern was serious and purposeful enough not to have spent all his time sightseeing and playgoing. What, then, did he do in this long stay? For the most part Kern remained determinedly silent about these months for the rest of his life. When interviewers pressed him, his responses tended to be somewhat coy. For American readers he often announced that Charles Frohman gave him his start; for English readers he just as frequently claimed George Edwardes deserved credit. Only years later, when he was firmly established and no longer needed to worry about his early image, did he confess that "his early musical-comedy training was successively with Sir Alfred Butt, Mr. Seymour Hicks, Mr. George Edwardes, and Mr. Charles Frohman, with whom he was retained by the year to supply music for their productions." Of course, in 1903 Butt had not been knighted. In fact, he was employed in a theatrical area that was not yet totally respectable—the music hall. Butt was tall, with a strikingly pink and white complexion and a habit of twisting his neck as if his collar were pinching him. He was assistant manager at the Palace, a house that had seen "better days" and would see them again, thanks to Butt himself. This was the period when rough-and-tumble music halls were struggling to evolve into more generally acceptable vaudeville theatres. While unlicensed, music halls by law were not supposed to present anything but singing and dancing—spoken dialogue was taboo. With few exceptions patrons were rowdy, hard-drinking members of the lower classes. Both the nature of the legal entertainment and the class of the patrons pointed to the music halls' origins in early-nineteenth-century taverns. Coincidently, in America Tony Pastor, Weber and Fields, B. F. Keith, and others were fighting a similar battle for respectability. Butt was in the forefront of the English struggle. Even as assistant manager he began to lure musical comedy stars into variety and to seek out promising new talent. On Charles Morton's retirement Butt was made manager.

Bills for the Palace in 1903–4 were long. The overture began no later than 7:55, and the first act came before the footlights at 8:00. Programs recorded the precise time each act would appear, although undoubtedly some deviations from so rigid a schedule were not uncommon. Many music hall favorites—such as Vesta Tilley and Daisy Jerome—appeared on bills, sometimes for just a week, sometimes for longer stays. Ominously for live vaudeville itself, all bills concluded with a Bioscope program—silent flickers depicting everything from a royal procession or a stag hunt to a tram moving along a London street. According to the programs, the musical background for these primitive films and most of the original musical material presented at other times during the evening were the work of the theatre's conductor, Herman Finck. Finck was a heavy-set, dark-haired, mustachioed man with the reputation for being a martinet at work, and a great wit, raconteur, and bon vivant after hours. Like Butt, he was to have a long association with Kern; the two remained friends until Finck's death in 1939.

No incontestable evidence exists for Jerry's first London stay. English trade sheets understandably make no mention of him, and an extensive examination of reviews for variety bills and West End musicals disclose no songs identifiable as his. The strongest arguments for Kern's visit are, first of all, the persistent stories, confirmed by him, that he did his earliest work in London. (Since Kern never again alluded to his songs for *An English Daisy,* he may have judged them not worthy of serious consideration.) Second, his revelation that he worked with Butt before he worked with Hicks, Frohman, and Edwardes argues in favor of a 1904 visit. But one story associated with this trip should be put to rest. Supposedly, Kern did encounter Frohman, who had been profitably offering English musicals to New York since 1895 and apparently had little time for American musicals or even American composers. According to the story, Frohman mistook Kern for an Englishman and invited him to accompany him back to America. Only as they reached New York did Frohman realize his Englishman was a Yankee. Frohman did make a west-bound voyage at this time—returning in July of 1904 on the *Kronprinz Wilhelm.* But no Jerome Kern is listed on the ship's passenger records. This does not preclude some casual, uneventful meeting in London.

If Kern and Frohman's meeting had occurred by then, it was nevertheless not Frohman who gave Kern his first major opportunity on the New York stage. That honor fell to Edward E. Rice, the man who had produced what may have been the first show Jerry saw. However forgotten he is today, Rice was one of the giants of the early American musical theatre. He was the co-author of *Evangeline,* which became one of the best-loved vehicles of the late nineteenth century. As producer of a troupe known as Rice's Surprise Party, he mounted many of the prototypical musical comedies of the era. He brought the earliest important black musical to a white legitimate stage when he presented *The Origin of the Cake Walk; or, Clorindy* as an afterpiece to his summer roof-garden entertainments at the Casino. But his greatest success was undoubtedly his 1884 hit *Adonis,* which he wrote with William Gill and Henry E. Dixey, and which became the first musical to run over 500 performances on Broadway. Rice was also responsible for giving stars such as Dixey, Lillian Russell, and Faye Templeton their first major opportunities in comic opera. His ability to spot young talent never deserted him. At the same time he was presenting Kern's material he gave Broadway its first glance at its greatest female impersonator, Julian Eltinge. Although no one, except possibly Rice himself, could know it, this latest offering was to be his farewell to the theatre. Since he survived for another twenty years, he could at least rejoice that the introduction of both Kern and Eltinge were added to his impressive list of achievements. Rice, who was moon-faced and pop-eyed, wore a large walrus mustache that made him look like a kindly old uncle.

As a producer, Rice had not done an original musical in nearly a decade. From 1896 on he had capitulated to the vogue for English musicals and had mounted only importations. His newest offering was no exception. At least it was written by an Englishman, Herbert Darnley, although it had failed of any success in its homeland two years earlier despite the presence of the music hall favorite Dan Leno at the head of its cast. That in no way discouraged Rice from proclaiming *Mr. Wix of Wickham* "the Latest English Musical Comedy" nor deterred the New Haven *Evening Register*, reviewing its American premiere at the Hyperion Theatre on September 12, 1904, from insisting "the play is English through and through with a fine lot of English shop girls, a scattering of nobility, and many more soldier lads and officers." The paper found every aspect of the show attractive, concluding, "It certainly gives promise of a good reception in New York. It deserves it." Yet Rice and his associates must have held the notice suspect. They paid little heed to the praise showered on two of the six songs the critic singled out for attention: "New York Way" and "Love Is King." Both were left behind when the musical moved on. Two other songs the reviewer noted, although he did not get the correct title for either one, were " 'Rub-a-Dum,' a military travesty; and 'Angling By A Bubbling Brook,' with real flyrods." In the latter case the staging seems to have delighted the critic as much as the melody.

Whether or not Rice trusted New Haven's judgment, *Mr. Wix of Wickham* had been booked to open the following Monday, September 19, 1904, at the Bijou in New York, and the showman saw no reason to delay the premiere. Accordingly, the curtain rose as slated with the following musical program:

Mr. Wix of Wickham

ACT I

1. Opening Chorus (George Everard)
2. Song, "A Handle To My Name" (Herbert Darnley) ....
    Maude and Chorus
3. Song, "Her First Can Can" (J. H. Wagner and Jerome D. Kern) .... *Madame and Chorus*

4. Trio, "The Important Man" (Jerome D. Kern) .... *Banks,*
Potter, Dodd and Chorus

5. Song, "One Thing Different" (J. D. Kern and Darnley) ..
Wix and Chorus

6. Song, "Saturday 'Till Monday" (J. H. Wagner and Jerome
D. Kern) .... *O'Scoot and Chorus*

7. Duet, "Cupid's Garden" (Max C. Eugene) .... *Lady*
Betty and Tom

8. Aria, "Raindrops" (George Everard) .... *Lady Betty*

9. Duet, "Waiting For You" (J. H. Wagner and J. D. Kern)
Wix, Madame and Chorus

10. Song, "Susan" (Jerome D. Kern) ....
Tom, Susan and Chorus

11. Finale (Herbert Darnley)

Between the acts Mr. Rice will conduct the orchestra in his latest composition, entitled "Pleasant Memories," dedicated to May Irwin.

ACT II

12. Opening Chorus (Herbert Darnley)

13. "Volunteers" (George Everard) .... *Chorus*

14. Trio, "Rub a Dub" (Jerome D. Kern) ...... *Banks, Potter,*
Dodd and Chorus

15. Song, "Angling By A Babbling Brook" (Jerome D. Kern)
Maude with Girls

16. Duet, "Googy-oo" (J. H. Wagner and Edward E. Rice) ....
O'Scoot and Mrs. O'Scoot

17. Solo and Chorus, "Military Maids" (Jerome D. Kern) ....
Tom

18. Song, "Because I Am A Duke" (Jerome D. Kern and J. H.
Wagner) .... *Duke and Chorus*

19. Song and Recitative, "Bluff" (Jerome D. Kern and J. H.
Wagner) .... *Madame*

20. Song and Specialty, "Not Like Other Girls" (Andros
Hawley) .... *John Smith, B.A.*

21. Aria, "The Dancing Kangaroo" (Jerome D. Kern) ......
David Abraham

22. Song, "Sergeant Wix" (Herbert Darnley) ...... *Wix with*
Chorus

23. Finale (Jerome D. Kern)

36

The show was staged by Tom Ricketts. Whitney Bennington conducted the uncredited orchestrations. Costumes were by Madame Ripley; scenery by Frank Rafter and Theodore Reisig.

As he had for *Little Christopher,* Rice complied with prevailing practice by including a synopsis of the plot in the program. It revealed the story to be typical period frippery. To escape a distasteful marriage Lady Betty (Thelma Fair), daughter of the Duke of Tadminster (Sydney De Grey), flees to Australia with her friend Maude Benton (Alice Maude Poole). Down under, the ladies accept positions as shop girls in a store managed by one Mr. Wix (Henry Corson Clarke). Musical comedy coincidence demands that the Duke hire a detective, Shamus O'Scoot (Frank Lalor), to find not only his daughter but a missing heir as well, and the detective comes to Australia in the belief Mr. Wix is the latter. Romances and complications ensue, only to be resolved happily before the final curtain. The "Tom" mentioned in the musical program was played by David Lythgow; Madame Marie by Laura Guerite; Banks, Potter, and Dodd by Arthur Wooley, Douglas Flint, and Andrew O'Neil. Comic characters included Mr. Jinks, of the Horse Marines (Fred Waters), and Drinkaweldry, an Aboriginal Chief (Milt Pollock), as well as a favorite of the period, a talking animal played by an actor, in this case David Abraham inside the Frolicsome Kangaroo. A chorus consisted of twenty-one women and ten men. There was just one set for each act.

Most New York critics found little to welcome in the new show. In the harshness of its judgment the *Times* typified the almost universal reaction. Heading its review "A Poor Show, Poorly Acted, with No Redeeming Features," it rated the evening as "not even fair theatrical hash" and condemned Rice's authors as "accomplices" in his crime. Not surprisingly in so dismissive a notice, no songs were accorded special attention. The *Dramatic Mirror* called the music "for the most part, reminiscent and commonplace," but it nevertheless gave passing mention to "One Thing Different," "Waiting For You," and "Mr. Wix," while dutifully recording that "Googy-oo" was "one of the few hits of the evening."

Yet one critic did have some especially kind words to offer, and in writing them secured an important place for himself in Jerome Kern's story. That critic was Alan Dale of the *American.* Dale, whose real name was Alfred Cohen, was a prissy little man with a meticulously waxed mustache and pince-nez. He had definite ideas of what directions the theatre should

37

take, directions often at odds with prevailing notions. He frequently expressed his ideas so acidly that at intervals he was prevented from entering theatres by irate owners or producers.

Dale admitted to mixed feelings about the evening. On a visit to England two years before, he had chanced to see the original. "It never occurred to me," he mused, "that anything could possibly be done with 'Mr. Wix of Wickham'—except forget it." Dale's faithful readers would have been amazed had he embraced a modern musical. By and large he found them little more than "tap-house fumes, and an unmuzzled low comedian," and in his latest review he wrote, "I respectfully submit that other times are infinitely preferable to those of to-day as far as the musical show goes." So while readers learned that Dale was disappointed by the offering—albeit "agreeably disappointed"—they may have been surprised to find him ultimately assessing it as "a pleasing entertainment, containing much that is pretty, and something that is humorous, a few good people, two or three 'dizzy blondes,' and a dozen catchy airs." In his satisfaction at these songs he devoted a whole paragraph to them:

> There are twenty-three numbers in "Mr. Wix of Wickham," and half of them are worth while, in an easy way. They are not "good," but they are catchy. That which is "good" plays tag with the average ear, and eludes it deftly. "The Important Man," "Saturday Till Monday," Max Eugene's pleasing "Cupid's Garden," "Angling by a Babbling Brook," "Because I am a Duke," "Googyoo" and "Rub-a-Dub" are a few of the things in this affair that beat the musical alleged entertainment.

But Dale went on to make one other judgment—a judgment that to a small extent demonstrated his taste and perspicacity and to a larger degree suggested that of the reviewers he alone read the program carefully; his colleagues seeming to have gone little beyond the large print immediately following the title. Indeed, the *Times's* critic quoted the program in order to list Rice's "accomplices." The playbill read: "Book and music by Herbert Darnley, additional musical numbers by George Everard and Jerome D. Kern, readaptation and many lyrics by John H. Wagner." Critics of 1904 and later students alike have all too readily accepted that the bulk of the score was by Darnley, with Kern's contribution minimal. Yet, as credits accompanying the list of musical numbers reveal, Kern had composed over half the score! The rather haphazard order of some of the credits, with

Wagner's name sometimes first and Kern's name sometimes first, is meaningless. While Kern did write some of the lyrics, Wagner composed none of the music. It was to this large share of composition that Dale addressed himself in a sentence that has been regularly misquoted: "There are so many bright features in the show at the Bijou, and its music, by Jerome D. Kern, towers in such an Eiffel way, above the average hurdy-gurdy, penny-in-the-slot, primitive accompaniment to the musical show that criticism is disarmed and Herbert Darnley's weak and foolish 'book' sterilized." For the remaining twenty-odd years of his career, Dale took a joyful, avuncular interest in Kern's development, remaining to the end a loyal advocate.

What did Dale actually hear in Kern's songs that left him so hopeful? In retrospect, precious little. Kern's songs for *Mr. Wix of Wickham*, like the plot, were typical period pieces. As songs they deserve study only because of Dale's remarks and because they represent the earliest large selection of theatre music by our greatest theatre composer. Kern published four of his contributions—the fifth song on the sheet music, listed as "Cupid's Song," turned out to be "Cupid's Garden" by Max Eugene, a pen name for none other than Max Dreyfus. "Saturday 'Till Monday" begins with a lithe verse in half time, changing in the chorus to a gently swaying, sentimental waltz. The melody's most interesting features are in its verse, especially the unexpected extension of the musical line in the eighth to tenth bars and the abrupt insertion of B-flat seventh and E-flat harmonies (the song is in the key of C) in the eleventh to fifteenth bars. The sole noteworthy point about the chorus is the printer's error in the eleventh bar, turning a *c* into a *d*. The error suggests Kern had not yet begun his insistent, careful proofreading of his songs, personal proofreading that was to keep most of his published material error-free. In its thirty-two bars the chorus offers just two slightly different variations of the same basic theme. The chorus of "Waiting For You" is only half as long and similarly presents just a single basic theme repeated once, although here with even less variation. The verse, with its mention of "little Annie Rafferty" in its lyric, has a distinctly Irish sound. Chorus and verse alike offer bland, tripping melodies made up almost wholly of eighth notes, without the merest syncopation, tempo changes, or untoward harmonies. Both songs, however, did employ dominant minors, a modulation Kern had used in "At The Casino" and one which would remain a life-long favorite. The shortest of the published songs was "Angling By A Babbling Brook," although Kern spread out the printed version by repeating the verse and the chorus. Both the chorus and verse contain unworded passages. The principal part of the chorus lasts just eight bars (with a two-bar tag). Bars three and four repeat the phrases in bars one and two, while the two unsung bars at the end echo the phrase in the seventh and eighth bars. It is pleasant—and was probably much more so when mounted with attractive young ladies toying with real rods—but not memorable. Possibly the best of the four songs is the ballad "Susan." Written entirely in 2/4, it moves from a dainty, innocuous verse into an ingratiating, soft-shoe refrain filled with warm harmonies, including one effective use of a supertonic minor.

Given Kern's celebrated idiosyncrasy of branding his choruses "burthens," it is interesting to note that none of these songs carries the term. "Saturday 'Till Monday" called its chorus a chorus, "Waiting For You" and "Susan" employed the common synonym "refrain," while "Angling By A Babbling Brook" left the passages unmarked. Fourteen years would pass before Kern would adopt the singular "burthen."

Quite possibly another song Kern copyrighted at this time was meant for *Mr. Wix of Wickham*. "He'll Be There!" is a thoroughly pleasant march with a lyric by Rice's old partner, J. Cheever Goodwin.

The reviews the musical received, which were cruel, though not unjustifiably so, had a deadening effect at the box office. Rice withdrew the show after only forty performances (plus one "professional matinee"). While the day's healthy theatrical economics allowed many a New York failure to have a profitable post-Broadway tour, Rice elected not to chance the road.

Coincidental with the opening of *Mr. Wix of Wickham*, Kern resumed interpolating random songs in other shows. His latest melodies were added to *The Silver Slipper*, and, anew, to *An English Daisy*. Both shows went into rehearsal at about the same time as *Mr. Wix of Wickham*, and *An English Daisy* played a Manhattan combination house, the West End Theatre, the very week *Mr. Wix* opened in New York. That Kern was approached for more material for *An English Daisy* no doubt reflected Weber and Fields's satisfaction with his previous contributions. *The Silver Slipper*, yet one more English musical, had first opened in New York in October of 1902 and quickly became one of the hits of its season. In September of 1904 it embarked on a third season of American touring with a stand at Manhattan Beach. Just when Kern's songs were added is uncertain. Significantly, Harms controlled the American rights to both *An English Daisy* and *The Silver Slipper*.

For *The Silver Slipper*, Kern collaborated with a songwriter who was to become one of Broadway's most successful producers, John Golden. Their joint effort, "My Celia," was a delicate, vaguely plaintive ballad. Working again with Edgar Smith on *An English Daisy*, Kern created "The Downcast Eye," a standard ballad with an optimistic melody that belies its title. If the song is noteworthy at all, it is solely because it represents the earliest known use by Kern of a device he would employ all through his career—inserting in his chorus phrases from his verse.

A month after the opening of *Mr. Wix*, Max Dreyfus took his broom and swept the cobwebs from Harms. Publicly, the most obvious change was a spic-and-span new office at 126 West 44th Street. But trade sheets hinted at a number of behind-the-scenes moves as well. Kern's purchase of an interest in the firm most likely occurred at about this time. He had, after all, shown Dreyfus how talented and energetic he could be. In any case, nine months later he was definitely a partner. Exactly how large a share he initially secured is unknown, though by the 1930s he held 25 per cent of the stock.

What Kern did next is lost to us. Given his interest in business, he probably remained close to the Harms offices for at least a month or so. But with no new shows to write or even to interpolate songs into, Kern was undoubtedly loath to dawdle. Soon enough he was on a ship for London. And this time there can be no doubt he met Frohman. The first important notice any trade sheet apparently took of the young composer occurred on July 15, 1905, when the *Dramatic Mirror* reported: "Jerome D. Kern, who, though not yet twenty-one, has composed several light operas and is a partner in a New York music publishing house, has just been retained by Charles Frohman and Seymour Hicks for three years. Mr. Kern is to write for them twelve songs a year. He sailed on the *Philadelphia* July 7 for New York." Actually, records show he was not on the ship when it sailed (a day late), nor was he aboard the *Kronprinz Wilhelm* on which Frohman returned on July 25.

Seymour Hicks, a nondescript figure of a man but for his conspicuously pointed nose, was a shining light on the turn-of-the-century English musical stage, something of an Edwardian Noel Coward. A performer, writer, and producer, he had enjoyed a string of hits such as *The Shop Girl, A Runaway Girl, Blue Bell in Paradise,* and *The Earl and the Girl* before teaming with Frohman to give London *The Catch of the Season* in September of 1904. This modern retelling of the Cinderella tale, with Hicks as Prince Charming in the guise of the Duke of St. Jermyns, caused a minor sensation on the West End not by virtue of any inherent excellences in its book or music, but by its brazen introduction of the bare shoulders, padded hips, and upswept hairdos of the newly stylish Gibson Girl. Women rushed to copy the fashions much as they had the innovative costumes of the Gaiety musicals. But the foppish Hicks went a step too far, attempting at the same time to persuade men to resume wearing knee breeches and silk stockings for formal occasions.

Hicks had collaborated with Cosmo Hamilton on the libretto, while Charles H. Taylor wrote lyrics to songs by Herbert E. Haines and Evelyn Baker. The British vocal score reveals that at least three other composers— W. C. Powell, Hugh Rumbold, and Theodore Morse—each interpolated a song. Additional interpolations may have been added at any time during the show's long London run, and at least one of these may have been by Kern. After their separate returns to America in the summer of 1905, Frohman and Kern's first order of business was mounting the work for Broadway. Much of the original lackluster score was discarded, to be replaced by songs that may have sounded more suitable for contemporary American audiences but which today sound as undistinguished as the English originals. Songs by Alfred Solman, H. E. Pether, and W. T. Francis were introduced, along with three by Kern. One of these Kern songs, "Won't You Kiss Me Once Before I Go?," had a lyric by Taylor, and so may have been composed while Jerry was still in England and added to the show there. Once again it is a typical period ballad with a long, twenty-five-bar verse and a short, sixteen-bar chorus. The chorus contains just four four-bar phrases, the second and fourth echoing the first and third. Even the harmonies are standard for the time. In this case the slightly pleading tone of the lyric matched the softly lugubrious melody played, in the first phrase, for example, above a progression of basic chords from F to A-seventh to D-minor. "Raining," with words by F. Clifford Harris, is a lighter piece. Although it is written in 4/4, it could easily and successfully have been transformed into a waltz. The chorus utilizes both syncopation and pizzicato to create a proper effect when "the rain comes pitter patter." Kern's third contribution had two titles, "Edna May's Irish Song" and "Molly O'Hallerhan." Kern wrote the lyric himself. The original English version had contained a song called "Molly O'Halloran." Kern paraphrased small sections of both its music and lyric, but essentially came up with an original number tinged with an Irish brogue—including a quotation from "The

Wearing Of The Green." *The Catch of the Season* premiered in New York at Daly's on August 28, 1905.

If Edward Laska's memory did not fail him—and some of his details from that 1955 broadcast are suspect—Frohman missed the chance to have Jerry's first big hit in *The Catch of the Season*. According to Laska, he had been asked by a producer to write a song with a lyric teasing the rage for the word "spoon." Laska went to Harms, where he found Kern, smoking away at a cigar while tinkering at the piano. Laska suggested they collaborate. Kern agreed. (The picture of Jerry puffing on a cigar is a jarring note. Kern smoked cigarettes and, later, pipes, but this is the only mention of his smoking a cigar.) When the song was finished, they hurried to the producer's office, only to be told to wait. Several later arrivals were seen first, which aroused Jerry's ire, and in high dudgeon he dragged Laska to Frohman's office. The producer was out, so his right-hand man, Alf Hayman, agreed to hear the song. The boys sang it, and Hayman applauded the melody. But he had reservations about the lyric. Laska began to say he would revise it when Jerry again pulled him aside, announced that they would make no changes, and stalked off with his increasingly dismayed lyricist to the Shubert headquarters. There Kern demanded to see none other than Lee Shubert, brazenly claiming he and Laska were protégés of Reginald DeKoven. Since the Shuberts had just opened a successful De-Koven show, they were ushered into Lee's suite. Kern and Laska once again played their new song. Shubert grabbed it, assuring the pair it would be inserted into an Eddie Foy vehicle then in rehearsal. That show was another of Seymour Hicks's London musicals, *The Earl and the Girl*.

The American version opened at the Casino on November 4, 1905. Audiences departed singing not Ivan Caryll's original score nor the other American interpolations, but Kern's playful little melody and Laska's appropriate rhymes for "How'd You Like To Spoon With Me?" The song had not been assigned to Foy; rather, Georgia Caine and Victor Morley exchanged offers of cutely worded affection ("How'd you like to . . . call me little tootsy wootsy baby") while chorus girls rocked back and forth on swings. In his *American Popular Song* Alec Wilder downgrades the song for its "doodling slightness." Yet this almost throwaway air seems to be precisely what Kern and Laska set out to achieve. If, apart from its historical importance, the song holds no major interest to musicologists, its gaily tripping syncopations caught a spirit, enchanted audiences, gave Kern his first big success, and, sixty-six years later, proved a show-stopper all over again when it was revived and interpolated into a 1971 London mounting of *Show Boat.*

One discordant note has been sounded here. Long after Kern's death, his cousin Walter Pollak told David Ewen, Kern's earliest biographer, that Jerry did not write the song in 1905 but rather lifted the melody from the score of his high school play.

At Christmas another Kern interpolation was incorporated into a second Shubert show, as with *The Catch of the Season,* one with a Herbert Haines score. Unfortunately no copy has come to light of "The March Of The Toys" from *The Babes and the Baron,* an extravaganza which opened a brief stay at the Lyric on December 25.

Some time soon after *The Babes and the Baron*'s premiere, Kern once more sailed for England. His first task there was to supplement a third Haines score. Hard upon his arrival Hicks brought a stranger to Kern's room, a tall, shy, balding young man whom the Englishman introduced to the American as "Plum" Wodehouse. Pelham Grenville Wodehouse was four years older than Kern. Like Kern he had just begun to call attention to himself with his work—humorous limericks and witty short stories. Hicks was convinced that the two working together could provide the spark Haines's otherwise suitable score lacked.

While Hicks sat listening, Kern played Wodehouse three melodies, at least two of which, "The Frolic Of A Breeze" and "Mr. Chamberlain," already had mediocre lyrics. Both songs had been published and copyrighted in America in July of 1905. Wodehouse accepted the task of revising the existing lyrics and of furnishing the remaining melody with words. The results were apparent when Hicks and Frohman's production of *The Beauty of Bath* opened at the Aldwych on March 19, 1906. The song with the totally new lyric had been discarded during rehearsals; in "The Frolic Of A Breeze," Wodehouse's delightful, infinitely superior lyric had supplanted much of F. Clifford Harris's turgid original; while "Mr. Chamberlain" (in 1905 "Oh, Mr. Chamberlain!") was the charmer of the show. Again, the revised lyric surpassed Harris's original. Neither melody has any real claim to special attention. Contemporary reviews disclose that "Mr. Chamberlain" was awarded some half dozen encores, but its success must have been the result largely of Hicks's rendition of the lyric—whose topical references are mostly meaningless today. The printed score credits the lyric to both Wodehouse and Kern. Kern was a stickler for accurate credits, generously acknowledging assistance when he received it and stubbornly demanding recognition for his share. So at least some of the applause belonged to him.

At *The Beauty of Bath's* rehearsals Kern also met another figure who would work happily with him for many years, the tiny, dapper English director, Edward "Teddy" Royce.

Even at this early date, Kern was beginning to be as much in demand in London as in New York. *The Beauty of Bath* was not the only West End musical he was asked to compose for. Indeed, he contributed the entire score—all of two songs—for a miniature revue that was part of a longer bill which opened at the Empire on April 17, 1906. *Venus, 1906,* was the closing item on the eleven-part program and was enlivened by "Won't You Buy A Little Canoe" and "The Leader Of The Labour Party." Pending discovery of a copy of the latter, we can only wonder if it attempted to balance the scales after "Mr. Chamberlain."

On this same trip Kern seems to have met George Grossmith, Jr., for the first time. Grossmith was a lanky, cadaver-faced heir to an old theatrical tradition. His father had been Gilbert and Sullivan's first patter-song singer. The younger Grossmith, like Hicks, was a jack-of-all-theatrical-trades. A leading high comedian, he was also an author and mounter of musicals. And, like Hicks, he was an almost ridiculously fastidious dresser. Grossmith's *The Spring Chicken* was nearing the end of its year-long run at the Gaiety, but that did not discourage him from collaborating with Kern on a new song for the show. The song, "Rosalie," is a fetching little march, almost Schubertian in its restraint and elegance.

With *The Beauty of Bath* playing to packed houses, Kern resumed his transatlantic shuttle, returning to his parents' Newark home and to Harms's New York office in time to contribute to the rash of fall openings. And a busy fall it was for him! Dreyfus saw to it that no fewer than four incoming attractions—all premiering within a ten-week period—contained Kern entries on their programs. One incentive to Kern may have been an increased interest in Harms, since Tom Harms's outstanding shares had been disposed of after his death on March 29, 1906.

The first of the new season's musicals to offer Kern songs was Charles Frohman's production of Owen Hall and Ivan Caryll's London hit, *The Little Cherub*. It opened at the Criterion Theatre on August 6, 1906, with cocky Hattie Williams as its star. Kern wrote three songs for the show, utilizing three different lyricists. Only one of the three, "Meet Me At Twilight," was deemed strong enough to retain its spot on the musical program throughout the Broadway run and subsequent tour. The less secure pair were "Under The Linden Tree" and "Plain Rustic Ride ('Neath The Silv'ry Moon)." No copy of the latter, which had a lyric by someone identified only as Gounard, seems available. The loss is unfortunate, because the surviving songs, while superficially no more than mere passing pleasantries, with hindsight appear to offer the earliest evidence of Kern asserting his own genius. For the first time careful, knowledgeable listeners can hear distinct hints of what would be called Kern's Princess Theatre style. The chorus of "Under The Linden Tree" (lyric, M. E. Rourke) presages the tempo and manner with which Kern would accommodate the fox-trot rage at the same time as its verse offers foretastes of other Kern techniques. These developments—a more gracefully fluid musical line and quietly modernized harmonies—are at their best in the verse to "Meet Me At Twilight" (lyric, F. Clifford Harris), a verse from beginning to end pure Princess Theatre. Kern sustained this advance for the first five and a half bars of the chorus before lapsing into the tritest of contemporary patterns.

Michael Elder Rourke, Kern's lyricist for "Under The Linden Tree," was born in Manchester, England, on July 14, 1867. Upon coming to America he set himself up as a press agent. Before long he had abandoned his agent's office and had begun to devote full time to lyrics. A burly cigar-chomper, Rourke resembled a Boston ward heeler more than a Tin Pan Alley rhymer. For now obscure motives, about the time of World War I he dropped the name M. E. Rourke and thereafter employed the nom de plume Herbert Reynolds.

By the end of September, Jerry was back in the Shubert camp. The brothers had imported still another English musical, *Lady Madcap*, and, under the title *My Lady's Maid*, presented it at the Casino on September 20, 1906. The show was slight, and Kern's single selection no more substantial. Glimmers of Kern's progressing artistry can be found in the sixteen-bar verse of "All I Want Is You" (lyric, Paul West), but the song's eight-bar chorus looks steadfastly rearwards.

Frohman may have been responsible for introducing Kern to the thin, gawky-eyed, nasal-voiced comedian Richard Carle, another of the musical theatre's multiple-threat men. Not only a star clown, he was often his own writer, composer, lyricist, director, and producer, working closely in this last category with Marc Klaw and Abraham Erlanger, manipulators of the nefarious trust that held a stranglehold on turn-of-the-century theatre. Carle generally portrayed a slightly salacious wiseacre. His brand of humor for some reason rarely pleased New York, so his Broadway runs were customarily short. But the road, especially Chicago, almost always embraced him, and for many years he did in fact make Chicago his base of operations. With his latest offering, Carle bowed to America's unquenchable craving for English goodies and revamped *The Spring Chicken* to Yankee tastes. The show opened at Daly's on October 8, 1906. Brought over from England with the show was the march Kern and Grossmith had written for it.

In one respect Kern's association with his next show, *The Rich Mr. Hoggenheimer*, marked a novel departure. For the first time in his professional career Jerry was adding songs to an American-made musical. Not that the piece was 100 per cent American. One of the 1903–4 season's more profitable attractions had been Frohman and Edwardes's importation of their London success, *The Girl from Kay's*. Much of its popularity in New York and on the road was attributed to the performance of the beloved "Dutch" comedian Sam Bernard as Mr. Hoggenheimer. So applauded was his characterization that Frohman commissioned Harry B. Smith and Ludwig Englander to create a sequel detailing Hoggenheimer's further adventures in America. The result was *The Rich Mr. Hoggenheimer*, which raised the curtain at Wallack's on October 22, 1906.

A secondary result was that for the first time in years the three biggest musical successes on Broadway were all more or less native. In 1906–7 the biggest hit of the season was the latest in the gigantic Hippodrome's mindless spectacles, *Pioneer Days,* followed closely by Victor Herbert's *The Red Mill*, with *Hoggenheimer* a rather distant third. Just how American these shows were is moot. Herbert was an Irish-born, German-trained musician, while Englander was Austrian-born and -trained. Yet from about the very time Jerry made his initial appearance on the theatrical scene other totally native artists had in fact been striving to create a truly native musical. The leader in this field was unquestionably George M. Cohan. But talented black authors were increasingly heard from, and the Russian-born but wholly American-styled Irving Berlin was, like Jerry, looking to interpolate his songs in any Broadway show that would take them. In Chicago, Joe Howard, Will Hough, and Frank Adams were creating a series of musicals as American as the proverbial apple pie.

Kern interpolated no fewer than five songs in *The Rich Mr. Hoggenheimer,* all easy on the ear. "The Bagpipe Serenade," for which Kern served as his own lyricist, carries a copyright date of 1905. It may have been intended for an earlier show or may have been used in a London production. Kern quotes both "The Campbells Are Coming" and "Comin' Thru The Rye" in the piece. Rourke supplied the lyric for "I've A Little Favor," Paul West that for "Don't You Want A Paper, Dearie?", while West and Kern combined to provide the words to "Poker Love" and "A Recipe," the latter added during the post-Broadway tour. All five songs received favorable notice from one critic or another, although some of their attractiveness undoubtedly stemmed from the excellent manner in which they were staged.

Paul West was born in Boston on January 26, 1871. He held a comfortable berth on the New York *World*'s editorial staff. Yet his newspaper chores never prevented his turning out a long list of plays, musical comedy librettos, lyrics, and books.

Kern may have spent the late fall and early winter of 1906–7 in London. Not until the spring was he definitely in the United States, and then his luck began to sour. Extant programs fail to list most of the songs Kern published from 1907 shows, although that does not preclude their brief insertion at some stand for which no playbill survives. And one of the most interesting songs was written for yet another English importation—one which languished a few weeks on the road, then folded before reaching Broadway. In fact, the next two years were to bring an unfair share of frustration, shock, and grief to young Jerry.

A hint of troubles ahead came with the out-of-town failure of *The White Chrysanthemum*, a failure which took with it "I Just Couldn't Do Without You" (lyric, West). What interests Alec Wilder in the song is only its final two-bar tag, which does demonstrate Kern's determination to break away from expected formulas and inventively extend his musical line. When *The White Chrysanthemum* folded, its star, vivacious, five-foot-short Edna Wallace Hopper, began a brief series of stands in Klaw and Erlanger's "advanced vaudeville" houses. Her act not only included "I Just Couldn't Do Without You" but also, at least at Philadelphia's Chestnut Street Opera, the composer himself as her accompanist.

At the same time *The White Chrysanthemum* was faltering, the Shuberts brought Eddie Foy into the Herald Square on April 8 with the Gaiety Theatre hit, *The Orchid*. Kern provided two numbers for the American version, the same "Recipe" sung in *The Rich Mr. Hoggenheimer* and "Come Around On Our Veranda" (lyric, Kern and West), a typical lighthearted waltz of the time, more interesting for its words than for its music. In its lyric the singer invites friends to come around not to spoon or chat, but to listen to the newfangled phonograph—to hear Blanche Ring sing and to play everything "From ragtime by Sousa, To songs by Caruso." Phonographs were the first of the technological devices to change both the nature of theatre music and, more urgently, its method of dissemination, with a concurrent change in composers' sources of income. Before phonographs replaced pianos as common household furnishings, turn-of-the-century sheet music sales reached figures that must leave modern readers incredulous—often in the hundreds of thousands for a popular song and not infrequently surpassing a million copies. One curious result for Kern would be that several of his earliest hits would quickly attain sales that his later, greater songs required decades to match.

A further indication of behind-the-scenes frustrations for the composer could be seen when *Fascinating Flora* premiered at the Casino on May 20, 1907. The musical was only the second on which Kern had worked that was an American original. It had a book by R. H. Burnside and Joseph W. Herbert, and a principal score by the Casino's conductor, Gustave Kerker. Burnside, who is best remembered as the creator of many of the Hippodrome extravaganzas, co-produced the show with a nervous, smiling young man who would loom large in Kern's career, Ray Comstock.

Comstock was born in Buffalo in 1880, and in his early teens he took employment at that city's Star Theatre. With the experience garnered there he moved to New York, accepting a job as assistant ticket seller at the Criterion. *Fascinating Flora* was his earliest production, so he most likely stood aside to allow his more knowledgeable associate to show him the tricks of the trade. But within a year he would be producing Bert Williams's musicals on his own and would ultimately play a crucial part in devising the Princess Theatre shows.

For this tale about an ambitious beauty torn between saving a dull marriage and embarking on an operatic career, Kern composed nearly a dozen songs and published at least five of them, yet programs of the New York run and subsequent tour reveal that only one of these songs was retained from beginning to end, while three others appeared in only one city apiece. The durable number was "The Subway Express" (lyric, James O'Dea), a quietly nimble melody that does anything but catch the propelling roar of a subway train. O'Dea, a sometimes composer, sometimes wordsmith, married a lyricist with whom Kern would often work, Anne Caldwell. New Yorkers also heard "Ballooning" (lyric, West), a song whose style and content ("How'd you like to go ballooning, And spooning, and mooning?")

strongly suggest it hoped to capitalize on the popularity of "How'd You Like To Spoon With Me?". Baltimore apparently heard "The Little Church Around The Corner" (lyric, Rourke), while Rochester listened to "Katy Was A Business Girl" (lyric, West). One published song that appears on no available programs was "Right Now." Interestingly, Kern wrote only the lyric, fitting his rhymes to a melody by Fred Fischer. Kern and Fischer collaborated on several songs in these early years before Fischer embarked on his own publishing career and found himself on the opposite side from his old associate in a landmark law case.

Just over three months later—early in the 1907-8 season—Kern had another sheaf of interpolations gracing the boards. This time they were sung in Charles Frohman's latest English importation, *The Dairymaids*, which opened a New York engagement at the Criterion on August 26, 1907. The musical had originally been done in 1906 in London with a score by Paul Rubens and Frank E. Tours. As with *Fascinating Flora*, the musical numbers on this side of the Atlantic varied from week to week. During *The Dairymaids'* relatively short New York run (86 performances) Kern's contributions ranged from a low of four songs to a high of seven. The Criterion's playbills were undated, so we cannot always be sure whether songs were added or dropped, although extant post-Broadway programs strongly suggest that most of Kern's material was slowly eliminated and that the high mark may have come at the opening. Loss of the songs leaves little to rue, since they are far from distinguished. The seven songs, all with lyrics by Rourke, were "Hay Ride," "I've A Million Reasons Why I Love You," "Never Marry A Girl With Cold Feet!," "Mary McGee," "I'd Like To Meet Your Father," "Cheer Up! Girls," and the finale, which may have merely reprised one or two of the better songs. By the time the show took to the road "Hay Ride," "Cheer Up! Girls," and Kern's finale were gone. The Library of Congress has a copy of a song called "Little Eva," which appears on no program and was apparently printed solely for copyright purposes. Of the published songs, "Never Marry A Girl With Cold Feet!" not only has the most striking title, but is the most interesting musically. The distinguished musicologist Alfred Simon remarked that the song unerringly captures a feeling of ragtime without once resorting to ragtime syncopation.

There is no way of knowing whether Kern met Frank Tours at this time or, if he did, whether it was their first encounter. The two would work together harmoniously for many years. More importantly, *The Dairy-*

maids was the first show for which Kern's leading lady was the petite, round-faced beauty, Julia Sanderson, who was to remain one of his most radiant interpreters.

On October 7, 1907, Kern inserted one song into the new Shubert revue, *The Great White Way,* when it opened at the Casino. "Without The Girl —Inside" (lyric, Kern and Rourke) is essentially another of the pleasant trifles he was churning out at this time, although one can hear in it tantalizing hints of his future Princess Theatre style.

But Kern's path, and that of everyone else associated with the era's musical stages, was dramatically and permanently changed two weeks after the revue premiered. On October 21 Franz Lehar's *The Merry Widow* opened, initiating a rage for anything Viennese and sweeping away forever the dominance of the London musical. The success and influence of *The Merry Widow* were world-wide. In America it was phenomenal. Only *H.M.S. Pinafore, Oklahoma!,* and, possibly, the Princess Theatre shows had, or would have, similarly potent influences. Kern got a quick taste of the show's importance when he learned that a new interpolation in *The Dairymaids,* a song by Vincent Bryan and Ray Goetz, was called "The Man Who Wrote The 'Merry Widow' Waltz."

The rush of Viennese operettas that followed set new standards for song-writing. The lightly jogging English style, a style which often carefully limited its range so that a singer could almost speak the lyrics, gave way to the dashingly florid, arioso waltz rhythms of Middle Europe.

There was no sign of these changes when Kern contributed a bit of minor pseudo-orientalia, "Eastern Moon," to a Frohman straight play, *The Morals of Marcus,* which followed *The Dairymaids* into the Criterion on November 18, 1907.

When Oscar Straus's beautiful operetta *A Waltz Dream* was rushed into the Broadway Theatre on January 27, 1908, to capitalize on the new rage for Viennese musicals, Kern was represented by two interpolations—apparently the only interpolations permitted. The chorus of one of these, appropriately entitled "Vienna," skillfully combined the fading English style with a suggestion of a Middle-European folk dance. But just before Kern began to digest the changes *The Merry Widow* necessitated, grievous personal losses intervened.

4

Family Matters
and a
Continuing Apprenticeship

Kern may have planned another trip to London, but domestic tragedies altered his plans. On December 30, 1907, his mother was rushed to St. Barnabas Hospital in Newark and died there the following night. Her death certificate listed the cause of death as "acute gastric dilatation and peritonitis." However, Kern's daughter recalls that her father told her his mother died after a cancer operation. Kern's memory and the official opinion are not necessarily incompatible, but may merely reflect the points of view of layman and professional. Whatever the explanation of her death, its effect on Kern was marked. He had lost not merely a mother, but a teacher, an advocate, and a friend as well. His career came to an abrupt, if momentary, halt. For the remainder of his life he honored his mother by refusing all invitations to New Year's Eve parties.

In his grief at his mother's death, Kern had an additional burden, for Henry Kern's health had long been failing. Pernicious anemia had sapped his energies, and the blow of Fannie's death further undermined his condition. Henry was forced to retire from the presidency of Wolff's. When hot weather signaled the onset of summer, Henry moved to the Kerns' summer home on Washington Avenue in Spring Lake, New Jersey. But the record-breaking heat proved killing. Henry died of "pernicious anemia and exhaustion" on August 13, 1908. Services were held in Spring Lake the next morning and his body then taken to lie beside Fannie's at Salem Fields.

Henry's obituaries disclose two interesting points. Papers called Henry "one of the incorporators of D. Wolff & Co." Since the house predated the arrival of the Kerns in Newark, the notice could mean one of three things: simply that before Henry's involvement the firm was unincorporated; that Henry had a financial interest in it while he was still on Broad Street in Manhattan; or that the statement is in error. The second point is even more interesting. As the Newark *Evening News* recorded, "Mr. Kern leaves surviving three sons, Jerome D. Kern, the well-known song writer; Edwin and Joseph Kern." That Jerry alone among the Kern boys was singled out for special mention attests to the celebrity attaching to him as early as 1908.

Until this time Jerry had lived at home, but with his parents gone he saw no reason for remaining on Nelson Place. Furthermore, his work lay in New York, and his associates and newfound friends all resided there. After Jerry and his brothers sold the Newark property, Jerry took an apartment at 107 West 68th Street in Manhattan.

With his father's passing both inevitable and imminent, Kern seems to have thrown himself back into his work. Fortunately, Frohman had two new musicals which required interpolations, an English importation, *The Girls of Gottenberg*, and an American-made piece, *Fluffy Ruffles*. Both were winding up their rehearsals and heading for tryout stands when Henry died. *The Girls of Gottenberg* reached the Knickerbocker Theatre on September 2, 1908. The program failed to give proper credits, but it seems a safe assumption in this case that the two songs Kern published were his only contributions actually used. "I Can't Say That You're The Only Girl" (lyric, C. H. Bovill) is commonplace enough, but "Frieda" (lyric, Rourke, although its cover says Joseph Loughry), while not memorably melodic, merits attention. It opens in D major with a long (19 measures), wordless, nervously rocking introduction in 4/4. When the lyric begins the tempo changes to 3/4 for a charming minuet. Midway in this section the key changes to F, and a countermelody is introduced. A final section, after the song has returned to D major, reverts to 4/4 for a pleasing period ballad. Even here, however, Kern was not finished. He once again ends a section by introducing a countermelody. Betty Kern Miller's collection of her father's manuscripts contains a light, Middle-European-style air, "Fraulein Katrina" (lyric, George Grossmith, Jr.), that was seemingly discarded.

If Kern felt peculiarly alone and depressed at this juncture, he was partially solaced by the sight of a dark-haired, hard-eyed, sensuous-mouthed beauty who played one of the principal female leads, Edith Kelly. Slowly or suddenly, Jerry fell in love. Details of this romance are nonexistent, but Jerry's daughter recalls her mother's confirming the account. Jerry squandered a sizable chunk of inheritance escorting his fiancée to the best night spots and shows.

His courtship would have had to be set aside briefly, for *Fluffy Ruffles* arrived five nights later, premiering at the Criterion on September 7, 1908. The musical was adapted by a dependable old hand, John J. McNally, from a popular cartoon series in the New York *Herald*. Fluffy was played by the same cheery brunette whom Kern had worked with in *The Little Cherub*, Hattie Williams. George Grossmith, Jr., was her co-star.

The first page of the program credited only W. T. Francis (listed elsewhere as "General Director of Charles Frohman's Musical Comedy Companies") with the music and Wallace Irwin with the lyrics. Kern and his songs were identified in small print at the back of the playbill. Of course, as a result of Jerry's influence at Harms, the sheet music told a different story, giving Jerry equal billing with Francis. Kern originally had five songs in the work. One, "Meet Her With A Taximeter" (lyric, Bovill), was dropped during the tryout. New York heard "There's Something Rather Odd About Augustus" (lyric, Bovill), "Won't You Let Me Carry Your Parcel?" (lyric, Bovill), "Sweetest Girl, Silly Boy, I Love You" (lyric, Irwin), and "Dining Out" (lyric, Grossmith). "There's Something Rather Odd About Augustus" and "Dining Out" hold scant musical interest. They were patter songs whose lyrics were primary. On the other hand, the refrains of "Meet Her With A Taximeter" and "Won't You Let Me Carry Your Parcel?" both contain ear-catching hints of the graceful Princess Theatre style, while the fifth and sixth bars of the latter disclose some particularly effective harmonic touches. "Sweetest Girl, etc." (called "Reckless Boy, I Love You" on the cover of the sheet music, and merely "I Love You" in the program) was, like "Frieda" in *The Girls of Gottenberg*, musically interesting while not memorable. An extended piece that moved in and out of time changes, it brought the lovers together at the end for a piano lesson. One passage is a Victor Herbert-like waltz. In another part Fluffy plays "Chop Sticks" to Augustus's countersong.

Most critics were unkind to the show, so it soon took to the road. As it traveled, more Kern songs were left behind. The Library of Congress owns a copy of a song called "Aida McCluskie," apparently slated for the show, but never used. A simple tune, it has some rather obvious fun quoting "Celeste Aida." Mrs. Miller has a manuscript of another song, one that was at least orchestrated, but apparently never used. "That's A Thing That's Really Wanted" is a tripping, inconsequential ditty.

Professionally and artistically, at least, 1909 brought no startling changes. Kern continued to do nothing more than interpolate two or three songs into scores written primarily by someone else. Of course, the effects of *The Merry Widow* were apparent. Of the five musicals to which Kern contributed, two were Viennese operettas, two original American endeavors, and only one an example of the British school on which Kern had first practiced his art. That English show came first. *Kitty Grey,* which opened at the New Amsterdam on January 25, 1909, had Julia Sanderson's charm and singing again captivating audiences. Sheet music covers and T. B. Harms's records show that Kern supplied three songs (all with lyrics by Rourke): "If The Girl Wants You," "Just Good Friends," and "Eulalie." No surviving copy of "Eulalie" has surfaced, nor does any *Kitty Grey* program I have seen include it among the musical selections. The remaining pair are attractive, unexceptional melodies.

Two weeks after *Kitty Grey's* premiere, *Havana* opened. Although the show was not graced by any Kern tunes, it nevertheless may have had a marked effect on his life. The darlings of the show were a bevy of comely young girls singing the hit of the evening, "Hello, People." Its popularity was not totally unexpected, since every Leslie Stuart score written after his "Tell Me, Pretty Maiden" became the show-stopper of *Florodora,* contained a similar song, generally performed as a sextette, although on occasion enlarged to an octette. One of those comely young girls helping to put across the number was Edith Kelly. All the young ladies of the famous *Florodora* sextette were purported to have married millionaires. Inevitably, the papers began to keep track of the romantic leanings of *Havana's* girls. But when Edith Kelly was mentioned her name was never linked with Kern's, but rather with that of Frank Gould, heir to the Gould fortune. Both Gould and Miss Kelly stubbornly denied any attachment. And just as stubbornly the papers continued to report a flourishing romance. Kern undoubtedly read the stories and drew his own conclusions, unless, of course, Edith had already made him privy to her secrets. Whether he was particularly anxious to put himself three thousand miles away from an awkward situation, or, as is just as likely, Kern hoped for more work on the West

End, the composer sailed for England in the spring or early summer. He found little more to do there than he had in New York. Yet enforced idleness may have been a disguised blessing. To pass a few empty days, Kern joined with two young theatrical friends, Lauri de Frece and Tom Reynolds, to boat down the Thames. Their objective was a small island favored by campers just above the village of Walton-on-Thames.

In 1909 Walton was a quiet, attractive little spot frequented by weekenders from London. It could be reached in half an hour by rail or several pleasant hours by water. Besides the river and camping areas, the village offered a number of fine small hotels and pubs. One of the most popular pubs and hotels was The Swan. Situated on Manor Road just above the river, it was constructed of brick and half timber, with a tiled roof and a small spire at its east end. The first floor had the various rooms common to all English pubs, while the second floor contained rentable bedrooms. But in Kern's time a second, slightly larger building, mostly wooden, ran from the back of the pub down the slope to the river. It seems to have offered additional rooms as well as space for storing boats. The pub and hotel were owned by Young and Co.'s brewery, which from 1907 to 1916 granted the tenancy to one A. A. Moore. No one in Walton remembers Mr. Moore. Conceivably his appearances there were rare. But they do recall the family Moore selected to manage the property. George Draper Leale was remembered as a jovial man with a military bearing despite his portliness. One lifelong resident, Miss Emily "Birdie" Higgins, described him as "the stout publican type," adding that occasionally "he tried to swank and people didn't like that." Still, when many villagers referred to him as "Lord Leale," they did so affectionately. His wife, Elizabeth Jane (née Hayward), was a small, reserved woman, universally respected. The Leales had three children. The eldest was Eva, a daughter much like her mother in build and manner, who had been born on June 16, 1891, at 98 Cornwall Road in Lambeth in the Waterloo sub-district of London.* At the time her father gave his occupation as "Beer Retailer (Master)," a designation James O. Young of Young and Co. insists he otherwise has never heard of. Two more children followed, Ethel and Albert.

Kern, de Frece, and Reynolds were apparently not prepared to spend all

---

* Mrs. Betty Kern Miller disputes the evidence of her mother's birth certificate, stating that her mother always celebrated her birthday on June 17 and that she was born at Farringdon Street. To corroborate this she offers the fact that several characters, especially in *Oh, Lady! Lady!!*, were named Farringdon in discreet bows to Eva.

their time on the island. Their plans included a visit with James Blakely, an actor friend who lived near by, and a visit to some pubs. Fortune took them to The Swan, where Eva was helping her parents. Whether, as legend has it, Kern fell in love at first sight is uncertain. But Eva Leale Kern, looking back after thirty-two years of marriage, recalled that the boys lingered for six hours, and that as they were leaving Jerry confided he wanted to marry her. At the time she accepted the confidence as a flattering sally. Jerry made several return trips to Walton, melting Eva's reserve with his superb piano-playing. "I had never heard such piano-playing in my life," she afterwards recalled, "and as he played I would float off into another world." Jerry was especially flattered at Eva's fondness for "How'd You Like To Spoon With Me?" and amused at her refusal to believe he wrote it. After he showed her the sheet music with his name printed boldly on the cover, her esteem grew by leaps and bounds. Some weeks later she received a telegram. "Leaving for New York tomorrow. Will see you next year. Love, Jerry." The telegram was the first she had ever received and made a deep impression, but even more touching was Jerry's acknowledgment of his love for her. Before he sailed, however, Jerry had worked on interpolations for another Viennese operetta, Leo Fall's *The Dollar Princess*. For England he wrote two songs: "A Boat Sails On Wednesday" (lyric, Adrian Ross and George Grossmith, Jr.) and "Red, White And Blue" (lyric, Ross). For the American production he wrote a third song, "Not Here! Not Here!" (lyric, Rourke).

Some idea of the excellence and efficiency of Frohman's producing organization can be gauged by the fact that it mounted the New York and London productions almost simultaneously. New York cheered the piece on September 6, 1909, at the Knickerbocker, London on September 25 at Daly's. In New York it competed with Oscar Straus's *The Chocolate Soldier* for honors as the runaway hit of the season (excepting the *sui generis* Hippodrome spectacle). Only the boat song appears in any of the programs. Its retention and durability in the show are surprising, since it is not an especially good song. "Not Here! Not Here!" is far more fascinating. A warm, caressing melody that somehow Kern was unable to put together effectively, it was stored away for future use. When he unpacked and revised it five years later, his growing artistry allowed him to turn it into one of his loveliest tunes, "The Land Of 'Let's Pretend.'"

Actually, New Yorkers had heard one other Kern song several months earlier when Henry Savage introduced Emmerich Kalman to American audiences. Kalman's *Ein Herbstmanoever* was presented as *The Gay Hussars* on July 29, 1909, at the Knickerbocker. New Yorkers were unreceptive to the Viennese master's early work. Failing with it was Kern's "Shine Out, All You Little Stars," another of the handful of published Kern material seemingly unrecoverable. If Kern was present for rehearsals, which appears doubtful, he probably had his first major encounters with Savage, a man with whom he would often work in later years.

Two nights after *The Dollar Princess* opened in London, the German dialect comedian, Sam Bernard, and the lovely singer with the famous back, Kitty Gordon, helped give Broadway a modest hit with *The Girl and the Wizard*. Kern helped, too. He added three of his melodies to a hodgepodge of a score the Shuberts had culled from works by no fewer than seven composers, including Louis Hirsch and Irving Berlin. All three of Kern's pieces had lyrics by the performer-writer Percival Knight. The best was probably "Frantzi," an engagingly cheerful, folk-dance-like melody that Kern nevertheless marked to be played slowly. Less interesting musically were "By The Blue Lagoon" and "Suzette And Her Pet," the latter published with the cryptic footnote, "Mr. Kern is indebted to M. George Krier for part of This Melody." Kern's songs, and possibly the whole score, were orchestrated by a now forgotten figure, G. C. M. Selling.

No sooner had *The Girl and the Wizard* settled in for a run at the Casino than the Shuberts again called on Kern, this time to help rescue a faltering production. The brothers had produced a new musical entitled *The Girl from the States*. Burdened with a trite story and bloodless songs by Glen MacDonough, A. Baldwin Sloane, and Raymond Hubbell, the entertainment had scarcely begun its tryout when its star, Lulu Glaser, walked out, forcing the show to close. Unwilling to waste their new scenery and costumes, the Shuberts called in Joseph Herbert to revise the libretto and hired Edward Madden to set lyrics to new melodies by Melville Gideon, Louis Hirsch, and Kern. Only a single number from the original score was retained. Beautiful, statuesque Louise Dresser was signed on to star. In less than a week the new package was unveiled at Washington's Belasco Theatre on October 26, 1909, as *The Golden Widow*.

The story both versions told was more typical period fluff. To escape a marriage her uncle and guardian is determined to impose upon her, the heroine runs away and assumes a fictitious name. At a railroad station in the imaginary principality of Berenna she falls in love at first sight with a dashing young man. In return, the young fan falls hopelessly in love with her. When the young man is shown to be the very groom her uncle planned for his niece the curtain can fall on general rejoicing.

Most likely in the impelling rush to put forward the "new" piece, little, if anything, was written specifically for it. All three composers no doubt scurried to their trunks for melodies that would not clash embarrassingly with the story's ins and outs. Indeed, the ensuing confusion was such that the Belasco Theatre's program reflected the fluster. Along with the credits and details of *The Golden Widow*, it listed among the coming attractions for the house none other than Lulu Glaser in *The Girl from the States*. The program failed to acknowledge who composed which particular songs. Only one minor number was published with Kern's name, "Howdy, How Do You Do" (lyric, Rourke). No reviewer seems to have mentioned it in his notice. The cover of the song's sheet music lists a second song almost certainly by Kern, "I Want You To See My Girl," but if it was actually issued, no copies have been found.

Washington's critics were only mildly diverted by the evening. Most of what praise they could dispense was awarded to Miss Dresser and her associates, notably three funmakers: Alexander Clark, Jobyna Howland, and the English favorite, Connie Ediss. From the capital the musical meandered desultorily westward, paying brief visits to such cities as Cincinnati and Cleveland before the Shuberts despaired of turning it into anything worthwhile.

Meanwhile, Joseph Herbert and Kern were rehearsing yet another Shubert show together. Herbert was directing, and Kern, as was to be expected, was interpolating new songs. Bucking the still fresh fad for Viennese operettas, the Shuberts had decided to import a 1908 London hit, *The King of Cadonia*. Sidney Jones had composed its original score; Adrian Ross its lyrics; and Frederick Lonsdale, not yet famous for his comedies, the libretto. Kern's share of the revised score was so large that the Shuberts granted him equal billing with the British writers. In unspoken tribute to Kern's growing artistry and fame, no one else was permitted to add new songs. Kern returned the courtesy by providing a selection of interesting melodies. The effort was in vain. Following an extended, troubled tryout, *The King of Cadonia* opened at Daly's on January 10, 1910. Greeted by generally disparaging notices, the show closed after a mere two weeks.

Harms's sheet music lists eight songs by Kern, although one of these, "Hippopotamus," appears on no extant programs, either for various tryout towns or for the New York run. Nor have any copies apparently survived.

Quite possibly the song was dropped while the show was in rehearsal, but too late to omit it from listings on song covers. Of the remaining pieces, "Mother And Father" (lyric, Rourke) is the least interesting, a pleasantly tripping, typical pre-World War I show tune. (The song, which most programs called "Father And Mother," begins much like the popular song of that same war, "Pack Up Your Troubles In Your Old Kit Bag.") The melodies for both the verse and chorus of "Come Along Pretty Girl" (lyric, Rourke) are especially inane and may possibly have been derived from some obscure folk dance. Nevertheless, by careful modulation of both tempos and harmonies Kern managed to imbue the chorus with his unique musical charm. The delightful ragtime verse of "Every Girl I Meet" (lyric, Percival Knight) may have provided Kern with the inspiration for the verse of a song he would write the following year, while the studied pacing of the chorus again gives real interest to an unexceptional melody. "The Blue Bulgarian Band" (lyric, Rourke) is an exhilarating march. Another lively dance, "Lena, Lena," employs a variation of its verse as part of its chorus, and, just possibly, may have provided Kern with the basic inspiration for "Drift With Me" years later. Buried in Mrs. Miller's manuscript orchestration for "Every Girl I Meet" is a handwritten piano part for a song called both "It's Always Been The Same Way" and "Oo-Oo" (lyric, Paul West). The nature of the lyric suggests that "Oo-Oo" could readily have been changed to "Coo-oo," and, if that be so, then "Coo-oo" is the sort of gay little thing that calls for a piccolo accompaniment. And Kern requested precisely that. Far and away the best number in the score is "Catamarang" (lyric, Knight). A romantic, pentatonic verse quietly evolves into a hauntingly longing chorus. It was too good a melody to waste, so Kern put the piece on the shelf for ten years until he was able to reuse the chorus as the title song for *Sally*. The surviving manuscripts for Kern's *King of Cadonia* music provide the earliest record of the composer's association with the great orchestrator who would handle all his major work for over a decade, Frank Saddler.

One consolation that must have gone a long way toward mitigating the pains of frustration and failure was Jerry's correspondence with Eva Leale, a correspondence not without amusing frustrations of its own. Eva's father insisted on opening her mail as well as reading her replies. But the resourceful young lady quickly found a way to slip in extra little notes before her letters were posted. These private asides had an immediate effect. By his third letter Jerry formally asked Mr. Leale for his daughter's hand in marriage.

Anxious as he must have been to return to England, Kern nonetheless had business to attend to first. Two August entries included his songs. The earlier arrival was *The Echo*, which opened at the Globe Theatre on August 17, 1910. It was a failure, but an interesting one. Meant to represent Deems Taylor's maiden effort as a Broadway composer, the show had been tried out first in 1909 and hastily removed for repairs. Revived in the spring of 1910, it proved still unready for New York's inspection. Yet its producer had sufficient faith to persist, even if much, possibly most, of Taylor's score fell by the wayside in the process. At least eight composers were called in to embellish the score. Kern's contribution was a single song, "Whistle When You're Lonely." Although by stretching a point one can hear a hint of "Ol' Man River" in the last four measures of the verse, the song was really no more than another of the many minor pleasantries Kern was turning out in that period. Just when the song was added and how long it remained in the production may never be determined. All extant programs fail to list musical numbers.

Yet however short and tenuous was Kern's connection with *The Echo*, the show marked his first professional association with the great producer who would mount more of his musicals than any other Broadway manager, Charles Dillingham. If Florenz Ziegfeld, Jr., had a more glamorous reputation—and deservedly so—Dillingham clung to the equally well-merited reputation of being the most gentlemanly of Broadway's major producers. He was distinguished in appearance and impeccable in his dress, his derbies becoming virtually a trademark. Dillingham was a Connecticut Yankee, born in 1868. The son of an Episcopal clergyman, he rejected his father's pleas that he attend college and instead selected a career in journalism. A stint as drama critic of the New York *Evening Sun* persuaded him his real love was the theatre. To prepare himself properly he spent several years as Charles Frohman's press agent and production assistant.

Twelve nights after the premiere of *The Echo*, *Our Miss Gibbs* opened at the Knickerbocker on August 29, 1910. The musical was Charles Frohman's latest importation, another London hit centering on another of the West End's beloved shop girls. The original London score had been by Lionel Monckton and Ivan Caryll. Kern's contribution to the American production was relatively slight, both in quantity and quality. The precise quantity is in some doubt, but was most likely a mere three songs. And for one of these Kern wrote only the lyric. Harry Marlowe created the music for "Come Tiny Goldfish To Me." Kern's lyric is ordinary enough, moving from some colloquial contractions ("I wonder if you're list'ning") to standard literary clichés ("Oh! hearken to my plea"). Kern's melody for "Eight Little Girls" (lyric, Rourke) was a daintily mincing period tune. Unfortunately, no copy of "I Don't Want You To Be A Sister To Me" (lyric, Frederick Day) has come to light. The song was dropped for the post-Broadway tour. Extant manuscripts disclose that "Betty's Advice" was a minor, concerted piece. Kern received no credit on the playbills for his effort.

By October young Jerry was in England, apparently staying with the Leales at The Swan, which he gave as his residence when signing the church register. On Tuesday, October 25, 1910, Jerry, Eva, the rest of her family, and their friends traveled the short distance from The Swan to old St. Mary's Parish church, where the vicar, W. Kemp Bussell, married the youngsters "according to the rites and ceremonies of the Established Church." Ethel was her sister's maid of honor; Lauri de Frece, Jerry's best man.

In conducting interviews with old friends and acquaintances of Eva and Jerry Kern, I found constant amazement that the marriage of two such very disparate people could work so well. Jerry was an American, a city boy, impish, mercurial, given to staying up all hours and sleeping till noon. Eva was English, city-born but village-bred, retiring, submissive, and steady. Yet virtually everyone who expressed amazement at the marriage agreed it was one of the happiest, most perfect they knew. For here was an instance where superficial opposites were clearly complementary. Furthermore, those who were able to get to know Eva realized she had a native intelligence, warmth, and a wit to match her husband's. In heeled shoes she appeared about an inch taller than Jerry's five foot six inches. She had a sweet face, a high forehead, and heavy-lidded eyes that brightened noticeably at Jerry's bantering. They took on a special glow at the prospect of seeing America. In time, Eva became as ardent an American as Jerry was an Anglophile.

The Broadway that Jerry and Eva returned to was still dominated by Viennese operettas, even if changes were in the wind. Significantly, while all three of the season's major lyric hits attested to the Continent's sway and offered music by foreign-born composers, all three were American-made and their composers adopted sons. Karl Hoschna's *Madame Sherry*, Ivan Caryll's *The Pink Lady*, and Victor Herbert's *Naughty Marietta* together suggested that America was quietly and irresistibly stamping its own imprint on Viennese styles.

If neither nature nor temperament allowed Kern to subscribe wholeheartedly to Middle-European manners, his background and inclination saw to it that his unique, developing signature was in no way inimical. Indeed, a few more enlightened critics, especially Alan Dale, continued to boost him, seeing correctly that he represented the best and most logical talent to provide a smooth transition from foreign to domestic influences. Producers increasingly understood that he could supply prompt melodic lifts to flatulent scores. Of course, as a married man with additional financial responsibilities, Kern was doubly eager for employment. In 1911 he assisted on six shows, in one instance providing the lion's share of the music for a major new American mounting.

Lew Fields called on him first, but only to add a single song to *The Hen-Pecks,* which opened at the Broadway on February 4, 1911. In an era when verses were important and often longer than choruses, "The Manicure Girl" (lyric, Frederick Day) heard Kern creating an inventive start for a less imaginative finish. The chorus is little more than a series of closely knit eighth notes. Nonetheless, like "Never Marry A Girl With Cold Feet!" from *The Dairymaids,* the song captures a ragtime lilt without ever resorting to syncopation.

Kern's biggest opportunity since *Mr. Wix of Wickham* followed. To open a new auditorium they planned as their flagship, the Shuberts assembled a gala, if somewhat pretentious, triple bill that was to include a ballet, a one-act opera, and a standard revue. Kern was signed to collaborate with Frank Tours on a score for the revue, to be called *La Belle Paree.* The new house was to be called the Winter Garden. Inevitably, postponements occurred. Not until March 20, 1911, were the show and the house finally ready for public inspection. *La Belle Paree* was the closing attraction on the bill. More so than most musicals, even in a day when musicals were subject to frequent changes, the program for the entertainment was revised week by week. The opening week program read, in part:

"La Belle Paree"

A Jumble of Jollity in Two Acts and Eleven Scenes by Edgar Smith. Lyrics by Edward Madden. Music by Jerome Kern and Frank Tours. Scenery by Arthur Voegtlin. Under the stage direction of J. C. Huffman and William J. Wilson. Costumes designed under the direction of Melville Ellis. Musical numbers under the direction of Wm. J. Wilson.

PART ONE

1. Opening Chorus . . . . *Guides and Tourists*
2. Song, "Susan Brown from a Country Town" . . *Susan Brown [Ray Cox]*
3. "The Human Brush" . . *Toots [Florence Tempest] and Artists*
4. Song, "Widows" . . *Mme. Clarice [Jean Aylwin] and Chorus*
5. Duet, "Paris is a Paradise for Coons" . . *Eczema and Sparkler*
6. "The Pretty Milliners" . . . . *Chorus*
7. Song, "Monte Carlo Moon" . . . . *Lady Guff Jordon*
8. Song, "That Deviling Tune" . . . . *Eczema*
9. Duet, "Teasing" . . . . . . *Toots and Susie [Marian Sunshine]*
10. Two-Step, "Bosphorus" . . . . *Chorus*
11. "The Edinburgh Wriggle" . . . . . . *Mme. Clarice and Chorus*
12. Russian Dance . . . . *Misses Hess and Chorus*
13. Song and March . . . . *Fifi and Chorus*

PART TWO

1. Violin Specialty by . . . . *Yvette*
2. Dance by . . . . *Mlle. Dazie*
3. Song, "Trovatore" . . . . *La Duchesse*
4. Specialty by . . . . *Sparkler*
5. Duet, "Goblins" . . . . *Tempest and Sunshine*
6. Song, "What Kind of a Place Is This?" . . . . *Eczema*
7. "The Duel" . . . . . *Mlle. Dazie, Grace Washburn and Chorus*
   INTERMISSION OF FIVE MINUTES
8. The Ballet of Pierrots and Harlequins
   [There was no number 9]
10. Finale . . . . *Ensemble*

A cast of characters and descriptions of those characters underscored the practice of older revues to tie their specialties together with a paper-thin plot, a practice retained well into the 1920s. *La Belle Paree* employed one of the oldest, most threadbare of stories, the city tour. Of course, in this case the city was Paris and the principal tourist ostensibly the Widow McShane. In sturdy burlesque fashion, the widow was portrayed by a man in drag. Bits and snatches of dialogue revealed that the rich widow was pursued by several ambitious young men. Her maid, Eczema (Stella Mayhew), and Eczema's self-assured boyfriend, Erastus Sparkler (Al Jolson), helped and hindered the romances as they saw fit.

64

Yet Arthur Cunningham, the man who clowned as the widow, was relatively insignificant in the theatrical line-up the Shuberts presented. Most 1911 theatregoers would have felt Kitty Gordon (as Lady Guff Jordon, a society modiste) was the major attraction with, perhaps, Miss Mayhew and Dorothy Jardon (who played "La Duchesse," Queen of Paris' "Bohemia") as runners-up. Barney Bernard (as Isadore Cohen, of Bridgeport, U.S.A.) and Lee Harrison (who portrayed Ike Skinheimer, a piker in the marts of trade) were also popular. Two names that meant little to most American legitimate playgoers were making their major debuts. The Shuberts had caught Mizzi Hajos (here in the character of Fifi Montemarte) either in her brief appearance in a summer roof garden production or in vaudeville. She was a tiny, Hungarian-born singer and dancer who had made a name for herself as a child star in Budapest and Vienna. In 1911 she was twenty years old. She would soon change the spelling of her first name to Mitzi and ultimately, dropping her patronymic, use it as her sole stage name.

Al Jolson had begun to call attention to himself in vaudeville and with Dockstader's minstrels. Jolson would quickly rise to become Broadway's greatest attraction, although he and Kern were never to work together professionally again. Yet it was in a Kern song that New York playgoers first heard the jazz singer croon. That song was "Paris Is A Paridise for Coons" (lyric, Edward Madden). Whether the misspelling of "Paridise," was an attempt at humor or simply an error cannot be determined with certainty. Since the word was spelled correctly in the lyric, the title's spelling was most probably a typographical error.

Although Kern undoubtedly appreciated that the new house would be the center of attraction, he nonetheless missed a notable chance to call attention to himself. His music for the new revue was far from his best. Nervousness may have prevented Jolson from making an opening night showstopper of "Paris Is A Paridise For Coons." Yet it was the best of the material Kern had submitted—or at least that the Shuberts had accepted. A delicious ragtime number, its verse may have been derived from *The King of Cadonia*'s "Every Girl I Meet." The chorus is original and zesty. When Jolson (and Mayhew) failed to propel it into the bestseller category, Kern stashed it away to reuse later. A similar, less fully realized piece was "De Goblin's Glide" (lyric, Frederick Day). Kern marked the song "Tempo di Rag." "The Edinboro Wriggle" (lyric, Rourke) opened with a vamp that echoed Scottish bagpipe music but quickly turned into something of a fox-trot, even though the lyric proclaimed the wriggle would be the new dance craze. "Sing Trovatore" (lyric, Madden) had sly fun with operatic bombast. "I'm The Human Brush (That Paints The Crimson On Paree)" (lyric, Madden) is of interest only because its chorus is a variation of its verse. Otherwise it is one of the dreariest pieces Kern ever released. Two songs were added later: a minor comic number, "That's All Right For McGilligan" (lyric, Rourke) and a pert love song, "Look Me Over Dearie" (lyric, Madden).

One point deserves discussion here. In Part I a two-step called "Bosphorus" was followed directly by "The Edinboro Wriggle." The pairing presaged the great dance craze that was about to explode across America. 1911 was the year of Irving Berlin's "Alexander's Ragtime Band." Its feverish popularity momentarily resuscitated the moribund ragtime rage, but more urgently sent young couples scurrying across the nation's dance floors. Two months after *La Belle Paree* premiered, Irene and Vernon Castle were married. They spent the summer performing in Paris, but, when they returned in the fall, their easy, elegant grace ignited the real spark for the phenomenal vogue of ballroom dancing. One-steps, two-steps, fox-trots, turkey-trots, and an assortment of oddly named dances swept the nation within a year. The rage affected not only social behavior but determined to no small extent the style of much show music in ensuing seasons. Kern had a feeling for this sort of music and readily secured a place for himself in the vanguard of dance melodists.

As for *La Belle Paree*, it played on merrily until the hot weather, recessed, and then had a brief road tour in the fall. A fortnight after the Winter Garden opening two Kern songs were heard in Nora Bayes's new vehicle, *Little Miss Fix-It,* which opened at the Globe on April 3, 1911. Even at this early date the first stirrings of the dance craze were evident. In conjunction with Dave Stamper, Kern contrived a melodically innocuous "Turkey-Trot." Like a classic waltz, the song was in several parts, each with a distinctive, but not distinguished, melody. The first theme returned in classic pattern at the end. Equally undistinguished was the Kern ditty for which Miss Bayes's husband, Jack Norworth, wrote the lyric, "There Is A Happy Land (Tale Of Woe)."

About this time Eva received an early lesson in how Jerry's absorption in his music could play havoc with her careful schedules. She had longed to see one of the great American circuses she had read about in England, and Jerry dutifully secured tickets. But shortly before they were about to leave their apartment for the circus an idea struck Jerry. He sat down at the piano to work it out. Eva's glances and hints were unavailing. The circus performance was long over by the time Jerry was satisfied. Eva quietly determined to be more forceful thereafter.

Shortly after *Little Miss Fix-It* opened, Florenz Ziegfeld put his annual *Follies* into rehearsal. Since one Kern tune was in the production, the show may represent the first professional association of these two theatrical giants. But it remains equally probable that any meeting, if one did occur, was casual and short. The lyric for "I'm A Crazy Daffydill" was by the young lady who sang it in the show, Bessie McCoy Davis. She may well have had the song written to order and brought it with her as part of her specialty routines. It was a trite, silly little piece, but undoubtedly just right for a performer who had often catered to the childlike instincts of her audience.

In the late summer—technically, at the beginning of the 1911–12 season —Kern supplied the Shuberts and Charles Frohman with songs for their latest Viennese importations. First to arrive was *The Siren,* opening at the Knickerbocker Theatre on August 28. Its star was Donald Brian, the dimpled, curly-haired performer who had been America's first Danilo in *The Merry Widow* and who would be on stage to share several of Kern's triumphs and failures. Brian's leading lady was Julia Sanderson. Programs credited only Leo Fall with the music, mentioning neither Kern nor Howard Talbot, who contributed a voguish two-step. Some uncertainty attaches to Kern's material for the show. American sheet music lists Kern as a collaborator with Worton David and George Arthurs for "I Want To Sing In Opera," but when the song was published a year earlier in England only David and Arthurs were credited. Kern seems to have done no more than make some minor changes in the lyric and melody of the verse. Covers of Harms's added songs also list a number called "Confidential Source," but the song was apparently never actually published and may never even have been performed. For "Follow Me Round" Kern merely revised Adrian Ross's English lyric to Fall's melody. That leaves just one or two songs as Kern's real contribution. "My Heart I Cannot Give You" (lyric, Matthew Woodward) is a lovely barcarolle. The same melody may have been used to a new lyric by Rourke and called either "In The Valley Of Montbijou" or "Maid Of Montbijou." Woodward's lyric spoke of Montbijou, while some sheet music covers superimposed "Maid Of Montbijou" over "My Heart I Cannot Give You." Since "My Heart I Cannot Give You" was assigned to a character called Lolotte in the sheet music and "In The Valley Of Montbijou" was assigned to her on programs, there is further reason to suspect the songs may be one and the same. "You're Just A Perfect Peach Beyond My Reach" exists in manuscript, but was probably never used. Its pleasant verse gives way to a difficult, singularly unattractive chorus.

Jerry and Eva probably had an especially happy time between rehearsals of *The Siren,* for Frohman had brought over Tom Reynolds to direct the production. Although Reynolds's name was tucked away in the rear of the program, Harms's sheet music featured it prominently on its covers, a move Jerry may have suggested in gratitude for the boatride that had first taken him to Walton-on-Thames.

Kern's share of the American score for *The Kiss Waltz* was more substantial and less arguable than his efforts on behalf of *The Siren.* Actually, Carl Ziehrer's operetta had been on American stages for some while, having been initially offered to New Haven the preceding May. Its reception had been cool, but not totally unpromising, so the Shuberts spent the summer whipping it into shape. Kern was called in for five songs and Louis Hirsch for two. Kern's collaborator on *La Belle Paree,* Frank Tours, conducted. The show reached the Casino on September 18, 1911.

Words were put to all of Kern's songs by Matthew Woodward, but his lyrics, like most of Kern's melodies, were indifferent. Most of the songs were meant to be duets or chorus numbers in which one or more voices sometimes sang simple countermelodies. "Ta, Ta, Little Girl," "There's A Resting Place For Every Girl," and "Love's Charming Art" can all be dismissed as lightweight. "Love Is Like A Little Rubber Band (Hoop Song)" is somewhat catchier. But "Fan Me With A Movement Slow" is a forgotten gem. Admittedly a period piece, its melody, tempo, and lyric seem to have been intentionally patterned after *Madame Sherry's* "Every Little Movement." Kern's tune had no cause to bow deeply before Hoschna's famous melody, but Woodward lacked Otto Harbach's skill with words, offering ungainly lines such as "Needless now for me my love to utter."

Broadway seems to have heard from Kern only once during the 1911–12 season after *The Kiss Waltz,* and even then we cannot be certain exactly what playgoers heard. On February 12, 1912, Marie Cahill and her husband brought the Viennese operetta, *The Opera Ball,* to the Liberty Theatre. Kern received no credit on playbills or in pre-opening publicity, but when piano selections were published in America, he was given equal billing with the original composer, Richard Heuberger. A comparison of these American selections with the German vocal score shows three songs not in the Continental version: two drill-like numbers, "Sergeant Philip Of

The Dancers" and "Nurses Are We," and the dulcet "Marie-Louise." All three exhibit traits that might well point to them as Kern's. But none of these songs is listed in extant programs.

When Kern songs did begin to reappear in the spring, they marked the beginning of a brief, new, and significant period. In a sense Kern till now had been progressing slowly but unobtrusively. The years 1912, 1913, and 1914 witnessed the first pronounced stirrings that led to 1915's major breakthrough. Actually, his spring offering was a lone song for Ziegfeld's *A Winsome Widow,* produced at the Moulin Rouge on April 11. Sheet music credits indicate that "Call Me Flo" was a totally collaborative effort, with Kern and John Golden working hand in hand on music and lyric alike. Two heads were not better than one, and the result was merely a pleasing if nondescript ditty. Its moment in the spotlight must have been brief indeed, since no available surviving program lists it among the songs.

Apart from this isolated offering no further Kern songs were heard until August. The show that broke the drought was *The Girl from Montmartre,* which opened at the Criterion Theatre on August 5, 1912. The musical was an Americanization of *Das Madel von Montmartre,* Rudolph Schanzer and Henry Bereny's musicalization of Georges Feydeau's 1899 hit, *La Dame de Chez Maxim's.* The small coterie of entrepreneurs and artists responsible for the era's better musicals meant that each new mounting was something of a reunion. The new show was no exception. Frohman was once again the producer, Hattie Williams and Richard Carle were starred, Tom Reynolds was directing, while a host of lesser performers and backstage figures were all by now more than nodding acquaintances to Kern. So was Harry B. Smith, who had adapted *The Siren* and who, with his brother Robert, had been assigned the task of translating and adapting the German original.

Despite his long and seemingly friendly association with Frohman, Kern still received no credit on Frohman's programs. Naturally, most critics accepted the playbill at face value, so Kern received no mention either in most reviews. Of the fifteen musical numbers (not including finales) Kern composed at least six, possibly eight. One song, "Half Past Two," was lifted from the English musical, *The Arcadians.* Bereny, then, composed no better than half of the American score, although he was given credit for everything.

Kern's six known songs were "Ooo, Ooo, Lena!" (another collaboration with John Golden), "I've Taken Such A Fancy To You" (lyric, Clifford Harris), "I'll Be Waiting 'Neath Your Window" (a collaboration with

James Duffy), "Hoop-la-la, Papa!" (lyric, Rourke), "Bohemia" and "Don't Turn My Picture To The Wall" (lyrics, Robert B. Smith). The first two hold little interest. Nor was "I'll Be Waiting 'Neath Your Window" noteworthy, although it was a particularly agreeable ballad. "Hoop-la-la, Papa!" is a lively, polka-like air that Alfred Simon believes may have been borrowed in part from a Bohemian folk song. Appropriately, "Bohemia" also suggests folk influences, especially at the end of its verse. The show's most delightful number was "Don't Turn My Picture To The Wall." Like "Fan Me With A Movement Slow," it is too much of its era to enjoy a general revival, but remains a cameo gem. Its glittering waltz verse gives way to a varsovienne-like chorus of exceptional charm. Harms's sheet music for the interpolations lists two other songs, "Oh, Doctor" and "Something Like This." Unfortunately, old catalogues fail to make clear whether Kern was in fact their composer.

By a fortunate chance, Harry B. Smith's contract for *The Girl from Montmartre* has been preserved, and is interesting for what it tells of the era's theatrical finances. The 1912 season was almost the end of a fifty-year period in which Broadway's top ticket had remained steady at $1.50 to $2.00, when $10,000 to $15,000 was a capacity gross for all but the Hippodrome spectacles, and when most shows could recoup their investments after four to eight weeks at capacity. Even making allowances for such low prices, the figures in the contract are strikingly small. The contract was signed by both Harry and his brother on March 4, although they previously must have been working under some sort of gentlemanly agreement, since they were called on to deliver their translation and adaptation six days later, on March 10. The brothers were to receive a flat $100 a week for every full week each company of the show played; incompleted weeks were to be prorated. If Frohman demanded further changes at any time, they were to be made free of charge. A $500 advance would be deducted from the first five weeks' royalties. Considering that the Smith brothers were major theatrical luminaries, one can only guess at how little Kern received. Of course, a number of shows to which he contributed were playing across the country, so royalties did become cumulative. Moreover, Kern shared in substantial royalties from sheet music sales. On the other hand, in these pre-ASCAP days, royalties from other sources were virtually nonexistent.

Even before *The Girl from Montmartre* premiered Kern was busy at work on his interpolations for another importation. The producers were two great Broadway figures with whom Kern had not worked until now,

George M. Cohan and Sam Harris. Cohan was reported to be delighted with Kern, hailing him as a future great. But these reports came long after the show had closed and been forgotten. Several of the new songs Kern contributed to the Cohan-Harris mounting were moving worlds away from material Cohan could be comfortable with.

For a week before *The Polish Wedding* opened at Syracuse's Empire Theatre on August 31, 1912, for a single performance, the Syracuse *Herald* carried a series of articles ballyhooing the show and noting, as did its advertisements, that "Europe's Reigning Musical Sensation" had been given 700 times in Berlin and 300 times in both Vienna and Hamburg. With Cohan busy elsewhere, Harris, the librettist, George V. Hobart, and Kern accompanied the performers upstate. In taking a bow after the cast sang a final reprise of the song everyone hoped would be the show's hit, "Let Us Build A Little Nest," Kern presented a striking picture. Led on by one of the company's most beautiful ladies, "He wore a neatly trimmed Van Dyke beard, his clothes were of the latest cut and altogether he presented a very artistic appearance." Appearances were all he presented, for he demurred at making a speech, preferring his music to speak for itself.

After a short stay in Detroit, the musical moved on to Cohan's Grand Opera House in Chicago, where it was booked for an indefinite run. Even before entering the theatre, audiences might have noticed one minor change. The definite article had given place to the indefinite. The musical was now *A Polish Wedding*.

The plot dealt with one of the many musical-comedy wills so cherished by the era's librettists. In this instance, Aunt Cordelia has bequeathed her vast estates to her beloved niece, Marga (Valli Valli), on the condition that Marga remain happily married for at least five years. To cement the marriage the niece and her husband must re-enact their wedding ceremony on each anniversary. Peter Puffle (Lincoln Plumer), who will inherit much of Cordelia's wealth if Marga forfeits it, manages to photograph Marga in a really innocent but seemingly compromising situation. It requires the rest of the evening for Marga to explain away the situation.

Chicago reviewers devoted most of their notices to the cast. The *Tribune* and the *Daily News* were typical. William Burress's comic shenanigans as the man with whom Marga is apparently cheating won the heartiest endorsements. None of the critics mentioned the tiny, dimpled-kneed nineteen-year-old who played Hansel or the little ten-year-old beauty who performed Gretel. In later years Ann Pennington became one of Broadway's dancing darlings, and Genevieve Tobin starred in Kern's *Dear Sir*. Of the performers' material the *Daily News* said merely that it was "not only laughable and melodious, but very quaint, out of the ordinary and entertaining." The *Tribune* found "almost all the tunes are pretty," although it gave credit for them to Jean Gilbert, who had composed the original score, and neglected to mention Kern. Critics could find little Polish about the evening.

No fewer than five of the songs were by Kern: "I Want To Be The One To Show Her That," which, while listed on the sheet music, may not have been published; "You're The Only Girl He Loves"; "He Must Be Nice To Mother" (both with lyrics by Hobart); "Let Us Build A Little Nest" (for which Hobart supplied the lyric to the verse and Kern that to the chorus); and "Bygone Days" (for which Kern served as his own lyricist). "He Must Be Nice To Mother" was another of the era's daintily prancing numbers. "Bygone Days" began as a dialogue in 4/4, then turned into a sweeping waltz for its chorus. It was in "Let Us Build A Little Nest" and "You're The Only Girl He Loves" that Kern indicated the direction in which he was advancing. The former's chorus is one of the earliest revelations of the attractively curvaceous melodies that would soon be a Kern trademark. "You're The Only Girl He Loves" was better yet, a sly, caressing, vaguely sad melody, hurt only by a weak ending. Kern clearly perceived these songs were a little ahead of their time and put both away to use later.

Among Mrs. Miller's manuscripts is a fascinating piece, a tarantelle designed for the show but apparently never used. It is a full-fledged orchestration, entirely in Kern's own hand. Enclosed inside the manuscript is a printed piano part of a 1907 tarantelle by Henri DuBois. In several places Kern has lifted passages for his own work. Given Kern's strict integrity, DuBois would undoubtedly have received his due had Kern published the work. But the show must have closed before the piece could be inserted. Names of Chicago and Milwaukee theatres are penciled in, with the Milwaukee house then scratched out—an indication of the haste and uncertainty besetting Kern and his producers. But the important point is that the manuscript proves Kern's ability to orchestrate his own material when a need arose. Mrs. Miller's manuscripts suggest that the other material in the show may have been orchestrated by Charles N. Grant.

A Polish Wedding had the misfortune to open in the middle of a late summer heat wave. When sweltering temperatures and cool notices immediately affected the box office, the show was withdrawn while it was still hundreds of miles from New York.

One consolation for the failure of *A Polish Wedding* was the pleasure of working with the fey, red-haired beauty, Billie Burke. Burke was Ziegfeld's wife, but she loyally maintained her professional allegiance to Charles Frohman. Miss Burke arrived at the Lyceum on September 9, 1912, in Arthur Wing Pinero's play, *The "Mind-the-Paint" Girl*. The play required two songs, which Frohman called on Kern to provide. One was "If You Would Only Love Me," a piece Kern wrote together with John Crook. The verse sounds like minor, contemporary Kern but the chorus, as softly sentimental as a Carrie Jacobs Bond melody, is atypical, so may have come from Crook. No less than Pinero himself wrote the lyric for "Mind The Paint," a melody every bit as graceful and gossamer as Miss Burke. In later interviews Kern said that one of these two songs had been written originally as his high school class song. The statement marks one of the rare instances on which Kern's memory failed him. In the next show he did with Miss Burke, he indeed went back to his school days for a melody, but it was one he had written for a class show, not as a class song. (For the record, the class song was composed by one Othelia M. Rauch. It was actually a poem, set to the music of "The Star-Spangled Banner.")

An instance of the era's freewheeling informality came when a second-rate Viennese operetta was mounted briefly as *The Woman Haters*. Produced by Al Woods at the Astor on October 7, it contained a number by Walter Kollo, "Come On Over Here," for which Hobart and Kern provided a lyric. When the show folded, the song was stored away to be used in a later Kern show. But Kern suddenly had something more important to think about. The Shuberts had approached him with an offer to do a complete score for a new musical. Here was the opportunity for a real breakthrough, and Kern jumped at the chance.

5

Whole Scores
and a
Scorching

It appeared briefly that Kern's first complete score would be for a third "Girl" show. When he, Paul West, and Rida Johnson Young sat down to sign their contracts, the new Shubert Brothers' musical was slated to be called *The Girl and the Miner*. (In an era that adored a "girl" in its titles, three other shows besides Kern's earlier two had already appropriated the word in the still young season—*The Girl from Brighton*, *My Best Girl*, and *The Charity Girl*.) This new musical was to be based on Mrs. Young's own failure of the preceding season, *Next*. The Messrs. Shubert, who had produced it, retained its original star, Helen Lowell.

Anxious to realize a return of their investment, the Shuberts penciled in a tryout at the Adelphi Theatre in Philadelphia beginning October 21, just three weeks to the day from the start of rehearsals. In mid-rehearsal the show was retitled *Look Who's Here*. By the morning of the opening, even the brothers could see the production was not in shape and grudgingly postponed the premiere. When three days and nights of hectic preparations still left some glaring rough spots, however, the producers brushed aside pleas for additional time and raised the curtain on the evening of October 24. If the music, the large chorus, and the colorful costumes and settings were a change from the year before, the story was essentially the same.

Otto Schmaltz, proprietor of the lone emporium in the roustabout mining town of Lost River, Nevada, is delighted when one S. Brush answers his advertisement for a barber to serve in his establishment. No matter that Brush confesses to being a graduate of a correspondence school. The unruly miners will appreciate the tone a "tonsorial artist" will lend to Otto's shop. But Otto's delight turns to consternation when S. Brush arrives and is seen to be a lady—one Sophie Brush, a lank, long-necked, popeyed hoyden with her own hair brushed primly back. She brings a band of manicurists with her, and she and her band promptly commandeer Otto's quarters as their own. Sophie does more than cut hair. With the help of a parrot she clears the gambler, Jack Warner, of a false charge of stealing and then engineers his marriage to the village schoolteacher, Phyllis Oldham. She even tames "Sage Brush" Kate, the local madam, and her flock of Red Palace beauties. Sophie's reward is Phyllis's handsome brother, "Brick." Jack's sister, Dora, was an important supporting role.

The helpful parrot was no trained animal, but an actress in costume. Performers in parrot costumes threatened to become the rage of the theatrical season. Just weeks before, an actor-parrot had kept squealing out the title in the musical *Oh! Oh! Delphine.*

Two changes of costume were high moments. One occurred at the end of the first act when the girls undressed for bed and Sophie was revealed wearing a red flannel petticoat. Later, just before the finale, Sophie and her girls threw off their practical Wild West garments (Sophie let down her hair as well), and they appeared in hoopskirts and crinolines.

Most Philadelphia critics courteously passed over any signs of unreadiness in the production. Virtually to a man they were enthusiastic. For several critics "originality" was the key to the show's success. The Philadelphia *Item* opened its notice excitedly, "At last we have broken from the stereotypedness of musical pieces. . . . One is not taken off into the decaying and imaginary spots of obsolete Europe; no, we are put right down in our own little America as the story begins." Such cries had been heard before, but they continued to fade away quickly, lost in the persistent strains of Viennese waltzes. Some saw the work as a lighthearted *Girl of the Golden West,* with the *North American* adding, "Mr. Kern, however . . . has not tried to imitate Puccini . . . for he has provided melodies of the simplest, orchestrated with no attempt at the grandiose and in the main quite rememberable because they are so much like many others. He has given a really beautiful song, however, in the 'Days of Granmamma,' of the last act [the song sung by the hoopskirted girls], and a very lively and unusual 'rag' in a restaurant song." Succeeding critics, in the remaining tryout cities and in New York, would find the Puccini comparison easy and convenient. Those critics willing to let Kern's music stand on its own were still kinder, the *Item* noting that "in the range from picturesque ragtime to beautiful melodies he reveals admirable taste." The *Item*'s critic, too, singled out "Since The Days Of Grandmamma"—the correct title—remarking, "it was charming and dainty, and was sung soft and low to entrance the ear; it was as fragrant as old lavender."

From Philadelphia the musical moved on to Trenton, New Jersey, and Albany, New York, earning more favorable reviews, although one Albany paper insisted the show was "An Operetta Worthy of More Romantic Title." Plans to transfer the show to Chicago for an extended run were hastily abandoned when the abrupt closing of a flop suddenly made Daly's Theatre available, and the show was rushed into New York. So hurried were the Shuberts' changed plans that even the trade papers were taken aback. To make matters worse, the producers had followed the Albany paper's suggestion and had given the work its third title in less than a month, *The Red Petticoat*. In the resulting confusion the *Dramatic Mirror* told its readers the new musical would be making "its first appearance on any stage." Much of the good advance word accorded to *Look Who's Here* was thus lost in the rush. Even the assignment of Daly's militated against the show. With new houses being constructed farther and farther north, Daly's, at Broadway and 30th Street, was, as *Variety*'s critic complained, "a long way out of the theatrical district."

Nevertheless, open it did on November 13, 1912, with the following musical program:

The Red Petticoat

ACT I

Opening Chorus of Miners
"Sing, Sing, You Tetrazinni" . . . . *Kate [Frances Kennedy]*
and Chorus
Duet, "I Wonder" . . . . *Phyllis [Louise Mink] and Warner*
[Joseph Phillips]
"The Correspondence School" . . . . *Sophie [Helen Lowell]*
and Chorus
"Dance, Dance, Dance" . . . . . . *Brick [Donald MacDonald], Slim*
[Allen Kearns], and Manicure Girls
Duet, "Little Golden Maid" . . . . . *Dora [Grace Field] and Brick*

ACT II

Opening Chorus . . . . *Kate, Schmaltz [James B. Carson]*
and Chorus
"Oh You Beautiful Spring" . . . . *Dora and Chorus*
Trio, "Where Did the Bird Hear That?" . . . . *Sophie, Schmaltz,*
and Parrot [Katherine Belknap]
Ensemble, "Peaches and Cream" . . *Phyllis, Warner, and Chorus*
"The Ragtime Restaurant" . . . . *Brick and Chorus*
Trio, "A Prisoner of Love" . . . . *Sophie, Phyllis, and Dora*

ACT III

"Walk, Walk, Walk" . . . . *Brick and Chorus*
Duet, "The Joy of That Kiss" . . . . *Phyllis and Warner*
"Oo-Oo-Oo" . . . . *Schmaltz and Girls*
"Since The Days of Grandmamma" . . . . *Sophie and Girls*
"The Waltz Time Girl" . . . . *Phyllis and Brick*

Joseph W. Herbert directed the production, and Clarence West conducted the uncredited orchestrations, which manuscripts in the possession of Mrs. Betty Kern Miller show to have been by Frank Saddler.

Between Philadelphia and New York, two early Kern numbers were dropped: "The Vigilantes," sung late in the first act by Kate and the chorus, and the opening chorus of the last act. The lone new song was "Oh You Beautiful Spring." Significantly, nowhere along the line was an interpolation injected. In an era careless of artistic integrity, this has to say something about either Kern's determination or the Shuberts' respect for their young composer, a respect they rarely displayed to more established names. Some suggestion that the brothers were taken with Kern comes in a final program change. All during the tryouts the program read:

Look Who's Here
by Rida Johnson Young
Lyrics by Paul West   Music by Jerome D. Kern

Programs at Daly's told a different story:

The Red Petticoat
Music by Jerome D. Kern
Book and Lyrics by Rida Johnson Young and Paul West

Many critics welcomed the show wholeheartedly. Kern's loyal booster, Alan Dale, began his review in the *American* with the same enthusiastic observation the Philadelphia *Item*'s man had made, hailing the switch from Europe's "sickly," "desiccated" courts to our own robust West. But Dale could not wait long to tell the world about his young wonder boy. Kern, Dale exclaimed, had

> . . . let loose a flood of toothsome, captivating and ultra-catchy music. And mark you—there was no suggestion of Lehar, or of Fall, or of Vienna. The music is perhaps prettier than anything in town. It is good enough to waft Kern on the crest wave of popularity. One song alone, called "I Wonder" . . . is charming enough to make a man famous. "Cuter" music has rarely been heard in this city and—let the foreign composers sit up and take notice—Mr. Kern is here to win.

Dale's fellow critics were less carried away, although most were kind to Kern. The *Evening World*'s Charles Darnton, for example, wished Kern had been permitted to insert still more songs. Whatever else they thought, critic after critic focused on "Since The Days Of Grandmamma" for special praise. However, no small part of this praise was lavished on the number's staging as much as on the song itself. There was considerably less satisfaction with the book. Trade papers, which had more time to ruminate on what they had seen and heard, came down especially hard on the show, with *Variety* concluding, "Emphatically it is not for Broadway."

From our vantage point, nearly seven decades later, the praise for "Since The Days Of Grandmamma" seems puzzlingly overblown. The verse, in 3/4 time, is marked "Tempo di Menuetto." Its melody, while stately, sounds like no more than a beginner's exercise. The chorus, in 4/4, is a gavotte with a nursery-rhyme-like melody that is pleasant but in no way commanding. A coda of eight bars reverts to the original tempo for a brief series of uninteresting progressions. Given the proper staging, the song might well have been impressive in the theatre, but it seems highly unlikely to have sent the audience away whistling. Nor are the remaining numbers much better, although "The Ragtime Restaurant" has an engaging lilt. "I Wonder" is a waltz that begins promisingly, then abruptly collapses. "Little Golden Maid" is interesting solely because of the length of the vamp that precedes the main song and of the dance melody that follows. Kern frequently attached little dance melodies to the ends of songs, melodies often quoting nothing from the songs themselves. But this one, thirty-two bars long, far exceeded the length of the song, where verse and chorus together amounted to only sixteen bars. "My Peaches And Cream" was an elaborate, concerted showpiece, passing through several key and tempo changes before ending as an innocuous waltz. The song that Kern added during the tryout, "Oh You Beautiful Spring" (lyric, Rourke), is a trite waltz whose bridge paraphrases Sullivan's "The Flowers That Bloom In the Spring."

By a fortunate happenstance Kern's working manuscripts for the unpublished material have survived. They reveal that the work was done under a fourth title, never announced to the public, *All After Sophie*. Kern began work in mid-April and finished one month later. Each song carries a single date while opening choruses and finales generally have two consecutive dates, suggesting that these took about twice as long to compose as the standard songs. "Sing! Sing! You Tetrazzini!" (with the artist's name spelled correctly and the more logical punctuation) is a rowdy, rangy number that eschews the obvious chance to incorporate operatic quotation. "Where Did The Bird Hear That?" is a delightful polka. "The Joy Of That Kiss" is an ingratiating Viennese-style waltz. As if to balance its Continental flavor, Kern created a charming American-style counterpart in "Waltz Me Up To The Altar, Walter," which, with apparent last-minute revisions, became "The Waltz Time Girl." (The manuscript folder contains another version of the Viennese style piece, entitled simply "Serenade.") The remaining numbers were pleasant, if minor, fillers.

Divided notices, lack of proper advance build-up, and an out-of-the-way house conspired against *The Red Petticoat*. Furthermore, the show had robust competition, including Victor Herbert's *The Lady of the Slipper*, Ivan Caryll's *Oh! Oh! Delphine*, Franz Lehar's *The Count of Luxembourg*, and the operetta that skyrocketed Rudolf Friml to fame, *The Firefly*. By the time the production was moved to the more accessible Broadway Theatre at 41st Street, the die had been cast. The Shuberts pulled the show after sixty-one performances, taking it to the West End Theatre for a week and then back onto the road, where it languished until spring.

Despite painful failures and lack of general recognition, Kern remained self-assured and optimistic. As if to underscore the bright future he hoped was his, Jerry and Eva relinquished their small brownstone apartment on 68th Street and moved uptown. Today 206 West 92nd Street is a dilapidated tenement, but it retains many telltale vestiges of the elegance and comfort it must have offered sixty-five years ago. An attractive tiled entranceway leads to a spacious, marbled hallway, which in turn leads to the elevator. Windows are large, suggesting the apartments must have been bright and cheery.

The first 1913 arrival to include a Kern song had a title every bit as bright and cheering. *The Sunshine Girl* was another Gaiety musical brought to America by Frohman. Julia Sanderson was its star, with Joseph Cawthorn its principal clown. If opening nighters at the Knickerbocker on February 3 left singing any song, it was most likely Kern's "Honeymoon Lane" (lyric, Rourke). The song was a real charmer. A two-step, it set the pattern that Kern would employ for this type of song all through these dance-mad years. A short, simple phrase would be repeated with the first note sustained slightly. Another brief phrase would complete the musical sentence by holding the final note for a measure. The whole process would then be run through again, usually a few tones higher. As often as not, a related release would then conclude by returning to the original sentence. This was not strictly the AABA pattern that was to become standard by the mid-1920s. In that pattern the initial musical sentence, or A, was repeated with virtually no variation, and a fresh theme or sentence followed before the song ended with a third statement of the opening theme. What Kern employed here was essentially an AA^{1}BA^2 formula, although in the case of "Honeymoon Lane" Kern added a second sentence, or, if one may use the term, musical clause, after each basic sentence. This early use by Kern—and others—in two-steps, fox-trots, and other dances of the day suggests the formula may have evolved as a response to dancers' needs for a predictable melody.

Programs for *The Sunshine Girl* give Kern no credit for the song, any more than he had received credit for his contributions in most other Frohman shows. But in this instance the oversight may have smarted, since John Golden and Cawthorn were singled out for credit for an inferior piece, "You Can't Play Every Instrument In The Band."

In April, Kern again supplied music for a Billie Burke vehicle. In her autobiography, *With a Feather on My Nose,* Billie Burke described Jerry's backstage appearances: "Often he would drop in to sit at a small piano in the wings strumming a special arrangement which sounded like mandolin music while Shelley Hull pretended to play on stage and while I sang." The show was Arthur Wing Pinero's *The Amazons,* which opened at the Empire on April 28, 1913. Kern's song was "My Otaheitee Lady" (lyric, Charles H. Taylor). The most interesting thing about it is its original copyright date, 1902! Obviously, this was the song Kern had salvaged from his high school show. Yet in clearing up one mystery, another appears. The 1902 copyright is solely in the name of Francis, Day, and Hunter, the English house affiliated with Harms. I am at a loss for an explanation.

Not until the end of summer, as the 1913–14 season was beginning, were more Kern songs broadcast across the footlights. And when they were, a small, mean brouhaha ensued.

Although opening night programs for Frohman's mounting of *The Doll Girl* credited only Leo Fall with its music, little more than half the songs sung at the Globe on August 25 were his. Kern had written four others, while four more composers were each represented by a single number.

Most New York critics enjoyed the show. They found Harry B. Smith's adaptation workable, and generally had high praise for the performances of two stars who were beginning to seem like Kern associates, Hattie Williams and Richard Carle. In passing judgment on the music they were equally approving. The *World,* accepting Fall as the sole composer, thought the music "simpler than Viennese musical shows usually present," yet replete with "dainty tunefulness." One song particularly caught the critic's fancy, "Come On Over Here." The *Herald* echoed the *World,* noting what "chiefly pleases . . . is Mr. Fall's music" and awarded special praise to " 'Come On Over Here,' which resembles 'Alexander's Ragtime Band,' a song about smoke . . . and a duet called 'On Our Honeymoon.' " Fall had composed none of these. As Kern might have expected, the most interesting notice appeared under Alan Dale's byline in the *American.* Dale wrote:

> . . . the music of "The Doll Girl" was better than its book. It is said to be the work of Leo Fall, but without first aid to the wounded, Leo would probably have taken—his last name. It was probably Mr. Jerome Kern (who was not made in Germany) who was responsible for the pretty things in "The Doll Girl"—such as "Come On, Over Here," "On Our Honeymoon" and "When Three Is Company."

If Kern had received no mention in the program he had at least received mention in most pre-opening publicity. But as soon as the run was under way, articles about him began to appear on all sides—articles that represented the first major publicity barrage he had ever enjoyed. All these articles took note that he had also contributed a song to a second Leo Fall operetta, *Lieber Augustin* (later called *Miss Caprice*), which the Shuberts had brought into the Casino on September 3, 1913.

Representative of the smaller articles that appeared was one in the New York *Review* for September 13, headlined "Jerome Kern's Songs Make the Big Hits of Two Productions." A sub-headline noted "Native Song Writer Gives Foreign Composers' Scores New Brilliancy." The article concluded, "Mr. Kern has firmly established his position as America's leading song writer." However farsighted the encomium was, in 1913 it smacked of presumption or press-agentry.

A far more extensive article, the result of an interview, appeared on Sunday, September 14, in the *World,* under the banner "New Maker of Melodies Talks About His Trade." The writer described Kern as "rather small of stature, slender and [with] a frank, keen face and a swiftness of speech and motion." Kern's music was described as "graceful, smart," and reflecting "good taste." The interviewer explained the sudden rash of publicity by noting that "[Kern's] wife had finally succeeded in convincing him that it would be as easy to accept fame and money as well as merely the latter for his work." If this statement is true, it confirms that in private Eva was not as quiet and retiring as she was in public, and that she may well have provided more than one effective goad. The article went on to list every one of the shows Kern had interpolated songs into, and then to discuss at some length his songs for the current season. But it also offered two interesting little lectures by Kern, one revealing why he had had to work on interpolations, the other telling why interpolating had come to seem a dead end to him. Both are worth quoting *in toto:*

> "To understand the work I have been doing," said Mr. Kern the other day in the study of his apartment, "a knowledge of the London theatres from which so many of our imported musical plays come, is necessary. In London the queue of people which stretches all day around a playhouse where there is a success is such an institution that the law requires the theatre owner to put up a glass or steel canopy around the building to protect the waiters for unreserved seats in pit and gallery from the weather.

The doors open at 7:30 o'clock and the crowd flocks in. At 8 o'clock the curtain rises with not a soul in the stalls. The fashionable part of the audience does not begin to arrive before 8:30, and it is 9 before most of them come.

"From 8 to 9 then the time is filled in with the most awful stuff in the world. Poor songs, worse comedy and stale jokes are used as padding till the audience in the stalls arrives. Then the play begins in earnest. The result is that when the play is brought to New York it has to be almost entirely made over. The first hour is usually tossed out bodily and scenes from the other acts are brought forward. This leaves holes in the show that must be filled, and the plugging of those holes has been my task.

"Sometimes, too, the nature of the music is such as to make it unfit for use here. This is particularly true of the music of the German composers. Their musical comedy singers usually can sing. They sacrifice looks to voice, and it is not uncommon to see a big, buxom woman of thirty-five playing the role of a girl of eighteen. However charming the majority of our musical comedy players may be, not many of them are prima donnas. So a great deal of the score has to be set aside or rewritten."

In effect, Kern had presented the best possible defense for the wholesale tampering with foreign works that was the common practice of the day. It was a history and a rationale he would reiterate often in later years. He changed some of his thinking about his second point, but never the heart of the matter, the need for more real native work:

"What I would like to see," Mr. Kern continued, "is an opportunity given American talent to express itself. It isn't so much the writing of music as the getting it produced that is difficult. I haven't a doubt but that there are plenty of young American composers and librettists who could do the work of the Viennese and London schools. I feel that M. E. Rourke, who often furnishes lyrics for my songs, and I could accomplish as much working with original versions as by patching up plays after they have gone through several adaptations. Let me illustrate by the case of 'The Doll Girl.' Originally it was a French farce by Caillavet and de Flers, called 'Miquette' [actually, "Riquette et sa Mere"]. Mr. Frohman owned the American rights. Along came two Germans who suggested they could make it into a musical play and get Leo Fall to compose a score for it. They were told to go ahead and 'Das Puppenmaedel' was the result. Then Mr. Frohman turned over 'Das Puppenmaedel' to Mr. Smith and me and we arranged the American version. Now, I contend that the producer might have saved the expense of all the middlemen and been given as good a product by letting Americans do the work to begin with."

Of course, Kern here was still talking about adaptations, and adaptations of foreign works with foreign settings at that. Whether he was acknowledging the prevailing mode or whether the sting of *The Red Petticoat*'s failure was still hurting is unclear. Nevertheless, Kern was in the vanguard of a host of American talents crying for a chance to be heard.

But for some reason now lost all this publicity rankled in trade circles. *Variety* opened its review of *The Doll Girl* with a snide vignette:

> Jerome Kern was in the lobby of the Globe Monday evening after the second act of "The Doll Girl," and confided to those present he had written the song hit of the piece—that is, it was the nearest approach to a song hit thus far developed in the three-act musical comedy. Then, just to disprove it, Hans Bartsch, foreign play-broker, hummed the German words of it.

But it fell to the *Dramatic Mirror* to launch a full-barreled attack on Kern and the attention he was receiving. Although the trade sheet had long held some inexplicable grudge against the young composer, its broadside is puzzling, since all through 1913 the paper had run full-page articles complaining that American music and the American musical theatre were both in desperate need of revitalization. Ostensibly, the paper was railing against unjustified publicity and self-aggrandizement. Its ire, or at least its suspicions, may have been raised by the number of articles that referred to Kern as rendering "first aid," a term it appropriated, wittingly or not. The *World*'s interviewer had used the expression, as had Dale in his notice. But given the persistent snipes the *Dramatic Mirror* had taken at Kern in early reviews, its motives were questionable. And, oddly, its editorial, run on October 1, probably did little more than further the attention Kern was receiving. The editorial was headed simply "THE SONG-SMITH."

> One of the Sunday papers recently contained an interesting account of Mr. Jerome D. Kern's work as an interpolative contributor to the musical plays of the day, a sort of musical ambulance surgeon extending first aid to the injured.
>
> As an example of efficient press work by Mr. Kern's press agent, we cannot withhold our unqualified tribute of admiration. Ac-

cording to the appraisement placed on Mr. Kern's activities as a songsmith, who hammers out "hits" on the anvil of his genius as easily as he can wink an eye, various successes, reputedly the work of Leo Fall, Reinhart, Henry Berniri, Carl Zierer [all three names misspelled!], and also Paul Rubens and others, were due to our own homegrown Kern's interpolation.

Truth of the matter is that, though we keep a vigilant guard over the matters of the theater and are counted among the genus of inveterate First-Nighters, we have failed to observe the uplifting influence of Mr. Kern's lilting muse. We will except "Come On Over Here" in *The Doll Girl,* for the sake of fairness; but we draw the line on "Will It All End in Smoke?" and "Don't Turn My Picture to the Wall."

We know the brand, sop to the gallery and pet of the music publisher.

The stuff that can be whistled after one hearing is for whistlers, and whistling is a practice avoided in good society. If Mr. Kern is ambitious to shine beyond its pales it is his concern.

But it can be no flattery to him to know that the various music factories in the vicinity of the tenderloin are grinding out, by a wholesale process, songs about pictures turned to the wall and "My Love Is Gone Up in Smoke."

When Mr. Kern has to his credit a song like "O Promise Me," "My Hero," "I 'Ave a Motter," "In the Merry, Merry May" and sundry song hits of Victor Herbert, De Koven, Caryll, Albini, Straus, or Sullivan, it will be time enough for him to lay aside his besetting modesty and enchant us instead with an epic of his accomplishments.

If Kern bothered to reply to this diatribe, the *Dramatic Mirror* never printed it.

No runaway hit emerged from *The Doll Girl,* not even "Come On Over Here." If *Variety* meant that as the song Kern supposedly was boasting about, it can only suggest that Kern took as much pride in his lyrics as he did in his music, since, as we have seen, Walter Kollo composed the music. Without the German original for comparison, there is no way of determining whether Kern also revised some of Kollo's work. But the probability is small. Had he redone the song musically, he would most probably have persuaded Harms to list him as co-composer as well as co-lyricist. Were Kern actually boastful on opening night, he could easily have been referring to several of his own melodies. "If We Were On Our Honeymoon

(Railway Duet)" (lyric, Smith) was another of his extended numbers moving through multiple changes of key and tempo. Individually the parts are attractive, and, taken together, particularly in a fine production, they must have been dramatically effective. Just how greatly Kern regarded it can be judged by his reuse of much of it fourteen years later—in *Show Boat!* "When Three Is Company (Cupid Song)" (lyric, Rourke) is equally attractive, the first four bars of its ballad-like chorus offering an exceptionally alluring musical idea. Kern filed it away alongside other good melodies he was loath to waste. "Will It All End In Smoke?" (lyric, Smith) begins in 4/4, but its curious swing hints at the change to 3/4 at the end of the verse and the graceful waltz that constitutes the chorus. It is pleasant, but minor. The least of the songs was "A Little Thing Like A Kiss" (lyric, Smith), a slightly regressive melody whose chorus nevertheless jogs along amiably. Kern's interpolation in *Lieber Augustin* was an expressive waltz he would also re-employ, "Look In Her Eyes" (lyric, Rourke). The song is written in classic Viennese style, utilizing several themes, or minithemes, each dramatically different in feeling and tempo. For example, the first theme of the chorus is graceful and tender, the second flashily brilliant.

Kern's coupling of his own name with Harry B. Smith's is significant, for while Smith had worked on *The Rich Mr. Hoggenheimer, The Siren,* and *The Girl from Montmartre, The Doll Girl* represents the first close and extended association for both men, an association that would prove meaningful in ways they could hardly imagine.

Smith was born in Buffalo on December 28, 1860, but was raised in Chicago. After the usual tribulations and failures, he achieved success, as we have seen, with *The Begum* in 1887. Smith was a heavy-set, kindly man. His long career, spanning fifty years when Broadway was at its most active, made him the most prolific lyricist and librettist in our history. He wrote the books for nearly 150 shows and words to several thousand songs. It may be cruel to call Smith a hack, even if some critics of his day did just that. By his own lights he was an intelligent, conscientious artist, acceptable as librettist and lyricist to most of the era's major composers. Indeed, a counterargument can be made that he was as good as or better than virtually any other of the period's writers. If his rhymes are remembered today solely because of the beautiful, enduring melodies they accompanied, in his own day Smith was highly enough thought of by many to be honored as the first American lyricist to have his material anthologized in hardback. It was an honor that must have been doubly prized by Smith, for his pride in his work was matched by his joy at book-collecting. Years later, when it came time to give his autobiography a title, he bowed to both, calling his book *First Nights and First Editions.*

Kern's profit from the relationship stemmed not from Smith's limited artistry. Instead, it came from Smith the man, by way of his warm personal friendship, Smith's wife, and Smith's hobby. Kern was hopelessly acquisitive, loving to collect for the sake of collecting and for what his collections could teach him. In time he developed impressive collections of silver, furniture, paintings, stamps, and coins. But his first great collection and the one that would remain his finest achievement was his collection of rare books and manuscripts. Smith provided the original inspiration. Smith discovered that Kern had already begun to pay two to seven dollars for composers' autographs. The older man pointed out that within a short while Kern could have all the signatures he could reasonably hope for. He spoke glowingly of the larger possibilities books and holographs offered, then suggested that Kern accompany him to one of the auction houses where he often unearthed the best buys. Kern accepted the invitation. The composer was flabbergasted when Smith bid $600 for a single volume. Smith got the volume. Apparently the excitement was contagious. Kern bid $100 for a copy of Keats's *Endymion* and was delighted when his bid held. He and Smith were even further astonished when they examined the book, for it contained a Keats signature the auctioneers and previous owners had not noticed. On his very first dip into strange waters Kern had struck a marvelous treasure. He was hooked.

If Smith thus markedly affected Kern's private life, Smith's wife influenced his public one. Mrs. Smith had been Irene Bentley, briefly one of the musical stage's most beautiful prima donnas. She had definite ideas about musicals, and she was as persuasive as she was beautiful. At a small dinner, she complimented the young composer on his work, insisting that he was on the right track and urging him not to deviate. For her the essence of any good musical was its charm, or, as she expressed it, "the odor of sachet." However gossamer and intangible charm might be, paradoxically it was what gave musicals their strength and durability. From the beginning, grace and charm had been strong points of Kern's art, so he listened sympathetically to Mrs. Smith's stricture. To the end, Kern employed "good taste, refinement, daintiness and charm" as "the keynotes of all musical plays." In more than one interview he acknowledged that Harry B. Smith's wife had really turned his unconscious approach into a philosophy.

Even while Kern was giving out his interview to the *World,* he knew his wish to devise a musical directly from a play had been granted. Once again the Shuberts were willing to gamble on the young composer. But before he could devote his full energies to the new show, he had to honor an obligation to Frohman. As might be expected, Frohman continued to play it relatively safe with another importation. However, this one was unique. It was a German operetta that was set in America, where, according to the Germans, wives could be bought at auction. *The Marriage Market* opened at the Knickerbocker on September 22, 1913. Amusingly, the *Dramatic Mirror* began its notice by rejoicing, "At last we have the cowboy in comic opera." Whether this was forgetfulness or whether the paper was archly ignoring *The Red Petticoat* (as well as a few other earlier works) is moot. Since Frohman followed his customary policy of allowing interpolations to go uncredited, the paper also unwittingly found itself singling out a Kern song as one of the three best from the show. That song, "A Little Bit Of Silk" (lyric, Rourke), was fittingly delicate, yet, by a stroke of irony that the trade paper took no notice of, the song was dropped shortly after the opening. So was "I'm Looking For An Irish Husband" (lyric, Rourke), a song which contained no hint of an Irish air but did quote "The Star-Spangled Banner." Only one of Kern's original contributions remained steadfastly in the musical program, "I've Got Money In The Bank" (lyric, Rourke), a gay, jaunty ditty.

Five days after *The Marriage Market* opened in New York, Kern hustled to Albany for the premiere of *Oh, I Say!*. He took the train, according to the Albany *Journal,* with Lee Shubert, J. C. Huffman (the show's director) and one unexpected companion, Alan Dale. The ethics of a New York critic accompanying a show's creators to a tryout when he would have to review that show in New York are open to question, but it most likely merely reflected the abiding avuncular interest Dale had shown in Kern ever since *Mr. Wix of Wickham* nearly a decade before.

The *Journal* was only mildly pleased with the new offering and gave it only a two-paragraph review, but one of those paragraphs was given over to a list of its favorite songs from the show, while the highest praise in the remaining paragraph was to call Kern's material "the tinkling, pleasing sort."

A month on the road followed, before *Oh, I Say!* opened at the Casino on October 30, 1913, with the musical program that read:

Oh, I Say!

ACT I

Opening Chorus .... *Guests of Hotel*
Dance Duet ... *Julie [Lois Josephine], Hugo [Wellington Cross]
and Gabrielle [Nellie King]*
Scene, "Each Pearl a Thought" .... *Suzette [Alice Yorke]*
Trio, "I Know and She Knows" ... *Portal [Walter Jones], Henri
[Joseph Phillips] and Marcel [Charles Meakins]*
Ensemble .... *Sydonie [Cecil Cunningham] and Guests*
Trio, "Well This is Jolly" .... *Sydonie, Henri and Marcel*
Reprisal, "Each Pearl a Thought" .... *Portal*

ACT II

Opening Chorus .... *Servants*
Dance Duet, "The Old Clarinet" .. *Claudine [Clara Palmer] and
Joseph [Tyler Brooke]*
Duet, "Alone at Last" .... *Marcel and Suzette*
Terzette, "A Woman's Heart" .... *Sydonie, Portal and Buzot
[Joseph W. Herbert]*
Duet, "Katy-did" .... *Julie and Hugo*
Supper Scene .... *Chorus*
Finaletto .... *Marcel, Portal, Sydonie, Henri, Buzot and Chorus*

ACT III

Opening Chorus .... *Guests of Laverdo*
Song, "I Can't Forget Your Eyes" ...... *Claudine and Gonzales*
Duettino, "A Wifie of Your Own" .... *Henri and Suzette*
Duel Bouffe .... *Portal and Buzot*
Finaletto, "Alone at Last"

Julian Alfred created the choreography and Melville Ellis the costumes.
Programs ignored the conductor (apparently Alfred Bendell), orchestrator,
and set designer, but extant manuscripts reveal that Frank Saddler provided
the orchestrations.

The story Sidney Blow and Douglas Hoare adapted from a French farce
by Keroul and Barre was standard Parisian puffery. Believing her mistress,
the celebrated actress Sydonie de Mornay, has embarked on an extended
tour, her maid Claudine sublets the actress's apartment to a honeymoon

couple. The groom turns out to be Sydonie's old lover. And if that is not complication enough, the bride's father engages Sydonie to give a special performance for the newlyweds.

New York reviews ran the gamut from disdain to mild enthusiasm, with a majority deeming the entertainment passable foolery. The *Times,* among the more severely critical, signaled its displeasure in its headline, where it branded the show a "Farce with Musical Interruptions." After sprinkling its notice with derogatory judgments ("commonplace," "vulgar"), it ruefully concluded, "nor does Mr. Kern's music provide any occasion for rejoicing." Not unexpectedly, Alan Dale's review in the *American* was one of the most favorable. Giving no hint he had accompanied the composer to the Albany tryout, Dale asserted that "Jerome Kern . . . writes all that score hits in the scores of Leo Fall and Franz Lehar." The critic saluted "A Wifie Of Your Own" as the show's best number, advised that "Alone At Last" had "a pathetic kink that gets you" and praised the "lovely tango" Clara Palmer danced to. Since "The Old Clarinet" is an unmistakable waltz, Dale must have been referring to "I Can't Forget Your Eyes," which would in fact make a beautiful tango, and did on period recordings.

Probably because the program took no notice of any orchestrator, critics ignored him and his contribution. Yet the orchestrations for *Oh, I Say!* are generally conceded to have brought a fresh sound to Broadway's theatre pits, a sound of saxophones that in a few years' time would be closely associated with jazz. This was Kern's suggestion to Saddler, and he remained proud of it. As future events will show, any pride Kern took in this progressive innovation was tempered by an eventual distaste for the abuses of jazz orchestras.

No tryout program seems to have survived, so we cannot say with certainty what songs were dropped or added. However, out-of-town notices mention three songs that failed to appear on New York or later playbills: "Good-bye, Everybody," "Have An Old Waltz With Me," and "Sidonie" (this last being either a misprint or suggesting the heroine's name was respelled en route).

Harms published seven of the surviving songs, although no copy of "A Woman's Heart" seems readily available. All had lyrics by Harry B. Smith. "A Wifie Of Your Own," a cutely mincing thing, and "I Know And She Knows," whose chorus is a banal polka, are the least interesting. "Katy-Did" is a thumping rag, with a chorus vaguely related to the chorus of "Paris Is A Paridise For Coons." "Alone At Last," probably slated as the hit of the show, opens with a recitative verse that moves from 4/4 to 2/4 before sliding into an intriguingly hippety-hop chorus in 6/8. Yet the loveliest melody by far was the lushly romantic "I Can't Forget Your Eyes." Kern liked the chorus enough to reuse it in two later shows, but then both "Katy-Did" and "Alone At Last" were also re-employed. In a turnabout, another composer's song, "The Old Clarinet," was interpolated into the score. The composer was Jean Gilbert, for whose *A Polish Wedding* Kern had added songs. Kern almost assuredly raised little or no objection. Unlike almost every other giant in his field, Kern permitted interpolations of one sort or another in virtually all of his Broadway shows, although most of these inserted melodies were either period or classical pieces designed to accentuate an atmosphere and not to bolster any weakness on Kern's part.

Oh, I Say! proved no more attractive to New York theatregoers than it had to Manhattan's critics. After sixty-eight performances it was returned to the road, where its name was eventually changed to *Their Wedding Night*. But even this more titillating title failed to lure playgoers in sufficient numbers, so by spring the attraction was withdrawn.

The Kerns' move uptown proved unsatisfactory, and after a single year they took a new apartment at 226 West 70th Street, closer to the theatre district. The apartment, which they retained for just two years, was to be their last Manhattan residence. Yet in those two years Kern leaped from being a relatively minor interpolator to being a leading musical figure on Broadway. His leap was not accomplished totally alone, for 1914 and 1915 marked a major turning point in the history of the American musical theatre.

6

Turning Points

If very little new Kern material was heard in 1914, the modern aphorism "less is more" could well apply to the songs he did publish. Two songs hurled his name before the public, so that anyone paying attention to sheet music covers or record labels could no longer be unaware of it.

February 2, 1914, witnessed the opening of a pair of musicals offering Kern interpolations. Vaudeville and Broadway's dynamic favorite, Blanche Ring, arrived at the small, unlucky 39th Street Theatre in a tailor-made vehicle, *When Claudia Smiles*. Among the numerous songs by an almost equally large number of composers was a lone Kern entry, "Ssh, You'll Waken Mr. Doyle" (lyric, John Golden and E. W. Rogers).

Frohman's latest importation, *The Laughing Husband*, which relit the Knickerbocker, offered three Kern contributions. All had lyrics by Harry B. Smith. A fourth song, "Take A Step With Me," had been dropped during the tryout. It was merely the 1906 "Rosalie," rerhymed. One surviving song, "Love Is Like A Violin," was a minor waltz that Kern nevertheless held in sufficient esteem to reuse, much as he reused an even fresher piece, "Bought And Paid For." But it was the third song, an irresistible appeal to dance, that was the hit of the show. It was added so late in the tryout that it was not even published with the show's other songs. In a brief article for *The Strand Magazine* of February 1916, Kern was able to supply some vivid details about its inception:

. . . the music of "You're Here and I'm Here" . . . was started at ten o'clock on the stage of the Lyceum Theatre in Rochester, New York, during the rehearsal of the late Mr. Charles Frohman's production of "The Laughing Husband." Twenty minutes later, the melody, scribbled on the back of a drum part, was sent to Mr. Harry B. Smith, the author of the American version of the play, at his hotel, and by eleven o'clock the completed duet was being rehearsed under the direction of Mr. Edward Royce, of Daly's Theatre, London.

The orchestration of "You're Here and I'm Here" I made at the nearest available piano. If memory serves correctly, it was the empty grill-room of a neighbouring hotel. The *matinée* performance had started before the band-parts were dry, so the duet was played as an *entr'acte* before the curtain rose on the second act. This, I may say, in lieu of a rehearsal. The same afternoon the number was sung in the second act, with great success, and has since been a featured hit in many revues and musical shows all the world over.

Kern's offhand remark about orchestrating the song is interesting. Few records exist of Kern's actually having orchestrated any of his songs, although as the tarantelle in *A Polish Wedding* shows, he could when necessary. But given the less sophisticated orchestrations that prevailed in the teens, and again, given the urgency of the situation, Kern may indeed have arranged the instrumentation. Certainly his training had provided him with at least the basic tools. His intelligence and innate sense of style would then have compensated slightly for any lack of experience.

In his 1948 study, *A History of Popular Music in America,* musical historian Sigmund Spaeth looked back on "You're Here And I'm Here" as "a practically perfect combination of words and music." For Alec Wilder, writing twenty-four years after Spaeth, the song marked "Kern's emergence from the operetta cocoon." Wilder examined it as a professional, recording that "The song is a series of imitations of the initial phrase, the principal characteristic of which is a pronounced syncopation at the end of the third, seventh, nineteenth, and twenty-third measures. It obviously seeks a native point of view . . . another bar sawed away from the cage of imported culture." In effect Kern had found the dance form he had struggled with in an earlier song such as "Honeymoon Lane."

And the nation swiftly found a dance song it wanted to step to. Advertisements acclaimed its success as "Unprecedented! . . . the big 30¢ song hit of six different $2.00-a-seat musical comedies . . . sold all over America . . . England, France and Germany. . . ." Appealing to holiday memories, advertisements added that the song "had captured Atlantic City, New York and Coney Island."

The Laughing Husband was a quick flop, so most of the sheet music for the song was published as part of *The Marriage Market*'s offerings. As a result the song is generally associated with the latter show, although, curiously, no extant program shows it actually among its musical numbers. Still, there is no reason to doubt the advertisements' claims that the song was sung in six shows. Surviving playbills for touring companies of *When Dreams Come True* and *The Queen of the Movies* include it in their synopses, so two other shows, no longer identifiable, probably did also. In London the song was presented in both *The Passing Show* and *Odds and Ends*. As late as the early 1920s Kern stated that among his works, sheet music sales for "You're Here And I'm Here" had never been surpassed.

Mention of Germany in advertisements brings up a minor but interesting point. ASCAP's record of Kern's works, admittedly incomplete and frequently inaccurate, lists him as composer of a song called "Die Susse Pariserin" for a German musical, *Die Ballkonigin*. ASCAP lists the lyricist as Fritz Luner and the publisher as W. Karczog of Leipzig. Quite possibly between the early February opening of *The Laughing Husband* and the July rehearsals of *The Girl from Utah* the Kerns spent some time in Germany and England, although their daughter, Betty, believes her parents never visited Germany together.

Although "You're Here And I'm Here" was such a tremendous success on stage as well as off that it became the only song in *The Laughing Husband* granted a reprise, Frohman continued to deny Kern any billing. As far as readers of the playbill were concerned, Edmund Eysler could well have written the song. Possibly wary of another spate of attacks on Kern, Frohman made no attempt to capitalize on the fanfare that had attended the composer's work on *The Doll Girl*. But by the time Frohman returned in mid-July from his "annual" English trip, either Kern's name had become too well known for him to remain neglectful or Kern himself demanded recognition. Whatever the reason, Frohman saw to it that advance publicity for *The Girl from Utah* gave the composer a fair share of attention.

George Edwardes had originally mounted *The Girl from Utah* at London's Adelphi Theatre on October 18, 1913. Its book was by James T. Tanner, with an assist from Paul A. Rubens. Rubens also collaborated in composing the score with Sidney Jones and on the lyrics with Adrian Ross and Percy Greenbank. The story told of Una Trance, an American girl who flees to London rather than become just one of a Mormon's many wives. The Mormon trails her, but Una is saved by the handsome leading man of the Gaiety Theatre, Sandy Blair. By curtain time Una and Sandy are betrothed. America's beautiful high comedienne, Ina Claire, was enlisted by Edwardes for the title role, while another American, by then permanently settled in England, Joseph Coyne, was the original Sandy. Edwardes's general manager, J. A. E. Malone, staged the London production. In New York, Frohman cast Julia Sanderson as Una, Joseph Cawthorn as the comic Mormon, and Donald Brian as Sandy. Harry B. Smith was summoned to provide lyrics for Kern's interpolations. The producer imported Malone to re-create his staging. He also hired Gustave Salzer as musical director.

Rehearsals had begun as soon as Frohman had returned. For one last time, Kern served as rehearsal pianist. Meanwhile, the assassination of the Austrian archduke at Sarajevo on the preceding June 28 had led the great European powers into war. If at first the battle seemed too distant to matter to Broadway, it was soon to have an incontestable effect on Kern, Frohman, and the American musical theatre. European artists volunteered or were drafted for their nations' armies. If they were lucky enough not to be killed, they were nevertheless kept from the stage for several years. Older talents, many of whom had shown signs of artistic exhaustion, were left to fend as best they might while the world they understood and reflected was savaged. As a result, the great European schools of light musicals were all but annihilated along with much of Europe's youth. Furthermore, writers still able to create stageworthy pieces found their American reception prejudiced by divided loyalties. As the war progressed and the Central Powers were seen increasingly as a potential enemy, German and Viennese importations were greeted with growing hostility. At the same time, a new generation was awaiting its chance on Broadway. Irving Berlin and Kern had already begun to make names for themselves. Within a few years they would be joined by Vincent Youmans, Cole Porter, Oscar Hammerstein II, and the Gershwin brothers, merely the brightest lights in a dazzling array of fresh genius. The European war, as much as any other circumstance, gave America its opportunity. America grabbed it, and held on to it tenaciously and rewardingly for the next half-century.

No man was more important in establishing this American dominance than Jerome Kern, and no song more important than his hit in *The Girl from Utah,* "They Didn't Believe Me." Yet either by design or because no one at the time realized its merits and significance, the song was given short shrift in advance publicity, although Kern himself was not. Coincidental with the show's American premiere at Atlantic City's Apollo Theatre on August 17, the Atlantic City *Press* featured an article headlined, JEROME KERN MUSIC DOCTOR, and subheaded, "'The Girl From Utah' Abounds With His Lilting Melodies." Noting that the composer was "a little man, who writes big hits," the paper continued:

> . . . In "The Girl From Utah" he has contributed a melody that it is believed will eclipse all of his former big successes for it is a tune of the same brand, yet distinctly different and absolutely contagious. It is programmed "Same Sort of Girl" and will soon be heard all over the country on dance floors everywhere, for it just makes your feet itch to dance to it. "Same Sort of Girl" will probably be used for one-step time on the dance floors, yet, it is one of those melodies of peculiarly fascinating rhythm that can be changed into time for Maxixe, Hesitation or mostly all of the popular dance vogues.

Virtually as an afterthought the article revealed that Kern had written four other songs for the show, including "a beautiful piece, 'They Didn't Believe Me.'" In his enthusiasm, the reporter or the publicist who gave him his information then proceeded to credit Kern with three more songs, only one of which, "You Never Can Tell," Kern actually wrote.

Conditioned perhaps by the pre-opening ballyhoo, the *Press*'s critic gave special praise to "Same Sort Of Girl" and "You Never Can Tell," hearing in them "the well-known Kern style of lilt." Later in the review, along with a second mention of "Same Sort Of Girl," the critic listed five superior songs from the entertainment. "They Didn't Believe Me" was the sole Kern number in the group. Of course, the playbill gave critics and audiences alike no clue as to who wrote specific songs. But the day when Kern could be passed over in the billing was gone forever, and the composer was credited with "Additional Songs" in type the equal of that given the original authors.

The Girl from Utah opened at New York's Knickerbocker Theatre on August 24, 1914. It was embraced as the first musical hit of the season. Surprisingly, New York's critics were no more swept away by "They Didn't Believe Me" than Atlantic City's reviewer had been. In fact, several critics failed to mention a single Kern song when they came to list their favorite numbers from the show. The *Dramatic Mirror* was typical, acclaiming "the chief song successes" to be "Florrie The Flapper," "Gilbert The Filbert" (both with music by Herman Finck and lyrics by Arthur Wimperis), and "At Our Tango Tea" (by Worton David and Bert Lee). The song the *Herald*'s critic felt "stood out above the other numbers with its popular swing" was "Same Sort Of Girl." In six reviews examined, not one contained the slightest hint of "They Didn't Believe Me." When Victor promptly recorded "Gems" from the show, it used only half of the song's chorus, while it included two full choruses of "Same Sort Of Girl."

Despite its relative critical neglect, "They Didn't Believe Me" nightly won audiences' affection and within weeks was the biggest musical hit in the country. Yet it was far from 1914's runaway song success. *Variety* recorded over half a dozen songs whose record and sheet music sales were larger. The list included such evergreens as "By The Beautiful Sea," "Can't You Hear Me Callin', Caroline?," "It's A Long Way To Tipperary," and "When You Wore A Tulip," as well as forgotten pieces such as "Sylvia" and "When You're A Long, Long Way From Home."

Alec Wilder is no doubt correct in dismissing "They Didn't Believe Me"'s light, charming verse as essentially unrelated to its chorus. The chorus is the strength and wonder of the song. Devoid of the trite, tinkly clichés that had marked so much popular show music up to its day, it progressed smoothly, freshly, and logically on its unhackneyed way. As Wilder has remarked:

> . . . the chorus is solid if unspectacular. Indeed the stronger Kern's melodies were, the less they needed interesting harmonic patterns, and well might have suffered from them. The melodic line of *They Didn't Believe Me* is as natural as walking. Yet its form is not conventional even by the standards of that time. In song writing parlance it may be broken down in eight-measure phrases as A-B-A^1-A^2. I can't conceive how the alteration of a single note could do other than harm the song. It is evocative, tender, strong, shapely, and, like all good creations which require time for their expression, has a beginning, middle and end.

For many the triplet in the seventeenth measure, over the rather awkward lyric "cert'n'ly am," remains one of the most intriguing inventions Kern ever employed. In interviews for this book, few comments have come up as often as the remark that this great song established the popular musical comedy number as it was to remain for the next half-century. However memorable Victor Herbert's or George M. Cohan's songs may be, they quickly betray their epochs. On the other hand, "They Didn't Believe Me" remains pristine and timeless.

It would have been impossible for Kern's four other original contributions to *The Girl from Utah* to be on quite so exalted and significant a plane. Nevertheless, there was not a weak piece among them. "You Never Can Tell" and, especially, "Same Sort Of Girl" must have been commanding invitations to the dance floor. Similarly, "Why Don't They Dance The Polka?" offered a melody that must have momentarily brought one-steps, two-steps, and fox-trots to a halt for a bit of Old World stomping. Yet the best of the four songs may have been "The Land Of 'Let's Pretend.'" In the show it served as both a prologue and an epilogue, with the principals stepping out of character (and dressed for a harlequinade) to invite playgoers to forget the problems of a war-wracked world. One of Kern's most romantic, fey melodies, the song assuredly deserves re-hearings.

With Kern's compositions clearly the real triumphs of the evening, Frohman decided to discard several more of the original songs and replace them with further Kern interpolations. None of these have the melodic invention or sense of high quality of his earlier contributions. "Alice In Wonderland" is a gentle, waltz-like affair, while "We'll Take Care Of You All (The Little Refugees)" was a more martial melody, whose lyric invited Europe's "little children" to "come over the sea." Despite his respect for Kern, Frohman followed the practice of the time by constantly adding other songs by other hands. However effective these may have been in the theatre, all but one failed to catch the public's fancy, and that one, Chris Smith's "Balling The Jack," was already a popular favorite by the time it was inserted to give Brian another dance. Some of these songs were added at the expense of Kern's additions, for not only did the refugee song soon disappear from playbills, but so did "You Never Can Tell."

The Girl from Utah enjoyed a New York run of 120 performances and then toured for two seasons. Wherever it moved, its songs and its publicity further acknowledged that from there on Jerome Kern was indisputably a composer to be listened to.

Tin Pan Alley and Broadway annals alike are strewn with ashen recollections of musicians who had meteoric careers, composers whose success or promise blazed briefly only to fade away forever. So the popularity and artistry of "You're Here And I'm Here" and "They Didn't Believe Me" could well have been greeted with skepticism. It remained for Kern to prove how determined, talented, and dependable he would be. To all but the most assiduous doubters, he gave his answer in the months following *The Girl from Utah*'s premiere. The material he wrote for a show that went into rehearsal in November proclaimed his new confidence and his well of melody. This show, *Ninety in the Shade*, would arrive in New York at the beginning of 1915, bearing with it a raft of melodies confirmed in Kern's new style. The style would ultimately be called his Princess Theatre style, and before the new year was over two shows mounted at the Princess would not only initiate a revolution in the American musical theatre but would reveal Kern as the revolution's fountainhead.

Richard Carle and Marie Cahill were the stars of *Ninety in the Shade*. Kern, of course, was by now well acquainted with Carle, but, if his interpolations for *The Opera Ball* are ignored, this musical would be his first professional experience with the "plump, pugnacious comedienne," Marie Cahill. Her reputation was fearsome. More than once she had engaged the most celebrated producers and composers in battle, and while she often came away licking her wounds (once she was fired), she was ever ready to re-enter the lists.

There was little chance Miss Cahill could be ousted from *Ninety in the Shade* since her husband, Daniel V. Arthur, was producing it. Indeed, following a 1905 contretemps with Victor Herbert, Arthur had mounted all his wife's vehicles. Their last show had been *The Opera Ball*. That dubious adaptation had been done by a rascally old-timer, Sidney Rosenfeld, in collaboration with a much younger lady who had written some popular songs and would go on to become a successful playwright, Clare Kummer. Miss Cahill was obviously pleased with Miss Kummer. At the same time she and her husband signed Kern to write the basic score for her new show, they retained Miss Kummer to compose several interpolations. Kern was to receive sole billing, but Miss Kummer's contributions would be acknowledged in the program. Kern no doubt offered little argument. The arrangement was clearly favorable to him, and he must have known that anything he would compose would necessarily outshine Miss Kummer's best attempts.

The new show's lyricist, possibly at Kern's suggestion, was Harry B. Smith. But the librettist was a name new to Kern. Guy Bolton quickly became not only one of Kern's closest friends, but one of his most important collaborators. Bolton was born in Broxbourne, Hertfordshire, England, on November 23, 1884. His parents were American, and his father a celebrated engineer. Bolton studied architecture in France. After moving to New York, where he helped design the Soldiers' and Sailors' Monument on Riverside Drive, he turned his hand to playwriting, at first with only middling success. If Bolton was hardly much taller than Kern, he nonetheless possessed an attractively masculine face and a deep, cultivated voice.

On Monday, December 28, Jerry entrained with the rest of the company for Syracuse, New York, where three days of dress rehearsals were slated prior to the opening. Advance press releases in Syracuse and later tryout towns, besides the customary glowing promises, presented some wildly imaginary tidbits, among them that "Jerome Kern, the composer went to the Philippines to make a study of their legendary airs" and that "the first fruit of his year's work there" would be the show's songs, songs that would establish a vogue capable of instantly supplanting ragtime.

Ninety in the Shade was first performed at the Empire Theatre, Syracuse, on New Year's Eve, and it elicited an enthusiastic response from its audience and the critics. The latter saw it not merely as a better-than-average musical comedy, but as one that was often refreshingly offbeat. The *Post Standard* recorded, "It is original in conception, its music is oddly interesting, it is consistent enough to rank as opera, it contains dramatic value and it displays superior comedians, singers, dancers and pretty girls, as well as several actors to good effect." Equally delighted, the *Herald* reported that the musical had enough comedy and talent for two or three shows and that the evening possessed "a distinct flavor of its own, and a very pleasant one." Then, neglecting to offer any credentials, but clearly led astray by the fictitious histories in the press releases, the *Herald*'s critic embarked on a remarkable analysis of Kern's music: "In most of the songs the composer, Jerome Kern, has introduced more than a hint of the plaintive sing-song note characteristic of Filipino melodies, but at the same time they are not without their modern qualities also. Filipino music, civilized, perhaps would describe it as well as anything."

If Syracuse reviewers gave accurate synopses of the plot, then a major change in emphasis occurred between the world premiere and the New York opening. According to upstate accounts a principal figure was the Philippine revolutionary, Mozi (Pedro de Cordoba), who is determined to marry the American heiress, Polly Bainbridge, for her money and her influence. Polly has come to the Pacific to wed Willoughby Parker, an executive in hemp, but Mozi shows her that Parker is a philanderer. When she is ungrateful enough still to spurn Mozi, he enlists Judge Splint, a temperance advocate, to wed them. Initially, at least, much of the plot consisted of Polly's ploys to keep the judge at a safe distance. Given his temperance leanings, inevitably, she succeeds in getting him drunk. But she does not marry Parker in the end, sailing away instead with Bob Mandrake, a charming sea captain. One thing not changed was the names given to chorus girls. Most were named after flowers, but one had the moniker Lettice Romaine.

Since Carle was Miss Cahill's co-star, the attention awarded to Mozi and the judge threw the evening out of balance. This must have been realized early on, for even at the Syracuse opening Carle performed with Miss Cahill an elaborate, lengthy spoof of a modern problem play, a spoof that had no real connection with the plot but gave Carle an extra chance to display his comic talents. By the time *Ninety in the Shade* reached New York's Knickerbocker Theatre on January 25, 1915, Mozi's and Judge Splint's roles had been reduced appreciably, prompting the original judge, Otis Harlan, to withdraw. The New York musical program read:

Ninety in the Shade

ACT I

1a. Scene Music
  b. "Where's the Girl for Me?" . . . . *Jerry [Victor Morley]*
2. "Jolly Good Fellow" . . *Parker [Carle], Jerry and Mandrake [Ed Martindel]*
3. "Lonely in Town" . . . . *Polly [Miss Cahill]*
4. "I Have Been About a Bit" . . . *Madge [Elenor Henry] and Jerry*
5a. "Rich Man, Poor Man" . . . . *Girls*
  b. "A Regular Guy" . . . . *Splint [Fred Walton] and Girls*
6. "Human Nature" . . . . *Polly, Parker and Splint*
7. "Whistling Dan" . . . . *Polly and Company*
8. "Where's the Girl For Me?" . . . . *Mandrake*
9. Finale

ACT II

10. Chant . . . . *Catti [Florence Dillon] and Natives*
11. "Package of Seeds" . . . . *Parker and Girls*
12. "Courtship de Dance" . . . . *Madge, Jerry, Dot [Dorothy Arthur] and Peter [Rollin Grimes]*
13. "My Lady's Dress" . . . . *Polly*

14. "Foolishness" .... *Parker*
15. "Peter Pan" .... *Dot and Peter*
16. "The Triangle" .... *Polly and Parker*
17. "Wonderful Days" .... *Madge, Jerry and Girls*
18. "My Mindanao Chocolate Soldier" .... *Polly*
19. Finale

Song, "Lonely in Town," and lyrics, "Jolly Good Fellow," "Rich Man, Poor Man," "Wonderful Days," and "My Mindanao Chocolate Soldier" by Clare Kummer.

John McGhie served as musical director. The production was staged by Robert Milton, with Julian Alfred designing the dances. No one was credited publicly with the orchestration.

New York critics welcomed the show politely. Few had harsh words for it, and fewer still glowing ones. Typical of the modest approval awarded the musical was *Theatre Magazine*'s assessment, which began, "'90 in the Shade' serves its purpose, useful enough, in entertaining the public," and concluded, "The opera has the merit of having less than the customary physical display. Its discreet choruses are nevertheless spirited, graceful and tuneful. Many of the songs are adapted to popularity. There are a few subordinate characters so individualized as to give opportunities for the players." When critics singled out a Kern tune, it was generally "Whistling Dan." Kern's growing renown was acknowledged when the *Dramatic Mirror* described him as "long famous as chief aid to anaemic scores," and, in what must have been a painful turnabout, confessed that Kern's work for the new show included "some very tuneful songs." Among the dailies the *World* echoed even the *Dramatic Mirror*'s metaphors and analogies. After comparing the show favorably with the old Gaiety musicals, the paper's critic suggested, "Jerome D. Kern, for many years Red Cross Society to imported musical comedy, qualifies as our own Paul Rubens. He has given the dance orchestras some new fox-trots and one-steps. . . . Rhythm and melody combine to make Mr. Kern's tunes the danciest, and to these requisites, deft orchestration always adds its allure."

Although *Ninety in the Shade* was a failure that precipitated personal tragedies, its score was a landmark in Kern's development—a breakaway that firmly established the patterns with which the composer would be identified for the next decade. The exact nature of this new style eludes definition. (However, there is nothing Philippine about it.) In essence it was little different from much popular music of the day—set apart by Kern's unique melodic gifts and impeccable taste. Much of it, however, did attest to the spread of the dancing craze. Song after song seemed designed as much to be danced as sung. Fox-trots and other voguish steps abounded.

If none of the new show's songs became immediately popular, all the surviving melodies—both those Kern published and those available in manuscript—were employed in later shows, many importantly in musicals of the Princess Theatre era that soon followed. "Where Is The Girl For Me?", the only song reprised in *Ninety in the Shade,* was eventually interpolated into a faltering importation, *The Lady in Red.* The song was then published as a bass solo, one of the few songs Kern released with the melody assigned to the treble clef. Like so many of his songs, it changed tempos and keys abruptly and dramatically, at one point moving from C to A-flat, and back again. "A Package Of Seeds," a lively 2/4 melody with a strange hint of melancholy, found its way into *Oh Boy's* great score. "It Isn't Your Fault" (lyric, Rourke) became "It Wasn't My Fault" when Kern and Smith collaborated on *Love o' Mike.* The song was also interpolated into a 1916 London mounting of Rudolf Friml's *High Jinks.* It remains one of Kern's loveliest, most neglected ballads. "Whistling Dan," which the Syracuse *Post-Standard* described as "a syncopated ditty with a whistling accompaniment," evolved into the title song for *Leave It To Jane.* "The Triangle" (lyric, Bolton) led into Miss Cahill and Carle's spoof of a modern problem play with a brief verse in 2/4, then an unworded waltz which underscored the action. It reappeared in *Very Good Eddie's* vocal score, although not on its New York programs. But audiences at *Very Good Eddie* did hear "Can't You See I Mean You" (lyric, Rourke), only it bore a new lyric and was called "Isn't It Great To Be Married?". With Clifford Grey slightly revising Rourke's original rhymes, the song was also heard in London's 1916 hit, *Theodore and Co.,* as "All That I Want Is Somebody To Love Me." The song's stay in *Ninety in the Shade* was brief. One Syracuse critic, noting it was not on the playbill, recorded that Miss Cahill had to be prompted, since she had not yet learned the song's words. Quite possibly both "Peter Pan" and "My Lady's Dress" were also reused. In any case, Kern did write songs that later reused the titles. *Ninety in the Shade's* sheet music further lists a song called "Love Blossoms." There seems to be no trace of a published copy, and neither programs nor reviews ever took note of the song. In passing we should mention that the songs for which Miss Kummer supplied only the lyrics did not have Kern music. For example, "My Mindanao Chocolate Soldier" had a melody by P. H. Christine.

Tepid notices and a spell of generally sluggish business combined to doom *Ninety in the Shade*. Audiences arriving for what should have been its fortieth performance on Saturday night, February 27, were given refunds, ostensibly because Miss Cahill was ill. Actually, four of her associates—Walton, Morley, Martindel, and de Cordoba—had refused to perform, claiming they had yet to receive their previous week's pay. Arthur had persuaded them to play the matinee, but by evening they were adamant. Erlanger stepped into the picture and offered to pay all the salaries if the performers would do the evening show and begin a road tour in Philadelphia the next week. Suspicious of Erlanger's word, the actors balked.

The losses incurred by *Ninety in the Shade* proved disastrous for the Arthurs. As Marie Cahill Arthur, the star entered a petition of bankruptcy on March 8, citing debts of $35,402 against assets of $23,827. She promptly went over to vaudeville to help regain solvency. Although she could not know it at the time, *Ninety in the Shade* was to be her last starring vehicle on Broadway, as it was for Carle as well. Both retained much of their popularity, especially on the road. But musicals of the day centered on young lovers, and Carle and Miss Cahill were no longer young.

Kern's failure to receive royalty checks for the last two weeks apparently rankled. After all, he was not yet securely established, even though "They Didn't Believe Me" was bringing in handsome returns. From here on Kern adopted a tougher stance on his royalties, a stance that would occasionally bring him into conflict with important colleagues.

Frohman again turned to Kern when he needed a song for a straight play he was producing, Porter Emerson Browne's *A Girl of Today*. The comedy opened in Washington early in February, received a critical drubbing and was hastily withdrawn. But Kern's song was too good to let die. "You Know And I Know" (lyric, Schuyler Greene) was one more of the delightful ballroom dance melodies he was pouring out with almost effortless abandon. Kern merely held the song in abeyance until his next major musical was ready.

At the same time, he permitted an older song a rehearing. When Klaw and Erlanger hurried a revue called *Fad and Fancies* into the Knickerbocker on March 8 to replace the failed *Ninety in the Shade*, its program included a Kern song sung on the same stage in *The Girl from Utah*, "We'll Take Care Of You All."

Whether Kern heard the song in the revue is moot. He may have been in London—although chances of this are small—to work on a West End show, *Rosy Rapture, the Pride of the Beauty Chorus.* The distinguished dramatist, Sir James M. Barrie, wrote the burlesque, while Kern, Herman Darewski, and John Crook combined to create the necessary songs. Kern published one number, "Best Sort Of Mother, Best Sort Of Child" (lyric, F. W. Mark). Pending discovery of a copy of the song, one can only wonder whether the melody was not that of "Same Sort Of Girl."

Even if Kern did rush hastily over and back—an especially tricky and dangerous feat in wartime—he could not have stayed for the March 22 opening or the last rehearsals, for he soon received a summons to discuss doing a new show for the Princess Theatre. Just when Kern began the work is lost, along with his contracts for the show, but news releases suggest he must have signed on about the same time *Ninety in the Shade* was in its death throes.

7

The Princess Theatre

For the most part the history of the Princess Theatre is drab, but its place in American theatrical history is assured because of the musical gems it sheltered while World War I raged.

In early 1912 the Shuberts, William A. Brady, and Arch Selwyn joined forces to erect a theatre on the south side of 39th Street, even then near the bottom of the theatrical map, but directly down the way from the Metropolitan Opera. The auditorium they planned for their site at 104 West 39th Street was to be far smaller than its neighboring theatres. Seating capacity was to be a mere 299. From the beginning the playhouse was called the Princess. William A. Swasey, who had designed the Winter Garden, was chosen as architect. Swasey created a nondescript, more or less modern, six-story façade that but for its electric signs might have passed for a swank apartment house. Four urn-flanked doors were the only entrance to the low-ceilinged, tile-floored lobby, which had homey lamps and a fake fireplace. But Swasey's tiny auditorium was a little jewel, vaguely Louis XV in style. The small balcony had just two rows, meaning that few cheap seats would be available and the theatre would be somewhat elitist by default. No seats were truly front and center, since the theatre's sole aisle ran down the middle of the house. Apart from fourteen rows that constituted the orchestra, there were four boxes, one box on each side, level with the stage, and a second box above each of the lower ones. Off-white plaster pilasters and moldings covered most of the walls, although two elegant blue tapestries hung between the balcony and the boxes. Carpets and upholstery picked up the blues of the hangings.

At intervals during the spring, summer, and fall of 1912, different projects were announced for the new stage. A group of New York's most prominent matrons was reported to have persuaded Annie Russell to form the Old English Comedy Company and book the as-yet-unfinished house as a home for classics fit for children. One persistent rumor had the new theatre becoming Broadway's Grand Guignol. Shortly before the house finally opened, Holbrook Blinn was appointed director and F. Ray Comstock manager. Blinn announced that the Princess would be devoted to one-act plays, primarily by aspiring new dramatists. The first bill of four short plays was presented, along with the new house, to the public on March 14, 1913. When the unknown playwrights and their short plays failed to draw, Selwyn and Brady grew discouraged. They sold their shares in the theatre to Comstock, and Comstock immediately set about finding a more acceptable sort of attraction for the Princess.

In seeking advice on how to move, Comstock turned to another figure who would loom large in Kern's future, Elisabeth ("Bessie") Marbury. "Loom large" is no figure of speech in Miss Marbury's case. Guy Bolton once described her affectionately as a "charming and benign elephant." She had been born in New York on June 19, 1856, daughter of a prominent attorney, Francis Ferdinand Marbury. Her father quickly became the guiding figure in her life. Before she was seven he had begun to teach her Latin, and as she grew older he directed her studies to such diverse reading as the Odes of Horace, Tasso, Kant, Samuel Johnson, Greek drama, and Shakespeare. She frequently accompanied her father to his office, where he allowed her to pore over his books and took time from his busy schedule to answer her questions about her reading. Her almost professional knowledge of international copyright, plagiarism, and piracy laws stood her in good stead when she set herself up as a literary and actors' agent. But her father had also passed on to her his business acumen. Bessie Marbury is generally credited with convincing playwrights to demand a percentage of the gross rather than accept a small flat fee and let the producer reap all future profits. It was Bessie who helped make Irene and Vernon Castle America's dancing darlings, and thus fuel what papers soon were calling "the dancing craze." Her success with the Castles led her to seek out composers as clients. Bessie had a deep voice and dressed as mannishly as the mores of the day allowed, but she often surprised her associates with the feminine warmth of her thoughtfulness. Marbury and Comstock had clashed in 1913 when she had brought suit charging that one of his short plays, *A Pair of White Gloves*, had been stolen from her client's *Au Rat Mort Cabinet*. Somehow the two came out of the scrape fast friends.

The idea for an intimate musical seems to have originated with Miss Marbury. But she and Comstock realized the venture would have to be watchfully budgeted, and so they ruled out leading librettists and composers such as Harry B. Smith, Henry Blossom, Otto Harbach, Ivan Caryll, and Comstock's first choice, Victor Herbert. (Years later Comstock learned Herbert was looking for just this sort of challenge and would have gladly minimized his demands for the opportunity to participate.) Miss Marbury suggested Kern. Whether he was then her client is uncertain, although by the next season he was listed in her roster. Jerry, for his part, suggested bringing in Bolton, with whom he had enjoyed working on *Ninety in the Shade*. Bessie replied she was aware of Bolton's works, adding, "He shows promise." Jerry's alleged riposte exemplified his quick wit and his growing assertiveness: "And now you're going to promise him shows." Comstock had already signed another librettist Kern had worked with before, although he soon disappeared from the picture. For the Princess's initial musical Comstock bought the rights to a ten-year-old English show. The earliest announcement appeared on March 3, 1915, in the *Dramatic Mirror*:

NEW PRINCESS POLICY
Paul Rubens's Musical Comedy
To Be Produced There on April 5

A radical change of policy is impending at the Princess Theater, on West Thirty-ninth Street, where the Barnes South African moving pictures are now being shown. F. Ray Comstock, manager of the Princess, has announced that in the near future he will present there a musical comedy, the book of which has been adapted from an English original of Paul Rubens, by Joseph W. Herbert. The music is by Mr. Rubens, with additional numbers by Jerome Kern. No title has been selected as yet nor has the cast been announced as yet. The piece is now in active rehearsal. The new offering will follow the Barnes pictures, probably on Easter Monday, April 5.

Cast members were revealed at intervals, as was the fact that Bessie Marbury's dearest friend, Elsie De Wolfe, would design the sets. Although the original title of the musical had been *Mr. Popple (of Ippleton)*, it was quickly changed in its American redaction to *Nobody Home*.

Rather than risk a tryout's unpredictable expenses, Marbury and Comstock decided to invite an audience of friends to a special dress rehearsal. The performance was a disaster. Many of the friends did not even wait for the final curtain before walking out. Now instead of merely facing the possibility of tryout costs, the producers were confronted with the uglier possibility of losing their entire $7500 investment. They decided to let Kern and Bolton rework the play, although they warned their writers they would have to confine themselves to the two existing sets and the existing costumes. All of Rubens's music was discarded and the story reset in America.

The action in Bolton's retelling began in the lobby of the Hotel Blitz. (The Ritz-Carlton was almost as new as the Princess, having opened in 1907.) Vernon Popple loves Violet Brinton, but their chances of marrying seem slim, since Violet's snobbish guardian, her aunt (Maude Odell), will almost certainly refuse to consent to her ward's marrying "a society dancer." Her refusal is virtually assured after she learns Vernon has been seen about town with the Winter Garden star Tony Miller. Vernon's dundrearyish brother, Freddy, appears. His behavior amuses Tony, so when she discovers he has no place to stay she lets him use a new apartment she has just rented but won't be using for a while, since her show is about to go on tour. Vernon arrives at the apartment to visit Freddy, Violet arrives seeking Vernon, her aunt and uncle arrive to consider subletting, and Tony arrives to create complications and, ultimately, to provide happy endings for everyone. In a salute to the dancing craze a number of chorus girls were given names honoring the latest steps—for example, Maria Maxixe, Tessie Trot, and Polly Polka, this last played by Marion Davies. Similarly, Quentin Tod was first listed in the program merely as a bell boy, but later as "Havelock Page, easily elevated to society overnight by his dancing."

The libretto was not always felicitously written. Much of the humor was outrageous, and had little or nothing to do with the plot. Furthermore, some of the writing was clumsy. At one point late in the second act, when the stage was suddenly and embarrassingly empty, the typescript reads "(Dance Specialty)."

As they rewrote, they rehearsed. Rehearsals often ran all the day and late into the night, prompting Miss Marbury not only to serve soup and sandwiches but to insist the performers receive at least some pay for the extra rehearsals. (In those pre-Equity days performers normally received no pay until the show opened.) At the same time Marbury and Comstock launched a barrage of publicity proclaiming their new offering was something strikingly different, and the last word in contemporary sophistication. Press releases, brochures, and inserts in programs at other houses in which the Shuberts held interest all heralded the forthcoming premiere. One brochure promised the "smartest musical offering of the New York season." Making virtues out of necessities, it continued, "It is said of 'Nobody Home' that there is a real story and a real plot, which does not get lost during the course of the entertainment . . . this particular offering seems especially appropriate to an intimate playhouse of the character of the Princess."

The revised *Nobody Home* was ready to receive the public and most critics on April 20, 1915. Most critics, but not all—since the Shuberts were having one of their intermittent disputes with a local daily. Programs warned, "This theatre does not advertise in the 'New York Times.'" In return, the *Times* sent no reviewer.

The musical program was:

Nobody Home

ACT I

1. Opening Chorus .... *Ensemble*
2. "Why Take a Sandwich to a Banquet" .. *Rolando D'Amorini*
   [Charles Judels]
3. Duet, "You Know and I Know" .. *Violet [Alice Dovey] and Vernon [George Anderson]*
4. "Cupid at the Plaza" .... *Vernon and Chorus*
5. "In Arcady" .... *Jack Kenyon [George Lydecker]*
6. "The Magic Melody" .... *Tony [Adele Rowland] and Chorus*
7. Military Dance .... *Bellboy [Quentin Tod] and Dolly Dip [Helen Clarke]*
8. "The Chaplin Walk" .... *Violet and Chorus*
9. Finale .... *Ensemble*

ACT II

1. Opening Chorus and Cakewalk ...... *Havelock Page [Tod], Dolly Dip and Chorus*
2. "Bed, Wonderful Bed" .... *Freddy [Lawrence Grossmith]*
3. Duet, "Another Little Girl" .... *Violet and Vernon*

4. "Any Old Night" .... *Tony and Chorus*
5. Dance .... *Havelock Page and Dolly Dip*
6. "The San Francisco Fair" .... *Tony and Chorus*
7. Finale .... *Ensemble*

Max Hirschfeld conducted Frank Saddler's orchestrations. The book was staged by Benrimo, and the dances by David Bennett.

The advance hoopla backfired. Critics were not overwhelmed. "Nothing remarkable" was how the *Herald* summed up its impressions. In a similar vein, the *Dramatic Mirror* concluded *Nobody Home* was "a good musical entertainment with nothing of special sensational interest." Critical comment on the music was sketchy, albeit generally favorable. The *American* categorized the score as "bright" without stopping to call attention to any one song. On the other hand, the *World* was particularly moved by one number, lauding "The Magic Melody" as "quite all its title implied." The *Dramatic Mirror* set down the songs as "bright and tripping," but added "only one song, 'In Arcady,' composed by Paul Rubens, makes any pretension to artistic dignity." Kern got the paper to acknowledge its error and give him proper credit two weeks later.

One reason he was so anxious to set the record straight was that he had not written all of the score. Although the program read "Music by JEROME KERN and Others," the interpolations were not properly credited. "You Don't Take A Sandwich To A Banquet" had words and music by Worton David and J. P. Long. Lawrence Grossmith wrote the lyric for C. W. Murphy and Dan Lipton's "Beautiful, Beautiful Bed." Otto Motzan composed the wordless "Nobody Home Cake Walk." Motzan and Kern combined their efforts on the music to "The Chaplin Walk" (lyric, Schuyler Greene), although just which part of the song which composer set down is uncertain. The composers combined, again inextricably, for a lively two-step, "Any Old Night," with Harry B. Smith assisting Greene on the lyric. But for the credit on the sheet music, the entire song could easily be ascribed to Kern. On the other hand, Kern clearly composed the verse to "At That San Francisco Fair" (lyric, Greene), while two celebrated blacks, Ford Dabney and James Reese Europe, created the chorus. Kern's driving introduction was a perfect lead-in to the joyously exhilarating chorus. "You Know And I Know," brought over from *A Girl of Today*, was an eminently danceable piece in the tradition and style of "You're Here And I'm Here."

The slightly raised harmonies of its bridge were especially refreshing. "The Magic Melody" was a marvelous rag, closely weaving around the principal notes in the main theme of its chorus. At the bottom of the sheet music the publisher made a startling statement: "This song is not a part of the Score of 'Nobody Home.'" Both songs had Greene lyrics. Herbert Reynolds supplied lyrics for Kern's other two songs. "Another Little Girl" was a pleasant, inconsequential ditty, composed in the period's popular 2/4 time. "In Arcady" had a verse in 4/4, but turned into a waltz for its chorus. Kern marked the verse "Moderato Pastoral. *In a dreamy and fanciful manner,*" but marked the chorus simply "Tempo di Valse Lente," although his adjective "dreamy" might well have applied here, too. The melody was sweet but unexceptional. Only the end was a surprise, for the waltz concluded not on its tonic but on a fifth. Later in the run, "Cupid At The Plaza" was replaced by "Keep Moving," neither of which seems to have been published. Eventually a Kern-Harry B. Smith song, "Wedding Bells Are Calling Me," was added about the same time it was also inserted into *Very Good Eddie*'s score.

In 1922, seeking the origins of commercialized jazz, Carl Engel suggested in the August *Atlantic Monthly* that "The Magic Melody" had provided the major breakthrough, recalling the evening in 1915 he first heard it, and continuing:

> I have not given the subject sufficient study to say definitely at what point the course of popular American music took a new turn, but unless I am very mistaken, "The Magic Melody," by Jerome Kern, was the opening chorus of an epoch. It is not a composition of genius, but it is very ingenious. While it is almost more tuneless than was "Everybody's Doing It"—if that be possible—and largely adheres to the short, insistent phrase, it stands on a much higher musical plane. Its principal claim to immortality is that it introduces a modulation which, at the time it was first heard by the masses, seized their ears with the power of magic.

The modulation Engel speaks of seems to be the characteristic jazz change from a tonic to a chord based on its fourth tone and raised to a seventh: in this case a B-flat seventh chording succeeding an F. This harmonic underscoring occurs in the seventh and twenty-third measures of "The Magic Melody"'s chorus. Without a study of all Broadway scores of the era there is no way to determine if any other important usages of such an identifiable modulation did occur earlier. But Engel took no note of some even more dramatic jazz harmonies Kern inserted into a song for his next Broadway offering.

Nobody Home caught on immediately, ending the season that had begun with "They Didn't Believe Me" on an equally triumphant note. But theatrical economics did not allow it to linger at the tiny Princess. In this respect it set a pattern all the so-called Princess Theatre shows would follow. The show could only gross a little over $6000 a week at the Princess, while its salaries alone exceeded $3500. (Just after the show opened the *Dramatic Mirror* ran an article on typical salaries, pointing out that "Few leading men get over $200 or $250 per week in the best attraction . . . leading women get the same or a little more." "Minor parts," the paper continued, "seldom pay more than $75 per week." Chorus players, of course, earned proportionately less.) With the prospect of realizing a profit of no more than $1000 a week at the Princess, the show was moved less than two months later across the street to the Maxine Elliott. Although the musical played only 135 performances in New York, three road companies were sent out, with one still touring the West Coast successfully during the 1917–18 season.

Eight nights after *Nobody Home* opened in New York, *Tonight's the Night* opened at London's Gaiety Theatre. In a curious turnabout, the show had been offered first to New York with many of the same English players who performed it for West End audiences. Like the source of *Nobody Home,* its principal score was by Paul Rubens. But the London version included two Kern songs: "Any Old Night," only recently introduced in *Nobody Home,* and "They Didn't Believe Me," the great hit that had been interpolated first into a third Paul Rubens musical. The song triumphed in England much as it had in America and helped secure Kern's reputation in Britain.

With *Nobody Home* successfully launched, Jerry apparently did agree to accompany Charles Frohman to England. In doing so he gave rise to the most famous of all Kern legends, one that probably has a strong basis in fact, although many years later Eva apparently told David Ewen the story was fabricated. (Betty Kern definitely recalls both parents confirming the story.) Certainly the existing void in his production suggests his schedule may have been purposely left open. Even the idea that he would have sailed without Eva seems plausible, given the rash of submarine attacks and the warnings published by the German government. One can only imagine Eva's frightened, private pleadings. But Jerry was tough-fibered, and conceivably offered what little consolation he could to his wife by assuring her he would spend as much time as possible with her family. Frohman had picked May 1 to sail—he customarily waited until the Broadway season was waning—and he picked a ship that was scheduled to sail at noon. He may have been aware of Kern's odd hours and may well have alerted the composer to what Jerry would consider an unsociably early sailing hour. Frohman's strictures were in vain. Even though the ship sailed from Pier 54 a few minutes late, Kern was later still. The ship had gone, and he could not arrange to overtake it. Frohman's reaction will never be known, for the ship was the *Lusitania*. Frohman went down with the ship, which was torpedoed by a German submarine and so helped turn American opinion against Germany.

Apart from the horror and compassion Jerry must have felt on learning of the news, one can only wonder what mixed feelings he harbored. While Frohman had indubitably given Kern many of his earliest chances, he had never, unlike the rival Shuberts, given the composer a chance to create a whole score. From beginning to end Kern was merely his principal American interpolator, and one to whom he apparently often begrudged even public credit. In later years, when Kern spoke of Frohman, he remembered the producer with respect, but also with a sense of reserve that implied his unspoken thoughts may not have been totally affectionate.

Missing the boat would have allowed Kern to attend the opening of *A Modern Eve* at the Casino on May 3, 1915, and hear two more of his interpolations: "I'd Love To Dance Through Life With You" and "I've Just Been Waiting For You" (both with lyrics by Smith). *A Modern Eve* was another importation, one with a checkered career on this side of the Atlantic. Originally mounted for Chicago at the height of the Viennese rage in 1912, the musical had failed to please the xenophobic Midwesterners. Now, after much rewriting, it was revived at a time of exploding anti-German sentiment. A good production, a first-rate cast, and Kern's two ballroom pleasantries could not overcome the spreading ill will.

With tragedy narrowly avoided and the Broadway season at an end, the Kerns could relax until rehearsals began for the fall offerings. His first two assignments were borderline affairs, shows that were neither full-blown musicals nor straight plays. Rather, they were vehicles for a pair of distinctive stars. Rehearsals began first for *Cousin Lucy* and reunited Jerry with Julian Eltinge, by 1915 at the peak of his career as America's greatest female impersonator. Although Jerry had only four songs to write, he clearly took their writing seriously and executed no fewer than two of them artfully. Perversely, the song that was apparently meant to be an outstanding ballad is the least interesting. "Those 'Come Hither' Eyes" (lyric, Greene) has a middling melody made difficult to follow by puzzlingly broken tempos. "Two Heads Are Better Than One" (lyric, Kern and Greene) is a lively waltz whose principal theme Kern later rephrased into an even better song for *Rock-a-Bye Baby*. But by far the most intriguing number is "Society" (lyric, Greene), an entertaining rag underscored by some startlingly advanced jazz harmonies. Kern elected not to publish his fourth song, "Keep Going," which may have employed the same melody as *Ninety in the Shade's* "Keep Moving."

Some suggestion of Jerry's steadily growing reputation was evident when the other vehicle, *Miss Information,* opened at Rochester's Lyceum on September 6, 1915. The show was billed as "a musical comedy and revue" with book by Paul Dickey and Charles W. Goddard, lyrics by John Golden and music by Jerome Kern. Actually, the show's star, slim, hoydenish Elsie Janis, had written most of the lyrics, so Golden's name was expunged from programs before *Miss Information* reached New York. But Jerry's contribution was not all that great either. He composed very few songs in the new piece. Of course, *Miss Information* had few songs to begin with.

Miss Janis played Dot from Nowhere, a telephone operator who suddenly discovers she must become a sleuth and assume any number of comical disguises. Her actions are prompted by Mrs. Cadwalder. The grande dame persuades her son Jack to hide her jewels so that she can enjoy the publicity the theft will bring. Her plan sours when a gang of crooks does steal the jewels. Dot not only recovers the jewels, she wins Jack.

By the time Dillingham's production reached the Cohan Theatre on October 5, 1915, more than Golden's name was gone. Instead of being called "a musical comedy and revue," the show was listed more honestly as "a Little Comedy with a Little Music." Indeed, there were no songs at all in the first act. Only one of the two songs in the second act may have been by Kern, the unpublished "Banks Of The Wye." The other, "Two Big Eyes," was by a man whose name Broadway had first heard earlier in the season, Cole Porter. But Porter received no credit on the program. Neither song was sung by Miss Janis. Irene Bordoni sang Porter's waltz, while Maurice Farkoa sang the other. Farkoa's third act solo, "Constant Lover," had words by Arthur Wimperis and music by Jerry's old friend, Herman Finck. Four more numbers from this act were unpublished: "Pianologue" (performed by Melville Ellis), a band number entitled "The Mix-Up Rag," and Miss Janis's "Dance Eccentrique" and waltz, "Driga Serenade."

The three published songs were Miss Bordoni's "A Little Love (But Not For Me)," "Some Sort Of Somebody," and one song dropped during the tryout, "On The Sands At Wah-Ki-Ki." Even though all three later found their way into *Very Good Eddie,* only "Some Sort Of Somebody" was moved over untouched. "On The Sands Of Wah-Ki-Ki" was a hula, for which Kern wrote only the verse to a 1913 melody by Henry Kailimai. Kern's refusal to write the hula itself was an early indication of a peculiar policy of his—a refusal to bow to the popular new dance beats that would sweep the nation. Although he wrote superb polkas, waltzes, two-steps, and fox-trots, these were dances he more or less had grown up with. But when Charlestons and jitterbugs and certain Latin-American rhythms became stylish, Kern abstained, insisting in several interviews that he had no feeling for such material. However reasonable such protestations seem on the surface, they would appear to mask an underlying arbitrariness rather than any lack of real ability. Given his genius, one suspects he would have written surpassing modern dance numbers had he put his mind to it. Some small proof of this is the success with which many of his songs have been given a Latin beat. Both the lyric and music in the verse of "A Little Love" had fun with the 1912 hit "Just A Little Love, A Little Kiss" before moving on to the engaging rag of the chorus.

A good many critics passed over the music entirely, and most had unkind words about the book. What small praise they could spare they reserved for Miss Janis. Although Miss Janis was unquestionably a star, she was not yet the wildly celebrated heroine World War I would make her. Her drawing power was still limited, as she learned when *Miss Information* closed after forty-seven performances.

For their second Princess Theatre show, Miss Marbury and Comstock introduced a new figure. Boyishly handsome, curly-haired Philip Bartholomae was a young millionaire who had left his family's business to try his hand at playwriting. His success was immediate, and nowhere more pronounced than with his farce, *Over Night.* Miss Marbury and Comstock quickly secured the rights to make the play into a musical, and the services of its author. Schuyler Greene was selected to create the lyrics.

Rehearsals for *Very Good Eddie* began on October 4, the day before *Miss Information*'s New York opening. On November 9, just over a month later, the musical gave its first public performance in Schenectady. Marbury and Comstock's astute publicity brought out a capacity crowd. The *Union Star* was delighted with the whole entertainment, noting of the music: "Among the numbers which proved highly popular with last night's audience were 'Babes in the Wood,' 'Hands Up,' 'An Ocean of Love,' which were of the cute variety; 'Nodding Roses,' Ernest Truex's comic song, 'When You Wear A 13 Collar,' and the dancing numbers and finales, which are pretty and snappy." The critic's only complaint was the weak timbre of the singing voices.

Even before truckers had removed the last of *Very Good Eddie*'s sets from the Van Curler the decision had been made to close the show after its second stand, Albany. Yet, unlike so many producers who announced they were closing for repairs when in fact everyone knew they were closing for good, Comstock and Marbury were aware they had a readily salvageable venture. By Saturday night the entire company was on a train to New York, not for the expected opening at the Princess, but for recasting, rewriting, and further rehearsing. Among the earliest casualties were the leading lady, Florence Nash, and the choreographer, Joseph C. Smith. Alice Dovey replaced Miss Nash, while David Bennett was called in to redo the dances. M. E. Rourke, now writing as Herbert Reynolds, supplemented Greene's lyrics, although his work was not particularly burdensome since a number of the songs apparently came from older shows and retained their original wording. Most important of all, Guy Bolton was asked back, to strengthen Bartholomae's book. He made no major changes. Rather, he cut out weak jokes, added better ones, and contrived a few minor additional complications such as inserting a new Elsie by renaming Caroline Powers, Elsie Lilly.

By the time *Very Good Eddie* was ready to resume its trek, Bolton and Bartholomae made the most of a fifteen-minute stopover in Poughkeepsie for the Hudson River Dayline's *Catskill*. Dick Rivers comes aboard. He has fallen in love with Elsie Lilly, Madame Matroppo's prize singing pupil. To be alone with Elsie he begs her teacher to let him interview the girl for a magazine article. Elsie is not easily wooed, for she is aware of Rivers's roving eye. Newlyweds Eddie and Georgina Kettle board the boat. Georgina is clearly determined to henpeck her tiny Eddie. The pair is followed by two more honeymooners, Percy and Elsie Darling. When the couples meet, Eddie and Percy turn out to be old schoolmates. Georgina leaves the boat to retrieve a bag Eddie has left behind on the pier. Percy accompanies her in order to send a telegram. The vessel sails without them. Eddie and Elsie Darling discover they do not have even enough money between them for one meal. Rivers appears, and Eddie, who knows him, is forced to pretend that Elsie is his bride. Rivers lends Eddie money. He also tells Eddie that Eddie's old flame, Elsie Lilly, is on the boat. As Eddie and Elsie Darling sit down to dinner, Rivers introduces them to Mme. Matroppo (Ada Lewis) as "Mr. and Mrs. Kettle." Eddie orders champagne for everyone. When they arrive at the Rip Van Winkle Inn, Eddie and Elsie discover there is no return boat or train. To the astonishment of the clerk they request separate rooms. Once they have signed the register, Eddie carefully spills ink over their signatures. Georgina and Percy arrive, but with the register ruined they cannot be sure they have come to the right hotel. Mme. Matroppo, who can never remember names correctly, assures them the only honeymooners are named "Fish." They take rooms and head for bed. But Georgina, remembering that Darling's wife is named Elsie, goes upstairs with the uneasy feeling that she was the Elsie Eddie had loved long ago. A mouse scares Elsie out of her room, and, when she knocks on Eddie's door he comforts her, advising her to be as brave as the babes in the wood. The next morning Rivers tells Georgina and Percy that Eddie Kettle and his wife are in the inn. But the Eddie who comes downstairs is a changed young man. He has learned how to handle himself, and, when he orders Georgina to sit down, she does.

As so often happened, names given chorus girls and boys were an entertainment in themselves. Some young ladies had relatively staid names such as Crystal Poole or Lily Pond, while others paraded about more flamboyantly as Miss Gay Ann Giddy and Miss E. Z. Morrels. Men answered to Dyer Thurst and Dustin Stacks.

Cincinnati papers, covering the musical's reopening at the Lyric on November 28, gave the show far more sophisticated examination than Schenectady's papers had. But they were not very encouraging. Typically, the *Enquirer* concluded its review by questioning "whether 'Very Good Eddie' will ever be as genuinely entertaining as 'Over Night.'" Of the songs, the critic wrote, "Jerome Kern has furnished the score, which is reminiscent of about every tune he ever wrote for any other piece. The music adds nothing to the enjoyment of the piece."

After a preview the preceding night, *Very Good Eddie* opened at the Princess on December 23, 1915. Its musical program read:

Very Good Eddie

ACT I

1. Opening Number, "We're On Our Way" .... *Victoria Lake [Julia Mills] and Ensemble*
2. Song, "The Same Old Game" .... *Dick [Oscar Shaw] and Girls*
3. Duet, "Some Sort Of Somebody" ...... *Dick and Elsie Lilly [Anna Orr]*
4. Quartet, "Isn't It Great To Be Married?" .... *Eddie [Ernest Truex], Elsie Darling [Alice Dovey], Percy [John Willard], Georgina [Helen Raymond]*
5. Finaletto, "Wedding Bells Are Calling Me"

ACT II
Scene One

6. Opening Number, "On The Shore At Le Lei Wi" .... *Elsie Lilly, Dick and Ensemble*
7. Song, "If I Find the Girl" .... *Dick and Ensemble*
8. Song, "When You Wear A 13 Collar" .... *Eddie*
9. Duet, "Old Boy Neutral" .... *Elsie Lilly, Dick and Ensemble*
10. Duetino, "Babes In The Wood" .... *Eddie and Elsie Darling*

Scene Two

11. Song, "The Fashion Show" .... *Victoria and Ensemble*
12. Song, "I Wish I Had A Million" .. *Al Cleveland [John E. Hazzard] and Girls*
13. Duet, "Nodding Roses" .... *Elsie Lilly and Dick*
14. Finale .... *Ensemble*

Max Hirschfeld conducted Frank Saddler's orchestrations. The second act set was by Elsie DeWolfe and costumes by Melville Ellis. No one was credited on the program with staging the show, although in his *Encyclopedia* Stanley Green lists Frank McCormick.

The careful, clever publicity Comstock and Marbury had showered on *Nobody Home* and the tryouts of *Very Good Eddie* was repeated in Manhattan. Even if the producers plugged their new offering as "the second annual Princess Theatre musical production," the series was by no means yet a genuine tradition. Nevertheless the first night audience was excep-

119

tionally chic. Vanderbilts, Havemeyers, Astors, Pulitzers, Baruchs, Elsie Janis, and dozens of other celebrities were on hand. Bolton and Kern crowded in among the standees. According to Bolton, he called Jerry's attention to "a large man in large spectacles . . . in the tenth row" who appeared to be having a singularly good time. Jerry replied succinctly, "Wodehouse," and, when Guy said he was unfamiliar with him, promised to introduce Guy to him after the performance. Their conversation became so animated that several other standees asked them to be quiet. Embarrassed and nervous, the pair retreated to the outer lobby and attempted to watch the rest of the show through a crack in the doors.

When the final curtain fell, Guy and Jerry left for a social supper at the Kerns' apartment. The flat was crowded not only with their associates at the Princess, but also, as Bolton and Wodehouse recalled, with friends and with many of the principals from a competing attraction, *Tonight's the Night*. The Grossmith brothers were present—brother George was in *Tonight's the Night*—as were Irene and Vernon Castle, Jerry and Eva's best man, Lauri de Frece, and his wife, Fay Compton. While Eva presided over the sandwiches, Jerry played the piano and Miss Compton sang. When Wodehouse arrived, Jerry saw to it that he and Bolton met, filling in details of the time he and Plum had worked together on *The Beauty of Bath*. To his death Bolton held with this story, and not even two interesting items in the *Dramatic Mirror* could shake him. The first, in the issue for September 8, 1915, announced that two new Kern musicals would play the Princess. One, written in collaboration with Harry B. Smith, was penciled in for an October opening. The other was scheduled for "the holidays" and promised to be "a new musical farce by P. G. Wodehouse and Mr. Kern." Long after October had gone by without any sign of the Smith-Kern opus, the *Dramatic Mirror* published a second item on November 27 which on the surface seemed to be an elaboration of the last part of its September notice:

> The Marbury-Comstock Company will produce during the Christmas holidays a new musical comedy called "Fully That." The book and lyrics are by Guy Bolton and P. G. Wodehouse and the music is by Jerome Kern. Maurice and Walton, Maurice Farkoa, and Melville Ellis will be among the principals.

Since the trade sheet had to receive the announcement several days before publication, it suggests it may have been released while *Very Good Eddie* was back in New York for revisions and may have meant that Marbury and Comstock were hurrying along another work should *Eddie* fail a second time. Bolton, whose memories, even in his middle nineties, were relatively clear and complete, insisted that he had absolutely no recollection of anything called *Fully That*. He suggested, by way of rebuttal, that the item may have been just another of the many irresponsible press releases issued by agents to gain public mention for their clients. By no small coincidence, every one of the names mentioned in the article was, in fact, Miss Marbury's client. Nevertheless, Bolton must certainly have been aware of the article at the time and so must have at least made some inquiry as to who Wodehouse was, if he really did not know it already. But the very fact that Wodehouse, and not any other of the dozens of possibilities, was coupled with Bolton and Kern's names suggests that there may well have been some earlier meeting, and, quite possibly, some tentative, abortive initial effort. One further fact tends to push the meeting toward an earlier date. Bolton and Wodehouse's recollection of guests from *Tonight's the Night* attending the party after *Very Good Eddie's* opening is chronologically impossible. *Tonight's the Night* ended its Broadway run nearly nine months before *Eddie* arrived, and its cast promptly sailed back to London. Of course, the show was playing when *Ninety in the Shade* opened. Quite possibly either Bolton and Wodehouse confused the openings, or else they felt *Very Good Eddie* was so much better known that no harm would be done by appropriating the show for their story.

Nor was Bolton wholly accurate when he recorded that *Very Good Eddie* was awarded an "excellent reception"—at least not if he was referring to the morning-after reviews. The notices were awash with quibbles. Of course, many of the critics were thoroughly pleased, and several, such as the *Evening World* and the *Sun*, took the easy way out of showing their approval by headlining their notices 'VERY GOOD EDDIE,' VERY GOOD INDEED (*Evening World*) or 'VERY GOOD EDDIE' PROVES TO BE A VERY GOOD SHOW (*Sun*). Many critics found parts more attractive than the whole, or the whole not at all distinguished. The morning edition of the *World* thought the show "was very, very good only in the acting," while the *Press* prophesied, " 'Very Good Eddie' is not going to set any fashions in musical comedies." Heywood Broun felicitously summed up the consensus of those taking a middle ground when he wrote in the *Tribune*:

> The music of "Very Good Eddie" is not pretentious, and no muses leaped and clapped their hands when the book was written, but for all of that it is an agreeable entertainment. Its charm lies

in the possession of more or less artless high spirits. Of course they are not really artless, but merely seem so. Clever work by accomplished players was needed to gain the effect.

Surprisingly, Kern came in for some of the harshest criticism. The *Mail* bemoaned, "The Kern songs sound all alike" and charged him with "melodious monotony." Such criticism was only partially fair. Songs in the period's musical comedies undeniably had a limited, similar texture. Almost all the songs were arioso, written for the full-throated projection so necessary in days before amplification. Ragtime had lightened textures slightly and allowed for a style of projection that was, perhaps, more shouting than singing. A decade had to pass before George Gershwin and his followers brought a truly fresh, different jazz style to Broadway and before Kern felt sure enough of himself and of Broadway theatregoers to expand his own style into equally fresh, different directions. In the meanwhile, to lament that Kern's songs all sounded alike ignores both the obvious fact that all great composers have readily identifiable styles and the incontestable fact that Kern's style, for all its period limitations, was far more artful and adventuresome than that of any of his contemporaries. Jerry could take solace in the *Sun*'s conclusion that he "had never provided a more tuneful score."

And a tuneful score it was! The show's hit ballad, "Babes In The Wood," quickly became a Kern classic. The infectious lilt of "Some Sort Of Somebody," moved over lyric and all from *Miss Information*, also caught the public's fancy. The chorus of a second melody from that earlier flop, the gay, raggy "A Little Love (But Not For Me)," was given a new lyric, and with a new verse became "Old Boy Neutral." The chorus was strengthened slightly by the addition of a few repeated quarter notes in the bridge that echoed the last part of the principal theme. The march-like "Wedding Bells Are Calling Me" was also probably extracted from Kern's trunk and apparently came from one of the pieces for which Kern worked with the song's lyricist, Harry B. Smith. (Or could it have been devised for that promised October show?) "Isn't It Great To Be Married," originally *Ninety in the Shade*'s "Can't You See I Mean You," catches the joyous exultation of its title, even if the song was sung tongue-in-cheek in the show. "If I Find The Girl" (for which the principal comedian, John E. Hazzard, collaborated on the lyric with Reynolds) was a vivacious two-step. Just as danceable was the show's best waltz, "Nodding Roses." Actually, only its chorus was in 3/4 time (with Kern slyly inserting a quotation from *Der Rosenkavalier* into his piano part); the verse was in 4/4.

Since the nation continued to be in the midst of "the dancing craze," another dance that was also the rage was added. "On The Shore At Le Lei Wi" was a hula, the same "On The Sands At Wah-ki-ki" sung in *Miss Information*. Reynolds put a new lyric to the music. Kern's juiciest dance number in *Very Good Eddie* was the captivating "I've Got To Dance," a number dropped during the tryout. The best and purest bit of ragtime in the show, it was wisely restored for the 1976 revival. After the show opened, "Old Bill Baker" was included for a time. Kern had written the song with Ring Lardner for the *Ziegfeld Follies*, but Ziegfeld had rejected the number. Comedy numbers are rarely meant to call attention to themselves musically, yet the only song from the show Alec Wilder found worthy of study was Eddie's show-stopping "Thirteen Collar." He remarks, "The many-noted melody of both verse and chorus [are] loose and casual, but the harmonization and voicing of the piano part is inventive and witty." Wilder's term "loose" is puzzling, at least applied to the verse, which is little more than another tightly fused series of alternating dotted eighths and sixteenths—a typical Kern device during this period. But he rightly points to the fifth and sixth bars of the chorus—an unsyncopated chorus consisting entirely of eighth notes—and perspicaciously compares the harmonies to the sound of "a Dixieland clarinet player." The show's vocal score contains a melodic, spirited waltz not included on any playbills, "Alone At Last" (lyric, Reynolds).

Despite the short-sighted crystal-ball-gazing of the *Press's* critic, Kern, Bolton, and the modern American musical comedy were slowly finding themselves. For Kern the process had been gradual but insistent. From the first fresh harmonies in "Susan" twelve years before Jerry had quietly yet steadfastly explored new possibilities, and grown in the very act of exploration. If nothing in *Very Good Eddie* represented the remarkable breakaway "They Didn't Believe Me" had, still, virtually everything in the musical was of a piece, in the better sense of the term. That is, the songs, regardless of their genesis, fit snugly into the story and unerringly caught its flavor. Bolton and Bartholomae's book was taut. The strained humor and awkward gaps of *Nobody Home* disappeared, and much of the evening's fun flowed directly from the legitimate characterizations. Although Bolton had employed the title of *Nobody Home* several times in its dialogue, he quickly picked up on Bartholomae's trick of using the title as a curtain line. All the remaining Princess Theatre shows would use the device.

In the spring, when business began to sag, *Very Good Eddie* moved down the street to the Casino, whose larger capacity permitted a lower scale. In the fall it moved briefly to another house on the block and then, shortly before it closed, back to the Princess. Two companies delighted the road, one traveling well into the 1918–19 season. Far more than *Nobody Home, Very Good Eddie* gave the Princess Theatre a cachet and began both a legend and a tradition.

8

An Intermission
and the Beginning
of the Annus Mirabilis

In Kern's life, 1916 was a quirky year. Ostensibly he had little new to offer his public. Actually he was extremely busy. But with *Very Good Eddie* appearing so late in 1915 and a rash of new shows not ready for New York until the beginning of 1917, Kern's 1916 calendar seemed bare. Yet even his private life in this year could have been branded quirky. Most of what we know about it we know indirectly or through hearsay, even if some of the hearsay comes from Kern himself. But incidents he and his associates recalled have an ongoing looniness about them. They are the comic small change of all our lives. That Kern remembered and retold several of them indicates how the assurances that come with success allowed him to sit back and savor day-to-day absurdities.

Myriad factors probably contrived to persuade the Kerns to give up New York and move to the suburbs. And in early 1916 they did relinquish their apartment and take a small house at the corner of Sagamore and Avon roads in Bronxville. Jerry and Eva rented the home from Edward A. Morange, who, as half of Gates and Morange, helped design and build many of the sets for Jerry's musicals. A fairly close friendship must have existed between the two men, for in later years Jerry bought other Bronxville properties in conjunction with Morange and Morange's wife. The Kerns' new home was a two-story stuccoed building that Jerry referred to as a bungalow and World War I realtors called "Dutch Colonial," although to later eyes it appeared neither Dutch nor Colonial. Jerry may well have been talking tongue-in-cheek when he insisted a minor incident brought about his decision to leave 70th Street. A policeman reproved him because he allowed his Boston terrier to run about unleashed and because it barked too much. Shortly after the dog began to enjoy the freedom of Bronxville's lawns it returned the courtesy by "assisting" Jerry after he slipped and fell into the Bronx River.

At the same time, Billie Burke had been lured from the stage to become one of the first major actresses to lend her glamour to the silent screen. Her voiceless vehicle, a serial, was to be called *Gloria's Romance.* Although screens were silent, orchestra pits were not. The smallest film houses offered a piano accompaniment to the flickering action while grander palaces had full-scale orchestras providing background music. Miss Burke convinced producer George Kleine and his backer, the Chicago *Tribune,* that Kern should compose the incidental music. On a visit to the film studio on Long Island Jerry was flabbergasted to see Miss Burke's beauty hidden under green face paint and purpled lips. The primitive orthochromatic film would have made her seem far more unnatural had normal make-up been employed. Jerry was happy to rush back to the relative sanity of the musical stage.

Kern, Bolton, and Wodehouse reached a verbal agreement to collaborate on a new musical for the Princess, but delays were quickly thrown in their path. Obstacles came from two sources: Erlanger and Savage on one side, and, of all people, Ray Comstock on the other. Erlanger and Savage had either picked up the small items about Bolton and Wodehouse in the *Dramatic Mirror* or else had heard of the new partnership on the street. How fully a crass money-grubber such as Erlanger appreciated Bolton or Wodehouse's clever craftsmanship is moot. Erlanger's dominant impetus may have been to deprive the Shubert-affiliated Princess of two obviously up-and-coming writers. To this end, he dangled a pair of immediate prizes. First, Savage's production of *Pom-Pom* was faltering, so Guy and Plum were asked to help Anne Caldwell rework her book and lyrics. Second, and more attractive, for the beginning of the next season Bolton was to adapt an Emmerich Kalman operetta, while Wodehouse could create new lyrics. (Only later did Wodehouse learn Erlanger had already commissioned Herbert Reynolds to do most of the lyrics.) To make the prizes all the more glittering, Erlanger agreed that Kern would compose whatever interpolations were required.

Meanwhile, down on 39th Street, Comstock unwittingly played into

Erlanger's hands. With *Very Good Eddie* successfully launched, Comstock proposed his new triumvirate apply itself to the next Princess vehicle, suggesting they adapt Charles Hoyt's 1894 success, *A Milk White Flag*. His writers were aghast when Comstock detailed a plot which centered on a funeral with a mock corpse. To their protest that songs could not be inserted into such a situation, Comstock is said to have replied, "The corpse has two daughters, and they have beaux. What more do you want?" The men responded, "But the daughters think their father is lying dead on ice in the next room. They'll scarcely be in the mood to sing." Comstock barked back, "That's up to you. I'm not writing the show." Kern insisted the story lacked the requisite charm for a Princess show or for any musical he cared to write. As alternatives, the writers revealed something about two musicals they were considering. One dealt with a girl who dreams of becoming a star while she drudges as a dishwasher. The piece had a working title, *The Little Thing*. Comstock was not interested. The second dealt with a young man who marries against the expressed prohibition of his rich Quaker aunt only to have his aunt appear on the scene. This piece also had a working title—*Oh, Boy!*. Comstock perked up a bit, but in the end insisted the trio redo *A Milk White Flag*. The men adamantly refused, so Comstock announced he would enlist other writers, thereby seeming to nip the projected Princess Theatre series in the bud. Whether or not the trio told Comstock of a third project is unknown. But if Jerry, Guy, and Plum had not begun work on that third musical, they must have started on it shortly afterward and put both *The Little Thing* and *Oh, Boy!* aside, for the first full-fledged Kern-Bolton-Wodehouse collaboration actually to reach the stage was initially announced in the *Dramatic Mirror* on July 8, 1916, when the paper reported succinctly, "'Have a Heart' has been selected as the title of the new musical comedy by Guy Bolton, P. G. Wodehouse, and Jerome Kern, which Elisabeth Marbury will present next season in New York." Quite possibly Miss Marbury planted the item to slap Comstock for abandoning her clients. In any case it certainly reflected behind-the-scenes controversy at the Princess and, significantly, Bessie Marbury's name was missing from credits on all future Princess shows.

All this while, ever since *Very Good Eddie*'s premiere, the public had heard no new Kern songs. Nearly five months later, on May 18, 1916, when new Kern music was again heard, many in the audience may not have associated it with the composer. For though the music was being played at the Globe, one of New York's leading legitimate theatres, it was played as accompaniment to a film. *Gloria's Romance* had been released. Kern provided a sixteen-part background consisting of an overture and fifteen themes for specific characters and situations. The themes were called Society Waltz; Gloria's Love Theme; Little Billie; Villainy; Gloria Theme; Automobile Ride; Gloria Serious; Judge Freeman Theme; Dr. Royce, The Hero; Friendship Theme; Conflict; Society March or One-Step; Gloria at Play; Treachery Theme; and Gloria's Father Theme. Some were brief. For example, the treachery theme took only seventeen bars. Others were much longer: the automobile motif ran seventy bars. The themes varied, as some of their names suggest, from waltzes to marches, two-steps, fox-trots, and even a gentle varsovienne. Not all were original. The Society Waltz was merely a development of the principal theme of *The Laughing Husband's* "Love Is Like A Violin." Moreover, some that apparently were original, such as Little Billie—which Kern did publish as a separate song at the time—and the Society March, were stashed away to be reused to better advantage later. Even though Kern conducted the Globe's orchestra on opening night, the music garnered little attention and was seemingly forgotten as quickly as the serial by all but the composer.

Less than a month later, however, a spin-off from his work with *Gloria's Romance* brought Kern a bit more attention, although not much. Ziegfeld had asked Jerry to write a few melodies for his latest *Follies*. Subconsciously or otherwise, Ziegfeld's very magnificence may have squelched inspiration. Composers knew in advance that the *Follies'* brilliant array of stars, its gorgeous Joseph Urban sets, and, most of all, its breathtaking line of beauties were what customers came to see and what they remembered when they left. Equally disheartening to the songwriters must have been Ziegfeld's indifference, verging on contempt, for the music in his mountings. Gene Buck wrote lyrics for Jerry's four contributions. Although all four of Kern's songs were sung for first nighters, several went by the wayside after a few weeks.

The *Follies of 1916* opened at the New Amsterdam on June 12, filled with a cast of names, many of which even then seemed magical: W. C. Fields, Fanny Brice, Bert Williams, Ina Claire, Justine Johnstone, Bernard Granville, Carl Randall, Ann Pennington, and Frances White. The edition had a theme, at least in some of its earlier scenes: a salute to Shakespeare. Kern's best song, "Have A Heart," was sung by Miss Claire and Granville as they spoofed Juliet and Romeo. The song is a gay little ditty in the style of the period. Heavily syncopated, small in range and tightly knit—the main part of the chorus ranges up and down only five full tones, from *c* to *g*—it suf-

An Intermission

fers, unfortunately, from a hasty, weak ending. Granville also came forward
to honor Cleopatra in "My Lady Of The Nile." The song begins in a
minor key with a resolutely pseudo-Oriental flavor, but switches to a major
key for a chorus sufficiently languid to allow a parade of Ziegfeld beauties.
Kern marked the song "Well-measured—but sensuous." Like his remaining
two contributions, it is pleasant but trite. The other two songs were not part
of the Shakespeare salute. Between changes of two lavish scenes, Miss
Claire and Sam B. Hardy sang "Ain't It Funny What A Difference Just A
Few Drinks Make?" The song is little more than a dreary series of exercises, made up almost entirely of eighth notes. Kern cannot have had his
heart in it. Miss Claire also sang the fourth song, "When The Lights Are
Low," again during a scene change. Beginning with an archly romantic
verse, it quickly moves into a sweet, innocuous ballad chorus. By the time
the show took to the road after fifteen weeks in New York both "When
The Lights Are Low" and, a little surprisingly, "Have A Heart" were gone.

First nighters next heard new Kern songs in two September openings—
an ocean apart. On the nineteenth *Theodore and Co.* premiered at London's
Gaiety Theatre, presenting not only a capital entertainment, but something
of a mystery. All the early announcements in the English trade papers mentioned only one name as composer, Ivor Novello. The suavely handsome
Novello had begun to make a small reputation by inserting interpolations
in West End musicals, much as Kern had before him. But it was the tremendous success of his war song, "Keep The Home Fires Burning," that
earned him a contract to write the new musical's score. Even when *Theodore and Co.* went into rehearsals at the end of July, the *Era* and the *Stage*
still listed him as the sole composer. But Novello's duties at the Air Minis-
try, actually not very burdensome, when coupled with his habitual laziness
took their toll. Although no public complaints were broadcast, Novello
apparently did not have a full score ready for Grossmith and Edward
Laurillard's new presentation. Still, not until the show began its tryouts in
Liverpool did Kern's name appear abruptly in the credits. Novello's fledgling aspirations must have taken a harsh slap when the *Era's* Liverpool man
reported one of Kern's songs, "365 Days," was "the hit of the evening."
London audiences agreed. The song's pleasant but unexceptional verse leads
into a catchy, devilishly insistent chorus. Its first four bars (which carry the
title in the lyric) offer a compellingly revolving phrase that is succeeded
by a four-bar halting, rocking theme. Both themes, with slight variations,
are then repeated. If these two themes are considered as a single sentence,

they are followed by a fresh theme of less obviously rocking quarter notes, punctuated with a bar of six unexpected eighth notes. The melody ends on a gay, roller-coaster of a theme recalling the first four bars. The song was followed immediately in the show by "That 'Come Hither' Look," a sweet, traditional ballad. Later in the act (all Kern's songs were in Act II) "The Casino Music Hall" gave the ensemble a vivacious rag. Its verse was interesting in that it was in two parts, with various principals singing one melody, while the company sang a lively countermelody. Just before the finale came "All That I Want Is Somebody To Love Me," obviously a Kern favorite. Except for the new title and some very minor changes in the lyric this was the same "Can't You See I Mean You?" that had been dropped from *Ninety in the Shade* and whose music Jerry had reused in *Very Good Eddie* for "Isn't It Great To Be Married?"

The mystery—if that is not too colored or theatrical a word—is where Kern was at this time. Was he on hand in England to write the new tunes when they were so urgently needed? After the *Lusitania*'s sinking, American papers became reluctant to print lists of sailings and notable passengers. Yet some ships did risk the crossing, and remembering Kern's refusal to be intimidated by earlier German warnings, there is no reason to believe he might not be brave and defiant enough to chance another trip. But several clues suggest that Jerry, after all, remained at home. Perhaps the most obvious one is the total absence of any mention by any newspaper or trade sheet of Jerry's being in London. In fact, the *Stage* in its review of the London premiere took space to list the writers making bows—noting proudly that both the show's co-librettist, H. M. Harwood, and Novello appeared in uniform—but nowhere mentioned Kern, a courtesy it would undoubtedly have extended had he accepted a curtain call.

Although Kern wrote only four songs to Novello's eleven (and two by Philip Braham) he received equal billing on the vocal score. Since the score was published by Ascherberg, Hopwood & Crew, Ltd., a house with which Kern had no connection, such prominent billing may well attest to his growing fame and influence, although it may just as likely have served as a polite way of reprimanding Novello for not completing the score on his own. Incidentally, Braham's name appeared only in direct connection with his two songs, and not on the cover or title page. In any case, Kern's melodic songs were put over by a first-rate cast that included George Grossmith, Jr., Leslie Henson, and Madge Saunders. This superior mounting helped *Theodore and Co.* prance merrily through 503 performances.

Across the Atlantic, Klaw and Erlanger's production of *Miss Springtime* gave its first New York performance six nights after *Theodore and Co.'s* London premiere. Even before the curtain rose Jerry became involved indirectly in an amusing contretemps with Erlanger. *Miss Springtime* was the Emmerich Kalman operetta Erlanger had dangled successfully before the new Princess Theatre team. Guy had informed Jerry that the title would be *Little Miss Springtime,* and Jerry duly passed the information on to Harms. As a result, the initial edition of the show's sheet music—both Kalman's and Jerry's—flashed the title on its covers. Erlanger summoned the authors to his office and curtly informed them that no show to play his great flagship, the New Amsterdam, could possibly be little. He issued an edict ordering the offending adjective expunged. It was—promptly.

Little or no, Jerry's contributions were interesting. Of the four published, three had Wodehouse lyrics; the other, words by Reynolds. Reynolds's lyric was for "Some One." Just why Reynolds wrote this lyric is lost. Quite possibly the song was from an older Kern-Reynolds collaboration, although the era's often Byzantine backstage machinations may have been responsible. The song is a solid, sweet ballad, without a hint of any voguish syncopation. Its sole novelty lay in that while its chorus was composed to what was essentially an ABAB pattern, the second A was entirely musical, no words attached. The nine bars are marked simply "(*Dialogue through music*) *delicato.*" The practice of dropping a lyric while the music continues under some dialogue was far from new, but that practice was normally confined to the theatre and published songs were generally provided with a full set of lyrics. Kern's issuing the song as it was performed was more than a little nervy.

"Saturday Night" (listed on programs as "A Very Good Girl On Sunday") is a mismatch of words and music. Most likely it was composed for another show and given to Wodehouse at the last minute for new words. The chorus clearly paraphrases the folk air "Molly Malone," even though the lyric makes no reference to the old song. Furthermore, the ninth to thirteenth bars shift abruptly from the 2/4 time used in the rest of the song to 4/4, and call for a broader tempo. Clever lyricist that he was, Wodehouse nevertheless was unable to use this change of pace to good effect. "All Full Of Talk" is a typical Kern pleasantry of the period, straightforward, if with little syncopation. Accordingly, Wodehouse provided an equally pleasant but ordinary lyric. The gem of the show is indisputably "My Castle In The Air." Alec Wilder devotes a full page to discussing the song in *American*

Popular Song, beginning, "This is the first time, in my opinion, that Kern not only wrote a fine verse, but wrote it, in a manner of speaking, at the same sitting as the chorus. The two belong together. The verse leads up to, and into, the chorus, as every proper verse should. In this instance, P. G. Wodehouse's lyric is as lovely as the music, and it works well from beginning to end." Such suppositions, however reasonable, can be dangerous. Manuscripts disclose that both the verse and chorus were substantially rewritten from an earlier, undated song called "Steady Little Girlie" (lyric, C. H. Bovill). In fact the song may have had yet another, lost reincarnation, for a penciled note on one manuscript copy says "Look up H. B. Smith's lyric." Nonetheless, although the entire song is short—only thirty-six measures—Wilder is right to suggest that "one does not feel cheated." Kern filled his lilting ballad with fresh tricks. For example, while the whole song is written in C, the verse ends and the chorus begins on the dominant chord, G seventh. If the song works even without its underlying harmonies, the reason may be a trick Kern employed in later years and may have used at this earlier date. When he finished with a piece, he would play the melody with one finger—for some reason he often used the eraser end of a pencil—to see if the basic melody was strong enough to stand on its own. Along with Kalman's "Throw Me A Rose," "My Castle In The Air" was the hit of the show. Its popularity, like that of "365 Days" in his English offering, played no small part in helping *Miss Springtime* achieve 224 performances in New York and great success on the road.

A month later Comstock's musicalization of *A Milk White Flag* was unveiled at the Princess on October 24 as *Go to It.* Kern's refusal to provide a score proved justified. The show was assailed from all sides and poor attendance forced its withdrawal after just three weeks. Undaunted, Comstock took the show on the road, where it quickly lost so much money that the producer threw in the towel. While Bolton and Wodehouse had stayed as far away as possible from the show, Kern sportingly permitted Comstock to interpolate two of his songs, "When You're In Love, You'll Know" (lyric, Golden) and the unpublished "Every Little While."

But Jerry had far more important things occupying his thoughts than the fate of *Go to It.* In the autumn of 1916 three new musicals, all with scores entirely by Kern, had begun or were about to begin rehearsing. The first to start practice sessions reunited him with the Shuberts (who were co-producers with Bessie Marbury) and his friend and lyricist, Harry B. Smith. Smith's son, Sydney, and Augustus Thomas, Jr., writing as Thomas Sydney, had created the book. Early announcements said the title would be *Strike the Lyre*, a pun stemming from the plot's centering on a man believed to be prevaricating, or *For Love of Mike*. But shortly before the musical took to the road for tryouts, it was given a title obviously dearer to the hearts of the Shuberts.

Girls Will Be Girls opened at Philadelphia's Lyric Theatre on November 20, 1916. The local critics were reserved, and several strongly criticized parts of the show. The *Evening Bulletin* suggested that the cast contributed more to the evening's success than did the authors. Turning to the music, the critic commented, "The score, by Jerome Kern, sounds rather thin. It is not orchestrated with great skill nor touched by many vivid dashes of tonal color. Some songs have a catchy swing, however, even when there is a lack of smoothness and no especial lure of melody." Nevertheless, the reviewer took time to single out six songs he felt had some chance of popularity: "Drift With Me," "It Can't Be Done," "Take The Eyes Of Mabel," "Dance Through Life With Me," "I Wonder Why," and "The Baby Vampire." In commenting on Kern's score the reviewer for the *Public Ledger* revealed that even at this early date Kern was employing music effectively to underscore the action. The critic found the score "light and graceful on the whole, never obtrusive, and in many passages a whisper of an accompaniment to what is taking place on the stage."

Critical reaction to the musical aside, the Shuberts and Miss Marbury apparently felt the public was not responding properly. After just two weeks they abruptly closed the show and hauled the company back to New York for revisions. Rehearsals must have been little short of frantic, for not only was the whole show, especially the second act, drastically revised, but a number of principals were replaced as well. Co-directors Julian Mitchell and William Collier gave way to Benrimo. The leading comedian's role was changed from "Billy the Goat, a Sentimental Burglar" to "Bif Jackson, the butler, a moving picture 'fan.'" But the central figure, as he had been from the start, remained Lord Michael Kildare, an English war hero who is the guest of Mrs. Marvin (Allison McBain). When all the local debutantes fall madly in love with him, their boy friends conspire, with the butler's aid, to expose him as a fraud. They succeed only in making him an even greater hero. In a further change, the title was altered to an abbreviated version of one of the two working titles. As *Love o' Mike* the musical reopened Christmas night in New Haven to hearty applause.

Jerry did not wait around to read the morning-after reviews. Instead, in a taste of the hectic schedule just beginning for him, he took a late train back to New York so that he could attend the final two dress rehearsals of *Have a Heart* the next day. Bessie Marbury was no longer the producer. When Henry Savage insisted that a technicality in their contracts with him and Erlanger gave him a right to the trio's next show, Bessie Marbury readily consented to turn *Have a Heart* over to him. Miss Marbury had enough irons in the fire and in any case preferred merely to act as agent.

On Wednesday Jerry and his associates joined the cast on the train for Atlantic City. Because another show was playing that night in the theatre they were to use Savage gave everyone a day off. But the next morning Savage ordered one brief run-through before the opening that evening, December 28, at the Apollo. Although Atlantic City had two newspapers at the time, both were run by the same management, which apparently saved money by hiring just one critic and printing his notice in both papers. Nevertheless, that notice must have thrilled Kern, not merely because the first two paragraphs were devoted to him, but because they treated his work so perspicaciously. The critic's by-line, Louis Cline, appeared only in the morning paper, the *Daily Press*. Cline hailed the score as "one of the best ever turned out by the prolific composer of that time-honored and country-sung 'You're Here And I'm Here.'" Admitting that "You Said Something" would probably be the hit of the show, Cline nevertheless lavished special praise on a song not in the playbill which he called "I See You There." To the critic's ear this was a real "gem." As for the rest of the entertainment, Cline was more reserved. He had only perfunctory compliments for the cast and reported that the book "dragged considerably in spots." Savage and his authors apparently shared the critic's reservations about the casting. When *Have a Heart* opened on Friday of the following week in Reading, Pennsylvania, for a one-night stand, an old Kern hand, Louise Dresser, had replaced Grace Field in a pivotal role, while New York newspapers carried announcements that Marjorie Gateson would supplant Leonora Novasio in another important role. Miss Dresser's entrance was so hurried that Reading programs still listed Miss Field in her role and a special announcement had to be made from the stage. Casting of the men's parts was apparently sounder. Thurston Hall, who had been brought over from *Girls Will Be Girls*, Billy Van, and another old Kern hand, Donald MacDonald, seemed secure in their roles. Some further idea of the pace of theatrical life when all small cities had legitimate theatres and when railroads could take you from one city to another with frequency and dispatch was offered when

Have a Heart opened the day after its Reading performance in Wilmington, Delaware—at a matinee! Jerry seems to have felt that he accomplished most of what he needed to do during the Atlantic City run, for Reading and Wilmington papers, which took particular notice of Savage, Bolton, and Wodehouse's presence, all failed to mention Kern's being in attendance. Puzzlingly, neither Reading nor Wilmington programs list "I See You There" or the title by which New York programs called it, "I Am All Alone." The omission is most likely an oversight resulting from haste since, again, both Reading and Wilmington critics took note of the song. Generally favorable out-of-town response allowed Savage to maintain his original schedule and to bring *Have a Heart* into New York's Liberty Theatre on January 15, 1917 with the following musical program:

Have a Heart

ACT I

1. Entrance, "Shop" .... *Salesgirls*
2. Duet, "I'm So Busy" .. *Lizzie [Marjorie Gateson] and Ted [Donald MacDonald]*
3. Musical Scene, "Have A Heart" .. *Ruddy [Thurston Hall]*
4. Duo, "I Am All Alone" .... *Ruddy and Peggy [Eileen Van Biene]*
5. Song, "I'm Here, Little Girls, I'm Here" .... *Ted and Girls*
6. Dance Duet, "Bright Lights" .. *Dolly [Louise Dresser] and Henry [Billy B. Van]*
7. Musical Scene, "The Road That Lies Before" .. *Ruddy and Peggy*
8. Finale .... *Ensemble*

ACT II

1a. Opening Chorus .... *Guests*
 b. "Samarkand" .... *Yussuf [Joseph del Puente] and Ensemble*
2. Song, "Honeymoon Inn" .... *Peggy and Ensemble*
3. Song, "Come Out Of The Kitchen" .... *Dolly*
4. Duet, "My Wife—My Man" .... *Peggy and Ruddy*
5. Duo, "You Said Something" .... *Ted, Lizzie and Ensemble*
6. Dance Duet .... *Ted and Georgia [Peggy Fears]*
7. Song, "Napoleon" .... *Henry, Flunkeys and Girls*

8. Song, "Peter Pan" .... *Peggy*
9. Finale .... *Ensemble*

Edward Royce staged the show and Gus Salzer conducted. Sets were by Henry Ives Cobb, Jr. No credit was given to any orchestrator, although he is known to have been Frank Saddler.

Have a Heart's plot recounted Ruddy and Peggy Schoonmaker's attempt to save their faltering marriage by going on a second honeymoon. The Schoonmakers come upon the husband's old flame, Dolly Brabazon, who makes waves, but Henry, a resourceful elevator boy, calms them.

New York failed to share the road's general satisfaction with *Have a Heart.* Critics were split. The *Times* judged it "a fine bit of fooling," while the *Tribune* complained it was no more than "passable." Most critics were content with Kern's songs. Among the more satisfied was the man from the *Post,* who reported that the music "tempts you longingly," while the *Mail* hailed the melodies as "charming [if] elusive." But perhaps the most enthusiastic notice was in the *Sun,* a notice which underscored Jerry's growing fame and the fact that, to some extent, this came from a more or less identifiable style: "a charming score, strictly in his own idiom." One particularly interesting comment was made by the *Dramatic Mirror,* which rejoiced that every Kern song "has always a direct bearing" on the plot. Although well-integrated musicals are not as recent as some people would like to believe, they were by no means commonplace then. But even at this date Kern was stating in interviews that he preferred to write songs only after he knew the situations into which they would be placed and something of the characters who had to sing them. Given the number of Kern melodies that moved from show to show with a certain cavalier ease, he was obviously still stating an ideal rather than a workaday reality.

Examined away from the faults and virtues of the original production, *Have a Heart's* score stands as one of Kern's better achievements, although obviously not one of his great ones. Its songs are variegated, inventive, and memorably melodic—and one of them is indubitably among the composer's neglected masterpieces. Of course, continuing a practice he was to employ virtually to the end of his career, Kern brought some of the songs over from earlier efforts. "Bright Lights" merely put Wodehouse words to a 1916 composition, "Toodle Oo," including the formerly wordless verse. "Look In His Eyes" (added after the New York opening) was the same "Look In Her Eyes" Jerry had interpolated four years before into a 1913 musical known both as *Lieber Augustin* and *Miss Caprice*. Only pronouns and the lyricist's credit were changed. Since M. E. Rourke had apparently decided to permanently adopt his pen name, Herbert Reynolds, the revised sheet music had to reflect the change. Songs not brought over whole were sometimes wittily hinted at. In "I'm Here, Little Girls, I'm Here" the melody the chorus boys sing while reassuring the chorus girls was clearly a sly paraphrase of the verse Eddie sang to console Elsie in "Babes In The Wood." "The Road That Lies Before" and "My Wife—My Man" are essentially the same song. As published in sheet form (under the former title) it is a pleasant, unexceptional piece, interesting perhaps only for its tempo changes. "I'm So Busy" is a friendly, old-fashioned American waltz, a bit reminiscent of "Meet Me In St. Louis." Its lyric is by both Wodehouse and Schuyler Greene. Since "Toodle Oo" also had a Greene lyric, the songs most likely were created for a show that never saw the footlights or even an advance notice in the trade papers.

"Honeymoon Inn" (employed in the 1976 *Very Good Eddie* revival) begins with four bars each containing a quarter note and two eighth notes. The first of the eighth notes remains the same, while the other two notes rise a whole or a half tone in each measure, and then are released for a jaunty end to the musical sentence. It makes a captivating chorus number. The title song is a middling ditty, far less attractive than the "Have A Heart" Jerry had written for the *Follies*. An equally lackluster melody is that used for "Napoleon," originally written for *Miss Springtime*. Kern professed to have conceived it while he was dummy in a bridge game. Admittedly, it was a patter song whose melody was trite by choice. In both "Have A Heart" and "Napoleon," Wodehouse's lyrics are the real strength.

The hit of the show was a charming, direct ballad, "You Said Something." The song is not only melodically infectious, but it displays Kern's careful attention to detail. Note, for example, the surprising, haunting chord suddenly injected under the last note (the *g*) of the chorus's third measure. But "You Said Something" was not meant to have been the hit of the show. That was reserved for another song, a song Kern had played throughout the evening and which his publishing house long afterward featured on the back of sheet music for other Kern songs. The song was one of the loveliest and most remarkable he ever wrote, as daring and appealing as "They Didn't Believe Me." Yet today the song is all but forgotten. The verse of "And I Am All Alone" begins on a high emotional pitch with a one-measure phrase that recurs at the climax of the chorus. Even the

ending of the fifteen-bar verse is unusual in that a sustained note is used
for the next to last word instead of the last one, which becomes the first
quarter note in a measure that also begins the chorus. This chorus develops
by revising rather than reiterating its principal theme. Over some remarkable harmonic progressions (which are detailed in Alec Wilder's *American
Popular Song*) it builds inexorably to a climax over the words "vision has
flown," at which point there is an abrupt stop and then the song resumes
only long enough to bewail at a lower pitch, "And I am all alone." The
intensity of the passion is striking, and it is probably significant that Kern
wrote much of the lyric himself. His deep devotion to his mother is almost
palpable in the phrase "mother's smile of tenderness." During the tryout
"Come Out Of The Kitchen," never published, replaced a song Jerry did
publish, "Polly Believed In Preparedness." Similarly, "Bright Lights" replaced "That's The Life." A song called "Why Can't It Happen To Me?,"
sung by Ruddy and the girls, gave way to a number for Peggy and the ensemble, "Daisy."

In the theatre Kern's songs were embellished by Saddler's superb orchestrations. Kern fully appreciated their artistry and was happy to give them
their due whenever he could. Especially gratifying must have been Saddler's practice of faithfully retaining a composer's harmonies and suggestions. No hint survives that Kern and Saddler ever locked horns in heated
intellectual debates such as those Kern and Robert Russell Bennett frequently enjoyed. Even the texture of Saddler's instrumentation urges that
he heeded Kern's plea for delicacy and charm. Blaring brasses, so common
in theatrical pits of the time, were all but eliminated, and when trumpets
were used they were customarily muted. The orchestra was far larger than
those at the Princess, with twenty-six instruments consisting of eight first
violins, four violas, two cellos, one bass viol, two flutes, one oboe, one
English horn, two bassoons, two trumpets, drums, and two harps.

Divided notices, plus the public's absorption with the country's obvious
move toward war, hurt business. *Have a Heart* ran only nine and a half
weeks in New York. But in 1917 the road was still willing to judge for
itself, so Broadway failures often prospered on post-New York stands. For
the show's tour Savage replaced all the female principals, while Jerry and
Plum added two songs: "What Would You Do For $50,000?" and "Whirl-
wind Trot." At the same time they dropped "Come Out Of The Kitchen"
and "Peter Pan." Tour programs also include a number, apparently in the
show earlier, called "Reminiscences." It was merely an orchestral version

of "And I Am All Alone," and so was probably billed as Jerry's way of calling further attention to the song. Savage's gamble paid off. *Have a Heart* flourished until it was finally withdrawn at the end of April 1919.

For Kern 1917 was to be his *annus mirabilis*, the year in which the extent of his prolificacy and the brilliance of his creativity were to establish him beyond any remove as Broadway's leading composer. Jerry got a further taste of how busy he would be the very day *Have a Heart* opened. He had spent the late morning and afternoon in Schenectady, supervising rehearsals for *Oh, Boy!*. That night he brought his suitcase with him to the Liberty, and when the final curtain rang down he did not stop to wait for the reviews but instead grabbed a late night train to Pittsburgh, where *Love o' Mike* was winding up its tryout tour. Jerry arrived in Pittsburgh on Friday morning and returned with the entire company on Sunday. The next night, January 15, 1917, *Love o' Mike* braved Broadway at the Shubert Theatre. Playgoers glancing at the program probably paid little attention to the names of several bit players—names such as Luella Gear, Peggy Wood, and Clifton Webb, that would soon command their own glamour.

The chorus was not listed by name, but only as "Boy Scouts, Camp Fire Girls and the Bronxville Volunteer Fire Department." Critics mentioned that the chorus was exceptionally small by the standards of the time. One might also note the private joke, Jerry and Eva having only recently settled in Bronxville.

Musical numbers were:

Love o' Mike

PROLOGUE

1. Scene Music
2. "Drift With Me" .... *Leone [Leone Morgan], Molly [Molly McIntyre], Vivian [Vivian Wessell], Luella [Miss Gear], Helen [Helen Clarke], Peggy [Miss Wood]*
3. Scene Music

ACT I

4. "How Was I To Know" .... *Molly*
5. "It Wasn't Your Fault" .... *Vivian and Lord Kildare [Lawrence Grossmith]*

6. "Don't Tempt Me" .... *Molly, Vivian, Leone, Helen, Peggy, Bruce [Alan Edwards], Ted [John Bohn], Phil [Quentin Tod], Vaughn [George Baldwin], and Alonzo [Webb]*
7. "We'll See" .... *Peggy and Bruce*
8. Dance .... *Phil and Helen*
9. "I Wonder Why" .... *Vivian*
10. Finale

ACT II

11. Scene Music
12. "Moo Cow" .... *Lord Kildare and Ensemble*
13. "Life's A Dance" .... *Helen, Phil, Leone and Alonzo*
14. "A Little Lonesome Tune" .... *Peggy*
15. "Hoot Mon" .... *Molly and Men*
16. "The Baby Vampire" .... *Vivian*
17. "It's In The Book" .... *Alonzo and Gloria*
18. "Lulu" .... *Vaughn, Alonzo, Bruce, Ted, Lord Kildare and Gloria*
19. Finale

The musical director was Jerry's old collaborator on *La Belle Paree*, Frank Tours. Frank Saddler provided the orchestrations, although again he received no program credit.

New York welcomed *Love o' Mike* politely. In its headline the *Tribune* labeled it a "SHOW OF CHARM." The *Tribune*'s man, Heywood Broun, usually among New York's most accurate as well as most readable critics, termed the show "agreeable, well mannered and dainty." *Theatre Magazine*'s appraisal was equally low-keyed: "A smart little show in spots is 'Love o' Mike,' with several captivating little tunes—if only there were somebody to sing them. A 'comedy with music,' it has both in reasonable quantities; but if it weren't for the orchestra, you'd never know about the music." The orchestra was largely identical to the one playing two blocks away at *Have a Heart*. One lone major difference was the replacement of the two harps by a baby grand piano and one upright, the latter with a "mandolin and banjo attachment." A press release noted: "The pianos are not employed as 'oompah,' but as solo instruments after the manner of modernists in the field of grand opera."

Love o' Mike's score falls a step or two down from the imagination and melodic richness of *Have a Heart*'s. Its best number, published as "It Wasn't

My Fault," had been cut from *Ninety in the Shade*. While Harry B. Smith was lyricist for *Love o' Mike,* the song retained Herbert Reynolds's lyric. A second ballad, "We'll See," was almost as good, although its attempt by Smith at humor somewhat marred Kern's graceful, flowing melodic line. "Drift With Me" is appropriately languid, but in no way distinguished. "I Wonder Why" is an effective rag crying for a few blues chordings such as those Kern inserted in *Cousin Lucy's* "Society." "Simple Little Tune," with a Smith lyric that professes to show how an Englishman might have written a "coon" song, is an indifferent melody with a slightly folksy, Western flavor. The *Dramatic Mirror* accurately described "Don't Tempt Me" as "a fox-trot of decidedly peppery quality." "Look In The Book" put new words to Jolson's number in *La Belle Paree,* "Paris Is A Paridise For Coons." "The Baby Vampire" is a novelty number colored with minor and diminished chords. Writing in 1929, in one of the earliest studies of Kern as a serious musician, Robert Simon saw in the chordings of the song's last measures a choice example of Kern's musical wit. Simon wrote in *Modern Music:* "The humor of Kern's music is an integral part of it. It does not depend upon obvious quotations. It is the humor of character. He can achieve his effect by short and yet not too broad strokes as in *The Baby Vampire* from *Love O' Mike.*"

Five songs were dropped during the tryout: "It Can't Be Done" (sung in the first act by Alonzo, Vaughn, Ted, and Phil); "Tell Me Why The World" (another first act song sung by Phil and a character eliminated on tour, Reine); "Who Cares" (Peggy and Phil's second act duet); "I Am Human After All" (Reine's second act solo); and, possibly, "Dance Through Life With Me" (which Reine, Vivian, Alonzo, and Phil romped through just before the finale). Kern published "It Can't Be Done" and "Who Cares." The first is uninteresting, but Kern may have found the seeds of "Good Morning, Dearie" in "Who Cares." The published music is noteworthy for another reason. Jerry had a reputation for carefully proofreading his printed material, yet the song contains a passage in 3/4 mistakenly marked 2/4. No doubt this rare carelessness reinforces the suggestion that Kern must have been almost frantically busy in these months. The songs added during the tryout were "How Was I To Know," "It Wasn't My Fault," "Life's A Dance" (which may be merely another title for "Dance Through Life With Me"), "Hoot Mon" (possibly an early example of Jerry's love of Scottish motifs), "It's In The Book" (published as "Look In The Book"), and "Lulu."

Love o' Mike far outran *Have a Heart* in New York—192 showings against the other's seventy-six. But on the road the story was quite different. Prompted by the musical's Broadway reception, Miss Marbury and the Shuberts arranged for a major touring company and a third troupe for one-night stands. A Canadian company was also franchised. The Canadian band folded after two weeks, while the principal road company played to disappointing grosses in city after city. Its Chicago stand, branded "a fizzle" by *Variety,* was abruptly cut short. By the end of the 1917–18 season the last of the troupes had been called in.

Hard upon the two openings, the *Times* Sunday theatre section ran a major article on Kern. Much of it was taken up in recapitulating his career with the obligatory praises. But one interesting paragraph purported to convey Henry Savage's amazement at his young associate. The paper recorded Savage as stating that Kern was "the most unusual composer he had ever dealt with, because he did not demand that the principals [in his shows] be good singers. That was because the composer believes that those who wish to hear really good singing will go to grand opera, and that in the lighter forms it is much more important that the lyrics be rendered effectively. Of course, if the soloist can sing, too, so much the better, but if he is only a moderately good performer and gets the words over the orchestra will attend to the rest. And Mr. Kern's orchestras usually do." Savage may have merely been rationalizing some critical complaints about singing in *Have a Heart,* yet in light of persistent critical cavils about singing in Kern shows all through the 1920s, the comment is revealing. Kern was not totally consistent. In later years he occasionally was to battle for superior voices and at least once, in his private correspondence, to bewail that one of his greatest singing stars had an overrated voice. Nevertheless, he preferred Fred Astaire's voice above all others.

9

A Perfect Little Show
and the Conclusion
of the Annus Mirabilis

Kern's decision to put a few finishing touches on *Love o' Mike* at its Pittsburgh tryout rather than attend *Oh, Boy!*'s maiden performance probably reflected more than his own evaluation. Everyone must have known from the start that they had a hit on their hands. Alone among the Princess shows *Oh, Boy!* moved so smoothly on its initially scheduled course that no delays were required. It opened as planned at Schenectady's Van Curler Opera House on January 13, 1917. Its first audience received the musical rapturously. The Schenectady *Gazette* hailed it as "a bully show" and assured readers that "Comstock and Elliott may congratulate themselves upon having secured another big winner for the Princess Theatre. . . . It is a tuneful success—a whirl of melody from start to finish." Critics in tryout towns that followed joined in the paeans. Like many of his colleagues, the *Gazette*'s man quickly alighted on "Till The Clouds Roll By" as the "most delightful" song in the show and its biggest potential hit. In his enthusiasm he also listed virtually every other song in the show.

Considering the cordial reception *Oh, Boy!* was accorded on the road, the number and variety of changes made was somewhat startling. Both male principals were replaced. The subplot was altered radically from a tale of a campus queen smuggled into the hero's house by a college football team to the one finally employed. Even the action was moved from upstate New York to Long Island, although the original setting in this case may have been merely a small bow to natives of the tryout territory. All typescripts but one show the same settings listed in New York. Yet for all the changes the work could not have been too laborious, and Kern (who returned to the tour after *Love o' Mike*'s opening), Wodehouse, and Bolton were easily able to have the show ready for the invitational preview at the Princess on February 19, 1917.

The official opening was the next evening. The musical program read:

Oh, Boy!

ACT I
Scene One

1a. Scene, Music
  b. Ensemble, "Let's Make a Night Of It" ...... *Jim Marvin [Hal Forde] and Ensemble*
2. Duet, "You Never Knew About Me" .... *Lou Ellen Carter [Marie Carroll] and George Budd [Tom Powers]*
3. Song, "A Package of Seeds" .... *Jim, Jane Packard [Marion Davies], Polly Andrus [Justine Johnstone] and Girls*
4. Song, "An Old-Fashioned Wife" ...... *Lou Ellen and Girls*
5. Duet, "A Pal Like You" .. *Jackie Sampson [Anna Wheaton] and Jim*
6. Duet, "Till the Clouds Roll By" ...... *Jackie and George*

Scene Two

7. Song, "A Little Bit of Ribbon" .... *Jane and Girls*
8. Trio, "The First Day of May" .... *Jackie, Jim and George*
9. Finale .... *The Company*

ACT II

10. Opening Number, "Koo-La-Loo" ...... *Jim and Ensemble*
11. Dance .... *Miss Dorothy Dickson and Mr. Carl Hyson* [Miss Dickson and her husband, Mr. Hyson, were not listed in the cast of characters and players.]
12. Song, "Rolled Into One" .... *Jackie and Ensemble*
13. Trio, "Oh, Daddy, Please" .. *Lou Ellen, George and Judge Carter [Frank McGinn]*
14. Duet, "Nesting Time" .... *Jackie and Jim*

15. Song, "Words Are Not Needed" ...... *Lou Ellen and Boys*
16. Trio, "Flubby Dub, the Cave-Man" ...... *Jackie, Jim and George*
17. Finale .... *The Company*
Frank Saddler's orchestrations were conducted by Max Hirschfeld. Edward Royce staged the work. Scenery was by D. M. Aiken; costumes by Faibisy.

Wodehouse and Bolton's story recounted the problems of a young man, George Budd, determined to marry his sweetheart, Lou Ellen Carter, without alienating his rich guardian Aunt Penelope (Edna May Oliver), a prim and proper Quaker. His difficulties are compounded when luscious Jackie Sampson climbs through his apartment window and demands to be protected from the clutches of an amorous old judge and the police. At one time or another Jackie is mistaken for either Lou Ellen or Aunt Penelope. All ends happily when the aunt is inadvertently made tipsy enough to give the wedding her blessing. Jackie settles for George's friend, Jim Marvin. Again, the librettists had fun with chorus names. Girls included Sheila Rive, Inna Ford, Annie Olde-Knight, and B. Ava Little, while among the men were Phil Ossify and Hugo Chaseit.

The cheering that had followed *Oh, Boy!* along its tryout trail grew louder and more persistent on 39th Street. There were very few dissenting voices, and even those were carefully muted. The *Times* rejoiced in its headline "NEW PRINCESS PLAY IS THE BEST OF ALL" and went on to suggest, "You might call this a musical comedy that is as good as they make them if it were not palpably so much better." The *Sun* exulted, "If there be such things as masterpieces of musical comedy, one reached the Princess last night."

Nor had the critics exhausted their superlatives by the time they came to discuss Kern, although by some curious coincidence virtually none singled out "Till The Clouds Roll By" as tryout reviewers perceptively had. In the *American*, Alan Dale exclaimed the evening offered a "BONANZA OF GOOD MUSIC," continuing:

> There are so many delightful musical numbers that it is next to impossible to mention all of them. Mr. Kern deserves more than a measure of praise for "You Never Knew About Me"; a charming flower song and chorus entitled, "A Package of Seeds"; "An Old-Fashioned Wife," with its lovely refrain; "The First Day of May"; "A Little Bit of Ribbon," delightfully sung by Marion Davies,

who, by the way, deserves her reputation as being the most beautiful girl in musical comedy; and "Wine, Women and Songs" [did he mean "Let's Make A Night Of It"?].

The *Times* elected not to pick any favorite songs, instead noting simply that Kern "was never better than in 'Oh, Boy!' "

Although "Till The Clouds Roll By" is the only great melody in the show and although Kern here displayed little of the musical daring and inventiveness he had demonstrated before and would show so often again, still, *Oh, Boy!* must surely rank as one of his finest achievements, certainly the apogee of his work at the Princess. If no song in the show approaches, say, "They Didn't Believe Me," "Smoke Gets In Your Eyes," or "All The Things You Are," there is, conversely, not a weak song in the score. *Oh, Boy!* is filled from its first curtain to its last with relatively straightforward but utterly beguiling period melodies. Inevitably, "Till The Clouds Roll By" takes pride of place. P. G. Wodehouse claimed that the song was "more or less a steal from an old German hymn" and Alec Wilder hears in it "a hymn-like purity." There is an old German melody, "Mendebras," to which the nineteenth-century Bishop Christopher Wordsworth set a lyric beginning "O day of rest and gladness," whose first six bars are strikingly similar. But even here the differences are marked and Kern's development is totally fresh. Wilder notes:

> It's forthright and uncluttered, employing a minimal number of notes, every one of which counts. It is typical of the great Kern "pure" melodies, which need nothing besides themselves to fulfill their task of pleasing, and also of delineating the characteristic elements of his style. It attempts no deviation from its key center; in fact, there is not a note outside its printed key. It is strong without being self-conscious, a completely natural and memorable melody, unmistakably his own.

Wilder's statement does call attention to a problem that exists in discussing this score. Apart from noting that the chorus never deviates from its key of E flat, it consists of generalizations that could apply to all the other songs in the show. Indeed, it reflects the fact that Kern did practically no experimenting in this score. Rather, he merely brought his unerring taste and uncanny, innate gift for melodies to the standard popular musical forms of the day. The melting sweetness of "Words Are Not Needed" (also published under its original title, "Every Day") gives place to the gentle pizzicato waltz strains of "An Old-Fashioned Wife," which in turn make way for teasingly rhythmic delights of "Rolled Into One." Aside from "Till The Clouds Roll By," the show's most popular song was undoubtedly "Nesting Time," a softly syncopated fox-trot. Two-steppers had a field day with the lively "A Package Of Seeds," brought over from *Ninety in the Shade*. Only two songs bear any study, and one of these for only a single bar. While readers may want to turn to Wilder's page-long discussion of a pleasant but essentially unexceptional ballad and dance number, "A Pal Like You" (also published under its original title, "We're Going To Be Pals"), the most interesting thing about the song is its next-to-last bar, where Kern works back toward the proper E-flat ending by means of two half note cs instead of the expected c and d. The startling flatness has pleased some but has clearly annoyed others, since several singers have recorded the song without Kern's repeated notes. Perhaps the most interesting melody musically is "You Never Knew About Me." Although the opening phrase of the chorus is repeated in the third bar, not a single musical sentence is repeated in all of the refrain's eighteen measures. Nevertheless the development is both logical and coherent. In almost all the songs, Wodehouse's literate, witty lyrics work effectively with Kern's melodies. When a few melodies are determinedly straightfaced or even, as in the case of "Words Are Not Needed," almost dangerously sentimental, Wodehouse's wit never clashes, but instead provides a dramatic surprise or at least some dramatic tension.

As with so many early Kern shows, no tryout programs of *Oh, Boy!* have surfaced, so we can only conjecture what changes were made in the musical program. However, in the case of *Oh, Boy!* a good chance exists that we can guess at virtually all the songs that were added or dropped. On the eve of the world premiere, the Schenectady *Union* printed a tentative list of songs, although it neglected to mention who was to sing them. The list discloses only two changes in the first act. "Ain't It A Grand And Glorious Feeling," sung early in the act, gave way to "A Package Of Seeds," and a late number, "The Bachelor," was replaced by "A Little Bit Of Ribbon." Neither "The Bachelor" nor "A Little Bit Of Ribbon" was published, but "Ain't It A Grand And Glorious Feeling" was. A joyously rousing melody, one probably meant for a full chorus, its omission could only represent a loss to those familiar with it. Either three or four songs were discarded from the second act, and two or three were added. The reason for the uncertainty here is that the *Union* failed to identify the opening number. In all surviving typescripts but one it is "The Land Where The Good Songs

Go." But that one is the earliest, indicating the song replaced "Koo-La-Loo" at some very late date. An undistinguished semi-ragtime number, "Be A Little Sunbeam," followed. Dorothy Dickson's dance specialty and "Rolled Into One" claimed its space. By an unintentional symmetry the two songs coming just before the finale, at the other end of the act, were also removed. The first, "When The Orchestra Is Playing Your Favorite Dance," was set aside only briefly, to reappear under a different title in *Leave It to Jane*. The second, "Why Can't They Hand It To Me?," was never published. In place of the last two cuts a rhythmic novelty number, "Flubby Dub," was inserted. Oddly, extant typescripts all include that song.

Curiously, Kern seems to have completely misjudged public response to his songs for the show. The original printing offered only four songs: the discarded "Be A Little Sunbeam," "An Old-Fashioned Wife," and two numbers performed from the beginning under different titles, "We're Going To Be Pals" and "Every Day." "Till The Clouds Roll By" and "Nesting Time," the show's two biggest hits and both in the entertainment from the start, were not published until later.

More than the superb songs contributed to the musical's success. Bolton and Wodehouse had contrived a story that was believable, if slightly far-fetched. Their characters were more three-dimensional than most (note that the comedienne was given the show's two best love songs, while the heroine was awarded its best comic number); their dialogue was literate and witty with a minimum of outlandish puns and gags; their characters and their situations interacted naturally, and the songs as often as not moved the action along. All the writing, and, apparently, the performance, too, had a consistent sense of style and tone. If there was nothing radically breakaway about *Oh, Boy!*, it was nevertheless patently a noticeable number of notches above the other musicals of its day.

Coming on top of enthusiastic notices, elated word-of-mouth spread like wildfire. The trade sheets—the *Dramatic Mirror, Variety,* and *Billboard*—quickly announced that *Oh, Boy!* was the hottest ticket in town. At a time when "hot" tickets usually remained so for only a week or two, *Oh, Boy!* retained its position for months on end, something virtually unheard of in the busy, competitive theatre of the era. Comstock and Elliot immediately announced plans for several road companies. By mid-April Elliot, Comstock, and their sometime silent partner Morris Gest took over Chicago's tiny La Salle Theatre to provide a base in that city for their shows. On June 2 the *Dramatic Mirror* reported: " 'Oh, Boy!' is in its fourteenth week at the Princess Theater. Not an empty chair has been known since 'Oh, Boy!' opened at this theater, and the house is absolutely sold out solid until the end of June." The producers' original estimate that the musical could run until July and then be moved to Boston had to be scrapped. Just over a month later *Billboard* announced that not only had "the advance sale of seats . . . broken all records ever known" but that in a totally unprecedented move tickets had been made available as far ahead as the coming Christmas. No outcry was heard when prices were raised to $3.50 for the best seats, the highest price in town. By the following fall five companies were criss-crossing the nation, playing everywhere to huge grosses, despite what *Variety* termed a "Country-wide Flop in Business." *Oh, Boy!*'s Chicago stay was twenty-three weeks, while in New York, where part of its stand was at the larger Casino, the musical played over fourteen months, tallying 463 performances. A company was still touring in 1922.

Because of *Oh, Boy!*'s success, the *Dramatic Mirror* felt compelled to send an interviewer to meet with Kern, much as other papers already had. Louis R. Reid, the interviewer, was most impressed with the composer's dismissal of voguish styles and fashions in musical comedy writing. He recorded Kern as saying:

> All this talk of the so-called intimate musical comedy being the prevailing style of musical production is mere nonsense. A comic opera, written according to new libretto standards, would undoubtedly find just as favorable a reception as "Love o' Mike" or "Oh, Boy!," provided, of course, the score was meritorious. I dare say, a comic opera, free from shallow characterization, obvious jests and impossible situations, and presented with a competent cast would prove extremely popular in New York. Plausibility and reason apply to musical plays as to dramas and comedies, and the sooner librettists and composers appreciate this fact the sooner will come recognition and—royalties.

A respect for tradition was implicit in Kern's remarks, but he became specific about his ideas of new standards when he turned to song cues:

> They are useless, unnecessary, and often glaringly inappropriate. It is my opinion that the musical numbers should carry on the action of the play, and should be representative of the personalities of the characters who sing them. In a scene of college life you would never to-day present students in songs which deal with

piracy or cheese manufacture unless the action of the piece demanded such activities. In other words, songs must be suited to the action and the mood of the play.

For the sake of introducing a catchy song, it was formerly the custom to prepare an elaborate cue, as nine times out of ten the number had no relation to the action of the piece. The very elaborateness of the cue showed the forced character of the number. In that way continuity of action was destroyed, and consequently interest in the play declined.

Kern had one more matter to get off his chest, one relating to tone rather than style or form. He spoke respectfully of Mrs. Smith's dictum—that "odor of sachet"—and advocated its promulgation.

The intelligent strictures that Kern spoke about were not new. Cries for integration of songs and text had been heard for decades, and in Gilbert and Sullivan as well as some of Victor Herbert's or Reginald DeKoven's better works, had been transformed from theory to practice. But they were by no means universal, and even Kern himself in ensuing years would occasionally have to look the other way. Indeed, it could have been argued that there was no good reason for bringing "Flubby Dub" into *Oh, Boy!*. But when it came to "good taste, refinement, daintiness and charm," Kern never swerved.

By June Kern had songs ready for two more shows. Actually he had only one song to interpolate in the *Ziegfeld Follies of 1917*, which opened at the New Amsterdam on June 12. Its insertion was probably more a gesture of friendship to the Ziegfelds, and the producer may never have realized it was merely an old song dressed in a new lyric. Nevertheless, Kern conscientiously reached back four years to one of his loveliest pieces, "When Three Is Company," from *The Doll Girl*. Retaining even the original piano part (and, unfortunately, the disappointing ending), Kern let Ziegfeld's right-hand man, Gene Buck, replace Rourke's original rhymes. The revised version was called "Just Because You're You."

For the second show Kern did have a full score ready, but New York was not slated to hear it for some while. Today, *Houp-La*'s presentation would be viewed as a summer stock tryout. Savage had persuaded the Hartford, Connecticut, Opera Players to allow his diminutive little star, Mitzi Hajos, to join them for a week while they interrupted their revival series with a new work. Kern's lyricist and librettist was a thirty-year-old redhead, Edgar Allan Woolf. Woolf's family was theatrical. His uncle, Benjamin

Edward Woolf, was an important, if now forgotten, figure in the nineteenth-century theatre, both in musicals and straight plays. Following the premiere performance on June 25 at Parsons' Theatre, Hartford critics agreed that the show would probably please New York. Nevertheless, they felt it was Mitzi who deserved the lion's share of credit. The *Times* merely observed that Kern wrote the score, without offering its readers the least hint of a comment, while the *Courant* fence-sat, appraising the score as neither "distinguished" nor "blaringly rampageous." At best it thought "several numbers likely to produce much popular effect." Savage and his star were clearly satisfied, and a fresh mounting was promised for the following season.

Kern stayed in Hartford only long enough to see the first two or three performances of *Houp-La,* since he was needed more urgently in New York, where another Kern-Bolton-Wodehouse opus began rehearsals the same week. In April Comstock had purchased the rights to George Ade's 1903 comedy, *The College Widow,* a play that had opened on Broadway the night after *Mr. Wix of Wickham*'s premiere. The musicalization had been scheduled to follow *Oh, Boy!* into the Princess, but, rather than disturb the hit's momentum, the new show was rebooked into a larger house uptown.

Leave It to Jane opened at Atlantic City's Apollo Theatre on July 30, a night of record-breaking heat stifling enough to daunt all but the most determined patrons. The reputation Kern, Bolton, and Wodehouse had built, however, was such that the theatre was packed. Many producers hold that theatregoers often read only the opening and closing paragraphs of reviews, especially the opening. Comstock and Gest must have breathed a sigh of relief when they saw Louis Cline's notice in the *Press*. It began, "Jerome Kern, Guy Bolton and P. G. Wodehouse added another hit to their growing list of successful musical comedies." Cline concluded his critique with praise for the producers and director, and just before this offered an entire paragraph extolling the score. He wrote, "The inexhaustible supply of Jerome Kern's music was never more pronounced than in 'Leave It To Jane,' for practically every one of the nineteen songs must be considered in the so-called 'hit' class." Cline called special attention to seven of these songs, including one, "I've Had My Share," that was abandoned on the road. Those readers who skipped the middle of Cline's review missed his serious reservations about the book, particularly his complaint that George Ade's distinct brand of humor had been scrapped and nothing worthwhile offered in its place.

Bolton and Wodehouse's book centered on Jane Witherspoon, daughter of Atwater College's president. Students know that if they have problems they need only bring them to her and she will somehow find a solution. A serious problem quickly develops for the football-mad school. Billy Bolton, an all-American halfback, signs to play for Atwater's arch-rival, Bingham. Jane is recruited to lure Billy away from Bingham and to persuade him to play for Atwater instead. She succeeds. Billy plays under an assumed name. While he helps Atwater win, he comes to believe Jane deceived him. It takes Jane all of the last love duet to make Billy trust her and love her.

After hopscotching Comstock and Gest's favorite tryout stands for nearly a month, *Leave It to Jane* opened at the Longacre Theatre on August 28, 1917. *Leave It to Jane*'s program is often thought to be the first to list the chorus as "Ladies and Gentlemen of the Ensemble." Musical numbers were:

Leave It to Jane

ACT I
Scene One

1. Atwater College Songs .... *Male Ensemble*
2. Duet, "A Peach of a Life" .. *Stub [Oscar Shaw] and Bessie [Ann Orr]*
3. Song, "Wait Till To-morrow" .... *Jane [Edith Hallor] and Boys*
4. Song, "Just You Watch My Step" .. *Stub, Louella [Arlene Chase] and Girls*
5. Trio, "Leave It To Jane" ..... *Jane, Stub, Bessie and Girls*
6. Duet, "The Crickets Are Calling" .... *Jane and Billy [Robert G. Pitkin]*

Scene Two

7. Medley of College Songs .... *Principals and Ensemble*
8. "There It Is Again" .... *Billy, Sally [Jane Carroll], Jane and Town Girls*
9. Song, "Cleopatterer" .... *Flora [Georgia O'Ramey]*
10. Duet, "What I'm Longing To Say" .... *Jane and Billy*
11. Finale

ACT II

12. Football Song .... *Bessie and Ensemble*

13a. Trio, "Sir Galahad" .. *Stub, Flora and Bub* [*Olin Howland*]
  b. Reprise of Football Song .... *Ensemble*
14. Duet, "The Sun Shines Brighter" .... *Bessie and Stub*
15. Duet, "The Siren's Song" .... *Jane, Bessie and Girls*
16. Trio, "I'm Going to Find a Girl" .... *Stub, Bub, Ollie*
      [*Rudolf Cutten*], *Louella, Marion* [*Helen Rich*]
                      and Cissie [*Tess Mayer*]
17. Finale

The show was staged by Edward Royce. John McGhie conducted Frank
Saddler's orchestrations.

A few New York critics shared Louis Cline's reservations about the book,
the *Sun* going so far as to headline its notice "'LEAVE IT TO JANE' A SAD
'COLLEGE WIDOW.'" But most accepted the libretto as up to or better than
the standards of the day. Some were downright enthusiastic about it. Alan
Dale began his review in the *American* with an old cry, one he himself
had employed in his review of *The Red Petticoat*, rejoicing at "rationally
American" material replacing creaky Ruritanian claptrap and exclaiming,
"The musical show has taken on a new lease on life." Yet the change, however clear, was in no way drastic. Kern, Bolton, and Wodehouse were not
scuttling old traditions, merely modernizing and improving them. The traditionalist in Kern must have been especially pleased when the *World* remarked, "This production again suggested, like 'Oh, Boy!,' the delicate
texture which once distinguished the George Edwardes musical comedies."
Kern must have been even more pleased to read the encomiums showered
on this score. The same *World* hailed his "delicate, tinkling and ingratiating airs, the mystery of which has made him the most popular of the
younger composers," while Dale saluted him as "the absolutely irrepressible
Jerome Kern, who seems to ooze sweet refrains from the pores of his skin."
The critics' favorite tune was plainly "The Siren's Song" (a curious title,
since the lyric refers only to sirens in the plural). Running close seconds
were "The Crickets Are Calling" and the title song. The strange punctuation of "The Siren's Song" is only one of several curious problems in the
titles of *Leave It to Jane*'s songs. Several songs were listed one way during
the tryouts and on opening night, but later were changed to match catchier
published titles.
  A hefty amount of revision occurred during the month on the road. At
least five songs were left behind and two added. "Why?", sung early in

the first act by McGowan, Flora, and the male chorus, was cut, as was Billy and Jane's "I've Never Found A Girl Like You," a duet placed just before the first act finale. Instead they were given "What I'm Longing To Say" in the same spot. Billy and Jane also lost their early second act duet, "I've Played For You." Flora lost her second act "Poor Prune" (a song restored for a 1959 revival), but by way of compensation was given a new song in the first act, "Cleopatterer." The final cut was the song the Atlantic City critic had praised, "I've Had My Share," done on the road by Billy and the chorus girls late in the last act.

In retrospect Alec Wilder branded the musical's score "solidly 'new Kern,'" although by 1917 the composer's new style was actually two years old. The verse of "The Siren's Song" is squarely written in 4/4 time and marked "Moderato." It leads naturally into the shorter, slower chorus. The fifteen-bar chorus is heavily syncopated, but when played properly in the "slow and dreamy" tempo Kern called for the syncopation falls swooningly on the ear, a far cry from common rags of the period. Apart from a three-bar vamp in 4/8, "The Crickets Are Calling" is in 2/4 and marked "Allegro." The lyric reflects the marking, employing words such as "merrily" and "chirping." Yet somehow the song works beautifully, possibly more beautifully, when done slowly. The basic melody of the title song looks stolidly four-square on paper, written as it is almost entirely in quarter and half notes. But the fact is that the melody is subtly syncopated. When played with Kern's superb harmonies (witness the diminished chord in the second bar) and coupled with its lively, more obviously syncopated counter-melody, it turns into one of the composer's most irresistibly fetching creations. Playgoers with good memories could recognize the principal theme as the main theme of *Ninety in the Shade*'s "Whistling Dan," although the countermelody had been revised. Theatregoers who had seen *Oh, Boy!*'s tryout could recognize another song, then called "When The Orchestra's Playing Your Favorite Dance," renamed for *Leave It to Jane*'s tryout "When The Orchestra's Playing Your Favorite Waltz," and finally titled "There It Is Again." The song is a lovely, yet unusual waltz in which Kern successfully captures a halting, groping attempt to recall a tune by bringing in two bars of unsung melody before each "There it is again." In fact the first four notes of the initial "there it is again" are pizzicato, as if to convey the singer's hushed, hurried exclamation as he continues to listen to the old song. The exclamations work cleverly into a lovely, flowing waltz. "The Sun Shines Brighter" (originally called "I'm So Happy") is indeed sunny and warming, with what Wilder rightly sees as containing "all the requirements of a swinging song," while "Wait Till Tomorrow" conveys its optimistic message by progressions of rising notes. "What I'm Longing To Say" is a gentle, rocking waltz with almost a nursery softness. For his peppy "I'm Going To Find A Girl," Kern reused his "Little Billie" theme from *Gloria's Romance,* making only minor changes but speeding the tempo. Wilder also praises a number that appears in none of the show's programs although it was published, "It's A Great Big Land."

Because the Longacre was triple the size of the Princess, Comstock and Gest wisely elected to charge no more than $2.50 for the best seats, a dollar less than they were asking for *Oh, Boy!.* These cheaper seats, coupled with the generally receptive notices, got *Leave It to Jane* off to a flying start. It regularly grossed $9000 a week, a thousand or two more than *Oh, Boy!.* Yet while *Oh, Boy!* ran over a year, *Leave It to Jane* ran only twenty-one weeks, or 167 performances. The record is somewhat deceptive. The newer show was forced to leave by a booking jam. Nevertheless the show would not have been forced onto the road if it had still been playing to capacity. For some reason it never caught the public's fancy the way *Oh, Boy!* had. In Chicago, where it followed *Oh, Boy!* into the tiny La Salle Theatre, it played eighteen weeks to the older show's twenty-three, and no booking problems forced it to close. Three road companies were sent out in 1918–19, but even there results were disappointing. One troupe closed in December of 1918, a second in April of 1919. *Variety,* looking for a reason for the unexpected lack of strength, could only suggest the musical had been "too expensively framed."

The rampant antagonism toward operettas from the Central Powers made it imperative that Kern (or someone of his ilk) interpolate a song or two into Klaw and Erlanger's latest importation, Emmerich Kalman's *The Riviera Girl,* which arrived for inspection at the New Amsterdam on September 24, 1917. Kern and Wodehouse combined to contribute just a single song, "Bungalow In Quogue." But this lone interpolation was a dandy. Possibly to call attention to Wodehouse's deliciously witty lyric Kern contrived a melody based largely on repeated notes. Normally this makes for a dull tune. But Kern found a uniquely felicitous blend of notes and tempo, and so turned out a compellingly engaging ditty. It became an immediate success both in the theatre and on the street, but it could not save *The Riviera Girl.*

Just over a month later, on October 28, Jerry had the bittersweet pleasure of helping to salute E. E. Rice's fortieth anniversary as a theatrical producer, a salute given eleven years and two months after the testimonial for Rice's thirtieth anniversary. So much water had roared over the dam since that last affair, and so much more since Rice had given Jerry his first real chance in *Mr. Wix of Wickham*. Yet if Rice and Jerry had time for a private *tête-à-tête* it must have been a little painful for both. In the intervening years Jerry had risen from being a minor tunesmith to the pinnacle of his profession, while Rice had slipped from the heights into virtual oblivion. His testimonial was, in fact, a benefit, designed to scrape together a small sum for the improvident, impoverished old man.

In late 1916 Dillingham and Ziegfeld had taken an extended lease on the Century Theatre. This huge, elegant house was far uptown, overlooking Central Park between 62nd and 63rd streets. Several popular managers there had found they were unable to lure patrons away from Times Square's convenient cluster of playhouses. Their failures could not daunt Dillingham and Ziegfeld, who knew that they themselves both represented a singularly potent glamour and occupied a unique niche in Broadway's pantheon. Their first offering suggested they could indeed break the house's jinx. *The Century Girl* opened in November of 1916 and ran six months. Neither producer ever did things by halves, and, when they combined, they brought together an almost unbelievable array of talent. *The Century Girl* offered a score by Victor Herbert and Irving Berlin, magnificent settings by Joseph Urban, and an all-star cast. By the time the producers were ready to consider their 1917 offering, the Princess Theatre shows were the talk of the town, so no one was surprised when Kern was selected to replace Berlin and when Bolton and Wodehouse were signed for sketches and lyrics. All through late summer and early fall an imposing line-up of performers was slowly compiled, a line-up that in retrospect seems incontestably more glamorous than even *The Century Girl*'s. Victor Herbert returned to provide his share of the score and Urban was again on hand to offer his strikingly imaginative designs. Lady Duff-Gordon (Lucile) created the costumes. Ned Wayburn was hired to direct and Adolf Bolm to choreograph.

When shows are in trouble, the troubles usually appear quite early. In the case of the new show, which Dillingham and Ziegfeld decided to call *Miss 1917*, the troubles began at the very first rehearsal. Jerry had been assigned to write a song that would frame the first-act finale, which was to consist of a medley of old favorites and a salute to then not-too-distant performers who had made them famous. Several of those performers were in fact in the show. Bessie McCoy had returned to the stage as Bessie McCoy Davis and would sing "The Yama Yama Man" much as she had nine years before in *Three Twins*. Elizabeth Brice and Charles King would revive "Be My Baby Bumble Bee" from *A Winsome Widow*. Other cast members were selected to impersonate famous artists not in the show and to sing their songs. For example, Marion Davies was to play Edna May and sing her "Follow On," from *The Belle of New York*.

When it came to assigning Vivienne Segal a song, Herbert promptly suggested that she do Fritzi Scheff's "Kiss Me Again." Jerry said he thought Miss Segal in no way resembled Herbert's old star but that she could easily impersonate Julia Sanderson and sing "They Didn't Believe Me." A mild argument ensued between the two composers, with each telling the young singer to go home and study his particular song. Miss Segal had only come to Broadway's attention two years before in *The Blue Paradise*. She rightly felt her place was not yet secure, but feared offending either Kern or Herbert. She took both songs home and sang each one carefully several times. Finally she concluded that Herbert was correct. His song fit her natural tessitura comfortably. Rather than make the ultimate decision herself, Miss Segal solicited Dillingham's advice. He told her, "Stick to your guns." Several days later when the time came for the first run-through of the scene, Miss Segal waited for her turn, then came forward and began to sing "Kiss Me Again." She had barely sung the first phrase when Jerry came running from his seat at the rear of the large house, demanding she stop. He repeated the arguments he had made earlier and insisted that Miss Segal sing "They Didn't Believe Me." Aware she now had Dillingham's backing, Miss Segal politely refused. The refusal was too much for Jerry. He blew his stack. He assailed not only Miss Segal and Dillingham, but "Kiss Me Again" and Herbert as well. This, in turn, infuriated Herbert, who had been sitting quietly in a seat on the other side of the house. He rushed to the defense of both Miss Segal and his song. Realizing he was outnumbered only fueled Jerry's fury. In no time each composer was running up and down the aisle on his side of the house, yelling insults and epithets at the other. For the moment Miss Segal was left standing dumbfounded on the stage.

Someone ran to get one of the producers and found Dillingham. As carefully as he could Dillingham pointed out to Jerry that besides a new Kern song framing the whole scene Jerry was to write a second dance tune that would be incorporated into the number. His two tunes would precisely balance two Herbert numbers in the scene (since Herbert's "March Of The Toys" was also included). Jerry parried that Herbert's numbers were already well known, almost classics in their field, while his would be unfamiliar and untested. Dillingham was unswayed. Exercising his rights as producer he bluntly told Jerry that Miss Segal would sing "Kiss Me Again." Jerry stormed out of the house, vowing to have nothing further to do with the show.

Other less publicized troubles obviously appeared, as the constant delays in opening hinted. The show had originally gone into rehearsal late in September with a promised October 21 opening. By the second week of October the opening had been set back to October 29, and ten days later it was set back again to November 5.

Little is known about one fascinating aspect of the rehearsals. The rehearsal pianist was nineteen-year-old George Gershwin. Gershwin had originally been impelled to write show music after hearing Kern's "You're Here And I'm Here" and songs from *The Girl from Utah.* Years later he still remembered his determination to compose music of "the kind Jerome Kern was writing." Published excerpts from Ira Gershwin's diaries suggested that George was awed to be working for his idol. But they hint at no special attention nor at any unusual problems. Still, it may be more than coincidental that shortly after *Miss 1917* closed, Gershwin resigned his job as a song plugger for Remick's and was taken on by T. B. Harms as a composer.

So elaborate was the mounting of *Miss 1917* that any thought of a tryout was out of the question. The show opened cold at the Century on November 5, one day short of a year after *The Century Girl.* Musical numbers were:

Miss 1917

ACT I

"The Mosquitos Frolic" (Herbert) ...... *Farmhands, Mosquitos
and Vegetables*
Song, "The Society Farmerettes" (Herbert) .... *Vivienne
Segal and Farmerettes*
Duet, "Crooks" (Kern) .... *Cecil Lean and Harry Kelly*
Song, "Papa Would Persist in Picking Peaches" (Kern) ......
*Andrew Tombes, Zitelka Dolores, Yvonne Shelton
and Peaches*

Song, "A Dancing M.D." (Kern) ...... *George White, Vera Maxwell, Marion Davies, Emma Haig*
Duet, "That's The Picture I Want To See" (Kern) .. *Elizabeth Brice, Charles King, Effie Allen and Albertine Marlowe*
A Movie Melodrama, "The Honor System" (Kern) .... *Harry Kelly, Andrew Tombes, George White, Ann Pennington and Vera Maxwell*
Duet, "Good-bye Broadway" [uncredited] .. *Lean and Mayfield*
Song and Dance, "The Old Man in the Moon" (Kern) .. *Bessie McCoy Davis*
Song, "The Land Where The Good Songs Go" (Kern) ...... *Elizabeth Brice and Charles King*
  (a) "Follow On" .... *Marion Davies and Double Octette*
  (b) "In The Good Old Summer Time" .. *Cleo Mayfield and Summer Time Girls*
  (c) "Dinah" .... *Cecil Lean, Emma Haig, Yvonne Shelton and Dinah Girls*
  (d) "Yama Yama" .... *Bessie McCoy Davis and Yama Yama Girls*
      [There was no letter e.]
  (f) "Sammy" .... *Misses Peggy Hopkins, Tot Qualters, Dorothy Klewer, Zitelka Dolores and Harry Kelly*
  (g) "Kiss Me Again" .... *Vivienne Segal*
  (h) "Bumble Bee" ...... *Elizabeth Brice and Charles King*
  (i) "March of the Toys"
  (j) "Toy Clog Dance" (Kern)

ACT II

Falling Leaves: Poem-Choreographic
Irish Jig (Arranged by Victor Herbert from songs by his grandfather Samuel Lover)
Song, "We Want to Laugh" (Kern) .... *Bessie McCoy Davis, Kathryn Perry, May Leslie, Lilyan Tashman, Tot Qualters*
Maja Dance .... *Tortola Valencia*
Duet, "A Dancing Courtship" [uncredited] .... *George White and Ann Pennington*
Dance .... *Irene Castle*
Song, "Who's Zoo in Girl Land" (Kern) .... *Andrew Tombes, Margaret Morris, Mlle. Dolores, Cecile Markle, May Leslie, Peggy Hopkins and Dorothy Klewer*
Songs .... *Gus Van and Joe Schenck*

Song, "The Palm Beach Girl" (Kern) . . . . *Cecil Lean*
and Cleo Mayfield
Finale

Performers who did not appear in musical numbers included Lew Fields
and Savoy and Brennan. Robert Hood Bowers, himself a Broadway composer, was musical director; no orchestrator was acknowledged in the
program.

Deprived of a tryout or even previews, the show inevitably ran overtime
on opening night—until nearly 12:30. Most critics were unfazed by the
show's length. Indeed, they may have been a bit overwhelmed. The *Times*
hailed the revue as "stupendous," while the *Tribune* suggested, "If there
are to be revues, let them be like the new one at the Century Theatre." As
always, *Variety* cast a knowing, dispassionate eye on the work. Noting that
"The performance started weakly and finished worse," the trade paper concluded that the revue's fate would be determined by how successfully
Dillingham and Ziegfeld pruned the excesses, but also noted the $3.00 top
(only three other musicals were charging as much or more at the time).

Kern's best contributions were probably "Go, Little Boat" and "The Land
Where The Good Songs Go." Both flow gently to romantically fey melodies,
and surprisingly poetic Wodehouse lyrics. "Go, Little Boat" does not appear
on any program, so was either dropped in rehearsal or else included on another program printing. The song was published rather bravely in the key
of E, a signature Kern preferred to avoid because of its four sharps. In
discussing the song Alec Wilder notes that the key was frequently employed
to create "a soft, passive, pavane-like mood." Although the quietly rippling
verse is in 6/8 and the more stately chorus in 4/4, the whole has a tonal
unity as if heeding the lyric's plea to glide serenely. "The Land Where The
Good Songs Go" was employed afterwards as the opening of the second act of
Oh, Boy! and was used years later, at Kern's suggestion, to open the finale
of Hollywood's film biography of the composer. A less venturesome piece,
it nevertheless caught the lovely, unworldly mood of its title. The rest of
Kern's contributions were attractive, if not outstanding. Most subscribed to
the easy syncopation of the time, with melodies regularly using progressions
of alternating dotted eighth and sixteenth notes. "We're Crooks," "Tell Me
All Your Troubles, Cutie" (another number either dropped or added late),
and "Peaches" all typified the style. "The Picture I Want To See" resorted
to a similar technique, but with a tightly knit theme concentrating on three

notes and thus foreshadowing the composer's tricky "Bull Frog Patrol." Another song published under a slightly different title was "I'm The Old Man In The Moon," a pleasant ballad. *Variety*'s review praised Miss Segal and Tombes's singing of "You're The Little Girl I've Looked So Long For," a song on no extant program. This, too, suggests that either two sets of programs were printed, or, more likely, that the program was not followed.

Divided notices, the Century's out-of-the-way location, and the $3.00 top ticket price quickly hurt sales. Only the first two performances played to capacity, and while the first week's gross was $39,000, attesting to the high-priced seats and the theatre's huge capacity, business quickly slumped. By the beginning of December a mass exodus of principals began. Irene Castle was the first to leave, followed by Bolm, his dancers, and their highly praised ballet. Brice, King, and George White also quit. When Dillingham and Ziegfeld saw losses hit $6000 a week, they withdrew the attraction after just forty-eight performances.

On March 28, 1918, as the Century Amusement Corporation, the producers filed schedules in bankruptcy, showing debts of $358,461 and assets of only $63,871. Although the stage hands and minor players had all been paid, many of the principal performers and writers were badly burned. Lew Fields, for example, was out $36,750; Herbert, $6400; Lucile (Lady Duff-Gordon), $10,857; Miss Castle, $4500; and Elsie Janis, who joined the show late in its short run, $225. One name noticeably missing from the creditors' list was Kern's. His costly experience with *Ninety in the Shade* had taught him a valuable lesson. If he had walked out on the new revue's rehearsals, he nevertheless clearly kept a watchful eye on its books. Somehow he demanded and received all his royalties. Curiously, when Dillingham and Ziegfeld relinquished control of the Century, Kern's other associates, Comstock and Gest, took over its management. But, apart from this fiasco, Kern's luck was holding out. One trade paper estimated his income for the year averaged $5000 per week. So large and steady an income probably prompted the Kerns to look for something they had never had—a home of their own.

10

A New Home,
New Hits,
and an Interesting Failure

In late 1917 Jerry and Eva Kern began to look for property in the Cedar Knolls section of Bronxville. The first piece of land the Kerns purchased was a plot shaped like the top of a grand piano at the corner of Dellwood Road and Gentian Lane. The deed was recorded on January 24, 1918. Over the next two years they also bought several adjacent lots as well as substantial property on the opposite side of Gentian Lane.* The Kerns commissioned Harry Leslie Walker, a leading local architect, to design a spacious, Colonial-style house fronting on Dellwood Road. The house was ready for the Kerns at the beginning of 1918. Walker had designed a large entrance hall leading directly to a stairway and a pantry. On the right was a comfortable dining room and on the left an even more commodious living room. Kern added to the room's magnificence by securing some beautiful English butternut paneling, which was skillfully adapted to the room's

* Being a landowner clearly appealed to Kern. As late as 1930 he was still buying up properties in Bronxville and Eastchester. In 1931 legal or financial considerations prompted Kern to convey most of these pieces to a holding company he had established. Kern named the company the J. E. B. Holding Corporation, the initials coming from his own and his wife's first initials along with that of their daughter.

measurements. The second floor was given over to the family's bedrooms and the third floor to servants' quarters.

Shortly after the house was built, Kern realized that his ever-growing collection of books would require additional space. Furthermore, his playing could be heard all through the house, giving Eva little privacy for her own affairs. Breaking through the far living room wall, he constructed a 24-by-24-foot sound-proofed, wormy-chestnut-paneled living room, lined with extra-deep shelves and cabinets. While the room was spacious and answered many of Kern's practical problems, its low ceiling and honey-colored, richly waxed woods gave it warmth and intimacy.

The house stood close to the road, so there was little area in the front for a garden or lawn. But the grounds extended on both sides and, more generously still, down the slopes at the rear. Jerry built a barn with a round, Norman-style turret that seemed a survivor of an older farm. He designed the barn's second floor for a workroom. After using it a few weeks, he concluded it was too isolated. Yet if no real farm remained within sight, the colony, as Cedar Knolls liked to call itself, retained an allegiance to its rural precedents, an allegiance that inspired Jerry to try his hand at animal husbandry. The experiment came to naught, except that it provided a droll incident which led to his meeting his neighbors, Mr. and Mrs. A. C. Lampke. Mrs. Lampke looked out her window one day to see a young man scampering awkwardly up and down her steep, rocky front lawn. She rushed outside to see what he was up to. Breathlessly, he told her he was her neighbor, Jerry Kern, and that if she would look to her right she would see a white lamb frolicking just out of reach. Mrs. Lampke helped Jerry catch the young animal, then invited her neighbor in for a cup of tea. Jerry, embarrassed at troubling her, apologized for the inconvenience but politely accepted her offer of refreshment. They sat together for a while before Jerry gathered the lamb in his arms and prepared to return home. As he was leaving, his mischievousness got the best of him, and he turned to Mrs. Lampke to apologize once more. But this second apology came not from any nervous awkwardness nor from any over-elaborate code of polite behavior. It merely offered Jerry an opportunity to confess the whole incident left him feeling "a little sheepish."

Jerry himself had been largely responsible for the decorations in the home he walked back to. One early visitor described them as "attractive and individual. In his travels he has picked up beautiful pieces of old furniture, paintings, antiques, rare vases, lamps with Buddha bases and lovely books.

He has daringly placed Colonial, Jacobean and Italian furniture together." But Jerry obviously could not allow his new house to monopolize his time. Several new shows were ready for the boards.

Back in the spring, when Woolf and Kern were collaborating on *Houp-La,* they most likely began work on a second project, a musical version of Rupert Hughes's farce, *Excuse Me.* At least Savage was able to announce in August that he had a satisfactory adaptation in hand and expected to have it ready for Broadway by mid-October. Early announcements made no mention of Berton Braley, the young writer and poet who would make his Broadway debut by writing the show's lyrics. The omission suggests that the version Savage announced was tentative at best. In any case, delays occurred. The show's rehearsals did not begin until a month after its initially projected opening. When they did start Woolf was in charge of the staging.

As *Toot Toot,* the musical was first presented to the public at Wilmington's Playhouse on Christmas night. The Wilmington *Star* and a second paper with the odd name *Every Evening* welcomed the new offering effusively, while the *Evening Journal* panned it. Kern probably received little consolation from any of the reviews, since all three papers singled out for praise the lone song in the score that was not his. *Every Evening* concluded its commentary on the music, " 'The Last Long Mile' promises to be a classic of the sort of 'There'll Be a Hot Time In The Old Town Tonight.' " The *Star* went further, predicting " 'The Last Long Mile' will be whistled and sung long after people have forgotten there was a song or place called 'Over There.' " Not a single Wilmington reviewer mentioned Kern by name.

Savage moved the show on to Baltimore and Washington, apparently growing more restless and dissatisfied with each move. By the end of the Washington engagement he had decided to close the show. The production was shipped back to New York, where Woolf was told to drastically overhaul the book. Savage then fired all the principals except Louise Groody. He also brought in Edward Rose to revitalize Woolf's staging. For any one of a number of reasons Kern was to do little additional work. Savage may have felt that Kern's score—which Baltimore critics had praised—was good enough. Or Kern, busy with a replacement for *Oh, Boy!,* may have balked, either because he deemed his commitment to the Princess more pressing or because he felt he could not overshadow Emil Breitenfeld's rousing march. Moreover, Jerry and Eva were occupied with settling into their new home.

Whatever his reason, he added only two unimportant numbers. Several of his songs that were retained were given new lyrics. In fact, one song went through three sets of lyrics before everyone was content.

While allowing Savage to revise *Toot Toot*, Kern turned his attentions to the Princess. Even before *Miss 1917* went into rehearsal, Kern, Bolton, and Wodehouse were discussing two new musicals. The need for at least one of these became urgent the week after *Miss 1917* opened, when the fading *Oh, Boy!* was moved from the Princess to the larger Casino down the street. The larger house promised to buoy returns by offering more cheap balcony seats. At the same time, Comstock, Elliot, and Gest announced that their dependable group would soon have a new work ready for the Princess. (Their original announcement failed to mention Bolton by name, but that was probably just an oversight.) The producers said the new musical was virtually ready and little more was needed than to finish casting and find "a title of the snappy sort." A few days before practice sessions commenced at the end of November the snappy title was revealed as *Say When*. Concurrently, the producers announced the team's other new work would be called *Here's Looking at You*.

For some reason, *Say When* would not fall comfortably together as readily as its authors and producers had hoped. A scheduled Schenectady premiere in late December had to be called off at virtually the last minute. So was the planned January 7 New York opening. As a result, to allow further work on *Say When*, *Here's Looking at You* was shelved, and in time was totally forgotten. Precisely what rewriting occurred is no longer remembered. Cast changes were minor. On the surface, the major change seems to have been the scrapping of the original title and the substitution of an even better one. For their new title Bolton and Wodehouse, two Englishmen, went back to American minstrelsy of a generation or two earlier. They seized on a popular burnt-cork exclamation that a black vaudeville act known as The Kemps had recently revived as a catch line: "Oh, lady, lady!". With the new title buttressed by some additional exclamation points, *Oh, Lady! Lady!!* finally was offered to the public at Albany's Harmanus Bleecker Hall on January 7, 1918. The Albany *Journal* found much to recommend in the evening—notably the excellent cast—but thought the show "too long by far" and particularly rued that "the last act flops." Since there were only two acts, the critic seemed to be saying that everyone had his work cut out for him. He observed that Kern's "delightful music . . .

is pretty and appealing, but not especially lingering." Songs the critic awarded high praise were "Not Yet," "When Ships Come Home," "Greenwich Village," and "Little Nest."

Comstock and his associates, anxious to relight the Princess but aware of needed revisions, decided to postpone a second scheduled opening date in New York—January 21—and to keep the show on the road for three full weeks. One stand was a then almost unheard of seven performances in Wilmington, Delaware. The result was that when New York's critics were invited to a January 31 preview at the Princess they were entertained by a show that pleased them mightily. So were playgoers on the official first night, February 1, 1918, although their judgment may have been prejudiced by the reviews. Preview and first night audiences enjoyed the following musical program for "The Fifth New York Princess Theatre Musical Production":

Oh, Lady! Lady!!

ACT I

1a. Scene Music
 b. "I'm to Be Married To-day" ..... *Mollie [Vivienne Segal] and Girls*
2. Duet, "Not Yet" .. *Mollie and Willoughby [Carl Randall]*
3. Trio, "Do It Now" ...... *Hale [Harry C. Browne], Spike [Edward Abeles] and Willoughby*
4. "Our Little Nest" .... *Spike and Fanny [Florence Shirley]*
5. "Little Ships Come Sailing Home" ...... *Mollie and Girls*
6. "Oh, Lady! Lady!!" .... *Will and Girls*
7. "You Found Me and I Found You" .... *May [Carroll McComas] and Hale*
8. Finaletto .... *Complete Ensemble*

ACT II

9. Opening, "Moon" .... *Clarette [Jeanne Sparry] and Ensemble*

 Dance .... *Parker [Constance Binney] and Stewart [Jack Vincent]*
10. "Waiting Around the Corner" .... *May and Boys*
11. "The Sun Starts to Shine Again" .... *Mollie and Girls*
12. "Before I Met You" .... *Will and Mollie*

13. Trio, "Greenwich Village" ...... *Will, Spike and Fanny*
14. "A Picture I Want To See" .... *Hale and May*
15. "It's a Hard, Hard World for a Man" ...... *Will, Hale and Twombley [Reginald Mason]*
16. Finale .... *Ensemble*

Max Hirschfeld conducted Frank Saddler's orchestrations, Robert Milton and Edward Royce directed, and sets were designed by Clifford Pember and costumes by Harry Collins.

Bolton and Wodehouse's story told how Mollie Farringdon marries Willoughby French despite her mother's objections and despite the larcenous machinations of Spike, Willoughby's valet, and the valet's old girl friend, Fanny. Character names demonstrated Bolton and Wodehouse again in a playful mood; they included May Ann Ayes and Cassie Roll, the latter done by Janet Velie, who later would have brief musical comedy stardom. Even Lettice Romayne was back, climbing the social ladder with a "y" in her name.

The *Globe* summed up the feeling of a majority of critics when its headline proclaimed *Oh, Lady! Lady!!* "a Worthy Successor to 'Oh, Boy!'." The *Times* harbored minor reservations, but noted, "If the offering lacks highly sensational features, it has the rarer virtue of being thoroughly well rounded and virtually flawless. The book . . . has a measurably novel plot that actually sustains interest for itself alone. The lines are bright and the lyrics well written. The music, by Jerome Kern, is in his familiar vein of easy gayety tinged at times with reverie and sentiment." Since no obviously outstanding hits emerged, critics varied widely in their choice of favorite songs. Typically, the *Tribune* hailed "Our Little Nest" as "one of the best songs of the evening" and gave honorable mention to "Little Ships Come Sailing Home," "Wheatless Days" and "Greenwich Village." More than one critic singled out no song at all.

Unfortunately, *Oh, Lady! Lady!!* is one of the shows whose tryout programs seem to have melted away without a trace, so that a comparison of musical numbers at its world premiere with those of the Broadway run cannot be made. Yet by one of history's odd quirks it is generally known that the most famous song to come out of the musical was discarded before the show reached Broadway, left behind either in a rehearsal hall or at one of the tryout stands. The song was, of course, "Bill." As originally planned it was to have been sung early in the first act by Mollie, attempting to explain to her baffled mother why she chooses to marry Willoughby. It was cut either because the ordinariness of the man described in the lyric did not depict the lively, handsome Carl Randall, who played Willoughby, or because the slow tempo required to put it across effectively was a drag so early in the evening. Alec Wilder notes that the music of the verse does not lead inevitably into the chorus and could just as easily have prefaced a different, faster melody. Yet both, when combined, have a singularly elusive undercurrent of sadness that Wodehouse obviously caught and perpetuated in his lyric. Taken without the lyric the song is a pleasant, minor ballad. Yet, even with the uncanny marriage of words and music, the song, if it was not eliminated earlier, failed to catch the attention of a single out-of-town critic. Indeed, as we shall see, virtually no reviewer of the original *Show Boat* thought it was worth so much as a line of notice. Actually, 1918 theatregoers could have heard part of the song, for Kern kept a substantial piece of it in the first-act finale.

If the remaining songs failed to blend rhymes and melody quite as demandingly, both Wodehouse's lyrics and Kern's melodies displayed a high level of imagination and taste. Perhaps the best was the sly "Not Yet." The song, a revised, improved version of the melody for "You're The Only Girl He Loves" from *A Polish Wedding*, was written in half-time, with an AABC frame. Its sweet, flowing melody changes abruptly in the C section, where rests underscore the warnings of the title. Two of Kern's most charmingly fey melodies were also in the score. The gently gliding "When The Ships Come Home" had a tune of almost Victorian sentimentality that only Kern's impeccable judgment saves from being cloying. "Moon Song" was more musically daring, moving from a willowy verse in 6/8 to a dignified chorus in 4/4 filled with exquisite phrases that for some strange reason never quite jell.

Two lightheartedly romantic numbers were equally interesting. "You Found Me And I Found You" had a gingerly tripping melody evocative of a country folk dance. Essentially it is another early use by Kern of the AABA formula, although Kern employed several twists. The second A, the first repetition of the principal theme, was set four notes higher—a pleasant eye-opener. Even more unconventional was the replacement of two eighth notes of the third bar by a quarter rest in the seventh. The unexpected pause was one of the few instances where Kern seems to have thrown Wodehouse off balance, for instead of using the break for dramatic or comic effect, Wodehouse left the line stand with an awkward gap. Wodehouse's revenge came in "Before I Met You," a sparkling little ditty that undoubtedly delighted fox-trotters and two-steppers. In this instance Kern did repeat the first musical sentence exactly, except for a grace note at the beginning. But Wodehouse stopped his second sentence three notes short, leaving Kern no choice but to utilize these last three notes merely as a passage in the musical piano part. Nonetheless, the device worked here.

A pair of exuberant chorus numbers were also superior: the title song, in which Willoughby led the girls, and "The Sun Starts To Shine Again," which Mollie sang with her friends. Kern put a series of repeated notes to effective, gay use in "Waiting Around The Corner" (also published, with the identical lyric, as "Some Little Girl"). The remaining songs are, musically at least, fillers, although Wodehouse's urbane lyrics and, no doubt, excellent staging, endeared them to audiences and critics alike.

For all the niggling reservations expressed in its reviews, *Oh, Lady! Lady!!* got off to a satisfactory start. Comstock's private records reveal he immediately set about planning two road companies. But it soon became apparent that the demand for seats was falling far short of *Oh, Boy!*'s runaway success. Reluctantly, Comstock canceled plans for one of the touring companies and kept setting back the date for the second. *Oh, Lady! Lady!!* ran only 219 performances in New York, or about ten weeks longer than *Nobody Home,* the first Princess Theatre show. The second company did take to the road, but only after the Broadway troupe had moved to Boston. Virtually everywhere both companies played, grosses were disappointing. For example, an open-ended Chicago stay was terminated after nine weeks.

Disappointment over the fate of *Oh, Lady! Lady!!* may have brought the Kern-Wodehouse-Bolton series to an end. The real cause of the break-up remains, regrettably, a mystery. At our first interview Bolton proffered one story on tape, but at a later meeting, off tape, told such a variant version that both must be highly suspect. Lady Frances Donaldson, who is currently writing an extended biography of Wodehouse and with whom I exchanged a considerable correspondence, wrote me on January 23, 1979: "In answer to . . . whether there is evidence of a row, I can only say I have seen none. There is some evidence that Kern was regarded as difficult in a prima donnaish way, but all the references are reasonably cordial. Then there is evidence of a long wrangle between Bolton and Kern about the lyric of *Bill* because Plum in an unguarded moment offered it to Kern in return for something less valuable and Bolton rescued it on the ground that, as it was half his, Wodehouse had no right to offer it." What is meant by "half his" is puzzling, since it is doubtful that Bolton had any hand in the lyric. Whatever the real reason, Kern wrote no more scores heard at the Princess, although Bolton and Wodehouse stayed on for one more show. Kern's departure terminated, for all practical purposes, the great series, even though Bolton and Kern did later write one musical earmarked for the theatre (but it folded on the road), and later still the producers did reunite the trio for a show initially announced to play the house. In the end it played elsewhere. If *Have a Heart* and *Leave It to Jane*, really Princess shows, are included, this great seminal series consisted of just six shows and spanned a three-year period virtually coinciding with the dates of World War I.

As we have said, the Princess Theatre shows were not radical departures for the American musical theatre. Yet, at the same time, they were clearly seminal in the genre's development. They assured that reasonably believable stories about reasonably believable people would provide the sturdy frame on which everything else would be hung. Royalty, supernatural beings, and grotesque clowns were shunted aside. Bolton and Wodehouse saw to it that the dialogue their characters spoke and the lyrics they sang were at once civilized and colloquial. Kern's graceful, warm melodies proved that raucous rags and grandly arioso pieces could give way to easily hummable, irresistibly memorable songs. Perhaps most importantly, these shows advanced the cause of musicals with a unifying elegance of tone, that "odor of sachet" that so delighted Kern. These musicals were of a piece, carefully selected, precisely polished, exquisitely mounted little jewels.

For Kern, the departure meant he must once again plunge into the crass commercialism of the Broadway musical theatre of the day. That it was a little less crass and a little more aware of tone and quality can be directly attributed to the Princess shows. But for the next several years, even though Kern would have a string of hits and produce some of his loveliest, most popular, and most memorable songs, there is evidence that he was never completely happy with his own achievement and that he longed to create a new, more coherent, more artistic musical theatre. Fulfillment lay nearly ten years away. Still, in the interim, for all its frustrations, life would be interesting and productive.

The first flush of *Oh, Lady! Lady!!*'s success once again sent interviewers knocking at Kern's door. Only this time, instead of receiving them in his spartan office at Harms, as had been his wont, Kern welcomed them in his Bronxville home, which was not quite finished. Much of what he expounded he had enumerated before. But two points were fresh. While he reiterated his stand that a first-rate composer must be both a knowledgeable traditionalist and an enlightened progressive, he noted specifically what path he hoped his own progress would take. As far as his musical comedy material was concerned he disclosed, "I'm trying to apply modern art to light music as Debussy and those men have done to more serious work." A quarter of a century later, shortly before his death, he returned to this idea of impressionistic popular song in a long letter to John Van Druten, when the two were dabbling with a possible Broadway musical. But at the same time Kern revealed his intention to modify his style he sprung a surprise by suggesting he might completely change his course. He startled the man from the *Musical Courier* by announcing that after his next three musicals—all breaking in or virtually ready—he planned to abandon the theatre temporarily, not only to refresh his own resources but to prevent theatregoers from resenting his domination of the field. "I am going to do serious work," he continued, "a symphonic poem with a choreograph accompaniment and a symphony. I suppose the people will laugh themselves sick. I wouldn't dare write that sort of thing while I'm still doing light music. People won't take a man's work seriously if they have been dancing to one of his fox trots."

The seeds of these ambitions never bore fruit. To no small extent pragmatic financial considerations saw to that. But a second reason must be that, however aware Kern was of his virtues as an artist, he was every bit as aware of his limitations. His genius and his security, luckily for him, both lay in the identical direction.

In mid-January Savage took his new company of *Toot Toot* to Philadelphia for two weeks of rehearsals before reopening. At the same time he made an unusual announcement in Philadelphia's papers. Since the outbreak of the war, ticket prices, which had remained virtually set since the Civil War, had been rising steadily. Savage announced that he would drop ticket prices to pre-1914 levels as "a war measure." Whether patriotism or the hope of packing the house during the tryout was the real motivation, Savage was able to use the cut to rebuff musicians when they asked that their $32.00-a-week salary be increased to $35.00.

Savage raised the curtain on his revised *Toot-Toot!* (with a hyphen and an exclamation point added) at the Forrest Theatre on February 4. To his dismay, Philadelphia critics judged his production more harshly than had earlier reviewers. The *Evening Bulletin* admitted, "Fun there is, but in homeopathic doses, widely scattered." The *Inquirer* found the show "missing the crackling, crisp touch that captures the auditor and holds him." However, the paper had special praise for lyricist Berton Braley: "He has the singing quality, the swing and dash and the grasp of popular humor that makes his debut in this field an auspicious one." For Kern the reviewer could find only mildly affirmative words, coupling them with the inescapable put-down, higher praise for Breitenfeld's interpolation. Disapproving notices failed to deter playgoers, however, and the musical enjoyed "big business" during its month's run.

Toot-Toot!'s libretto took an ordinary farce plot and clothed it in khaki. When Lieutenant Harry Mallory is called up, he and his sweetheart, Marjorie Newton, decide to marry at once. Unable to find a minister, they bank on one being aboard the train so they can travel as man and wife. On board they encounter a couple bound for a Reno divorce and a troupe of Isadora Duncan-like "Greek" dancers, led by a wildly swishy Hyperion Buncombe. Another passenger is a gentleman determinedly searching for a fling. A train robbery and other complications beset the lovers. Luckily, the man on a fling proves to be a minister in disguise, so all ends happily. A real Indian, Oskenonton, played himself. A large chorus—twenty-four girls and twenty boys—included eight "classical dancers."

Toot-Toot! opened in New York at the George M. Cohan Theatre on March 11, 1918, with the following musical program:

Toot-Toot!

ACT I

1a.	Scene Music	
b.	"Toot-Toot!"	*Ensemble*
2.	"Quarrel and Part" .... *Mr. and Mrs. Wellington [Edward*	
	Garvie and Flora Zabelle] and Ensemble	
3.	"Runaway Colts" .... *Mr. and Mrs. Colt [Earl Benham and*	
	Louise Groody]	
4.	"Kan the Kaiser"	*Military Ensemble*
5.	"Every Girl in All America" .... *Mallory [Donald*	
	MacDonald], Marjorie [Louise Allen] and Ensemble	
6.	"Shower of Rice"	*Ensemble*
7.	"Let's Go"	*Mallory and Marjorie*

8. "It's Greek to Me" .. *Pandora [Florence Johns], Hyperion
[Billy—later, William—Kent] and Pupils*
9. "The Last Long Mile" (Plattsburg Marching Song, 1917.
Words and Music by Lieut. Emil Breitenfeld, 153
Depot Brigade, Camp Dix, N.J.) .... *Captain Jones
[Greek Evans] and Ensemble*

ACT II

1. Scene Music
2. "When You Wake Up Dancing" .... *Ensemble*
3. "Girlie" .... *Mallory and Marjorie*
4. "Smoke" .... *Ensemble*
5. "Cute Soldier Boy" (Music by Anatol Friedland. Lyric by
Edgar Allan Woolf.) .... *Mrs. Wellington and
Military Ensemble*
6. "It's Immaterial To Me" .... *Porter [Harry Fern]*
7. "If" .... *Mallory, Marjorie, Hyperion and Sally*
8. Indian Folk Song .... *Oskenonton*
9. "Indian Fox Trot" .... *Peter Deerfoot [Greek Evans] and
Ensemble*
10. Finale

Anton Heindl was musical director. No one was publicly credited with
the orchestrations. Robert Marks devised the choreography.

New York's critics were kind to *Toot-Toot!*. Still, many held serious reservations about the wisdom of musicalizing Hughes's farce. Readers who
read further discovered the critics nevertheless enjoyed themselves. Several showered the one principal to escape Savage's purge, Louise Groody,
with special praise. Braley's lyrics garnered handsome kudos. Once again
Breitenfeld's march won most of the attention and admiration, but Kern's
work was not ignored, even if some of the praise was faint. The *Tribune*
called it "regular Kern music, whistling music"; the *Times* thought it
"tuneful, although as a whole, it is slightly below his standard."
A collation of the show's programs indicates that three songs performed
in Wilmington never made it to New York—an opening ensemble called
"Good-By And Good Luck"; Mallory and Marjorie's duet late in the first
act, "Honey Moon Land" (published as "Honeymoon Land"); and the

Wellingtons and Colts's number just before the finale, "I Will Knit A Suit Of Dreams" (also published as "Teepee"). By Philadelphia "Toot-Toot!" had been added, as had "Indian Fox Trot," while the song "If You Only Cared Enough" (the song with three changes of lyrics) ended up simply as "If." Late in the Philadelphia tryout "Shower Of Rice" was introduced along with the interpolated Indian song and Friedland's "Cute Soldier Boy."

If the score was hand-me-down Kern, it was not without interest. For example, the verse of "I Will Knit A Suit Of Dreams" moved startlingly, yet effectively, from G major to G minor to E flat to D major. "When You Wake Up Dancing" is a sweet, lively, although unexceptional romp; "Girlie" a pleasant, minor waltz. "If" has a chorus that begins with offering one of Kern's most beguiling inventions, but fails to develop it imaginatively. One puzzle is the copyright date of "Every Girl In All America"— 1909. Obviously, the song represents a reuse of an old tune, one that seems to elude identification. The scuttled "Honeymoon Land" was too good a melody to forget. Kern stashed it away until he found a place for it two years later.

The public sensed a lack of enthusiasm in the reviews. What was more telling, theatregoers had an amazing abundance of musical riches to choose from. At the time *Toot-Toot!* premiered, 1917-18 lyric hits still going strong included Romberg's *Maytime* (the biggest success of the season); the Hippodrome's *Cheer Up*; Fred Stone's vehicle, *Jack O'Lantern* (sending its audiences away singing "Wait Till The Cows Come Home"); the great London hit, *Chu Chin Chow*; Silvio Hein's now forgotten *Flo-Flo*; Louis Hirsch's *Going Up*; Al Jolson in *Sinbad*; *Oh, Look!* (with Harry Fox crooning "I'm Always Chasing Rainbows"); and Kern's own smash, *Oh, Lady! Lady!!*. The competition overwhelmed *Toot-Toot!*. After just five weeks, Savage sent the show back out on the road, where wartime prosperity and less competition kept his train on the track well into the next season.

A further sign that Jerry was ineluctably drifting away from the Princess Theatre appeared the very week *Oh, Lady! Lady!!* opened. The Selwyns announced that come March they would offer a musical version of Margaret Mayo's farce, *Baby Mine*, under the title *Rock-a-Bye Baby*. Jerry was to do the music, while his *Toot-Toot!* associate, Edgar Allen Woolf, would adapt the play. Herbert Reynolds signed to provide lyrics. Optimistically, the Selwyns further announced that the musical would be the initial attraction at their new 42nd Street theatre, a theatre they were going to call, with no false modesty, the Selwyn. Archie and Edgar Selwyn were both well known to the public. On stage and in films, Edgar had early on become a minor matinee idol, but his assets were not confined to his good looks or his acting ability. He was a competent theatrical craftsman who would write several straight play hits—and later would do the libretto for Jerry's worst New York flop. He and his burly, more vulgarian brother were also active, successful producers. *Rock-a-Bye Baby* was to be their first venture into musical comedy.

Their celebrated theatrical acumen deserted them when they set out to do *Rock-a-Bye Baby*. Even their preliminary announcement was unrealistic. Their new house was far from finished and, in fact, would not open until the following fall. But their claim that the new musical would begin rehearsals in a few weeks and still be ready sometime in March was almost as farfetched. Quite likely even the brothers did not really believe the promises, viewing them merely as a way to get the name of the new show before the public. These bits of misinformation meant little. One bit of news the public never learned and that would have meant little or nothing to it if it had was the fact that George Gershwin was again Kern's rehearsal pianist. This time they worked closely together and a warm friendship began to develop. Kern advised young George to seek his counsel before taking on any major assignments. Some time later, when he learned Gershwin had signed to write a musical without first consulting him, Jerry's feelings were hurt. For several years thereafter he was noticeably cool to George. (Kern often took a paternal interest in talented young composers. He sent Lewis Gensler small checks until Gensler received sufficient recognition to support himself.)

What did begin to count with theatregoers were reviews and word-of-mouth once the show reached the boards. From the moment the curtain fell on the first performance at New Haven's Shubert Theatre on April 8, *Rock-a-Bye Baby*'s real problems became Broadway gossip. What had been planned as a short shakedown cruise soon evolved into an extended tour. Road critics generally enjoyed Kern's music. One Atlantic City reviewer found it "exceptionally charming," but then went on to say the book was inept. Similarly, *Variety*'s man in New Haven rejoiced that the show offered "a musical score that bordered on the edge of light operetta and is perhaps the best Jerome Kern has composed," but he, too, went on to dismiss the libretto as "weak." The Selwyns hurriedly called Miss

Mayo back to help bolster Woolf's revisions. Their story was typical musical comedy foolery.

To get her mind off her disintegrating marriage, Zoie Hardy decides to buy a new car. On a test ride with Jimmy Jinks the car breaks down and the two are stranded at the Rock-a-Bye Baby Inn, where, coincidentally, Zoie's philandering husband, Alfred, also has an engagement. Learning of Zoie's marital problems, Jimmy has a suggestion that he promises will solve everything. He advises Zoie to tell Alfred she is about to have a baby. Jimmy assures her he will find a suitable one somewhere. In his zeal he finds not one infant, but three. The babies' parents appear to reclaim their tots, and Alfred, realizing the lengths to which Zoie will go in order to keep him, swears he will reform.

Just as the new show was winding up its tryout, an older Kern show received a London hearing. Unfortunately, the *Very Good Eddie* that opened at the Palace Theatre on May 18 was an atrociously emasculated version of the Princess original. Only five numbers from the New York production were retained. At least four other composers, including Cole Porter, had songs interpolated, while many older Kern songs, reaching as far back as "Don't Turn My Picture To The Wall," supplanted his 1915 melodies. The piece was sourly received and survived for only forty-six performances.

After nearly two months on the road, *Rock-a-Bye Baby* opened on May 22, 1918, at the Astor Theatre, which fronted on Broadway in the heart of Times Square, with the following musical program:

Rock-a-Bye Baby

ACT I

1a. "Bella Mia" .... *Pasquale [Arthur Lipson], Finnegan [Gus Baci] and Waiter [Bert Pullaney]*
 b. Ensemble, "Hurry Now" .... *Girls*
 c. "Motoring Along the Old Post Road" .... *Archie [Carl Hyson] and Girls*
2. Song, "One, Two, Three" .. *Dorothy [Dorothy Dickson], Archie, Monte [Alan Hale], George [Eddy Meyers] and Girls*
3. Duet, "I Never Thought" .... *Zoie [Edna Hibbard] and Alfred [Frank Morgan]*

4.   Trio, "I Believed All She Said" .. *Monte, Archie, George and Girls*
5.   Song, "A Kettle is Singing" ...... *Aggie [Louise Dresser]*

ACT II

6.   Ensemble, "Stitching, Stitching" .... *Aggie, Zoie, Monte and Girls*
7.   Song, "Rock-a-Bye Baby Dear" ...... *Madam Tentelucci [Edna Munsey] and Girls*
8.   Song, "Little Tune Go Away" .... *Aggie and Girls*
9.   Quartette, "According to Dr. Holt" ...... *Aggie and Zoie, Jimmy [Walter Jones] and Alfred*
10. Trio and Dance, "There's No Better Use for Time Than Kissing" .... *Zoie, Dorothy and Archie*
11. Song, "The Real Spring Drive" .... *Zoie, Monte, Archie, George and Girls*
12. Finaletto .... *Ensemble*

ACT III

13. Song, "My Own Light Infantry" ...... *Zoie and Kiddies*
14. Song, "I Can Trust Myself with a Lot of Girls" .. *Monte, Archie, George and Ensemble*
15. Finale .... *Ensemble*

Frank Tours conducted the orchestra, but no credit was given to any orchestrator. Edward Royce directed, while Robert Marks devised the choreography. Lucile (Lady Duff-Gordon) created the costumes, and Joseph Physioc designed the sets.

As far as most critics were concerned, the labors to improve the book had been wasted. Just why Jerry did not see the problem in advance or, if he did, why he did not realize how much it would hurt the show's chances is puzzling. Nonetheless, he produced a score that delighted the critics and that he himself for many years afterwards, until *Show Boat* came along, insisted remained his personal favorite. The *Times* noted, "There are four or five high spots in the Kern score—his best, undoubtedly, since 'Oh, Boy!.' . . . For that matter, there was not one tune in the fifteen which is not good to hear." Most other critics agreed, the *Evening Sun* noting, "The music has the magically melodious Jerome Kern lilt, especially 'There's No Better Use for Time Than Kissing,'" while the

World heard "Kern's usual agreeable sound." Obviously Kern had established a distinctive standard, if critics could resort to a word such as "usual" or employ his name as a meaningful adjective. With more time to consider, *Theatre Magazine* concluded that "the music proved to be one of the best scores Broadway has heard in many a day." A pianissimo chorus of dissent came from two sides. The *Tribune,* bucking the consensus, liked the book better than the music, and Alan Dale in the *American* complained, "The Kern music was very like some of the other Kern arrangements—quite tuneful and frolicsome, but not at all inspired."

Substantial changes occurred in the musical program between New Haven and New York. Six songs were discarded—three from the first act, two from the second, and one from the last. Curiously, high hopes must have been held for two of the numbers cut from the first act, for they alone were reprised in New Haven. One was Madame Tentelucci's "Signorina Adelina," a song never published and therefore unidentifiable and indescribable. The other was Zoie and Jimmy's "Not You." The third first act cut, "Just One Kiss," was also sung by Madame Tentelucci, along with two minor male figures. The second act lost "Cretonne," assigned to several unimportant characters, and the mawkish "My Boy," performed by Zoie, Aggie (Miss Dresser, but Adele Rowland during the tryout) and Alfred, while Aggie's "Think Of Where You Might Be Instead Of Where You Are" was eliminated from the last act. The added numbers were "I Believed All She Said," "Little Tune, Go Away," and "There's No Better Use For Time Than Kissing." The last, as well as one of Miss Rowland's numbers, was awarded, at least in part, to Dorothy Dickson. Miss Dickson was not in the show in New Haven, but Jerry insisted she be brought in from *Oh, Boy!,* thereby continuing a relationship that would soon make her one of his brightest interpreters.

One reason Kern was probably so satisfied with the score was that it was so much of a piece and so befitting the play's theme. Many of its melodies had either a soft, nursery-like air or a jingly, childishly playful beat. The dainty "Kettle Song" and the self-descriptive "Lullaby," two especially lovely melodies, best exemplify the nursery airs. "My Boy" may also fall into this category, although its melody is not particularly inventive or memorable and Reynolds's lyric employs much the same treacly sentiment and heavy sentimentality as Al Jolson's "Sonny Boy" does. The jaunty syncopations and jazz harmonies (moving, for example, from G natural to B-flat seventh) of "Little Tune, Go Away" gave it an almost unique gamine gaiety among Kern's pieces. The raggy march of "My Own Light Infantry" foreshadows the later "Bull Frog Patrol." (The song was published under the title "Nursery Fanfare," possibly so that potential buyers would not think it a war song.) "There's No Better Use For Time Than Kissing," which so many critics called attention to, is actually a catchy if squarish ballad whose musical sentences consist largely of tightly knit quarter notes brought to a period by one or two half or whole notes. The melody was adapted from "Two Heads Are Better Than One," the waltz in *Cousin Lucy*. "I Never Thought" and "I Believed All She Said" are both far more commonplace ballads, exhibiting weak endings that plagued this score. Probably the best ballad from the show was "Not You," so rightly reprised on the road and then so inexplicably dropped. The primary theme, like that of "There's No Better Use For Time Than Kissing," was closely knit, but in this instance utilized a long line of pleasantly rocking eighth notes, vaguely recalling the verse of "The Siren's Song." Among the dance numbers the compelling lilt of "The Big Spring Drive" stands out.

With publication of *Rock-a-Bye Baby*'s sheet music, Kern embarked on a peculiar practice he employed for the rest of his life—designation of what heretofore had been called a song's "chorus" or "refrain" as a "burthen" (which the composer always pronounced "burden"). The term was then obsolescent if not obsolete, and Kern's motives for adopting it are baffling. Some have suggested that Kern concluded the word was English. But this argument is weak. Kern was well aware of contemporary English practice and would have realized how rarely even the English called the chorus a "burthen." Edward ("Teddy") Holmes, the retired head of Chappell in London, who knew Kern well, has suggested that Kern may have thought the term was German. But Kern would surely have avoided reviving a German term when his country was at war with Germany and when even harmless Viennese operettas were discriminated against. No truly incontestable answer emerges, although other possibilities exist. Dictionaries note that a burthen (or burden) was a repeated refrain. While they are clearly talking about entire choruses, Kern may have sought to borrow the term to underscore increasing use of shorter, repeated themes in the more and more frequent AABA formula. Of course, the counterargument here would be that Kern employed the word indiscriminately, using it even where he did not employ the formula. Perhaps his daughter Betty has the answer. She suggests he employed the term because his sure theatrical instincts told him it would pique interest.

Tepid notices hurt business. By late June *Variety* reported that the principals had been asked to take pay cuts, prompting Walter Jones to leave. The only performers not asked to take less pay were members of the chorus, who were each receiving $50 a week. But the cuts failed to keep the piece afloat. *Rock-a-Bye Baby* closed on August 2 after chalking up a mere eighty-five New York performances.

Of course, as with *Toot-Toot!* and so many other shows, a New York failure seldom precluded a post-Broadway tour. Even before the Broadway run ended, the Selwyns announced that a cross-country trek would begin September 9 at the Majestic Theatre in Brooklyn and that Jefferson De Angelis, the beloved old favorite, would assume the role of Jimmy. The injection of so popular an old name often gave a prolonged welcome on the road to shows New York had rejected. *Rock-a-Bye Baby* was not among the lucky. Grosses were disappointing when they were not downright disastrous. Shortly after the musical opened what was hoped to be a four-week stand in Philadelphia, *Variety* reported the show was in deep trouble. Four days later it folded.

But *Rock-a-Bye Baby's* closing did not allow Jerry to put the show from his mind. In mid-March he was slapped with a nasty suit by the Selwyns. Their vice president, Crosby Gaige, alleged that Jerry had bought a one-sixth interest in the show and thereby was responsible for covering one-sixth of the losses. The complaint revealed that as of January 4, 1919—a little over a month before the musical was withdrawn—losses had amounted to $61,447.21. This meant Jerry's share was something over $10,000. Gaige stated that Jerry had paid $5000, just short of half his liability, not including interest and court costs. Jerry's lawyer, Max D. Josephson, sat down with the Selwyns' attorney and apparently settled the matter out of court, for it quickly disappeared from the records.

When *Houp-La* was ready for the big time, Savage announced it would be retitled *Head over Heels.* He also disclosed that Mitzi Hajos had been encouraged to drop her patronymic. Hereafter she would be merely Mitzi. The show first opened at Boston's Tremont Theatre on Saturday, May 25, 1918. For many years the house had harbored popular summer musicals, no small number of them under Savage's aegis. As a result, *Head over Heels* was made especially welcome. Unlike the case in Hartford Mitzi and Kern were equally acclaimed. Mitzi surprised many critics with acrobatic feats. The Boston *Post* delighted in music so "modern," so "rhythmic," and so danceable. Since the illustrious *Evening Transcript* published no Sunday edition and could wait an extra day before pronouncing its verdict, its reaction was most eagerly anticipated. To everyone's joy, the long review, which occupied almost two whole tightly printed columns, was generous with its praise. It said of the music:

> Alike for her [Mitzi], for the other "principals" with occasion to sing, and for the ensembles usually allotted to women's chorus, Mr. Kern has made a lighter, fresher, more graceful music than has come of late from his pen unless it be in the equally recent and no less praised "Rock-a-bye Baby." He is less dependent now upon rag-time rhythms, indeed he uses them but sparingly, deploying others with ease, familiarity and skill as the design of the music warrants. His melodies gain in charm and in character to the personage and the moment in the play; he paces and modulates them more artfully and elegantly. More and more he shuns the heavy hand, the mere noise-making for the sake of theatrical excitement; more readily than of old, he escapes mere space-filling commonplace. Throughout "Head Over Heels" he writes lightly, fancifully, tastefully, transparently in his orchestra, almost elegantly in the curve of some of his melodies. Not another composer for our musical plays has his light fingers.

Besides his excellent notices, *Head over Heel's* tryout brought Kern a restful change of pace from the hectic packings and movings of so many recent pre-Broadway tours. The musical settled in comfortably at the Tremont, staying there nearly through the hot weather before Savage transferred it to New York's George M. Cohan Theatre on August 29, 1918.

Woolf's story was neither very complicated nor original. Little Mitzi Bambinetti is the "top-mounter" of her family's acrobatic troupe. She persuades her family to come to America so that she may be near Edward Sterling, whose gift of a ring has convinced the innocent girl that he loves her deeply. Her arrival brings a rude awakening, for Sterling is revealed to be an incorrigible philanderer, who has completely forgotten both the acrobat and his gift to her. In time for a happy ending Mitzi learns that Edward's friend and partner, Robert Lawson, will be both loving and loyal.

Musical numbers were:

Head over Heels

ACT I
Scene One

1. Opening, "With Type a-Ticking" .. *Misses Graham [Fan Haggerty], Wentworth [Martha Bowes], Collins [Florence Browne] and Hammond [Eleanor Livingston]*
2. "Today is Spring" .... *Muriel [Dorothy MacKaye] and Girls*
3. "Any Girl" .... *Sterling [Irving Beebe] and Girls*
4. "Mitzi's Lullaby" .... *Mitzi*
5. "The Big Show" .... *Mitzi and Girls*
6. "The Moments of the Dance" .... *Edith [Jean Mann], Mrs. Montague [Margaret Linden], Lawson [Boyd Marshall], Sterling and Baron [Paul Oscard]*
7. "Head Over Heels" .... *Mitzi and Lawson*

Scene Two

8. "At the Thé Dansant" ...... *Mrs. Montague, Muriel, Edith, Baron and Girls*
9. "Vorderveele" .... *Mitzi and Squibbs*
10. "All the World is Swaying" .... *Mitzi and Girls*
11. "Me" .... *Bambinetti [Charles Judels], Toni [Joseph Dunn], Oscar [James Oliver], Buxaume [Andy Bennett] and Henri [Edward Mathews]*
12. Finale (Houp-La)

ACT II

13. Opening (The Charity Bazaar) .. *Mrs. Montague, Muriel, Edith, Baron and Girls*
14. "Every Bee Has a Bud of Its Own" (Music by Harold A. Levy) .... *Mitzi*
15. "Ladies, Have a Care!" .. *Squibbs [Robert Emmett Keane], Lawson, Sterling and Girls*
16. "I Was Lonely" .... *Edith and Sterling*
17. "Funny Little Something" ...... *Mitzi, Squibbs and Muriel*

Harold A. Levy served as conductor, but no orchestrator was credited publicly. Julian Mitchell staged the musical numbers, while George Marion directed the book. The costumes and scenery were by a number of artists, with Joseph Urban assisting in the Garden set.

New York's critics were nearly as enthusiastic as Boston's, although several noted that Mitzi was not performing any real acrobatics. Whether this meant a change in staging had occurred or whether New York merely viewed her feats with less awe is now probably lost in history.

Differences between the Boston and New York programs suggest no more than the normal tryout difficulties. One song, "The Big Show," was added to the first scene, and if "Any Girl" is not a retitling of "A Girl For Each Day In The Week," then a second change occurred. Neither song has been published. In the next scene, the opening "Butterflies Of Fashion" was dropped, while Lawson and Squibbs's "Twenty-Five Years Ago" gave place to "Me." "Let Us Build A Little Nest" was also left behind in Boston, although it was restored for part of the post-Broadway tour.

Time has not been as rewarding to Kern's score as were 1918's critics. In this instance time's dissenting vote was well cast. Once Kern hit his stride he was incapable of offering Broadway a bad score, but his songs for *Head over Heels* are among his least likable and least memorable. As was so often the case, not all the songs were originally created for the show. Kern reached back to 1912 and *A Polish Wedding* for "Let Us Build A Little Nest." George V. Hobart's lyrics for the verse were jettisoned in favor of Woolf's new rhymes, but Kern's own lyric for the chorus was retained. The title song is a toe-tapping fox-trot coupled with a polka verse, yet the equally inviting two-step melody for "'The Big Show" is marked to be played "slowly." "Mitzi's Lullaby" has a Middle-European air that Kern may have recalled from his youth. Perhaps the most interesting feature of some of the other songs, such as "I Was Lonely" and "Funny Little Something," is their use of jazz chordings and of suddenly imposed minor, augmented, and diminished chords. Kern generally gave special and careful attention to the proofs of his sheet music, so it is interesting, if puzzling, to find two of his melodies are not marked with his traditional "Burthen." "Let Us Build A Little Nest" follows the 1912 sheet music in employing the term "Refrain"; and "All The World Is Swaying" goes a step further, using the popular term Kern professed to disdain, "Chorus." This suggests that the latter song is an older, unidentified melody set to new words.

Shortly after *Head over Heels* opened, *Town Topics* published an interesting bit of gossip:

> One of the intense Liberty Loan drives took place the other evening at a performance of "Head Over Heels." Mitzi and the

official speaker had finished their remarks, the latter concluding with the urge that "someone please start the proceedings with a good-sized pledge so that the tone of the contributions shall be set in the pitch of high figures." A small, very young-looking chap in a gray lounge suit, who was seated in the middle of the parquet, said very quietly; "I pledge twenty-five thousand dollars!" After the applause had died down, the drive started with a rush and whenever there was an odd $1,000 or $2,000 or more needed to round off a big total, the bidder of the original $25,000 was on hand with the additional donations, until he had signed altogether for $46,000. He did not allow his name to be used, and all those in the audience who did not know him were agog with curiosity to discover his identity. Finally a fashionable lady in the front row leaned over to the first violinist and asked: "Who is the young man who has given all that money?" The fiddler replied: "Oh, just one of the musicians." It was Jerome Kern, composer of "Head Over Heels," "Very Good Eddie," "Oh, Lady, Lady" and other shekel-producing successes of the past few years.

If the story is not apocryphal or exaggerated, Kern's largesse was not cruelly pinching. *Head over Heels* alone continued to provide him with handsome royalties until early fall of 1919, although its Broadway run was only one hundred performances.

Since most of *Head over Heels*'s score had been written a year earlier, while *Toot-Toot!* and *Oh, Lady! Lady!!* also began their tryouts in 1917, Kern apparently did little fresh composing in 1918. Revisions and rehearsals occupied what time was not absorbed in setting up the Kerns' new home and other family matters. One other family matter occupied much of Jerry and Eva's time and thought. After nearly eight years of marriage, Eva was expecting a child.

Nonetheless, in November Kern was able to resume his old practice of interpolating songs into other men's scores. When Dillingham offered Julia Sanderson and Joseph Cawthorn in Ivan Caryll's *The Canary* at the Globe on November 4, two Kern melodies added immeasurably to the evening's pleasures. "Take A Chance" (lyric, Smith) was one more peppy, heavily ragged invitation to the dance floor. By contrast, "Oh Promise Me You'll Write To Him To-day" (lyric, Harry Clarke) was a straightforward ballad in which the opening of the chorus quoted Reginald DeKoven. The lyric urged listeners to write to their boys "over there." When the war ended a week after the show opened, the song was eliminated. But Kern liked the melody and stored it away for later.

At the end of the month, on November 26, Comstock and Elliot presented their latest Princess Theatre show, the second without a Kern score. Instead, *Oh, My Dear!* had a score by Louis Hirsch, although both Bolton and Wodehouse were at their old stands. Possibly as a gesture of goodwill, Kern allowed his old associates to insert "Go, Little Boat" from *Miss 1917*.

But Kern soon had a new little princess to dote over. On December 16 Eva gave birth to a girl. The baby arrived at home, in the Kerns' own antique Italian bed, and she was named Elizabeth Jane, after Eva's mother. At home she was always called Betty, the same epithet by which Jerry's grandfather Seligman had addressed his beloved Bertha.

11

Delights
and
Disappointments

Circumstantially, the hiatus of more than ten months between the world premieres of Kern's last 1918 score and his first for 1919 would suggest the possibility that the Kerns went to England for business and pleasure. Indeed, if *Head over Heels* is really considered a 1917 opus, then a full year elapsed between the maiden performances of *Rock-a-Bye Baby* and *She's a Good Fellow*. The London premiere of *Oh, Joy!*, the transatlantic title of *Oh, Boy!*, at the Kingsway Theatre on January 27, 1919, would appear to bolster the conclusion that the Kerns were away. But Eva's pregnancy gives the lie to these suppositions.

Why, then, did the feverish activity of the preceding months end so abruptly? Perhaps the most obvious answer is that by making his mark Kern had made his point. At the opening of 1919 Kern was undoubtedly the glittering hope of the American musical theatre. There also remains the small possibility that Kern took some of his loftier pronouncements seriously and did try his hand at more extended composition. No records of such attempts survive, although many years later Kern made a few tentative stabs at more extended writing, but only with the help of friendly orchestrators.

A more probable answer is that Kern was not asked to write so many shows. Despite his newfound reputation and the impetus his successes had given to the musical theatre in general, producers had suddenly grown wary. In March of 1919 *Variety* ran a gloomy article headlined, "MUSICAL COMEDIES HAVE HAD THEIR DAY FOR THE TIME BEING." A subheading assured readers that no lack of talent was to blame, rather that post-war inflation was squeezing out any hopes of a reasonable profit. Over-all costs, the trade sheet noted, had jumped 25 per cent in four years, adding that transportation charges had become "prohibitive"; salaries, "sky-high"; and demands of the newly recognized Actors' Equity and other unions, "impossible." Authors were now sharing 6 or 7 per cent of the show's weekly gross, and composers were refusing to give producers a cut on sheet music sales. But producers soon found that increased costs could be passed on to the playgoers, who would complain, but pay.

If Kern failed to see the London version of *Oh, Boy!*, he missed little. For the most part it was faithful to the American original, although the action was moved to England and some of the lyrics changed accordingly. Even Tom Powers was brought over to re-create his original role. One song by another composer was interpolated, but it hardly detracted from the luster of Kern's score. All Kern really missed was the clowning of a youthful Beatrice Lillie as Jackie. Londoners were more welcoming to *Oh, Joy!* than they had been to the emasculated *Very Good Eddie*, but they were not as taken as New Yorkers had been. *Oh, Joy!* compiled a satisfactory but modest 167 showings.

In late February of 1919 Dillingham began releasing publicity bulletins for a new Kern and Caldwell musical. Anne Caldwell was a plump, sometimes dowdy, but inveterately jolly woman, eighteen years Jerry's senior. Early on she had tried her hand at composing, but she had soon abandoned the effort. For the rest of her career, she confined herself to writing lyrics and librettos. While Jerry and Miss Caldwell had met socially, their first, loose professional association was either at practice sessions of *Go to It!* or *The Canary*, for which Miss Caldwell provided lyrics to the original scores. Rehearsals for their initial collaboration got under way on the first Monday of March with a cast led by Douglas Stevenson and Helen Shipman. Only at the end of the month did Dillingham announce the title would be a *A New Girl*. Advertisements for its world premiere at Washington's National Theatre on Sunday, April 6, informed potential ticket buyers that the production would offer a chance to ogle the "Famous Globe Beauty Chorus." Dillingham may have been attempting to borrow Ziegfeld's mantle. The advertisements also proclaimed Kern "America's Most Popular Composer." The advance notice in the *Star* promised "a consistent story" despite the many musical numbers (more than a dozen). Interestingly the paper saw the show's plot as a carryover or development of the all-soldier vehicles that had been voguish during World War I and in which "bass-singing chorus girls and classic dancers as husky as stevedores" romped. In fact, the plot was of a sort that easily predated the war. Julian Eltinge had time and again delighted audiences in similar pieces all through the preceding decade. Miss Caldwell's hero is Robert McLane, who marries Jacqueline Fay against the wishes of her conniving guardian. Jacqueline is a pupil at a seminary and under age. When the guardian attempts to annul the marriage and to have McLane arrested, the hero disguises himself as a girl and pretends to be his wife's classmate.

The audience for the premiere was far from capacity, but it displayed the ardor that made Washington's Sunday night crowds legendary. On the whole, the city's critics shared the enthusiasm, although they held several important reservations. The *Herald* found the libretto "gossamer," the *Post* praised it as "fresh and sparkling," while the *Star* called it "dangerously clever." The production itself was deemed "impressive" by the *Post*. Since Kern, in a pre-opening interview, had impishly challenged critics and playgoers to detect musical quotations "hidden throughout the score," critics had a field day, sometimes unearthing only fool's gold. The *Post,* for example, insisted Kern "seems to have edited one of the song hits of that eminent Princess Theater hit, 'Oh, Lady! Lady!!'—'I Found You and You Found Me,' to be exact—and reissued it in 'A New Girl' under the title of 'Teacher, Teacher.'" Besides misquoting the correct title ("You Found Me And I Found You"), the critic confused the similar tempo and slightly reminiscent melody with outright quotation.

What bothered several critics was the apparent miscasting of the principals. Few reviewers could find kind words for either Stevenson or Miss Shipman. Dillingham obviously agreed, for by the end of the first week, *Variety* reported that Joseph Santley and his wife, Ivy Sawyer, were being rushed in as replacements. At the end of the month a second major replacement was announced, the original title giving way to the snappier *She's a Good Fellow.*

The show opened at Dillingham's Globe Theatre on May 5, 1919, with the following musical program:

She's a Good Fellow

ACT I

1. Ensemble and Song, "Some Party" .... *Lavinia [Ann Orr]
and Girls*

2. "The Navy Foxtrot Man" .... *Billy [Scott Welsh] and Girls*
3. "The First Rose of Summer" .... *Jacqueline [Miss Sawyer],*
   Robert [Joseph Santley] and Girls
4. "A Happy Wedding Day" ...... *Jacqueline, Lavinia, Billy,*
   Robert and Admiral Franklin [James C. Marlowe]
5. "Jubilo" (founded on "Kingdom Comin'" by Work) ......
   Lavinia and Girls
6. Finale

ACT II

7. Opening Chorus, "Faith, Hope and Charity" .... *Ensemble*
8. "Just A Little Line" .... *Jacqueline and Lavinia*
9. "Teacher, Teacher!" .... *Lavinia and Billy*
10. "Bullfrog Patrol" and Songs .... *Duncan Sisters*
11. "Oh, You Beautiful Person!" .... *Robert and Chester Pollard*
    [Olin Howland]
12. Finale, "Snip, Snip, Snip" .. *Jacqueline, Robert and McVey*
    [Jay Wilson]

ACT III

13. "I Want My Little Gob" .... *Lavinia and Girls*
14. "The Bumble Bee" .... *Chester and Girls*
15. "I've Been Waiting for You All the Time" ...... *Jacqueline,*
    Robert, Billy, Lavinia, Chester, Duncan Sisters and Chorus
16. Finale

William Daly was musical director, although no one was publicly credited with orchestrations. Fred G. Latham and Edward Royce directed. Gladys Monkhouse designed the costumes.

New York's critics greeted the show with modified rapture. Typically, the *Morning Telegraph* called it "agreeable, diverting and generally pleasing." The *Sun*, confessing that the audience left "feeling that it had seen a good show," nevertheless thought much of the book "quite dull" and still badly miscast. The *Times* even qualified its satisfaction with Kern's score, noting that "the music . . . is sprightly and tuneful, but by no means above his best." Kern's old admirer, Alan Dale, seemed discreetly evasive, writing light-heartedly in the *American*, "Toons were from the factory of Mr J. Kern of large industry and conviction." Significantly, virtually no critic bothered to mention any special favorite among the songs.

Comparing the Washington first night program with the Broadway playbill discloses how lopsided the changes were. Two songs were cut from the first act: Jacqueline and Admiral Franklin's "A Little Pep" and Horatio and Chester's "Wine, Women And Song." Zizi (played by Elsie Lawson) and Billy's "Ginger Town" was dropped from the second act. No new songs were added to either act, suggesting the cuts were time trimmers. But the third act was totally revamped. All three songs heard in Washington were scrapped: Lavinia's "I Believe In Signs," Jacqueline and Billy's "Over The Hills," and Lavinia and Chester's "Semiramis."

"Sprightly and tuneful" neatly described the surviving songs. John McCormack's recording of "The First Rose Of Summer" quickly made it the hit of the show. The song is at once dashingly romantic and endearingly nostalgic. Although its range is only slightly more than an octave, several small but artful jumps and a series of rising phrases beginning with the line "the first song heard" give it an unusually open, arioso quality. Its quotation of "The Last Rose Of Summer" in its twenty-fifth to twenty-eighth bars tied the song squarely to the beloved "art" songs of an earlier day. Kern lifted the twelfth to sixteenth bars of his verse from the twelfth to sixteenth bars of the chorus of his own "Where's The Girl For Me?." With its sustained opening note followed by a series of shorter notes, "Some Party" presages "Who?". The song was one of the first in a rash of party songs that soon became a commonplace in the musicals of the day. Kern insisted that he quoted "no less than three familiar songs of the South" in the melody, but apart, possibly, from "Old Black Joe" they remain unidentified. "I've Been Waiting For You All The Time" is a sweet, flowing ballad, a rewrite of "Oh, Promise Me You'll Write Him Today" from *The Canary,* and perhaps deserving a revival. "The Bull Frog Patrol" is an odd, clever gimmick song. Four tightly knit melodies, all cutely ragged, are repeated over and over again. The result is a capital minstrel song. Kern may have been mischievously paraphrasing Caryll's "My Beautiful Lady" from *The Pink Lady* in "Oh, You Beautiful Person," a waltz with an identical tempo and similar melody. In the show Chester Pollard sings it to Robert (Robert is gorgeously gowned as a girl). "Jubilo," a real rouser in the production, admittedly leans heavily on Henry Clay Work's "Kingdom Comin'." "Faith, Hope And Charity," besides jazzing Chopin, Debussy, and Chaminade, begins with a passage culled from a Gregorian chant.

In an interview shortly after the musical opened, Kern said, "When I write the score of a musical play I try to get into the spirit of the book." He went on to deny that he was, as he professed his critics had claimed, trying to create a new school of music. He readily admitted taking increasing pains with his scores and suggested an urgent reason why all composers should. If his reasoning betrayed a certain unfortunate antipathy to the latest American musical sounds, it nevertheless demonstrated that he was a thoughtful, incontestably progressive artist.

> I believe that theatregoers are going to demand better musical plays when prohibition comes into effect. They will not be satisfied with the jazzy type of entertainments that are holding the boards in many Broadway playhouses. I wrote this music with a view of having it appreciated by people who come to the theatre without any alcoholic stimulation. I don't insinuate that people come to the theatre that way at the present time. I merely believe that people will be more exacting after July 1. And I hope, therefore, that "She's A Good Fellow" will have a longer run after July 1 than before it.

One reason Kern granted the interview was that his latest musical had gotten off to a discouragingly slow start at the box office. *Variety*, reporting on the disappointing grosses, shared Kern's hope, adding that business should pick up since *She's a Good Fellow* was "regarded as a class show." Kern got his wish, but only by a hair's breadth, for the musical never really caught the public's fancy and was withdrawn after 120 performances.

A week after *She's a Good Fellow* opened, a single Kern song was offered in *The Lady in Red*. The musical, a failure, had another set of Caldwell lyrics, but the lyric for Kern's song was by Harry B. Smith. New Yorkers had first heard "Where Is The Girl For Me?" four years earlier in *Ninety in the Shade*.

Stories of a Bolton-Wodehouse split began circulating in April and were confirmed in May. Further confirmation followed in August when announcements served notice that Bolton would develop a new Princess Theatre libretto on his own. Reverting to a practice he had employed before Plum had entered the scene, Bolton chose not to create a story out of whole cloth, but rather to adapt a popular old play. The play selected was *Brewster's Millions*, a 1906 hit about a young man who must spend a million dollars in a single day in order to inherit seven million.

Buddy De Sylva, then a rising, relatively unknown writer, was hired to provide lyrics. Ziegfeld's old standby, Julian Mitchell, took on the task of directing the dancing and a chorus of twenty girls and ten boys, while a rather unimportant name, Oscar Eagle, was called on to stage the book. A favorite from *Oh, Boy!*, Marie Carroll, was signed as leading lady.

For many the biggest news was that Harry Fox would star. Fox was something of a musical matinee idol. He had recently finished a long, successful tour in *Oh, Look!*, in which he had introduced "I'm Always Chasing Rainbows." His co-stars on tour had been the Dolly Sisters, and his celebrity had skyrocketed after he married one of the sisters. Although he could not know it, his career had just peaked.

Word of who would compose the score was withheld for some time. No doubt the disappointing reception accorded *Oh, My Dear!* prompted Comstock and Gest to press Jerry for another score. Their argument may well have been that Jerry had gone on to bigger but not better things. Whatever his reasoning, Jerry agreed to return to the Princess. Already committed to Dillingham for a new musical, Jerry tossed off this latest score in just short of a month.

Jerry's signing forced a delay in the schedule. The new musical had originally been slated for a late October opening at the Princess, an opening now put ahead to January 5. A second change occurred at the same time. Comstock and Gest originally had called their new show *Maid of Money*, but when George Tyler, another producer, claimed to have prior rights, they agreed to come up with a second title. They were probably glad to do so. Indeed, they would most likely have revised the title in any case. Not only was it unattractive, it called attention to the female lead, although only Fox was to be given prominent billing. Their new title was a happier choice, *Zip Goes a Million*.

The show opened at the Worcester Theatre in Worcester, Massachusetts, on December 8, 1919. Although no other show competed for first nighters, the town's critics gave it short shrift. Neither the *Morning Telegram* nor the *Evening Post* seems to have reviewed it, while the *Evening Gazette* said all it had to say about the offering in three skimpy paragraphs. The paper found the show "gives promise of taking its place with other successful musical shows" and noted in closing, "The performance last night ran considerably over time, but the audience evidently enjoyed every minute of it, as it remained until the final curtain dropped, a few minutes before midnight." Only two songs, both sung by Fox and his leading lady, Marie Carroll, were singled out: "Whip-Po-Will" and "You Tell 'Em." From Worcester *Zip Goes a Million* moved to Springfield and then to Providence.

Variety's man caught the show in Rhode Island. He was none too happy with it, suggesting its dancing was its best asset and singling out only the same two songs the Worcester critic had. Two more stops were scheduled before New York—Washington and Newark. But tepid notices in the capital prompted Comstock and Gest to cancel both the Newark and New York engagements. Not even a surprisingly strong Washington gross of $14,000 would change their minds. They gave out the customary explanation that nobody took seriously—the show had been closed temporarily for rewriting. The musical was Kern's lone show ever to fold during its tryout.

Given the speed with which Jerry turned out the score, his music was quite remarkable. In fact, two songs were later transfered to *Sally*, where they entered his canon of classics. One was a song dropped during *Zip*'s rehearsals, "Look For The Silver Lining." The other was "Whip-Poor-Will" (which a number of programs and reviewers for both shows spelled "Whip-Po-Will"). "A Man Around The House" and "Little Backyard Band" are pleasant waltzes, the latter with a curious, yet appealing hurdy-gurdy quality. "A Business Of Our Own" is a ballad, whose lyric offers a novel twist on the "cozy-little-bungalow-of-our-own" theme, a theme soon to be the rage of Broadway and Tin Pan Alley. De Sylva had even cleverer lyrics ready for "Telephone Girls," lyrics which managed to incorporate the names of all the major New York City telephone exchanges. Jerry provided an appropriately light, syncopated melody.

Jerry had once again found himself shuttling back and forth between a show breaking in out on the road and a second rehearsing in New York. But after it became obvious that Comstock and Gest were to close *Zip Goes a Million*, Kern remained in New York to devote his full time to another musical that reunited him with Dillingham and Anne Caldwell.

The Night Boat was launched on December 29, 1919. If the launching occurred closer to Chesapeake Bay than to the Hudson River, no matter. Audiences at Baltimore's Academy of Music hailed the new ship as beckoning to the eye and superbly manned. Yet for all the elation, reservations quickly surfaced as to the excellence of the ship's construction. Both the *Morning Sun* and the *American* preferred to salute the good news first. "It is a beautifully staged and costumed production," the *Morning Sun* began, "fresh and charming, and having throughout the Dillingham stamp of good taste." The *American* said simply that the show was "beautifully mounted." The papers vied with each other to shower encomiums on the cast, with both critics taking special note of the chorus, which the *Morning Sun*'s man praised as "the freshest, most youthful" in many months. One novelty that delighted critics and public alike was the young chorus girls interrupting the action during the first act to recapitulate the plot for the benefit of latecomers. That plot centered on Bob White, a man whose foundering marriage is being directed straight for the rocks by his harridan mother-in-law. To escape his stormy home life and enjoy a few tranquil evenings, White pretends to be the captain of an Albany night boat. When Mrs. Maxim, his suspicious mother-in-law, with her unmarried daughter, Barbara, and Mrs. White in tow, books passage on the boat, complications ensue, especially after the real captain of the boat turns out to be named Robert White also. By the time everything is resolved at the home of a lady with whom White (the hero) had flirted, Mrs. Maxim had been sufficiently subdued to present no further threats to the Whites, although she casts an ominous eye on young Freddie Ides, who would marry Barbara.

Somehow, a plot that might have served a straight play adequately seemed insufficient to hold together an evening larded with song and dance. As the *Morning Sun* advised its readers, the story "is not presented in a particularly new way, nor is it irrepressibly funny, and it scarcely balances the spontaneity of the cast." The libretto seemed its most feeble in the second act, just when a crowd of specialty performers came aboard the boat. Indeed, only one thing seemed more feeble to Baltimore's critics, and that was Kern's score. The *Morning Sun* ignored the composer and his melodies entirely, while the *American* could only note that "the music is pretty and lively, although not free from the usual musical comedy brand of reminiscence." No doubt a lack of familiarity with Kern's new tunes clouded the critics' judgments, but it is especially hard to see how they could be so deaf to the delights of this irresistible score. Philadelphia and Rochester's critics were more alert, and by the time *The Night Boat* opened at the Liberty Theatre on February 2, 1920, the cheering was virtually universal. New York firstnighters heard the following musical program:

The Night Boat

ACT I

1. "Some Fine Day" ... *Barbara [Louise Groody] and Ensemble*
2. "Whose Baby Are You?" .. *Barbara and Freddie [Hal Skelly]*
3. "Left All Alone Again Blues" .. *Mrs. White [Stella Hoban] and Ensemble*

4. "Good Night Boat" .... *Bob White [John E. Hazzard], Mrs.*
   White, Barbara, Freddie, Mrs. Maxim [Ada Lewis]
   and Ensemble
5. Plot Demonstrators ...... *Misses Curtis, Chase, E. Conway,*
   Leigh, Sinclair and Wendell
6. "I'd Like a Lighthouse" .... *Barbara and Freddie*
7. Buffo Finale

ACT II

8. Opening, "Catskills, Hello" .... *Ensemble*
9. Jug Band and Dance .... *Mr. [Hansford] Wilson and*
   Jug Band
10. Maid's Sextette .... *Misses Alexander, Scott, Sinclair,*
    Wendell, Leigh and Chase
11. "Don't You Want To Take Me?" ...... *Barbara and Freddie*
12. "I Love the Lassies" .. *Robert White [Ernest Torrence], Miss*
    Chase, Miss Leigh and Misses Wendell, Curtis, Sinclair,
    Hollis, Alexander, Wilson, Conway, Gates, Daniels,
    Cavanagh, Appleton and Burns
13. River Song Medley
    "The Quadalquiver"
    Dances by Cansino Brothers
    "Saskatchewan"
    "On the Banks of the Wabash"
    "Congo Love Song"
    "Down by the Erie"
    "M-i-s-s-i-s-s-i-p-p-i"
    "Good Night, Boat"
14. Plot Demonstrators .... *Misses Curtis, Chase, E. Conway,*
    Leigh, Sinclair and Wendell
15. Laundry Duet .... *Bob White and Miss Cooper*
16. "A Heart For Sale" .... *Barbara and Boys*
17. "Girls Are Like a Rainbow" .... *Freddie, Misses Chase,*
    Leigh, Sinclair, Wendell and Chorus
18. Finale .... *Ensemble*

Victor Baravelle was musical director. Once more, no orchestrator was credited. The book was staged by Fred G. Latham, the musical numbers by Ned Wayburn. O'Kane Conwell designed the costumes.

For the most part, New York critics were jubilant. The *Times* began its notice with what seems like a paraphrase of the Baltimore *Morning Sun:* "The stamp of Mr. Dillingham's taste and showmanship is imprinted even more deeply than usual on 'The Night Boat.'" But unlike his Baltimore colleague, the *Times's* man had ample praise for "several insidious melodies by Jerome Kern," prophesying they would soon "be popular in the song shops—'Left All Alone Again Blues,' for example, and 'A Heart For Sale.'" The *Tribune* commented, "For the trip up the river Jerome Kern has furnished some whistleable tunes, which are sung and danced with real Cohanlike speed." A few critics had reservations about Miss Caldwell's libretto and lyrics, but the men expressed them with gentlemanly tact. For the cast they had only the highest praise, with the "cute and dimpled ingenue," Miss Groody, and Hansford Wilson's "knockabout" dancing earning the choicest adjectives.

Despite Baltimore's reservations about the book and songs, Dillingham and his authors had concluded that the show was in such good shape that few changes were made during the tryout and these consisted largely of minor rearranging of the songs' order of presentation. Three songs were cut, one from each act. The Whites's duet, "Bob White," was dropped from the first act; "She's Spanish," at the end of Act II, was axed, as was "Jazz," the opening of Act III. "Rip Van Winkle And His Little Men" was used briefly in Philadelphia. The only additional Kern song heard on Broadway was "Girls Are Like A Rainbow," although Miss Caldwell gave the "plot demonstrators" new lyrics at the start of the last act. The lyrics this time summarized the rest of the plot for the benefit of those who had to catch an early train. The elimination of "Jazz" and the addition of the river song medley are telling. While "Jazz" may have been discarded because it was weak—no tryout review mentions it—its removal may also have been prompted by Kern's growing discomfort with the new idiom. Although Kern was advancing the art of popular song and would continue to do so until his death, he rarely felt at ease with the more blatant, strident side of jazz and almost never attempted to write but superficially in the style. Similarly, the insertion of interpolations into what had until then been a totally Kern score reflected his tolerance of other men's music, albeit inferior, and his realization that they could help establish a mood. Note, though, that however "old" some of the interpolations now seem, most of the songs were then relatively fresh. For example, Marie Cahill had introduced "Congo Love Song" in *Nancy Brown* seventeen years before; "Saskatchewan" came from the 1911 hit, *The Pink Lady;* while "Down By The Erie" (actually about a canal, not a river) was from George M. Cohan's 1914 revue, *Hello, Broadway!*

Kern's own sunlit score sparkled from beginning to end. After a pleasant opening number that moves along gracefully in 6/8 time, Kern followed with his three best numbers for the show. Alec Wilder rightly terms "Whose Baby Are You?" "a rouser," adding, "From the first note of the verse this song drives. And it leads marvelously into the chorus." He notes that in the last four bars of the verse Kern quotes the first four measures of "The Down Home Rag." (Kern would employ quotes all through this score, much as he had in *She's a Good Fellow.*) The song is harmonically simple. "The tune and the rhythm," as Wilder concludes, "are all important." A principal device used by Kern was syncopation of the last eighth note in seven of the thirty-six bars. The song's odd length stems from a rare use by Kern of a tag at the end. "Left All Alone Again Blues" wears its contemporary harmonies lightly. Its lilting jog and catchy melody spotlighted it as the hit of the show. In performance the melody was sung over a countertune, "The Blue Bells Of Scotland," whose lyric Miss Caldwell had quoted in her own. It was this counterpoint that Kern referred to in a 1924 assault on jazz when he stated, a little ambiguously, "There is no legitimate objection to the use of countermelody on occasion. I used it myself in 'The Night Boat' in the case of 'Left All Alone Again Blues,' where I opposed a modern melody to 'The Blue Bells Of Scotland,' but there was a characteristic reason for this course in the personal nature of the song involved." "Good Night Boat" could also be hailed as a rouser. Essentially a small group of half (sometimes quarter) notes alternating cleverly with a longer string of eighth notes, it seems quite danceable. The 4/4 time of its chorus suggests a fox-trot, but the song's rhythm seems better suited to a gay, tricky two-step. "I Love The Lassies" offers a theatrically Scottish melody that sneaks in a quote from "Annie Laurie." (Torrence sang it in the show with a broad Scottish accent.) "A Heart For Sale" is a pleasant ballad that moves back and forth between repeated notes and, a Kern favorite, cascading thirds. Another engaging number, "I'd Like A Lighthouse," coupled a straightforward melody which Kern had employed for "Honeymoon Land" in *Toot-Toot!* with lyrics that spoofed the "cottage-of-our-own" type of song. A note of longing, reflecting the lyric, creeps into the lovely 4/4 melody Kern wrote for "Don't You Want To Take Me?."

The Night Boat quickly became one of the season's smash hits, rolling up 313 performances in New York and touring successfully. For several weeks running *Variety* reported the show had established new house records and was the "hottest ticket in town." Dillingham's publicity manager, Mark Luescher, whetted passersby's appetites by mounting a miniature replica of an Albany night boat on the Lyric's canopy. The boat contained a revolving light that described an arc around 42nd Street. The construction reminded old timers that Dillingham had given Broadway its first moving electric sign only fourteen years before when he had produced Victor Herbert's *The Red Mill*. Sales were further stimulated when Victor's back-to-back recordings of "Left All Alone Again Blues" and "Whose Baby Are You?" became national best sellers in May. Sheet music sales failed to keep pace after publishers suddenly tripled the price of show music. For several years a price war had cut the price to a dime. Now the publishers decided to let theatre music, with its special associations and cachet, lead the way back to "normal" prices. How long *The Night Boat* might have run had it been left alone, like its heroine, is uncertain. But a booking jam forced it to close. Ironically, the show that forced it out was a failure. By that time, however, *The Night Boat* was setting house records in Boston. It continued to tour successfully for three seasons.

A lone Kern song adorned a comedy that began to tour in the spring, although it did not reach New York until mid-summer. Alice Duer Miller and Robert Milton's *The Charm School* told of the problems that beset a handsome young headmaster at a ladies' seminary. Kern's contribution was "When I Discover My Man," a gently rocking if undistinguished melody, for which Mrs. Miller wrote the lyric. The show seemed a natural for musical treatment and perfectly apposite for Kern's graceful style. Yet when it was turned into a musical several years later, Kern was not asked to do the score. Not until he set music to her *Gowns by Roberta* thirteen years later did Jerry work with Mrs. Miller again.

While *The Charm School* was on the road, Jerry and Eva were invited to a dinner at the home of Rabbi Stephen Wise, probably the most famous Jewish cleric of his day. Franklin P. Adams and his wife were also among the guests. Adams was a famous columnist, raconteur, and wit, remembered by a later generation for his expertise on radio's *Information Please*. The rabbi told his guests that he had come into possession of some rabbits and had decided to present them to his nieces. But on phoning them he learned they had been given a pair of baby rabbits that very day. Kern and Adams exchanged amused glances. When the guests adjourned to the rabbi's living room, Kern headed straight for the piano, with Adams beside him. Before the evening was over they had composed a not-quite-immortal opus, "Keep Your Rabbits Rabbi [,] We've Rabbits Of Our Own." Kerns had Harms publish it privately, sending the rabbi and his nieces copies.

By the time *The Charm School* reached the Bijou on August 2, Kern was occupied with rehearsals for the last revue he would ever write. The show was another in the series that Raymond Hitchcock, "a lanky, raspy-voiced comic with sharp features and straw-colored hair," had produced with himself as star. The shows were called *Hitchy-Koo*. For his 1920 edition Hitchcock enlisted Anne Caldwell and Glen MacDonough to provide sketches and lyrics. Julia Sanderson was Hitchcock's co-star. It was her last important association with Kern.

Hitchy-Koo had its world premiere at Boston's Colonial Theatre on September 6, 1920. The sixth was Labor Day, the traditional big gun for out-of-town theatrical seasons. As a result the opening competed for attention with first nights at nearly half of Boston's other playhouses. Although the opening attracted a large and elegant crowd, the Hub's leading critics saw fit to attend other offerings. Reactions of the second-stringers ranged from runaway enthusiasm to bilious disdain, with most critics awarding the revue guarded approval. No doubt much of this wait-and-see tolerance came from the very fact that the show was not a book musical, whose final shape and fortune were often easier to predict. Almost to a man, the critics praised the costumes. When they arrived at the evening's humor the reviewers shaved their adjectives a bit. A few regretted that for the first time Hitchcock had abandoned his practice of addressing extended monologues to his audience. Julia Sanderson was praised for her light dancing, her lovely voice, and, most of all, simply for her winsome charm. Having devoted much time to the cast, the comedy, and the production, reviewers found little to say about Kern's music, and what they did write was not particularly kind. The *Globe,* without mentioning any outstanding song, judged the music to be of "surpassing excellence," but the *Evening Transcript,* offering, as usual, Boston's longest and most thoughtful notice, mentioned neither Kern nor his songs. Perhaps the *Herald* best summarized the general sentiment when it concluded its review: "The music—but why discuss that; it is wholly adequate for the varying occasions, yet after all is a minor part of the bewildering, anatomical agglomeration that makes 'Hitchy-Koo, 1920' what it is."

One change in the non-musical part of the evening bears some looking into. The *Herald* lauded the revue as "up-to-the-minute," while the *Evening*

Transcript devoted considerable space to a number in the second act, "Costumes For 1950," which purported to show how "progeny of the profiteers" would dress "thirty years hence." *Hitchy-Koo*'s prognosticators employed cloth of gold and cloth of silver to "swathe . . . comely bodies from top to toe." By the time the revue reached the New Amsterdam on October 19, 1920, the number was gone, as were several other bits that had suggested a modishly contemporary tone.

Here are the musical numbers and their principal performers:

Hitchy-Koo, 1920

ACT I

1. Dance .... *Marion Wilbanks and Girls*
2. "The Military Mannequin" .... *Florence O'Denishawn*
3. "I Am Daguerre" .... *Tyler Brooke and "Rainbow Girls"*
4. Old-Fashioned Dances
5. "Sweetie" .... *Ruth Mitchell and "The Balloonatics"*
6. "Ding Dong, It's Kissing Time" .... *Julia Sanderson and Douglas Stevenson*
7. "Moon of Love" .... *Grace Moore and Chorus Girls*
8. "Canajoharie" .... *Douglas Stevenson and Chorus*
9. "Buggy Riding" .... *Julia Sanderson and Mr. Hitchcock*
10. "Old New York" ...... *Mr. Hitchcock, Mr. Freeborn, Miss Moore and Mr. Cunningham*

ACT II

11. "We'll Make A Bet" .... *Ensemble*
    Dance by Florence O'Denishawn and Tyler Brooke
12. "I Want To Marry" .... *Julia Sanderson*
13. "Treasure Island" .... *Grace Moore*
    Dance by Florence O'Denishawn
14. "Bring 'Em Back" .. *Douglas Stevenson and Miss Sanderson*
15. "The Star Of Hitchy-Koo" .... *Miss Sanderson, Mr. Huntley and Mr. Hitchcock*

Ned Wayburn staged the entertainment. Cassius Freeborn was musical director. Programs listed no orchestrator, but surviving material at the Library of the Performing Arts in New York reveals the orchestrations were the work of Frank Saddler. Costumes were by Madam B. Rasimi.

Its glance at the future discarded, the show seemed determinedly old-fashioned, with numbers entitled "At The Maison Daguerre," "A Little Bit Of Yesterday," "Old New York," "Buggy Riding" and "Old-Fashioned Dances." This last included Florence O'Denishawn's "Serpentine Dance . . . invented by Ida Fuller in 1890, and . . . reproduced with her supervision." If so much nostalgia represented a reversion to the crackerbarrel Americana typical of Hitchcock, it struck New York critics as an unfortunate throwback. Heywood Broun branded the entertainment "undeniably old and frayed." Without mentioning Kern at all, he named just one song in passing, "Buggy Riding," and then merely to comment on Hitchcock and Miss Sanderson's interpretation.

If the score was unquestionably minor Kern, it was nevertheless pleasant. From beginning to end it was so patently out of step with new sounds beginning to be heard that one suspects Kern ransacked his trunk to find melodies with genuine period flavor for songs such as "The Star Of Hitchy Koo," "The Old Town," "Ding Dong, It's Kissing Time," "Moon Of Love," "Chick! Chick! Chick!," "Girls In The Sea" (the last two published, but cut during tryout), and "Buggy Riding." Knowing Kern's violent distaste for the word "cupid," his almost defiant use of a few more modern harmonies in "Cupid, The Winner" suggests his impishness at work. He published the song, although it, too, was discarded before the New York opening. A manuscript copy of "Treasure Island" at the Library of the Performing Arts reveals it to be an unexceptional ballad.

Hitchy-Koo, 1920 had a disappointing nine-week run and on the road encountered early signs of the post-war recession. The poor grosses hurt Hitchcock, who claimed to have spent $125,000 on costumes alone, and precipitated a crisis in his personal finances that caused him to abandon the series and, shortly, to declare himself bankrupt. But Ziegfeld himself was now knocking at Kern's door, coming to bring about a major change in Kern's life.

12

The Great Glorifier

Almost from the moment Ziegfeld hired Marilyn Miller for his 1918 *Follies* he began to plan bigger roles for her. She was, of course, as ravishing a beauty as ever paraded into a Ziegfeld spotlight. Enchanted critics described her as "spritelike" and compared her delicate features to those of Dresden china figurines. But unlike so many of the producer's gorgeous mannequins, this entrancing blonde could dance divinely. Ziegfeld quickly determined that she also had a passable singing voice, small but sweet and on pitch. Only her abilities as an actress remained untested.

Ziegfeld's interest in Miss Miller was not entirely professional, and his emotional attachment soon created problems that nearly nipped his plans in the bud. In the producer's possessive eyes, his newfound star did an inexcusable thing. She fell in love—and not with him. In fact, she fell in love with another player featured in the *Follies,* a handsome young man who could both step and sing, Frank Carter. Ziegfeld threw every conceivable obstacle in their path. But neither obstacles nor enticements cooled their ardor, and Miss Miller and Carter were married in May of 1919. Although he was furious, Ziegfeld nevertheless signed both performers for his new 1919 edition of the *Follies*. Whether he had decided they were too talented to lose or whether he all the while planned a mean trick is uncertain. But as soon as the tryout started, the producer noisily fired Carter. Miss Miller threatened to quit, while Ziegfeld in turn threatened to haul her into court for breach of contract and to ruin her career. A loud, squalid battle ensued, with four-letter gutter words exchanged between the impeccably dapper producer and his dainty, feminine star. Miss Miller stayed. Her decision probably secured her career, for Ziegfeld realized that not only could she swear like a trouper, but that she would put her own advancement above even her marriage.

Shortly after the 1919 *Follies* went on its post-Broadway tour, Ziegfeld decided to take a working vacation in Palm Beach. He booked a suite at the Breakers until he could find a suitably grand house and also made arrangements to charter Leopold Replogle's luxurious yacht, the *Wench*. Ziegfeld rarely used the phone. He had a special contract with Western Union allowing him to send a total of three million words a year at a special reduced, but prepaid, rate. Three of the earliest cables he sent once he was comfortably unpacked went to Bolton, Wodehouse, and Kern. He invited them to join him. Not only did Ziegfeld provide a complete staff, he provided unexpected company as well. Fellow guests included producer Messmore Kendall, newspaper executive Paul Block, automotive heir Walter Chrysler, and novelist Arthur Somers Roche and his wife, singer Ethel Pettit. Also lolling about were a number of typical Ziegfeld beauties, including one of his many favorites, Olive Thomas. Ziegfeld's itinerary called for them to sail along the Indian River and possibly to run up the Loxahackie in one of the launches.

Despite the crowded guest list, lavish cocktail parties, and extended dinners, Ziegfeld did manage to get down to business. What he wanted was a vehicle for his new star, Marilyn Miller. Could the boys suggest anything?

They recalled a piece they had worked on in the now passed Princess Theatre days, that piece with the unpromising title of *The Little Thing*. It was about a waif who washes dishes at an actors' boardinghouse. Because she was found in a telephone booth, she was given the phone's exchange as a patronymic, and so she was known to all the old-timers at the home as Sally Rhinelander. Sally dreams of being a great dancer. Her dreams are encouraged by one of the boarders, an old harridan named Esmeralda, who once had been a ballet star. Esmeralda's decrepit but loyal lover dutifully takes a similar interest in the orphan.

When, to Wodehouse's surprise, Ziegfeld saw possibilities in the work,

Plum added that there were some lovely Kern songs already written for it and that two of them contained some of Plum's own favorite lyrics. One celebrated the very church in which he had been married, The Little Church Around the Corner; the other was a song they had dropped from another Princess Theatre show—a song called "Bill." There was a piano on the yacht, so Jerry played the songs. (In *Bring on the Girls,* Wodehouse and Bolton imply that the melody for "Bill" was actually written as early as 1906.) Ziegfeld did have one immediate suggestion. He hated older woman comedians. The part of Esmeralda would have to be rewritten to fit a young lady or a man. And as a seeming afterthought he added in his curiously melancholy tone that the dishwasher does not just want to become a great dancer, she wants to become the dancing star of the Follies.

In the meantime, Miss Miller's husband had been killed in an automobile accident. The sudden death of her husband made it imperative in Ziegfeld's mind that a vehicle be found quickly. He was determined to keep his star's mind off her woes. Although she was clearly distraught, Ziegfeld demanded she return at once to the tour of the *Follies* in which she was appearing.

Within a week the producer announced with great fanfare that he had at last found the proper book show to serve as Miss Miller's first starring vehicle. Jerry and his associates were startled to learn the show was to be a musical version of *Captain Jinks of the Horse Marines.* A quick call to Ziegfeld's office brought assurances that no such musical existed. The producer was simply trying to distract his star-to-be with publicity. Such reassurances might have calmed the writers had not they discovered by accident that several other composers and librettists were also working at Ziegfeld's suggestion on a new offering for Miss Miller. In any case, less than a month later Ziegfeld did announce that plans for *Captain Jinks* had been shelved, but all he would add was that he would be searching for another property while Miss Miller and her mother-in-law vacationed in Europe.

Ziegfeld was not the only one who was changing his plans. Wodehouse took on commitments that forced him to sail for England and remain there for several months. With Wodehouse unable to return, the book became solely Bolton's charge. Clifford Grey was called in to write additional lyrics. For some reason Wodehouse took umbrage at other men's rhymes sung side by side with his. That he had often interpolated his own into competitors' shows suddenly seemed immaterial. He sent off what he himself described as "the sort of cable that the Kaiser might have sent to an underling."

Astounded and annoyed, Jerry wired back snappishly, "You have offended me for the last time."

Bolton's story opened at the Elm Tree Alley Inn, a chic Greenwich Village bistro. Wealthy Mrs. Ten Broek brings a group of orphan girls to tour the place just when a dishwasher is needed. One of the young girls, Sally, is selected. A fellow employee is "Connie," the exiled Duke Constantine of Czechogovinia. He soon befriends the new girl. Blair Farquar, scion of the Long Island Farquars, arrives to book a party. He is momentarily captivated by Sally, but quickly moves on to other business. Connie, as Duke, is to attend a gala at the Farquars'. A theatrical agent, Otis Hooper, who was to supply the principal entertainment for the soirée, arrives at the inn and confesses that his prima ballerina has backed out. Hooper notices little Sally dancing and decides to pass her off as his leading lady. At the gala Sally is nervous, and when Blair fails to recognize her she is crestfallen. She has an argument with Blair, he berates her, and, nonplussed, she drops her disguise. Connie quietly offers to take the humiliated little girl home. Otis, however, soon discloses that he has arranged for Sally to dance in the Ziegfeld Follies. She triumphs there in a Butterfly Ballet. Hooper and his girl friend, Connie and Mrs. Ten Broek, and Sally and Blair head for a triple nuptial at the Little Church Around the Corner.

In raising a poor girl from rags to riches, Bolton's story fell in line with two other hits then running on Broadway, *Irene* and *Mary*. Together these three musicals established a vogue for similar stories and led to the early years of the 1920s being looked at as the Cinderella Era of American musicals.

When Ziegfeld finally did get around to announcing the show, only days before rehearsals began in mid-October, he created a certain confusion either by giving out two titles or by offering one that suggested the other. Papers called the new work both *Sally of the Alley* and *Sally in Our Alley;* some papers even spelled the heroine's name as "Salley." Just before the world premiere at Baltimore's Academy of Music on November 29, 1920, the producer officially shortened the title to *Sally*. The change came so late it caught several critics unaware. Baltimore reviews of the period were generally among the skimpiest in any major city, and since *Sally* opened along with three other new shows, it received scant attention. The *Morning Sun* devoted most of its brief notice to praising Ziegfeld. Without so much as mentioning Kern, it stated simply, "The music is light, and while it does not make heavy demands upon the vocalists, it is catchy and contagious."

After a week in Baltimore, the show moved on to Newark, New Jersey, a desperation booking after no other suitable road house was found to be available anywhere. Word of mouth quickly spread across the river, and hundreds were turned away for opening night at the New Amsterdam on December 21, 1920. *Sally's* musical program was:

Sally
ACT I

1. Opening Ensemble
   Violin Solo .... *Sascha [Jacques Rabinoff]*
2. Song, "Way Down East" .... *Rosalind [Mary Hay]*
   and Ensemble
3. Song, "On with the Dance" .... *Otis [Walter Catlett],*
   Rosalind, Betty [Betty Williams], Harry [Jack Barker]
4. Song and Dance, "This Little Girl" .... *Mrs. Ten Broek*
   [Dolores], Pop [Alfred P. James], Misses Kingsley, Otis,
   Maude, Henderson, Freeland and S. Vernon
5. Song, "Joan of Arc" .... *Sally and Misses Kingsley, Otis,*
   Maude, Henderson, Freeland and S. Vernon
6. Duet, "Look for the Silver Lining" (Words by B. G. De
   Sylva) .... *Sally and Blair [Irving Fisher]*
7. Dance .... *Sally and Connie [Leon Errol]*
8. Song, "Sally" .... *Blair and Ensemble*
9. Dance .... *Sally*
10. Finale .... *Sally, Connie, Rosalind, Otis and Ensemble*

ACT II

1. Opening, "The Social Game" ...... *Jimmie [Stanley Ridges]*
   and Ensemble
2. Song and Dance, "The Wild Rose" .... *Sally and Diplomats*
3. Song, "The Schnitza Komisski" ...... *Connie and Ensemble*
4. Duet, "Whip-poor-Will" .... *Sally and Blair*
5. Trio, "The Lorelei" (Words by Anne Caldwell) ...... *Otis,*
   Rosalind and Jimmie
6. Duet, "Little Church Around the Corner" (Words by P. G.
   Wodehouse) .... *Rosalind and Otis*
7. Slavic Dance .... *Sally*
8. Finale .... *Entire Company*

ACT III
(No new songs were introduced in the last act, which was devoted largely to the Butterfly Ballet, with Victor Herbert's music.)

The show was staged by Edward Royce and conducted by Gus Salzer. No one was credited with the orchestrations. Sets were by Joseph Urban and costumes by a long list of designers.

Programs also gave several pieces of information whose import would be lost on audiences. If Bolton and Wodehouse's memories of *The Little Thing* are accurate, then the heroine had undergone a name change. She was no longer Sally Rhinelander, but Sally of the Alley. On the other hand, a number of Ziegfeld's beauties paraded about as Miss Rhinelander, Miss Vanderbilt, Miss Worth, and other telephone exchanges of the day. No doubt there is some connection between the original Sally Rhinelander, "The Telephone Girl" of *Zip Goes a Million,* and the chorus girls of *Sally.* Nor could audiences know that supporting players such as Mary Hay, Jack Barker, and Stanley Ridges would move on to more important roles in other shows.

Inevitably, Ziegfeld and Miss Miller monopolized the morning-after reviews. Typically the *Graphic* welcomed *Sally* as "the most imposing musical comedy of the year. In fact, Florenz Ziegfeld, Jr. in 'Sally' has eclipsed all his former productions, even the most famous of the 'Follies.'" Alexander Woollcott went so far as to end his review in the *Times:* "it is of none of these, not of Urban, nor Jerome Kern, not of Leon Errol, not even of Marilynn Miller that you think first as you rush for the subway at ten minutes to midnight. You think of Mr. Ziegfeld. He is that kind of producer. There are not many of them in the world."

Miss Miller was hailed as Broadway's indisputable musical comedy queen, and her associates all came in for their share of kudos. A number of critics compared the show favorably to *Irene.* As for Kern's music, only the *American* seems to have forgotten to comment on it. The *World* suggested it "had the pleasing cadence of the period," while the *Herald* called it "Kern's buoyant music of the spheres." When it came to singling out favorite tunes those critics who elected to pick winners almost to a man selected "Wild Rose" and "Whip-Poor-Will." One of the few to comment on another song was Heywood Broun in the *Tribune.* He wrote: "Jerome Kern seems to have set his heart on popularizing a tinkling tune called 'Look For the Silver Lining' which is ingratiating enough in its own mushy way to fulfill this purpose admirably, but our favorite is another more comical ditty called 'The Schnitza Komisski,' which is a merry melody of a spirited, dashing quality not often found in our musical plays." Still, despite quibbles here and there, Charles Darnton of the *World* summed up the consensus when he labeled *Sally* "nothing less than idealized musical comedy."

A comparison of Baltimore and New York playbills discloses that only minor changes were required in the musical program. While several numbers were repositioned, only three were cut and one added. The opening scene music gave way to a song originally sung later in the first act, "It's The Nighttime." The melody captures the glamour and mystery that was once New York's. Connie and Hooper's only comic duet, "Nervous Wrecks," was replaced in Act II when "Church 'Round The Corner" was moved up from the last act. "At The Play" was also cut from the last act. The lone addition was the title song. It was not a new melody. Even at this early date Kern apparently had lost interest in the show and had developed a passionate disdain for it. Many years later, when Edwin Lester planned a West Coast revival, Jerry gave the producer free rein to make whatever changes he chose, asking only that he not be required to attend, and confessing to Lester that of all his hits *Sally* was the only one he "hated."

Admittedly, few of Kern's better songs for *Sally* were actually written for the show, but this in no way gainsays their excellence. In his *American Popular Song* Alec Wilder waxed ecstatic, calling "Look For The Silver Lining," "Wild Rose" and "Whip-Poor-Will" three "phenomenal songs." Wilder continued,

> The three songs from "Sally" were a big leap forward in invention, style, and experimentation. They were markedly distinctive, wholly detached from his operetta writing, and suggestive of an awareness, a sudden awareness, of the musical world around him. Should one keep in mind that by 1919–1920 a revolution in dance band arranging had begun? Had Kern been listening to the new sounds, new instrumentation, new harmonic and rhythmic devices? It must be assumed so.

Wilder may have been a little unfair to Kern in suggesting that his music from *Sally* was his earliest breakaway from operetta and especially in emphasizing a new awareness on Kern's part. Even when Kern was inserting interpolations in Viennese operettas, he rarely attempted to parrot Continental styles, although he undoubtedly tried to prevent his additions from being as jarringly antagonistic to the original composer's style as many of his lesser competitors' ragtime ditties were. As for awareness, there was rarely a composer as aware both of musical trends around him and of just how far he ought to go in subscribing to these trends.

Nevertheless, Wilder is unerring in sensing that *Sally* marked for Kern the end of one era and the beginning of another, and clearly the new jazz influences helped bring about this change. Actually, despite the triumph that it was, *Sally* signaled a six-year interval in which Kern marked time while he groped for a new form. The light, airy, dance-based graces of his Princess Theatre shows were put behind, and Kern did indeed lend an attentive ear to the more pronounced tempos and strident harmonies of the burgeoning jazz era.

Wilder is not alone in calling "Look For The Silver Lining" "a great tried-and-true folk song or hymn-tune." When *Sally* reached London, its West End star, Dorothy Dickson, told Jerry the song had a hymn-like quality. He responded that well it might, since he loved to play hymns and hoped his music reflected his pleasure. (One of Kern's least known songs is "An Evening Hymn," published in 1905 with a lyric by Arthur Platt Howard.) "Look For The Silver Lining" is simple harmonically, with few jumps and written mostly in quarter, half, and whole notes. Two features stand out. One is the fifteenth and sixteenth measures, where a series of dotted quarter and eighth notes, sung over the words "do is make it shine for you" leads fetchingly back to the main theme. Wilder points out that many who cannot sing the whole song invariably join in for these two bars. The other feature is less obvious. It is the small jump in the sixth bar over the second syllable of "appears." Until this point the song has moved with amazing tightness, only once skipping more than a full tone. If one of the period's hacks had by chance stumbled on the same theme he most likely would have gone not from *b* flat to *e* flat (the song is in E flat) as Kern did, but rather would probably have kept the tight-knit melody by going only to *c* natural and then letting the phrase echo the similar phrase in the second bar. It is probably farfetched to call so small a leap arioso, but it nevertheless hints at the broader phrases the composer would later employ.

"Whip-Poor-Will" (whose De Sylva lyrics, incidentally, were not credited as such in the sloppily prepared program) is filled with what Wilder calls "wonderful novelties." It begins with an octave jump dropping to a minor third, proceeding from there through unexpected harmonies and even re-iterating the main theme, originally in a minor key, in a major one. When Kern was asked why he did not utilize a real whip-poor-will call for his principal melody, he responded, as the true bird lover he was, that if he had, the song would have sounded too much like George M. Cohan's "Over There." He was right, naturally. Kern knew his birdcalls. Of course, by the time *Sally* reached New York, "Bill" had once more been relegated to his trunk, but the other survivor of *The Little Thing*, "The Church 'Round The Corner," is a lively waltz written entirely in quarter notes except for the last note of each musical sentence. But Kern went further back —far beyond either *The Little Thing* or *Zip Goes a Million*—for the plaintive title song. The chorus of "Sally" merely put new lyrics, with trifling musical alterations, to the chorus of *The King of Cadonia*'s "Catamarang."

Of the songs apparently written specifically for *Sally*, "Wild Rose" is far and away the best. Wilder writes, "*Wild Rose* is a perfect instance of a song which would suffer from any other harmonization than its own. As it stands, there are literally only four chords in the entire song. . . . The song is so pure that it needs no harmony." Wilder also mentions that a third composer, Eubie Blake, was able to play the piano part from memory after fifty years. This compliments Kern, for while he was never able to successfully orchestrate his own shows, he did write almost all his own piano parts. "The Schnitza-Komisski," like "The Church 'Round The Corner," was a lively, squarely written waltz again utilizing virtually nothing but quarter notes, while "On With The Dance" was a more syncopated waltz. "The Lorelei," which had been dropped during *The Night Boat*'s rehearsals, was another song laden with quarter notes, with a gently rocking melody. "Joan Of Arc" (published as "You Can't Keep A Good Girl Down") was a sprightly march.

Sally immediately became the biggest Broadway musical hit up to its time. Week after week the show pulled a capacity $32,500 ($35,000 if taxes were included). On several occasions Ziegfeld announced that Mary Eaton would head a road company, but he finally announced that his stars wanted to play all the major road stops and so no tour would take place until after the show finished its Broadway run. By May 11 tickets were placed on sale for the entire summer. At a time when seats were rarely available more than a month in advance, *Variety* termed Ziegfeld's order "unheard of." By the end of July the show had grossed over a million dollars. In New York alone the show compiled 570 performances. The legendary *Florodora* faded into history, and while *Irene* had run thirteen weeks longer, it had played at a house half the New Amsterdam's size and at a lower top. Miss Miller was especially aware of the importance of the show to her career, and most of the other principals apparently looked on it as money in the bank. As a result, despite Miss Miller's often violent battles with Ziegfeld, the cast held together for what by the standards of the time was a remarkably prolonged tour. Miss Miller played the role nearly 1500 times, except when Mary Eaton replaced her briefly during an illness. She did not leave until just before Christmas of 1923. Even then only a seemingly irreparable break with Ziegfeld prompted her to withdraw. Most of the remaining cast held on until Ziegfeld closed the show late in the 1923–24 season. By that time it had brought him over $5 million. Yet even then *Sally*'s career was not finished. In September of 1924 Ziegfeld sold the rights for one-night stands to George H. Nicolai of Nicolai-Welch-DeMilt, who kept the show on the boards for another season.

On March 28, 1921, Frank Saddler died. More than one critic credited Saddler's fine work—far above the commonplace rooty-toot of most musical comedy orchestras—with advancing Kern's popularity. Not until Robert Russell Bennett provided the scoring for *Stepping Stones* two years later did Kern find another orchestrator he was happy to work with.

At the end of April Jerry and Eva sailed with little Betty for England, planning a prolonged visit with the Leales, a spate of London showgoing, and a brief sojourn on the Continent. The trip meant that Jerry would not be on hand for the opening of the *Ziegfeld Follies of 1921* at the Globe on June 21. Ziegfeld was forced to book the Globe because *Sally* was so firmly entrenched at the New Amsterdam. The producer hired Hitchcock and Florence O'Denishawn from the defunct *Hitchy-Koo,* as well as casting such Ziegfeld regulars as Fanny Brice, W. C. Fields, Ray Dooley, and Van and Schenck. Victor Herbert, Rudolf Friml, and Harry Carroll joined Kern in providing melodies, but only Miss Brice's numbers, "My Man" and "Second Hand Rose," were runaway hits. Kern's staid ballad, "You Must Come Over" (lyric, De Sylva), was lost in the shuffle.

The Kerns had planned to stay in Europe until *Sally*'s London opening, but a semi-comic mishap altered their plans. No sooner had Jerry and Eva unpacked their bags in Paris for a week of sightseeing than Jerry felt ill. A doctor was called, and before the physician left, Jerry learned he was to spend the next ten days in the darkened bedroom of their suite. Jerry had the measles, which in an adult can have serious consequences. Luckily, he weathered the storm without apparent complications. But he suffered from double vision, from an unidentified problem that often forced him to keep his head at a tilt, and from a fear of the pernicious anemia that had helped kill his father. Seemingly frightened that French and English doctors might have overlooked some problem, he returned alone August 9 to New York on the *Olympic.* On landing Jerry revealed that even while on vacation he had been hard at work and that he had the score of *Good Morning, Dearie* ready to go.

But Dillingham and Miss Caldwell were not so well prepared. Rather than hang about idly, once his own doctor had given him a clean bill of health, Jerry rejoined Eva and Betty in England. A brouhaha had developed there in his absence, a brouhaha Jerry played a large part in creating and one that theatened briefly to nip in the bud a series at what became his London theatrical home for the next several years.

London's Winter Garden stood on Drury Lane, in 1921 a deteriorating back street of minor shops and warehouses. The theatre had been built in 1910 as the New Middlesex Theatre of Varieties. Less than nine years later George Grossmith and Edward Laurillard (soon superseded by J. A. E. Malone) acquired the theatre and renamed it the Winter Garden. They redecorated it in a manner befitting its new name, utilizing a "treillage style of architecture," painted in nature's greens and embellished with flowers and birds. Parrots, often considered unlucky in the theatre, were bravely carved into the proscenium. The auditorium was large by both London and New York standards, seating 1800. Since the theatre had only one balcony instead of the customary two, extra capacity was obtained by fanning out to create the widest seating area of any major West End house. The Winter Garden's opening show, first performed on May 20, 1919, was *Kissing Time*, with music by Ivan Caryll to lyrics and dialogue by Kern's old collaborators, Bolton and Wodehouse. It was followed by a second musical, *A Night Out*, in which Willie Redstone's music was coupled with Grossmith and Arthur Miller's words. Another success, like its predecessor, its principal male roles were assumed by Grossmith and Leslie Henson.

Henson was a genial, pop-eyed comedian who prided himself on the cleanliness of his smiling humor. The warmth of his clowning was matched by the warmth of his offstage personality.

Grossmith had returned from America in July (1921) with the script of *Sally* and a problem. Kern was opposed to his choice for the leading role, Dorothy Dickson. The problem seems to have arisen from Kern's recalling Miss Dickson only as a dancer who walked away with rave notices for her brief appearances in *Oh, Boy!* and *Rock-a-Bye Baby*. Kern felt that as a singer Marilyn Miller had not done full justice to his songs. He was determined to fend off a second disappointment. What happened next is confused. Grossmith insists that Kern had somehow auditioned Miss Dickson, found her flat, and "put a definite embargo" on her. To further protect his interests, the composer had convinced Ziegfeld, who also retained a financial interest, to cable Grossmith threatening "an injunction, cancellation of contract, and action for damages: if you put Dickson in the part you are imperilling my property." Guy Bolton remembered matters differently. He had arrived in London ahead of Kern with Kern's instructions to give Miss Dickson a discreet audition. Kern trusted Bolton's judgment. Bolton persuaded Grossmith to have Miss Dickson sing a few numbers from the Winter Garden's stage while he sat hidden in darkness. Everyone agreed the results were satisfactory. Miss Dickson remembers no audition whatsoever—although this may simply attest to Bolton's thoughtful discretion—rather, she recollects Grossmith took her to lunch, assured her that her performance in the recently closed *London, Paris and Broadway* convinced him she could handle the role, and promised her that she would be on stage for opening night.

Grossmith's choice was doubly bold, for not only was he possibly bucking Kern and Ziegfeld, but he was facing one of those periodic bursts of anti-Americanism that beset our Allies. As a result, when Kern returned in late August he found that Dickson had been signed, but that her casting had not been announced. In fact, London trade papers were coyly announcing, "A search for a suitable Sally is now being made among our leading musical comedy ladies." Not until the end of August, less than two weeks before the opening, was Dickson's casting made public. Even then it was carefully paired with the notice that Heather Thatcher would be featured.

Throughout rehearsals Kern spoke not so much as a single word to Miss Dickson. Instead he sat morosely at the back of the house. If she or anyone else concluded that he was sulking, they were probably wrong. What most likely prompted such behavior from the generally gay and jumpy composer was the news he had received on disembarking. His old friend and best man, Lauri de Frece, lay dying of stomach cancer. De Frece's agony ended a few days later when he died on August 25 at the age of forty-one.

Sally opened at the Winter Garden on September 10 without benefit of a tryout. Miss Dickson, of course, was Sally; Grossmith, Otis Hooper; Henson, Constantine; Miss Thatcher played the slightly expanded role of Rosalind Rafferty, a manicurist. Gregory Stroud, a good singer but a stiff actor, was Blair Farquar. To Grossmith the opening night fell "curiously flat." Happily, critics and public never noticed. The show was an immediate hit.

Dorothy Dickson's fondest memory of the first night reveals a special reason why the show was so readily accepted, as well as attesting to Kern's fairness. After the curtain fell on the second act—the act in which the seemingly triumphant Sally is sent home exposed and disgraced—Miss Dickson rushed back to her dressing room. She had begun to change into her costume for the Butterfly Ballet when an urgent knock sounded on her door. Her dresser let Kern in. He pointed to his cheek and showed Miss Dickson a tear. Miss Dickson had accomplished something Marilyn Miller never had: she had made Sally a truly believable, heart-breaking waif. Indeed, although the production lacked Ziegfeld's electrifying opulence and was played out in a relatively gigantic house, the English performers had captured a warmth and intimacy the original production had missed.

Sally ran 387 performances at the Winter Garden. For a brief time three companies regaled England with Kern's delightful score. The show began Miss Dickson's decades-long reign as one of London's musical comedy queens. Kern and Grossmith starred her in the next two shows they were to create for the Winter Garden. Everyone connected with this *Sally* had cause to rejoice, even Ziegfeld. As Grossmith recorded, "The play made £40,000 profit [over $200,000 in 1920 dollars] and put something like four or five hundred pounds a week for many months into the pockets of both Kern and Ziegfeld." But that tally became evident only with time. Meanwhile, Jerry was westward bound.

13

Transatlantic Shuttle

By the time *Good Morning, Dearie* finally began rehearsals on September 19, Kern was once again in New York. Dillingham's press release that week indicated the new musical would have its name changed to *Good Night, Dear*. The new name may well have been a press agent's slip, or possibly merely a device to obtain attention. The original title was clearly catchier, and the revised name was never mentioned again. Dillingham was especially anxious to give the new show all the publicity it could get. As early as mid-September *Variety*'s banner proclaimed: "BROADWAY BAD/WORST SEASON IN YEARS." Business was down, and producers were caught in a profit squeeze brought on by increasing union demands and the public's determination to resist higher ticket prices. For some reason, even plays of first quality seemed suddenly scarce. Although no one could foresee it at the time, the musical theatre was entering into three seasons of generally inferior shows, most given over to imitating the poor-little-girl-makes-good plot that had served *Sally, Mary,* and *Irene* so well.

Good Morning, Dearie was one of the season's better offerings, as the Atlantic City *Press* reported the day after its October 12 opening at the Apollo, calling it "one of the most satisfying musicals that has graced the boards in years." *Variety* failed to discuss the show until it moved on to

Washington, but its D.C. man was equally enthusiastic, declaring the entertainment "a knockout."

The story the *Press* labeled "well-devised" was essentially another of the era's many Cinderella fables. Society's Billy Van Cortlandt is engaged to Ruby Manners, but he has fallen in love with a couturier's assistant he has seen from his tailor's window. The girl in question, Rose-Marie, had once been the pet of a crook, Chesty Costello—an attachment she would dearly like to forget. Rose-Marie's crusty employer warns her to be careful. But when Chesty, just out of prison, attempts to steal Mrs. Greyson Parks's jewels while Mrs. Parks is busy with a large soirée, Billy and Rose-Marie foil the robbery and let Chester escape on condition that he give up his old girl friend. Ruby finds a fiancé in Billy's cousin George. A large chorus of twenty-three girls (not including Sunshine dancers) and twelve boys enlivened the musical numbers.

After an additional week of tryouts in Pittsburgh, *Good Morning, Dearie* opened in New York at the Globe on November 1, 1921, with the following musical program:

Good Morning, Dearie

ACT I
Scene One

1. "Every Girl" . . . . *Billy [Oscar Shaw] and George [John Price Jones]*
2. "Way Down Town" . . . . . . *Rose-Marie [Louise Groody] and Chesty [Harlan Dixon]*
3. Musical Scena
   a. "Rose-Marie" . . . . *Rose-Marie*
   b. "Didn't You Believe" . . . . *Billy*
4. Finaletto

Scene Two

5. Coolie Dance . . . . *The Sixteen Sunshine Girls*

Scene Three

6. "The Teddy Toddle" . . . . *Girls and Men*
7. "Sing Song Girl" . . . . *Steve [William Kent] and Six Fan-Tan Girls*

8. Musical Scena
   a. Entrance of Sailors
   b. "Blue Danube Blues" .... *Rose-Marie and Billy*
9. Trio, "Easy Pickins" .... *Chesty, Steve and Gimpy*
   [John J. Scannell]
10. Finale

ACT II
Scene One

11. "Melican Papa" .... *Steve, Darling Twins and Girls*
12. "Niagara Falls" .... *Rose-Marie and Billy*
13. Pas de Deux .... *Chesty and Cutie [Marie Callahan]*
14. Toddle Quartette .. *Rose-Marie and Ruby [Peggy Kurton]*,
    Steve and George

Scene Two

15. Dance du Fragonard .... *The Sunshine Girls*

Scene Three

16. "Kailua" .... *Billy and Girls*
17. "Good Morning Dearie" .... *Rose-Marie and Men*
18. Dance .... *Chesty and Cutie*
19. Maurice and Leonora Hughes
20. "Le Sport American" .... *The Sunshine Girls*
21. Reprise .... *Rose-Marie and Billy*
22. Finale

Stephen Jones orchestrated the score, and Victor Baravalle conducted.
Leo Reisman's orchestra played on-stage. Edward Royce staged the work.
Costumes were by Herman Patrick Teppe; sets by Gates and Morange.

New York critics, delighted with the show, eagerly returned the title's greeting. The *Herald*, saluting the musical as a "lalapaloosa," insisted it "would entertain any one, even before breakfast." The paper reserved some of its happiest judgments for the music, "which can be smoothly lilting and again so engagingly tricky it would make a pup wiggle his ears with joy. Kern is about the only composer who can write 'blues' that ought to be allowed in the home—he proves it again in 'Blue Danube Blues'—and in 'Way Down Town,' 'Every Girl,' 'Good Morning, Dearie,' and 'Melican Papa' he has tunes that are bound to find their way over the whistle route to the very desert places." The *Times* felt the whole score was "so good that it isn't possible to select any one song," and then promptly selected the title song. The *Daily News* voted for "Easy Pickin's" and "Blue Danube Blues." Virtually no critic called attention to "Ka-lu-a," the song that would quickly become the most popular and, unfortunately, the most notorious song from the show.

Musical changes made between Atlantic City and New York were not significant, except for the final scene. New York programs fail to list the "Scene Music" that originally opened each act. More than likely, this was retained, but dropped from the playbill for the sake of brevity. The original second scene of the second act had been recorded as "My Lady's Dress in the Making (Tableaux)." When it was discarded, the song "My Lady's Dress" went with it. The "Dance Du Fragonard" was inserted in its place. Only the final scene was radically revised. Its opening number, "Fragonard Dances," was expanded and made into the second scene. "Green River Glide," sung by Kent, and "Rose Ruby," sung by Miss Groody and the male chorus, were both eliminated. "Le Sport American," the title song, and Maurice and Hughes's dance specialty were all added. The Atlantic City program also helpfully identifies the Quartette as "Wedding Bells Are Ringing" and the unspecified reprise as "Niagara Falls."

The evening's applause winner, "Ka-lu-a," was a pseudo-Hawaiian song, capitalizing on the fad for Hawaiian music that had begun six years earlier and was still far from passé. The verse is in 4/4 and in D minor. Lushly romantic, it begins with an attractive melody strikingly like a theme used three years later in Friml's "Indian Love Call" from another show with a heroine named Rose-Marie. The chorus, in D, is an alluringly languid melody set above a rocking basso ostinato precisely like the one employed in the great 1919 hit, "Dardanella." "The Teddy Toddle" (published simply as "Toddle") uses a device that Vincent Youmans was soon to fall back on— a simple phrase repeated over and over, and modulated largely by changing chordings. "Blue Danube Blues" coupled a tightly knit, syncopated jazz melody with Strauss sung in counterpoint. The title song, added so late in the tryout, is a lively tune that may, in fact, be a rewrite of "Who Cares" from *Love o' Mike.* Conversely, "Way Down Town" is a swinging waltz whose first eight bars Kern may have redeveloped into "The Enchanted Train" for his 1924 *Sitting Pretty.* The first half of "Easy Pickin's" is attractive, if melancholy. But Kern seems to have lost interest in the song, leaving the last half a mere series of scale exercises. Although "Didn't You Believe" is largely a hippety-hop of alternating dotted eighth notes and sixteenth notes, its melody has an irresistible childlike innocence and charm.

The public was in no way daunted by critics' ignoring "Ka-lu-a." By late January 1922, *Variety* announced the song led the nation in sales of music rolls, while it was the second most popular record. In mid-March the trade paper could report it was still a best-selling record, although it had dropped from the music rolls list.

Good Morning, Dearie racked up 347 performances in New York and toured under Dillingham's aegis until April 21, 1923. At that time Dillingham sold the rights for one-night stands to Leffler and Bratton. They sent a less elaborate version out for the entire 1923–24 season. *Variety* rarely paid attention to such troupes; there were simply too many of them criss-crossing the country. However, *Good Morning, Dearie* did occasionally make news. Often it was reported to have broken house records in towns such as Flint and Bay City, Michigan, and in Johnstown, Pennsylvania. On the other hand, in Columbus, Ohio, it met with skepticism and resistance when the press assailed it for dishonestly advertising "original New York cast."

More so than any other Kern show, *Good Morning, Dearie* earned some dubious publicity for itself during its New York run when it ran into legal problems. The first problem was more comic than significant. The musical had been sailing along gaily until January when municipal authorities suddenly took umbrage at a line in "Easy Pickin's." The offending line was "The biggest fall guys of them all are working down in City Hall." A hint that trouble was brewing came when the city refused to renew the permit for two children, the Darling Twins, to work in the show. Apparently other hassles were promised. Only when the line was changed to "The boobs who are the first to fall are selling stocks at Broad and Wall" was the permit reissued and further threats removed.

A month later a more serious problem developed. If the critics had paid scant attention to "Ka-lu-a," Fred Fisher watched its success with growing fury. On January 2, 1920, the publisher of "Dardanella" had purchased the entire front page of *Variety* for a declaration of war. It read:

WARNING!
THIEVES AND PIRATES!
and those who live on the efforts of other people's brains
DON'T IMITATE, COPY OR STEAL
any part of
"DARDANELLA"
The Biggest Musical Hit of the Past 20 Years
We give you notice we will prosecute to the fullest extent of

the law, criminally and civilly, any infringement on the melody or lyric of "Dardanella." This notification is intended for anyone and everyone who may infringe or attempt to infringe the above song, copyrighted by

McCARTHY & FISHER, Inc.

224 West 46th Street   New York City

NATHAN BURKAN, ATTORNEY

By June of 1920 *Variety* recorded that Fisher had seven suits in court. In February 1922 Fisher brought suit against Kern, T. B. Harms, Dillingham, Caldwell, and Royce, alleging that the recurrent bass theme in "Ka-lu-a" had been pirated from "Dardanella" and demanding one million dollars in damages. In March, Dillingham and Kern's attorneys filed an answer. The trial was delayed until the fall, and Dillingham set sail for Europe.

With *Good Morning, Dearie* sturdily on the boards, Kern and Miss Caldwell set to work on a new musical. It was to be the first of several musicals they would write with star performers in mind, even if, ironically, the star they wrote this show for refused to play it. Their recalcitrant leading lady was the beautiful comedienne Ina Claire, who had been London's girl from Utah. Until 1917 her career had been entirely in vaudeville and musicals, but after none other than Guy Bolton had persuaded David Belasco to star her in *Polly with a Past* she devoted herself to farce and high comedy. Miss Caldwell's story apparently made her reconsider her decision to abandon musicals. As late as mid-March of 1922 Dillingham's office was distributing releases announcing he would mount the new show in the fall with Miss Claire as star. Then Miss Claire was handed a comedy she fell in love with, *The Awful Truth*. Reluctantly, Dillingham released her from her contract. Her withdrawal foreshadowed problems Dillingham, Caldwell, and Kern would have with *The Bunch and Judy*.

Meanwhile, in late March, George Grossmith arrived in New York with the rough draft of *The Cabaret Girl*, a new show he planned to mount at London's Winter Garden after *Sally* had run its course there. His arrival coincided not only with Miss Claire's change of heart, but also with Dillingham's and Kern's first moves in Fisher's law suit. Editions of *Variety* that took notice of the Englishman's coming detailed the defendants' response to Fisher's charges. Kern was confident and in no mood to be intimidated. Defiantly, he and Dillingham sold Grossmith the rights to *Good Morning, Dearie.* When Grossmith later decided the show was too American to be adapted, Kern suggested to Grossmith that they utilize "Ka-lu-a" in the new show, and Grossmith agreed.

With much of *The Bunch and Judy* and the London show written, one would think Kern might have spent the summer in England. But the records show he did not, even if they give no clue to his whereabouts. So perhaps it was at this very time that the Kerns took a trip with their neighbors, the Nathan Newmans. Mrs. Newman remembers the trip well, especially its amusing, revealing conclusions, but she is no longer certain in which year it occurred. Mr. Newman was a businessman, with large asbestos interests in Canada. He made frequent trips there to oversee the operation, traveling either alone or with his wife. But on one occasion he casually suggested to Jerry and Eva that they join him. To his surprise and delight the Kerns accepted. The trip was pleasant and uneventful, except that Mr. Newman was taken aback by the number of probing questions Jerry asked about the plant. Jerry was especially struck by the large amount of waste the operation produced, waste for which Newman assured him no use could be found. Several weeks after the party returned home, Newman came back from his office waving a rather thick report at his wife. He rarely bothered her with workaday details, but he insisted she look at the report. Mrs. Newman remembers it as running to something like forty pages. It discussed a number of possible uses for asbestos waste, uses that Mr. Newman assured her were within the realm of possibility. Of course, the report was from Jerry, although whether he compiled it alone or with professional help is unknown. But it nevertheless alerted the Newmans to the startling breadth and depth of Jerry's interests.

The Cabaret Girl went into rehearsal in mid-August. Grossmith directed, with Jack Haskell staging the dances. Wodehouse sat inconspicuously in the rear of the house, occasionally proffering a shyly couched suggestion. Kern arrived only after rehearsals were well under way. His presence really was not needed, since matters seemed to be proceeding with unaccustomed smoothness. By the first week in September Grossmith and Malone felt confident enough with the results to announce the musical would open on September 14, 1922. In keeping with the theatre's practice, a tryout was eschewed. *The Cabaret Girl* would open cold. Only on the morning of the opening did trouble become apparent. Acting on medical advice, Leslie Henson temporarily relinquished his part. To give his replacement, Norman Griffin, time to fully learn the part, the premiere was set back two days; and when two days in intense rehearsal proved inadequate to allow Griffin to master the role, opening night ticket holders had to be turned away for a second time. On Monday, September 18, the *Times* announced the show would definitely open the next night.

Grossmith and Wodehouse's libretto told a tale suspiciously close to *Sally*'s. Once again a poor working girl dreams of wealth, love, and fame, and once again a masquerade helps her attain them. Even the settings followed *Sally*'s pattern. The first act took place at a superficially glamorous commercial establishment—in this case the showroom of Messrs. Gripps & Gravvins, Music Publishers on Bond Street. Act II carried the cast to The Pergola, Woollam Chersey, a luxurious estate; while the last act moved from the Entrance to the "All Night Follies" to The Cabaret itself. Only a British equivalent of the Little Church Around the Corner was missing. The authors even had recourse to a private joke none but the more knowledgeable British playgoers would appreciate. They named their heroine Marilynn Morgan. (Marilyn Miller had originally spelled her first name with two "n's.")

Miss Morgan comes to the publishing house looking for employment. She is pursued by a handsome young man, James Paradene, a nephew of the Marchioness of Harrogate. James's father has willed him a fortune, provided his choice of a bride meets with the approval of the Marchioness and her son. Mr. Gripps, a friend of Paradene, suggests a ploy. He will borrow Mr. Gravvins's estate and throw a swank party for James and Marilynn, inviting all the neighboring elite to impress the Marchioness. Unfortunately, the neighboring elite all turn out to be away on holiday, so Gripps hurriedly enlists a cabaret troupe to impersonate the local notables. Gripps himself will pretend to be the vicar. Of course, the real vicar appears in time to expose the hoax for a second act curtain. However, Marilynn's Hawaiian routine at the cabaret helps convince everyone that she and James—as well as the Marchioness's son and Ada, a chorus girl—are meant for each other.

The musical numbers, unlisted in the program, were:

The Cabaret Girl

ACT I

1. "Chopin Ad Lib" .... *Chorus*

2. "You Want the Best Seats, We Have 'Em" . . . . . *Effie [Vera Lennox] and Girls*
3. "Mr. Gravvins—Mr. Gripps" . . *Gravvins [Norman Griffin] and Gripps [George Grossmith]*
4. "First Rose of Summer" . . . . *Jim [Geoffrey Gwyther]*
5. "Journey's End" . . . . . *Marilynn [Dorothy Dickson] and Jim*
6. "Whoop-de-oodle-do" . . . . *Gravvins and Cabaret Troupe*
7. "At the Ball" . . . . *Quipp [Leigh Ellis]*
8. "Dancing Time" . . . . *Marilynn and Gravvins*
9. Finaletto

ACT II

10. "The Pergola Patrol"
11. Entrance Scena
12. "Shimmy With Me" . . . . *Marilynn and Girls*
13. "Those Days Are Gone Forever" . . . . *Gravvins*
14. "Looking All Over For You" . . . . *Marilynn and Jim*
15. "Nerves" . . . . *Ada [Heather Thatcher], Gravvins and Gripps*
16. Finale

ACT III
Scene One

17. Opening Music
18. "London, Dear Old London" . . . . . *Jim and Chorus of Men*

Scene Two

19. Opening Music (a) Tango (b) Fox-Trot
20. "Ka-lu-a" . . . . *Marilynn and Chorus of Girls*
21. Finale, "Oriental Dreams"

John Ansell led the pit orchestra, as he had for the London production of *Sally.*

Almost all the critics pronounced the show delightfully entertaining. Praise was showered on Grossmith's fast-paced staging, on Joseph and Phil Harker's brightly colored sets, on Dolly Tree's tasteful costumes, and on the cast. Miss Dickson, the *Play Pictorial* noted, "sustains the reputation she made in 'Sally.'" Grossmith and Griffin won high praise. Geoffrey Gwyther, a strikingly good-looking youngster who was also an accomplished musician and composer, was lauded as "a pleasant baritone" who sang "fervently." For the statuesque comedienne Heather Thatcher, the show continued a five-and-a-half-year stint as the Winter Garden's principal soubrette. Inevitably, some critics did express reservations—about the book and score. The *Morning Post* felt the "story does not rise above the level of a good West End show" and concluded, "Some may prefer 'Sally.'" The *Daily Sketch* damned Kern with faint praise, predicting, "All London will soon be humming Jerome Kern's music, largely because all London will have nothing new to learn. It is catchy stuff, but 'reminiscent' would be a euphemism." Happily, most reviewers disagreed. The *Referee*, a Sunday paper, observed, "As elsewhere, Kern's melodies are touched with a certain dreamy and haunting wistfulness, even at their gayest . . . a refreshing holiday from jazz."

Kern had indeed presented London with a pleasant, readily hummable score, although not all the songs were written specifically for *The Cabaret Girl*. "First Rose Of Summer" (with a new Wodehouse lyric) had been heard in *She's a Good Fellow*, as had "Chopin Ad Lib," where, with minor differences, it had been "Faith, Hope And Charity"; "Ka-lu-a" (with the litigated bass dropped, apparently on legal advice) had come from *Good Morning, Dearie*. Apart from "Ka-lu-a," the biggest hit of the evening was incontestably "Dancing Time." The basic melody of the chorus was initially sung "Slowly, a la Varsoviana" by the piano tuner, Quipp (Quibb, in programs), in his "At The Ball" number. Then, in an expanded and varied version, employing syncopation and trilled eighth notes where quarter notes had sufficed, Marilynn and Gravvins sang increasingly accelerated reprises until, in the finale of the first act, it was being performed with "joyous abandon." "Mr. Gravvins—Mr. Gripps," with its "Are you with me, Mister Gravvins/Absolutely, Mister Gripps!," spoofed the song Gallagher and Shean were even then singing in the *Ziegfeld Follies* in New York. (If the "G's" in Grossmith, Griffin, Gravvins, and Gripps are not coincidental, then this number may have been inserted just before the opening.) "Journey's End" was a solid ballad that never caught the public's fancy.

In the four years since Grossmith and Laurillard had taken over the Winter Garden, London had slowly grown aware of a new theatrical phenomenon. The *Play Pictorial* wrote,

> The Winter Garden is within a stone's throw of the Gaiety, and the traditions of the Gaiety had not far to travel for a new home

when the Gaiety lost the Edwardes "touch." One feels the presence of the old Gaiety spirit immediately the curtain rises at the Winter Garden, and one never loses it even when the curtain drops on the final scene. . . . "The Cabaret Girl" is in the direct line of descent to those wonderful girls who maintained for so many years the prestige of the popular Strand house.

Looking back over nearly two-thirds of a century, survivors of the Winter Garden's heyday—Miss Dickson, Miss Thatcher, Stanley Holloway, and the box office head, Frank Sleap—all seized on the very same word to epitomize the house and its reputation. That word was "glamour." "Glamour in the front; glamour in the back," Miss Thatcher insisted, recalling, "If you saw three men in black ties, they were bachelors. They were all in white ties." And Miss Thatcher was not merely recalling opening nights! This ubiquitous glamour, coupled with consistently high quality, resulted in yet another manifestation peculiar to only a handful of houses in theatrical history—a sense of loyalty, again on both sides of the footlights. Embroidering only slightly, Miss Thatcher went on to suggest that "No girl left unless she married. No chorus girl ever left." With the success of *The Cabaret Girl* following on *Sally*'s heels, Kern seemed about to join the illustrious ranks of the Winter Garden's regular men and women. The new offering, helped by Henson's return for most of the run, compiled 361 showings at the house, just twenty-six short of *Sally*'s. When the show closed, it was recast, its physical production cut down slightly to allow for easy moving, and the new company sent out to become the second troupe singing and dancing its way about the provinces.

Jerry quietly chalked up another hit and grabbed the *Olympic* for New York, prepared to plunge anew into rehearsals.

The Bunch and Judy opened on schedule November 6, 1922, at Philadelphia's Garrick Theatre. Critics were not only divided sharply on all aspects of the show, but they seemed baffled and uncertain. The *Ledger* found it "a show of many moods . . . apt to inspire quite as many on the part of prospective audiences." The *Bulletin*'s reactions see-sawed, regarding the first hour "so good . . . that enthusiasts in the big audience were almost convinced they were witnessing the birth of a new record-breaker," then concluding the final two and a half hours "weren't good enough to bear out the promise of the auspicious beginning." Almost all the critics were delighted to discover the production displayed the taste and largesse expected of Dillingham. Comedian Joseph Cawthorn, Ray Dooley, and her vis-à-vis, a local boy named Delano Dell, were generally applauded, while several critics stopped to mention that Roberta Beatty called attention to herself with her fine singing—she possessed the only really good voice in the cast—even though her part was minuscule. Surprisingly, although the musical had been rebuilt (with Hugh Ford's assistance) around Fred and Adele Astaire, critics gave them no more attention than they gave the other principals. The *Inquirer* even got their names wrong, while the *Bulletin* complained they danced too much. The same papers seemed similarly thrown off balance by Kern's music. Those critics who discussed Kern's contribution were not overwhelmed. For example, the *Record* decided, "Some of it has 'catchiness' and some of it is remindful of other melodies," while the *Ledger* saw the score as "out of Mr. Kern's own well-beaten paths . . . on occasion quite grandiose, again sparkling and lilting, but rarely are there heard any of those wistful strains characteristic heretofore of this gifted composer."

The critics' discomfort with the book was understandable, for while the plot was elementary it was handled in a singularly odd, lopsided fashion. The story centered on musical star Judy Jordan. As soon as she gives her final performance in *Love Will Find a Way*, she abandons her career and sails for Scotland to marry a laird. The marriage fails when she and her husband's snobbish friends cannot reach an accommodation. She heads for London, discovering her old leading man, Gerald Lane, there. In no time she realizes that Gerald has always been her true love. What was so curious about Caldwell and Ford's treatment was the first act, virtually monopolized by a representation of *Love Will Find a Way*. The main story's progress was shunted aside for over an hour. Even the denouement was ineptly contrived. In Philadelphia the last scene was set in Paul Poiret's famous London salon to allow Judy and Gerald to swear eternal love surrounded by mannequins in chic, eye-filling gowns. The setting, however attractive, proved deadeningly constricted and was left behind when the company headed for New York. A cabaret set was introduced in its place (with the female customers still in Poiret's dresses). The setting allowed the insertion of specialty acts, such as the saxophone pyrotechnics of the Six Brown Brothers, specialties that enlivened the entertainment while further debilitating the development of the main plot.

During the final week of the Philadelphia stay, the Astaires' co-star, Joseph Cawthorn, tripped rushing down the stairs from his dressing room to the stage. He smashed his kneecap so badly that there was no chance of his returning to the show for several months. Ray Dooley's brother, Johnny, was summoned from New York. He rehearsed each day with the cast while they performed with Cawthorn's understudy at night. To make sure everything was in order Dillingham postponed the New York opening from Monday, November 27, 1922, to Tuesday, November 28. Monday was given over to two full dress rehearsals.

When the curtain did rise at the Globe the musical program was:

The Bunch and Judy

ACT I
The Operetta

1. Minuet .... *Ensemble*
2. Duet, "Silenzio" .. *Beppo [Carl McBride] and Lizetta [Ray Dooley]*
3a. Entrance of Duke .... *Ensemble*
   b. Song, "The Naughty Nobleman" .. *The Duke [Augustus Minton]*
4. Duettino, "Pale Venetian Moon" .... *Antonio and Paulina [Fred and Adele Astaire]*
5. Finaletto .... *Ensemble*
6. Song .... *Jack [Carl McBride]*
7. Duet, "Peach Girl" ...... *Judy [Adele Astaire] and Gerald [Fred Astaire]*
8. Song, "Morning Glory" .... *Judy and Ensemble*

ACT II

9. Pastoral, "Lovely Lassie" ..... *Lady Janet [Roberta Beatty] and Ensemble*
10. Duet, "Every Day in Every Way" ...... *Judy and Gerald*
11. Septette, "Times Square" .... *Judy, Evie [Ray Dooley] and Hazel [Patrice Clark]*
12. Clansman March and Fling .. *Judy, Lord Kinlock [Philip Tonge] and Ensemble*

The Cabaret

13. Song, "Have You Forgotten Me" Blues .. *Miss Grace Hayes*

14. Duet, "How Do You Do, Katinka?" .... *Judy and Gerald*
15. The Six Brown Brothers
16. Dance a la Russe .... *Evie and Otto [Johnny Dooley]*
17. Finale

 Victor Baravelle conducted. Fred G. Latham directed. (In his auto-biography Fred Astaire seems to imply that Edward "Teddy" Royce may have assisted with the choreography, but if Royce did, he was given no credit in any of the programs.) The most celebrated of the many hands contributing designs for sets and costumes was, of course, Poiret.

Broadway's critics were not bowled over. Although many headlines im-plied reviews would be raves, notices themselves were filled with qualifi-cations. Most of the real enthusiasm was reserved for the Astaires. When it came to Kern's score the critics were generally unhappy, but they did follow their Philadelphia counterparts in saluting the orchestrations.* One of the more satisfied reviewers, James Craig of the *Evening Mail,* wrote: "Jerome Kern has fitted it with a musical score of unusual quality. It has more body and there is more substance to the orchestration than is ordinarily expected in productions of the kind. In a play-within-a-play scene in the first act there is a minuet that is one of the most delightful bits of fugitive music that has come to Broadway in a long time." At the other end of the scale, Alan Dale, Kern's old advocate, wrote dejectedly in the *American*: "The music was ascribed to Jerome Kern, who seems to have lost his individuality. Although the worst of his music was perhaps better than [that of] many of his colleagues, it was a disappointment. It lacked the original phrases and the quaint mellifluous ideas that this composer used to put forth so agreeably." The songs most critics singled out were those sung in the cabaret and only loosely connected with the plot.

 Musical changes between the Philadelphia and New York first nights were few. In Act I, an eccentric dance specialty was replaced by Judy and Gerald's "Peach Girl." In the second act Judy and Gerald's bow to Coué, "Every Day In Every Way," filled the gap left by the cutting of Caw-thorn's only number, "And Her Mother Came Too."** The chorus of

---

* Regrettably, these orchestrations were uncredited. Survivors of the show can no longer recall who was responsible. The composer Milton Ager, a friend of Kern's, suggested either Saddler's protégé, Maurice De Packh, or Harms's Stephen Jones might have provided them.
** This was the lone number in the production not written by Kern. It had been composed by Kern's onetime collaborator, Ivor Novello, to a lyric by Dion Titheridge.

"Every Day In Every Way" appears to be a reworking of "Katy-Did" from 1913's *Oh, I Say!*. A marvelous polka, "Hot Dog," sung by Jack and Evie, was also eliminated. Several songs were repositioned and one song was taken from Judy and Gerald and assigned to Grace Hayes, a singer who was not given a character to play, for the cabaret, with its title changed from "Why-Don't-You-Write-To-Me Blues." The lyric apparently was unchanged, since it asked both questions.

Critics who gave the score short shrift were probably justified. Darnton's adjective, "pleasing," is totally accurate, for while nothing truly memorable or noteworthy emerged, none of the published material was unattractive. Unfortunately, the minuet which so many critics enjoyed was not published. "Pale Venetian Moon," clearly slated to be the show's hit, is pallid stuff indeed. It is written in 2/4, as is "Morning Glory," a simple melody of the order critics loved to brand "tinkly." Although " 'Have You Forgotten Me?' Blues" employs some striking harmonic progressions, it represents a rare "cop-out" for Kern, since it primarily belabors phrases based on repeated notes. In the theatre "How Do You Do, Katinka?" was the big applause-getter, thanks in no small part to the Astaires' celebrated "run-around" routine in which they made increasingly larger circles until they disappeared from sight. It is a trivial "oom-pah" melody, like so much of the score, in 2/4 time. The lyric had fun at the expense of "The Parade Of The Wooden Soldiers" from the imported hit revue, *Chauve Souris*. Since the song was in the score from the beginning, it may have suggested the revised setting for the final scene. Music lovers no doubt owe a vote of thanks to Alfred Simon, who suggested interpolating "Hot Dog" in the 1976 revival of *Very Good Eddie*. The polka is probably the catchiest, gutsiest number in the score.

When it quickly became obvious that Broadway playgoers were not going to endorse the musical, Dillingham pulled the show after sixty-three performances. Once again, in this era of relatively healthy theatrical economics, a New York failure did not preclude a subsequent road tour, so Dillingham moved the production to Boston. There, the *Evening Transcript*, which continued to give Bostonians their most thoughtfully considered reviews, looked on Kern's music with a unique slant: "The chorus throughout is a large factor in the pleasures of 'The Bunch and Judy.' To them Mr. Kern has allotted the best of the melodies, and with good reason, since theirs are the voices."

The Astaires had not yet become the irresistible attraction they soon would be, so the show was not able to override the lukewarm reactions of the road's critics. After a few weeks Dillingham finally withdrew it.

While Dillingham was rehearsing *The Bunch and Judy,* Ziegfeld was rehearsing *Rose Briar,* a Booth Tarkington comedy that was to star Billie Burke. Just before tryouts began Ziegfeld announced Victor Herbert had been signed to compose background and cabaret music for the show. Whether the music was actually written or employed is uncertain. Edward Waters makes no mention of it in his thorough, definitive study of Herbert. But when the show gave its first performance at Wilmington's Playhouse on November 16, Miss Burke was singing a Kern song, a watery ballad called "Love And The Moon," for which Tarkington had provided a lyric.

The year ended with Kern quietly backing away from what might have been a noisy, futile law suit. In September the Shuberts and Eddie Dowling had produced a show brazenly capitalizing on three other musical hits. With no attempt at subtlety they called their offering *Sally, Irene and Mary.* Allusions to all three earlier musicals were rampant and obvious throughout the new work. The piece had originally been a vaudeville sketch in one of the New York Winter Garden's entertainments. When it first appeared, the Vanderbilt Producing Company, producer of *Irene,* had approached George M. Cohan, *Mary's* producer, and Ziegfeld, asking them to join in a suit against the Shuberts and Dowling. Ziegfeld demurred. But when *Sally* was playing in Boston, Ziegfeld caught the show and immediately decided a suit was in order. When, however, he advised the Vanderbilt organization that he was now ready to cooperate, he learned it had cooled to the idea. Ziegfeld then asked his writers for their thoughts. Kern was furious at what he saw as a cheap attempt to ride other men's coattails, but he counseled prudence. His colleagues agreed, so Ziegfeld dropped the matter. Yet the affair may have rankled. Even though the Shuberts had given Kern some of his earliest important opportunities, Kern thereafter retained a distaste for the opportunistic brothers. Years later, when Oscar Hammerstein and Otto Harbach were seeking a Broadway producer for *Gentlemen Unafraid,* a musical they had written with Kern, Hammerstein wrote Kern that he would not submit it to the Shuberts, knowing Jerry's displeasure with them. Quite possibly other matters had arisen to deepen Kern's distrust, but *Sally, Irene and Mary* must have played no small part in Kern's feelings.

The first half of 1923 is another of the many extended periods during which Kern's life remains a closed book.* Newspapers and trade sheets on both sides of the Atlantic are largely silent on his activities. Even the obviously optimistic projects so often sprinkled through theatrical gossip columns are left unannounced. Of course, Kern must have been working on his two fall shows, one for London and one for New York. A safe supposition is that Wodehouse made a number of little trips from Long Island to Bronxville to work with Kern on their contributions to *The First Prize*. Similarly, Jerry and Anne Caldwell could have spent pleasant hours whipping into shape a vehicle Dillingham required for the beloved clown, Fred Stone. But Kern, at heart so private a person, must have relished the lack of publicity as much as he enjoyed his creative labors. He probably was aware that the fall would change matters drastically, not only because of the two openings, but also because Fisher refused to consider an out-of-court agreement on "Dardanella" and would settle for nothing less than a trial, which he hoped would bring him a substantial financial benefit.

Sometime in the late spring or early summer Jerry probably sailed with his family to England to spend a summer with his in-laws and his old friends, and merely to enjoy, as he always did, being in London. He was definitely in London by the beginning of August, staying at the Savoy, when three thousand miles away New York papers published Robert Milton's announcement that Kern and Bolton were to write several intimate musicals for him. Milton had co-directed at least one Princess show, so the paragraphs were happy news. Nothing, however, came of the announcement, unless it planted a seed in Comstock and Gest's minds. Meanwhile, back in England, Wodehouse arrived on the *Homeric* on Sunday, August 5. Rehearsals began in earnest the next day, the same time London papers carried their earliest mention of the new musical, still called *The First Prize*. Preparations proceeded with exceptional smoothness, partly because Grossmith, Wodehouse, and Kern were skillful professionals who had often worked together harmoniously before and partly because of the semi-stock nature of the troupe. Not only were the three stars of *The Cabaret Girl* and *Sally*—Dorothy Dickson, Leslie Henson,

---

* A letter brought to my attention as this book was going to press sheds some light on the Kerns's whereabouts. Written on stationery headed "The Nuts," Bronxville, New York, and dated February 10, 1923, the letter was addressed by Kern to John Henry Nash, a San Francisco printer. In thanking Nash for a copy of Nash's *Life of Dante,* Kern disclosed that he had just returned from an extended vacation in Palm Beach. "The Nuts" was Kern's early name for his Bronxville home, a name he eventually discarded.

and Grossmith—back in the fold, but many of the secondary performers reappeared as well, notably the fast-rising Heather Thatcher. Even Miss Thatcher's account of the Winter Garden chorus girls' loyalty seemed to hold true. Eleven of the new musical's twenty-one girls remained from the previous show, as did five of the eight chorus boys. Not until August 30 did the *Times* inform its readers that the show had been retitled and would thereafter be known as *The Beauty Prize*. In the same notice the paper recorded that the production would open "about" September 8. Two days later, satisfied that everything had fallen into place beyond their most optimistic expectations, Grossmith and Malone officially advanced the premiere to September 5, 1923.

Wodehouse and Grossmith's story reflected the transatlantic origins of the work. Wisely, the plot departed in several important respects from similar, overemployed Cinderella motifs used in the preceding two musicals. Still, some basic themes reoccurred. Once again Miss Dickson was cast as a heroine involved in a deception and unmasked. Only this time she was a rich American girl, Carol Stuart, pretending to be poor. Her equally rich English boy friend, John Brooke, is equally deceptive, pretending to be every bit as impoverished as Carol. Both, of course, are determined to be loved for themselves and not for their wealth. Each has a loyal friend of lower station. John's is his secretary, Flutey Warboy; Carol's is a milliner's assistant, Lovey Toots. The doting Lovey sends Carol's photograph to a newspaper contest in which the first prize is the hand in marriage of oddball Odo Philpotts. Carol's picture appears in the paper, with word that she has won the competition, on the very morning of her marriage to John. When John furiously and publicly berates his bride-to-be for such puerile behavior, Carol impetuously announces she will accept the astonished Odo. Fate contrives to place all the principals on a great ocean liner speeding westward. (The ship was wryly named the *Majestania,* after the *Majestic,* the liner on which Grossmith and Wodehouse did their original blocking out of the plot.) John and Carol's horrified friends bribe the wireless operator to send each a telegram announcing to them that they have lost their respective fortunes. This seemingly mutual ill luck brings about a reconciliation. At her father's Florida mansion Carol finally weds John, while Lovey and Odo are also paired.

The opening night musical program was as follows:

The Beauty Prize

ACT I
Scene One

1. Opening Number
2. Melodrama

Scene Two

3. Opening Number . . . . . . *Kitty Wren [Vera Lennox], Maids and Midinettes*
4. Entrance Scene
   [Listed in vocal score as performed by Carol, Kitty and Midinettes]
5. Melodrama and Song, "Honeymoon Isle" . . . . . . *Carol Stuart [Dorothy Dickson]*
   [The vocal score lists this song as sung by Carol with Kitty]
6. Melos . . . . *Entrance of Lovey Toots [Heather Thatcher]*
7. Melos . . . . *Entrance of Odo Philpotts [Leslie Henson]*
8. Duet, "I'm a Prize" . . . . *Carol and Odo*
9. Song, "It's a Long, Long Day" . . . . . . *Flutey Warboy [George Grossmith]*
10. Sextette, "Joy Bells"
11. Finale

ACT II

12. Opening Number, "Mah-Jong"
13. Duet, "You Can't Make Love by Wireless" . . . . . . *Carol and Flutey*
14. Song, "Non-Stop Dancing" . . . . *Odo and Chorus*
15. Duet, "For the Man I Love" . . *Carol and John [Jack Hobbs]*
16. Melos
17. Duet, "A Cottage in Kent" . . . . *Lovey and Odo*
18. Finale

ACT III

19. Ballet
    [Listed in vocal scores as Opening Chorus; clearly same number]
20. Duet, "Meet Me Down on Main Street" . . . . *Flutey and Odo*
21. Song, "Moon Love" . . . . *Carol*
22. Finale

Fred Leslie was the choreographer, the settings were again by the Harkers, and the costumes were by Comelli. John Ansell conducted his third Kern score at the Winter Garden.

As usual at the Winter Garden the show opened without a tryout, but technically everything was in readiness. Pacing was swift, sets and costumes colorful, and performers all at top form. The *Daily Mail* could proclaim: "Not since the old Gaiety days has any musical comedy theatre known such a sequence of success as the Winter Garden." The reviewer further rejoiced to find "there is really a story." Yet, tellingly, the critic mentioned Kern only in passing. The *Daily Express* stated bluntly that Kern's tunes were "below the level of 'The Cabaret Girl' "

Discreet or blunt, the papers were correct in judging the score patently inferior Kern. Part of the problem may have been the absence of one outstanding number—the sort of superior melody that somehow infuses something of its cachet into the rest of the score. Except possibly for a few bars of a pleasant waltz theme, the four opening numbers are especially drab—a series of repeated notes and of progressions that sound like hastily thrown-off exercises. Yet the last of these—the entrance scene for Carol, Kitty, and the Midinettes—suggests how even such a seemingly nondescript passage, placed in the proper context, could indeed develop strangely moving undertones. Kern, with some revisions, employed the melody from the verse of this number four years later as Magnolia's piano exercise in *Show Boat* where, surrounded by magnificently inspired themes, the simple phrases took on a peculiar poignancy. There is also the small chance that the first bar and a half of Lovey's entrance contained the germ of a theme Kern developed in *Sunny*. "A Cottage In Kent" provides an interesting glimpse at one songwriting technique Kern apparently resorted to on occasion. The melody, without being imitative, nonetheless clearly manages to recall an earlier Kern-Wodehouse collaboration, "Bungalow In Quogue"—and for good reason. The lyrics are interchangeable. In fact there are some striking echoes, beyond the similar pictures evoked by the titles. At the identical bars in each song Wodehouse promises to "pluck tomatoes from the trees" and to "grow tomatoes on the trees." Most likely, having decided on the type of song they required for Lovey and Odo in the second act, Wodehouse used Kern's existing tune to hang his new lyrics on, while Kern, in turn, used Wodehouse's *Riviera Girl* rhymes as a framework for another melody. Disregarding a pair of ornamental sixteenth notes at two points where the later song employs single eighth notes, the melodies, while quite different, give each note precisely the same value in the same place. Of the remaining numbers, the best was probably the luringly vivacious "Non-Stop Dancing," although for a while one ballad, "Moon Love," enjoyed a passing popularity.

The loyalty that Grossmith and his Winter Garden shows had carefully nurtured paid off after the mixed notices. While the run of *The Beauty Prize*—213 performances—fell far short of those accorded *Sally* and *The Cabaret Girl*, the show was neverthless deemed a success. When it closed, Grossmith brought in a revival of *Tonight's the Night*, retaining Kern's interpolations in that 1915 hit. But by the next season George Gershwin's *Tell Me More* was filling the Winter Garden with a newer, steelier sound, a far cry from Kern's sweet romanticism. Whether an argument or merely an urge to be voguish prompted the change is uncertain.

Rehearsals for *Stepping Stones* were announced to begin on Monday, September 3. The production would be the seventh Dillingham had mounted for his genial star, Fred Stone. When the first week of September passed without any signs of the preliminary readings, rumors of an ailing Stone circulated up and down Broadway. Dillingham's office was forced to issue emphatic denials, even going so far as to publish letters Stone had sent to friends indicating he was in the pink of health. The real explanation is probably the simplest. Dillingham and his performers were awaiting Kern's return from London.

Rehearsals finally did get under way immediately after Kern's return, on Monday, September 17. Coincidental with the start of rehearsals Dillingham made public his intention to give Stone's daughter, Dorothy, who was making her debut, billing over the title. For the most part rehearsals ran smoothly, although two problems gave Kern some trouble. At first the composer wanted to reuse "The First Rose Of Summer" as a first-act finale, set in a lavish "Garden of Roses." John McCormack's recording had made the song popular shortly after *She's a Good Fellow* opened, but Kern seems to have felt it deserved a further hearing. The song was assigned to Helen Glen, playing the minor but appropriately titled part of Rose. After Miss Glen's initial singing of it, Kern turned to young Louis A. Lotito, one of Dillingham's assistants, sitting across the aisle, and asked the startled young man what he thought of it. The youth decided to give a candid reply, suggesting he liked it better when Joseph Santley and Ivy Sawyer had sung it. He added quickly that he thought the song was already established. Kern glowered and snapped back in apparent anger, "I suppose you'll go far." He then broke out in one of his irresistible grins, so the youngster realized he had not offended the composer.

Despite his antic response, Kern must have agreed, for the song was gone by the next rehearsal. In its place was a melody Kern had set to a Herbert Reynolds lyric, "I Saw The Roses And Remembered You." The song was more complicated and conspicuously artful than Kern's typical work of the period, changing tempos frequently and jumping back and forth between D flat and E, two keys customarily eschewed in more popular releases. The melodic line was as florid as the piano part Kern later published. The song's sheet music emphasized the artful nature of the song by giving it what might be called the "art song treatment." It was issued in the simple, austere black-and-white printed cover most classical music employed at the time. Its first page was given over entirely to a poem—a soppy one, left uncredited. Only the ending was interesting—a ravishingly beautiful two-bar tag that Kern may have recalled years later when he came to write "The Night Was Made For Love" for *The Cat and the Fiddle*. Whether Kern reestablished contact with Reynolds to write the song or whether he pulled it from his trunk is uncertain. The quickness with which he offered it as a replacement suggests it had been composed some time before, although the musical line more often than not argues against this. One rehearsal was enough to convince everyone that the song contrasted jarringly with its surroundings. Not until the tryout was under way did Kern find a suitable "Rose" song.

A tall, lanky, dignified young man, slightly handicapped by the effects of polio, ambled into Kern's life at this point. Robert Russell Bennett was an orchestrator who had recently begun to work with Harms. Although Dreyfus had great faith in the man, Kern was uncertain. He decided to grasp this opportunity to try his own hand at orchestrating some of his songs. After Victor Baravelle, the musical director, had dutifully played them through, Kern asked his impressions. Baravelle babbled a few kind words, but his embarrassment was obvious. Kern, who had quickly drawn his own conclusions, was not fooled. He insisted his own orchestrations were inadequate and, gathering up the music, handed it over to Bennett for revision.

Stepping Stones gave its first public performance at the Shubert Theatre in New Haven on October 16. The *Journal-Courier* saved its headline and opening sentence for its praise of Dorothy Stone, noting the applause for her was "thunderous." Calling the elder Stone "king of entertainers," the critic reported the musical was typical of the star's "good wholesome shows." "Added to this," the reviewer continued, "is a musical score with several numbers of the hit variety. Mr. Jerome Kern is responsible for the score and the pieces that are hits are 'Wonderful Dad,' 'In Love With Love' and 'The Dolls.'"

The plot was the beloved childlike nonsense that Stone had always employed and excelled at. Prince Silvio loves a little shopgirl, Rougette Hood, but the villainous bandit, Otto DeWolfe, demands the prince marry his daughter instead. By way of a concession DeWolfe offers all the spoils of his years of thievery as a dowry. The prince refuses, and with the aid of an ingenious plumber, Peter Plug, foils DeWolfe's myriad machinations.

After additional stands in Hartford and Providence, *Stepping Stones* opened at Dillingham's Globe Theatre on November 6, 1923. Always a leader in raising prices, Dillingham brought the show in with a nightly top of $5.50. The opening night musical program was:

Stepping Stones

ACT I

1. Descriptive Music, "The Nursery Clock"
2. Trio, "Little Angel Cake" . . . . . . *Radiola [Primrose Caryll], Richard [Harold West], Mary [Lucille Elmore] and Girls*
3. Dance . . . . *Tiller Sunshine Girls*
4. Buffo Trio, "Because You Love the Singer" . . *Lupina [Evelyn Herbert], Otto [Oscar Ragland] and Remus [John Lambert]*
5. Ensemble and Song, "Little Red Riding Hood" . . . . *Rougette [Dorothy Stone], Widow Hood [Allene Stone] and Girls*
6. Duet, "Wonderful Dad" . . . . *Peter Plug [Fred Stone] and Rougette*
7. Trio, "Pie" . . . . *Peter, Otto and Remus*
8. Ensemble and Song, "Babbling Babette" . . . . *Lupina and Ensemble*
9. Duettino, "In Love with Love" . . . . . . *Rougette, Prince Silvio [Roy Hoyer] and Principal Characters*
10. Dance, "The Wood Nymphs" . . . . *Tiller Sunshine Girls*

11. Song, "Our Lovely Rose" .... *Lupina*
12. Rose Potpourri Finale

ACT II

13. Trio, "Once in a Blue Moon" .... *Prince Silvio, Lupina,*
Remus, Charlotte [Lilyan White], Eclaire
[Ruth White] and Girls
14. March, "The Mystic Hussars" .... *Tiller Sunshine Girls*
15. Dance, "The Skeleton Janitor" .. *Landlord [George Herman]*
16. Song, "Raggedy Ann" ...... *Peter, Rougette, Remus, Tiller*
Sunshine Girls and Globe Theatre Ensemble
17. Dance Duet, "Dear Little Peter Pan" .... *Peter and Rougette*
18. Palace Dance .... *Tiller Sunshine Girls*
19. Coronation March, "Stepping Stones" .... *Lupina, Otto,*
Remus and Ensemble
20. Finale .... *Peter and Rougette and Entire Company*

R. H. Burnside, who collaborated with Anne Caldwell on the libretto, was stager. Sets and costumes were designed by numerous artists.

Rushing back to her dressing room after her final curtain call, Miss Stone found the room lined with orchids and gardenias and jammed with well-wishers. But the mob seemed particularly numerous and cramped. Only as they parted to make space for her did she realize why the congestion seemed so extraordinary. In the corner of the dressing room was a shiny new piano, a gift to her from Kern.

While the opening night performance was progressing, electricians at the Globe put Dorothy Stone's name up in lights alongside her father's. The spontaneity of the gesture was tarnished slightly by Dillingham's earlier promise of equal billing, but the stardom was nevertheless deserved. Most critics devoted their opening paragraphs to extolling the seventeen-year-old. Few gave more than passing mention to Evelyn Herbert, who possessed probably the finest voice of any Broadway singer of her era. Stone's clowning and acrobatics were applauded (he parachuted down for his first entrance), and Dillingham's lavish, tasteful hand was complimented as well. Alexander Woollcott always found especially felicitous phrases for things he liked. In the *Herald* he reported that the evening was "abrim with sweet melodies by Jerome Kern," adding, "The loveliest of them is the song called 'Once In a Blue Moon,' so beautifully, so coolly and so daintily staged that it becomes an epitome of all the sweet songs he ever wrote." Even German language papers joined the cheering. In a one-paragraph review the *New Yorker Staatszeitung* proclaimed Kern's music "einschmeichelnde" (ingratiating).

A number of changes in the musical program inevitably occurred between New Haven and New York, although in the case of *Stepping Stones* several may have been merely title changes. "When I Went To School" was dropped and the same singers given instead "Little Red Riding Hood." "The National Dish" may simply have been the original title of "Pie," sung in the same spot by the same performers. The song's lyric associates the dessert with our American blessings. Fred Stone's number late in the first act, "Little Gypsy Lady," was left behind, while a new first-act finale opened with "Our Lovely Rose" and ended with a medley of old favorites about the flower—"My Wild Irish Rose," "Ma Blushin' Rosie," and "The Last Rose Of Summer," but not Kern's "First Rose" or, for that matter, "Wild Rose" or "Nodding Roses." Gone from the second act were two Fred Stone numbers, "The Magician Does His Stuff" and "The Growing Men." Two other songs again seem to have been simply retitled, "The White Cavaliers" becoming "The Mystic Hussars" and "Dolls," "Raggedy Ann."

While Kern's score was charming, it was singularly curious. Many of the songs seem to foreshadow the styles of other popular composers of the 1920s. Almost certainly the best number is "Once In A Blue Moon," a song Mabel Mercer has attempted to rescue from an unmerited oblivion. It is, as Alec Wilder has said, "a short, very simple lullaby . . . a song of extreme harmonic simplicity and a narrow melodic range." But Wilder sees the piece as falling "in the pure area of Kern's writing." Actually its warm harmonies and the insistent return within each basic musical sentence to a single basic note could easily allow the melody to be mistaken for early Richard Rodgers. Miss Caldwell's equally sweet and simple lyric underscores this when, in the last line, it turns abruptly cynical in Lorenz Hart's best fashion. On the other hand, the stomping melodies for "Raggedy Ann" and "Wonderful Dad," inspired by little more than obvious chord progressions, could readily pass for something out of a De Sylva, Brown, and Henderson show. The title song is a melodic, if unexceptional, march, while "In Love With Love" (which Kern would use again) is a jauntily pleasant ballad. "Pie" 's bouncy syncopation in a way jumps far ahead to the lighthearted melodies of later children's movies. As he did with "Nodding Roses," Kern had fun sneaking a quotation from *Der Rosenkavalier* into his piano part for "Our Lovely Rose," but the song, written in half-time, is nondescript and reminiscent of melodies Kern threw off in the teens of the century. For the most part Kern's writing for *Stepping Stones* reveals him a composer of his period, rather than, as he usually was, above it.

The demand for seats became so pressing that within three weeks of the opening Dillingham raised ticket prices still further, asking a $6.60 top for Friday and a whopping $7.70 for Saturday night. Such then-exceptional tabs failed to discourage eager playgoers, so week after week the musical set a new house record of $37,000. The Stones romped through their vehicle 241 times in New York, until closed by an actor's strike, and then delighted the road until early 1926.

On November 21 the long-awaited trial began. The setting was the United States District Court, located, oddly, in the Woolworth Building in lower Manhattan. Kern, wearing a conservative gray suit, arrived early in the company of his lawyer, Nathan Burkan. Burkan had also been Fisher's counsel, but when a conflict of interest developed, he chose to side with Kern. Dillingham, Dreyfus, and Miss Caldwell, all co-defendants, were also on hand, although papers failed to mention the presence of the fifth defendant, Edward Royce. Fisher, dressed more nattily and bubbling with confidence, arrived accompanied by his attorney, Julian T. Abeles. Spectators may have done double takes on entering the courtroom and wondered if they had not come to a musical comedy's rehearsal instead. On one side of the room an eight-piece jazz band was tuning its instruments. Next to the orchestra stood an upright piano, and beside the instrument was a large "victrola."

The trial promised to be a grand show indeed, and to no small extent kept its promise. *Variety* headlined its first report of the proceedings "DARDANELLA SUIT TURNS COURTROOM INTO 'CAB' [cabaret]." Before the week-long action was finished, the court heard not only several versions of both "Dardanella" and "Ka-lu-a" but a toccata by Schumann, "The Mermaid's Song" from Weber's *Oberon,* a brief excerpt from Wagner's *Der Fliegende Hollander,* and a cello piece by someone named Kummer, with none other than Victor Herbert as cellist. Fisher even attempted to sing several of his points, but courtroom laughter and Abeles convinced him to let others handle the music. If spectators were more amused than surprised to learn a composer was not necessarily a good singer, they were nevertheless given some eye-openers about Fisher. Burkan got Fisher to admit that he had not really written "Dardanella" but had bought the rights to the music. Still more dramatically, when Burkan handed Fisher a song by Chopin and asked him to play it, Fisher was required to confess he could not sight-read. If Fisher was a dismally inept witness, the defense produced a stellar one. *Variety* recorded, "Victor Herbert's testimony at the trial seemingly swung the tide for the defense. Herbert set forth that the bass is neither original with Jerome Kern or with Black and Bernard [the actual composer], tracing its history back to the classic which makes it properly public domain." Indeed, the tide had seemingly swung in Kern's favor when the judge dismissed the writ off the bench. Abeles immediately announced he would move for a new trial or would appeal.

Some confusion exists regarding one major matter. Judge John C. Knox had originally refused to grant Fisher an injunction when Fisher first brought action in 1921, and all papers agree that Judge Knox was sitting when the trial began on November 21. Yet the papers are similarly unanimous in recording that the distinguished jurist Judge Learned Hand was presiding at the end and rendered the decision. What, if anything, happened is uncertain. In any case, it was to Hand that Abeles appealed. On January 26, 1924, Hand published a carefully reconsidered opinion. Kern learned that the judge, on a technicality, had reversed himself. However, he refused to punish the defendants with more than an obligatory slap on the wrist.

Hand's decision took into account nine points. He noted that (1) "Plagiarism of any substantial component part of a musical copyright, either in melody or accompaniment, is proper subject of suit" but that (2) "The law imposes no prohibition on those who, without copying, independently arrive at precise copyrighted combinations of words or notes." On those two points Hand insisted the plaintiff "must show that Kern, the composer, used 'Dardanella' as the source of his accompaniment." He further agreed that the plaintiff had a strong argument in stating that (3) "Where [a] figure in [the] defendant's piece of music was exactly like [a] figure in [the] plaintiff's copyrighted piece of music, and both parties used it as an 'ostinato accompaniment,' and defendants have not been able to discover either figure or 'ostinato accompaniment' in either earlier popular music, [it must be] held to show infringement." Branding the figures "not only . . . exactly alike, but used in the same way" and suggesting the defendants failed to discover an earlier such figure, Hand asked, "Can I suppose that such parallelism could be the result of coincidence only?" He then attempted to answer in a long, remarkable passage worth quoting in its entirety:

> Mr. Kern swears that he was quite unconscious of any plagiarism, and on the whole I am disposed to give him the benefit of the doubt. For this I rely, not only upon the impression which he made upon me, but upon the insufficiency of motive. I cannot agree that the accompaniment was at all as important to the success of "Dardanella" as the plaintiff would ask me to believe. I admit that it was a good bass, and helped; but I think the piece won its success substantially because of the melody. It is of course possible that Kern might have lifted it bodily, hoping to escape detection. However, he has an established place among composers of light opera, and has succeeded more than once. Certainly detection would be a matter of some moment to him. No producer willingly invites the suits which follow musical piracy. Once convicted in such a case, Kern's market might suffer. With the profit small and the price high, it seems to me unlikely that he should have set about deliberate plagiarism.
>
> Whether he unconsciously copied the figure, he cannot say, and does not try to. Everything registers somewhere in our memories, and no one can tell what may evoke it. On the whole, my belief is that, in composing the accompaniment to the refrain of "Kalua," Mr. Kern must have followed, probably unconsciously, what he had certainly often heard only a short time before. I cannot really see how else to account for a similarity, which amounts to identity.

Point Four confirmed an author's right to protect himself from copying. The fifth and sixth points were highly technical, essentially dealing with whether Fisher actually was the author of "Dardanella" and, if he was not, did he as copyright owner have the right to sue? Even the defense agreed to let this matter pass. The seventh point was looked on by Hand as crucial. "The most important point of law in the case is whether it is a defense that there was in prior art substantially the same figure." Hand continued, "I think there is a clear difference between its use at intervals, as in Wagner, Schumann, or Kummer, and its use by Bernard as an 'ostinato.' . . . For the purposes of this case it must be deemed to be original, if by original one means that it was the spontaneous, unsuggested result of the author's imagination." For the eighth point Hand spoke to the question of whether an "original" work may be copyrighted if an identical work had existed before. The very arguments the defendants had employed to show similar pieces here came back against them for these arguments also demonstrated the differences among the pieces. "I conclude," wrote Hand, " . . . that the existence of Landon's 'ostinato,' though substantially the same as the 'Dardanella' accompaniment, did not invalidate the copyright pro tanto, there being no evidence, or, indeed, any reasonable possibility, that it was the source of Bernard's conception." Kern and his associates must have quailed on hearing this.

In essence, Hand had upheld Fisher's copyright, had dismissed the defendants' claims to prior use in public domain, and had agreed with Fisher that Kern's basso ostinato employed the same musical sentence for the same purpose as "Dardanella"'s basso ostinato. Only one point remained, the ninth, "the matter of relief." On this Hand seems to have changed his tack, writing, "As for damages, it seems to me absurd to suggest that [Fisher] has suffered any injury. 'Dardanella' had faded out before 'Kalua' appeared; but if it had been at the peak of its popularity, I do not believe that the accompaniment to the chorus of 'Kalua' would have subtracted one copy or one record from its sales. The controversy is a 'trivial pother' . . . however, [the law] fixes a minimum of $250, which is absolute in all cases. . . . Therefore I must and do award that sum as damages. The plaintiff is likewise absolutely entitled to a full bill of cost, but I will make no allowance for counsel fees, since that is discretionary. Such victories I may properly enough make a luxury to the winner." It was now Fisher's turn to be crestfallen. Visions of significant monetary damages were gone for good.

Judge Hand's decision became a landmark. It established the important rule that a bass could be plagiarized as readily as a principal melody. But Hand wisely saw that there had been no malice on the part of Kern and his associates and no real injury inflicted on Fisher. For once the scales of justice were balanced with an impeccable precision.

14

Two Fascinating Failures

If the outcome of the trial was good news to Kern, his devotees could rejoice in another welcome announcement. The same issue of *Variety* that discussed the end of the court sessions recorded that Comstock and Gest were planning a revival of the Princess Theatre series. The producers revealed that Bolton, Wodehouse, and Kern were hard at work on a musical called *Sitting Pretty* and playgoers would be able to enjoy the results early in 1924.

In the late spring or early summer of 1922 Bolton and Wodehouse had agreed to provide a vehicle for a pair of popular vaudevillians, the Duncan Sisters, with Irving Berlin doing the songs. Berlin's admiration for Wodehouse was such that he consented to a rare departure in his customary policy, allowing "Plum" to write several of the lyrics. Berlin's partner, Sam Harris, was to produce the piece. Bolton developed an outline of a plot, featuring, as so many of Bolton's stories did, a lovable crook circulating in high society. In this instance the crook would receive his comeuppance from two beautiful twins. The Duncan Sisters would play the twins, of course. Wodehouse and Bolton wrote the show in London at Wodehouse's home on Onslow Square. But when they returned to New York after Wodehouse's

Winter Garden opening and presented themselves at Harris's office, they were dismayed to learn that rehearsals had been postponed to allow Harris and Berlin to devote additional time to their next edition of their *Music Box Revue.* The Duncan Sisters were equally disappointed, especially when they were advised they were not even being considered for a temporary berth in the new revue, since any appearance they might make in that show would detract from the freshness of their material in the Bolton-Wodehouse work. Fearing that last-minute vaudeville bookings, if they were available at all, would force them to hopscotch inconveniently all over the country, the girls asked to be allowed to fill the time by appearing in a show they had worked out for themselves. Harris quickly acquiesced, and he later informed his writers, "It's a sort of half amateur affair. *Topsy and Eva* they're calling it. It's a sort of comic *Uncle Tom's Cabin.*"

Topsy and Eva was one of the runaway hits of the 1920s, playing nearly a year in Chicago alone and securing the Duncan Sisters' paychecks for nearly four years. With the Duncan Sisters no longer available, both Harris and Berlin requested releases from their commitments. Neither Bolton nor Wodehouse was at a loss on how to move next. While they had been working on the show in London, Wodehouse and Kern had been applying finishing touches to *The Cabaret Girl,* and Kern had read their script. He was enthusiastic and suggested that if Berlin ever dropped out of the project he would like to try his hand at it. Without a celebrated sister team for the leads, some rewriting was necessary, but this was an easy matter.

From the beginning Bolton and Wodehouse apparently had plump Frank McIntyre in mind for Uncle Joe, and his casting was the first to be announced. Filling the roles of the two sisters took a while longer. Bolton and Wodehouse were elated to learn that Gertrude Bryan was available. Miss Bryan—"an unexpected blend of Ethel Barrymore, Maude Adams and Rebecca West"—had won the hearts of playgoers a decade or so before, especially in *Little Boy Blue,* only to marry and retire from the stage. Kern had originally proposed her and had argued forcefully to sweep aside Comstock and Gest's reservations. But having first won over his producers, Kern had next to win over Miss Bryan's wealthy husband. Comstock and Gest made his task all the harder, for they demanded he obtain written assurances from the husband to the effect that he would not compel his wife to leave the show during its New York run. Kern succeeded in getting what he sought, but quickly came to rue his success. While Miss Bryan's husband made no problems, Miss Bryan did. Her lovely contralto voice and graceful presence were unimpaired, but she had picked up some haughty airs that would cause backstage difficulties, particularly after the youngster brought in to play her sister walked off with the notices. That second young lady was a tiny dynamo who had begun her career as a dancer at the Metropolitan Opera and garnered acclaim uptown in *Helen of Troy, New York,* Queenie Smith. (Miss Bryan was replaced shortly after the New York opening by Eleanor Griffith.)

When *Sitting Pretty* was finally ready to face its public, Comstock and Gest joyfully advertised it as "The Seventh of Their Series of the Princess Musical Comedies." So well known were its authors that both the programs and sheet music simply said the work was by "Bolton, Wodehouse and Kern," much as if it had been by Gilbert and Sullivan.

The Sunday night audience that packed Detroit's Shubert Theatre on March 23 was highly receptive, an enthusiasm shared by the Detroit *Free Press* in its long, carefully weighed review. The critic, who praised the production as "a visual feast," rejoiced that Kern's score was "evenly excellent" and that the music "fit to the story instead of being dragged in whenever someone decides to break into song." Initiating a long line of ecstatic notices for Miss Smith, the reviewer exclaimed, "When she was in sight nothing else mattered." Yet a hint of trouble to come could be read into his comment on the book. "It was not," he recorded, "one of those violently funny affairs. Many of the best lines went over the heads of the opening audience, but that wasn't the fault of the lines. It is the sort of humor that calls for some thought to fully appreciate it." A week later Buffalo responded with much the same pleasure Detroit had shown.

In absolute terms the theatrical economics of 1924 were relatively healthy. Financial pressures did not dictate small casts and large houses. Yet little consideration was apparently given to offering this seventh Princess musical comedy at the bandbox Princess Theatre. Apart from the earliest announcements, this "Princess Theatre show" was never slated for the tiny house. Instead it was booked at a theatre not only more centrally located, but capable of allowing more sizable grosses. Although the Fulton was one of Broadway's smallest playhouses, it seated three times as many patrons as the 39th Street auditorium. *Sitting Pretty* opened there on April 8, 1924. Firstnighters heard tell of how rich Mr. Pennington adopts May Tolliver, hoping to have her marry his adopted son, Horace, and never dreaming Horace is casing the Pennington estate for his real but crooked Uncle Joe. But in typical

Jerome David Kern
(Photograph by Walter Pollak.   Courtesy, Mrs. Davis Zimmerman)

Fannie Kakeles Kern.
(Courtesy, Mrs. Betty
Kern Miller)

Henry Kern.
(Courtesy, Mrs. Betty Kern Miller)

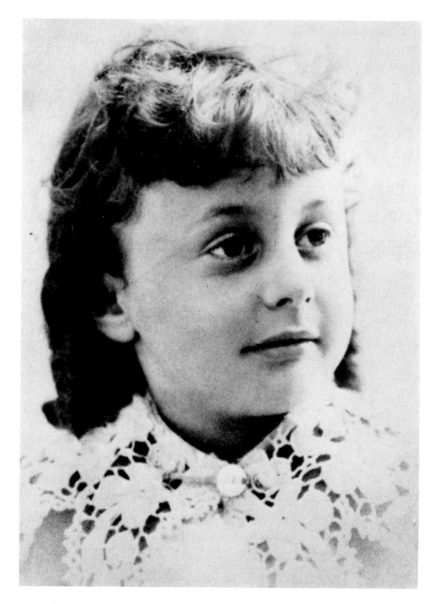

Jerome Kern at age four.   (Courtesy, Mrs. Betty Kern Miller)

The Swan Hotel, Walton-on-Thames, England, where Kern met Eva Leale.
(Weybridge Museum, Weybridge, England)

Kern at age twenty-five, the photograph he lovingly signed and gave to
Eva during their courtship.   (Courtesy, Mrs. Betty Kern Miller)

Eva and Betty Kern in the early twenties.
(Courtesy, Mrs. Betty Kern Miller)

Seligman Kakeles looks down from his portrait on his grandson, Jerome Kern, and his great-great-grandson, Steven Kern Shaw. (Courtesy, Mrs. Davis Zimmerman)

Eva, Betty, Jerry, and Steven on the rear patio at Whittier Drive, several months before Kern's death. (Courtesy, Mrs. Betty Kern Miller)

The final scene of *The Girl from Utah,* depicting the London Arts Ball. Here, bathed in artificial moonlight, Julia Sanderson and Donald Brian introduced "They Didn't Believe Me." (Theatre and Music Collection, Museum of the City of New York)

The three Princess Theatre collaborators: Bolton, Wodehouse, and Kern. Wodehouse is probably seated so as not to tower embarrassingly over his much shorter colleagues. (Theatre and Music Collection, Museum of the City of New York)

A fine and rare formal portrait of Kern about the time of the Princess Theatre shows. In both this and the preceding photograph Kern was still favoring traditional ties. (Courtesy, Mrs. Davis Zimmerman)

The exterior of the Princess Theatre, its simple, undistinguished façade giving little hint of the elegance and beauty on both sides of the footlights inside. (Theatre and Music Collection, Museum of the City of New York)

The interior of the Princess Theatre. A color photograph would reveal an auditorium done largely in whites and blues. (Theatre and Music Collection, Museum of the City of New York)

The last act of *Oh, Lady! Lady!!* with its then-novel setting of a Greenwich Village roof garden. An imbalance of chorus girls over chorus boys was minimized by pairing girls in the back row. (Theatre and Music Collection, Museum of the City of New York)

Hammerstein, Ziegfeld, and Kern outside Washington's National Theatre just hours before the first performance of *Show Boat*. (Courtesy, Mrs. Matilda Clough)

Otto Harbach at the time of his collaborations with Kern. (Theatre Collection, Free Library of Philadelphia)

"Where'd you get that smile from?" Clifton Webb seems to be asking Marilyn Miller in a posed publicity photograph for *Sunny*. Kern had a copy of Miss Miller's costume made for Betty. (Theatre and Music Collection, Museum of the City of New York)

With the "Cotton Blossom" behind it, the chorus sings "Happy The Day" in Act One of *Show Boat*. (Theatre Collection, Free Library of Philadelphia)

Georges Metaxa accompanies Odette Myrtil's fiddling in a scene from *The Cat and the Fiddle*. (Theatre and Music Collection, Museum of the City of New York)

Irene Dunne singing "Smoke Gets In Your Eyes" in Hollywood's version of *Roberta*. Miss Dunne starred in more Kern films than any other artist. (Courtesy, Joellyn Ausanka)

Undoubtedly the happiest development stemming from the filming of *Roberta* was the beginning of Kern's collaboration and warm friendship with Dorothy Fields, shown here working in Kern's Beverly-Wilshire suite. (Edward Jablonski Collection)

Kern's pixyish charm is caught in a photograph made about the time *I Dream Too Much* was being filmed. In this and the preceding photograph Kern has adopted his unique mode of ties. (Academy of Motion Picture Arts and Sciences)

Edwin Knopf, Irene Dunne, and the Kerns attending some long-forgotten premiere. (Courtesy, Mr. and Mrs. Edwin Knopf)

Georges Metaxa seems more interested in Fred Astaire and Ginger Rogers than in leading his band, and no one seems to appreciate *Swing Time*'s art deco surroundings. (Courtesy, Joellyn Ausanka)

Cornel Wilde, Jeanne Crain, Dorothy Gish, Walter Brennan, Linda Darnell, and William Eythe in a scene from Kern's last film, *Centennial Summer*. (Movie Star News)

musical comedy fashion Horace loves May's twin sister, Dixie, who has been left behind at the orphanage, while May falls in love with the scapegrace who is Pennington's real nephew.

In keeping with the old Princess Theatre tradition, there were two acts, with only one set for each.

Musical numbers were:

Sitting Pretty

ACT I

Overture
1. The Charity Class .... *Charity Girls*
2. Song Scene, "Is This Not a Lovely Spot?" ...... *Pennington [George E. Mack], Bill [Rudolf Cameron], Judson [Eugene Revere], Coaching Party, Girls, Gardeners, etc.*
3. Trio, "Worries" ..... *May [Gertrude Bryan], Dixie [Queenie Smith] and Bill*
4. Trio, "Bongo on the Congo" .. *Horace [Dwight Frye], Judson and Uncle Joe [Frank McIntyre]*
5. Duet, "Mr. and Mrs. Rorer" ..... *Dixie, Horace and Cooking Class*
6. Song Scene, "There Isn't One Girl" ...... *Bill, Roper [Harry Lillford] and May*
7. Duet, "A Year From Today" .... *Bill and May*
8. Song, "Shufflin' Sam" .... *Dixie and Ensemble*
9. Finaletto .... *Ensemble*

ACT II

Prelude
1a. Chorus, "The Polka Dot" .... *Ensemble*
 b. Scene Music
 c. Aria, "Days Gone By" ...... *Dorothy Janice and Ensemble*
2. Duettino, "All You Need Is a Girl" .... *Bill and May*
3. Buffo Duo, "Dear Old Fashioned Prison of Mine" .... *Horace and Uncle Joe*
4. Duet, "A Desert Island" .... *May, Dixie and Girls*
5. Duet, "The Magic Train" .... *Bill, May and Ensemble*
6. Song, "Shadow of the Moon" .... *Dixie and May*
7. Finale .... *Ensemble*

Max Steiner was the musical director, while Robert Russell Bennett orchestrated the score. Fred G. Latham and Julian Alfred staged the work; P. Dodd Ackerman designed the sets; Charles Lemaire and Alice V. O'Neill, the costumes.

The show set New York's reviewers to reminiscing about the old Princess shows, and while few agreed with the *Telegram* that *Sitting Pretty* was "a bigger, better and brighter show than its predecessors," most saw it as a worthy companion to them. Still, the fact that many of the reviewers saved their most glowing adjectives for Queenie Smith did not pass unnoticed. While there were generally kind words for the rest of the cast, several stopped to complain about an absence of good singers. E. W. Osborn in the *World* noted, "Having regard to Mr. Kern's lovely score, a great deal more might be asked for the vocal part of the performance. There were more times than not, last night, when it was a case of music, music everywhere and scarce a voice to sing." When they did turn to the material at hand virtually every critic praised the melodies of the man the *Times* dubbed "America's best writer of light music." "A Year From Today" was most frequently singled out, although almost every other song found a place in one review or another. Wodehouse's lyrics proved equally impressive. Mantle noted that "the love lyrics are soft without being mushy," but most critics centered their attention on his two comic numbers, "Bongo On The Congo" and "Dear Old Fashioned Prison Of Mine" (published, inexplicably, as "Tulip Time In Sing Sing"). They received so many encores they "threatened to ruin the audience." Even when they held reservations about the "workmanlike" libretto, a number of critics were delighted enough to pass on such bits of wit as, "A chafing dish is a frying pan that's gotten into society." Perhaps the harshest judgment came from *Variety*. Casting a cold, commercial eye on the show, it noted that the musical "somehow misses the fun of its predecessors" and concluded, "'Sitting Pretty,' if it had a moderate operating cost, would stand a good chance for a long run. The impression is it will not draw capacity, though good business is sure for about three months."

The score Broadway heard was not much changed from the Detroit premiere. For the most part, changes were made to bring the show down to standard running time. Six songs were cut. Three—"Roses Are Nodding," "Coaching," and "You Alone Would Do"—had been sung in succession at the beginning of the first act, the first two by the chorus, the last by Bill and Babe (Myra Hampton). "Just Wait," performed by the male principals

248

in mid-act, also disappeared. A trio from the middle of the second act, "Ladies Are Present," performed by Horace, Bill, and Dixie, was cut, as well as the act's final number, the show's title song. If Miss Smith's recollections were correct, this pleasant ballad was cut not because it was inferior or because it failed to fit into the story (in fact, it brought Horace and Dixie's romance to a head), but because Dwight Frye had a slight speech impediment and his singing of the words "sit and sit and sit" sounded embarrassingly different. One new song, "Is This Not A Lovely Spot?" supplanted the first three cuts.

Whatever was lost, the score that remained was one of Kern's finest and perhaps his most unjustly neglected except for *Oh, Boy!* and *Three Sisters.* (In a 1977 interview Robert Russell Bennett, who has been so often publicly contemptuous of many fine Broadway scores, agreed this one deserved a rehearing.) "A Year From Today," which Kern marked to be sung "a l'antique," has a beguiling nostalgic sweetness. The song was sung first by Bill, then in harmony by Bill and May. "Shadow Of The Moon" was marked "Moderato misterioso." Its elegantly languid melody makes haunting use of diminished chords. "The Magic Train"—a second song from this score published under a different title, in this instance "The Enchanted Train"—was as irresistibly gentle as a lullaby. On the livelier side, "All You Need Is A Girl" was a spirited waltz with a distinctly Hibernian flavor. Kern would salvage this tune and reemploy it in *Sweet Adeline.* "Shufflin' Sam" was a rollicking invitation to dance that Bennett underscored somewhat eccentrically in his orchestration with themes from Dvorak's New World Symphony. Arguably, there is not a weak song in the published material.

Kern's feelings about the score are unrecorded, but one incident shortly after the show opened suggests he not only was fond of it but felt quite strongly about it. With the show drawing good, but somewhat disappointing, attendance, Kern unleashed a broadside at the musical world, announcing he would not allow the score to be played in cabarets or on primitive, but burgeoning, radio stations, nor would he permit phonograph recordings. His statement was lengthy and impassioned, and worth quoting in considerable part.

> None of our music now reaches the public as we wrote it except in the theatre. It is so distorted by jazz orchestras as to be almost unrecognizable.
> A composer should be able to protect his score just as an author

does his manuscripts. No author would permit pirated editions of his work in which his phraseology and punctuation were changed, thereby giving to his work a meaning entirely different from what he intended.

The psychological moment has arrived not only for the revival of the tuneful, melodious and mannerly musical play which had its vogue several years ago with such pieces as "Nobody Home," "Very Good Eddie," "Oh, Boy!," "Oh, Lady! Lady!!" and "Leave It to Jane," but also for a revolt against the manner in which all music, even classic, is currently rendered through the sources which reach the popular ear. The public, through the cabaret and radio broadcasting, is not getting genuine music, only a fraudulent imitation.

There is no such thing as jazz music per se, at least nothing that may honestly be called original and characteristically American. The Gypsy orchestra of Hungary knew and used similar methods years ago, but they were artists and knew how and when to apply these methods.

The trouble with current popular musical rendition is that it runs everything into the same mold, utterly heedless of the original nature of the score and of the right of the composer, whether living or dead. Increasingly in the course of the last five years, I have noted when taking English friends out to see New York that this debasement of all music at the hands of cabaret orchestras has grown by leaps and bounds.

No doubt some of these statements are unnecessarily petulant and reactionary. Surely any dispassionate student of the American musical scene in 1924 would have observed elements of jazz that were indeed original and characteristically native. Nonetheless, abuses were flagrant. Kern was not alone among responsible composers in resenting the desecration of his carefully constructed melodies. But he was among the first to speak out bravely against excesses.

How much of this public annoyance reflected heartfelt disgust and how much represented a calculated attempt at calling attention to *Sitting Pretty* is moot. As clever businessmen, Kern and his associates may have felt it worth a gamble to try to lure playgoers by precisely the opposite method customarily utilized. Instead of allowing a song's popularity to act as a magnet to the box office, they may have attempted to create an air of mystery to intrigue potential ticket buyers. If so, it was a chancy, dubious ploy. In any case, Wodehouse, Bolton, Comstock, and Gest all professed to support Kern's sentiments. No recordings of the songs were made, and by extension it seems safe to assume that the music was not heard on radio or in clubs.

A peculiar quirk in the law prohibited Kern from granting permission to carefully selected exceptions. A composer had a right to withhold a song entirely, but once he allowed a single artist to perform or record a song (except, of course, to perform it in the show itself) that song became available to any other artist willing to pay a royalty.

Strategem or no, the failure of *Sitting Pretty*'s songs to receive a wide hearing probably hurt the show. *Variety*'s astute reviewer had called the shot exactly. *Sitting Pretty* was withdrawn after ninety-five performances —a three-month run.

From New York the show toured throughout the fall of 1924 in a desultory fashion. Of the original principals, only Frank McIntyre and George E. Mack remained. But at the beginning of 1925 the show enjoyed a brief resurgence when two minor producers, A. L. Jones and Morris Green, bought into the show and moved it to Chicago. For the occasion, two new stars were hired, the Dolly Sisters (whom Bolton had suggested as replacements for the Duncan girls). *Variety*'s review of the Chicago opening is interesting on two accounts—the two faults the critic mentioned in an otherwise highly favorable review. Like his Detroit colleague at the show's first performance, he recorded that the "fresh, breezy and original lines . . . fall flat." He continued, "One other criticism applies . . . and that is the special jazz orchestra, billed as a Vincent Lopez outfit, although splendid as a jazz band, detracts from the value of several excellent songs. . . ."

On May 28, 1924, Kern had a sad duty to perform, acting as an honorary pallbearer at Victor Herbert's funeral. Kern surely recalled the happy aspects of their long association—Herbert's generous and accurate prediction that Kern would inherit his mantle, their work together in ASCAP, and Herbert's helpful testimony the preceding year. With Herbert's passing, Kern became the most venerable, distinguished composer in the American musical theatre. He was only thirty-eight years old.

Two months later, at the end of July, *Variety* announced another of those intriguing little projects that never saw the footlights. The forthcoming *Ritz Revue* promised to include a miniature Kern operetta, "The Lamplighter." If Kern ever completed the piece, no known trace survives. But he was already deeply involved in another project—one he came to rue.

Philip Goodman was a hulk of a man who at times seemed to have no neck.

His round, dark face was crowded with his heavily Semitic features. The same age as Kern, Goodman had moved from Philadelphia to New York to try his luck at publishing and advertising. He was well read, almost determinedly cultured. If much of his work kept him close to the garment district, he nevertheless loved the theatre and harbored theatrical ambitions. In 1922 he had been responsible for Don Marquis's developing a character from his *Evening Sun* column into the hero of a hit play, *The Old Soak*. A year later Goodman's production of *Poppy* with W. C. Fields had been one of the major box office attractions of the season. Success spawned the inevitable jealous rumors, to the effect that Goodman was an especially nasty Broadway type. Kern, ever up on the ins and outs of theatre gossip, was well aware of the scuttlebutt. In response to Goodman's overtures Kern appeared one morning at Goodman's office at 33rd Street and Broadway. The composer's greeting entered the canon of his legends: "Good morning, Mr. Goodman. I'm Kern. I hear you're a son-of-a-bitch. So am I!"

Although the gambit may have eased the trip ahead for two difficult men, in one respect Kern need not have been too worried. Goodman's heart was in the right place. The musical he hoped to offer Broadway as *Vanity Fair* was not to be just an ordinary boy-meets-girl or Cinderella lark with the customary outlandish jokes and tinkly songs. Goodman was seeking a stylish, witty commentary on modern life embellished with superior melodies. Of course, as a solid businessman, Goodman would only reach out so far ahead of the crowd. The frame of the new show would be steadfastly conventional.

But Kern's nagging doubts persisted. They focused not only on the producer, but, perceptively as it developed, on Goodman's choice of librettist as well. Goodman had written Kern in early March asking Jerry to use his influence to obtain Teddy Royce for director. Busy with preparations for *Sitting Pretty*, Kern failed to reply until May 12. His reply was couched in a mock formality that may have been meant to suggest a certain reserve. After promising to speak with Royce and noting the tryout schedule Goodman proposed (and which was later set back a full month), Jerry concluded the letter, "If you hear any rumors about material for the libretto of your musical comedy, please don't hesitate to let me know. Hoping you are not the same, I am, Dubiously, Jerome Kern."

Goodman's choice of librettist reflected his concern with box office imperatives. He chose Edgar Selwyn, that jack-of-all-theatrical-trades who had co-produced Kern's *Rock-a-Bye Baby* of unhappy memory. By 1924 the

Selwyn brothers owned several of New York's choicest legitimate theatres, including the Times Square, where *Vanity Fair* was slated to play. The musical was said to be Edgar's first solo attempt as a librettist.

Selwyn's basic plot was simple, and not radically new. Laddie Munn is a rich man-about-town frequently at loggerheads with Dorothy Fair, a charming young socialite who has publicly broadcast her contempt for his playboy ways. When she puts herself up at a charity auction as a maid-for-a-week, Munn buys her services and sets about to humiliate her. Andrew Bloxom, a down-at-the-heels vaudevillian masquerading as a millionaire, enters the picture to set things right.

Goodman's suggestion to Kern for a lyricist was even more venturesome than his choice of Selwyn as librettist. Howard Dietz had just turned twenty-eight. He looked like an amiable tough guy. After a stint in the navy during World War I. Dietz had tried his hand at both advertising and journalism, with what proved to be equal luck. His first boss had been none other than Goodman, one of whose accounts was Sam Goldwyn. Dietz began working on publicity for Goldwyn and followed the colorful film-maker to become chief of publicity for MGM. Some of Dietz's light verse had appeared in New York papers when early in the summer his phone rang.

"Is this Howard Dietz, otherwise known as Freckles? Well, this is Jerry Kern, and I'm a fan of yours. I keep up with your stuff in F.P.A.'s 'Conning Tower.'"

Stunned, and not a little disbelieving, Dietz could only retort, "Is this really Mr. Kern?"

Kern was amused, replying, "Take a chance on it. Is this really the author of 'I've A Bungalow In Babylon On Great South Bay'?" Dietz warned Kern he felt like fainting. "Well, don't faint yet," Kern urged, "not until you hear this. Phil Goodman thinks you're a better light-verse writer than an advertising man. We want you to write the lyrics to a show that Goodman says he'll produce. Is it a deal? Come up to Bronxville tomorrow and we'll go over the whole thing. Take the 11:22 train and get a taxi at the station. Charge the taxi to me."

The next morning the dream became the reality. Dietz was ushered into the great Kern library he had heard so much about, and within moments Kern was standing before him in a brocaded smoking jacket. Dietz noticed Kern's hair was conspicuously gray at the sides. Kern plunged directly into business, advising Dietz, "Goodman wants to produce a musical from a book by Edgar Selwyn with a score by you and me. I intend to use some numbers I wrote for a few English shows that didn't come off, or rather didn't get on. Do you think you can put words to tunes, or being a poet, you might prefer to have me set the words to melody. Either way will suit. Autoxinus said that music was in the ear."

For all Dietz knew, Autoxinus might have been the New York *Times*'s third-string critic.

Kern informed Dietz that he never ate lunch while working, but the composer did offer the young writer some tea, which Dietz was too nervous to accept. For the next four hours Kern played a variety of tunes he had pulled from his stock, discussing the type of song it was and generally suggesting how it might be employed in the show. As always, Kern retained his sure instincts for theatrical placement, although he was considerate enough of his untried colleague to assure him he would listen to any alternate suggestions. When it came time for Dietz to catch the 4:54 back to New York, Kern asked him if he could return two days later with some trial lyrics, and Dietz promised him he would.

If Dietz's recollections are precise, then there may have been an undertone of hurt or even bitterness in Kern's words, an undertone the inexperienced and euphoric Dietz need not have been expected to catch. "A show that Goodman says he'll produce" carries with it the unstated hint that Goodman might renege, while the remark about London shows that "didn't get on" could refer to some disappointment at not having a new Winter Garden show on the boards. September 1924 was the first September in four years without a Kern musical raising its curtain on Drury Lane. Kern must have confessed to himself that he was in something of a slump. An occasional tune aside, Kern had not produced a hit-filled score since *Sally,* and even most of *Sally*'s better melodies had been salvaged from earlier shows. Kern was to come up with a remarkable answer for the new musical, although the answer was to contribute to the show's failure. And the answer suggests Kern really did not pull too many pieces from his trunk. Up to a point, Goodman must have been aware of what Kern intended, and he courageously acquiesced.

Given the inescapable confusion with both Thackeray and Frank Crowninshield's popular magazine, *Vanity Fair* could only serve as a working title. Just before the show premiered on September 3 (after a last minute two-night delay) at Philadelphia's Forrest Theatre, its name was changed to *Dear Sir*. With the new title some of Goodman and Kern's original high aims began to slip away. Of course, Philadelphia critics could only judge what they saw and heard. Virtually without exception they were ecstatic. Selwyn's book was lauded for its "intelligence and good taste," encomiums rarely lavished on the era's inane plots and dialogue. *Dear Sir's* three stars were also praised, particularly Walter Catlett for his brash comedy. Oscar Shaw was commended as "ingratiating" and Genevieve Tobin as "lovely," although a number of critics regretted their voices could not do justice to the music. Shaw's singing was termed "agreeable but uncertain," while Miss Tobin labored under "the handicap of a 'parlor' voice." Among lesser performers, Clair Luce was singled out for her "thistledown" dancing. Raymond Savoy's settings were applauded as "extraordinary in their beauty and in the subtle harmony of colors." Most critics passed over Dietz, although Arthur B. Waters in the *Public Ledger* welcomed his verses as "more than ordinary." Waters also typified the attention and admiration awarded Kern, but his special insights into and fondness for Kern's art would make him, next to Dale, probably Kern's most articulate advocate.

> Jerome Kern has written oodles of music, come these many years, but his present score is as musicianly as anything he has ever done. Of jazz there is little, but of haunting melody, vivid outstanding strains, and expert arrangement there is much. Some day America is going to wake up to the fact that Mr. Kern is capable of doing big things.

Rehearsals just before the Philadelphia opening and during the tryout were marred by a ghastly accident and by heated rows. A chorus girl broke her back in a dancing mishap and looked to be permanently crippled. Although the cast and others associated with the show took up a collection, Jerry felt the sum was grossly inadequate. He arranged for a special benefit performance of *Stepping Stones* to be given when the show reached Philadelphia in January.

Charity was nowhere to be found when disagreements on how to rewrite the show flared. Goodman, Kern, and Selwyn had adjoining suites at the Ritz Hotel, and to keep their arguments out of the cast's ears met regularly in the producer's rooms. Several times the shouting matches grew so loud the hotel's desk was forced to phone up and warn the men of the disturbance they were creating.

His funds dwindling and his best efforts to polish the show accomplished, Goodman hustled the musical into the Times Square Theatre on September 23, 1924.

Musical numbers were:

Dear Sir

ACT I
Scene One

"Grab a Girl" ...... *Oliver [George Sweet], Clair [Clair Luce],*
Boys and Girls
"What's the Use?" .... *Laddie [Oscar Shaw] and Girls*
"I Want to Be There" .... *Dorothy [Genevieve Tobin] and Boys*
"A Mormon Life" .... *Bloxom [Walter Catlett] and Girls*
"Dancing Time" .... *Dorothy, Laddie and Ensemble*

Scene Two

"To the Fair" .... *Ensemble*
"My Houseboat on the Harlem" ... *Bloxom and Sukie [Kathlene*
Martyn]

Scene Three

Opening Chorus .... *Ensemble*
Dance .... *Mr. [Ritchy] Craig*
"All Lanes Must Reach a Turning" .... *Dorothy and Laddie*
Finale .... *Ensemble*

ACT II
Scene One

Opening Chorus .... *Ensemble*
"Seven Days" .... *Dorothy and Laddie*
"If You Think It's Love You're Right" .. *Bloxom, Sukie, Oliver,*
Gladys [Helen Carrington] and Ensemble
"Weeping Willow Tree" .... *Laddie and Ensemble*

Scene Two

Scene .... *Dorothy and Laddie*

Waltz .... *Ensemble*
Dance .... *Miss [Lovey] Lee*
Finale .... *Company*

The production was staged by David Burton, who had replaced Clifford Brooke during the Philadelphia tryout. David Bennett devised the choreography. The orchestra leader, Gus Salzer, was also a replacement, in this instance for Max Bendix. *Dear Sir's* highly praised orchestrations were by Allan Foster. Kiviette and James Reynolds joined ranks to design the costumes.

Only minor cast changes occurred during the Philadelphia tryout, but the musical changes, while unexceptional in number, are interesting. Three songs were cut. Miss Tobin and Mr. Catlett's duet early in Act I, "There's Lots Of Room For You," was dropped, as was "Follow Handy Andy," in the middle of the first scene of the second act, when its performers were assigned "If You Think It's Love You're Right." This number had been moved up from its place just before the final curtain. Also discarded was the song so many critics had singled out, "Gypsy Caravan." Nothing filled its place. Only two songs were added, both at the end of the first scene of the first act. The first was "A Mormon Life" (in which Dietz impudently rhymed "bigamy," "polygamy," and "make a pig 'o me"). Curiously, Dietz's working papers reveal that a version of this song, under the title "I'll Lead You A Merry Song And Dance," had been slotted for this spot from the beginning. But for some reason it was not used until well into the Philadelphia run. The concerted finale to this scene, reusing parts of "Gypsy Caravan," gave way to "Dancing Time," which failed to repeat the success it had enjoyed in *The Cabaret Girl.*

Given the history of New York's cool reception to plays the road had embraced, no one was probably too taken aback when Broadway's critics greeted *Dear Sir* with considerable restraint. For the most part the reviews were favorable. New York critics continued their tolerant acceptance of all but the most obviously inept musicals until the end of the 1920s. Several critics suggested the show fell squarely into the Princess Theatre tradition, with the *Times* adding, "Dietz is a most capable substitute for P. G. Wodehouse as lyricist in chief to Mr. Kern." And although the same critic found Kern's music "beautiful," he passed over it with that single adjective, much as the majority of his fellow critics did. Virtually no critic gave Kern more space, nor called attention to any particular song. As far as the performances and the show itself were concerned, expressions such as "graceful and polite," "courteous and prim," and "restrained charm" were sprinkled throughout the notices. They were not the sort of words calculated to send tired businessmen rushing to their ticket brokers.

Yet Kern's music (as well as Dietz's better lyrics) deserved more. Although Kern's score may have invited failure, he did not merit such thoughtless dismissal. In some ways, *Dear Sir*'s score was Kern's most audacious up to this time, now and again bravely breaking away from easily accessible patterns and presenting audiences with departures obviously too studied and involved to be immediately retained—or, for that matter, to be grasped —after just two or three hearings. It was, in effect, a breakthrough score, signaling the style Kern would employ from *Show Boat* onward. Kern's feeling about the music was revealed in a dramatic moment that Goodman's publicist, Marian Spitzer Thompson, could still recall vividly more than half a century after the event. Frustrated by Bendix's inability to properly phrase the longer musical lines Kern was employing, the composer stood on the street outside the theatre helplessly reduced to tears. He finally demanded that Goodman replace Bendix with a conductor capable of handling the more difficult, progressive material. Gus Salzer was rushed in.

"Weeping Willow Tree" has a range of just short of two octaves, leaving one to wonder if limited singers could handle it as written. Eighty-five bars long, with no verse, it displays a curiously extended form. A principal theme, languid and falling, is varied, repeated, then varied again, to the point where it barely seems a variation, and is finally returned one last time. It could be considered AAA^1AAA^2AA or, with equal justification, AABAACAA. "I Want To Be There," a simple love song in its lyrics, has a verse in waltz time that jumps startlingly from D flat and C major and back again. Its seventy-five-bar chorus has a main theme in 4/4 time and a bridge in 2/4 time. The last note is sustained for nine beats, with the final quarter note appearing at the beginning of a bar. Even a trite ditty such as "If You Think It's Love You're Right" does not escape without a few uncommon harmonies. By the time the show reached New York, the hit of the evening was clearly intended to be "All Lanes Must Reach A Turning" —the last major song, according to Dietz's work papers, written for the show. Since it contains a leap of just under an octave, it too may have presented difficulties. The melody foreshadows the more supple, arioso line that Kern would soon begin to employ regularly. Yet, curiously, it was almost certainly developed out of a single passage from the Society March theme in *Gloria's Romance*. Too good a song to waste, it would be reused by Kern as the title song for his next London work, *Blue Eyes*. But by that time, with *Show Boat* behind him, it would fit comfortably into his new style of writing. One glaring false note in the score was "Gypsy Caravan," with a pseudo-romanticism not unlike the Tin Pan Alley Orientalia the great spectacle revues so loved. The decision to drop it despite Philadelphia's praise was enlightened. For the most part, however, Kern seemed to be almost defiantly testing the limits of a 1924 audience with his *Dear Sir* score. He should have understood it was a score incongruously juxtaposed against a trite, if highly aimed, libretto.

The polite reviews had immediate and disastrous consequences at the box office. While Goodman had apparently been willing to take an initial risk with something a bit out of the commonplace, he was not prepared to throw good money after bad. Sensing there was no way to save *Dear Sir,* he closed the show abruptly at the end of its second week. An attempt by the Selwyns to take over the show came to naught. Goodman, who had sunk his own money in the show, hurriedly sailed with his family for Europe, leaving a pile of unpaid bills behind. Kern's reaction is unrecorded, but Goodman's daughter recalls that a perceptible coolness remained between Kern and her father for many years.

Kern's obviously conscious attempt to introduce a new artistry to popular song may not have been merely a response to inner, aesthetic urgings. Good businessman and realist that he was, he probably comprehended external forces working a change on the theatre as a whole, and foresaw the direction those changes would take. While films had been altering the complexion of the legitimate stage for nearly two decades, a more recent technological development was compounding the theatre's problems and luring away more and more potential patrons. Sales of radios had grown so large that Sol Bloom, a New York Congressional Representative and a man with a deep interest in the theatre, predicted in September that "radio will kill off theatres in towns of 75,000 or less within 5 years." He added that the number of playhouses in New York itself would probably shrink as well. Of course, although it was no inexpensive toy, radio, like films, first of all drew away the less monied classes. This left the richer generally better educated elements of society as a theatregoing elite. The demands of a so much more knowledgeable group would not be the same as the mass of older theatregoers. By once again being in the vanguard of more sophisticated musical tastes, Kern would be assured of retaining his position in the musical theatre of his day.

Curiously, his last offerings for 1924 went against the trend, but with good reason. Dillingham had lured Marilyn Miller away from Ziegfeld and on November 6 presented her in a revival of James M. Barrie's *Peter Pan* at the Knickerbocker. Kern was asked to provide a pair of melodies. To match the innocent, slightly old-fashioned tone of the piece, Kern resurrected two of his old songs, "Won't You Have A Little Feather" (lyric, Paul West) and "The Sweetest Thing In Life" (lyric, De Sylva). The latter melody had been used both as "When Three Is Company" in *The Doll Girl* and "Just Because You're You" in the *Ziegfeld Follies of 1917*.

If, as *Dear Sir* had demonstrated, Kern was eager to reexpand the boundaries of popular theatre music, his ambitions nonetheless had sensible limits. On November 18 the *Times* disclosed that Otto Kahn, chairman of the Metropolitan Opera, had made overtures to Kern, Irving Berlin, and George Gershwin, hoping to persuade one or more of the composers to provide the company with a thoroughly contemporary "jazz" opera. As Kahn described it, the work would have to be "a grand opera, not of the old sentimental type, but some modern American type—[featuring] the shop girl, stenographer, bobbed-hair flapper or the like—after the manner of Parisian life shown in Charpentier's 'Louise.'" The article revealed that Kahn had solicited Kern's aid first; indeed, he had written him six years before while the Princess shows were the talk of the town. Nothing had come of the discussions, so Kahn had let the matter rest. But now, with new American musical styles not only coming to the fore, but enjoying a vogue across the western world, Kahn felt the moment especially propitious for a serious plunge. He met with respectful regrets. Berlin informed him he would "give his right arm" to compose a syncopated opera suitable for the Met, but realized he lacked the technical equipment. Professionals who recalled Berlin's pronouncements a decade earlier when *Watch Your Step!* premiered probably recognized in the term "syncopated opera" a steadfast allegiance to the ragtime opera Berlin had spoken about in 1914. Kern was equally honest in grasping and admitting his limitations. He acknowledged that he could not seriously consider writing one at the moment, but added that "he believed an American opera on the popular sort of music a possibility, and would champion such an enterprise, no matter whether he or someone else should compose it." The article hinted, and time proved it correct, that Gershwin was the most likely candidate to write this great American opera—although when the time came for him to do it, the Met was not prepared to mount it.

15

A Circus Queen,
a City Chap,
and Christopher Cross

The exciting offer extended by the Met and even Kern's venturesome compositions for *Dear Sir* opened bright possibilities for the new year. But the glittering, hopeful lights were quickly dimmed. As a result early 1925 repeated the pattern of the preceding several years. The winter, spring, and early summer were spent at Bronxville, working on the fall's new musicals. Once again the Kerns may have spent some while in England, although the papers make no special mention of their sailing.

Both 1925 offerings were to be mounted by Dillingham. One was a musicalization of *The Fortune Hunter*, Winchell Smith's 1909 comedy that had helped make a star of John Barrymore. Smith had been co-adaptor of *Brewster's Millions*, the source of *Zip Goes a Million*. But no one took that as an ill omen. Plump, cheery Anne Caldwell was once again to serve as Jerry's lyricist and librettist.

The second musical was to be totally original. More importantly, it introduced two new figures into Jerry's Bronxville study. One was an owlish-looking man, twelve years Jerry's senior, Otto Harbach. Harbach had come to the theatre several years after Kern, and then only when failing eyesight forced him to abandon the scholarly and journalistic pursuits he had preferred. But whereas Jerry had waited eleven years for an outstanding success, Harbach's very first effort, his lyrics for *Three Twins*, brought him fame and money. Harbach took with him to Bronxville a tall, handsome, if pock-faced, youthful-looking man, ten years Jerry's junior. Oscar Hammerstein II was the scion of a celebrated theatrical family. His grandfather, the first Oscar, had been a flamboyant impresario and had on several occasions turned his hand to writing musicals. The younger Oscar's father and uncle were both active theatrical managers. Harbach had taken him under his wing five years before and had guided him through his apprenticeship. In the fall of 1924 they had been collaborators with Rudolf Friml in one of the greatest of all Broadway triumphs, *Rose-Marie*.

From the beginning the authors knew they were writing a vehicle for Marilyn Miller, who had fought with and left Ziegfeld after he had made her a star in *Sally*. When Dillingham's mounting of *Peter Pan* fizzled embarrassingly at the box office, the producer realized he had to find a suitable hit for his new star or relinquish her to his rival. Kern and Harbach had suggested a circus motif, with elaborate sets, real animals, and a story that would find excuses for moving the action into other spectacular situations—an ocean liner, a ballroom, a fox hunt. Accepting the outline, Dillingham told them to go full speed ahead.

So complex and cumbersome a production created myriad problems, forcing Dillingham at the eleventh hour to set *Sunny*'s Philadelphia premiere at the Forrest back from Monday to Wednesday, September 9. Even then the *Evening Bulletin* found "the need of further rehearsals still in evidence." Performers were jittery, lines were flubbed, and, perhaps most embarrassing of all, at one point the first act had to be halted completely for an unwieldy scene change. Making allowances for opening night difficulties, critics still could discover little to celebrate. Only the *Inquirer*'s man liked everything he saw. Comparing the show to earlier Kern musicals such as *Good Morning, Dearie*, and *The Night Boat*, the *Ledger*'s critic found the entertainment "pretty puny." The *Evening Bulletin* rued the "labored" book, "struggling for humor that does not materialize." Even Miss Miller was not immune from critical reproach. To a man, critics praised her beauty and delicate dancing, but the *Evening Bulletin* spoke for more than one disgruntled patron when it saw her as "showing little ability as an actress, speaking her lines rather amateurishly." The *Ledger* noted that Jack Donahue won "the evening's biggest reception" and ended its review, "But, Oh, Mr. Donahue, don't get sick or decide to retire! 'Sunny' needs you very badly." When it came to Kern's score, Philadelphia's critics were divided, although they generally moved into Kern's corner. If the otherwise complacent *In-*

quirer passed over the songs with the bloodless adjective "good," the *Evening Bulletin* offered one of its few cheering judgments, remarking, "Mr. Kern has written a very melodious score that greatly enhances the piece." The *Ledger* discussed the music at slightly greater length, concluding somewhat startlingly, "Jerome Kern's score bore out the promise found in 'Dear Sir,' a promise of semigrand opera of far less melody and far more of the discordance of the modern school . . . but there seemed not to be a single catchy number or even haunting piece of melody throughout." None of Philadelphia's major critics took special note of "Who?," "Sunny," or any of the other songs from the show.

The critics, of course, were unaware that *Sunny* had gone into rehearsal without a second act. But the slight storyline apparently needed all the help Dillingham and his crew could muster. Sunny Peters is a bareback rider in an English circus. She falls in love with a young American, Tom Warren, whom she had known briefly when they were children. Intending to see him off when he returns to the United States, she discovers she has missed the last call and has become an inadvertent stowaway. Aboard ship she is forced to marry Tom's friend, Jim Deming, but ultimately arranges a divorce and weds Tom. George Olsen and his popular band played on stage. There were forty chorus girls and twenty-eight chorus boys.

Less than two weeks after its Philadelphia premiere, *Sunny* opened at the New Amsterdam on September 22, 1925, to draw to a close the most remarkable seven nights in the history of the American musical theatre. The biggest musical comedy hit of the 1920s, Vincent Youmans's *No, No! Nanette!* had opened on September 16, Rodgers and Hart's *Dearest Enemy* followed two nights later, while the night before *Sunny*'s premiere Rudolf Friml's magnificent swashbuckler, *The Vagabond King*, began its long run.

Sunny's opening night musical program at the New Amsterdam read:

Sunny

ACT I

1a. Opening .... *Ensemble*
  b. Marilyn Miller Cocktails
2. "Sunny" .... *Tom [Paul Frawley] and Boys*
3. "Who?" .... *Sunny [Marilyn Miller] and Tom*
4. "So's Your Old Man" .... *Harold [Clifton Webb] and the*
                                       Marilyn Miller Cocktails

5. "Let's Say Good Night Till It's Morning" ...... *Jim [Jack Donahue] and Weenie [Mary Hay]*
6. "Do You Love Me?" .... *Sunny*
7. Dance .... *Jim*
8. "The Wedding Knell" .... *Sunny and Boys*
9. "Two Little Blue Birds" .... *Harold and Weenie*
10. Finale

INTERMISSION
George Olsen and his Orchestra

ACT II

1. Opening .... *Ensemble*
2. "When We Get Our Divorce" .... *Sunny and Jim*
3a. "Sunshine" .... *Elsa Peterson*
  b. Dance .... *Linda*
4. Reprise, "Who?" .... *Sunny and Tom*
  Dance .... *Sunny, Jim, Harold and Weenie*
  Dance .... *Ensemble*
5. "Ukelele Ike" .... *Cliff Edwards*
6. The Chase
7. "Strolling, Or What Have You?" .... *Harold and Weenie*
8. "Magnolia in the Woods" .... *Magnolia [Pert Kelton]*
9. The Hunt Dance .... *Sunny*
10. Finale .... *Sunny and Entire Company*

Gus Salzer was musical director and Robert Russell Bennett, orchestrator. The production was staged by Hassard Short, while three men shared choreographic chores: John Tiller for the Cocktails' dances, Fred Astaire for Miss Miller's numbers, and Julian Mitchell for the remaining routines. (For Mitchell, as for co-star Joseph Cawthorn, *Sunny* represented the last show in a long, distinguished career.) James Reynolds designed the sets and costumes.

A week and a half of arduous revising and replaying in Philadelphia had clearly worked wonders for *Sunny*. Although the *Times*'s unnamed critic insisted that Donahue was still responsible for "most of the merriment," and Robert Coleman in the *Mirror* went so far as to proclaim Donahue "the hit of the show," most critics singled out Miss Miller. Not content with extolling her golden beauty and her light-as-air dancing, they also praised her acting and singing. Kind words saluted all the supporting performers. Dillingham's taste and largess received prominent attention. E. W. Osborn of the *Evening World* carped that "the things which caught last night's ready laughter might not be so funny served cold to-day," but even he fell in line with his colleagues who discovered no glaring inadequacies in the libretto. Kern's score was highly praised. Percy Hammond of the *Herald Tribune* dubbed it "aristocratic." Osborn wrote, "'Sunny' proceeded to music by Jerome Kern, most of which was joyous, all of which was melodious, and some of which was exquisite." Three songs—"Who?," "Sunny," and "Do You Love Me?"—were singled out by critic after critic. In the *Daily News*, Burns Mantle summed up many firstnighters' reactions by exclaiming that the show was better than *Sally*.

A comparison of Philadelphia and New York programs hints at what hectic rewriting had occurred. Six of the original twelve numbers from the first act were dropped. Miss Miller lost her first two songs, "Dream A Little Dream" and "To Think He Remembered Me." The reprises initially slated for "Dream A Little Dream" (published as "Dream A Dream") imply high hopes were held for it. "Heaven's Gift To The Girls," done by Webb and the Cocktails, disappeared, although it may simply have been retitled more modishly "So's Your Old Man." The latter's lyric, after all, begins: "I'm Heaven's gift to the girls." Weenie and Tom's "Under The Sky" was cut. Poor Joseph Cawthorn was deprived of his only comic number, "Tonsils." Late in the act Sunny, Tom, and Jim had a trio called "It Won't Mean A Thing." It, too, got the axe, although it was restored for the London version. With three of the six numbers originally assigned to the star, the suspicion remains that the cuts may have been prompted as much to protect Miss Miller's limited voice as for any other reason. The only number to disappear from the second act was Harold and Weenie's "Two Total Losses." But this seems to have resurfaced as "Two Little Bluebirds."

Kern's score was, indeed, superb. "Who?" and, to a slightly lesser extent, the title song remain high in his canon of classics. Both, as Alec Wilder notes, retain "the same direct, driving quality of *Whose Baby Are You?*." "Who?" is deceptively simple. Beginning on a sixth interval that is sustained for a remarkable two and a half measures, it moves forward with a series of totally unconventional skips. Sigmund Spaeth has remarked on the similarity of the last half of the chorus to "The Siren's Song." Kern himself often credited Hammerstein's choice of the word "who" for the repeated sustained note with catching the public's fancy and making the song the enduring success it has become. Any other word seems to drag down the held note. "Sunny" was less daringly inventive, but equally catchy. Like "Who?" it benefited from congenial lyrics, most likely Hammerstein's. The rhyming of "Tom Boy" with "Where'd you get your smile from, boy?" reflects the sunlit glee of the melody and the title.

Time has been less kind to "Do You Love Me?" (published as "D'ye Love Me?"). A small, gently rocking tune of almost lullaby sweetness, with a second melodic part reflecting the principal theme in its answer, the song was sung in the show both as a waltz and as a fox-trot. "Sunshine," an unappreciated Kern gem, has a curiously persistent beat that suggests it would work well even with modern rock and roll. Kern himself must have thought fondly of it. The melody for the chorus was the same one he had used twelve years earlier for "I Can't Forget Your Eyes" in *Oh, I Say!*. A year later, with *Sunny* still going strong, he would employ it a third time in *Criss Cross*. Passages in "The Wedding Knell" have a distinctly Middle-European sound, suggesting Kern may have once again returned to his Bohemian roots. The gay lilts of "Let's Say Good Night Till It's Morning," "Two Little Bluebirds" and the somewhat giddier 3/4 tempo of "When We Get Our Divorce" provided capital dance numbers and might have enjoyed a more general vogue had their lyrics been less specialized.

Notice must be taken of "Dream A Dream." If Kern really expected the song to be *Sunny*'s hit, he was indeed brave, for the song presented several difficulties. For one, a countermelody in the chorus made two singers necessary to fully realize Kern's intention. Second, the chromatics Kern employed were anything but typical of the period, reflecting instead the moodier harmonies that would not be fully voguish until the 1930s. Yet Kern had time and again led the way musically, sometimes to great success as with "They Didn't Believe Me," sometimes to marked disappointment as with "And I Am All Alone." Significantly, when the song's harmonies would have been more readily understood several years later, Kern made no attempt to revive it in the way he did so many other melodies. Once again, Kern's judgment was sound. Apart from its daring strides for 1925, "Dream A Dream" was not one of his demandingly melodic inventions.

Despite impressive competition, *Sunny* quickly became the town's hottest ticket. Its run of 515 performances fell slightly short of *Sally*'s, but a $5.00 top compared with the earlier show's $3.50 allowed it to gross over $2.4 million during its Broadway stay alone. Even a subway strike and ten days of record-breaking summer heat failed significantly to dent grosses, which averaged $43,000 a week. Miss Miller embarked on an extended tour, and when she and her original fellow players left, *Sunny* still held the boards in less glittering productions well into 1928.

Sunny had barely left Philadelphia when *The City Chap* arrived at the Garrick on September 28. The story Philadelphians watched unfold was much the same as one Barrymore had played out sixteen years earlier. Nat Duncan, a big-city cut-up, accepts a dare to spend six months on good behavior in a small town. If he succeeds his reward will be the village heiress. Nat grabs a train to a backwater whistlestop called Radford and hires himself out at Graham's Drug Store. Although he manages to behave himself—just barely—and court Josie, the local banker's daughter, in the end he succumbs to the small-town charms of his employer's daughter, Betty Graham.

So solid was Smith's old play it seemed to defy musicalization. One Philadelphia critic insisted the musical had retained "too much plot," while *Variety's* man reported, "As far as story interest is concerned there is an embarrassment of riches, the problem being how to eliminate enough to allow the songs and dances to be interpolated." One reason critics begged for more songs was they liked the ones they heard. Several reviewers judged Kern's score "greatly superior" to *Sunny's*. "When I Fell In Love With You" elicited the largest number of favorable comments, with "Why?" (in the style of *Sunny's* "Who?") and "June Bells" (a rewriting of *The Beauty Prize's* "Joy Bells") not far behind in critical esteem. Curiously, in the frantic reshufflings to follow, all but "When I Fell In Love With You" were gone by the time *The City Chap* reached 42nd Street, and even this ballad, after failing to receive special attention from Broadway's critics, was dropped during the New York run. Critics and playgoers alike relished the humor of "Skeet" Gallagher, "one of the few good-looking young men on the stage who is willing to be first, last and always, a comedian." The critic who so summed up the star—he was *Variety's* man again—went on to note that Gallagher could not sing, adding ruefully that it seemed "a shame" since he had been awarded "three or four corking numbers." However, at least in Philadelphia, Gallagher did not steal the show; rather, "the hit that bowled over the audience completely was that of George Raft . . . the fastest stepping Charlestonian who has been on a local stage." By the time the show reached New York, Raft's routine had been so shortened that critics either ignored him or complained he was not given enough to do.

Plainly a number of clashes were besetting *The City Chap*—clashes of priorities, of style, and of egos. Dillingham sensed this. His answer was to cancel the penciled-in third week in Philadelphia and spend the time in extensive rewriting and rehearsal. Yet even when the show reopened for a week in Brooklyn, followed by a week in Newark, the problems remained despite generally welcoming notices. Reshuffling and rewriting went on.

Hindsight allows us to see the problem in a way Dillingham and his associates were denied. Curiously, Kern's work for this show suggests he did, indeed, understand the situation, but chose either not to make his thoughts known or else was unable to convince others. It had been only a year or so since the jazz craze, slowly budding since the end of World War I, had exploded full force on the American consciousness, and, more urgently, in the American musical theatre. The metallic, citified sounds of the new idiom were alien to Kern and to the bucolic setting and story. Furthermore, jazz-age Broadway, while beginning to rebel against over-elaborate productions of the Ziegfeld school, nonetheless at heart still felt cheated without its tinsel and glitter. The simple rustic sets and costumes of *The City Chap* went out of vogue with the Cinderella plots that had dominated Broadway in the early 1920s. Kern clearly opted for stylistic and tonal integrity, as one Philadelphia critic noted with satisfaction when he reported: "Jerome Kern reverts to his more rhythmic and less pretentious style of 'Oh, Boy!.' "

Dillingham almost certainly disagreed with Kern, seeing rewards in precisely the opposite direction. During the one-week hiatus, Dillingham had a gaudy, sumptuous ballroom set built to replace the relatively plain ballroom set used in Philadelphia. To make assurances doubly sure, when the production moved across the river to the Liberty, Dillingham had George Olsen and his band as well as the ballroom dancers, Marjorie Moss and Georges Fontana, dash over from *Sunny* down the street at the New Amsterdam to enliven the last scene. (They left shortly after the premiere.)

The program for October 26, 1925, the opening night at the Liberty, listed the musical numbers:

The City Chap

ACT I

1. Chorus, "Like the Nymphs of Spring" .... *Grace [Irene Dunne*] and Girls*
2. Song, "The Go-Getter" ..... *Steve [John Rutherford], Grace and Girls*
3. Song, "Journey's End" .... *Nat [Richard "Skeet" Gallagher]*

* Who still at this date spelled her last name "Dunn."

4. Finaletto .... *Ensemble*
5. Duetino, "Sympathetic Someone" .. *Betty [Phyllis Cleveland]*
and Nat
6. Quartette, "The City Chap" ...... *Pete [Robert O'Connor],*
Watty [Eddie Girard], Roland [Hansford Wilson]
and Josie [Ina Williams]
7. Song, "He Is the Type" .... *Josie, Betty and Girls*
8. Quartette, "Journey's End" ..... *Nat, Betty, Josie and Angie*
[Mary Jane]
9. Trio, "If You Are as Good as You Look" .... *Nat, Josie*
and Angie
10. Finaletto .... *Watty, Pete, Betty [Betty Compton], Roland*
and Ensemble

ACT II

1. Chorus, "The Fountain of Youth" .... *Lucy Monroe*, Miss*
Sperry [Helyn Eby Rock], Angie, Danzi Goodell* and
Mound City Blue Blowers [a comb band]
2. Duo, "A Pill a Day" .... *Roland and Josie*
3. Song, "Walking Home With Josie" ...... *Nat, Josie, Tracy*
[Francis X. Donegan], Watty, Pete, Betty, Pearl and Boys
and Girls
4. Chorus, "Bubbles of Bliss" .... *Ensemble, Dances by Angie,*
Roland and George Spelvin [George Raft]
5. Song, "No One Knows" .... *Betty, Steve, Nat and Grace*
6. Dances by Marjorie Moss and Georges Fontana with George
Olsen and His Band
7. Quartet, "When I Fell In Love" ...... *Steve, Betty, Nat and*
Grace, and Dance by Roland
8. Finale .... *Ensemble*

*Not assigned a character.

R. H. Burnside directed. Victor Baravalle led the pit orchestra. Robert Russell Bennett devised the orchestrations. David Bennett was choreographer; James Reynolds, set designer.

Suspecting that the show would not be seen as fully or successfully integrated and would be considered a bit old-fashioned to boot, Dillingham had the program call *The City Chap* "a comedy of country life with musical numbers." By and large, New York's critics were pleased with the results, but not overwhelmed. They viewed the musical as pleasant, unimportant entertainment, and centered their notices on Gallagher. When they finally turned their attention to the music most were content simply to note that Kern had composed it (although the *Times* questioned whether Kern had written George Olsen's material). Unlike their Philadelphia colleagues, none was willing to see the score as superior to *Sunny*'s.

The short shrift the critics gave Kern is understandable, but regrettable. No doubt an inescapable sense of *déjà entendu* pervades Kern's songs for *The City Chap,* as if the small-town, bucolic story had sent the composer scurrying back to his trunk to unearth his songs from a simpler day. "No One Knows" was a melodic two-step that could have felt at home in any of the Princess Theatre shows. It presented distinct echoes of "Morning Glory" from 1922's *The Bunch and Judy.* "Walking Home With Josie," a sweet song with a gentle swing, properly evoked country lanes. Of course, if any of the critics had visited London three years before they could have heard "Journey's End" sung in *The Cabaret Girl.* Perhaps the most "up-to-date" of Kern's major songs for the show was "Sympathetic Someone," with its blues-like chording.

Knowing that critics were lenient, the public made up its own mind. It decided it had better things to do, so Dillingham withdrew the show after nine weeks.

With *The City Chap* a sorry failure and *Sunny* a rousing hit, Kern could settle back into a customary winter and spring routine. Only one new show was on his 1926 fall schedule, although *Sunny* was slated for a major London production. At Dillingham's request, Harbach and Miss Caldwell joined forces to design a new vehicle for Fred Stone and his daughter Dorothy. The pair began to make regular trips to Cedar Knolls to work with Jerry. The collaboration would be Miss Caldwell's seventh and final one with Jerry. Thereafter all of Kern's Broadway shows would be written either with Harbach or Hammerstein.

Because rehearsals for both the new show, *Criss Cross,* and *Sunny* coincided, Kern elected to supervise the American piece. Yet he may have made a brief trip in the spring or early summer to England, a trip again unnoticed by the press. In any case, when *Sunny* did open to critical acclaim in London, it contained one song not in the original New York production. "I've Looked For Trouble" was a jazzy restatement of "Bought And Paid For" from *The Laughing Husband.* With another lyric the same revised melody would become one of the hits of *Criss Cross.*

In company with Dillingham, Max Dreyfus's brother, Louis, and Louis's wife, the former prima donna Valli Valli, Kern checked into New Haven's Taft Hotel on Sunday, September 19. Monday and early Tuesday were given over to runthroughs next door at the Shubert Theatre.

The plot was characteristic Fred Stone never-land nonsense. After an extraneous prologue that managed to bring in villains and heroes of older Stone musicals, the story told how a clownish aviator, Christopher Cross, acrobatically rescues Dolly Day from the snares of the evil Ilphrahim Benani and restores her to her true love, Captain Carleton.

From the start *Criss Cross* was rarely perceived as a Kern show. Stone dominated any of his vehicles with his homey clowning and lively acrobatics. The new musical was no exception. Only in Philadelphia was Stone briefly shunted to second place. There the play opened a magnificent new legitimate theatre, the Erlanger, so most critics devoted a paragraph or two to extolling the house before turning their attention to Stone's antics. But once they came to Stone, they stayed with him. Kern and his associates hardly ever received more than a perfunctory mention. And those who did linger on Kern's contribution were generally none too happy. Arthur Waters was typical. Waters had been one of the few critics alert to Kern's attempt to create an enlarged musical idiom in *Dear Sir*. But on hearing Kern's music for *Criss Cross*, he wrote dejectedly in the *Public Ledger*: "Jerome Kern's score is only so-so. 'In Araby With You' and 'Rose of Delight,' neither sung by the 'leads' of the show, seemed most melodious, and there were a number of lively dance steps. There is no use talking, Mr. Kern is not tuneful as he used to be in the days of 'Sally' and 'Good Morning, Dearie.'"

With Stone the be-all and end-all of the evening, such criticism mattered little. *Criss Cross* was able to open on schedule on October 12, 1926, at the Globe with the following musical program:

Criss Cross

PROLOGUE

1. Opening

   a. "Indignation Meeting"
   b. "Hydrophobia Blues"

   { Misses [Carolyn] Nolte, Scott, Monroe, Caryll, [Marietta] Sullivan, and Messrs. Ragland, Lambert, Herman, Shannon, [Willie] Torpey, with Ensemble }

2. "Cinderella Girl" .... *Dolly [Dorothy Stone], with Sunshine*
Girls and Ensemble
3. "Cinderella's Ride .... *Dolly*
4. "She's on Her Way" ... *Messrs. Shannon, Thomson, Lambert*
and Truscott, with Girls

ACT I

1. "Flap-a-Doodle" ...... *Christopher [Fred Stone], with Misses*
Meakins, Eaton, Donahue, Franck, Goodell, Bate,
Leet, and Breslau
2. Dance of the Sunshine Girls
3. Opening of School Scene, "Leaders of the Modern Regime"
Renee [Primrose Caryll], Fifi [Beth Meakins] and Girls
4. "You Will—Won't You?" .... *Dolly, Capt. Carleton [Roy*
Hoyer] and Girls
5. "In Araby With You" .. *Yasmini [Dorothy Francis], with Girls*
6. Travelogue .... *Christopher, Dolly, Sunshine Girls and*
Soldier [Charles Baum]
7. Finale

ACT II

1. Opening
   a. "Dear Algerian Land" ⎱
   b. "Dreaming of Allah" ⎰ *Dorothy Francis, with Ensemble*
2. "The Dancers of the Cafe Kaboul"
   a. Dance of "The Rose of Delight" .... *Dolly and*
   Capt. Carleton
   b. Dance of "The Golden Sprite" .. *Christopher and Curé*
   [George Herman]
   c. Dance of the Camel Boys .... *Sunshine Girls*
3. Trio, "Rose of Delight" .... *Yasmini, Ilphrahim [Oscar*
   Ragland] and Prof. Mazeroux [John Lambert]
4. "I Love My Little Susie" ... *Christopher, with Susie, a camel*
   [Joseph Shrode and Thomas Bell]
5. "The Ali Baba Babies" .. *Curé, with Goldie Digger [Dorothy*
   Bate] and Girls
6. Dance of "The Four Leaf Clovers" .... *Sunshine Girls*
7. The "Portrait Parade" ...... *Christopher, Dolly, Countess de*
   Pavazac [Allene Stone], Yasmini, Capt. Carleton, with
   Carolyn Nolte, Lydia Scott, Phyllis Pearce, Lucy Monroe,
   Kathryn Burnside, Cynthia Foley, and Marietta Sullivan

272

Al Newman conducted Maurice De Packh and Robert Russell Bennett's orchestrations. R. H. Burnside staged the production, while David Bennett provided those dances not devised by Mary Read for the Sunshine Girls. James Reynolds created the sets.

Like their out-of-town colleagues, New York's critics reserved most of their space and most of the kudos for Fred Stone and, to a lesser extent, Dorothy Stone. But several let their pleasure with Kern's work be known. Kern's old rooter, Alan Dale, after confessing in the *American* that nobody but Stone really mattered, relented enough to suggest that "Jerome Kern mattered a bit, of course. His music was pleasant and one air, 'In Araby With You,' recalled other days to those with hideous memories like myself." Dale's somewhat cryptic remark, besides suggesting Kern was on the decline, seems to reveal he alone recognized the provenance of the song. Writing in the *World,* another Kern friend, Alexander Woollcott, extolled Kern's "running stream of sweet music." But hours before, Woollcott had played a brief, monumental role in Kern's life.

Three songs were cut between New Haven and New York, all from the first act: a title song, sung by the chorus; Miss Stone and Hoyer's "Bread And Butter"; and Miss Francis's "Kiss A Four Leaf Clover." "You Will—Won't You?" was brought forward from the second act for Miss Stone and her leading man, while Miss Francis (as the Arabian, Yasmini) was given the only added number, "In Araby With You," as a replacement.

Despite the critical approval awarded "Cinderella Girl" and despite Kern's plugging it on the back of much of Harms's sheet music, the public quickly expressed preferences for "You Will—Won't You?" and "In Araby With You," although neither became a Kern standard. Nonetheless, the popular choice no doubt underscored a problem for the composer, since both of these songs were older melodies rehashed. "You Will—Won't You?" was the same revised "Bought And Paid For" that was then being sung at London's Palace in *Sunny* as "I've Looked For Trouble," while "In Araby With You" had first been heard as "I Can't Forget Your Eyes" in *Oh, I Say!* and was currently being offered as "Sunshine" in *Sunny* on both sides of the Atlantic. Both were, in fact, superior tunes that Kern obviously hoped to find a successful home for. He was never to do so. "Cinderella Girl" was an uneven ballad, offering hints of the broader, more flowing musical line Kern was beginning to employ. The cut "Kiss

A Four Leaf Clover" was a more ingratiating ballad, but apparently failed to work on stage. "Bread And Butter," also cut, was a rhythm number, probably best suited for a loudly tapping chorus. "Susie" was a vapid ditty whose verse contains some distinctly Gaelic references. Since the song's lyric addresses a camel (played in the show by two men), the melody was probably brought over from an earlier, unidentifiable work. After the post-Broadway tour was under way Kern published "That Little Something" as part of *Criss Cross's* score. As we shall see, it was salvaged from Kern's next show. But no obtainable program shows it was actually sung in *Criss Cross*.

Although *Criss Cross* was admittedly one of Kern's weakest efforts, his failure to come up with a superior score hardly hurt the musical. Legions of Fred Stone fans saw to that. *Criss Cross* played 206 performances in New York, then toured successfully until mid-1928.

16

Show Boat

If *Criss Cross* was of little moment in Kern's development as an artist, a meeting at intermission on opening night was one of the most momentous of his career. Kern had been reading a novel that struck his fancy, and learning that Alexander Woollcott was a friend of the author, asked the critic to arrange an introduction. Kern was anxious to secure rights to the book. At intermission Kern spotted the critic, who had just wandered away from a tiny lady he was accompanying. He reminded Woollcott of his promise to secure a meeting with the novelist. Woollcott coyly replied he thought he could do it if he played his cards right. Kern thanked him and was about to walk away when Woollcott bellowed across the lobby to the lady he had just left: "Ferber. Hi, Ferber. Come on over here a minute." He then introduced the novelist and the composer. And a musical version of *Show Boat* was under way.

How quickly Jerry went to work on *Show Boat* soon became evident in the flood of news releases. Yet even before these came pouring out, Jerry had been busy. Only after he won over Ferber and obtained her formal permission did the novelist learn that Jerry and Oscar Hammerstein were already busy on the musical. Hammerstein recalled a phone call from an excited Jerry. Jerry advised him he was halfway through the book and determined to make a musical out of it. He urged Hammerstein to rush to buy a copy. Jerry's arguments in *Show Boat*'s favor began with its title—"a million dollar title," as Kern saw it. Of course the richly romantic plot played out against such colorful backgrounds remained the principal impetus. Hammerstein and Kern agreed to make independent outlines for a stage version and then compare their sketches. As Hammerstein remembered, he and Jerry were amazed and pleased to discover they had developed virtually identical plans. Both these plans put slightly too much emphasis on the last half of the story, but that was quickly realized and amended.

Attending a performance of an intimate revue called *Americana*, Jerry was smitten by Helen Morgan's sitting atop a piano and mournfully singing "Nobody Wants Me." Jerry knew he had found a Julie. A small problem developed when Oscar's uncle, Arthur, felt he was entitled to produce the show. However, from the start the authors seemed to prefer Florenz Ziegfeld. Given Ziegfeld's frequently demonstrated contempt for texts and writers as well as his perpetual emphasis on his beautiful chorus girls, the decision was brave. Time proved it was also perspicacious. By Thanksgiving the producer's office disclosed that Elizabeth Hines had been signed for Magnolia. The release neglected to mention that Ziegfeld himself had signed no contracts with Kern or Hammerstein. That signing occurred over two weeks later, on Saturday, December 11. Their contract called for Kern and Hammerstein to deliver a first draft by January 1 and for Ziegfeld to place the work on a stage by April 1. Kern received a $1500 advance and Hammerstein $1000. Kern was to be paid 4.5 per cent of the weekly gross, from which he was to pay Edna Ferber her 1.5 per cent of the gross. Hammerstein's take was to slide between 2.5 and 2 per cent, depending on weekly figures. On the Monday after signing, December 13, the producer announced the signing of the second major figure, Paul Robeson. This suggests how early Hammerstein hit on the idea of elevating the character of Joe to something of a one-man Greek chorus.

Excitement over the show was generated immediately. No better example could be offered of this excitement than *Variety*'s confusion about rehearsals. For three weeks early in 1927—January 17 and 19, and February 2—the trade sheet eagerly anticipated Ziegfeld by listing the musical in active rehearsal. For some inexplicable reason it added an article to the title, calling the musical *The Show Boat*. The announcement was as premature as Ziegfeld's own casting releases. Neither Miss Hines nor Robeson were to be in the cast of the first production, and Miss Hines later involved the producer in an unpleasant law suit, insisting he had reneged on his agreement.

But while *Show Boat* had not begun rehearsals, *Lucky* had, on January 31. Its production would juxtapose the nadir of Kern's career alongside what is generally considered to be its acme.

Although the gentlemanly Dillingham and the flamboyant Ziegfeld were friendly competitors, occasionally cooperating in joint ventures and frequently lending each other artists under exclusive contracts, in the public's eye Ziegfeld was indisputably the more glamorous and important. Dillingham was well aware of his rival's edge, and, being human, his secondary position sometimes galled him. Actually, changing tastes were passing both men by, even if neither could see it at the time. Ziegfeld's great *Follies* were a thing of the past, and two editions of the revue he would mount in the future were to seem pale shadows of his earlier triumphs. A few major book shows were to be his last great successes. Similarly, Dillingham's biggest hits were all behind him.

When Ziegfeld announced the opening of his magnificent new theatre, promising a lavish mounting outdoing anything he had offered before, Dillingham's pride rankled. He determined to present New York theatregoers with a spectacle that would outziegfeld Ziegfeld. He held discreet conferences with a number of composers and librettists, but he was particularly taken with an idea Jerry suggested. Somewhere in his omnivorous reading Jerry had learned about young ladies in Ceylon who wore newly found pearls close to their skin to give the pearls added luster. Only certain girls were reputed to have the proper skin. They were called "pearl feeders." Dillingham appreciated the novelty of both the setting and the heroine's occupation. He was thrilled at the opportunity Ceylon would offer his scene and costume designer. One of his first moves was to sign James Reynolds, the closest person Joseph Urban had to a rival, to create sets and clothes. Since Jerry was hard at work with Oscar Hammerstein on *Show Boat,* both the composer and the producer quickly settled on Otto Harbach, their *Sunny* and *Criss Cross* collaborator, to develop the story.

When Harbach came to Dillingham's office to discuss the project, he was dismayed to learn that Jerry demanded a hefty slice of the librettist's royalties for having suggested the basic idea. There was nothing unethical or uncommon about such a demand, and Otto would have been happy to cut Jerry in. But Jerry's imperious insistence on a huge percentage took Otto aback. (*Variety* nonetheless reported Jerry was getting only the "usual 3%.") Mild and genial, the librettist acquiesced, keeping his unhappiness about the matter to himself. However, he was further shocked to hear Jerry's second demand. Jerry wanted credit for the principal score, although, busy with *Show Boat,* he would actually write only two or three songs. Bert Kalmar and Harry Ruby would provide the rest. Apparently, Jerry was not unwilling to have a note in the program giving his associates proper credit. What he seems to have wanted was the lion's share of the publicity. *Variety*'s first notice tends to confirm this. Obviously following a Dillingham release, it noted, "Otto Harbach and Jerome Kern are doing the libretto and score, with interpolated numbers and scenes by Bert Kalmar and Harry Ruby."

By design or accident several advance announcements in Philadelphia attributed the music solely to Kern, crediting Ruby and Kalmar only with a hand in the book and lyrics—seemingly a further move toward Kern's usurping full credit. These same releases listed Monday, March 7, as the premiere's date at the Garrick. For Philadelphians who might have heard that Paul Whiteman was in the cast the announcements did offer some disappointing news. The celebrated orchestra leader was confined to New York by commitments and so would be represented merely by "a special Paul Whiteman Unit Band of 36 musicians." Not unexpectedly, the elaborate mounting proved unwieldy, forcing a one-night delay in the opening. Even a twenty-four-hour postponement was insufficient to allow all of Dillingham's gaudy pieces to fall into place.

Establishing a pattern New York's critics would follow two weeks later, the Philadelphia reviewers dwelled principally on *Lucky*'s eye-filling spectacle and on Mary Eaton. While they were kind to the supporting cast, most dismissed the book as a hopeless hodgepodge, seemingly contrived to fit James Reynolds's sets and costumes. By the time they came to discuss the music their charity had been exhausted. The *Public Ledger* asserted bluntly, "The musical features are not only far below the standard of Jerome Kern, but actually flat and tawdry as compared to the tunes of 'Leave It To Jane,' 'Good Morning, Dearie,' 'Sally' and 'Oh, Boy.'" Because *Variety* often printed its out-of-town judgment a week late and because its pronouncements were aimed at a more professional readership, the trade paper was frequently the hardest hitting and most perceptive. Its evaluation of *Lucky* was no exception. Its Philadelphia man concluded, "Jerome Kern's score is the most disappointing feature of the whole show. If 'Sunny' and 'Criss Cross' marked a falling off in originality and catchiness, this one registered a startling drop. There is not a sure fire number in this show, and it is hard to see where any can be plugged."

Dillingham took gravely ill just before the premiere and was confined to bed. When Otto went to the theatre the next morning to start work on revisions, he was told he was not welcome. Stunned and unbelieving, he asked who had shut the doors to him, and was informed the instructions came from Kern. He demanded to see Jerry. The composer came out and tartly advised his collaborator that he, Kern, and Hassard Short, the director, had taken over. They would make all the changes. Jerry insisted the show had been his idea, and, with Dillingham effectively out of the picture, he was going to revise and save the show his own way. As a parting shot, Jerry warned Otto not to bother Dillingham with his problems. If he went to see the producer, he was to say only that audiences were receptive and the show was being turned around. Harbach had no intention of disturbing Dillingham. Instead, he simply walked away from the show in disgust. Dillingham inevitably got word of *Lucky*'s problems and, against doctor's orders, entrained to Philadelphia to see for himself. The exertion proved too much. After a night at Jefferson Hospital the producer returned to New York in an ambulance.

With its myriad plots and counterplots removed, *Lucky*'s story was revealed as little more than another Cinderella tale, a sort of continent-spanning *Sally*. This time instead of working as a dishwasher in Greenwich Village, the young lady of the title earns her keep pearl diving in Ceylon for a treacherous slavedriver and thief whom she believes is her father. A handsome American pearl buyer, Jack Mansfield, falls in love with the girl and succeeds in bringing her to New York, where she triumphs as a cabaret dancer. When it turns out her real father died at sea and left her and her brother two million dollars, even Jack's snobbish sister, Grace, agrees to his marrying Lucky. In fact, Grace accepts the proposal of Teddy Travers, the pusillanimous nance of a tea house owner who is discovered to be Lucky's long lost brother.

Lucky opened in New York at the New Amsterdam Theatre on March 22, 1927, asking $6.60 for its top seats. Musical numbers were:

Lucky

ACT I

1. Opening, "The Treasure Hunt" .... *Ensemble*
2. "Cingalese Girls" .. *Jack [Joseph Santley], Albertina Rasch Girls and Ensemble*
3. Quartette, "Without Thinking of You" ...... *Grace [Ivy Sawyer], Mazie [Ruby Keeler], Charlie [Walter Catlett] and Teddy [Richard "Skeet" Gallagher]*
4a. Entrance of Lucky .... *Ensemble*
 b. "Lucky" .... *Lucky [Mary Eaton] and Ensemble*
5. Duet, "That Little Something" .... *Lucky and Ensemble*
6. Finaletto .... *Ensemble*
7. Cocoanut Dance .... *The Albertina Rasch Girls*
8. Duettino, "When the Bo Tree Blossoms" .... *Lucky and Ensemble*
9. Keller Sisters and Lynch
10. "Dancing the Devil Away" .... *Lucky and Ensemble*
11. The Elida Webb Girls
12. Finale .... *Lucky and Ensemble*

ACT II

1a. Opening
 b. "Pearl of Broadway" .... *Mazie and Ensemble*
2. "Spring Is Here" .... *Lucky, Charlie, Teddy and Male Ensemble*
3. "Same Old Moon" .... *Grace and Jack*
 a. "If the Man in the Moon Was a Coon" .... *Mazie and Show Girls*
 b. "Shine On Harvest Moon" .. *Keller Sisters and Lynch*
 c. "By the Light of the Silvery Moon" .... *Charlie, Teddy and Dancers*
 d. "Once in a Blue Moon" ...... *Lucky and the Albertina Rasch Girls*
4. Paul Whiteman and his Orchestra
5. Ballet, "The Pearl of Ceylon" ...... *Lucky, Premiere, the Albertina Rasch Girls*
6. Finale .... *Ensemble*

Gus Salzer was musical director and Robert Russell Bennett the orchestrator. Hassard Short staged the work, while David Bennett and Albertina Rasch were its choreographers.

Reversing a common pattern, Broadway's critics were more lenient on *Lucky* than Philadelphia's had been, although the difference was largely one of degree. Once again Mary Eaton and the evening's spectacle monopolized both the headlines and the praise. Some sympathy was extended to the rest of the cast, lost in the vastness of the production and in the large number of their associates. Miss Sawyer and Gallagher seemed particularly wasted. A curious thing occurred when critics reached the music. Because the program had coyly listed *Lucky* simply as the work of "Otto Harbach, Bert Kalmar, Harry Ruby, Jerome Kern," neglecting to specify which man wrote what, most reviewers blithely assumed Kern had composed the whole score. Reaction to the score was respectful—either tactfully critical or politely welcoming. Unlike their Philadelphia colleagues, the New York critics did stop to single out favorite songs. Some sign of how Kern, even in his lesser efforts, towered over his fellow composers, was revealed when the songs most critics devoted special attention to were the only two songs from the show published under Kern's name—"When The Bo-Tree Blossoms Again" and "That Little Something." A few critics heard distinct hints of Kern's "rippling and ingratiating quality" in "Spring Is Here." Unfortunately the song was never published and appears to have been lost. Perhaps responding to *Variety's* Philadelphia reviewer who saw a certain unpleasant significance in Paul Whiteman's band not playing any of the show's tunes, Whiteman, on joining the show for its New York run, led a medley of *Lucky's* tunes—but to everyone's delight, quickly continued with Gershwin's "Rhapsody In Blue."

The musical changes between the Philadelphia and Broadway openings were all but nil. Given the unpromising Philadelphia greeting, they suggest Kern and Short were willing to rely on the beauty of the mounting and the expertise of the performers. Clearly, the material was of secondary importance, a mere starting point and not an end in itself. Only a single song was dropped—"Pearl of Ceylon," from early in the first act—and even its main theme remained heard in the final ballet. For the rest, changes consisted of eliminating a few reprises and some reshuffling in the songs' order of presentation.

Despite the readiness of some papers to credit the composer with all of the evening's music, Kern seems to have composed little of the score. Three of the five published songs are by Kalmar and Ruby—"Cingalese Girls," "Dancing The Devil Away," and "The Same Old Moon." Only the two mentioned before are definitely known to be Kern's. Although they are minor, pleasant tunes, in their warmth and sweetness both are un-mistakably Kern. Yet even in such relatively indifferent numbers Kern could be full of surprises. By 1927 the thirty-two-bar AABA formula was generally established. Nevertheless, the chorus of "When The Bo-Tree Blossoms Again" lasts just sixteen bars, with the twelfth bar of its simple, tinkly, *fausse-Orientale* melody abruptly punctuated with jazz chordings. "That Little Something" is less interesting, an innocuous ballad, tritely pretty, but not truly memorable. The waltz theme from the ballet, pub-lished in the piano selections, also has a pleasing loveliness that suggests it came from Kern's pen.

The basically unenthusiastic notices, the show's gargantuan weekly costs, and the commanding excellence of the competition all hurt *Lucky*. Dillingham confessed he had an expensive failure and closed the show after seventy-one performances.

Kern's deplorable behavior, so unkind and so atypical, never perma-nently alienated those he offended. Although Ruby spoke of it in his cor-respondence, he regarded Kern with affection; and Harbach, of course, remained a steadfast collaborator. Both men undoubtedly understood the circumstances behind Kern's meanness. First of all, Kern was at the lowest point in his career. His recent offerings, *Sunny* excepted, had not produced major song hits; and critics on all sides were scolding him for his lackluster melodies. At home he had a second problem. Eva had suffered a nervous breakdown. Confined to bed and under the care of nurses, she had totally withdrawn from society. What prompted the trouble is unknown. Some suggest Kern's erratic hours, busy schedule, and often imperious attitudes had worn her thin. Betty Kern Miller believes the breakdown was triggered by her mother's grief over the death of her dear friend Edna Kern, the wife of Jerry's brother Joseph. Regardless of the cause, the effect was to bring Eva and Jerry closer together than ever.

Niggling nuisances most likely exacerbated the situation. Certainly Zieg-feld was no help. Four days before *Lucky* was scheduled to open in Phila-delphia, Kern had returned home from rehearsals to find a telegram from the producer, then vacationing in Palm Beach. In effect the cable must have confirmed any fears Kern held that Ziegfeld might sooner or later attempt to over-commercialize and prostitute *Show Boat*. Ziegfeld had written:

> I feel Hammerstein not keen on my doing Show Boat. I am
> very keen on doing it on account of your music but Hammerstein

book in present shape has not got a chance except with critics but the public no, and I have stopped producing for critics and empty houses. I don't want Bolton or anyone else if Hammerstein can and will do the work. If not, then for all concerned we should have someone help. How about Dorothy Donnelly or anyone you suggest or Hammerstein suggests. I am told Hammerstein never did anything alone. His present lay-out too serious. Not enough comedy. After marriage remember your love interest is eliminated. No one on earth, Jerry, knows musical comedy better than you and you yourself told me you would not risk a dollar on it. If Hammerstein will fix the book I want to do it. If he refuses to change it or allow anyone else to be called in if necessary, you and he return the advances. You yourself suggested you would and let someone else do it. If Hammerstein is ready to work with me to get it right and you and he will extend the time until Oct first let's do it together. I really want to if O.H. is reasonable. All we want is success. Answer.

This mixture of threat and cajoling is interesting on several points. Ziegfeld clearly viewed the show as "musical comedy" and not as operetta or, as he was ultimately to bill it, "an American musical play." His mention of Kern's refusal to invest in so experimental, path-breaking a work implies Kern's own nervousness about the attempt.

Striving for verisimilitude, Kern and Hammerstein journeyed to Maryland, where they spent a day examining an old showboat. Succeeding months brought further public announcements. In May Arthur Hammerstein, accepting the inevitable, withdrew from contention. In mid-July Erlanger promised that his new theatre, then nearing completion on 44th Street and to be named for himself, would offer *Show Boat* as its initial attraction. Helen Morgan returned from a London engagement on Septmber 6. The same day she was signed for the company. A week later—if *Variety* was not again premature—*Show Boat* went into rehearsal.

Norma Terris, who was to play Magnolia, would appear to confirm the lengthy rehearsal time. While she cannot be specific, she recalls that the rehearsals, held in a large room high up in the Ziegfeld Theatre, were far longer than customary. Although Hammerstein was actually directing, Kern was careful to instruct the principals on his interpretation of their roles. He informed Miss Terris that he looked on Ravenal and Magnolia's meeting much as he did on Romeo and Juliet's—love at first sight. The comparison may well have been called to mind by Magnolia's first appearing on an upper deck of the ship. Kern saw Magnolia as "a genuine little girl—not coy, not a flirt." And he told Miss Terris to play the scene without ever taking her eyes off Ravenal. His interpretation led to a run-in with Robert Russell Bennett. Bennett's orchestration of the lovers' first song, "Make Believe," had strings under the hero and wood-winds supporting the heroine. Kern insisted the opposite should prevail. His argument was that strings were warm and feminine while the cooler woodwinds were more masculine. Bennett challenged the composer, see-ing Ravenal as the more immediately impassioned of the two, and Mag-nolia as more reserved, even teasing. As Bennett recalls, he won his point.

Show Boat gave its first public performance at Washington's National Theatre on Tuesday, November 15. Although the premiere ran somewhere between four and four and a half hours, the musical was instantly recog-nized as a superior achievement. Understandably, given their perspective, Capital critics viewed the entertainment more as a Ziegfeld production than as a Kern and Hammerstein opus. Harold Phillips, writing for the *Times,* kept referring to the musical as "Flo Ziegfeld's 'Show Boat'" and nowhere mentioned Kern or Hammerstein. Phillips saw great potential in the musical, predicting: "There are three music hits in the making here." Songs he held high hopes for were "Can't Help Lovin' That Man," "Make Believe," and "Old Man River." (From the beginning *Show Boat*'s music listed the songs as "Ol' Man River" and "Can't Help Lovin' Dat Man," but programs, and therefore the era's critics, used the more "correct" spellings. Many early programs called "Make Believe," "Only Make Believe.") Lee Somers in the *Herald* also looked on the mounting as "Ziegfeld's 'Show Boat,'" although he was careful to properly credit the authors. He noted, "The book by Oscar Hammerstein, 2nd has been skillfully adapted from Miss Ferber's novel," and he awarded even more space to Kern, reporting that he "has written a rather exceptional score, even for Kern, with two songs—'Old Man River' and 'Can't Help Lovin' That Man'—that seem destined for instantaneous, hit popularity." With several extra days to digest matters, John J. Daly, in his Sunday retrospective for the *Post,* nonetheless totally ignored Kern and Hammerstein, and implied instead that Ziegfeld's unique largess and flair were responsible for *Show Boat*'s success.

By that Sunday, however, Ziegfeld, Kern, Hammerstein, and all their associates were on a train for Pittsburgh. They were probably gleeful at Washington's reception. Later in the week *Variety*'s Washington corre-spondent reported the musical "took all the dough in town, getting every-thing the National would hold at the $3.50 top scale, $27,500." As soon as all were settled in at Pittsburgh's William Penn Hotel, Jerry summoned Robert Russell Bennett to his suite. When Bennett arrived, he found Jerry at the piano absorbed in finishing a new piece. Jerry asked Bennett to wait a few minutes and resumed trying out different, if similar, phrases. He finally turned to his orchestrator and complained that he had lost a phrase he would desperately like to retrieve. Bennett replied he thought it was a waste of time for Jerry to dawdle at the piano when he could just as easily pull the recalcitrant phrase from the recesses of his mind if he really wanted to. Jerry gave Bennett an impish smile, grabbed his sheet music, and finished the melody in his head. At the same time he gave a copy to Hammerstein. Oscar came back with a set of lyrics filled with all the words and expressions, notably "Cupid," that he knew Jerry detested. Jerry grew angrier and angrier as he played, until he suddenly realized Oscar's game. He laughed so hard tears ran down his cheeks. Oscar then handed him a second set of lyrics, one whose chorus asked, "Why do I love you?" Shortly afterward Jerry and Oscar entered the William Penn ballroom, where the cast was rehearsing. Jerry made a low bow to Miss Terris, who had requested a more comfortable song for the second act, and, handing her the sheet music, remarked, "We sat up all night writing this."

Although the song could not be readied in time for the Pittsburgh opening, the pruning that had begun as soon as the first Washington curtain was run down had a telling effect. The new musical was clearly emerging as a masterpiece. No matter that Karl B. Krug of the *Press,* like his Washington colleagues, failed to salute Kern or Hammerstein. Krug's enthusiasm was contagious and obviously meant to include them. After opening his review by quoting the lyric of "Ol' Man River," he continued, "Playgoers in this, the week of Thanksgiving, are ordered to drop to their knees and offer up their most fervid gratitude for Florenz Ziegfeld's 'Show Boat.'" Krug concluded his review by perceptively predicting that the musical "marks a milestone in musical comedy production." Pittsburgh's other papers joined in the rejoicing.

As *Show Boat* moved on to Cleveland and Philadelphia, critics there fell into line, hailing the work but seemingly handing Ziegfeld a disproportionate share of the credit. One notable exception was Arthur B. Waters, who had been following Kern's work with special interest ever since *Dear Sir.* Although he opened his notice in the *Public Ledger,* "Say simply that Mr. Ziegfeld has surpassed himself, and you've given the best description of 'Show Boat,'" he devoted a whole paragraph to Kern:

It is a pleasure to record that Jerome Kern has staged a definite and certain comeback. His score is a thing of many delights, in orchestration, in tunes, and in the manner he has caught the atmosphere of the "mauve decade." For once, there doesn't seem to be a single "filler" song number in the entire list of twenty-six.

But Waters saved his big guns for his Sunday follow-up. Remarking that he could rarely think of a single new thing to say about most musical comedies, he noted happily, "We are not exaggerating when we say that we could devote two or three of our Sunday 'second-thoughts' comments to the production of 'Show Boat.'" He then continued:

> There have been a number of note-worthy operettas during the last few seasons which have attained a high level of excellence, but "Show Boat" is not simply an operetta, although Jerome Kern's distinguished score can easily be ranked with the best of them. No, Mr. Ziegfeld's production, styled in the program "an American musical play," has many of the finer attributes of musical comedy, operetta, even of revue, with a definite suggestion of legitimate drama that is not dragged in by the heels and never falls into the customary mawkish channels that mistake bathos for pathos.

This might have sufficed for most other critics, but Waters launched into a seven-paragraph discussion of Kern's art. No New York review, not even Alan Dale's, nor any New York Sunday follow-up devoted so much attention to Kern and his music. Philadelphia theatregoers took the show to heart, leading *Variety*'s local man to report, "Oldtimers don't remember anything like this for a show without a Broadway rep[utation]."

After three weeks in Philadelphia, *Show Boat* moved to New York, opening at the magnificent Ziegfeld Theatre on December 27, 1927, with a cast that by itself amply demonstrated Ziegfeld's prodigality and taste. A chorus of 96 included 36 white chorus girls, 16 white chorus boys, 16 black male singers, 16 black female singers, and 12 black girl dancers.

Musical numbers were:

Show Boat

ACT I

1. Opening, "Cotton Blossom" . . . . *Entire Ensemble*
2. "Only Make Believe" . . . . *Ravenal [Howard Marsh] and Magnolia [Norma Terris]*

3. "Old Man River" .... *Joe [Jules Bledsoe] and Jubilee Singers*
4. "Can't Help Lovin' That Man" ..... *Julie [Helen Morgan],*
Queenie [Aunt Jemima], Magnolia, Joe, Windy
[Allan Campbell]
5. "Life On The Wicked Stage" ... *Ellie [Eva Puck] and Girls*
6. "Till Good Luck Comes My Way" ...... *Ravenal and Boys*
7. "I Might Fall Back On You" .. *Ellie, Frank [Sammy White]*
and Girls
8. "C'Mon Folks" .... *Queenie and Jubilee Singers*
9. "You Are Love" .... *Magnolia and Ravenal*
10. Finale .... *Entire Ensemble*

ACT II

1. Opening, "At The Fair" .. *Sightseers, Dandies, Barkers, etc.*
2. "Why Do I Love You?" .. *Magnolia, Ravenal, Andy [Charles*
Winninger], Parthy [Edna May Oliver] and Chorus
3. "In Dahomey" ...... *Jubilee Singers and Dahomey Dancers*
4. "Bill" (Lyric by P. G. Wodehouse) .... *Julie*
5. Song, "Can't Help Lovin' That Man" .... *Magnolia*
6. Service and Scene Music, St. Agatha's Convent
7. Apache Dance, "First Time in America" ...... *Sidell Sisters*
8. "Goodbye, My Lady Love" .... *Frank and Ellie*
9. Magnolia's Debut in Trocadero Music Hall
10. "Ol' Man River" .... *Old Joe*
11. "Hey, Feller" .... *Queenie and Jubilee Singers*
12. "Why Do I Love You?" .... *Kim and Flappers*
13a. Kim's Imitation of her Mother
b. Eccentric Dance .... *Constance McKenzie*
c. Tap Dance .... *Una Val*
14. Finale .... *Entire Ensemble*

Victor Baravalle conducted. John Harkrider did the costumes, and Urban the sets. Hammerstein staged the work, even though he was not given program credit.

Reduced to essentials, Ferber and Hammerstein's story told of a bittersweet romance between a river gambler, Gaylord Ravenal, and a showboat captain's daughter, Magnolia. Their marriage is destroyed by Ravenal's gambling. After Ravenal leaves, Magnolia is forced to sing in night clubs to support herself and their daughter. She eventually decides to return to the family boat, and years later Ravenal appears and brings about a reunion in time for the final curtain.

New York critics, like their tryout town brethren, gave Ziegfeld pride of place in their notices, but virtually to a man they were sufficiently sophisticated to understand that, for all the producer's panache, Kern and Hammerstein were really responsible for the show's greatness. A few, such as Burns Mantle in the *Daily News,* complained that "Mr. Ziegfeld's musical entertainment" was too long. (Despite cuts on the road the show still ran until nearly 11:40.) But then Mantle was almost the only critic who failed to mention either Hammerstein or Kern, although he did single out "Ol' Man River." In company with his colleagues, Mantle lavished kudos on the principal players and on Ziegfeld's great set designer, Joseph Urban. Those critics who did call attention to Kern's work often breathed an audible sigh of relief that he had recovered from his slump. His oldest booster, Alan Dale, writing in the *American* what proved to be his last review of a Kern show, rejoiced:

> It is all set to pleasant, rhythmic music, composed by Jerome Kern, who is always musicianly and has outgrown his adolescence of mere tune. He has written in "Show Boat" some particularly relevant and harmonious stuff, some of it seeming to suggest the great Mississippi and its turgid depths. That there are tunes, too, need not be overlooked, but what I say is that this new score is not designed for lovers of thick molasses. There isn't a drop of treacle in its make-up.

The *Times* praised the "exceptionally tuneful score—the most lilting and satisfactory that the wily Jerome Kern has contrived in several seasons." The *New Yorker* rated the score "triple A." *Variety,* one of the mild dissenters, did employ the much quoted phrase "a Leviathan of a show," but seemed to be talking about Ziegfeld's brilliant production and the rich panorama of Ferber's tale as much as anything. In fact, it proclaimed that the show was "muchly overrated," suggesting "it's almost a pity the Edna Ferber novel wasn't dramatized 'straight,' sans the musical setting." While most critics, if they selected any favorite songs at all, picked "Ol' Man River," "Can't Help Lovin' Dat Man," and, surprisingly, "Life On The Wicked Stage," *Variety* prophesied that "You Are Love" would be "the dark horse of the show." However, the trade paper offered the only major review to comment on one other song in the show. It wrote:

> Miss Morgan, from the nite clubs, could have made her impression a wow click, instead of passably fair, with a song specialty

instead of the mild "Bill" number. Striving hard for a "Mon Homme" type of song, Hammerstein and Kern just missed out in that reach. Were it not for a natural desire against an interpolation, the song from George Gershwin's flop, "Strike Up The Band," comes to mind as an ideal number for Miss Morgan. It is the nearest approach to an American "My Man" yet, and Harms, Inc., Gershwin's as well as Kern's publishers, knows the title referred to. Still, Miss Morgan, perched atop the upright, registered with this serenade to her "Bill." [The Gershwin song was "The Man I Love."]

A comparison of tryout programs with the New York playbill shows that four songs were added during the pre-Broadway tour and a larger number were dropped. Perhaps the saddest loss was "Mis'ry's Comin' Aroun'," a beautiful, plaintive piece from the middle of the first act. Later in the act, "I Would Like To Play A Lover's Part" was discarded in favor of "Be Happy, Too," and that in turn gave way to "I Might Fall Back On You." Early in the second act, "Cheer Up" was replaced by "Why Do I Love You?" Two minor numbers, "Coal Black Lady" and "Bully Song," were cut, while late in the act "It's Getting Hotter In The North" was eliminated. "Hey, Feller" was added to follow up the first of the second act's two reprises of "Ol' Man River."

It seems almost cruel to dissect so glowingly romantic and cherished a score. Virtually every note in the score is familiar to theatregoers, and no fewer than half a dozen songs have enjoyed a steady, wide popularity for over fifty years—and give every promise of remaining beloved for at least another half-century. Today "Ol' Man River" is practically a folk song. Sigmund Spaeth on several occasions hinted darkly that the melody was suspiciously similar to one a minor composer named Maury Madison had published in Paris earlier the same year with the title "Long-Haired Mamma." "The opening lines of both choruses," Spaeth observed, "are almost identical." Maury apparently thought so, too, for in June of 1928 he brought a plagiarism suit against Kern, Harms, and Ziegfeld. The issue must have been settled quietly out of court, for nothing more was heard about the matter. Although the melody covers an octave and a sixth, it has no wide jumps and is of a piece harmonically. The fact that it remains one of the few songs whose verse singers still regularly perform is a tribute not so much to Kern—although he did tie the verse and chorus together by using the theme of the chorus's release as part of the introduction—as to

Hammerstein's compelling lyrics. A persistent legend has it that Kern originally wrote the principal theme as a fast banjo number. In this connection it should be noted that the Cotton Blossom theme is essentially the beginning of "Ol' Man River"'s chorus played in reverse and accelerated. Of course, Kern employed variations of principal themes all through the score. Bits from the verse of "Ol' Man River" were sung in the opening. Other echoes will be discussed later.

"Can't Help Lovin' Dat Man" is headed with the curious marking "Tempo di Blues." In *American Popular Song* Alec Wilder pointed out that, while the song is rhythmically and structurally unexceptional, it does employ unusual harmonies that nevertheless cleverly convey accepted blues sounds.

If "Ol' Man River" and "Can't Help Lovin' Dat Man" use the AABA formula that had become commonplace only a few years earlier, the rest of *Show Boat's* major songs ignore this standard framework. All of the musical's great love songs resort to distinct formulas. "Make Believe" is built on an $ABAB^1A^1$ skeleton, "Why Do I Love You?" on ABAB, and "You Are Love" on ABB. "Make Believe" is indisputably the best of the three, pouring forth not just lovely melody but rhythmic and harmonic surprises, such as the triplet over "that you love" in the sixth bar of the chorus, or the fresh chordings over "Might as well make believe I love you" near the end. A number of commentators have remarked that the words and music fail to fit tightly. The verse affords several examples of two notes used for a single syllable. Depending on whose side one chooses to take, the fault can be laid on Hammerstein's not respecting Kern's excellent melody or on Kern's refusing to bend to Hammerstein's excellent lyric. In truth, the discrepancy is minor and not worth quibbling about. "Why Do I Love You?," written under the pressure of the tryout, is a more straightforward work, yet the subtle variations of its gently rolling five-note phrase should not be given short shrift. In the extended version sung in the show, Kern tellingly worked in references to "Can't Help Lovin' Dat Man." "You Are Love" was the evening's main waltz. The varying tempos of its several waltz themes suggest Kern was harking back to the traditions of the classic Viennese waltz. But Kern himself, in a number of interviews and in conversations with friends, confessed to never liking the song, apparently accepting charges that both his music and Hammerstein's lyric were overblown. Those who like both the melody and the appropriate lyric see the piece simply as the most arioso moment in the show.

The lilting melodies of both "Life On The Wicked Stage" (whose lyric always insists it is "upon" the wicked stage) and "I Might Fall Back On You" (a marvelous polka) recall the infectious gaiety of Kern's Princess Theatre days. Given Kern's practice of reviving good, neglected melodies, the possibility exists that both were written years before. The plaintive little theme Magnolia plays on the piano in Act One was borrowed from entrance music in Act One, scene two of *The Beauty Prize*. Indeed, Kern went further back than his English or Princess Theatre shows for several themes. Curiously, two separate passages in *Show Boat* have music culled from a single song, "If We Were On Our Honeymoon," which Kern wrote in 1913 for *The Doll Girl*. The waltz theme underscoring part of Act One, scene four, uses the beginning of the song, while the accompaniment to "Mis'ry's Comin' Aroun'" was derived from bars 68 to 75.

Kern also went further back, to use three or four songs that were not his. The opening of Act One, scene six is a violin solo, setting the mood for the performance of *The Parson's Bride*. To create the right atmosphere, Kern used Lange's old salon favorite, "Blumenlied." Kern used both "After The Ball" and "Good Bye, Ma Lady Love" for period flavor. But Kern also demonstrated the universality of some folk themes when he returned to his Bohemian roots and used an old Bohemian melody for Captain Andy's entrance. The melody was clearly dear to Kern, for he used clever variations of it throughout the score. For example, in the "Te Deum" during the convent scene, little Kim's relationship to the captain is noted by the orchestra's playing his theme under the organ melody.

Shortly after *Show Boat* opened, Robert Simon, the noted musicologist, gave Kern his first extended treatment as a serious musician with a long article in *Modern Music*. He remarked: "The action is accompanied by a great deal of incidental music—although 'incidental' is a misleading trade term, for Kern's music heightens immeasurably the emotional value of the situation." He cites the passage that accompanies Julie's second appearance and records how it "foreshadows, in the midst of a gay scene, her forthcoming disaster." Simon continues, "Themes are quoted and even developed in almost Wagnerian fashion throughout *Show Boat*." He lists several other uses of Captain Andy's theme to make his point. He then concludes:

> An examination of the full score will reveal dozens of interesting passages which testify to the composer's skill. They may not be apparent to the casual customer, who does not know what it is that is gripping him; but the musician will find much to admire. . . .

Kern seems to be at the turning point of his career. If he makes the transition from a sort of opera-comique—and *Show Boat* is exactly that, in the classic sense of the term—to "leit-opera" we may finally have opera which is thoroughly and indigenously American.

As he had with *Sally,* Ziegfeld early on promised a road company, but, again, as with *Sally,* the company never materialized. Sound films had arrived to lure more and more theatregoers and theatres themselves away from the legitimate fold. Nevertheless, the New York run of 575 performances (five more than *Sally*) represented the longest run Kern was ever to see a show of his achieve. Shortly after the original company embarked on its post-Broadway tour the stock market collapsed, and the Depression began further thinning the ranks of playgoers and playhouses. As a result, *Show Boat* became Kern's first musical hit to play only a handful of major cities, ending its tour in March of 1930.

The onset of the Depression both minimized and underscored the importance of *Show Boat.* It minimized it by leaving it in a theatrical limbo when Broadway desperately sought more escapist lyric entertainment. No similar works appeared in the following seasons. It underscored the greatness of the work when this same rush to lighter, more frivolous musicals left *Show Boat* standing apart as a unique breakaway until the arrival of *Oklahoma!* And breakaway it was—the first truly, totally American operetta, even if fashion has dictated that the word "operetta" is unstylish and that these new American operettas were to be called "musical plays." *Show Boat* took a piece of beloved Americana and treated it with appropriate romanticism and yet with a theatrical seriousness. And despite some borrowings of European musical themes it clothed the work in a distinctly native lyricism. Identifiable American types—the river gambler, the showboat crew, the black workhand—sang American sentiments in an American musical idiom.

17

London and Literature; Boats and Broadway

Even before *Show Boat* had opened in New York, Kern's old associate and friend, Alfred Butt, decided to mount it in London. On January 13, 1928, the Kerns sailed with Hammerstein on the *Majestic* to oversee the production. By coincidence, P. G. Wodehouse was a passenger on the same sailing. Kern and Hammerstein prepared two new songs for the London show. "Me And My Boss" was conceived for Paul Robeson, whose commitments finally allowed him to accept the role of Joe. But the song was cut before the London first night. The second song was "Dance Away The Night." It was required at the end of the second act to fill a void left when no other performer could match Norma Terris's celebrated imitations. The song was serviceable, a light, tripping melody with a hint of melancholy. Alfred Simon has suggested that Kern may have adapted its verse from a similar verse in *The City Chap*'s "Sympathetic Someone."

Kern had no sooner landed than he was asked to supply a single song for a new London musical, *Lady Mary*. Kern obliged, so when the show opened at Daly's on February 23, audiences could hear "If You're A Friend Of Mine" (lyric, Graham John). Knowledgeable transatlantic travelers may have recognized the melody as "In Love With Love" from *Stepping Stones*. Both the play and the song enjoyed a modest success. Better things were in the offing.

Before work began in earnest on London's *Show Boat,* Kern had another project to attend to. Lee Ephraim, who had mounted *Sunny* in England, asked him to compose a score for a musical designed around the talents of one of the West End's most beautiful leading ladies, Evelyn Laye. Miss Laye was then in the throes of an emotional divorce. Ephraim felt hard work would provide the most salutory diversion for his troubled star. Far less glamorous than Miss Laye were the three men with whom Kern worked, co-librettists Graham John and Guy Bolton, and director John Harwood.

On Sunday, April 8, the entire company boarded a train for Portsmouth. Miss Laye continued to brood privately, all the while keeping a brave public front. If Kern harbored any doubts, he, too, kept them hidden. For most of the trip he played cards.

The next night the audience at the Kings Theatre, Southsea, seemed more than satisfied. *The Stage's* local man prophesied, "London is likely to give a warm welcome to 'Blue Eyes.'" The *Hampshire Telegraph* recorded, "No new play that has been 'tried out' at Portsmouth in recent years has created such an impression." Even more enthusiastic than *The Stage's* critic, the *Telegraph's* reviewer went on to proclaim that the show would take London "by storm." Yet reading between the lines with hindsight one can realize all was not truly well. Both critics gave inordinate space merely to detailing the plot, without actually commenting on how successfully or unsuccessfully the story had been developed. Much of their remaining notices were taken up in describing—and praising—the performers. *The Stage* did go on to note that Kern had done "so well with the music that it is impossible to pick or choose," but then promptly chose the title song and "Nobody Else But You" for special mention. The *Telegraph* mentioned neither Kern nor any individual song.

Apparently, like its beautiful leading lady, *Blue Eyes* was deeply troubled. The problems were obvious to those working with it. Although it was sumptuously mounted and wisely cast, the show lacked humor and an outstanding melody. It also ran far too long, a minor problem common to tryouts. Paring and rewriting began as soon as the first night curtain fell. Confident that Hammerstein could handle *Show Boat* alone, Kern elected to remain in Portsmouth to help with the changes. Yet curiously, when *Blue Eyes* opened London's brand-new Piccadilly Theatre on April 27, 1928, after a fortnight in Portsmouth, only a single new Kern song was listed on the program. The very newness of the house was to cause serious opening night difficulties.

Bolton and John took for their heroine a real eighteenth-century actress, George Anne Bellamy, who had played a well-received Juliet to David Garrick's famous Romeo. They presented her with a beloved, if imaginary, brother, a fervent partisan of Bonnie Prince Charlie, with whom he shared in the débacle at Culloden. To carry a message to her brother, George Anne, whom everyone calls "Nancy," dresses in his clothes. Her masquerade forces her into a duel with handsome Captain Sir George Fairmount of the 3rd Royal Dragoons. When the Duke of Cumberland, known affectionately to his troops as "The Butcher," appears on the scene he engineers a trial at which George Anne is tried for high treason, but acquitted. The Duke makes clear to her the favor he expects in return for the verdict. Only when one of George Anne's fellow troopers, the blustering Henry Horatius Pilbeam, alerts the Duke's mistress to the Duke's plan is Nancy able to escape unscathed. By that time Sir George has learned the true identity of his dueling rival and fallen in love with her. A secondary romance enmeshes Nancy's brother, Jamie, and Flora Campbell.

Musical numbers were:

Blue Eyes

ACT I
Scene One

1. "The Good King James" . . . . *Boots [Trevor Glyn]* and *Ensemble*
2. Air, "Charlie is the Darling of My Heart" . . *Jenny [Carlito Ackroyd] and Chorus*
3. March, "His Majesty's Dragoons" . . . . *Sir George [Geoffrey Gwyther] and Men*
4. Scena, "Little Feet That Lightly Beat" . . . . *Nancy [Evelyn Laye] and Sir George*
5. Duet, "Blue Eyes" . . . . *Nancy and Sir George*
6. Trio, "The Trouble about the Drama" . . . . *Pilbeam [W. H. Berry], Jenny, Moll [Ethel Baird] and Chorus*
7. Chorus, "Praise the Day" . . . . *Ensemble*
8. Finaletto . . . . *Nancy*

Scene Two

9. Medley of Old Scottish Airs . . . . *Male Chorus*

Scene Three

10. Chorus and Burthen, "Prince Do and Dare" .. *Flora* [*Sylvia Cecil*] *and Ensemble*
11. Air, "The Curtsey" .... *Nancy and Girls*
12. Burthen and Dance, "Bow Belles" .... *Nancy and Girls*
13. Finale

ACT II
Scene One

14. Ballad and Gavotte, "Fair Lady" .... *Ensemble*
15. Duettino, "Back to the Heather" .... *Flora and Jamie* [*George Vollaire*]
16. Air, "In Love" .... *Nancy and Girls*
17. Catch, "In Vodeodo" .... *Pilbeam and Girls*
18. Duet, "No One Else But You" .... *Sir George and Nancy*
19. Finaletto .... *Sir George and Nancy*

Scene Two

20. Buffo Solo, "Romeo and Juliet" .... *Pilbeam*
21. Scena, "When I Marry Mr. Pilbeam" .. *Moll and Dragoons*

Scene Three

22. Finale Ultimo .... *Nancy, Sir George, and Ensemble*

The musical director was Kennedy Russell.

Backstage everything went wrong on opening night. Miss Laye attempted to imbue her role with her customary gaiety and fire, but still overwhelmed by her personal problems, her heart was not in it. Worse, with construction workers busily hammering away until just before the overture, there had been no time to give the stage a proper cleaning. Dust and grit pervaded the air, forcing the performers to marshall all their professional know-how to keep from choking. Singing became almost painful. Furthermore, double doors between the stage and the dressing rooms impeded movement, turning costume changes into desperate races with time.

Reviews suggest critics were most taken by the beauty of the production. Praise for Joseph and Phil Harker's sets and for B. J. Simmons and Co.'s costumes was virtually universal. Praise, too, was accorded the cast, who successfully hid their breathing problems. If any critics were sharp enough to notice, they tactfully ignored it. Inevitably, Miss Laye received the best notices. Her handsome leading man, Gwyther, and the principal comedian, Berry, a portly low comedian, were especially welcomed. At least one paper singled out Bertram Wallis, himself a dashing leading man a decade or so before, for his role as a properly "harsh and forbidding" villain.

When it came to the book and music the critics were less enthusiastic. Most still viewed musicals as distractions to soothe the tired businessman. The *Times* was typical. While it noted that "a musical comedy whose 'book' is in the manner of a Waverly Novel is something of a novelty, and it would seem to require a more respectful greeting than is generally afforded to entertainments of this kind," it continued, "Alas that the tale is meant to be taken so seriously." Discovering "no concerted dances, no feats of smiling enthusiasm or athletic precision," the critic insisted that Highland reels and flings "are not compensation enough." "Even the sentimental songs," he continued, "are weighted by the general solemnity." Returning to the songs later in the review he concluded, "Mr. Jerome Kern's music is neither very striking nor very obtrusive; no doubt it serves its purpose very well." Several other critics pounced on Kern's failure to write real Scottish music—a failure underscored by the medley of genuine old Scottish airs Kern introduced into the first act.

A comparison of the first night programs from the tryout and from the Piccadilly shows that one of Kern's songs, "Fair Lady," which had originally been sung by Sir George and the girls in Act I and reprised by the ensemble in Act II, was now performed only in the second act. "Some Day," a duet for Flora and Jamie just before the first act curtain, was gone. Three Kern numbers from the last act had also been dropped: Sir George's quintet with four chorus men at the end of scene 2, "What Can I Say"; and the last two numbers in the show, Nancy and Pilbeam's lighthearted "Henry" and Nancy and George's "You Are There." One new song, "When I Marry Mr. Pilbeam," was sung by Moll and the Dragoons late in Act II.

The vocal score, published several weeks after the show opened, tells a remarkably different story, suggesting drastic changes after the opening. Five more Kern songs are missing, along with Moll's recently added melody. The original opening number, "Good King James," gives place to what had been the show's second song, "Charlie Is The Darling Of My Heart," sung by Jenny and the chorus. Nancy and George's meeting, "Little Feet That Lightly Beat," has been cut, as has the air Flora and the chorus sang to open the third scene, "Prince Do And Dare." An anachronistic ditty Pilbeam performed with a bevy of chorus girls, "In Vodeodo," and the lovers' duet mentioned in the tryout review, "No One Else But You," are also gone. Three new songs are added, one of which was not by Kern! Flora and Jamie's "Some Day" was given new, more comic lyrics, slightly retitled as "Someone," and assigned to Pilbeam and Moll in the very same spot. Kern's oldtime associate, Frank Tours, composed music to Clifford Grey's words for "Women," which Pilbeam romped through instead of "In Vodeodo." Replacing "No One Else But You" and reprised, significantly, as the finale was the most enduring melody to come from *Blue Eyes,* "Do I Do Wrong?". The song became fairly popular, as its record and sheet music sales attest, but not until five years later, when it was given new words and sung in *Roberta* as "You're Devastating," did it truly enter the canon of Kern classics.

Just when these last changes were incorporated into the production is uncertain. Miss Laye, looking back over a half-century, recalls that "Do I Do Wrong?" was sung on opening night, but the testimony of the program and the fact that not a single first night critic seems to have taken notice of it suggest it may have been some while later. Robert Russell Bennett's recollections, as a rule encouragingly accurate, tend to confirm this. Bennett orchestrated the original production and remained in London until *Show Boat*'s premiere. He is certain "Do I Do Wrong?" was not in the show on opening night, and insists it was not in the show in the weeks before he returned to New York. Driving the point home, he adds the first time he heard the song was when Kern handed him *Roberta*'s score.

If Kern's work for *Blue Eyes* was not among his most felicitous, it nonetheless remains a landmark in his development, for it confirmed that the more flowing arioso line to which he first gave free rein in *Dear Sir* and *Show Boat* was to dominate his theatrical and, to a lesser extent, his film writing for the rest of his life. The verse of "Bow Belles," which Nancy and the ladies' chorus sang late in the first act, recalls a similar verse for "Look For the Silver Lining," but Kern has gently stretched both the melodic line and the range. The chorus of Flora and Jamie's second act duet, "Back To The Heather," evokes memories of Magnolia and Ravenal leading into their chorus of "Why Do I Love You?." The title song, Nancy and George's principal first act duet, could only be sung by thoroughly trained voices. It ranges over an octave and a half, with several jumps a half note short of an octave. Arpeggio-like phrases in George's countermelody for the chorus frequently lie several tones above Nancy's. Tellingly, the melody of "Blue Eyes" was the same Kern had employed for "All Lanes Must Reach A Turning" in the pioneering *Dear Sir,* although Kern added the countermelody for the new version. Yet Kern was equally willing to go back to earlier days for Nancy's light, bantering number, "In Love." Bringing in only minor variations, Kern reached back for the melody to "Alone At Last" from *Oh, I Say!.* Yet, such an exception apart, with his writing for *Show Boat* and now *Blue Eyes* Kern resumed moving away from the more restricted world of popular musical comedy toward a new style of Anglo-American operetta. He would rarely turn back.

Despite its failings and its reserved reception, *Blue Eyes* was a modest hit. Although it moved out of the Piccadilly to make way for the first major talking picture, *The Jazz Singer,* it finished its run at Daly's lovely little theatre on the edge of Leicester Square with a record of 276 performances.

Yet despite the musical's success, critical rejection of Kern's Scottish themes must have rankled. Several weeks after *Blue Eyes* opened the matter came up at a party Jerry, Eva, and Miss Laye were attending. Moments after Miss Laye realized Jerry had disappeared, a loud parody of Highland music began to emanate from a piano in the next room. Miss Laye opened the door and saw a sight to match the sounds. Jerry had removed his pants and had improvised a kilt from one of the Spanish shawls that decorated pianos in the 1920s. Jerry looked up at his star and calmly assured her that his kilt made him a bona fide Scot, so he could thus compose genuine Scottish music.

Show Boat opened at London's Drury Lane on May 3, 1928, with a cast every bit the equal of the New York original. The American-born Edith Day, who had delighted Broadway in *Irene, Wildflower,* and *Orange Blossoms,* and the West End in *Rose-Marie* and *The Desert Song,* was Magnolia. London's student prince, Howett Worster, was Ravenal. Paul Robeson, at last available to play the role conceived with him in mind, sang Joe. Cedric Hardwicke brought his distinguished dramatic skills to the part of Captain Andy, while beautiful, fine-voiced Marie Burke played Julie. Both the musical itself and Butt's production received general critical approval. As a result, the work compiled 350 performances at the large house. The composer's decision to trust Hammerstein with the London staging proved sound.

Yet the acclaim Jerry fully expected to win and his own realization of his accomplishments left his perceptions unaltered in one respect. After a rehearsal he did attend, Jerry startled his old friend and associate, Herman Finck, who was conducting the English production, by reasserting his affection for the long-gone Gaiety musicals. "I still like the George Edwardes school," Jerry told him. As his next show would suggest, the past meant more to Jerry than possibly he himself was aware.

By the time the Kerns and Hammerstein returned home, Jerry and Oscar had agreed to work on a new show. But there was neither a definite story nor any urgency to find one. A change in Jerry's attitude had surfaced. The days when Jerry would create two or three shows in a single season were gone forever. In fact, the forthcoming 1928–29 season would be the first since Jerry came to Broadway a quarter of a century before without so much as a single new Kern song gracing some show. Age can hardly be an explanation for the sudden slow-down. At forty-three Kern had reached a time when many musical talents mature and flourish. No doubt a sense of more determined artistry prompted some hesitation. Kern, at least for Broadway, would no longer consider producing a score by creating one or two possible hits and pleasant collection of "fillers."

The principal explanation for the sudden, marked change in Kern's pattern, however, may have been his desire to devote more time to his family. Eva's breakdown had made him painfully aware of how much attention she needed and of how little he understood his wife and daughter's requirements. Betty presented another instance. Wanting his daughter to grow up as normally as possible, Jerry had insisted she attend public school. But his affection and concern led him to unwittingly make a normal reception impossible. Jerry insisted Betty be escorted to school each day by her governess. In rainy or snowy weather, the pair were chauffeured in the family Rolls. Fellow students who failed to catch the arrival or departure could still see that Betty's clothes were several cuts above average. Enough envious youngsters made life so miserable for Betty that she ultimately prevailed on her father to let her attend Brantwood, a near-by private school. But in both public and private schools Betty found herself often taken out for weeks at a time to accompany her parents. Although she later matured into an exceptionally intelligent, gracious lady, she admits her schooling was anything but complete or normal. Hearing her tell of it, one suspects she has particularly painful recollections she does not care to share.

In one or two earlier interviews Jerry had jokingly suggested his evergrowing collection of books was driving his wife to despair. In retrospect he may have discovered how serious the joke was. Perhaps in hopes of mollifying Eva, Jerry authorized a sale of 347 books and autographs in November of 1927. Writing a preface for that catalogue Jerry noted Harry B. Smith's dictum that "one should not truthfully call himself a collector until he has acquired his first duplicate." Many of the items disposed of in this small sale were indeed duplicates, even if they included such treasures as first editions of *Robinson Crusoe* and Gray's *Elegy*. The sale brought in $28,100. The highest price was paid for the *Elegy,* the so-called Clawson copy. It was knocked down at the Anderson Galleries for $4000. The successful bidder was a Philadelphia book dealer from whom Jerry had made several purchases, Charles Sessler.

The success of the small sale may have prompted Kern to consider selling more of his collection, or the impetus could have come from elsewhere. Quite possibly Eva was still unhappy. In several later interviews, just before the larger sale, Kern again alluded to his wife's concern, although Kern's tone was no longer as bantering as it once had been. Most likely, Mitchell Kennerley, Anderson's president, underlined the advantages— familial and monetary—that would almost certainly accrue. Whatever his precise reasons, Kern agreed to dispose of his great collection.

In his autobiography, *Dukedom Large Enough,* the distinguished bookman David Randall described Kern's collection from a professional point of view:

> The Kern library was typical of the collecting era in which it was formed, guided and directed by A. Edward Newton's *Amenities of Collecting, and Kindred Affections* (Boston, 1918). Almost entirely English literature of the eighteenth to the twentieth century, it was heavy in Johnson, Goldsmith, Lamb, Shelley, Dickens, Thackeray, the Brownings, Conrad and Hardy, with a small sprinkling of seventeenth-century English and nineteenth-century American books.*

The 1920s' prosperity had created a bull market for rare books, especially those by authors Randall mentioned. Indeed, by the late 1920s the market

---

*A note in the Rosenbach Archives reveals that at least at one time Kern hoped to branch out into more esoteric areas. The note, in Kern's hand, contains an extended description of a fourteenth-century French manuscript copy of a late *chanson de geste, Voeux du Paon.* At the bottom of the page another, unidentifiable hand has written, "Of the greatest importance to Mr. Kern." Rosenbach was apparently unable to procure the rare item for the composer.

had become so feverish and buying so desperate that the *Times* reported: "For the last two years the whole book world had been informed that there were no more good books to be had." Kern put his collection under the gavel at a most propitious moment.

At the first announcement of the sale Kennerley remarked, "I do not know of a more delightful and valuable private library." Kennerley went on to list choice items, concluding with "the longest manuscript in existence in the handwriting of Oliver Goldsmith." The auctioneer could not know this would be the one item in the sale to wind up in bitter litigation.

Standing beside Kennerley, Kern chose to give him credit for the sale. Noting that his collection had grown so large he was forced to leave a full staff at home even when his family was away, he informed reporters, "In spite of this, it would not have occurred to me to sell my library if my friend, Mitchell Kennerley, had not suggested that within a short time he would give up the management of the Anderson Galleries. Somehow I could not think of my books ever being sold by anyone else, even after my death, and in a flash I saw an escape from my slavery." Since Kennerley at the time seems to have been planning quietly to expand rather than divest his auction house interests, Kern's statement was to some extent merely a public courtesy.

The sale offered 1488 items. With so much to digest, Kennerley divided the sale into two parts. The first 748 pieces would be offered in five sessions beginning January 7, 1929; the remaining pieces in a series of sessions starting January 21. Kern and Kennerley were hopeful the sale would bring somewhere near a million dollars. Headlines in the *Times* were soon disclosing how conservative their estimates had been.

On January 9 the *Times* recorded:

BURNS COPY BRINGS
$23,000 AT AUCTION
Sum, Believed More Than Poet
Got in Lifetime, Paid for
Inscribed Volume
KERN SALE YIELDS $166,363

The next evening's sale was more remarkable still, prompting the *Times* to give it front page coverage.

BOOK PRICES SOAR;
$615,387 IN KERN SALE
World Record of $28,000 for
"Pickwick Papers," That Sold
for $3,500 in 1920

The paper noted that the $273,952.50 take represented a new high for a single session in American auctions. Of the total, $252,540 was paid for 113 Dickens items. It was clear, the paper continued, that the total figures for the sale would be well above the expected million. The fourth session raked in an additional $176,400, with a first edition of *Tom Jones,* uncut and in the original binding, establishing a record $29,000.

When sessions resumed later in the month, Sessler paid $48,000 for a manuscript of Lamb's contribution to the *Table Book* and Gabriel Wells spent $68,000 to obtain Shelley's personal copy of "Queen Mab." By the time the final gavel fell on the evening of January 24 the sale had brought in $1,729,462. How much Kern earned from the sale is unknown, since most records of his purchases are lost. But Charles Sessler had his assistant, Mabel Zahn, keep tabs on the prices of books Kern had purchased from him. Her records show that Kern had paid Sessler's Philadelphia firm just over $20,000 for volumes that brought in just over $100,000. His earliest purchase had been made only nine years before.

Interviewed after the sale, Kern revealed one reason his collection had brought such a handsome return—his insistence on quality. It was an insistence he believed foreign dealers did not expect from Americans. The composer stated, "I have returned more books sent me on approval by foreign dealers than I have bought. The foreign dealer seems more interested in the title of books, while the American dealer also stresses the condition of preservation."

Kern went home the night after the final sale to confront a library with forlornly empty shelves. One of his first actions on returning to New York the next day was to stop by Temple Scott's Neighborhood Book Shop at 73rd Street and Madison Avenue and buy a rare book—the first in a new collection. Far less ambitious than his earlier collection, it was not disposed of until after his death.

Even before the auction brought him additional cash, Jerry had decided to realize an old dream—to own a yacht. One can only wonder if, as he ordered it, he thought back to the days of the Newark Yacht Club and

Uncle Tom's Cabin. The vessel was named *Show Boat* and duly christened by Edna Ferber. Although Jerry used it for cruises on Long Island Sound, he quickly decided it would better serve as transportation to Palm Beach. Kern had a number of prominent friends in the area, and his social life was active. At a party thrown by the Donahues, Woolworth heirs, Jerry met a former Philadelphia society belle with Gibson Girl features, Kathleen Ritter. At the time she was managing a dress shop. Kern came in one day, bringing George Gershwin with him. Before long the two were busy at some impromptu composing, singing their material for each other. Work at the shop came to a halt while Kathleen and her customers listened. Soon afterward Miss Ritter became Mrs. Joseph Cooper. Kern was never to see Mrs. Cooper again; their relationship became, as Mrs. Cooper wrote, "entirely an endless correspondence." But it persisted until Kern's death. Mrs. Cooper was a trained musician and an accomplished pianist, so Kern would often send her snatches of his work and ask for her opinion. He also filled her in on theatrical gossip, occasionally pouring out to her things he could not say about his associates publicly. His letters were warm and witty. Once, when Mrs. Cooper had described the extreme religiosity of her devoutly Catholic mother-in-law, with whom she was living in Baltimore, Kern addressed his reply to her care of "The Vatican, Baltimore, Md." Mrs. Cooper swears she received the letter.

Another of Jerry's pleasures in Palm Beach was gambling at Bradley's. Whenever he won enough chips he would pocket them and thumb his nose dramatically at the staid dealer before heading to the cashier.

But more serious work was at hand. Kern and Ziegfeld had had a number of heated arguments in the producer's office when royalty checks were not promptly forthcoming. So Kern was not anxious to allow Ziegfeld to produce his next work. Moreover, Kern and Hammerstein were probably sensitive to Arthur Hammerstein's chagrin at not being awarded *Show Boat*. They decided he would produce their new work, a vehicle tailored around Helen Morgan's talents. The exact approach for the piece eluded them, until one morning Oscar received a call from Jerry. He had dreamed of people on old-fashioned bicycles, wheeling around while carrying Japanese lanterns. Had Jerry dreamed of his boyhood New Jersey? Did he recall his own entrance atop a velocipede for a high school show or the highly praised effect of Oriental lanterns in *Uncle Tom's Cabin*? Did these vague, probably unrecognized remembrances of a bygone Newark suggest setting the opening scene of the new show in a bygone Hoboken? Be that as it may, the picture created the mood that allowed the men to move ahead with the work, a work they tentatively called *Just the Other Day*.

The title hinted at the feeling the authors hoped to convey. Much of the work was done aboard the *Show Boat* while the Kerns and the Hammersteins cruised Long Island Sound. The story soon became filled with what a later generation would label "in" bits. For example, Jerry and Oscar saluted Miss Morgan's omnipresent mother, Lulu, by naming an important character after her. By mid-July rehearsals had begun, and a week later the title was changed to *Sweet Adeline*.

Time and again runthroughs were punctuated by Jerry's demands for historical accuracy and by his determination to discard threadbare conventions of the musical stage. He sensed that racial and religious stereotypes were increasingly offensive, and so locked horns with Arthur Hammerstein on just how the character of the Jewish impresario should be played. Jerry persuaded the producer to remove the exaggerated mannerisms that had long been stock-in-trade for portraying Jews. Nor did minute details escape his cultivated eye. He startled his associates by stopping the first dress rehearsal, running down the aisle and shouting, "No, no, no, that's not right." The object of his displeasure was not a performer's interpretation, but a spittoon that had no rubber mat under it. Insisting spittoons of the era always had small mats beneath them, he made an assistant rush out to buy one.

Sweet Adeline opened at Atlantic City's Apollo Theatre on August 19. Curiously, little had been made in its advance notices of its connections with *Show Boat*. Only one release, centering on Miss Morgan, mentioned the show and then only to note she had appeared in it. Possibly because of this strange silence (was it that *Show Boat* was not an Arthur Hammerstein production?) or possibly because of the rush of musicals 1920s' critics took for granted, Atlantic City reviewers made no attempt to relate the two shows, but judged *Sweet Adeline* on its own. They liked what they saw and heard. Critics on both daily papers seemed to sense that Kern and Hammerstein were attempting a work several notches above the commonplace. The *Evening Union* hailed the result as "different and as tuneful and colorful as it is unusual, well-acted and full of substance. It is like reviewing history by taking sugar-coated pellets." The *Daily Press* also praised *Sweet Adeline* for its didactic virtues, seeing it as "an education to the younger generation." The men on both the resort's papers clearly felt honors of the evening went to Oscar Hammerstein. The *Evening Union* labeled the entertainment "Oscar Hammerstein's new musical" and nowhere in its review so much as mentioned Kern. Scenery and costumes were noted not merely for their beauty but for their historical accuracy as well.

That historical accuracy gave some verisimilitude to a story set, as the title hints, in the Gay Nineties. The era's tawdry small-time burlesque troupes, the limelit glamour of its Rialto, and the Spanish-American War provided background color. Kern and Hammerstein's Addie was not Adelina Patti of the beloved old barbershop song but Addie Schmidt, daughter of the immigrant proprietor of a Hoboken beer garden. She loses Tom, the sailor she loves, to her younger sister, Nellie. By way of compensation she realizes her dream to be a Broadway singing star. Three friends help her climb the ladder to success: Ruppert Day, a yokelish drama-lover; Lulu Ward, a boisterous backwater prima donna; and James Day, a man whose love she is finally able to understand and reciprocate.

Sweet Adeline opened at Hammerstein's Theatre in New York on September 3, 1929, with the following "Programme of Music":

Sweet Adeline

"Fin De Siecle"
Based by Jerome Kern on melodies of the period

ACT I

1. Song and Dance, "Play Us A Polka Dot" .... *Dot [Violet Carlson], Boys and Girls*
2. Folk Song, " 'Twas Not So Long Ago" .... *Addie [Helen Morgan] and Ensemble*
3. Song, "My Husband's First Wife" (Words by Miss Franklin) *Lulu Ward [Irene Franklin]*
4. Air and Scene, "Here Am I" .... *Addie and Dot*
5. Entrance and Chorus, "First Mate Martin" .. *Tom [Max Hoffman, Jr.], Ruppert [Charles Butterworth] and Ensemble*
6. Buffo Duo, "Spring Is Here" .... *Dot, Ruppert and Girls*
7. March Ballad, "Out of the Blue"
    (a) *Jim [Robert Chisholm], Tom and Boys*
    (b) *Dot, Nellie [Carly Bergman] and Girls*
    (c) *Drill, Gus and Will*
8. Song, "Naughty Boy" .... *Lulu, Ruppert and Girls*

306

9. Rehearsal
   a. "Oriental Moon" ...... *Sultan [Thomas Chadwick], Jester [George Djimos] and Ensemble*
   b. "Mollie O'Donahue" ...... *Maizie O'Rourke [Helen Ault] and Girls*
10. Air, "Why Was I Born?" .... *Addie*
11. Finale .... *Ensemble*

ACT II

1. Scene, Music and Reprise, "'Twas Not So Long Ago" .... *Schmidt*
2. Scene, Music and Ensemble, "Winter In Central Park" .. *Ensemble*
3. Waltz Ballad, "The Sun About To Rise" .... *Sid [John D. Seymour] and Addie*
4. Song and Chorus, "Some Girl Is On Your Mind" .... *Jim, Tom, Sid, Thornton [Jim Thornton, an old vaudevillian and composer] and Male Ensemble*
5. Duet, "Don't Ever Leave Me" .... *Addie and Jim*
6. Reprise, "Here Am I" .... *Dot*
7. Finaletto .... *Addie*
8. "Miss Lulu Ward's Specialty" (Words and music by Miss Franklin and Jerry Jarnagin)
9. Duettino and Dance, "Take Me For A Honeymoon Ride" .. *Dot, Ruppert, Gus and Will and Bicycle Girls*
10. Harbor Scene
11. Scene .... *Addie, Sid and Jim*
12. Reprise, "'Twas Not So Long Ago" .... *Chorus*
13. Finale .... *Ensemble*

Reginald Hammerstein staged the show and Robert Russell Bennett orchestrated the score. Gus Salzer conducted. Danny Dare did the choreography. Costumes were by Charles Le Maire; sets were by Gates and Morange.

New York's critics were delighted with *Sweet Adeline*, although their delight, or at least their manner of expressing it, was not the sort to compel readers to rush to buy tickets. For example, Percy Hammond began his review in the *Herald Tribune* by calling the show "a gentle opera with appropriate music" and ended his notice by branding the entertainment "one of the politest frolics of the new year." In between, much of his praise, not unlike that of his Atlantic City colleagues, centered on the affectionate and accurate sense of period captured by the authors and designers. The only song he singled out was "Why Was I Born?," a song he labeled "Kern's wailing obbligato." In contrast to tryout critics, Hammond and several other New York reviewers seemed to regard Kern's efforts as pivotal. Hammond mentioned Kern three times without once taking note of Hammerstein. Some reviewers failed to mention either Kern or Hammerstein. *Theatre Magazine*'s critic devoted virtually all of his essay to lauding the performers, although he did mention "Here Am I" and "the rather lugubrious 'Why Was I Born.'" His lone sally at judging the texture of the show itself was aimed not at the music or lyrics, but at the dancing. He concluded his notice: "And I am not at all sure that it was not a relief to sit through a musical evening without having long lines of mechanized dancing preëmpting the stage from time to time for no good reason at all." Of course, by indirection the comment flattered Kern and Hammerstein's good taste.

Some indication of how harmoniously and skillfully Kern and Hammerstein's partnership worked can be seen by comparing the Atlantic City and New York programs. Changes in the score were clearly minimal, setting a precedent for the pair's remaining efforts, even the troubled *Very Warm for May*. Between the Boardwalk and Broadway only four changes occurred. Two songs were dropped and two added. Since the songs that were discarded were both in the second act, while the additions were awarded to the first act, there must have been a slight structural imbalance that the tryout critics failed to mention but which Kern and Hammerstein discerned. Tom and Nellie's "I've Got A New Idea," sung just before "The Sun About To Rise," and Addie and Jim's "I'm Dreaming," sung just before "Don't Ever Leave Me," were the cut numbers. The new songs were "My Husband's First Wife" and "Spring Is Here." One minor, if interesting change, remembering Jerry's vision of bicycles and Japanese lanterns, was the renaming of "Take Me For A Bicycle Ride" to "Take Me For A Honeymoon Ride."

More than merely good taste, Kern's melodic invention and musicianship elevated *Sweet Adeline*'s score. Still, the critics' choice of epithets—"lugubrious," "wailing"—suggests a minor flaw in the score. Except for, possibly, "The Sun About To Rise," a certain bittersweet sameness pervaded all the better songs, written as they were for Addie—or, more specifically, for Helen Morgan. Taken one by one these songs are marvelous; and examined closely, quite different. Nonetheless, "Here Am I," "Don't Ever Leave Me," and "Why Was I Born?" are like three sweet, long-faced sisters. Still, their differences and their artistry are telling. In many ways, "Here Am I" is the most interesting. Kern marked the song "Moderato," except for a brief, six-measure passage in the verse marked "Allegretto (*alla barcarolle*)." The song is remarkable harmonically from beginning to end. Alec Wilder has detailed Kern's musicianship in his study. Suffice it to note one example here. The song is written in E flat, yet begins rather startlingly on an *f sharp* held for three beats and resolving on the fourth quarter to a *g*. This move, or a variation of it, is used repeatedly throughout the song. "Don't Ever Leave Me" is marked "Moderato (*slowly*)." The qualification seems governed by the lyric, for the truth is that if the melody (at least of the chorus) can be totally dissociated from the words, the music is quite optimistic. Except for the gently falling phrases of the first two measures (repeated twice later in the song), the musical sentences rise happily throughout. Clearly, Hammerstein's masterful lyric has colored the song indelibly. The hit of the show, "Why Was I Born?," is essentially a series of progressive phrases based on repeated notes and underscored with light blues harmonies. Wilder seems to have discovered the key to the song's success in "the alternation of single and double-note cadences." That is, phrases ending in "born," "get," "try," and "cry" alternating with phrases ending in "living," "giving," "near me" and "hear me."

"The Sun About To Shine" is a gay, sweeping waltz, one of Kern's most neglected charmers. "'Twas Not So Long Ago" is a dainty piece, employed as a sort of leit-motif throughout the play, and one that Kern was not far-fetched in labeling a folk song. Sigmund Spaeth, after some musical snooping, says it is indeed borrowed from a Viennese song, *"Es was schon damals so."* But that is the very title Hammerstein gave to the secondary German lyrics. "Out Of The Blue" is an interesting song with a pleasant melody. It is too enervated to be a ballad, but does not quite seem to work in the semi-march tempo that Kern suggested. Perhaps the most fascinating piece in the score is "A Girl Is On Your Mind," a grippingly effective concerted number for the principal men and one that uses blues colorings for its languid soliloquies. "Play Us A Polka Dot," a lively dance number, is noteworthy largely for its clever quotation of von Suppé. (Did Kern use the same melody he had for "Polka Dot" in *Sitting Pretty* and, for that matter, did he reemploy *Lucky*'s "Spring Is Here" for *Sweet Adeline*'s song with the same title?) As he so often did, Kern went back to his trunk for several tunes—in this case the two songs used in a rehearsal scene. England had heard "Oriental Moon" earlier, in both *Fun of the Fayre* and *The Cabaret Girl,* where it was called "Oriental Dreams." "Mollie O'Donahue" had been "All You Need Is A Girl" in *Sitting Pretty.* "Naughty Boy" has the lilt of a Princess Theatre song and distinct echoes of "The Sun Shines Brighter," so it too may have an earlier provenance.

For its first two months *Sweet Adeline* was the hottest ticket in town, selling out at every performance. *Variety* confidently forecast that the show would run out the season and possibly even span the warm weather. Then the stock market collapsed. Initially the crash seemed to have less effect on *Sweet Adeline* than on many other shows. Weekly grosses remained at capacity, although advance sales steadily dwindled. By the new year, however, the musical could not escape the slump. Box office figures fell dramatically, and the show was running at a slight loss when it closed after only 234 performances.

Shortly after *Sweet Adeline* opened and as the year was drawing to a close, Ziegfeld gave theatregoers hope of hearing a second Kern score before summer. In mid-November he announced that the composer would write the score for a new Ed Wynn revue. The announcement was not totally chimerical, as so many of Ziegfeld's promises were. Come February Ziegfeld did offer *Simple Simon* with Wynn as star. But no Kern songs graced the score. However, on February 11, 1930, a week before *Simple Simon* premiered, Dillingham brought Fred Stone into the New Amsterdam in *Ripples* with one spicy Kern interpolation, "Anything Can Happen Any Day" (lyric, Graham John).

If the Wall Street fizzle had been 1929's most conspicuous event, other events were nevertheless quietly determining Kern's future. In 1925 a silent screen version of *Sally,* with Kern's music played as an accompaniment by theatre musicians, had proved a box office failure, even though First National had prevailed on Leon Errol to recreate his Broadway antics and had starred the popular Colleen Moore. But in 1929 the studio had lured Marilyn Miller to Hollywood to make a sound version, with Joe E. Brown in the Errol role and T. Roy Barnes in Catlett's part. Released at a time when Hollywood's earliest outpouring of musicals were inundating the market, it proved a strong contender against tough competition. The film's success signaled that Kern's songs could be as much at home on the screen as on the stage.

18

The "Talkies," and New Producers

With the craze for "all talkie" musicals sweeping Hollywood, First National signed Jerry and Otto Harbach to compose songs for a musical to be called *Stolen Dreams*. The story concerned a subject popular with screenwriters at the time—aviators in World War I. Principals were to include Irene Delroy, Jack Whiting, and Bramwell Fletcher.

The Kerns rented a bungalow at the Beverly Hills Hotel, and Jerry and Otto set to work. But the balmy air frequently offered irresistible distractions. Lunch was often turned into a gala production, with Jerry personally seeing to his secret salad dressing. Jerry sometimes joined Otto and his young son, Bill, at miniature golf, a pastime that had suddenly exploded all over the map. While Jerry was delighted to watch the youngster play, he grew concerned as a polio scare developed. He feared that clubs, handed from one player to another, might somehow carry polio germs and infect little Bill. One morning as the three set out to a miniature putting range, Jerry presented an attractively wrapped, elongated package to Bill. On opening it Bill discovered it held his own monogrammed club. Jerry accompanied the gift with a stern if loving warning not to allow anyone else to use it.

Work on the film proceeded apace. Filming began in mid-July and concluded on September 15, 1930. Coincidently, Marilyn Miller was shooting *Sunny* at the same time, although the film only employed a handful of the top songs from the show. A week after *Stolen Dreams* was finished, the Kerns returned to New York. By that time the film's title had been changed to *The Man in the Sky*. In a short while Kern began receiving ominous news about the picture. Hollywood's outpouring of musicals in 1929 and early 1930 had sated its public. Singing and dancing suddenly became anathema at the box office. Even air battles had momentarily had their day, although there was little First National could do about that. But it could attempt to save its new film, finally called *Men of the Sky*, by releasing it as a songless drama, and that was precisely what the studio did in 1931.

Cutting of the songs was tragic, for Kern had composed one of his sweetest, most ingratiating scores. Had the music remained, several new songs might well have been added to Kern's list of standards. "Every Little While" (later published separately) is a gently flowing, tender ballad. Written to an ABA¹C pattern, the song concludes with an effective series of rocking, cascading triplets. "All's Well With The World" is a charming waltz whose first four bars offer a melody identical to that in the first four bars of *Fiddler on the Roof*'s "Matchmaker." But whereas "Matchmaker" continues in much the same vein, "All's Well With The World" proceeds with lightly dropping, nostalgically tinged phrases. "Stolen Dreams," a second ballad, possesses a quiet, stately dignity. A sprightly canzonetta was given two titles: "You've Got To Meet Sweet Marguerite" and "I'll Share Them All With You," while a gay tyrolean asked "What's Become Of Spring." Page after page of incidental music offered equally gracious, attractive material. One can only wonder why Kern never attempted to buy back the whole score and reuse it. Perhaps he tried, unsuccessfully. It may be significant that, apart from additional songs he created for the film version of *Sweet Adeline*, which First National's parent company, Warner Brothers, released in 1934, Kern never worked for the studio again.

Kern's presence on the West Coast spared him the tedium of court proceedings in Philadelphia that stemmed from the auction of his library. The manuscript copy of Goldsmith's translation of Vida's "Game of Chess" had been returned to Kern, its authenticity questioned. Kern had purchased it from Sessler in March of 1928, while Sessler was in London on book business and Kern was working there on *Show Boat* and *Blue Eyes*. Kern had paid Sessler the same £5600 Sessler had paid for it, plus a 5 per cent agent's commission and 15 per cent that was to represent Sessler's profit. Now Kern demanded Sessler offer either indisputable credentials for the manuscript or repay him the full purchase price with interest. Kern may have been piqued not only at the challenge to the piece's authenticity, but by the recollection that it was one of the few items that had not brought a profit at the sale. In fact, knocked down at $27,000, it had actually represented a slight loss. Sessler, like Kern, was no doubt doubly annoyed. His reaction seems to have been not merely a defense of his own knowledgeableness, but a meanly motivated response to the tremendous returns Kern had realized. When both parties remained adamant, litigation was inevitable. Sessler corralled the more distinguished authorities, renowned bibliophiles Benjamin A. Maggs and Charles Geoffrey Des Graz. But both of these witnesses had at one time or another sold the manuscript and so had vested interests in preserving their own reputations. Kern's attorney, Mark Holstein, obtained the opinions of Katherine C. Balderston, a Goldsmith scholar and assistant professor of literature at Wellesley, and the respected bookseller, Temple Scott. They spoke with equal authority and were untainted by any earlier connections with the holograph. Unfortunately, neither side's evidence was truly conclusive. In the end Sessler was ordered to take back the book and return the purchase price—but without interest.

On their return from California, the Kerns did not remain in Cedar Knolls for long. After little more time than it took them to repack their bags they sailed for a European holiday. They returned on Jerry's favorite ship, the *Olympic,* reaching New York on November 11. But Jerry returned home with little to do. Hollywood had dropped him for the time being and so, seemingly, had a Depression-hit Broadway. In early December Jerry wrote Harry B. Smith that "Eva has been equally pressed what with no governess and then a new governess and then no governess etc." He also advised Smith that for want of work he was taking his family to Palm Beach on December 9. While they were in Florida, Ziegfeld announced Kern and Hammerstein would provide a new vehicle for Evelyn Laye. He added that Hammerstein would soon leave to join Kern in Palm Beach. Hammerstein did go, but the project came to naught, ending an unsatisfactory year on a weak note.

The year 1931 began as sourly. In February Kern was slapped with a nasty law suit. One Regina Mermel demanded $50,000 damages, alleging that in 1928 Kern had engaged her to exploit him as a composer for films. She claimed she "stimulated competition" only to have Kern exclude her from a private $500,000 deal he then made with Warner Brothers. Nothing further seems to have been heard of the affair, so it is reasonable to conclude that the lady's charges were apocryphal at best. Certainly, given the figures in Kern's later contracts, the half-million sum seems distinctly suspect.

Relief from inaction and nuisances came from an unexpected corner. In 1930 a young vaudeville agent, all too aware that two-a-day was virtually dead, began to look about for a new source of revenue. Mechel Salpeter had been born to immigrant parents in New York on June 28, 1892, but early on had begun to use the name Max Gordon for professional purposes. Small, slightly professorial in appearance, Gordon combined a sure eye for talent and a rare refinement of taste with a mercurial temper and a histrionic emotionalism. He once stood on the ledge of an open window threatening to jump if money he needed was not forthcoming. His first two producing ventures had been triumphs. *Three's a Crowd* and *The Band Wagon* were brilliant revues, gorgeously mounted, memorably cast, and filled with insistently melodic music. They helped establish the mold out of which the thoughtfully intimate revues of the 1930s were cast.

Once *The Band Wagon* had been successfully launched in June 1931, Gordon grew anxious to try his hand at book shows. He casually mentioned to Max Dreyfus that he would like to do something as daring and well-integrated as *Show Boat* had been, suggesting to the publisher that nothing quite so artful had been attempted since. Gordon carefully omitted mentioning Kern by name, but he knew Dreyfus would shrewdly read his message and, he hoped, act on it. He was right. A few weeks later he received Dreyfus's invitation to dinner at Dreyfus's Bronxville home. "Kern would like to see you," Dreyfus told him, adding by way of reassurance, "He will be there." To impress the composer, Gordon read up on everything he could discover about Jerry, poring over old clippings and reviews and going so far as to have a friend play him all of Kern's published music. Sitting with his wife on the train to Bronxville, he was perturbed by second thoughts. Fears that he might appear too forward or brazen prompted him to weigh the alternative of remaining almost mute, allowing his shows to speak for him. As they rode up to Dreyfus's house, set far back from the road and surrounded by stately trees and huge shrubs, Gordon decided simply to let the conversation take its own turns. Since Gordon himself was so short he saw Kern as "of medium height," remembering more accurately that "his hair was graying and receding, his nose strong and sharp, his clothes well tailored and immaculate. Through his heavy spectacles I saw eyes that were alert and impish, while his mouth spread in a warm smile illuminating his whole countenance."

Kern probably sensed Gordon's nervousness, so he opened the meeting by warmly congratulating Gordon on *The Band Wagon*. Gordon responded by saying how much he had enjoyed *Sweet Adeline* and how sad he was that Kern had been unrepresented on Broadway by any subsequent effort. Kern dominated the talk at dinner, awing the producer with his deep, broad-ranging interests. After a while this nimble display of knowledge started to worry Gordon. He suddenly felt inadequate, comparing his limited schooling and humble beginnings to Jerry's extensive learning and comfortable roots. He saw his chances of working with so erudite an artist slowly fading away. As soon as dinner was over and Dreyfus had passed cigars around, Kern asked Gordon to follow him to an upstairs bedroom. Shutting the door behind them, Kern explained,

> I did not wish to say this downstairs in front of the others because I thought I might embarrass you. However, Dreyfus knows how I feel. I think you are going to mean a great deal to the theatre. These are bad times, and the old producers are falling away. You can be the theatre's white hope. No, don't protest, there is no need for modesty here. I have seen *Three's a Crowd* and, as you know, *The Band Wagon*. It is clear to me that you are in the tradition of Ziegfeld and Charles Frohman. You are like me, a devil on details. You spare nothing to make a production as right and as attractive as possible.

When Gordon tried to thank Kern for the compliments, Jerry silenced him with a wave of the hand and continued,

> Dreyfus tells me that you are now interested in producing a musical and that you would like to do one by me. It happens that I am working on one with Otto Harbach. I would like very much to invite you to my home next week—I live here in Bronxville, too—and we'll discuss it further. You can listen to some of the music I have completed. If you approve, we can talk terms. I am thinking in terms of another musical which, like *Show Boat*, would attempt to explore new paths. I think the American public is ready to accept musical theatre that is more than routine claptrap. *Show Boat* has encouraged me to think that it is possible to work artistically and with greater integrity in the medium than we have imagined. Otto has an idea for a musical that lends itself to serious treatment. You should know that we have been talking about eliminating chorus girls, production numbers and formal comedy routines. We are striving to make certain that there will be a strong motivation for the music throughout.

Contracts were signed after Gordon's first hearing. For the next two and a half months Gordon was a familiar figure on the Bronxville train, going up several times each week to listen to Jerry and Otto's latest material. Rehearsals got under way at the end of August.

Gordon learned quickly that Kern was not joking when he labeled himself a devil on detail. Hardly a rehearsal passed without Kern demanding some adjustment or other that almost any other artist might have ignored. Even the color of men's ties did not escape his attention. A Kern ploy infuriated Gordon. As the producer recalled, "He could be maddeningly irritating, constantly countering almost any suggestion with an impertinent 'Why?'—a deliberate tactic calculated to unnerve the questioner." Since no one else recalls this tactic it may well be that Kern employed it specifically to rile Gordon. But Kern just as readily found witty outlets for his deviltry. Bettina Hall affected an exaggeratedly trilled Continental "r." In an unguarded moment she once asked Jerry how she could get from one side of the stage to the other. Not about to lose a golden opportunity, Jerry instantly retorted, "Just roll over on your Rs." Miss Hall apparently did not catch his double meaning.

The Cat and the Fiddle was first offered to the public at Philadelphia's Garrick Theatre on Tuesday, September 23, 1931. Several local critics opened their reviews by praising Max Gordon, with both the *Inquirer* and the *Evening Ledger* saluting his courage in mounting so off-beat a musical. The *Evening Ledger,* virtually alone in harboring reservations, rued that the book was "uninteresting, flat, pallid and . . . lethargic." But this complaint aside, the paper joined in the paeans for the production, the cast, and, most of all, for Kern. Indeed, its critic was not alone in concluding, "Jerome Kern's music . . . is something to be cheered. He has wrought better than in 'Show Boat,' 'Sweet Adeline,' and his other recent hits."

In the paper's morning sister, the *Public Ledger,* Arthur B. Waters prefaced his praise by offering an extended list of earlier Kern works, demonstrating how Kern was at long last securing an unshakable reputation. Still, it was not merely his impressive string of successes that was marking him out as unique. Circumstances were also in his favor—circumstances that critics may have been too close to to ignore, but that Kern himself may have alluded to in his initial conversation with Gordon. In suggesting that the American public was ready to accept more serious lyric theatre, Jerry was tacitly acknowledging the changing audience brought about by the lure of talking films and the agony of the Depression. The factory hand and his date in the last row of the balcony, that imaginary pair whom George M. Cohan had often professed to play to, had, for the most part, deserted live entertainment. Grinding economic necessity had discouraged many once marginal white-collar patrons. The theatre was never again to be an entertainment for the masses, and this was especially true of the 1930s, when Kern's last four musicals were to premiere. What remained was largely an affluent, well-educated, and relatively discerning coterie of loyalists. Their tastes were still channeled by a group of superior critics and columnists. Further, many of his lesser competitors had rushed away to Hollywood. Kern was the right man at the right time.

Kern's deviltry manifested itself in another way during the Philadelphia tryout. Gordon detested off-color material so often employed in musicals. At times he deleted even slightly suggestive lyrics and scenes. He had often proclaimed that the best entertainment was clean entertainment. Knowing this, Kern quietly drafted a new scene filled with wild scatalogical jokes, and carefully coached the comic secondary leads, Doris Carson and Eddie Foy, Jr., on the way to play it. He emphasized how important it was for the two players to present the new scene in as natural and straight a manner as possible, so that it would flow undetected as part of the play. At the first obscene reference Gordon "went through the ceiling of the Garrick Theatre in indignation." Now it was his turn to stomp down the aisle demanding a halt in rehearsals. Only when he noticed Jerry "beside himself with laughter" and saw tears streaming down the composer's face did he realize that he had been the butt of one of Jerry's practical jokes.

Even if Gordon had been a boorish, foul-mouthed variety of producer he would have immediately understood that the inserted scene clashed with the show's moonlit romanticism. *The Cat and the Fiddle*'s story moved starry-eyed through the boites and by-ways that were lovers' worlds in Brussels. On a July night two young composers meet on a moonlit quay. One is a handsome young Romanian, Victor Florescu; the other is an attractive American, Shirley Sheridan. Despite their shared youth and love of music, their ambitions are markedly disparate. Victor is a highbrow, floating in dreams of art for art's sake. Shirley wants only to write good popular songs. When Victor suspects Shirley of attempting to tamper with his opera the two have a falling-out. Of course, by curtain time they have been reconciled and work together on music for a Pierrot and Pierrette story.

By the time *The Cat and the Fiddle* opened at the Globe on October 15, 1931, the Depression had been under way for just short of two years and was fast approaching bottom. The days when Ziegfeld or Dillingham could demand a top price of five or six or even seven dollars were gone. Gordon dared not ask more than a $4.40 top. He even had to rescue the Globe from films, although the rescue was short-lived.

Programs in Philadelphia and Newark had listed Robert Russell Bennett as Orchestral Partitur and continued with the following somewhat pretentious announcement: "No attempt is here made to do more than indicate a list of numbers which may be readily disassociated from the complete musical fabric." By the time the musical reached New York the synopsis of music read simply:

The Cat and the Fiddle

ACT I

"The Night Was Made For Love" .... *Pompineau [George Meader]*

"The Love Parade" .... *Pompineau and Maizie [Flora LeBreton]*

"The Breeze Kissed Your Hair" .... *Victor [Georges Metaxa]*

"Try To Forget" .. *Shirley [Bettina Hall], Alec [Eddie Foy, Jr.] and Angie [Doris Carson]*

"Poor Pierrot" .... *Compere and Commere*

"Episode in Victor's Play, 'The Passionate Pilgrim'" ..... *Odette [Odette Myrtil]*

Finaletto ...... *Claudine [Lucette Valsy], Constance [Margaret Adams], Colbert [Peter Chambers]*

ACT II

"She Didn't Say 'Yes'" .... *Shirley*

"A New Love Is Old" .... *Victor*

"One Moment Alone" .... *Shirley and Victor*

"Hh! Cha! Cha!" .... *Shirley and others*

Cafe Scene .... *Pompineau, Victor, Shirley*

Finale

Dance in Phantasy by Albertina Rasch Dancers

One unusual feature of the program was its careful listing of every member of the orchestra along with instruments the musician played. The list disclosed the orchestra was composed of a concert master, two pit pianos (with one pianist alternating on a celeste), one on-stage piano, two violins, a viola, a cello, a bass (whose player doubled on a tuba!), a flute and an oboe (with the artists doubling on saxophones), a clarinet (with the clarinetist playing the bass clarinet and a third saxophone when necessary), three trumpets, one trombone, a musician who moved from marimba to xylophone to glockenspiel as needed, and a final musician who served as both tympanist and drummer. The eighteen musicians, termed "soloists" on the playbill, constituted a noticeable drop from the twenty-odd players then required by the musicians' union. Gordon, Bennett, and Kern, assisted by a popular composer-conductor, Al Goodman, had prevailed on the union to make an exception for *The Cat and the Fiddle,* granting in return substantially higher pay to the hands retained. Goodman, who knew every musician on the street, was given a free hand in selecting the best available players.

Kern's dependable standby, Victor Baravalle, conducted, while Bennett did the orchestrations, even though the New York program noted, "The orchestration devised by Jerome Kern was scored by R. Russell Bennett." Kern, of course, had made numerous suggestions on which instruments to employ and had presented Bennett with an unusually elaborate outline to serve as guide. But as he had with the orchestration for "Make Believe" in *Show Boat,* Bennett drew his own conclusions and went his independent way without serious opposition.

The Cat and the Fiddle was directed by José Ruben, who also played a principal part. Henry Dreyfuss provided the settings.

New York's critics were harder on the show than reviewers in Philadelphia and Newark had been. This was a common enough occurrence, especially after critics adopted a tougher stance with the onset of the Depression, but in the case of the new musical several of the unhappy reviewers betrayed some guilt feelings at not judging more softly. What disturbed objectors was the libretto and much of the casting. Robert Garland of the *World-Telegram* found Harbach's effort "workmanlike and not overly inspired." A less tactful *New Yorker* critic suggested that "Mr. Harbach had really outdone himself in banality." Nevertheless, with so much else in the show to admire, the critic ended his notice a bit apologetically, concluding, "When you come to count your blessings at 'The Cat and the Fiddle,' you find that you have more than had your money's worth. It is just that you *think* you're being bored, I guess." *Time* magazine's man berated the principals: "Unhappily, neither Miss Hall nor Mr. Metaxa have very attractive voices. Miss Hall belongs to that school of musicomedy prima donnas which signifies its charm and purity by assuming too, too graceful postures, willowing all over the stage." Similarly, the *Times* assailed Metaxa, regretting that he had "a metallic quality in his singing that destroys the ardor of his full-voiced numbers." Both the magazine and the paper joined forces to salute Foy and Miss Carson, who played Shirley's brother and sister-in-law. The *Times*'s Brooks Atkinson recorded that Foy, "the most likeable india rubber clown on the stage, is paired with Doris Carson, who is elastic and droll and beaming." Atkinson was equally delighted with Lawrence Grossmith, who had first worked with Kern on the initial Princess Theatre show, *Nobody Home,* and who now played suave Major Sir George Wilfred Chatterly. But of the comedienne who played Odette, Victor's leading lady, he could only write, "Odette Myrtil brings us back to the workaday theatre with the hackneyed mannerisms of her overacting and the harsh tone in her singing." Tellingly, Atkinson devoted his entire first paragraph to Kern.

> Since Jerome Kern is not only a song writer but a composer of music, they have made another attempt to break free of the stereotyped musical comedy patterns in "The Cat and the Fiddle," which was acted at the Globe last evening. It is a gallant attempt with considerable achievement, and it gives Mr. Kern greater scope than he has had before. As a song writer in good Times Square standing he touches off a torch-song again. But he also writes tinkling ballads like "She Didn't Say 'Yes,'" love serenades like "The Night Was Made For Love," a variable score for a Pierrot ballet, to say nothing of a ravishing piano fugue. Among the Broadway show shops, Mr. Kern is the man who is not afraid of hurdy-gurdy melodies and who demands something more than a thump and a squeal from his orchestra. "The Cat and the Fiddle" may not be his best score, but it is genuine and infectiously romantic and a joy to the last double piano note.

A comparison of Philadelphia and New York programs reveals that the only major change in the first act's musical program was a reversal in the order of two songs. One number, "Don't Ask Me Not To Sing," was cut in the second act, although phrases of its melody were retained and employed throughout the orchestral accompaniment. Two songs were added in the act, "A New Love Is Old" and "Hh! Cha! Cha!"

There can be no question that this score was Kern's most ambitious work to date. A device he had used timidly before, the extended musical lead-in, was utilized from beginning to end. Orchestral passages accompanied much of the action, and there were a number of recitatives. Kern ranged broadly, and often wittily, in searching for melodies to provide the proper atmosphere. In the opening scene he resorted to Belgian and Bohemian folk tunes to set a proper mood. To suggest that Shirley was not the most original of composers, he paraphrased Grieg in one of her purported compositions. He even borrowed material from himself, using *Show Boat's* "Why Do I Love You?" as a countermelody for "Hh! Cha! Cha!"; and the opening measures of Angie and Alec's dance at the end of the first act were lifted from a passage in *The Beauty Prize's* "Meet Me Down On Main Street." However, the *New Yorker's* critic went too far when he accused Kern of stealing "Try To Forget" from Richard Rodgers's "My Heart Stood Still." If the first seven notes are similar (actually, one moves from a dominant, the other from a tonic), the development is unique, and unfortunate, some would add, for the song moves from one felicitous invention to another, only to end disastrously on an abrupt, flat phrase. The *New Yorker* critic might have been on surer ground had he suggested that Kern possibly drew his ideas for "The Night Was Made For Love" from the curious tag to "I Saw The Roses And Remembered You," that obscure, arty song he had written in 1923. The newer song's sweeping arpeggios and decorative triplets give it an arioso quality, even though its range is safely under two octaves. The lush romanticism of its melody proved especially effective in the theatre, where the song was introduced shortly after the first curtain and reprised in one form or another whenever it became necessary to establish a soft, silvery mood. Because "She Didn't Say 'Yes'" persists in accenting the fourth beat in each measure of its cute little ascending and descending basic theme, Alec Wilder sees it as foreshadowing more "swinging" melodies Kern would later write for films. Actually the accents, at least in the vocal score, do not occur when Shirley first sings the song, but only in a reprise. Similarly, Wilder's remark that the song is one of Kern's earliest to discard the verse is technically correct, but, again, in the show, where it was part of a more extended musical number, this would have almost certainly been lost on the audience.

Lunching at Dinty Moore's the Monday after the show opened, Jerry defended his collaborator, noting, "The reviewers were not kind to Otto Harbach but I think the libretto is magnificent. It provided the setting for the music, just as dark velvet makes a jewel shine brighter. The characters are so normal and understandable. They might be at the next table." If there was an unwitting hint of arrogance in his gem-fabric analogy, Kern was clearly sincere in his respect for his dependable, likable librettist. He quickly moved on to a philosophy of composing he had expressed before: "A composer never should compose unless he has something to say. The characters wrote the music; I only placed the notes on the paper. That is why it is the most direct, uncompromising thing I have accomplished—the audience is not the target; it sits on the sidelines." This dangerous indifference to an audience's reaction was not typical of Kern. What he was really saying, of course, was that an artful work with inner integrity could have a life of its own.

His hopes for *The Cat and the Fiddle* remained high. Friends had suggested that the show could be turned into "the greatest musical moving picture ever filmed," and Jerry thought such optimism not too farfetched, insisting there were "no wide gaps" in the work. Although he kept a watchful eye on royalties, he wondered out loud what really made a hit song—and many of the same friends had crowded around him on opening night assuring him that such and such a tune would soon be the rage. "What do they mean," he asked, "that it will sell many copies? Or that the boot-black on the street will whistle it?" His own answer was simple and took a long-range view: "To me a hit is something that will endure." Jerry closed the interview on a wryly amusing note, feigning concern about the musical's future. Most of his major hits of the 1920s had titles beginning with the letter "S." Citing *Show Boat, Stepping Stones, Sally, Sunny,* and *Sweet Adeline* (but conveniently leaving out *The Night Boat, Good Morning, Dearie,* and *Criss Cross*), he mused whether he had a lucky letter.

No one knew better than Kern that he had little to worry about. Of the season's musicals only *Of Thee I Sing* ran longer, and that played at a house far smaller than *The Cat and the Fiddle*'s. Still, the Depression did create problems. As the financial picture darkened, receipts began to fall off with the advent of Lent. At the beginning of May, with everyone involved with the show agreeing to accept pay cuts, Gordon lowered the top ticket price to $3.30. Three weeks later a ghastly incident occurred.

No Broadway producer had a more glowing reputation than Charles Dillingham. Only Ziegfeld rivaled him in the excellence of his productions. The two customarily led the way as well in increasing ticket prices, something their reputations often allowed them to accomplish with impunity. But where Ziegfeld was rude, undependable, and sometimes downright treacherous, Dillingham was the consummate gentleman—unfailingly courteous and trustworthy. If he had a flaw, it was one he also shared with Ziegfeld. He lived up to his last penny—he had homes and apartments everywhere and sported only the finest hand-tailored clothes. Starting in the late 1920s, with *Lucky,* in fact, his heretofore sound judgment eluded him, and he suffered a string of costly flops. After the stock market collapse wiped out most of his holdings, he remortgaged his sole remaining asset, the Globe. Nonetheless, his financial picture continued to darken. When Gordon went to the theatre to collect his part of the receipts for the week of May 16 he made a sickening discovery. Dillingham had absconded with virtually the entire gross. In desperation, Gordon prevailed on the company to wait an extra week for payment. The show was hastily transferred to the Cohan, where Gordon kept it afloat until he could take it on the road at the end of September. It had rolled up 395 performances. The original company remained on tour until mid-March of 1933. Meanwhile a second company played the West Coast. London welcomed the show at the Palace Theatre on March 4, 1932, and kept it on the boards for 219 performances.

Although Kern was understandably furious at Dillingham's behavior, he was forgiving. In the two years that remained to him Dillingham was forced to live off charity. The same Louis Lotito whom Jerry had teased at the first *Stepping Stones* rehearsal quietly began collecting small sums from old Dillingham associates, enough to give the forlorn producer $100 a week. This may have seemed a vast amount to many pounding the pavements for work, but to Dillingham it was a tragic comedown. Jerry was one of the men who regularly added something to the pot.

The deepening Depression had hurt Oscar Hammerstein far more than it had disturbed Kern. It had early on destroyed *Sweet Adeline'*s chances of a long run. Even before the musical had closed Oscar went to Hollywood. But the work he was asked to do there stifled his freedom and imagination. Hoping to put so many unsatisfying months behind him, he returned to New York, only to be confronted with further failures and even tragedy. He worked on three successive flops and, worse, had to sit by helplessly while his family lost its theatre, *Sweet Adeline'*s old home. Undaunted, Hammerstein purposefully set aside all of 1931 to work on just one project. His original plan for a libretto, somewhat nebulous, centered on a music publisher's office. Early outlines called for a contemporary setting, depicting the noisy excitement of Tin Pan Alley. Exactly when Jerry first heard of Oscar's new work is lost, but when he did finally see the material he quickly made a crucial suggestion to his friend, urging him to tell his story in a more escapist setting, one comfortably distant in time or place from a troubled world audiences were anxious to forget. Since both men were half German, some place in that musical land clearly presented an attractive alternative. Both were steeped in its melodic traditions, and they knew how appealing the setting could be to the large number of successful immigrants and first-generation Americans who still looked back affectionately at the motherland. History was shortly to throw the pair a cruel, ironic curve, but naturally neither foresaw it.

Shortly after *The Cat and the Fiddle* was launched, Kern turned his full attentions to the new show.* Without his realizing it, Kern had jotted down the principal theme for the show's hit song a year or so before. He had jotted it down because of his fascination with bird calls, a fascination, like so many of Jerry's broad interests, that he pursued with scholarly determination. In this instance the pursuit was aided by one of the Kerns's friends and neighbors, Dr. Oliver L. Austin. Austin was a respected ornithologist who maintained large bird sanctuaries on Cape Cod and in Bronxville. Learning of the composer's curiosity, he invited him to spend time at both places with him. Kern accepted with alacrity. Whenever his schedule permitted, Kern passed hours in the fields, often netting birds to better record their songs.

But his inspiration for "I've Told Every Little Star" came not on one of his trips with Austin, but while he and Eva were at a house party in Nantucket, at the home of his cousin, Walter Pollak. Kern was awakened one morning by a bird singing just outside his window. The warbling so enchanted him that he awoke Eva, and they listened together. When the bird flew away, Jerry sang the melody over and over to himself. Then, since he and Eva had not gone to bed until shortly before dawn, he went to sleep. When he awoke again late in the morning he set about writing down the theme. To his dismay he could not recall it correctly. Nor could Eva sing it for him. He dressed and went downstairs to the piano, but soon gave up in frustration. The song that had seemed so memorable and simple just a few hours before eluded him completely. The incident spoiled his whole day. But by a stroke of luck the bird obligingly reappeared near his window ledge the next morning. Kern grabbed a pencil and an index card that was

* On October 18, 1931, the New York *Times* noted that Hammerstein and Arthur Hopkins were completing their version of *Camille*, for which Kern would provide the score. Helen Morgan apparently was to star. However, nothing came of the work.

near by and stole downstairs. As quietly as he could in the sleeping house he put the tune on paper, writing below it, "6 a.m. Bird song from the willow tree outside east window. J.K." As Kern noted, "It was a complete phrase and a perfectly rounded melodic treatment." Returning home, he played the melody for Austin, who identified the bird as a Cape Cod Sparrow with the happy Latinate name of *Melospiza melodia*. The grateful composer presented the ornithologist with the index card, which Austin kept tacked above his desk until he died.

Just who would produce the new musical became a matter of some delicacy. Oscar's uncle had done a fine job with *Sweet Adeline,* but Arthur Hammerstein had lost more than his theatre. His finances were in a shambles and his zest for producing was gone. Max Gordon took an off-hand remark by Jerry to mean that he would be allowed to bring the piece to New York. He assumed the prickly little tensions that had arisen between him and Jerry to be just commonplace irritants between two tough-fibered associates. Ziegfeld's plans to revive *Show Boat* turned attention to him. In February 1932 Jerry and Oscar sent Ziegfeld registered letters canceling their old arrangements. New details were agreed to and signed on April 26, eight days after rehearsals had actually gotten under way. Yet all the while both Jerry and Oscar quietly entertained grave doubts about Ziegfeld's ability to mount their new piece. Ziegfeld was aging and rumors were rife about his failing health. Worse, like most of the 1920s' high-living, glamorous managers, Ziegfeld was trapped in the financial maelstrom. In his attempt to rise above it he had mounted a string of costly failures that cast doubts on his theatrical acumen. Some of the doubts faded after the revival opened on May 19 to joyous notices. The show quickly became a smash hit all over again. Ziegfeld had given it his customarily lavish treatment and, more importantly, had brought back virtually all of the original players—paying premiums to rehire several performers he had helped make stars. The only two principals not returning were Howard Marsh and Jules Bledsoe. Paul Robeson assumed the role originally designed with him in mind, while the 1920s' leading male musical star, Dennis King, portrayed Ravenal. The consensus was that they were improvements over the excellent originals.

Despite his new triumph, with its promise of redemption, the task of piloting the musical claimed a heavy toll on Ziegfeld's health. His physical deterioration became conspicuous. A late June heat wave sent ticket sales plummeting. The sudden collapse of business coupled with the producer's constant wild partying proved too much. Ziegfeld suffered a severe attack of pleurisy. When his doctors prescribed a complete rest, his wife, Billie Burke, rushed back from California to be with him. Stories of his late night carousings and one glimpse of his gaunt appearance convinced her he would be better off at her Santa Monica home. Even before she and his loyal staff could get him on a train the producer became incoherent for long stretches. On the train ride west he grew delirious, talking forlornly of his Chicago boyhood and early successes. He rallied briefly, but shortly after he reached his wife's home he suffered a relapse. Rushed to the Cedars of Lebanon hospital, he died there on July 22.

With the revival threatened with shuttering, A. C. Blumenthal offered to keep the production alive. Blumenthal was a successful developer of motion picture palaces who had married one of Ziegfeld's greatest beauties, Peggy Fears. Inevitably, discussions about keeping *Show Boat* on the boards led to talk about Jerry and Oscar's new work. Blumenthal was given a typescript of the libretto. His own reaction was favorable to everything except the working title, *Karl and Sieglinde*. Yet for all his theatrical dabbling, Blumenthal did not trust his lone reaction. He handed the typescript to both his wife and to his manager, Nick Holde, lest his own enthusiasm be misguided. They shared his feelings. Blumenthal then told Holde, "Call up Jerry and Oscar. Let's get some action." Jerry and Oscar were to learn that Blumenthal brought an unyielding businesslike efficiency to all his enterprises. Blumenthal made only two demands. One was that a better title be chosen; the other was that the show could not cost more than $100,000. Since his name meant little to the theatregoing public, he also suggested that his wife be credited as producer. Jerry and Oscar readily acquiesced. By default and by courtesy a producer had been found.

Apparently in deference to Blumenthal's dislike of the working title, the contracts he signed with Kern and Hammerstein on August 9, 1932, left the musical momentarily nameless. The contracts also specifically gave him the right to credit his wife, Miss Fears, as producer publicly while he worked anonymously behind the scenes.

Harking back over the years, Miss Fears has only pleasant memories of working with Kern. Surprisingly, it was with the tactful, pacific Hammerstein that she encountered difficulties. Her recollections include a fearsome battle with Hammerstein, when he wanted the aging concert artist, Reinald Werrenrath, for the role that ultimately went to Tullio Carminati. Werrenrath was later awarded a smaller role.

A second encounter between the pair led to Oscar grabbing a train for Atlantic City and pouting there for several days. More certifiable than any backstage bickerings is the principal change made during the tryout, the disastrous insertion for a single performance of a ballet in the second act. Miss Fears couples Oscar's brief departure with a second change papers took no note of, his insistence that the opening scene be cut. Miss Fears protested to him and to Jerry that it was "the most touching scene" she had ever witnessed and backed up her argument with the nightly tears of the little old lady who was the powder room attendant. The scene was cut for one night, then promptly restored—at which point, according to Miss Fears, Hammerstein took off.

Music in the Air opened at the Garrick Theatre in Philadelphia on October 17. Most of the city's first-string critics preferred to sit through Jane Cowl's new offering, premiering down the street. Philadelphia society was divided, with its sportier element electing to brave an incessant rain to sample Kern and Hammerstein's latest offering. Celebrities from New York were also on hand, including Arthur Schwartz, whose wife, Katharine Carrington, had a prominent role, and two old *Show Boat* hands, Charles Winninger and Howard Marsh. Although Kern's reputation was untarnished, while Hammerstein no doubt felt at this point he had to prove himself all over again, it was Kern who betrayed the worst first-night jitters. In fact, his trips to the Garrick's water cooler became so frequent that several critics took note of it and commented on it.

He need not have worried. Even critics who found something or other to displease them acknowledged that their reservations would be lost in the cheering. The cast was uniformly praised. Only the *Inquirer* had doubts about Hammerstein's book, branding it "loosely woven," but predicting it would be tightened before the show moved away. The same man called the music "ingratiating," but professed to discern "no one dominating number." The *Record*'s critic, a man named Robert Reiss, was a faddist determined to be accepted as a loyal member of the swelling brigades crying for the obliteration of operetta. But if Mr. Reiss was prejudiced, he was gentlemanly enough to admit it and to report that spectators around him obviously did not share his disdain. In fact, he remained sufficiently honest and objective to suggest that *Music in the Air* was superior to *The Cat and the Fiddle*. The *Bulletin* and the *Public Ledger* were ecstatic, praising not only the cast and the authors, but giving Robert Russell Bennett due credit for his fine orchestrations.

Jane Cowl's Monday opening was not alone in keeping Philadelphia's first stringers from *Music in the Air*. The following night saw the premiere of a new left-wing musical, *Forward March* (which finally arrived in New York as *Strike Me Pink*, with a new cast and watered-down book). As a result, Philadelphia's finest critic, Arthur B. Waters, was unable to see the new show until its third night. His review appeared in the *Ledger*'s Sunday edition. Readers expected his notice to be the most detailed and perspicacious Philadelphia could offer. They were not disappointed. He rarely lost an opportunity to remind his readers of Kern's long list of melodic hits. He did so again in his Sunday notice, moving on to call the newest addition "a great musical show" and "epoch-making." He continued by suggesting that Kern had become something more than our finest composer of light opera.

> As a matter of fact, Kern no longer writes "light opera" music, just as he no longer writes "musical comedy" music. The latter phase, he outgrew several years ago; the former one he passed definitely beyond with that highly musicianly score of "The Cat and the Fiddle."
>
> In "Music in the Air," there is not one, single superfluous tune —not even an extraneous bar of music. In this remarkable offering . . . Mr. Kern has thrown the idea of "set arias" in the ash-heap just as the great maestros of grand opera succeeded in doing a half century ago. Instead of insisting on a complete divorce between the musical sequence and the dramatic action, he has seen to it that they are welded in perfect unison.
>
> When any one bursts into song during the course of "Music in the Air," that song is a logical and normal function of the plot. . . .

That plot transported audiences to a tiny Bavarian village. Edendorf's lovable old music teacher, Dr. Walther Lessing, has collaborated with the town schoolmaster, Karl Reder, in writing a song called "I've Told Every Little Star." They have taken its melody from a bird song. Accompanied by Karl's sweetheart, Sieglinde, and a local walking club, they head for Munich to find a suitable publisher. Once in the big city, Karl and Sieglinde find temptations and seducers at every turn. Frieda Hatzfeld, a leading prima donna, wheedles her way into Karl's life, while the composer Bruno Mahler proposes to write an operetta for Sieglinde. He is chagrined to discover she prefers to play on a swing. Undeterred, Bruno keeps on writing music for her. His efforts go for naught when Sieglinde makes a totally unimpressive debut. Her failure and all Munich's vaunted charms leave the villagers cold. With Karl and Sieglinde they head back for their mountain hamlet.

Hammerstein's careful, year-long labors and Kern's equally loving efforts produced remarkable results. The show was in such ready shape at its first playing that virtually no work was needed during the Philadelphia stay. Apart from the problems Peggy Fears recalls, the tryout was exceptionally serene.

Typical of how minor the other adjustments were was a story told by Reinald Werrenrath. Until *Music in the Air,* the six-foot-one baritone had been "backed into a piano for thirty years in the most hideous costume ever devised by man." Yet discarding his dress suit made the concert singer strangely uncomfortable on stage. Bare-kneed, in lederhosen, Werrenrath saw himself as "a glorified boy scout." The consoling applause that recognition might have offered was denied him by a hat that partially concealed his face. Sensing this, Jerry suggested that as soon as he came on stage, Werrenrath should remove his hat and mop his brow. In his nervousness Werrenrath kept forgetting this small bit, and his nervousness grew. Jerry's answer was simple. He went to the singer's dressing room, took the hat, and threw it away.

With little more than such minor tinkerings required, the show was spared extensive rehearsals for revisions that beset so many musicals. As a result, *Music in the Air* was the season's lone musical to earn even a small profit during a tryout.

When the operetta opened at the Alvin on November 8, 1932, its program contained several unusual features.

The chorus of sixty was divided into three parts. Twenty-two were "Members of the Edendorf Choral Society," thirty-one were "Members of the Edendorf Walking Club," and six were listed solely as "Edendorf Girls." In a rare departure, members of both the society and the club were listed according to voices. The choral society was divided equally between ladies who sang soprano, mezzo, or contralto and men who sang tenor, second tenor, baritone, and basso. On the other hand, the division of the walking club was lopsided, having only four men.

The synopsis of scenes set a pretentious note by giving each scene a title. For example:

ACT I

Scene One   *Leit Motif,* Dr. Walther Lessing's Home, Edendorf, Bavaria.
Scene Two   *Etudes,* Karl Reder's Classroom—two weeks later.
Scene Three   *Pastoral,* Stony Brook, on the road to Munich—that afternoon.
Scene Four   *Impromptu,* Ernst Weber's Office, Munich—three days later.

The seven scenes of the second act were called Sonata, Nocturne, Caprice, Rhapsody, Intermezzo, Humoresque, and Rondo.
Musical numbers were:

Music in the Air

ACT I

Dr. Lessing's Chorale
   a. "Melodies of May" .... *Edendorf Choral Society*
   b. "I've Told Every Little Star" ...... *Karl [Walter Slezak]*
Prayer ... *Karl, Sieglinde [Katherine Carrington] and Ensemble*
"There's A Hill Beyond A Hill" ..... *Hans [Edward Hayes] and Walking Club*
   a. Scene Music
   b. "And Love Was Born" .... *Cornelius [Werrenrath]*
Dance .... *Hulde [Desha]*
"I've Told Every Little Star" .... *Karl and Sieglinde*
Scena from Bruno's Play "Tingle Tangle"
   a. Letter Song, "I'm Coming Home" .... *Bruno [Tullio Carminati]*
   b. Aria, "I'm Alone" .... *Frieda [Natalie Hall]*
   c. Duo, "I Am So Eager" .... *Bruno, Frieda and Ensemble*
Finaletto ..... *Marthe [Dorothy Johnson], Ernst [Nicholas Joy] and Walther [Al Shean]*

ACT II

"One More Dance" .... *Bruno*
"Night Flies By" .... *Frieda*
"When Spring Is In The Air" .... *Sieglinde and Ensemble*
Excerpt from "Tingle Tangle" .... *Orchestra*

"I'm Alone" .... *Frieda*
Duo, "The Song Is You" .... *Frieda and Bruno*
Scena, "We Belong Together"
Finale

Victor Baravelle was once again Kern's conductor. John W. Harkrider designed the costumes. Joseph Urban created the settings. Kern and Hammerstein were listed as co-directors.

Most readers probably took their time about getting to the reviews. Papers on Wednesday, November 9, filled their front pages with details of the presidential election, an election that brought Franklin Delano Roosevelt into the White House for his first term. When they finally reached the theatre pages, readers learned that critics were overjoyed. A few reviewers hinted at the growing disdain for operetta. For example, Richard Lockridge in the *Sun* confessed some fears early in the evening when it seemed that the show might turn out "to be another operetta of old Germany." But his concern was soon swept away. A few critics, the *Herald Tribune*'s Percy Hammond among them, expressed marked unhappiness over Tullio Carminati's inability to do justice to Kern's lovely music, but, this apart, they hailed all the players. The *Times*'s Brooks Atkinson typified the aisle-sitters' delight with Hammerstein's libretto, noting: "Without falling back into the clichés of the trade he has written sentiment and comedy that are touching and tender. It is an amusing story and an effortless piece of craftsmanship, and it provides a perfect setting for Mr. Kern's score." Since they were working against hectic deadlines, no critic devoted the thoughtful attention to this score that Waters had in Philadelphia. Still, they were lavish in their praise. The distinguished John Mason Brown, writing for the *Evening Post,* began his review: "If you had no other reason for journeying to the Alvin these nights, Jerome Kern's entrancing score for 'Music in the Air' would provide one. It abounds in the sort of soft, insinuating melodies which are rarely heard along Broadway and of which Mr. Kern is past master."

The raves Kern received were well earned. Many students of popular music, such as Alfred Simon, consider his score for *Music in the Air* the peak of his career. Since Kern had been an exquisite, prolific melodist from the beginning, the show's wealth of gorgeous song could not have exalted it by itself. In the case of *Music in the Air,* this explosion of magnificent melody was coupled with a thoroughgoing unity of tone and style far more consistent than the composer had ever achieved or, indeed, would ever achieve again. *The Cat and the Fiddle* had hinted that this was Kern's aim. *Music in the Air* fulfilled the ambition. To a large extent this remarkably expressive cohesiveness probably stemmed from Kern's writing, for all practical purposes, the entire score directly for the operetta. He appears not once to have gone to his trunk for a forgotten melody. Only the first two songs seem to owe anything to earlier inspiration. In the case of "Melodies Of May" the inspiration was Beethoven's, not Kern's. He simply made a vocal arrangement of a principal theme from the piano sonata in C (opus 2, No. 3). How much of the complete "I've Told Every Little Star" Kern put on paper immediately after jotting down the sparrow's song is moot and immaterial. Simon has pointed out a third possible borrowing, noting the similarity of the "Prayer" to "It Won't Mean A Thing" from the London versions of *Sunny*. Both even employ the rarely used four-sharped key of E. A careful search of all Kern's apparently extant material uncovers no other borrowing, not even for the supposed excerpts from Bruno's tinselly-titled musical, "Tingle Tangle." A few passages in these excerpts momentarily recall Kern's style from the Princess Theatre period, but leave no reason to assume Kern was not simply purposely reverting to older patterns to separate this material from the rest of the score. The extended songs for "Tingle Tangle" are as artful as anything else in the show.

All through the score its charm was evident, while its artfulness was often cleverly concealed. As Alec Wilder has noted, "I've Told Every Little Star" is "in the conventional A-A-B-A, thirty-two measure form, very simply designed, but containing, in the release, an unexpected interval, *e* flat, held for a full measure, as well as a startling drop of a seventh from *e* flat to an *f* natural. In an innately simple song this difficult relationship of melody notes comes as a big surprise. . . . Kern must have been pleased with the release as he repeats all but the final note of it twice in the verse." Wilder is less happy with "The Song Is You," dismissing it as "one of Kern's self-consciously elegant 'art songs.'" He proceeds to note, "It attempts too dramatic a statement on too small a stage." What Wilder neglected to take into account was its employment within the story. In the original it was sung by the weak-voiced Carminati as Bruno in Frieda's dressing room while the prima donna was having a gown fitted by her dyspeptic maid. Watching the scene during rehearsals, Arthur Schwartz came to the conclusion that the song was "the outstanding song in that score" and was dismayed to see it thrown away in an essentially comic scene. He approached Kern and asked, "How can you sacrifice this sensational melody which will not be heard by anybody with all this physical stuff going on?" Jerry's reply was terse: "The scene calls for it." The ballad is a lovely flowing affair that in its first part gently rocks and cascades by turns, after which the cascading phrases turn and move beautifully higher and higher. The release begins with effectively repeated notes that suddenly give way to a new, dramatic melody utilizing unexpected harmonies. "When Spring Is In The Air" is a rapturous upbeat melody that also makes telling use of repeated notes. "One More Dance" is an infectiously swirling waltz. Although "There's A Hill Beyond A Hill" is in 6/8, it makes a sunny march, while "Egern On The Tegern See" glows softly and nostalgically. The only song added during the tryout, "We Belong Together," is a jaunty theme, gaily plummeting in a way quite distinct from the development of "The Song Is You." (There is a possibility that "I'm Alone" was also inserted in Philadelphia. Tryout programs call it "Alone With You," but no one seems to be able to recall whether the title change was merely that or whether it reflected either new lyrics or an entirely fresh number.)

Although *Music in the Air* cost $100,000 to mount in the depths of the Depression and employed a large cast as well as a full orchestra of twenty-six, plus thirty stagehands, the show paid off in just twelve weeks, even though with a top of only $4.40 it could gross no more than $34,000 a week. The fast payback was a compliment not only to Blumenthal's efficient organization, but to Kern and Hammerstein's initial craftsmanship, which required so little reworking and thereby allowed the show to begin to make money while it was still in Philadelphia. Before it left Broadway it rolled up 342 performances.

The euphoria brought on by the show's success prompted announcements that not one, but two Kern-Hammerstein musicals would be offered New York in the coming season. Either would have meant a departure from the semi-European material Kern had been working with, and a return to an earlier America Kern and Hammerstein had treated so successfully in *Show Boat* and *Sweet Adeline*. One musical promised to unfold its romantic tale against a background of the Erie Canal's most roistering days, while the second would be played out against the equally rough-and-tumble background of the 1849 Gold Rush. Blumenthal and Fears were announced as prospective producers for the latter. Sadly, both shows quietly slipped into the ever burgeoning list of "might-have-beens." A decade later Kern did compose music for a story set in the Gold Rush era, but it was for a film and Hammerstein was not his collaborator. Nor was Hammerstein co-author of the next Kern work actually to see the footlights.

19

A Near Miss
and a Sad Failure

All winter long Jerry and Otto Harbach worked assiduously on a new show. Jerry had read Alice Duer Miller's *Gowns by Roberta* and saw in it possibilities for a sumptuously bedecked musical romance. When Mrs. Miller readily assented to Kern's plans, Jerry urged Harbach to read the novel. Otto liked it, and the two set to work. When spring came and the London version of *Music in the Air* went into rehearsals, Jerry stayed home to continue his writing, trusting in Hammerstein to supervise the English performers. With America's first Rose-Marie, Mary Ellis, starred, the show began a 275-performance run at His Majesty's Theatre on May 19. But Jerry's allegiance to an even older associate also remained alive. In late May Jerry sent Harry B. Smith a check for $21 to cover the cost of six copies of Smith's privately printed *A Sentimental Library*, concluding his letter: "With kindest regards to the author, editor, bookkeeper and shipping clerk and their wife." Only after the principal writing on the new show was finished did Jerry, Eva, and Betty sail for Europe to catch the London plays and visit with the Leales. When they returned August 1 on the *Olympic*, Jerry, probably at some press agent's behest, walked down the gangplank arm in arm with Ramon Novarro. The resultant publicity advised readers that Novarro would be starred in the film version of *The Cat and the Fiddle*. (The film was released early in 1934 with more of Kern's score intact than in any earlier filmings of Kern's Broadway hits and with Jeanette MacDonald and Vivienne Segal in important roles.)

A letter of Alexander Woollcott's, written two weeks after Kern's return, reveals an interesting side of the composer's private life, a side Kern generally saw was kept truly private. Woollcott wrote to a friend, D. G. Kennedy, that Kern was going to pay for his (Kern's) nephew's college education. Woollcott added flippantly that the composer, "made irrational by the broadcasts of the Hamilton Choir," had elected to send the boy to Woollcott's alma mater.

Jerry meanwhile was putting finishing touches on his new work and settling on a producer. Although Jerry had paid several courtesy calls on Max Gordon when the producer was hospitalized in 1932, Gordon refused to put aside festering resentments after having been passed over when it came time to mount *Music in the Air*. They met several months later at a party given by mutual friends, and Gordon confronted Jerry with his grievances. Jerry was taken aback, assuring the producer he had no idea Gordon had felt slighted. By way of explaining his actions, Jerry pointed out that Gordon had already announced his intention of putting on *Flying Colors* and Jerry had simply assumed Gordon could not or would not want the burden of mounting two shows simultaneously. To Gordon's riposte that Jerry at least might have let Gordon make that decision for himself, Jerry merely shrugged his shoulders and professed not to have thought of it. Although every Kern reply only fueled Gordon's fury, he kept his temper. While he was emotional and capable of harboring prolonged and unreasonable grudges, Gordon was also a practical businessman, willing to live and let live whenever profits were involved. As much as he disbelieved Kern, Gordon kept the conversation open with bits of theatrical shop-talk. One bit of shop-talk Kern passed on was that he and Harbach were at work on their musical version of *Gowns by Roberta*. Gordon asked Jerry who was to produce the new piece. Jerry's response was evasive—only, as Gordon recalls, "a mysterious smile." He knew the Blumenthal-Fears divorce had effectively eliminated them, so Gordon surmised that the composer was playing hard to get. Since his relationship with Harbach had been far sunnier, Gordon got on the phone the next morning and asked the librettist what the real picture was. Harbach told him the work was still in its early stages and no producer had been selected, but he added that as far as he was concerned he would be delighted to work with Gordon again. Gordon quickly concluded the best policy would be to leave everything in Harbach's hands, and told him as much. It proved a wise move. The producer let drop that Kern could direct, something Gordon suspected was the composer's secret ambition. A month or so later Otto called the producer back and informed him he had persuaded Kern to let him mount the new work. And Kern agreed to direct.

In a casting coup, Gordon lured Broadway's turn-of-the-century prima donna, Fay Templeton, out of retirement.

Even before rehearsals began Kern and Gordon were at loggerheads again. The show required a comic who could also handle an M.C.'s glib patter. A few performers who came immediately to mind all turned out to be unavailable for one reason or another. When every one of the original candidates had been crossed off, Gordon heard of a young comedian then featured on the vaudeville bill the Palace was offering in conjunction with its weekly film. The comedian was not totally unfamiliar to Broadway theatregoers, having played a few minor parts in some quickly forgotten failures. Gordon was delighted with his work and rushed back to inform Kern, "The problem is solved." Looking back over the years Gordon has insisted that Kern's voice became acid when the composer replied rudely, "What are you trying to do, palm off one of your old vaudevillians on me?" Unless Kern was teasing and Gordon failed to sense this, the story sounds preposterous. Kern spent several early years on or near vaudeville stages and he not infrequently took Eva to see old favorites on a bill. No record at all exists of his ever belittling the form the way he did, say, jazz or swing.* Misunderstood joke or not, Gordon demanded that Kern go to the Palace to see for himself. Jerry did so and returned to agree the comedian had talent. Thus was Bob Hope signed.

Other auditions had a quieter, wrier tone. Jerry naturally demanded that he personally audition the actress who would sing what eventually became his favorite song from the show, "Smoke Gets In Your Eyes." When a beautiful Ukranian named Tamara Drasin was chosen, Jerry and Otto brought the song to her and asked her to sing it. The song presented few difficulties, even though Kern may have originally written it in a different tempo—first as a tap dance bit for a scene change in *Show Boat,* then as a march for the theme song of 1932 NBC radio series of made-for-broadcast

* A malevolent spirit seems to have hovered over Gordon whenever Kern walked into his presence. Nearly half a century after they worked together Gordon continued to flail vituperatively at Kern's ghost, although his own archives at Princeton and surviving records elsewhere show that his accusations were either unfounded or exaggerated.

musicals Kern was to write but that never got on the air. Dutifully, if nervously, Tamara sang the song for its writers. When she was finished neither commented. With a certain trepidation she asked if she had done something wrong. "Oh, you were all right," Jerry explained, "We were just wondering about the song."

Gowns by Roberta opened at the Forrest in Philadelphia on October 21. Reviews were discouraging. The *Record* began its notice, "Filled with the best material the American musical comedy stage can offer, 'Gowns by Roberta' got off to a lugubrious and slow-paced start." The critic was not referring to the opening scenes, since he found only the early and last moments of the show at all satisfactory. In between these better moments he lamented that the show displayed a "lack of spontaneity" and offered no more than "a kind of labored excellency." The *Public Ledger* was happier. Building its review around a score that "comes very nearly being Kern's best" and that offered an "illustration of the admirable technique that Kern is bringing to perfection," the paper could even pass off Harbach's "good libretto" as adequate to the occasion.

Harbach's plot remained faithful to the essentials of Mrs. Miller's novel. All-American halfback John Kent and a flippant debutante girl friend, Sophie Teale, have a violent quarrel and separate. Both seek solace in Paris. John's old Aunt Minnie lives there, running a successful modiste shop under the name Roberta. Shortly after his arrival his beloved aunt dies and John learns he is heir to the shop. With Minnie's young, winsome assistant, Stephanie, John sets about running the establishment. Sophie appears, hoping to retrieve John, but John concludes she is too fiery and irresponsible for his tastes. In time he and Stephanie fall in love. Only after their engagement does John discover Stephanie is a princess. Harbach's primary additions were theatrical figures, a hoofer and a crooner, who could provide action should his book threaten to bog down.

As soon as the rewriting was under way, Harbach mentioned that his nephew, Bernard Dougall, wanted to enter the theatre and would like to try his hand at lyrics. Kern promptly handed Harbach a new melody and suggested Dougall put words to it. The song became "I'll Be Hard To Handle."

When the show drew disappointing grosses and lost $3000 in its first week, Gordon made a decision that brought his relation with Kern almost to a breaking point. He phoned Hassard Short and asked him to hurry down from New York to restage the entire show. Short had been responsible for the fine mountings with their unique stamp of elegance Gordon had given his earliest revues, and was, indeed, probably the finest director on Broadway at the time. He arrived the next morning, and Jerry found himself abruptly dismissed from his first directorial assignment. Jerry exploded and stalked out of the theatre, but his good sense prevailed, so he soon returned.

Gordon also made a second decision, a very expensive one. He ordered most of the costumes and several of the sets redone. These changes helped increase the cost so that what had originally been a carefully tight budget of $80,000 fell apart. By the time these additional charges had been added to losses for the three-week tryout plus a week of further rehearsals and revision back in New York, *Gowns by Roberta* had cost $115,000.

Short's revisions began to be inserted during the third week in Philadelphia. At the same time the title was shortened, although Philadelphia programs for the final week, printed in advance, still retained the old name.

Roberta reached the New Amsterdam on November 18, 1933, with the following musical program, slightly abridged:

Roberta

PROLOGUE

1. Scene Music, Song, "Let's Begin" .. *Billy [George Murphy] and Ensemble*
2. Fraternity Song, "Alpha Beta Pi" ...... *Huck [Bob Hope] Billy, John [Raymond Middleton] and Ensemble*
3. Scene, "You're Devastating" .... *Huck*
4. Trio, "Let's Begin" .. *Billy, John, Huck and Male Ensemble*

ACT I

1. Reminiscence, "You're Devastating" ... *Stephanie [Tamara]*
2. Air, "Yesterdays" .... *Aunt Minnie [Fay Templeton]*
3. Trio, "Something's Got to Happen" .... *Scharwenka [Lyda Roberti], Huck and John*
4. Prose Recital .... *Huck*
5. Duettino, "The Touch of Your Hand" ..... *Stephanie and Ladislaw [William Hain]*
6. Scene and Pas de Seul .... *Sidonie [Berenice Alaire], Marie [Mavis Walsh], Mme. Grandet [Marion Ross] and Luella [Nayan Pearce]*
7. The Showing at Roberta's

8. "I'll Be Hard to Handle" (Words by Bernard Dougall) ....
                                                    Scharwenka

ACT II

1. Scena, "Hot Spot" ...... *Scharwenka, Billy, Marie, Angele*
                            [Bobette Christine], Valerie and Luella
2. Proverb, "Smoke Gets in Your Eyes" .... *Stephanie*
3. Reminiscence, "Let's Begin" .... *Huck and Stephanie*
4. Dance Finaletto .... *Billy and Sophie [Helen Gray]*
5. Duettino, "Something's Got to Happen" ...... *Scharwenka*
                                                    and John
6. Scena, "Let's Begin" ... *Huck, John, Scharwenka and Lord*
                            Henry [Sydney Greenstreet]
7. Roberta's Employees' Entertainment
     a. Sewing Department Dance .... *Girls and Boys*
     b. Travesty, "Don't Ask Me Not to Sing"
        Huckleberry Haines and His Orchastra
        Bing Crosby .... *Neil Wood*
        Ruth Etting .... *Herb Montei*
        Ethel Merman .... *Lou Wood*
        Rudy Vallee .... *Fred MacMurray*
        Morton Downey .... *Alan Jones*
        Arthur Tracy, the Street Singer .... *Ray Adams*
        Helen Morgan .... *Rene Du Plessis*
     c. Scene and Duet, "The Touch of Your Hand"
        Natcha, the Peasant Girl .... *Tamara*
        Volodya, the Officer .... *William Hain*
8. Finaletto
9. Scena, Dressing Stephanie ...... *Stephanie, Luella, Mme.*
                                                    Grandet, Marie
10. Scene Music
      Singer .... *George Djimos*
11. Entrance of Clementina Scharwenka
      Impromptu, "I'll Be Hard to Handle"
12. Entrance of Stephanie
13. Finale

The score was orchestrated and conducted by two old Kern favorites, Robert Russell Bennett and Victor Baravelle, although Baravelle left shortly after the opening. Clark Robinson designed the sets and Kiviette the costumes. Tellingly, no one was credited on the programs with direction, an indication of how bitter behind-the-scenes fighting may have been.

339

Neither feuds nor painstaking revisions seemed to count for much when morning-after reviews appeared. Richard Lockridge told the *Sun's* readers that *Roberta* was "handsome, but not funny; the plot offers numerous opportunities, few of which are accepted and the music is sweetly forgettable, although entirely pleasant to hear." Bernard Sobel of the *Mirror* began his notice by lauding Kern's music, but went on: "It is my regretful task to state that the book is a somewhat monotonous rewriting of an old theme, with the humor only intermittent." Returning to the music, he continued, "[Kern's] score, in this instance, has his customary melodiousness, graceful motif recurrences, graceful song numbers. . . ."

Broadway's smart money read the reviews and promptly pronounced *Roberta* as good as dead. *Variety's* weekly reports of the show's grosses seemed to confirm every gloomy prognostication. Running expenses were between $18,000 and $20,000, rising a little more if the take increased. Gross receipts for the first week were a disappointing $16,500, well in the red. Business jumped promisingly the second week to $21,500. But thereafter it dropped week after week. Even as his losses piled up, Gordon was determined to keep the show on the boards, convinced that word-of-mouth would turn it around. Christmas week was always a boom time, and Gordon decided to stick it out until the new year. To the amazement of cynics, Gordon's tactics proved sound. Slowly but ineluctably, lines at the box office grew longer.

Three reasons for the upswing in business became obvious in retrospect. From the very beginning *Roberta* had attracted the carriage trade. On December 10 the *Herald Tribune* carried a small paragraph that implied as much, while incidentally recording the pervasive decline on 42nd Street: "The showiest Rollses and Isottas may be parked in front of the New Amsterdam Theater of an evening while their proprietors are at performances of 'Roberta,' but really smart and conservative folk, the sort who have old Lincolns and 1924 Packards, park their motors at the back exit in Forty-first Street, and make their getaway of an evening without running the gamut of Minsky's Burlesque patrons." Mere mention of glamorous men and women flocking to the New Amsterdam unquestionably prompted an even larger crowd of less lordly men and women to rush to follow in their footsteps.

A second circumstance was a piece of remarkable luck. Although *Die Fledermaus,* playing under the assumed name of *Champagne Sec,* was doing modest business at the tiny Morosco, only two lyric works had appeared since the season's start to establish themselves as solid hits. One was Earl Carroll's revue-cum-mystery play, *Murder at the Vanities* (which had moved from the New Amsterdam to make way for *Roberta*); the other was Irving Berlin and Moss Hart's witty, song-filled and star-laden revue, *As Thousands Cheer*. Like *Champagne Sec* it was housed at a tiny theatre that nightly had to turn patrons away, this time Berlin's own Music Box. Both hits had a top price of $4.40, while Max Gordon shrewdly asked only $3.30, despite costs that vastly exceeded his careful estimates. Amazingly, just two more musicals won popular acclaim later in the season. Once again both were revues. In short, Gordon and his associates had the only book show and the cheapest musical in town, and less than expected competition.

Yet most authorities discounted both luck and upper-class patronage as the source of *Roberta's* surprising turnaround. To them the lone explanation lay in the runaway popularity of "Smoke Gets In Your Eyes." By January 21 the *Herald Tribune* cited *Roberta* as "the latest and one of the best examples of a show profiting immeasurably by a sudden outburst of public whistling, humming and crooning of its score." The paper added that "Smoke Gets In Your Eyes" "has swept the dance floors, radio studios and glee clubs of the country." The paper went on to lament that Kern practically threw the number away in the show by letting it be sung so casually and softly. However, recalling "The Song Is You" in *Music in the Air*, it decided Jerry was an old and knowing hand at this.

Privately, Jerry may have had mixed feelings about the success of "Smoke Gets In Your Eyes." Shortly before his death, Otto Harbach remembered a series of potentially explosive incidents stemming from the song's genesis. As Harbach recollected it, he himself had seen the melody on Kern's piano, but Kern insisted the tempo (still in one of its older forms) was wrong for the show. Harbach begged Kern to play the piece slowly and smoothly, and when Kern did, immediately recognized the tune for the gem it was. But Harbach insisted Kern snapped at him whenever he reminded the composer of this, and the lyricist soon found it politic to ignore the subject. Whether or not Harbach's recollections are accurate, another matter may have irritated Kern even more. In February Woollcott had written Jerry inviting him to "join me in murdering Eddie Duchin." Woollcott's gripe stemmed from the pianist's recording of "Egern On The Tegern See," which the humorist found offensive. Kern may have shared Woollcott's sentiments, but he certainly resented the arrangements he was hearing of "Smoke Gets In Your Eyes." By December *Variety* was reporting Kern's threats to remove the song from the air. That the threats were never carried out may have reflected Kern's relative financial situation. He was no longer as prosperous as he had been when *Sitting Pretty* was on the boards. He had alluded to this in a 1931 interview with Ward Morehouse, while in a March 1933 letter he wrote of "what was once the great Kern fortune."* By a particularly cruel irony, Kern had invested much of the profits of his 1929 book auction in bank shares.

Of course, the verseless "Smoke Gets In Your Eyes" was merely the most popular song in another superlative Kern score. Its warm, appropriately "smoky" main theme is punctuated with a surprisingly arioso release. Two other songs had been written for earlier productions. The sprightly "Don't Ask Me Not To Sing" came from the first-act finale of Kern and Harbach's previous collaboration, *The Cat and the Fiddle*. The haunting "You're Devastating" put new words to Kern's late addition for *Blue Eyes*, "Do I Do Wrong?". A soft, compassionate waltz, "The Touch Of Your Hand," was an unusual, small gem—unusual in that it ignored that prevailing AABA formula; small in that it said all it had to say in just twenty-three bars. Another song that abandoned the AABA formula, but took thirty-two bars to run twice through its lovely nostalgic theme, was "Yesterdays" (first published as "Yesterday"). Like "Smoke Gets In Your Eyes," the song is verseless. Wilder has correctly described it as "an extraordinarily evocative song, simple in construction, narrow in range (a tenth), and unforgettable." It provided a glorious note on which sixty-eight-year-old Fay Templeton could close a career that had begun at the age of five. In the long run it became the second most popular of all songs from the show. For example, in May 1957, when "Smoke Gets In Your Eyes" still sold over 1800 copies, "Yesterdays" sold 179. All the other songs combined sold little more than 100. Percentages remained about the same in other years. "I'll

* Ward Morehouse's "Broadway After Dark" column in the *Sun* on December 14, 1931, quoted Kern as saying, "Funny about Wall Street. Before that smash-up business happened I was just too rich, too fat, too prosperous. . . . Well, well, Wall Street blew up. Now I'm working and I've regained my soul." Kern also sensed that his work would have to be different, but not radically so. He added, "The old-fashioned musical comedy form is as dead as the dodo. In its place? I wish I knew. What we need is a form that will appeal to adolescents as well as adults. It should be sophisticated, but also gay and charming. It should be such that it won't need an $8000 a week star. It will stand on its own feet." Modesty, or an amazing misjudgment, made him ignore *Show Boat*, for he concluded, "The big one hasn't been written. The real one, one that will be revived from year to year." The March letter was to Mrs. Cooper.

Be Hard To Handle," "Let's Begin," and "Something's Got To Happen" all reflected the trippingly light jauntiness of the 1930s that had replaced the more pronounced beat of the 1920s, while "Alpha Beta Pi" was a joyful anthem any institution might be proud of.

Three songs were left behind in Philadelphia. "You Inspire A Mad Desire" and "Armful Of Trouble" were both dropped from the first scene, although the latter was still retained in the show's incidental music. "Clementina" was dropped from its spot immediately before the final curtain when it was discovered Lyda Roberti couldn't master the almost patter-song rapidity the melody and its lyric demanded. "I'll Be Hard To Handle" was the lone new song added in Philadelphia.

From January on *Roberta* did successful business until the heat set in. When business fell and Gordon again asked the cast to take cuts, several balked. Miss Roberti and Hope both left for better-paying assignments. The show closed on July 21 after 295 performances. Gordon took it on tour the following season, but when RKO released its movie version the producer decided not to buck the film and closed the show permanently in Montreal on March 16, 1935.

With Kern somewhat soured on both Gordon and Harbach, it was inevitable that he would once again turn to Oscar Hammerstein. Oscar and Jerry had both read and enjoyed Donn Byrne's highly praised novel, *Messer Marco Polo.* They agreed the adventurer's exotic itinerary would provide strikingly novel settings and his curiously cerebral love affair with a Chinese girl, Golden Bells, could be adapted to provide a unifying thread for the myriad, diverse incidents the explorer encountered. From the first they took the heroine's name as their working title. Oscar was always to remember a conversation they had at the start of their work on the piece. "Here," he remarked to Jerry, "is a story laid in China about an Italian and told by an Irishman. What kind of music are you going to write?" Jerry looked at Oscar and replied, "It'll be good Jewish music."

Certainly he had no intention of filling the new score with Jewish motifs. What would seem to be the few surviving scraps from the work show an attempt to give it a slightly Oriental flavor. But after a spell Jerry and Oscar concluded the story line was not strong enough to support a full-length musical. They put *Golden Bells* aside, but its appeal was such that as late as 1944 they toyed with the idea of reworking it. They never did.

On December 19 the New York *Times* announced that Kern and Hammerstein were at work on a new musical to be called *Three Sisters*. The paper noted that the show would be ready the following season, but made no mention of a London presentation, thus suggesting that it might have been first conceived of for New York. The paper offered the information that the pair had started work the previous spring, but ignored the fact that the germ of the story had come to Oscar and Jerry while they were in England attending the Derby at Ascot. Neither the *Times* nor any other paper made public another project the pair considered briefly. The Theatre Guild had approached them asking them to make a musicalization of DuBose Heyward's *Porgy*. The Guild hoped to lure Al Jolson back to Broadway by offering him the title part.

In late January 1934 the Kerns and the Hammersteins sailed for England. After a shipboard argument with Dorothy Hammerstein, Jerry, realizing he was in the wrong, presented her with a George III silver saucer. It was an omen. A few years later, when the incident was long past, Jerry helped Dorothy establish herself in the antique trade.

Rehearsals for *Three Sisters* began on March 12. Jerry was probably still smarting over his directorial débacle with *Roberta* and no doubt felt relieved that his trusty collaborator was again at the helm, although both were to share program credit. Jerry took a special interest in a ballet that Ralph Reader was staging. The ballet revolved about Derby Day and was the most ambitious piece Reader had ever attempted. The choreographer confessed his fears to Jerry, and Jerry not only warmly reassured him that he need not worry, but promised him he would be there as often as possible. Dance rehearsals were not held at Drury Lane, but at the Palace Theatre a few blocks away. Reader always knew when Jerry had arrived first. A large box of bonbons would be sitting conspicuously on the piano. They were Jerry's daily present to the chorus. Reader's fears were not entirely unfounded. Some of the ballet music was complex and, at least to Reader's mind, difficult to dance to. Whenever he came to one of these passages he simply advised the dancers to go "back to the sway" and everyone would simply sway in unison. But Reader also knew which routines especially pleased Jerry. From the back of the theatre he would hear a pair of hands applauding fervently. Quite often, when rehearsals had concluded for the day, the choreographer would sit at the back of the house with the composer reminiscing, much as Jerry had with Finck after the *Show Boat* rehearsals. Reader was amazed not only at how much Jerry recalled, but at how fondly he recalled it.

Sentiment could sometimes be leavened with humor. An old horse was required in the plot, and someone informed Jerry that the horse the producer had rented was a doddering old beast which in its more youthful days had been ridden by Binnie Hale in *Sunny*. Jerry was intrigued, but skeptical. When the horse appeared on stage for its first run-through, Jerry sat down at the piano and played the circus music from *Sunny*. Responding to memories long recessed, the horse performed to perfection the entire bit it had done hundreds of times eight years before.

One small contretemps did develop when the entire cast assembled at Drury Lane. Kern came in a minute or two after rehearsals had begun, took one look at the stage and brought the run-through to a halt. Jerry had spotted a girl with brightly bleached hair. He announced that no girl with hair like that would ever be in one of his shows. He demanded she go home and restore her hair to its natural color. Bleached blondes had, of course, been in many of his shows, but this young lady apparently was in the vanguard of platinum blondes, a type thoroughly inappropriate to the tenor and period of the musical. When she promised she would, the rehearsal continued.

A week or so before the opening, when the show had been virtually set, Jerry was riding to the theatre with Edward ("Teddy") Holmes, an executive of Harms's English branch, Chappell. Holmes mentioned how happy he was with the score, but he thought Jerry's response was perfunctory; Jerry seemed preoccupied. The composer finally turned to him and said, "You know, that girl Adèle Dixon has a million dollar personality. We have to get her a single." Holmes agreed, but suggested it might be too late. The next morning Jerry came to the theatre with a new song in hand. It was not a single, but it was the song that would prove to be the most enduring from the show, "I Won't Dance."

The vastness of the production, with its complicated turntables, precluded a tryout. *Three Sisters* opened cold at London's Drury Lane on April 19, 1934. The opening was clearly one of the season's biggest theatrical events. So eager were many theatregoers that they had begun queuing up days in advance, leaving owner's cards on their stools when they went to eat. Like *Roberta,* the new work drew a well-heeled, glamorous crowd of first nighters. They seemed all to converge at once, causing a traffic jam as far back as the Strand. Mobs of celebrity chasers aggravated matters, massing in front of the house and cheering everyone they recognized. For some reason, Tallulah Bankhead's sweeping entrance elicited the loudest shrieks.

Hammerstein's story centered on three daughters of Will Barbour, a poor, itinerant photographer. Mary, the youngest, is deserted by her gypsy groom. Dorrie, the second and most ebullient of the lot, determines to marry a peer, while tall, lanky Tiny, the eldest, is the most down-to-earth and settles for a policeman, Eustace Titherley. World War I breaks out and all three men meet near the front. They meet again after the war at Boulter Lock, where reunions and reconciliations allow a happy ending.

The opening night musical program read:

Three Sisters

ACT I

1. Impromptu Concert Party
    a. "Roll on Rolling Road" . . *Gypsy [Esmond Knight], George [Albert Burdon], Ensemble*
    b. "Now That I Have Spring Time" . . *Gypsy, George, Mary [Victoria Hopper], Ensemble*
    c. "My Beautiful Circus Girl" . . . . *Gypsy, George, Tiny [Charlotte Greenwood], Mary, Will [Eliot Makeham], Ensemble*
2. Chorus, "What's in the Air, To-night?" . . . . *Ensemble*
3. Quartette, "There's a Joy That Steals Upon You" . . . . . *Mary, Tiny, Gypsy, George*
4. Serenade, "Hand in Hand" . . . . . *Eustace [Stanley Holloway]*
5. Lullaby, "Somebody Wants to Go to Sleep" . . . . *Tiny*
6. Scena, "While Mary Sleeps" . . . . . . *Mary, Gypsy and Dancers*

ACT II

1. An Impression of the Derby . . . . *Entire Company*
2. Duet, "You Are Doing Very Well" . . . . *Tiny and Eustace*
3. Fantasy, "Lonely Feet" . . *Dorrie [Adèle Dixon] and Ensemble*
4. Finaletto, The Tryst Duet, "What Good Are Words?" . . *Mary and Gypsy*
5. Air, "There's a Funny Old House" . . . . *Eustace, Mary, Gypsy, Male Sextette*
6. Buffo Chorale, "Welcome to the Bride" . . . . *Eustace and Ensemble*
7. Scena, Pastorale
    a. "Before The Wedding"

    b. "The Wedding"
    c. "And After"

ACT III

1. Reminiscence, "There's a Funny Old House" .... *Mary*
2. Ballad, "Keep Smiling" .... *House*
3. Fox-Trot (1917), "I Won't Dance" .. *Dorrie, John [Richard Dolman], Chorus*
4. Rehearsal in Khaki, "The Gaiety Chorus Girls" .... *Gypsy, George, Eustace, Pony Ballet, Male Ensemble*
5. "August Bank Holiday"
    A Medley .... *Mary, Gypsy, Tiny and Will*
6. Finale .... *Ensemble*

Charles Prentice conducted Robert Russell Bennett's orchestrations. Scenery and costumes were designed by G. E. Calthrop.

Even before the reviews appeared, Jerry and his associates had a nasty indication of what they would say. The gallery had booed frequently throughout the evening, although Stanley Holloway suspected much of the vocal unhappiness stemmed from Miss Dixon's admirers, chagrined at how little she had to do. Given their unfamiliarity with the songs, they could not grasp that she had been given two of the best numbers in the score. Miss Dixon, who had starred in the preceding Drury Lane vehicle, recalled the booing, but hoped none of it had been on her account.

So the bad reviews came as no surprise. Several critics, their English up, openly resented Americans attempting to write about Englishmen for English audiences. Indeed, there may even have been a gentlemanly hint of anti-Semitism when the *Daily Herald* chose to call attention to Jerry's middle name, a practice Jerry himself had discarded years before. The paper complained that "Oscar Hammerstein, the American author-producer and his composer, Jerome David Kern, have tried to be terribly English." In the paper's eyes they failed embarrassingly. Taking much the same tack, the *Morning Post* decried that "everything rings false." For many the nub of the problem lay in Hammerstein's book, which the *Daily Mail* saw as attempting to pour "a pint into a quart pot." When it came to the music the critics were noticeably divided. The *Times* thought there were too many "lugubrious sentimental songs of the kind that one had supposed to have vanished long ago even from those back parlours in which pianos are still preserved." On the other hand, the *Morning Post* proclaimed: "Jerome Kern's music is again and again lovely in its dreamy way," while the *Evening Post* flatly asserted that "Mr. Jerome Kern, the composer, is the hero of 'Three Sisters.'"

Unfortunately, in this instance the composer was a hero whose feat remained uncelebrated. Along with *Sitting Pretty* and, possibly, *Oh, Boy!*, *Three Sisters* remains Kern's most regrettably neglected score, and since alone of the three it offers Kern in his later, richer vein the neglect is especially sad. Only the lively, jumping "I Won't Dance" joined Kern's canon of favorites, but even that song did not catch the public's attention until it was used in the movie version of *Roberta*, with revised lyrics. (Fred Astaire, who had closed his London run of Cole Porter's *Gay Divorce* just before *Three Sisters* opened, caught the show and suggested to RKO that it buy the song for the film.) One remarkable feature of "I Won't Dance" is the tricky release that follows the simple, catchy principal theme. Alec Wilder has called it "perhaps the most difficult release Kern ever wrote." Leaving the main key of C, it jumps in wide steps from A flat to D flat to B before returning to the tonic. "Hand In Hand" is a meltingly beautiful ballad with an unusual form. The main phrase takes only four bars and after a repeat leads into an eight-bar release, following which the main phrase is again brought in twice, the second time with minor harmonic variations. An eight-bar tag introduces a gentle new melody to close the song. Kern quoted similar themes in both verse and chorus. "Lonely Feet" is another mellow, poignant ballad, with a soaring release. A third lovely, if lesser, ballad was "What Good Are Words?" (Since the song was the only one reprised in the piano selections—where the reprise came as the finale—there is the possibility that Kern hoped it would be the hit of the show.) "Roll On, Rolling Road" is another superior Kern number, this time a rousing anthem. "Now That I Have Springtime" and "You Are Doing Very Well" are both jaunty and likable, while "Somebody Wants To Go To Sleep" is a pleasant waltz. Nothing from the show appears to have been taken from older Kern material, suggesting again that the composer was determinedly exploring new musical horizons.

The heady excitement that preceded opening night quickly dissipated. Bad reviews and bad times told at once at the box office. By late May *Three Sisters* was announcing "last weeks." It closed on June 9 after a mere seventy-two performances.

Just after the show opened, Kern himself conducted a recording of the show's songs, featuring several of the principals. Released on two sides of a twelve-inch disc by the English Decca, the record was soon out of print. But it demonstrated once more the debt music lovers and scholars owe English recording houses.

Packing to leave for America, Oscar asked Jerry what his plans were. Jerry's reported reply was succinct: "Hollywood, for good!" Private letters reveal Jerry was actually not at all that certain about writing for films. Still, the failure of *Three Sisters* and *Roberta's* near miss suggested that Hollywood offered better security in those troubled times. He was even willing to overlook the shabby treatment he and his scores had been given on occasion, no doubt convinced his still growing stature would offer additional protection against abuses dealt so many behind the scenes creators.

20

Hollywood, for Good!

Kern returned to New York at the beginning of May on the *Majestic*. Before leaving for a month of trout-fishing and bird-watching in Wellfleet, on Cape Cod, he wrote his old friend, Kathleen Cooper, that his own high estimate of *Three Sisters* was in no way tarnished by its failure. "I think it's swell," he exclaimed, and promised it would be done on Broadway in the fall. It never was.

Indeed, Broadway was to see no new Kern show for five years, for Jerry's attention was diverted by the renewed solicitations from Hollywood. Musical films were again coming into vogue and Kern was asked to compose additional songs for picture versions of *Sweet Adeline* and *Roberta*. For the first, a Warner Brothers release, he composed a shimmeringly nostalgic ballad, "We Were So Young." The song makes effective use of a favorite Kern device, triplets, and ends with a surprising barcarolle tag. Hammerstein wrote the lyric. The two also brought over "Lonely Feet," from *Three Sisters*, a good indication that Jerry knew in his heart Broadway would never see the show.

At RKO, because of *Roberta*, Kern met two figures with whom he would work frequently in later years. Pandro Berman was a small, darkly handsome twenty-nine-year-old dynamo, one of Hollywood's brightest producers. He had bought *Roberta* for Fred Astaire and Ginger Rogers, but felt some new songs were needed. To write the new lyrics he hired a tall, well-dressed girl, Dorothy Fields. She came from an old theatrical family. Her father, Lew, and her brother, Herbert, had long since made names for themselves, while Dorothy's lyrics for *Blackbirds of 1928* and *The International Revue* assured everyone she had neither the intention nor the need to coast on her family's reputation. She had a warm smile, a quick wit, and a sharp intelligence. Her first assignment was to come up with a lyric that could be used both for a fashion show and as a love song. Her answer was the lyric for "Lovely To Look At." A favorite Kern legend has it that the studio brass were aghast when they first heard the melody, insisting that a chorus of just sixteen bars could not possibly represent a complete song. Kern was reached and responded, "That's all I had to say!" The song stayed as it was. Later in life, Miss Fields could no longer recall whether she and Jerry had met earlier. Her lyric was put into the picture without Kern's approval. He did not hear the finished song until after the sequence was shot. Everyone waited with some trepidation for his pronouncement. But he came away from the viewing entranced. Dorothy and Jerry became fast friends. Because of his often impish behavior, and because of the disparity in their heights, Dorothy soon took to calling Jerry "Junior." That he raised no protest testified to the respect and affection Jerry quickly grew to hold for her. Her second lyric for *Roberta* was a revision of Hammerstein's rhymes to "I Won't Dance," further proof that *Three Sisters* was being dismantled and would never be produced again.

The failure of *Three Sisters* was not the only black cloud in the year. Jerry became ill with the first of those many protracted sicknesses that would plague him for his remaining years. His worst fears were realized when his physician, Dr. Forster Kennedy, confirmed that Jerry had the same sort of pernicious anemia that had helped kill his father. Among the more painful but less lingering problems were kidney stones. After medication soon resolved (or dissolved) this matter, Jerry celebrated by composing an "Ode To A Passing Kidney Stone."

In January 1935 Metro Goldwyn Mayer commissioned Kern and Hammerstein to write a musical for Jeanette MacDonald ("La Jeanette," as Jerry called her) and Nelson Eddy. The story line concerned a sophisticated lady who takes refuge from her problems in a mountain retreat only to find romance there. "It'll probably be called *Champagne and Orchids*," Jerry wrote a friend, "unless the bright boys in the sales and distributing dept. consider that censorable these pure days." Work progressed slowly, so in

April when Jerry took Eva and Betty to a desert retreat called La Quinta, Oscar came down to continue the collaboration there. Further casting was announced from time to time—Constance Collier, Wallace Beery, Clifton Webb. But announced postponements followed with equal frequency, and by late summer the project had definitely been dropped.

Surviving manuscripts suggest Kern's music for the film was not as readily embraceable as some of his other unpublished film work, but it was still both artful and attractive, and it might have grown on listeners with repeated hearings. "Singing A Song In Your Arms" was a glittering waltz. Its chromatics bear a slight resemblance to those Kern would employ a few months later in the superior "I Dream Too Much." The pulsating "Dance Like A Fool" (Kern marked it "Tres sauvage") and the more ordinary ballad "When I've Got The Moon" both have slightly "torchy" melodies, although Hammerstein's effective lyrics for the latter took little note of the torchiness. Jerry may have been particularly fond of the latter song. A note, apparently in his handwriting, scribbed across the top of the manuscript reads, "Oscar   Get this released from MGM." Three other songs, all dated April 29, 1935, seem to have been composed at MGM for a film called *The Flame Within*. A title song, "Lazy But Free," and "Dream Of A Ladies Cloak Room Attendant" exist with fully worked out piano parts, but nevertheless seem incomplete. Whether they were meant as sections of songs, background music, or were merely suggestions is unknown. Kern's daughter has commented: "I have the recordings in storage—there were more than three pieces of music involved. My father felt terrible that *Champagne and Orchids* was never produced. He believed that he and Oscar had taken money under false pretenses. He volunteered to do the underscoring for *The Flame Within*, a straight dramatic picture with Brian Aherne (I've forgotten who else). He wrote and *orchestrated* it all for no recompense."

With *Champagne and Orchids* dropped, Hammerstein determined to return to New York, disheartened by a series of Hollywood failures. Solicitous of Hammerstein's predicament, Jerry proposed writing a musical on the order of the old Princess shows. Hammerstein was amenable. Only when both men soon found their schedules crowded was the plan set aside for four years.

Jerry and Oscar's stay at MGM was not totally fruitless, for when the studio released Jean Harlow's starring vehicle *Reckless* later in the year the title song carried their names on its credits. The song is a satisfyingly smooth blend of Kern's gracefully flowing sweetness with blues phrases and harmonies. One aspect of the song may have given Kern some trouble. Kern concluded the published version with a more heavily chromatic blues arrangement of the chorus, an arrangement he apparently decided he could not bring off successfully without assistance. The song was issued with the blues reprise "Arranged by Roger Edens and Jerome Kern."

January 27, 1935, marked Kern's fiftieth birthday, an event his friends determined to celebrate on a national scale. Arrangements were made to assure that Kern would be in his Beverly Wilshire suite when Alexander Woollcott went before his Columbia Broadcasting Company microphone at 7 p.m. in New York. Woollcott announced that his entire program would be a tribute to Kern. Following the announcement the orchestra launched into a medley that ranged, chronologically, from "Babes In The Wood" to songs from *Music in the Air*. Woollcott then announced Alice Duer Miller, who read a poem Franklin P. Adams had written for the occasion, after which Julia Sanderson stepped out of the past to sing "They Didn't Believe Me." A parade of celebrities came forward to extend greetings, including Ethel Barrymore, Kathleen Norris, and Noel Coward, who hailed Kern as "my favorite composer." But Woollcott saved his biggest surprise for last. As the ensemble sang "Happy Birthday," someone knocked at Kern's door. Kern was prevailed upon to answer it himself, and when he did he discovered Irving Berlin standing there with a bouquet of flowers. Berlin confessed to Woollcott that the tribute had left him teary-eyed, and when Jerry opened the door, Woollcott later wrote, "They fell on each other's necks. 'Just a couple of old Jewish pansies' was the way Irving described it to me over the telephone."

Despite vestiges of his illnesses (Jerry informed a friend he was probably doomed to take "30 drops of dilute hydrochloric per meal from now on forever"), the Kerns continued to have an active social life. Except for Jean Harlow's mother, Kern was not especially fond of anyone he met on the MGM lot. But he was truly irked when he met Igor Stravinsky and discovered Stravinsky could not talk intelligently about Wagner.

Thinking his own picture work was at an end, Jerry and his family returned East. They had hardly returned when Kern was headed West again, having accepted a new offer to write music for opera star Lily Pons's film debut. Kern apparently stipulated that Dorothy Fields serve as lyricist. Accordingly, Pandro Berman wired her in New York on May 28 offering her the Kern assignment at $1000 a week. Because she had to begin her collaboration by June 5, Berman provided air fare. Dorothy accepted with alacrity. Kern signed on June 3. In forwarding the signed contract to Kern's lawyer, Howard Reinheimer, RKO's Daniel O'Shea let drop two interesting points. One was that Kern and Harbach had signed an earlier contract with RKO on June 8 of the preceding year.* Second, O'Shea advised Reinheimer that Kern had already written eight melodies from which RKO would probably select the four songs required by the contract.

RKO gave Kern generous terms. The composer was to be paid $5000 per week for four weeks. If additional work were necessary Kern would be available for a fifth week at no compensation, but thereafter any further weeks would again be at the rate of $5000 each. Kern retained publishing and "small performance" rights—"small performance" being the trade term for individual radio, vaudeville, or other presentations. Since Kern was still officially based in Bronxville, RKO also paid for his and Eva's transcontinental train trip.

As always, work with Dorothy proceeded pleasantly apace. However, one behind-the-scenes problem did develop. While nothing in their contract forced RKO to bow to Kern's selection of an orchestrator, the studio's respect for Kern was such that they agreed to employ Robert Russell Bennett. This precipitated a dispute with Max Steiner, who was to conduct and had also apparently hoped to orchestrate the music. Nothing survives to indicate that Kern lacked confidence in Steiner. The two had worked together amicably when Steiner was conductor for the ill-fated *Sitting Pretty*. But Kern's sense of loyalty and his comforting trust in Bennett prevailed. Poor Steiner received a second slap when, as star of *Love Song*, Lily Pons demanded that André Kostelanetz conduct the operatic arias she was to sing in the picture. His job done, Kern did not wait to supervise the filming, although he probably attended some recording sessions. On July 11 he and Eva boarded the Chief to return home. (In September Reinheimer had to remind RKO the train bill was still unpaid.)

James Gow and Edmund North's screenplay was based on an unpublished story by Elsie Finn and David G. Wittels. In Gow and North's redaction the heroine, Annette (Miss Pons), is a young French girl with a fine voice but no ambition. Her singing career flourishes only because her composer-husband, Jonathan (Henry Fonda), promotes it. His efforts backfire. Before long Annette has totally overshadowed Jonathan, and he walks out in disgust. But Annette contrives to have one of his operas turned into a successful musical comedy. That, plus news Jonathan is to be a father,

* A contract now lost. Lost with it are details on the projected film.

brings the film to a happy conclusion. Supporting players included Osgood Perkins, Eric Blore, and Lucille Ball.

Berman came to have such high hopes for one song that he decided to rename the picture after it. On September 19 he telegraphed Kern informing him the film would thereafter be called *I Dream Too Much*. He urged Kern to begin promoting the song six or seven weeks before the picture was released about Thanksgiving. Kern cabled back the next day, congratulating Berman on *Alice Adams* and the "synonymal success" of *Top Hat* (which, he confessed, he had yet to see), approving the new title, and agreeing to start exploitation in mid-October. On October 29 Berman again wired Kern, this time to report the preview "clicked like a million."

I Dream Too Much opened at the Radio City Music Hall on November 28, 1935. John Cromwell directed; Hermes Pan created the choreography.

Variety predicted the film would be "a winner at the b.o., without breaking any records," a prediction that proved accurate. While the trade sheet found kind words for almost everything except the photography, its comments on the music were guarded. Beginning with its reservation that the "songs are not too well spotted," it mentioned in passing Miss Pons's operatic arias and the title song. Only "Jockey On The Carrousel" received extended comment. The paper branded it "a honey" and saw "dark-horse" possibilities for it, but at the same time confessed it was the best song in the picture largely "from the standpoint of fitting Miss Pons." The *Times* was reserved in its appraisal, summing up both the songs and the film as "agreeably unimportant." Typical of the more enthusiastic responses was that of Eileen Creelman in the *Sun*. She welcomed the film's arrival as "a happy occasion," delighted, as she was, with every aspect of it. She translated some of her pleasure into a more extensive notice of Kern's work than a majority of critics gave: "The most tuneful and most typically Kern is 'Jockey on the Carousel,' a gay sentimental lullaby sung by the little dark-eyed soprano as she whirls about on a merry-go-round. 'I Got Love' has Miss Pons doing a hot number in an Apache costume. 'I'm the Echo' and 'I Dream Too Much,' the last a brilliant waltz, are very evidently written to show off Miss Pons's sparkling tones."

Time has not been good to Kern's songs for the film. Only the title song remains among his standards, and even it clings precariously to the edge of that charmed circle. In the waltz Wilder sees Kern reverting to "the European manner," but he adds forgivingly, "It is, however, a much less overt plunge into the theatrical wisteria mists of the past." The forlorn little tale of the merry-go-round horse whose young jockey could never make it catch the horse on which his sweetheart sat was a showpiece for the great coloratura. "The Jockey On The Carrousel" jumped through several moods and key changes, including the five-sharped key of B, a key which Kern knew discouraged sheet music sales. "I'm The Echo (You're The Song That I Sing)" and "I Got Love" are distinctly minor Kern.

A month after *I Dream Too Much* was released, *Show Boat* went before the cameras at Universal. Kern and Hammerstein created five new songs for the film version, although two, "Negro Peanut Vender's Street Cry" and "Got My Eye On You," were dropped. "I Have The Room Above Her" was a lovely ballad that was probably deprived of deserved acceptance because it was overshadowed by the superior original songs. As Magnolia, Irene Dunne strutted in blackface as she sang a peppy banjo number, "Gallivantin' Around." Paul Robeson was awarded a humorous defense of shiftlessness, "Ah Still Suits Me."

On January 1, 1936, Harry B. Smith died. Although he and Jerry had not worked together for years and Kern had moved on to bigger and better things, Jerry still remembered him. He wrote a loving, personal eulogy that Christopher Morley printed in *The Saturday Review*. Calling "Hank Smith . . . my friend and mentor," Jerry noted that "with the soul of a real poet, he fashioned jingles for Broadway." But it was as a fellow bibliophile that Jerry best remembered Smith. He paused to praise *A Sentimental Library* as "perhaps the most charming book about books ever compiled." Smith's passing, he concluded, deprived the theatre of "a notable figure and the world of a gallant gentleman." The sentiments were clearly heartfelt.

Even before Kern had returned East he had begun negotiations with Berman and RKO to do the score for a Fred Astaire and Ginger Rogers film, *I Won't Dance*. Negotiations were anything but smooth. In early July Berman offered Kern an advance of $35,000 against 5 per cent of the gross to one million and 7.5 per cent between a million and a million and a half. Through Reinheimer Kern advised Berman he would not consider such terms, even though he had accepted considerably less for *I Dream Too Much*. His grounds for the abrupt rejection are unrecorded. Apart from using it as a negotiating ploy, his reasoning may have been twofold. For one, Berman was now asking him to compose a full score instead of merely four melodies. Moreover, the earlier picture, with its star making her film debut, had represented something of a gamble. On the other hand, Astaire and Rogers had become two of Hollywood's hottest attractions and were virtually assured of a huge box office. Kern justly felt he was entitled to considerably more.

Berman let the matter ride over the summer and into the fall. Not until after *I Dream Too Much*'s preview did he again wire Reinheimer. He professed to have not checked the wording of his July telegram and only now realized that he should have offered the $35,000 not as an advance but in addition to the percentages. Rather puzzlingly, Reinheimer's reply two days later does not reject this, but rather an offer of a flat $50,000. Whether an intervening telegram is lost or Reinheimer was employing yet another gambit, the stakes were effectively raised. Several more missing telegrams must have crossed the country before terms were settled on October 30. Kern was to receive $50,000 plus a percentage of the gross up to an additional $37,500. Berman assured Reinheimer that Jerry would probably realize the full amount since all three earlier Astaire and Rogers films had grossed between two and three million dollars. Jerry also agreed to be available for work on the film from December 1, 1935, to March 1, 1936. Once again Jerry requested that Dorothy Fields provide lyrics. Miss Fields signed her contract on November 12; Jerry signed his on November 19.

The Kerns left for the Coast on Thanksgiving, expecting to remain only as long as it took Jerry to compose the score for *I Won't Dance* and for a Universal film, *Riviera*. Kern's private correspondence shows he had no suspicion that he and Eva would never again live in the East. They continued to retain a full staff at Cedar Knolls. For their stay in Hollywood they booked what Jerry called "a vulgar, hideously over-done pent-house at the Beverly-Wilshire." The suite had a balcony, and the mischievous imp in Jerry soon discovered he could stop traffic on Wilshire Boulevard below by standing out on the balcony and ranting in the best Mussolini fashion. On one occasion he confounded patrons leaving the fashionable Brown Derby across the street by delivering them a mock temperance lecture.

As with *I Dream Too Much*, tempers soon flared behind the scenes. And once again Kern's loyalty to Robert Russell Bennett was at the heart of the disagreement. Kern was expected to provide seven songs, at least two of which Astaire wanted to be thoroughly contemporary, imaginative dance numbers. The request daunted Kern. His strong traditional streak that had rebelled at writing hulas in 1915 and had refused to allow jazz orchestras to play havoc with his melodies in the 1920s again surfaced to befuddle his attempts. Yet he clearly respected Astaire's artistry and realized the reasonableness of the dancer's request. Unable to oblige, he decided to work with

Bennett in providing suitable material. But a youngster named Hal Borne, who had worked with Astaire and Astaire's assistant choreographer, Hermes Pan, had aggressive ideas of his own. The two songs involved were "Waltz In Swingtime" and "Bojangles Of Harlem." Borne insists he found the original of the latter was in 2/4 time and filled with what he terms "corny" syncopation. Borne's first recollection is undoubtedly correct. The song was even published with Kern's marking the burthen "Tempo di Marcia (*not too fast*)." But his reactions to Kern's syncopation seem unnecessarily cruel and faddish. Borne states that he added a section that "I played on an upright piano. It was based on a vamp idea that kept going up different keys. That was not a harpsichord, it was a doctored piano, and that was not Kern, it was me." Since Kern material T. B. Harms donated to the Library of Congress contains the manuscript for this section, Borne's recollections are suspect, although Borne no doubt did write some music. Kern got wind of this and in a fury called RKO's David Dreyer, warning that Borne was not to compose any music for the film and demanding RKO not pay him for any composition. If Borne thought Astaire required any special rewriting, Borne was "simply to prepare a dummy for tempo, number of bars, and whatever other information that Mr. Kern would need." Since Kern's intellectual integrity always allowed him to give credit for any help he received, the absence of Borne's name on the sheet music is telling. That same intellectual integrity did let him credit Robert Russell Bennett for his assistance on "The Waltz In Swing Time." The sheet music reads: "Music by JEROME KERN Constructed and arranged by R. Russell Bennett." Bennett has told me that Kern provided some basic themes and then told him to put them together in any way that would satisfy Astaire. Obviously, Bennett had to devise some extended phrases to join Kern's themes. Alone or with Bennett, Kern provided the seven songs, turning in the last, "Pick Yourself Up," shortly before shooting began. The public heard only the melody of "It's Not In The Cards," the lyric having wound up on the cutting room floor.

During most of its shooting the film was known by a second title, *Never Gonna Dance,* but in May Kern suggested that both *I Won't Dance* and *Never Gonna Dance* might lead to confusion with *Roberta* and thus hurt attendance. He suggested calling the picture *Swing Time* and promised Berman if the name were changed he would publish "The Waltz In Swing Time," which until then he had not intended to issue. Berman was delighted with the suggestion and passed it on to RKO's top brass, who readily acquiesced.

Swing Time was based on an unpublished story by Erwin Gelsey. Howard Lindsay provided the original screenplay, a text substantially revised by Allan Scott. The film was directed by George Stevens. Nathaniel Shilkret was musical director and Hermes Pan staged the ensemble dances.

The story centered on John "Lucky" Garnett (Astaire), who arrives so late for his wedding to a rich heiress (Betty Furness) that his prospective father-in-law (Lander Stevens) sends him away with instructions not to return until he has earned $25,000. While looking for a quick way to win the sum, Lucky meets a dance instructress, Penny Carrol (Miss Rogers). Before the film ends the two are dancing together and the heiress is forgotten. Georges Metaxa was cast as the man Penny jilts for Lucky, while Victor Moore, Helen Broderick, and Eric Blore handled the comedy.

Following *Swing Time*'s opening on August 27, 1936, at the Radio City Music Hall, critics were virtually as one in approving the film, even if many expressed picayune reservations. *Variety* typified that school of criticism which found the film's major failing was that it fell a notch or two below Astaire and Rogers's earlier films. Performances were universally admired, especially Moore and Miss Broderick's comic bits and Astaire's superb dancing. *Variety* praised Kern's tunes for their "substance and quality," adding, "Paradoxically, too, unlike many Kern scores, where the hit songs assert themselves long after the premiere, this particular sextet of songs is consistently fetching and a good variety of material, certain to command general radio and other exploitative attention." The *Times* agreed with *Variety* that the film was not as good as its Astaire and Rogers predecessors, labeling it "a disappointment." But in seeking reasons for its disappointment, the paper took a stance directly opposed to that of the trade sheet. "Blame it," it suggested, "primarily upon the music. Jerome Kern has shadow boxed with swing, when he should have been trying to pick out a few companion pieces to 'Smoke Gets in Your Eyes' and 'I Won't Dance.'" Later the reviewer concluded, "Right now we could not even whistle a bar of 'A Fine Romance,' and that's about the catchiest and brightest melody in the show. The others . . . are merely adequate or worse. Neither good Kern, nor good swing." Among the more totally satisfied critics, Kate Cameron in the *Daily News* rejoiced that Kern's music was "entrancing."

Kern's marvelous score represented the third important breakaway in his musical writing. Just as *Ninety in the Shade* firmly established his Princess Theatre style and *Dear Sir* announced the form his later show music would take, so *Swing Time*'s melodies broadcast the nature of his compositions for Hollywood. *Variety* touched on a key to this new style in lauding its instant appeal. To this extent, in the immediacy of their appeal, Kern's Hollywood songs were much like his Princess songs. Gone were the subtleties that made some of his later show songs sleepers. Gone, too, were many of the broader, more arioso musical lines. Remaining was Kern's artistry, his grace, and his unquenchable musical invention. Like the Princess songs, Kern's film tunes were close in form to the popular Tin Pan Alley songwriting of the day, but usually miles above it in accomplishment.

Because of Astaire and Rogers's dancing, "Pick Yourself Up" is rarely perceived as the superlative polka it is. It employs a Bohemian motif used by Smetana and by Jaromir Weinberger in "Schwanda, the Bag-Pipe Player." "A Fine Romance," subtitled "A Sarcastic Love Song," is a delightful, seemingly simple ditty. Written without a verse, it utilizes an ABAB[1] pattern. Wilder has analyzed the clever devices Kern employed to help smooth the song's path. Of "The Way You Look Tonight" he writes, "It's a lovely, warm song," and goes on to note, "The song flows with elegance and grace. It has none of the spastic, interrupted quality to be found in some ballads, but might be the opening statement of the slow movement of a cello concerto." The song gave Kern the first of his two Academy Awards. "Never Gonna Dance" is a smoky, sometimes wailing, rhythm number that resorts to the tempo and key changes Kern so loved. It suggests how thoroughly Kern was attuned to all but the wildest musical usages of the mid-1930s. Another major rhythm number, actually a subtle march, is Kern and Fields's affectionate, dignified salute to the greatest of contemporary black dancers, Bill Robinson, "Bojangles of Harlem." Kern did not publish the section Borne professes to have written, and, in fairness to Borne, this may suggest a certain truth to his story. Yet, as I have mentioned, its existence in the Kern papers, manuscripts going back to his earliest days, suggest it is just as probably Kern's. This section, unlike the printed parts, is in 4/4. Referred to as a "Jig Piano Dance" by whomever was responsible for the manuscript, it closely reflects the scoring used in the film. In her discussion of Astaire and Rogers films, Arlene Croce described "The Waltz In Swing Time" as "all in one tempo, seemingly one breath—a wide, white stream flowing in agile cross-rhythms, flowing without pause through so many intricacies and surprises." Miss Croce has also noted a pervasive strain of sarcasm, not merely in many of the film's lyrics, but in the relation of the songs to the story: Fred Astaire, for example, exclaiming "Never Gonna Dance" when the audience knows he will.

However stubborn he could often be, Jerry was always open to honest, thoughtful criticism. When his old pen-pal, Kathleen Cooper, wrote him to complain about the harmonics in the first bar of "Never Gonna Dance," Jerry readily confessed he had erred. Acknowledging that "you make me want to bite holes in myself for not doing it so," he sent her a revised, more effective version which supplanted the original G-minor coloring with a G-seventh, and he accentuated the G-sharp diminished chord that underscored the second half of the measure. The distinguished musicologist, Dr. Orin Suthern, has suggested the notes Kern added in the treble clef constitute a new voice that noticeably "spices" the piano part.

But some implicit criticism from more distinguished circles did hurt him. The Kerns often met Dorothy Fields and the Sigmund Rombergs at parties where George Gershwin was also a guest. Time and again either Gershwin alone was asked to play, or if George usurped the piano, as was his wont, no one protested that Jerry or Romberg should be given their hour. Dorothy long afterward remembered driving home from such an affair with Jerry, and Jerry poignantly complaining that he and Romberg were never asked to play. He wondered out loud whether they no longer liked his songs, or thought he could not play well. Of course, neither Kern nor Romberg was the pyrotechnical pianist that Gershwin or Rudolf Friml was, but both clearly deserved more courteous treatment.

For all the piddling hurts, Hollywood seemed determined to keep Kern busy. His successful work for Lily Pons made it natural that Kern's name should head the list of prospective composers when songs were needed for a new Grace Moore vehicle, *Interlude*. The film was produced by Edward Riskin with a screenplay and direction by Robert Riskin. Riskin took his tale from an "idea" by Ethel Hill and Cedric Worth. Leon Leonidoff staged the musical numbers, and Alfred Newman conducted the studio orchestra.

One can only wonder exactly what Miss Hill and Worth's "idea" was, since the basic story had been a standby of comic opera and musical comedy for longer than most people could remember. In its simplest terms it recounted a marriage of convenience that blossoms into a real romance. In this case the heroine is Louisa Fuller (Miss Moore), an Australian opera star stranded in Mexico and denied entry into the United States. To cross the border she marries Jimmy Hudson (Cary Grant), an American citizen. Expected complications and snide comedy follow before a happy ending comes as no surprise.

As with Kern's two earlier films, a working title was discarded prior to its release. By the time *Interlude* was ready to open at the Radio City Music

Hall on February 18, 1937, the musical was called *When You're in Love*.

Variety looked on the work as a "nice Grace Moore musical with a fair quota of giggles." Significantly, the trade sheet all but passed over Kern and Fields's pieces, stopping only long enough to note that "of the numbers 'Our Song' seems best." The *Times* and the *Daily News* characterized the reaction of New York's principal papers, finding the film passably entertaining but giving Kern the shortest possible shrift. The *Times* elected not to mention his specific songs, let alone evaluate them. It noted only that they were poorly recorded. All the *Daily News* would say was that "the new Kern songs lack the popular appeal." Two reasons for this slighting treatment were obvious. Among the other songs Miss Moore sang were such immediately familiar pieces as "In The Gloaming," Schubert's "Serenade," and arias by Gounod, Verdi, and Puccini, as well as such lighter favorites as "Siboney" and "Minnie The Moocher." Their familiarity gave them an instant advantage over Kern's previously unheard songs. But the second reason was clearly that Kern's songs were second-rate Kern.

Still, second-rate Kern was better than most other composers' best. Both melodies were waltzes: "The Whistling Boy" and "Our Song." Both moved from tightly knit, syncopated verses to broader, vaguely plaintive choruses. "Our Song" was the more plaintive and, as *Variety* suggested, the more appealing of the two.

However, Jerry himself was pleased with his work. Shortly after *When You're in Love* was finished Jerry wrote Mrs. Cooper that he hoped the scores for two forthcoming films, Universal's *Riviera* and Paramount's *High, Wide and Handsome*, would turn out as well. *Riviera* was never made, although its score was used by Universal for another film four years later.

With Broadway withering and Hollywood booming, the Kerns decided to pick up stakes and move permanently to Beverly Hills. They bought a plot on newly developed North Whittier Drive—the official address was 917—and accepted the developer's basic French Provincial design—a two-story house of whitewashed brick. Although the house was smaller than their Cedar Knolls home had been and the grounds substantially less, it was in keeping with real estate Hollywood giants were buying on all sides of them. Most of Hollywood's elite would live within walking distance—even if custom dictated one rarely walk. But Jerry could never settle totally for a developer's plans, no matter how individual and exclusive those plans might be. With Dorothy Hammerstein's help Jerry located a master carpenter named Hammond Ashley who could panel several of the rooms with the style and elegance Jerry demanded. Jerry made several trips to Irene Dunne's home to study patio flooring he especially admired. Unlike the Cedar Knolls house, Jerry's library and workroom was on the other side of the entrance hallway from the living room, giving Jerry and Eva greater freedom of action. The entrance hall itself had a beautiful spiral staircase.

In settling into the Whittier Drive house, Jerry did more than settle into a new home. Consciously or not, he inaugurated as well a new approach to his daily living, an approach far more relaxed and hedonistic than he had allowed himself until this time. Always fun-loving, he now found that his humor and zest for life permeated as never before every aspect of his day-to-day world. His 1935 illness may have promoted something of a *carpe diem* philosophy, and when a ghastlier illness nearly killed him shortly after the Kerns occupied their new residence, he seemed all the more determined to enjoy fully his remaining days once his health was restored.

Up to a point, his new attitude may have been imposed upon him by a second consideration. Writers were rarely treated by Hollywood executives with the respect Broadway producers extended to them. Even as famous and admired an artist as Kern was not exempt from this relative disdain. On Broadway a composer worked with his associates day and night through a show's writing, rehearsals and tryouts, adding, eliminating, or emending after conferences in which all major figures connected with a show had a significant voice. Hollywood's ways were different. Customarily, a composer's contract called for him to deliver a determined number of songs by a specified date. Thereafter, as far as their use in the film was concerned, a studio's word was law. One result of this attitude was that many composers took little interest in the films their songs were written for. Important survivors of Kern's films are in agreement that he virtually never appeared on sets during filming (despite the evidence of publicity photographs), although he often came to recording sessions for soundtracks.

Furthermore, a film never used the number of songs a Broadway musical required. Even making allowance for the sheaves of songs written but never presented, Kern's entire output during his dozen or so years in Hollywood probably never added up to the total he created in any one busy year on Broadway—say, 1917 or 1918.

In effect, the futility of attending rehearsals and filming, coupled with a need for fewer songs, freed Kern for hours of additional leisure time. He took happy advantage of it. Many a morning was spent with other songwriters—Harry Warren, Ira Gershwin, Harold Arlen—at a "pitch and putt" miniature golf course near by. Lunches at the Farmers' Market were a frequent diversion. In the evening, dinner parties and parlor games passed the time.

Whenever Mildred Knopf, one of Hollywood's best cooks, invited Jerry and Eva, Jerry would play a little game before entering. Jerry was especially fond of the Middle-European dishes Mrs. Knopf prepared so well—dishes redolent of his mother's cooking. He insisted that whenever he and Eva were invited the menu be composed of those dishes, and he devised a little way of seeing to it his demand was met. When the butler answered the Knopfs' door, Jerry insisted on talking with Mildred. Before he would move any farther she had to advise him what the appetizer was. If he was satisfied, he took a single step into the house, but refused to continue until another item was mentioned. Item by item, step by step, the Kerns crossed the threshold, arriving safely in the foyer only when Jerry had approved the dessert.

And Jerry loved after-dinner games. In bridge, his partner was frequently Romberg, and one of their hands has entered into Kern's legends. When Romberg could not figure out how many trump cards Jerry held, Jerry began to whistle Romberg's "One Alone." Romberg failed to catch the hint, advising Kern after the hand, "Who knows from lyrics?" But Jerry's most celebrated game was his own invention, Guggenheim. Essentially, it was a game of categories. Jerry would distribute pads printed with classifications (Furniture, Authors, Automobiles, etc.) and would then have someone pick a word at random from a newspaper or magazine. If the classification was furniture and the word was chalk, players would have to think of famous furniture makers whose names began with C, H, A, L, and K. Jerry's name for the game came about in this way. One night the category was printers or publishers and the word selected included the letter G. Jerry alone thought of Gutenberg. One disgruntled and not very sharp player snapped that he would continue only if Jerry did not pull any more obscure names such as Guggenheim out of his hat. Amused, Jerry thereafter had a title for his game. He sometimes used variations. For example, he would pass around photos or offer trivial details about obscure figures, and challenge his guests to identify them. Jack Cummings, a Hollywood producer who after Kern's death married his daughter, Betty, remembers the intensity with which Kern played the game and Kern's amazement and joy when Cummings alone among a party of guests identified a minor European aviator in one of the games.

Jerry's love of games went hand in hand with a passion for gambling. He once remarked, "It's a poor roulette won't work both ways." His losses at the Thanatopsis Literary and Inside Straight Club often amounted to thousands of dollars a night, although, of course, that group dated back to his New York days. But most of all he loved the horses. As a fledgling composer in Hollywood, Jule Styne was thrilled when Kern praised his songs and invited him to breakfast the next morning. He blithely assumed Kern wanted to hear more of his music away from the noise of the party they were attending. Eager and not a little nervous, he appeared promptly the next day at Whittier Drive and was led into the breakfast room. Jerry, all warmth and charm, launched directly into the reason for the invitation. Styne discovered he had not been asked because of his promising gifts as a composer, but because of his reputation as a handicapper. Jerry merely wanted his selections for the day's races.

Sartorially, Kern's individuality asserted itself in theatrical style, giving rise to two memories of him especially cherished by friends. His ties, which often had been daringly colored, gave place to highly chromatic scarves— generally ordered from Liberty's in London—that Jerry carefully knotted four-in-hand fashion. His custom-tailored jackets had sleeve buttons that actually functioned, allowing Jerry to unbutton them and roll up his jacket sleeves whenever he sat down to play. John Green, the noted composer and orchestrator, once got up enough nerve to ask Jerry why he did it. Jerry turned to him and, with all the mock disdain he could muster, replied, "Because I choose to."

One incident connected with the move west may have savagely affected Kern's health. Jerry owned two pianos, a Steinway and a Bluthner, but the German instrument was by far his favorite. He arranged for Steinway to ship both pianos from New York. The American piano arrived in pristine condition, but on uncrating the Bluthner Jerry discovered that Steinway had secured it in its shipping crate by means of screws and one of the screws had pierced through the sounding board. The realization of how badly damaged his beloved instrument was made Jerry almost apoplectic. His daughter remains convinced that this incident contributed to his heart attack several days later.

No sooner had the Kerns moved into their new home than Oscar Hammerstein brought over Rouben Mamoulian, who was to direct their next picture, *High, Wide and Handsome*. While Eva took Oscar out to show him the garden, Jerry played the songs for Mamoulian, including one he said he had just completed and had not yet given to Oscar. When Jerry finished he noticed Mamoulian was perturbed. With proper deference, the director pointed out that eight bars were a direct copy of a Gershwin melody—one which, at forty years remove, he recalls being from *Porgy and Bess.* Jerry emphatically denied any similarity, so the two agreed to let Hammerstein be the judge. Jerry played the song for Hammerstein, and Hammerstein sang the Gershwin song. Jerry's response was to go to the phone and telegraph Gershwin for permission to steal eight bars of his music.

Hammerstein's story begins when a nineteenth-century Pennsylvania farmer, Peter Cortlandt (Randolph Scott), shelters an itinerant medicine man, Doc Watterson (Raymond Walburn), his daughter, Sally (Irene Dunne), and their sidekick, Mac (William Frawley). Peter finds oil on his land, but a villainous railroad magnate (Alan Hale) attempts to gain control. Although Sally has had a falling out with Peter, she remembers her debt to him in time to help him defeat the magnate's hired goons. Dorothy Lamour had an important role as a night-club hostess, while Helen Lowell, who had starred a quarter of a century before in Kern's first complete musical, *The Red Petticoat,* played a bit part. Behind the scenes, Boris Morros conducted Robert Russell Bennett's orchestrations.

High, Wide and Handsome opened at the Astor on July 21, 1937. Critical reception was sharply divided, although a careful count would probably reveal a tilt in favor of the film. Few were as harsh in their evaluation as *Variety.* Nothing and no one escaped its displeasure. It condemned Miss Dunne as "too coy," Scott as "too forthright," and Mamoulian's direction as "heavy-handed." The trade sheet berated Hammerstein's screenplay as "a cross-section of Americana tinged with too much hokum," while Kern's score was listed "among the major disappointments." Yet *Variety* always attempted to be objective and fair, so it concluded that despite its displeasure the film should enjoy "nice returns." Some of those returns were assured by the *Times*'s review, which once again found itself substantially opposed to *Variety.* In its enthusiasm the *Times* drew a comparison that must have startled many readers. Proclaiming the film "probably as good all-around entertainment as we are likely to find on Broadway this summer," the paper continued, "Against it 'Show Boat' was an effeminate piece, nostalgic and sentimental." The review hailed the film and Kern's score alike as "picturesque, folksy and brimful of Americana."

Kern composed a rich, lovable score for *High, Wide and Handsome.* If it just misses the greatness of his finest efforts, it does not merit the neglect or dismissal it has long suffered. The music is sweet without becoming saccharine, memorably melodic, and, reflecting Kern's acute ear, captures a period flavor while remaining contemporary. Only "Can I Forget You" still enjoys some popularity. A lovely ballad with a slightly arioso release (which Kern marked "Piu cantabile ad espressivo"), it is written in the standard AABA frame and is composed solely of quarter, half, dotted half, and whole notes—except for two exquisitely placed pairs of eighth notes in the seventh and twenty-fourth measures of the chorus. The title song is a stirring anthem. Lively pieces include the unpublished "He Wore A Star," a sprightly reel, and "Will You Marry Me Tomorrow, Maria?," which Kern published as a march, while suggesting it be played almost as a polka. Besides a paraphrase of von Suppé at the start, the trio section may have been derived from a Bohemian theme. "The Things I Want" introduced blues into the score, while "Allegheny Al" offered a fetching sample of old-fashioned minstrelsy. "The Folks Who Live On The Hill" provided a pleasantly minor interlude. Unlike most of the rejected material for other Kern films, some of the discards for *High, Wide and Handsome* remain extant and identifiable. They reveal Kern also composed a pleasant waltz, a canzonetta (marked "a la tarentelle"), and an extended number tentatively entitled "Grandma's Song." The last not only employs some dissonances untypical of the composer, but contains passages highly reminiscent of Gershwin's "Looking For A Boy." Could this be the song Mamoulian remembered?

At the same time the Kerns moved into Whittier Drive, Jerry signed with RKO to compose six songs and incidental music for a new Irene Dunne film. The contract, signed on February 4, called for Kern to receive $35,000 with a complicated clause extending the possibility of an additional $5000. Dorothy Fields was to serve as lyricist. Miss Fields and her brother Herbert had conceived the story for the film, but in Hollywood's typically grotesque fashion two other writers were called upon to devise the screen play, although this may have been forced on the studio by subsequent events.

For some reason work on the songs proceeded slowly, and by March 21, just over six weeks later, the songs had not yet been finished. That morning Jerry prepared to play bridge, but then complained of feeling ill. Moments later he collapsed. By the time his doctor, Samuel Hirschfeld, arrived the composer was obviously in serious condition. Nor could the doctor's diagnosis encourage Eva and Betty. Jerry had suffered a heart attack, possibly complicated either by a mild cerebral hemorrhage or an embolism. Thoroughly frightened, Eva wired the Hammersteins, who were in England, to come back and help. The Hammersteins caught the first westbound ship. Not until May could Oscar announce that Jerry was out of danger, and Jerry's doctor forced him to keep to his bed until July. Jerry wrote to Mrs. Cooper of his convalescence and its imaginary results:

> I had more prohibitions imposed upon me in my condition than you have dreamed of in your cloister. Also, I have completely lost my manners. Able-bodied men and women rush to pick things up for me, and I pass through doors, ignoring waiting women and children, with complete and unconscious imperturbability. If there is no one to answer the telephone for me, it remains unanswered.
>
> I hasten to add that the medicos have lately pronounced my physical condition better than it has been for years [Kern was writing on March 24, 1938], but from the very beginning of my illness the wretches forgot to mention that one of the chief ingredients of a protracted convalescence was the horrible and devastating despondency that a patient inherits. So for the last seven or eight months, I have had periodic drops into the indigo that make Hamlet a giggling, buoyant acrobat.
>
> They wouldn't let me read a paper or listen to the radio for months and months, so I was spared most of the ghastly horrors of of the past year. George Gershwin had gone for weeks before they intimated to me that he was ill.

Jerry's references to telephones and Gershwin tell only half stories. Once he himself was on the road to recovery, Jerry was told that Gershwin was ill when he remarked that he was surprised not to have had at least a letter or call from his old friend. He was not, however, told of George's death in July. Innocently, he wrote Gershwin, "They have been keeping me in cellophane and absorbent cotton, and shielding me from all distressing news. So it was only yesterday that I heard of your trouble. I hasten to send you my best wishes for the speediest and completest recovery." But hearing a broadcast of Gershwin music, Jerry caught the announcer's use of the past tense in speaking of the composer. When he asked Eva if George was in fact dead, Eva had to reveal the painful truth. On the lighter side, Eva found Jerry on the phone one morning placing bets with his bookie; she knew then he was recovering rapidly.

In July he was well enough to give at least some thought to working again. In any case, he went looking for his RKO contract and, unable to find it, requested a copy as well as a list of payments made to him by the studio. Reading the studio's response Kern may have had second thoughts about his commitments or he may have advised the producer, Felix Young, that while he was better he was not well enough to resume work. Whatever the reason, on August 17, anxious to have Kern complete the score, Young granted the composer 40 per cent of his own income from the film. However, Kern's debility caused the studio to move gingerly, and serious consideration was given to presenting the film, entitled *The Joy of Loving*, as a songless farce. This consideration had lasting effects, conditioning everyone's thinking even when the picture went before the cameras at the end of the year. Filming was completed in February of 1938, but before the results were released for public inspection the title was slightly changed, apparently in response to the censors. The seemingly harmless, if vaguely suggestive, "loving" gave place to the wholesome "living."

Joys of loving and living—and their problems, too—propelled Gene Towne, Graham Baker, and Allan Scott's screenplay. (Edward Chodorov and Samson Raphaelson were among a number of uncredited contributors to the final version.) In the story, a handsome, rich man-of-the-world, Dan Brewster (Douglas Fairbanks, Jr.), opens the eyes of the musical comedy star, Margaret Garret (Miss Dunne), to the thralldom her greedy, grasping family has imposed upon her. A superb supporting cast included Alice Brady, Guy Kibbee, Jean Dixon, Eric Blore, Lucille Ball, Billy Gilbert, and Franklin Pangborn. Tay Garnett directed, and Kern's old collaborator, Frank Tours, conducted Robert Russell Bennett's orchestrations.

As *Joy of Living* the film opened at the Radio City Music Hall on May 5, 1938. More than one critic ignored Kern's songs entirely or mentioned them only in passing. Kate Cameron explained to her *Daily News* readers, "The picture is straight comedy but, since the heroine plays a musical comedy star, the role gives Irene Dunne an opportunity to use her lovely soprano voice on a number of Jerome Kern tunes." *Variety*, adding a judgment on the quality of the music, said much the same thing: "[The songs] are melodious and spotted effectively without interrupting the farce tempo of the film." A dissenting voice came from the *Times*, which was not particularly amused by a picture it found "forty joyless minutes too long." On the other hand it heartily enjoyed one feature, advising, "The saving grace is Jerome Kern's score."

Either the studio discarded two of Kern's songs or else Kern provided

only four of the six his contract called for. None is among his best, but
considering his condition they remain remarkably attractive. Clearly they
are not the composer's most readily whistleable. Yet, as Wilder's analysis of
two demonstrates, they are otherwise every bit as artful as Kern's songs are
expected to be. At the same time, they have a peculiarly indefinable "show
music" quality; they cannot be instantly categorized as belonging to Kern's
corpus of film material. Perhaps knowledge that Miss Dunne was to play a
Broadway singing star prompted Kern to envision privately these songs as
being sung on a real stage, and to write them accordingly. Wilder examines
"You Couldn't Be Cuter" with some amazement, incredulous that the song
could actually be by Kern. Exclaiming that the song "really swings," he
continues, "The song not only swings, but it builds in the last section of
twelve measures (as opposed to the other, eight measure sections) to perfection." His conclusion is that the song is "irresistible." In the film the
song was anything but swung, presented as it was with a light, carillon airi-
ness marred perhaps by moments of sugary cuteness. Wilder describes "Just
Let Me Look At You" as "a beautiful, uncluttered song which proceeds
from melodic point to point in one long flowing line and doesn't bother to
repeat sections, as is customary in the best of theater songs. Its form is
A-B-A¹-C-D, which may give you an indication of how prodigal Kern
could be with his material." Conversely, repetition is a key to Kern's plan
for "A Heavenly Party," where not only are short phrases repeated as soon
as they are uttered, but measures of the chorus refer back to measures in
the verse—a practice Kern increasingly applied. Alone of the film's songs,
"What's Good About Good-Night?" has no verse to refer to. A lovely,
straightforward, ABA¹B¹ melody, it utilizes another favorite Kern device
by hanging on to the repetition of a short phrase (over the repeated words
"take the dreams") in order to lead into a new section.

Although *Joy of Living* was no failure, it brought to a close the long
association between Miss Dunne and the composer. Miss Dunne elected
to follow the path of so many talented musical comedy stars by moving on
to conquer the worlds of straight comedy and drama. In his fifties and
not in the best of health, Kern, for his part, was simply slowing down.

But as Jerry's strength began to rally he embarked on a project he hoped
would put his name once more on a Broadway marquee. He took extra
pleasure in the work because for the first time since *Sunny* it united him
with both Hammerstein and Harbach at once. Their libretto was based on
a story an ex-West Point cadet, Edward Boykin, had sold to films but which

was never used. Early letters show that Boykin had a hand in some of the initial drafts. The piece promised to offer another glorious bit of Americana.

Before theatregoers knew anything about it, they could read in their papers news that seemed to bring Kern's year to a happy end. Only the public could not know the tragedy behind the innocent, optimistic paragraphs they scanned. On December 18 the Kerns announced that their daughter, about to turn nineteen, would marry Richard Green. Green was the younger, handsome brother of John Green (the composer of "Body And Soul") and was hoping to find himself as secure a niche in the picture industry as his brother had. Even before the wedding Betty realized that the marriage would not work. But Green pleaded with her that he would find a broken engagement more humiliating than a later divorce. Luckily for Green, not only Betty but her parents as well were understanding. Although they were clearly in some state of shock, they agreed to honor young Richard's wishes.

Meanwhile work continued apace on the new musical, *Gentlemen Unafraid*. Kern's absorption in it was such that he rejected MGM's offer to do a musical version of *The Wizard of Oz*. Early on its authors determined that *Gentlemen Unafraid* would have to be sufficient unto itself. As Kern wrote his loyal correspondent, Kathleen Cooper, "The piece has not been fashioned for any stars or even featured players of note. It shall have to stand or fall on its own merits, dramatically and musically." To give themselves a certain artistic freedom, away from Broadway's cold, commercial eye, Kern and his librettists agreed to try the work out not on the usual pre-New York routes but at the prestigious, independent St. Louis Municipal Opera Company. The decision was reasonable and not a little courageous, but in the long run it led to Broadway's never seeing the show, since no Broadway producer had money in it and therefore none felt an obligation to struggle with it until it might be whipped into shape. By late winter it was announced that the show would open St. Louis's summer season.

Of course, Jerry was still too weak to travel far, so final preparations of *Gentlemen Unafraid* had to be left to Oscar and Otto. Oscar himself was not in the best of health, having only recently recovered from a severe attack of bronchial pneumonia. But the men knew their latest work was being carefully assessed. St. Louis papers recorded the long list of New York and Hollywood notables arriving in the city for the premiere. Max Gordon, who hoped to present the musical in New York in the fall, was among the earliest to detrain. With him came John Kenneth Hyatt, man-

371

ager of Rockefeller Center, anxious to determine if the show would be suitable for his white elephant, the Center Theatre. Louis A. Lotito, manager of the Martin Beck, also arrived with an eye to booking the show. MGM sent Kenneth McKenna. Other leading theatrical figures, with less immediate interests in the show, included Laurence Schwab and a man who would ultimately inherit Kern's mantle, Richard Rodgers.

At the last minute, a problem Jerry, Oscar, and Otto were unaccustomed to threatened to wreck the opening—the weather. The St. Louis Municipal Opera performed out of doors, and as patrons began to arrive for the Friday, June 3, 1938, premiere, the rain came down in torrents. As late as 9:30 the management delayed a decision on postponing the first night. Then the rain slackened, so the order was given to proceed. It continued to rain off and on throughout the evening. Nevertheless, the papers reported, most of the audience remained for the whole performance, following the example of Secretary of War Harry H. Woodring and other political notables sitting in a special box.

Musical numbers were:

Gentlemen Unafraid

ACT I

1. Opening
   a. "Virginia Hoe Down" . . . . . . *Polly [Kay Picture], Don [Kirk Alyn], Ensemble, Dancers*
   b. "Our Last Dance" . . . . . . *Linda [Hope Manning] and Singing Ensemble*
2. "Gentlemen Unafraid" . . . . . . *Don, Bob [Ronald Graham], Linda and Male Ensemble*
3. "What Kind of Soldier Are You?" . . . . *Betsy [Vicki Cummings], Bud [Richard "Red" Skelton] and Male Ensemble*
4. "Your Dream is the Same as My Dream" . . *Linda and Bob*
5. Reprise, "Hoe Down" . . . . *Joe [Avon Long] and Ensemble*
6. "De Land o' Good Times" . *Liza [Minto Cato], Linda, Bob, Polly, Don and Entire Ensemble*
7. Finaletto . . . . *Linda, Bob and Singing Ensemble*
8. "Abe Lincoln Has Just One Country" . . . . *Male Ensemble*
9. "What Kind of Soldier Are You?"
10. Fantasie . . *[Female Singing Ensemble and Corps de Ballet]*

11. Finale .... *Entire Company*

ENTRACTE

ACT II

1. Opening .... *Singing Boys*
2. "When You Hear That Humming" ...... *Betsy, Bud and*
   Singing Ensemble
3. "It's Gayer Whistling as You Go" .... *Betsy, Bud, Bob and*
   Male Ensemble
4. "Mister Man" .... *Linda*
5. "How Would I Know?" .... a. *Liza and Colored Ensemble*
   b. *Male Ensemble*
   c. *Linda and Female Ensemble*

ACT III

1. "What Kind of Soldier Are You?" ...... *Bob, Jim [Harry*
   Sullivan] and Male Ensemble
2a. "Little Zouave" ...... *Betsy, Bud, Pignatelli [Ralph Riggs]*
   and Male Ensemble
b. Zouave Drill .... *Dancing Girl*
3. Finale .... *Entire Company*

George Hirst conducted Robert Russell Bennett's orchestrations. Zeke Colvan directed. Theodor Adolphus and Al White, Jr., were choreographers. Sets were by Raymond Savoy and costumes by Billi Livingston.

A note in the program read: "The music is interwoven throughout the play in the usual fine style of Messrs. Kern, Hammerstein and Harbach. The musical numbers come out of the dramatic situations, and have a pertinent bearing on the plot."

The libretto told of Bob Vance, a West Point cadet from Virginia, who finds himself in a dilemma at the outbreak of the Civil War. His sense of duty urges him to fight for the Union, but his sweetheart, Linda Mason, begs him to return home and aid the Confederacy. He elects to remain in the North. After the war is over he learns Linda has remained loyal to him.

Out of courtesy or out of a lack of experience with tryouts (St. Louis had long ceased being a break-in city), the critics seemed hesitant to pass detailed judgment. Yet even their reserved comments hinted at trouble. Without specifying what problems and virtues prompted its conclusion, the *Post-Dispatch* noted mechanically that "the show has a really strong first act, a fair second act ending in a tremendous climax and a third act that takes only a little bit too long." The *Globe-Democrat* was even less precise, early on calling the work "somberly sincere" and later noting reiteratively, "What the dignitaries witnessed was no flippant, flag-waving treatment of war and of soldiers after musical-comedy fashion, but a serious, solemn and dignified attempt to set a crisis in United States history to music." When it came to Kern's music, both critics were more obviously enthusiastic. According to the *Globe-Democrat*, "Kern has provided music that is at least up to the standard of his previous work and has included songs that may come to be regarded as surpassing it when repetition makes them more familiar. There is an ample supply, too, an abundance of music calling for the services of the chorus." The *Post-Dispatch* went into greater detail, stopping to discuss songs that particularly impressed it. Hearing Kern's "trademark" in the songs, the paper continued by listing and evaluating the better numbers:

> "Gentlemen Unafraid," the title of which was taken from a Kipling poem; "Our Last Dance," "Your Dream Is the Same As My Dream" and "What Kind of Soldier Are You?" are exciting, romantic or comic things needed to fill out a show, but "How Would I Know?" a Negro anti-war spiritual is one of the greatest songs of Kern's career.
> Beginning "How Would I Know, Why They Made My Man a Soldier?" and ending "I Wish There Weren't No War," the number is a perfect combination of rousing music and lyrics. Woven in with a flash history of the war, called after the fashion of the movies, a "montage," it builds up to the second act climax. It seems to be the song of "Gentlemen Unafraid" that may bring fame to the entire show.

Beautiful as the music was, one aspect apparently caused problems, prompting the *Post-Dispatch* to report: "The only difficulty of the evening seemed to come when the choruses were wrestling with some of Kern's more intricate modulations, but this feature was only slightly noticeable."

Two of *Gentlemen Unafraid*'s songs remain vaguely familiar to the public: "Your Dream," because it was reused in the film *One Night in the Tropics;* and the stirring "Abe Lincoln Has Just One Country." "What Kind Of Soldier Are You?" is a lilting, slightly old-fashioned number. More old-fashioned still, "De Land O' Good Times" was patently meant to recall classic Negro spirituals and Stephen Foster's songs about blacks. At once

374

contemporary and anachronistic, "Mister Man" is a languid torch song. "It's Gayer Whistling As You Go" (called "Gayly I Whistle A Song" in the manuscript of the vocal score) enchants as one of Kern's sweet, lithesome bonbons.

If he was not well enough to travel to St. Louis, Jerry was sufficiently recovered and sufficiently anxious about opening night reaction to remain up late accepting phone calls from those who saw the show. Everyone had kind words for Jerry's score, but a telegram he sent to Oscar in the early hours of June 4 foreshadowed the ultimate discontent with the new piece. Jerry wired:

> Max Dreyfus telephoned most enthusiastically about score. He complained about dialogue amplification going over his head owing to pocket he seated in. McKenna's report . . . was also enthusiastic, stating story very powerful up to last 30 minutes which he said went down hill. This may have been caused by thin third act. McKenna very complimentary about score and considers entire piece positive natural for pictures. The big New York manager didn't trouble to phone. Maybe he does not like it for Center after all. Goodnight and heartfelt thanks and congratulations to you and Otto.

Although most playgoers and critics clearly felt Kern's score represented the redeeming strength of the show, the composer was not about to let his colleagues and friends accept blame for its disappointing reception. Several weeks before the show opened, Edwin Lester, the West Coast producer, had visited Kern with plans for a summer revival of *Roberta*. When he returned to work on the revival after the St. Louis premiere, the subject of *Gentlemen Unafraid* crept into the conversation, and Lester diplomatically remarked, "Too bad that 'Gentlemen Unafraid' didn't go on; the music was awfully good." As Lester remembers Jerry's riposte: "He answered me very sharply (as was his wont), 'A musical show is a collaboration and if the show doesn't turn out well all the collaborators are equally responsible.'" Lester cannot recall any other composer so self-effacing in a similar situation. (Lester recalls a second occasion in which Kern's reply was similarly tart and similarly indicative of his sense of professionalism. Learning that Kern had signed a contract for a new film, Lester inquired who would serve as lyricist. "He answered," Lester remembers, "with an emphasis designed to correct me, 'My *collaborator* is Johnny Mercer.'")

Letters of Hammerstein to Kern show that Hammerstein persisted for some while in attempting to move the show to Broadway. Meanwhile both he and Harbach worked diligently to fortify the book. No Broadway production was ever forthcoming, although during World War II the play was released for amateur presentation in a revised and retitled form, as *Hayfoot, Strawfoot*. By that time "Your Dream" had been sung in *One Night in the Tropics*, and so was replaced by a lovely, rangy ballad, "When A New Star." "Boy With A Drum," a thumping tattoo, was also added. Unfortunately, its apparent anti-war sentiments necessitated the elimination of "How Would I Know?" and no copy seems to have survived. At the same time, "Abe Lincoln Has Just One Country" was employed by the government at patriotic rallies. Jerry was determined not to be depressed by *Gentlemen Unafraid*'s failure to move on to New York. But thoughts of New York seemed more and more to cry for attention.

21

Broadway, Briefly—
and New Horizons

As he recovered his strength, Jerry grew restless. Even California's comforting balminess palled. Old ties, and New York's glitter and excitement, seemed once more especially salubrious. Jerry and Eva came East in November and began to catch up on their theatregoing. Some idea of Jerry's tastes in straight plays can be gathered from his reactions to the plays he saw. He was deeply moved by *Oscar Wilde, Abe Lincoln In Illinois,* and *Our Town,* but dismissed *Kiss the Boys Good-Bye* as "the world's tedious waste of time." His visit led the Shuberts to announce that the composer would collaborate with Fannie Hurst on a new musical. Once more, nothing came of the project. However, Kern did use some of his time to insert a single song in a drama of Negro life then in rehearsal, *Mamba's Daughters.* The bluesy "Lonesome Walls" had a lyric by the play's co-author, DuBose Heyward.

The Kerns were back in Beverly Hills by the beginning of December. But the outlook for work was bleak. Jerry wrote Oscar Hammerstein:

> The situation now is past the pleasant, joshing point, and you and I both have got to bang through with something powerful for the stage. We have both been much too long off the boards. While we naturally do not want to roll up on Broadway with just a

show, I find the prospect very encouraging. Upon analysis, there was never a thoroughfare more naked of competitive traffic. When you think that only somewhat more than a handful of seasons ago plenty of entertainment was provided by Friml, Romberg, the Gershwins, Berlin, Youmans, Hirsch, us and the Europeans, not to mention the current limited group, the target for a bull's-eye has pretty good visibility.

Together, Jerry and Oscar revived the idea of a Princess Theatre style show. But despite a marked improvement Jerry still was not in the best of health, so work proceeded at a snail's pace. Even playing the piano had become an ordeal. Jerry complained to Kathleen Cooper, "I can no longer strike a simple C-Major tonic chord without faltering. My left hand is inept and my memory gone completely." Yet Jerry's ear and his receptiveness to genuine new talent remained as acute as ever. In the same letter he rejoiced that he had been "reintroduced to YESTERDAYS by Mr. Artie Shaw, a virtuoso, if I ever heard one." The praise of Shaw is ironic, since Betty's unfortunate marriage to Richard Green was followed during World War II by an equally unhappy one to Shaw.

In March Dennis King announced that he and Vincente Minnelli would bring to Broadway a musical with a book by Sam and Bella Spewack, lyrics by Ira Gershwin, and music by Kern. The project was no sooner announced than it was forgotten.

If Jerry's initial idea for his and Oscar's next effort never bore fruit, it led to the story Oscar finally used. That initial idea set the ailing Kern to recalling more vigorous, halcyon days and Elisabeth ("Bessie") Marbury. Long out of both the theatre and Kern's life, Bessie had died in January of 1933. Kern had always remembered her affectionately, not merely for her perspicacity and for her kindness to him, but for her dramatically vital life. Kern several times mentioned the possibility of a stage biography to Hammerstein. Nothing came of it, but their talks did lead them to think about a theatrical background for their new show. It was a comfortably familiar theme. Consciously or not, all their Broadway efforts had featured heroines who performed in one way or another. Sunny rode in a circus, Magnolia worked on her showboat and at a night spot, Addie and Sieglinde in the theatre.

By the late 1930s Hammerstein was at the nadir of his career, disillusioned with Hollywood and smarting from a string of Broadway failures. A new musical with Kern, one dealing with theatre folk he knew and loved, must have seemed especially reassuring.

Perhaps Kern's persistent hope of bringing Bessie Marbury to life on stage suggested as much as anything that they could at least revive the Princess Theatre's lovingly remembered style of intimate musical comedy. Indeed Bessie's then recent death may have prompted Kern and Hammerstein's thoughts about a Princess show five years earlier. The Princess itself was still standing, although when the pair began work on their new show the house was occupied by *Pins and Needles* and appeared to be committed indefinitely. But even by the end of 1938 theatrical economics were such that so small a theatre was no longer truly feasible.

Early announcements confirmed that the new musical would be "reminiscent of the song and dance fun-fests that used to tenant the Princess Theatre." Plans called for the show to open in Los Angeles during the winter, tour the West, and arrive in New York in spring, or the following fall. When spring arrived there was still no sign of the show, although in March announcements informed readers that the musical would be called *Very Warm for May*. Curiously, when contracts were signed three months later, the title had been changed to *In Other Words*.

Hammerstein persuaded Kern to allow Max Gordon to produce the show, despite the unpleasant contretemps that had developed on both occasions Gordon and Kern had worked together before. Kern was probably convinced that Hammerstein's warmth and tact would calm any angry waters that might rise. Gordon himself, in Hollywood, working on a movie, had been hounding Kern with letters and phone calls, begging to produce his next work. In May Kern played him melodies meant for the new show and Gordon left, confident he was about to have a smash hit.

Come July, Hammerstein rented Norma Talmadge's beach-front home in Santa Monica, and he and Kern set to work finishing the musical. For the most part they worked steadily, although one day the romantic lyricist presented Kern with a lyric he had been inspired to write the evening before during a moonlit walk along the shore, where he had watched an elderly, white-haired couple walking hand in hand. He set the lyric to a melody he and Kern had written for *Show Boat,* but discarded. The two spent the day revising and perfecting it, although "Sweetest Sight That I Have Seen" (called merely "I Have Seen" in the manuscript) was never used in *Very Warm for May* and remained unpublished until after Kern's death.

Hammerstein arrived in New York on August 28 to complete casting and schedule rehearsals. Kern was slated to arrive September 18, two days before the first rehearsal. At the last minute he took sick again. Confined to bed for a week, he finally reached New York on September 25.

When rehearsals began at the Music Box the show was still without a New York berth. The 1939–40 season had gotten off to a surprisingly bullish start. Of course, Gordon was unconcerned, knowing full well that his name, Kern's, and, despite his recent setbacks, Hammerstein's still were magical enough to assure a first-rate house. As if the names were not sufficient, a barrage of publicity was launched.

The show opened at Wilmington's Playhouse on October 20 and immediately received the first of the glowing notices it would garner all along its tryout path. William P. Frank began his review in the *Evening Journal* by joyously proclaiming, "Happy days are really here again!" Although the initial performance ran well past midnight, Frank was certain that after careful pruning the musical would be "an unqualified success." He showered virtually every facet of the show with raves, pausing only long enough to lament that the story was "pretty thin." Turning to the score he advised readers, "For your hit-parade list, add such new songs as 'In Other Words, Seventeen,' 'All the Things You Are,' and 'All in Fun.' They'll be around a long while."

In retrospect, the story *Very Warm for May* told in Wilmington was not especially thin. If it was not strikingly novel, it nevertheless was dramatic and capable of eliciting an audience's compassion. William Graham carelessly allows himself to fall into the clutches of gangsters who threaten his daughter, May, if he fails to do their bidding. She flees, finding refuge at a summer stock playhouse run by a flamboyantly artistic director, Ogdon Quiler. The theatre is on the property of a slightly batty matron, Winnie Spofford, whose son and daughter both have dramatic ambitions. For all her eccentricities, Winnie proves a motherly, understanding protector to May. The gangsters appear, kidnappings occur, and the police arrive to add to the confusion. In the end, the gangsters are thwarted, May falls in love with Winnie's son ("Sonny"), and May's widowed father discovers in Winnie a long-lost flame.

When his Hollywood commitments ran overtime, Max Gordon had allowed his office, Hammerstein, and Vincente Minnelli to whip the show into shape. He himself never saw it on stage until he appeared in Wilmington the morning after the premiere. The city's cordial reception meant nothing to him. He disliked almost everything he saw and heard; he found the book weak, the direction limp, the dances dreary. Even Kern's songs had somehow lost their enchantment for him. Although the second night audience was every bit as enthusiastic as the first, the performance merely served to reinforce Gordon's displeasure. As soon as the curtain fell Gordon was on the phone enlisting Hassard Short to aid Hammerstein and persuading Albertina Rasch to fly in from California to revise Harry Losee's choreography. He badgered Hammerstein to make drastic revisions on the book, most importantly eliminating all references to gangsters and crime, and toning down Quiler's outlandish pretensions. Short began work with the company when it opened in Washington the beginning of the next week. With Short on hand, Gordon sent an emissary to tell Minnelli he was fired. Miss Rasch appeared on Thursday, October 26. On October 30 the show moved to Philadelphia, and one week later, on November 6, it opened in Boston. Hammerstein's rewritten book went in during the Boston visit. Whether the new book was tighter is moot, but there is no question that all the color had been drained from Hammerstein's original conception. What survived was a pale, trite, backstage story. For example, when Winnie originally reprised "In Other Words, Seventeen" to a frightened, befuddled May as a first act finale, the situation gave the song a devastating poignancy. The same song sung with May's terror vanished seemed simply watery, or, worse, treacly.

With its reworked plot, reworked dances, and reworked staging, *Very Warm for May* trundled on to New York for its premiere at the Alvin Theatre on November 17, 1939, with this musical program:

Very Warm for May

ACT I
Scene One

1. Duettino, "In Other Words, Seventeen" ...... *May [Grace McDonald] and Mr. Graham [Donald Brian]*
2. Stop Dance, Finaletto .... *Jackson [Avon Long]*

Scene Two

1. Characterization .... *Ogdon [Hiram Sherman]*
    Babbling Brook Dance, Kay Picture
2. "All the Things You Are" .... *Ogdon, Liz [Frances Mercer], Carroll [Hollace Shaw] and Charles [Ralph Stuart]*
3. Winnie's Audition (Accordionist, Milton Delugg)
4. May Tells All .... *May*

5. "Heaven in My Arms" ..... *Johnny [Jack Whiting], Liz and Carroll*

Dance by Evelyn Thawl, Sally Craven and Kate Friedlich
6. Finaletto, "In Other Words, Seventeen" .... *Winnie [Eve Arden]*

ACT II
Scene One

1. "That Lucky Fellow" .... *Raymond [Robert Shackleton]*
2. Gavotte: "L'histoir de Madame de la Tour" .... *Carroll, Miss Wasserman [Virginia Card], Jane [Evelyn Thaw] and Andre [Andre Charise]*
3. "That Lucky Lady" .... *May*
4. The Strange Case of Adam Standish .... *Ogdon*
   a. Song, "In The Heart of the Dark" .... *Carroll*
   b. Ballet Peculiaire .... *Walter [Walter Long] and Honey [Maxine Barrat]*

Scene Two

1. Audition .... *Matty Malneck's Orchestra*
   [Songs played here included "Liebestraum" and "Swing Low, Sweet Chariot"]
2. Dance .... *May*
3. Reprise, "In the Heart of the Dark" .... *Liz*

Scene Three

1. The Deer and the Park Avenue Lady .... *Andre Charise and Miss Hyde [Kay Picture]*
2. "All in Fun" .... *Liz and Johnny*
3. Schottische Scena .... *Johnny and May*

Scene Four

Reprise, "All the Things You Are" .... *Kenny [Ray Mayer]*

Scene Five

1. Dance Da Da
   a. Lady in Red .... *Sylvia [Kate Friedlich]*
   b. The Blackbird and Lady in White ...... *Smoothy [Don Loper] and Honey*

382

2. Reprise .... *Liz and Johnny*
3. Interlude .... *May and Sonny*
4. Finale

Robert Emmett Dolan conducted Robert Russell Bennett's orchestrations. Short received no mention in the program, but Minnelli was credited with designing and staging the production and Hammerstein with staging the book. Miss Rasch and Losee shared choreographic honors.

Most critics found kind words for the cast and for Minnelli's production, but when it came to the revised book Gordon had demanded they resorted to their harshest epithets. Among the more gentlemanly comments, *Cue* saw the "inconsequential plot . . . forever slowing things down." *Variety* thought Hammerstein's basic idea "dandy," but "never well developed" and often "a confused jumble." In the *Times*, Brooks Atkinson wrote, "The book is a singularly haphazard invention that throws the show out of focus and makes an appreciation of Mr. Kern's music almost a challenge." But Stanley B. Whipple in the *World-Telegram* and John Anderson in the *Journal-American* pleaded with their readers to ignore the libretto, insisting Kern's music alone made a trip to the Alvin worthwhile.

A comparison of the Wilmington and New York programs shows that no major songs were added during the tryout, but that several numbers were dropped. The original openings of both acts disappeared: May's "Me And The Roll And You" from Act One and a rumba-tango-paso doble from the second act. A minuet from the first act was also cut, while several specialties were inserted for Jackson and Winnie. The dance numbers from the last half were severely shortened.

Despite Atkinson's figure of speech it was really not difficult to appreciate Kern's score, although it is generally known that even Kern doubted "All The Things You Are" would gain much acceptance. It was not so much the single key change in the verse he feared—a change from G to A flat— but the unexpected notes and harmonic progressions that for all purposes represented hidden key changes all through the song. Arthur Schwartz, on first hearing the song, shared Kern's doubts, but he has since come to consider the piece "the greatest song ever written," an opinion more or less shared by such fellow composers as John Green and Harry Warren.

In his *American Popular Song* Alec Wilder discusses five of six published songs. This in itself is noteworthy, since even in many of Kern's biggest hits Wilder could not find so many numbers deserving special attention. He considers "All The Things You Are" "not only very ingenious, but very daring," noting in particular the startling note and chord that "Kern thought . . . beyond the public ear. The melodic note at the end of the release . . . a g sharp with an E-major chord supporting its first measure." (Remember, the chorus is in A flat!) For "Heaven In My Arms" Kern returned to a device he had begun to employ regularly in his film musicals, repeating part of the verse as part of the chorus—in this instance, the end of the chorus. The verse and the chorus are so of a piece that Wilder guessed they were composed at a single sitting. "In The Heart Of The Dark" uses repeated notes and quarter note triplets in a fashion that clearly suggests Cole Porter. While Wilder records "some curious melodic moves" in "In Other Words, Seventeen" he correctly concludes that the melody's real strength lies in its charming innocence and naturalness. "All In Fun" comes the closest of any of Kern's songs from the show to recapturing the straightforward gaiety of the songs he was creating one World War earlier, yet it does so with bittersweet chordings and a few unusual turns that were clearly contemporary. The only published song Wilder neglected was "That Lucky Fellow," whose chorus opens with a progression of repeated notes that suggest George Gershwin as much as "In The Heart Of The Dark" suggests Porter. Good as the rest of his melodies for the show were, there can be no gainsaying the public's making "All The Things You Are" Kern's last masterpiece for Broadway. Fifteen or more years after Kern's death the song was still selling about a thousand copies a month, while all the other tunes from the show could sell little more than a dozen combined. His marvelous harmonies have made it a jazz standard.

The disparaging reviews coupled with the flock of hits that preceded and followed *Very Warm for May* into New York quickly told against the show. Gordon hoped to stimulate sales by offering excerpts from the show on a still primitive television. Union demands scuttled the broadcast, but the producer did receive some briefly helpful publicity from the attempt. Even though Gordon lowered ticket prices from a $4.40 top to $3.30, he was unable to attract patrons. The road had long since virtually died and the day when a Broadway flop could still look ahead to a season or two in the hinterlands had died with it. *Very Warm for May* closed after just fifty-nine showings.

Returning discouraged to Hollywood, Kern found there were still no new films to compose for. But shortly after Paris fell on June 14, 1940, Kern received a special request from Hammerstein to put a melody to a lyric he had written nostalgically recalling the City of Light in happier times. Kern readily complied, marking on the manuscript of "The Last Time I Saw Paris" the direction, "not sadly," an admonition many singers of the song obviously never saw. Indeed, there is a gay lilt to the melody with just a tinge of melancholy that needs no underscoring. Even in such dismal moments Kern kept his wit, appending a second message on the song advising Oscar to phone Ira Gershwin to see if George's celebrated Paris taxi horns (orchestral, of course) could not be borrowed for it. Kern won his second Academy Award when the song was interpolated into the 1941 film *Lady, Be Good!* Jerry sympathized with outcries that the song should not have been selected since it was not written for the film. He helped lobby to change the rules.

The immediate success of the song may have prompted Nick Holde (Blumenthal and Peggy Fears's former assistant) and Albert Johnson to promise Broadway two Kern and Hammerstein shows in the fall. One was to be a revival of *Show Boat,* the other a new work "about life in San Francisco during the years 1865 to 1875." Neither production materialized.

The lone Kern score to be heard in a new film was one the public did not know he had written several years before. By 1940 Universal Pictures was deep in financial trouble and desperately seeking a success to bolster its shaky position. Studio executives decided to take a chance on a promising young talent, Leonard Spigelgass. They made him producer and gave him virtually free rein in unearthing a property. Spigelgass approached the studio's director of music, Charles Previn, asking for his suggestions. After a few moments' thought Previn went to the shelf and pulled out a musical score, which he told Spigelgass was one Jerome Kern had written for the studio for a film (*Riviera*) that was never produced. The score was available, provided Kern's consent was forthcoming. Spigelgass had read a book, Earl Derr Biggers's *Love Insurance,* that he had enjoyed and felt would be readily adaptable. So all that remained was to obtain Kern's consent.

Kern was called and arrived for a meeting with Spigelgass and his associates. The producer informed Kern of his plans and told him of the story he planned to use. Spigelgass was appalled at Kern's reaction, which he described as one of "icy rage." But before Kern could fully articulate his anger the phone rang. It was a message for Spigelgass, advising him his mother had been rushed to the hospital. Kern's rage melted abruptly. He became solicitous and concerned, offering to take the producer to the hospi-

385

tal in his own car. By the time discussions resumed, Kern was at least partially mollified, or else he had decided on the tack he would take. He
agreed to authorize the use of the score for a substantial additional payment.
Universal acquiesced.

Dorothy Fields's original lyrics were retained, but Oscar Hammerstein
also received recognition in the official credits, since one song was brought
over from *Gentlemen Unafraid.* Curiously, no mention was made of Harbach, even though that song's sheet music lists him as Hammerstein's collaborator.

Spigelgass turned the book over to Kathryn Scola and Francis Martin
for an outline and then turned their outline over to Gertrude Purcell and
Charles Grayson. An old Mack Sennett gag writer, A. Edward Sutherland,
was chosen as director. Charles Previn conducted Frank Skinner's orchestrations. Larry Ceballos was choreographer.

The story told how an insurance agent named Jim (Allan Jones) sells
his pal Steve (Robert Cummings) an insurance policy on Steve's marriage
to Cynthia (Nancy Kelly). But Jim and Cynthia soon fall in love. The
complications are ironed out on a lovely West Indian island. Supporting
roles went to Mary Boland and one of Kern's earliest stars, Richard Carle.

One Night in the Tropics opened December 19, 1940, at the Roxy. Most
critics could muster little enthusiasm for the film. *Variety* lamented the
"stilted story," and production values it deemed merely "adequate." The
weekly magazine, *Time,* saw it as "no more than a jumbled exaggeration of
the Boy Meets Girl motif." In New York the *Times* dismissed it as "a mild
sedative." With two exceptions performers were handed at best perfunctory
praise. Those two exceptions elicited the sole gleeful responses. According
to *Variety,* Abbott and Costello provided "the brightest spots in the picture." The *Times* elaborated, reporting: "Abbott and Costello, as a pair of
undercover men, account for whatever hilarity there is in the film—and
that is strange because the plot stalls in its tracks whenever they appear."
The paper was among the minority that enjoyed "Kern's lilting melodies."
The *Hollywood Reporter* agreed, hearing "five pleasing melodies." But most
critics seemed to concur with *Variety* when it rued that "Kern fails to reveal
one tune that will be remembered."

All of Kern's songs for the film exhibited his customary sweet gifts, yet
remained undeniably second drawer. Alec Wilder completely ignores Kern's
material for *One Night in the Tropics,* although he does comment in passing on the one song Kern brought over from elsewhere. That song was

"Your Dream (Is The Same As My Dream)," originally conceived for *Gentlemen Unafraid*. Wilder felt the song "wanders all over the lot." In his discerning analysis of Kern, Alfred Simon draws a similarly unhappy conclusion about "Remind Me," which Simon observes is "one of the rare instances in which Kern started with a lovely theme, rather overdeveloped the song and then seemed to have trouble finding his way back." The song is also one of the few in which Kern explicitly calls for a rhumba beat (beginning in the chorus's bridge). Spiegelgass remembers the song was not initially conceived in a Latin tempo, but that the setting of the film suggested the change. To Spiegelgass's surprise, Kern was delighted. "You And Your Kiss" is a nondescript ballad, while "Back In My Shell," presented in its sheet music as "A Song of renunciation in the Negro manner," is an equally nondescript blues. The unpublished "Farandola" is, as the title suggests, a lively farandole. But a certain haunting sadness in its melody partially belies its lyric's claim that it is gay.

Looking back over thirty-eight years, Spiegelgass says he has come to share Jerry's disdain for the film, although he adds that Jerry rather unfairly held the film against him and often cold-shouldered him because of it. For all its faults, the film made stars of Abbott and Costello, and their stardom helped save Universal.

On September 24 Jerry gave the lie to his own laments that he could no longer play well when he appeared at a special program at the San Francisco World's Fair. The program, arranged by ASCAP, gave visitors a unique chance to see and hear most of America's greatest composers play their own beloved melodies. Irving Berlin, George M. Cohan, and a host of other celebrities entertained admirers. Kern played two compositions, "All The Things You Are" and "Smoke Gets In Your Eyes." As recordings of the event disclose, Kern played them in a slightly florid style marked by some unexpected tempos, a style Saul Chaplin has labeled the "Viennese Concert Style."

The year ended sadly, but foreseeably, for the Kerns when Betty obtained her divorce at the beginning of December. Betty's problem may have monopolized the Kerns' attention in the early months of 1941. Although Jerry complained to Mrs. Cooper in June that he was "water-logged due to being swamped in professional duties," vestiges of any writing he did at the time have failed to survive, or at least are no longer identifiable. Not even the customary false hopes were raised to hint at the nature of his labors. Kern did make occasional visits to camps to entertain draftees. And with his faithful amanuensis, Charles Miller, he did transcribe old hits from "Bill" to "All The Things You Are" for string quartet. These may have been merely an exercise for what followed. Solid confirmation of renewed activity did not come until July.

On July 18 the conductor of the Cleveland Symphony Orchestra, Artur Rodzinski, made public Kern's acceptance of the orchestra's invitation to compose a symphonic poem based on his themes from *Show Boat*. In earlier years Kern had sometimes promised he would attempt such extended pieces, and just as often disclaimed either the interest or technical proficiency to do so. Now Kern agreed to have his composition ready for an October premiere. Kern worked throughout August on the piece, assisted possibly by Miller and Harms's Emil Gerstenberger. If, as Robert Russell Bennett suspects, Kern received help on the construction and instrumentation of the new work, then it represents virtually the only instance in which he failed to give open recognition for such assistance. Reluctant to offer the public so important a departure without something like a theatrical tryout, Kern arranged for the Los Angeles Youth Symphony to play him sections as he finished them. In gratitude, Kern generously donated all performance royalties to the youngsters' orchestra.

Cleveland heard the first performance of "Scenario For Orchestra" on October 23 and 25. The following month Rodzinski and his musicians headed East to repeat their interpretation at New York's Carnegie Hall. The Kerns also came East for the occasion. As the Carnegie Hall rehearsal began, Jerry quietly took a seat in the middle of the empty auditorium. Rodzinski alerted his men to the composer's presence, and at the end of the first reading they tapped their instruments in salute. Visibly moved, Jerry whispered to a reporter seated beside him, "I don't belong in Carnegie Hall. This is the greatest thing that has ever happened to me." Later in the day he spoke at greater length in his suite at the St. Regis, explaining what he saw as the principal distinction between his work and standard symphonies or tone poems: "The object of many of the older symphonies was to say as little as possible in the most grandiloquent, ponderous and intellectual forms. What I tried to do was to say as much as I could as briefly as I could."

After the November 19 performance several critics questioned the validity of Kern's comparison. The piece was certainly not all that long, running only about twenty minutes, and it made no claims to intellectual profundity, but it seemed to many, if not grandiloquent and ponderous, at least over-ornamented and often sluggish. Virgil Thomson, writing in the *Herald Tribune,* used a homey figure to convey his disappointment: "If your sister came out on a concert stage got up like that you would tell her she looked like a Christmas tree or ask her if she hadn't forgot the kitchen stove." Despite all their reservations about the work's aesthetic achievements, critics reflected the universal respect and love for the themes on which the work was based.

Kern's private correspondence shows he failed to subscribe to the pervasive critical complaints. He called the work "musically exciting" and hailed Rodzinski's performance as "masterly." When the Ford Hour broadcast a truncated version the following January, Jerry wrote his faithful correspondent, Kathleen Cooper:

> I have a sneaking notion, knowing the instrumental requirements of the deleted portions, that perhaps it was not only due to those inexorable seconds ticking themselves off on the studio clock, but to a certain amount of orchestral virtuosity which may have been lacking.

Kern framed the "Scenario" in two motifs—excerpts from "Ol' Man River" and "Mis'ry's Comin' Aroun'." Indeed, the opening in the muted strings (marked "Andante sostenuto ma non troppo") is hauntingly beautiful and gives promise of a masterful composition. But Kern simply could not sustain the artistic development. Several of the most beloved songs are simply presented whole, in straightforward instrumental versions inserted boldly but unimaginatively into the text. Still, as critics noted, Kern's melodies are so great that the work succeeds as an entertainment even where it fails as a piece of high art.

Yet Kern was an artist ever striving for new approaches. When he confined himself to the miniature form at which he was second to none, few could complain. So it is particularly sad that another work Kern was tinkering with at the time never came to fruition. Kern's correspondence discloses that while he was working on the "Scenario" he was collaborating with the popular playwright John Van Druten on a musical deriving from Leonard Merrick's short tales of Paris life. Merrick was an Englishman whose once-popular works have slipped into obscurity. Kern had definite ideas about how both the libretto and music should be handled and did not mind telling Van Druten how the librettist should go about his business. He was particularly anxious to avoid what he called "those ze, zis and zat horrors," suggesting instead that an occasional literal translation of a French idiom would serve the same end more effectively. When he turned to his own chore, his ideas were equally firm and quite startling, unless one recalled his earlier comments about impressionistic music. He gleefully told Van Druten: "I'm bubbling over with fervor over the pattern I know the music should follow. In a nutshell, the music *must* resemble the exciting technique of the post-impressionist and modern boys and gals—you know—from Cezanne, Van Gogh, and Gauguin, through Utrillo, Rouault, Laurencin, Pascin and Chagall, etc.—must employ this technique even though we depict the genre of our particular, pleasant, placid period." He continued, at once exuberant and thoughtful: "This really ought to be a cinch. If successfully expressed, it will serve two masters, the youngsters and the oldsters, and above all, should satisfy our own critical selves." He signed off on an optimistic note, hoping that Van Druten shared his "enthusiasm for this approach." Van Druten apparently did, for while other commitments claimed both men, correspondence on the work continued almost to the day of Kern's death.

Kern's public never learned about his labors with Van Druten, but early in 1942 expectations were lifted once more when Billy Rose announced that Kern and Hammerstein were working on a musical translation of a second Edna Ferber novel, *Saratoga Trunk*. Richard Rodgers had asked Hammerstein to collaborate with him on the same project a year before. There is no evidence that Hammerstein and Kern ever sat down to begin work. Hammerstein was fearful that Rose, who had a reputation for running hot and cold on projects, might suddenly change his mind. Hammerstein reminded Jerry that his music could always be used for another story, but that a Rose rejection would mean all Hammerstein's efforts had been for naught. Jerry's attorney, Howard Reinheimer, suggested the writers demand Rose take out an insurance policy against any change of heart. Rose apparently demurred, for the musicalization seems to have been quietly dropped.

In March Jerry received a rude slap from his ASCAP associates, losing an election that would have allowed him to remain on ASCAP's board. Jerry had served on the board from 1924 to 1929 and then again from 1932. If he was disappointed by the balloting he kept his peace, perhaps content that his old colleague, Max Dreyfus, was elected to represent the publishers.

A seemingly happier March event was Betty's marriage to Artie Shaw. Kern had long admired Shaw as a musician, although Shaw's wide-ranging and probing fascination with all sorts of nickel knowledge sometimes confounded his new father-in-law. In a few years the marriage was to fall apart, but it would leave Jerry with the only grandchild he lived to cradle.

As projected new stage projects fizzled out, Kern busied himself with three endeavors that were eventually realized—a new concert piece, a major West Coast revival of *Music in the Air,* and a new film. Soon after the United States entered the war, André Kostelanetz solicited a number of prominent American composers for works on native material. Most of these writers had reputations in loftier branches of music than Kern did, so he was probably thrilled to find himself in Aaron Copland and Virgil Thomson's august company. He wrote to Kostelanetz, "All else is laid aside in my tremendous enthusiasm for our project, which for the past forty-eight hours or so has made me well-nigh breathless." Kern elected to base his tone poem on Mark Twain's life and writings, telling amused listeners, "The book was first issued in 1885—so was I." The composition was divided into four parts—"Hannibal Days," "Gorgeous Pilot House," "Wanderings, Westward" and "Mark In Eruption." Kostelanetz played the work in Cincinnati and Toronto in May and on June 7 broadcast it across the nation, with Kern himself, speaking from Hollywood, delivering his own program notes. A diffuse, meandering work, lacking even Kern's usual melodic invention, "Mark Twain (Portrait For Orchestra)" created few ripples and was soon forgotten.

Kern had frequently profited from revivals of his older works, but he rarely worked as closely on them as he did with Edwin Lester for his revival of *Music in the Air.* Two interesting matters came up. With the war raging and Germany an enemy, Hammerstein suggested changing the show's locale to Bohemia. Jerry naturally approved, and so did Lester. But they balked at Oscar's other suggestion, replacing "I Am So Eager" with "All The Things You Are." "Lester and I both yell bloody murder in disagreement," Jerry responded in a long, detailed letter. They felt Irra Petina's flamboyant interpretation of the original would be a show-stopper. Later in the letter Jerry suggested he was amenable to letting the newer song replace "The Song Is You" (which he referred to as "I Hear Music"). But this may have been a ploy on Jerry's part to allow Hammerstein to persuade him to retain the song. As Lester recalls, it was retained, although "All The Things You Are" was interpolated along with a new song for Sieglinde. Somehow, everyone was even persuaded to retain the original setting.

In May, when Hammerstein came out to the Coast, he suggested yet another collaboration with Jerry. Oscar had become excited by the possibilities of making a musical out of Lynn Riggs's old play, *Green Grow the Lilacs*. Kern remembered the drama, but he reminded Hammerstein that the 1931 production had been a failure. Turning a hit play into a musical was difficult enough; musicalizing a flop loaded the dice against the writers. Hammerstein dropped the subject. Just how Kern's reluctance affected the American musical and Kern himself will never be known. As all theatre lovers are aware, a year later Hammerstein joined forces with Richard Rodgers to adapt the work, which came to Broadway as *Oklahoma!*.

Neither "Mark Twain" nor the revival of *Music in the Air* offered Kern's music the wide exposure his next film permitted. Kern signed with Harry Cohn, the feisty head of Columbia Pictures, for his first wartime picture. A Latin-American setting meant that Kern would have to compose some songs in a style he often claimed he could not do justice to, but he took the plunge anyway. In the end, he and his associates apparently reached a compromise. The picture was to star Fred Astaire and Rita Hayworth, and was looked upon as a sequel to their successful *You'll Never Get Rich*. Almost from the start, the new film was called *You Were Never Lovelier*. Kern was given a screenplay that in accepted Hollywood fashion had passed through many hands. Michael Fessier, Ernest Pagano, and Delmer Daves had written the dialogue for a story suggested by Carlos Olivari and Sixto Pondal Rios. Once again the basic storyline was not original. More than one Broadway musical had dealt with a father who must marry off his daughters in order of their ages. As usual, one of the older ones proves recalcitrant, creating problems for her younger sisters. In this case the difficult daughter is Maria Acuna (Miss Hayworth), whose father, Eduardo (Adolphe Menjou), owns vast hotel interests. The father writes romantic love notes and sends them with orchids to his daughter, hoping she will believe they come from one of her suitors and will fall in love with him. An out-of-work hoofer, Robert Davis (Astaire), attempts unsuccessfully to obtain work from Acuna. But a mix-up leads Maria to conclude he is the source of the letters and flowers. A romance ensues.

William A. Seiter directed Louis F. Edelman's production. Leigh Harline was musical director, while Conrad Salinger orchestrated all of the score except "The Shorty George," for which Lyle Murphy received credit. Val Raset assisted Astaire with the choreography.

Wartime shortages of personnel, material, time, and space beset the film from the start. For example, Astaire could not wangle a place on the Columbia lot to rehearse. He rented an auditorium blocks away for practice sessions. When prior bookings made even this undesirable site unavailable, the cast was reduced to rehearsing in a funeral parlor at Hollywood Cemetery. Their lone consolation was that the cemetery was close to the studio.

Filming occupied much of the late spring and early summer (June 2 to August 7). New Yorkers could see the results when *You Were Never Lovelier* opened at the Radio City Music Hall on December 3, 1942. Although complaints were aired about an insufficient number of dances and about the triteness of the story, most critics agreed with the *Times's* assessment of the film as "light and winsome fare." If Astaire came in for the bulk of critical attention and praise, most reviewers were equally interested in Miss Hayworth. Even though it was generally known she did not do her own singing, her radiantly inviting glamour exerted a patent fascination on the critics, a fascination that prompted many of them to devote far more space to her than they had to the colder, aloof Rogers or the more mechanical Irene Dunne. Unfortunately, the critics' preoccupation with the stars left them little room for examining Kern's score. *Variety* recorded that the music lent "additional strength" to the picture, and dropped the matter there, while Archer Winsten of the *Post,* writing in a similar vein, gave the score a single sentence. He included it in his list of the film's good points and singled out "the familiar 'Dearly Beloved'" as the "most easily remembered number."

According to the *Times,* "Dearly Beloved" was more than familiar, it was "inescapable." Actually it was merely the most immediately hummable of three exceptional ballads Kern composed for the film. As is the title song, it is built on an uncommon ABAB[1] frame, and it combines a superb melody with some remarkable chromatics. While written in the key of C, the principal theme is introduced over alternating G and F chords. The entire progression from then on is diatonic except for the last two measures of the first B theme. Alec Wilder objects to this abrupt transposition, but he forthrightly acknowledges most music lovers look on the song with a certain reverence. Claims that the song was suggested by a passage in Puccini's *Madame Butterfly* are unprovable. Wilder is also annoyed by what he hears as an unnecessarily abrupt ending for the title song. Granting the last two measures are unexpected in light of the long, easy sweep of the rest of the song, they still, as the popular expression goes, "work." Wilder remarks that "I'm Old-Fashioned" employs an ABCA[1] formula with "the last section being extended to twelve measures." An equally strong argument could be made for reading the construction ABA[1]A[2]. Essentially, the song is an imaginative series of theme and variations, all played out in a range of just over an octave. Inside the principal theme (in 4/4) there seems to reside a happily entrapped waltz, adding a certain tension to the melodic appeal. By 1942 Kern was able to compose two swing numbers without a hint of outside assistance. The results—"On The Beam" and "The Shorty George"—ably satisfied Astaire's dance needs. "Wedding In The Spring" sent Kern back to his roots for an attractive piece patterned after a Middle-European folk dance. "These Orchids If You Please" moves with a rippling grace and even lent itself in the film to Xavier Cugat's Latin beat. Cugat's showpiece in the picture, "Chiu Chie," was an interpolation, composed by Nicanor Molinare.

Jerry's most private thoughts about the runaway success of *Oklahoma!* following its March 31, 1943, premiere are unknown. He was a generous enough friend to rejoice in Oscar Hammerstein's triumph, but his perceptive and competitive nature must have unleashed some deeply disturbing emotions. He must certainly have realized that Rodgers was now more than his probable heir, and had in fact effectively eased him aside as the leading mover in the American musical theatre. Guy Bolton recalled a luncheon at which Jerry asserted he would not let Rodgers usurp his place for long. But Bolton's predilection for remembering so many unkind stories about Jerry leaves the tale open to suspicion. Jerry's age and, more importantly, his somewhat precarious health made it inevitable that he would be superseded sooner or later.

Even as *Oklahoma!*'s success became a legend and its songs swept the nation, matters closer to home diverted Jerry and occupied his attention. On June 30 Betty gave birth to a son, Steven Kern Shaw, and Jerry immediately had another outlet for his bubbling-over affections. The baby's arrival was not without its problems, although, happily, not for Betty or young Steven. Jerry lamented in a letter to Otto Harbach that a couple who had served the Kerns for many years gave notice when the baby was due, and for several months the wartime help shortage turned Eva into a "nursemaid."

Oklahoma! sounded the gun that unleashed a wild race to musicalize stories of an earlier America. For many the great new musical play represented an audaciously pioneering achievement, but more enlightened commentators, those with a requisite sense of history, understood that *Oklahoma!* was essentially reviving a style which Kern and Hammerstein had actually pioneered with *Show Boat.* Hardly anyone seemed to remember that Kern and Hammerstein had attempted to transfer something of this style to the screen with *High, Wide and Handsome.*

Falling in with the vogue, Universal asked Jerry if he was willing to compose the music for a film based on Samuel J. and Curtis B. Warshawsky's novel, *Girl of the Overland Trail.* Jerry read the book and accepted. John Klorer and Leo Townsend reshaped the story to fit the screen, but left the final screenplay to Lewis R. Foster and Frank Ryan. The story that passed through so many hands centered on Caroline Frost, the headstrong daughter of a United States senator. To prevent her marrying a cavalry officer he dislikes, the senator arranges to have the soldier sent west. Caroline determines to follow her sweetheart and joins a wagon train heading for Gold Rush-mad California. On the way she is bilked out of her money, but a handsome card-sharp, Johnny Lawlor, wins it back for her, and appoints himself her protector. The high-born gal and the lowly hustler fight and fuss and, eventually, fall in love. Deanna Durbin and Robert Paige were signed for the romantic leads, while important secondary roles went to Akim Tamiroff, David Bruce, and Ray Collins. Out of Kern's past came Andrew Tombes for a minor bit.

With Kern's favorite collaborators, Hammerstein and Dorothy Fields, committed elsewhere, the film's producer, Felix Jackson, assigned E. Y. Harburg to supply rhymes for the songs. The same Frank Ryan who helped on the screenplay was director. H. J. Salter conducted Frank Skinner's orchestrations.

Goaded by the runaway success of *Oklahoma!* Kern seems to have had ambitious plans for *Caroline,* the working title for the picture. Even the simplicity of the working title, coupled with its similarity to the nickname of two Southern states, suggests the studio may have wanted the public to make some sort of connection between the Broadway hit and the film. In any case Kern began to move in astonishing directions that might have left him uncomfortably ahead of popular acceptance. Discarded songs are filled with remarkable harmonies that thirty-five years later are still too advanced for general usage. For example, in one extended number, "There'll Come A Day," a hymn of hope the heroine sings to encourage the children in the wagon train, the principal section begins with the lyric, "There'll come a day—There'll come a day—When magic carpets rise again to castles in the skies again." The song is in E flat, and with two exceptions the tender melody accompanying the words is played out over E-flat chords and uses only notes natural to the key. Both exceptions occur above the words "again," where Kern jolts the listener out of a comfortable reverie. The first "again" is sung to two g *flats* played above an A-flat seventh chord, while the second is sung to two e *naturals* played above an E seventh chord. Even more daring are the totally untoward harmonic progressions Kern employed for what was clearly meant to be a standard love song, "Once In A Million Moons," where the melodic line moves along one adventurous path while the bass moves in an equally novel but separate line. In the end, pragmatic considerations prevailed and the more avant-garde melodies gave place to readily hummable ones. Even the simple working title was rejected in favor of a more exuberant one.

As *Can't Help Singing* the film was first offered to New Yorkers on December 25, 1944, at Loew's Criterion. The *Times* was only one of many papers to note the film's resemblance to *Oklahoma!* Most reviewers who made a comparison felt the film easily stood its own ground, enhanced as it was by beautiful outdoor photography no stage mounting could hope to match. Miss Durbin was universally admired, although some critics had reservations about her leading man. But the *Times* characterized one overwhelming sentiment when it wrote: "The songs . . . are fair reason for taking off to see the show. Jerome Kern is the author of them, and they range from the lyrical title song to a rousing choral number called 'Californ-i-ay.'" As much as anything else, that song's lyric, with its reflection of the clever spelling trick Hammerstein had inserted into "Oklahoma!" elicited comparisons between the two works. *Time* magazine considered Kern's material "solid enough," but predicted, incorrectly, that it was "a touch too operatic for the winter's juke boxes." If the critics concurred in any major complaint it was that the screenplay was not on a level with everything else in the film.

At least two, possibly three, of Kern's superior songs for the film remain popular. The ballad "More And More" never repeats itself, moving along on an ABCD frame. Yet the song is tied together by variations of the initial theme that begin the C and D sections. The title song is a lusty, straightforward waltz. An equally spirited waltz, "Californ-i-ay" uses an AABA[1] frame in which the release revives the main theme of the verse.

Only its unexpected sudden and weak ending has probably deprived it of the ongoing popularity it deserves. Several critics singled out for praise a gay reel Kern chose not to publish, "Swing Your Sweetheart 'Round The Fire," but the composer did issue a second ballad, "Any Moment Now." The song opens with sweet, simple phrases of the sort Kern had employed often in earlier days but quickly resorts to the darker, more advanced harmonies he preferred at the close of his career. "Finale Ultimo" (not a closing recapitulation of other songs) and the charming, slightly old-fashioned "Elbow Room" rounded out the score.

In early 1943 the great Broadway composer, Arthur Schwartz, decided to buy back a property he had sold Columbia Pictures and to turn it into a stage musical. He was in New York at the time, so he called Columbia's New York office to ask when Harry Cohn could be expected in town. A secretary advised him that Cohn happened to be in Manhattan at that very moment. She took the composer's name, promising Cohn would return the call. Schwartz had barely hung up when Cohn's call came in. Cohn informed him that by coincidence Schwartz was on his own list of people he wanted to talk to and he invited Schwartz to his suite at the Sherry-Netherland. When Schwartz arrived, Cohn waved aside any discussion of Schwartz's old property and, to the composer's amazement, asked him how he would like to produce Rita Hayworth's next vehicle, a film musical to be called *Cover Girl*. Schwartz told Cohn what Cohn already knew, that he had never produced a film before and that if he did this one it would be at Cohn's expense. Cohn raised no objections, but he did add that he assumed Schwartz would also compose the songs the film required. Not wanting to assume two burdens at once, Schwartz demurred. He countered with the suggestion that they get "the very best"—Kern for the melodies and Ira Gershwin for the lyrics. Cohn accepted the suggestions. Schwartz called Kern in Hollywood and was delighted when Kern accepted. Nevertheless, Schwartz was somewhat fearful of working with a man whom he idolized, but also whom he had heard could be "provoking." He soon found that Kern could indeed be irritating, but more often than not was amiable, understanding, and accommodating. He remembers getting a call from Kern, who was especially excited by a new song he had tossed off. Schwartz drove over to Whittier Drive and Jerry played the melody. Sensing a negative reaction on the producer's part, Jerry scribbled "A.D.L." on the manuscript. Schwartz asked what the initials meant, and Jerry replied, "Arthur doesn't like." Kern immediately discarded the song. The very next day he had a replacement ready, a song that ultimately became "Long Ago And Far Away."

Kern was increasingly interested in chromatic invention, in what Schwartz calls "the inner workings" of his songs. So, when he played the second new song for Schwartz, Kern leaned so heavily on the under-chordings that Schwartz was unable to make head or tail of the piece. He asked Jerry to play the melody with one finger. Jerry did, and Schwartz instantly recognized the song for the masterpiece it is. But problems followed. The lackadaisical Gershwin, possibly showing early symptoms of the lethargy that soon deprived both Broadway and Hollywood of his unique talent, procrastinated about providing suitable rhymes. Kern was particularly fond of the genial, lovable lyricist, so rather than yell in anger he took another tack. He composed his own lyric and sent it off to Ira. Jerry's dummy lyric began, "Watching little Alice pee . . ." Ira was amused and shamed. He rushed back a lovely lyric for a song he called "Midnight Music." Good as the lyric was, he later replaced it with the one finally employed. ("Long Ago And Far Away" later brought Gershwin more royalties than any single lyric he wrote with his brother.)

But if Ira was giving Jerry troubles, Jerry in turn was showing Schwartz his irritating side. George and Ira Gershwin had written a number called "Put Me To The Test" for *Damsel in Distress*. The song was cut before the film was released. At Gershwin's suggestion, Kern put a new melody to the original lyric. Kern was delighted with the result. But his joy turned to dismay when he learned the song was not to be featured in a big production number. Schwartz pointed out that Gene Kelly was supposed to be managing a small night club, where any such massive mounting would be patently ridiculous. Kern walked away in a huff. The next day Schwartz received a call from Jerry, who advised him that he was at MGM and that if Schwartz didn't want to give "Put Me To The Test" a properly lavish staging, MGM would put it in a new picture and do it justice. Schwartz casually told Jerry that was all right with him. The producer's indifference deflated Jerry. No more was said about the matter, and the song remained in *Cover Girl*.

Gene Kelly, who was signed to co-star with Miss Hayworth, has only pleasant recollections of the composer. At recording sessions for "Long Ago And Far Away" Kelly sang in a soundproof booth, all the while watching Kern, who sat stiffly in a straightbacked chair and gave no sign of his reaction. Coming out of the booth, Kelly was nervous and apologetic, fearing he had displeased Jerry. The singer said he thought he ought to make several more takes, but, to his happy surprise, Kern warmly assured him he had done just fine and that there was no need to rerecord. They did anyway. But, as Kelly remembers, Kern's judgment was sound, and the first recording was the one employed. When filming was complete Kelly requested a photo of Kern. It came in the mail, inscribed "To G.K who's O.K. with J.K." The flippancy masked the respect of one determined perfectionist for another.

For a story, Virginia Van Upp worked with an older, unused screenplay by Erwin Gelsey. It was trite but serviceable. Rusty Parker (Miss Hayworth) is a Brooklyn girl who dreams of seeing her photograph on the cover of all the fashionable magazines. But Danny McGuire (Kelly), the proprietor of a Brooklyn night club, has greater ambitions for her, telling her she has diamonds in her feet. A rocky romance follows, ending with Rusty not just a cover girl but a dancing star. Lee Bowman, Phil Silvers, Eve Arden, Otto Kruger, and several then-famous cover girls, lent their support. Thurston Hall, thirty years before, one of Kern's leading men, appeared as Tony Pastor.

Under Charles Vidor's direction, the film was shot in the late summer and early fall. Val Raset and Seymour Felix combined to devise the choreography. Maurice Stoloff conducted Carmen Dragon and Saul Chaplin's orchestrations. It opened at the Radio City Music Hall on March 30, 1945. Without being overwhelmed, New York's critics clearly enjoyed the film. In the *Sun* Eileen Creelman hailed it as "A Fine and Dandy Musical," while the *Post's* banner greeted it as "A Most Colorful Dish for Jaded Musical Appetites." Neither passed judgment on Kern's score. The *Times* saw the film as balm for the tired businessman, but growled that Columbia "should have tried for something more original and cinematic." Of Kern's music the paper could find no stronger epithet than "rather nice."

Because Kern's last great masterpiece, "Long Ago And Far Away," towers over everything else in the score, the danger remains of minimizing the total achievement. (Technically, Kern may have considered the actual title simply "Long Ago," since the rest is printed in the sheet music in smaller type below and in parenthesis.) In his discussion of Kern's picture music for *Films in Review*, R. V. Tozzi has epitomized the song as "transfixing." It employed a daringly original form, AA^1AA^2, as well as a typical Kern device of restating the principal theme on different tonal levels. The ever-rising "Make Way For Tomorrow" is a superlatively up-lifting anthem. Virtually every scholar who has touched on the score has evinced a special fondness for "Sure Thing." Tozzi termed it "tender, but deceptively titled." Stanley Green, emphasizing its turn-of-the-century flavor, joined it with the title song and "Long Ago And Far Away" as one of the score's "three musical pieces of enduring value." Alec Wilder viewed it as an "endearing and melodically interesting song . . . one of the most American-sounding of Kern's later ballads," although he confessed he could not wholly fathom the song's construction. Cognizant, perhaps, of its history, Kern's new melody for "Put Me To The Test" was mildly Gershwinesque. The smoothly rising and falling title song is a neglected gem, while the un-published "Who's Complaining," with its lyric's comic capitulation to war-time rationing, is a sprightly, minor piece. In their excellent survey, *The Gershwins*, Robert Kimball and Alfred Simon list several songs that were never used.

Phil Silvers's appearance in *Cover Girl* must have been especially pleas-ing to Kern, for many a night Kern took his family and friends to Charley Foy's popular night club to watch Silvers perform a skit in which Kern was a central figure. The skit had Kern teaching Paul Robeson "Ol' Man River." Much of the fun derived from contrasting the grammar and rhetoric of the unlettered black who is supposed to sing the song in the show with the college-educated Robeson's meticulous English. Robeson, for example, demands to know what "taters" are and when he is told then attempts to sing the line in his impeccable Rutgers grammar. But even Robeson must admit that "He doesn't plant potatoes and doesn't plant cotton" fails to work. The composer can only apologize, "Well, I didn't write the lyric." Kern saw the skit so often he came to know it by heart, so one night when he met Silvers at a party he had no trouble playing himself to Silvers's Robeson.

His satisfaction with his work on *Cover Girl* (he asked Mrs. Cooper, "Don't you purr to Long Ago?") and the success it enjoyed proved a tonic to Kern. He wrote that he had not felt better in years. His newly refound exuberance made him anxious to join in the battle against "the world's greatest paranoic," and he pleaded with influential friends in Washington to find some significant way he could contribute to the war effort. Mindful of his medical history and age, his friends assured him his continued out-pouring of magnificent melody was a contribution few could match.

Actually, not all of the war effort was to Kern's liking. Unlike many of his fellows, he remained level-headed enough to resent some of its excesses. He bridled at the extremes of wartime propaganda that saw every Japanese and German as villainous and all enemy culture as corrupted. He refused to appreciate rationing of items he knew were not in short supply simply to further a sense of wartime urgency.

Nor could he find the war sufficient reason for tampering with the artistic integrity of his works—at least not beyond a certain point. When soldiers at Camp Roberts requested permission to mount *Roberta*, he readily assented, going so far as to suggest that for patriotic considerations they add "The Last Time I Saw Paris" and "And Russia Is Her Name." The latter was a song, as much Semitic as Slavic in its melody, that Kern had composed for a 1944 film, *Song of Russia*. On receiving a program he was dismayed to discover the soldiers had scrapped most of his original score, interpolating such diverse numbers as "Siboney," Cole Porter's "Begin The Beguine," and Gershwin's "The Man I Love." As a result, when Maurice Evans and Max Gordon asked to be allowed to mount a similar production for the troops overseas, Kern begged them not to.

> Naturally there is no disposition on my part to withhold anything from any branch of the service anywhere, and you would have my unqualified approval to release ROBERTA without fee, were it not that I am solicitous about any performance of any work bearing my name. Roberta, with its many scene changes, and consistent fidelity to the original Alice Duer Miller "Gowns for [sic] Roberta" story is, I think, too much of a nut for the average service boys' camp entertainment to crack.

Arguing that the Camp Roberts treatment resulted in a "musical hodge-podge, more of a revue than a consistent score," Kern continued:

> Rather than have the same thing happen again I would just as soon that the boys overseas took a more loose-jointed type of show, easier to produce and with more musical plums for popular consumption than is the case with our property.

Kern then gave Gordon and Evans a list of great revues—headed by *The Band Wagon*—he felt would be suitable.

The year 1944 ended on a sweet note when, just before Christmas, the National Institute of Arts and Letters elected Kern to membership. Honored with Kern were such notables as Booth Tarkington and Edward Hopper.

At the beginning of 1945 Kern signed with 20th Century Fox to create songs for a screen musicalization of Albert E. Idell's novel, *Centennial Summer*. Idell's story was set in Philadelphia in 1876. Against a background of the great centennial exhibition, it recounted the rivalry of two sisters, Julia and Edith, for the attentions of a dashing Frenchman, although Edith has been expected to marry a Philadelphia scion, Benjamin Franklin Phelps. Jeanne Crain and Linda Darnell were assigned to play Julia and Edith to William Eythe's Phelps. Walter Brennan, Constance Bennett, Dorothy Gish, Cornel Wilde, and Charles Dingle were prominent in the supporting cast, while Avon Long was brought in for a specialty dance.

No doubt the success of two earlier fair musicals, *Meet Me in St. Louis* and the homier *State Fair,* whetted the studio's eagerness. The latter film had helped translate the vogue for "integrated musicals" from the stage to the screen. Of course, knowledgeable theatregoers knew that integration of song and story had long been a goal of even much older musicals—a goal more often achieved than publicists of the period were prepared to admit. Regardless of how old or new integration really was, 20th Century Fox press releases promised that no song would be sung from a stage (a ploy often used to introduce a number), and that the action would never be stopped to bring in a song, since all songs would advance the plot's development. But, privately, Kern and his lyricist were asked to find a way to include a railroad song that might match the vogue of Judy Garland's "On The Atchison, Topeka And The Santa Fe."

Leo Robin, a small man with a face as impish as some of Kern's pranks, was selected to devise the lyrics. Always a slow, careful worker, he was so in awe of Kern that he was determined to be especially careful in collaborating with a man he clearly idolized. His determination soon led to problems. Kern initially came forth with a striking proposal. He suggested the entire score be composed in waltz time to enhance the period flavor. Hollywood's workaday approach soon scuttled so artful a plan. (Years later Stephen Sondheim was to accomplish the feat in his score for *A Little Night Music.*) Kern and Robin settled down to compose the more common variety of songs film producers expected. Robin took Kern's material home with him and began to labor over the rhymes. Before long he was receiving phone calls from Jerry, demanding to know where the lyrics were. Robin assured him he would have them in good time, but Kern indicated he was not satisfied. Privately, Kern concluded Robin could not deliver. To this day, Jerry's daughter, Betty, remembers it as "the worst time my father ever had with a collaborator." When Robin arrived at the studio one day, he was horrified to learn that Kern had submitted additional material with lyrics by other lyricists. One of these was a song he had salvaged from an earlier collaboration with Hammerstein; the others had words by E. Y. Harburg and Johnny Mercer. For a brief time the studio considered calling the film *Cinderella Sue,* which was the title of one of the songs Harburg had worked on, a change which would have been particularly humiliating to Robin. Cooler heads prevailed, so the original title was soon restored. Looking back over three decades, Robin attributes Kern's impatience to some instinctive awareness of how little time remained to him. Indeed, by the time *Centennial Summer* opened at the Roxy on July 17, 1946, Kern had been dead for more than eight months.

Otto Preminger directed Michael Kanin's screenplay. Alfred Newman conducted the studio orchestra, using orchestrations by Herbert Spencer, Conrad Salinger, and one old Kern hand, Maurice De Packh. Dorothy Fox supplied what choreography was required.

Kern, of course, never read the largely favorable reviews. A modest dissent was offered by the *Times,* which observed, "The Jerome Kern score, while sometimes pleasant, is very poorly used, since the show is neither blessed with voices nor sparked with fresh musical numbers. Best of the songs is a choral, entitled 'Up With The Lark,' although the popular-tune detectors seem to prefer a chant called "All Through The Day.' One specialty in the whole show, by Avon Long, to 'Cincinnati [*sic*] Sue' is a wise little touch of variety. But there the favors cease."

It was not a truly topflight score. No doubt some of the praise reflected regret at a master's passing, and a realization by many critics that they had often passed hasty, unkind judgments on his songs later recognized as superior. Happily, at least two of the pieces are excellent. "All Through The Day" is a warm ballad in traditional AABA form that reveals both Kern and Hammerstein at their best. One unusual feature is Kern's final statement of the A theme, begun with harmonies that effectively transpose four measures into a fresh key. The use of rests after the initial notes in his phrases for "Up With The Lark" (lyric, Robin) add to the catchy appeal of this ingratiating waltz. A second ballad, "In Love In Vain" (lyric, Robin), is at once solid and stolid, sounding much like the perfunctory tunes lesser 20th Century Fox composers churned out for that studio's Betty Grable films. "Cinderella Sue" (lyric, Harburg) has a pleasant lilt and seems perfectly suited to Avon Long's bouncy dance (with five urchins joining in). The distinguished historian of the American musical theatre, Stanley Green, has hailed one unpublished waltz, "The Right Romance" (lyric, Robin), as a "gem." Certainly it deserved a better chance. Green has written of Kern's late work: ". . . his music had now become increasingly more complex both chromatically and harmonically. Although during this period Kern seldom ventured beyond the standard thirty-two bar form, he was constantly coming up with imaginative structural innovations that helped make so memorable this final phase of his musical creativity." Some of his complex harmonies may have been responsible for the elimination of one song that was nevertheless published, "Two Hearts Are Better Than One" (lyric, Mercer). Curiously, it is the only song written for the picture that Wilder felt worthy of analysis. Wilder was fascinated by the song, particularly its use of repeated note triplets, but he concluded, "Kern indulges in his predilection for raising (or lowering) the melody a third by doing it twice in this song. It's clever, to be sure, but it makes the song extremely difficult to sing. And I must suggest that, in his enthusiasm, he carried himself harmonically too far out to get back comfortably in time to restate his theme in the original key." Studio releases listed Kern's other songs for *Centennial Summer* as "Railroad Song," "Centennial," and "Long Live Our Free America," all with Robin's lyrics.

During the war, Hollywood discovered the public would flock to film biographies of famous Broadway composers. Of course, Hollywood's respect for fact was minimal, so the Gershwin and Porter stories that started the trend were wildly untruthful. Inevitably, Hollywood saw irresistible material in Kern's melody-rich career. Having so long guarded his private life from public scrutiny, Kern was not especially eager to consent. He suggested his scandal-free life was not an interesting subject anyway. MGM's top brass disagreed, persisting in their entreaties until Jerry softened. He finally granted permission, but with the stipulation that the story be largely fictitious, using only his better melodies and a few well-known anecdotes about him. The stipulation presented no problems to the Hollywood mentality. Jerry's old friend, Guy Bolton, was entrusted with blocking out the screenplay.

The film's musical numbers were shot first. Another friend, Jerry's neighbor and fellow composer, Harry Warren, who was working at MGM at the time, drove Jerry to the lot for recording sessions. Jerry was displeased with the way the musical numbers were being handled. He complained to Warren about myriad infelicities, such as the way the orchestrations went from the verse into the chorus of "Who?". Warren retorted that Jerry should protest, but Jerry replied he had all but given up fighting Hollywood's strange ideas and ways. He missed the authority Broadway granted him to impose his taste on his material. In fact, he missed Broadway.

As if in answer to an unspoken prayer, Hammerstein asked Jerry to join him in a revival of *Show Boat* and to compose the score for a musical he and Richard Rodgers hoped to mount in New York. The new musical was to be called *Annie Oakley,* after its leading figure, the most famous of all lady sharpshooters. He advised Jerry that Herbert and Dorothy Fields would do the book and Dorothy the lyrics. Rodgers lent his support by wiring Jerry: "It would be one of the greatest honors in my life if you would consent to write the music for this show." Jerry's affirmative acceptance was prompt and enthusiastic.

The night before the Kerns left for New York, they attended a farewell party given for them by the Edwin Knopfs. Jerry's spirits were bubbling over. Friends had not seen him so effusive and confident for months. He confessed to several that if the show succeeded he might move back to New York permanently.

Jerry and Eva arrived in New York on November 2, taking a suite at the St. Regis. He had brought with him a new song for the revival, "Nobody Else But Me." Freed from the restraints and compartmentalization of Hollywood, Jerry took an immediate interest in every aspect of the *Show Boat* revival. He amazed Lucinda Ballard by his visit to the costume-makers, where he posed careful questions. Certain that the production would enjoy a long run, he asked Miss Ballard if she felt the costumes would last. She called his attention to an inner lining that could be removed and laundered separately, thus adding to the life of the garments. Such details delighted Jerry. Of course, he had an important say in the casting. He was particularly charmed with the Magnolia, Jan Clayton, patting her on the shoulder and assuring her she was the sort of performer he loved to write songs for. But since there would be no need to attend rehearsals until the following Monday afternoon at 2 p.m., Jerry could spend the long weekend relaxing with old friends and associates. Ominously, some of the vigor he had displayed at the Knopfs' suddenly drained away. He canceled plans to attend the theatre on Saturday night. But he did keep a luncheon engagement with Guy Bolton, pay a loving visit to his parents' graves at Salem Fields, and travel to Scarsdale on Sunday evening for a dinner party the Lee Hartmans gave for his most intimate circle. Mark Holstein was there as were Walter and Elsie Pollak. Not even such cameraderie could dispel his uneasy fatigue, and Jerry, who so loved staying up until the small hours, asked to be excused. He had no sooner left than he was back, apologizing for not giving Elsie a farewell kiss. "I love you," he told her, but his remark seemed addressed to the whole gathering.

On Monday morning, November 5, Kern proposed to shop for antiques. He left Eva a note, scribbled in soap on the bathroom mirror, reminding her of her luncheon date with Dorothy Fields. Shortly after noon he walked north to the southwest corner of Park Avenue and 57th Street. Stopping at the corner for a light, he suddenly collapsed on the street. Patrolman Joseph Cribben saw him fall and radioed for an ambulance. The composer, still unconscious, was taken by automobile and ferry to the City Hospital, then still on Welfare Island. Authorities were disconcerted to discover the patient carried no clear-cut identification. But a card identified him as a member of ASCAP. ASCAP notified Hammerstein's office. Hammerstein's assistant, Leighton Brill, took the call and promptly phoned his boss at the Dramatists' Guild. Hammerstein summoned his physician, Dr. Harold Hyman, and the two rushed to Welfare Island. They found Jerry had been placed in a corridor at the edge of a ward for indigent patients and derelicts.

Somehow, Jerry's fellow patients had learned who their neighbor was. Hammerstein and Dr. Hyman were struck by the awe-filled silence the others maintained on Kern's account. Hammerstein's office located Eva and began a series of frantic calls to locate Betty in California. At 3:15 Jerry regained consciousness and briefly recognized his friends. But his conscious moments proved intermittent. Hyman and the other doctors concluded Jerry had suffered a cerebral hemorrhage. Privately, Hyman concluded there was no hope, but he warned Eva only that even if Jerry lived he might not recover all his functions. On November 7, despite the seriousness of his condition, it was decided to remove him to Doctors' Hospital, where he could receive better attention. Jerry was ferried back to Manhattan and placed in a private room, in an oxygen tent. Oscar, Dorothy Fields, Eva, and Betty were given rooms near by.

Apart from occasional optimistic moments, Jerry's condition slowly deteriorated. He lapsed into a coma, and his breathing grew difficult. On Sunday, November 11, Oscar came in to resume his bedside vigil. Desperate and grasping at any hope, Oscar remembered Jerry's special affection for "I've Told Every Little Star." Lifting the oxygen tent, Oscar began to sing it softly in Jerry's ear. The song finished, Hammerstein glanced at his beloved associate. There was no movement. The clock on the wall read 1:10 p.m. For the moment, Oscar alone knew what a saddened world would shortly learn.

Index

For the reader's convenience we have divided the Index into two parts. The first lists only songs; the second, everything else of interest. In the first part will be found all Kern songs mentioned in the book. Thus the reader will have an alphabetical catalogue of virtually every known Kern piece (the exceptions are the handful published posthumously). Wherever possible the official, published title is given; this sometimes differs from the title listed in the program or cited in a review. We have also listed songs by other composers which figure importantly in the text. These songs are marked by an asterisk. In the case of a few songs from very early shows, we have not been able to determine conclusively whether or not they were Kern's. Such songs are marked with a †. I thank Mrs. Carol Bower for her assistance on this section.

In the second part will be found shows, figures, theatres, books and such that are given significant attention in the text. People and things mentioned only in passing or as background have not been included.

G.B.

PART I

Songs

Abe Lincoln Has Just One
    Country, 372, 374, 376
According to Dr. Holt, 177
* After The Ball, 291
Ah Still Suits Me, 356
Aida McCluskie, 55
Ain't It A Grand And Glorious
    Feeling, 147
Ain't It Funny What A Difference
    Just A Few Drinks Make?, 129
* Alexander's Ragtime Band, 66, 81
Ali Baba Babies, 272
Alice In Wonderland, 98
All Full Of Talk, 131
All I Want Is You, 46
All In Fun, 380, 382, 384
All Lanes Must Reach A Turning,
    256, 258, 299
All That I Want Is Somebody To
    Love Me, 103, 130
All The Things You Are, 146, 380,
    381, 382, 384, 387, 388, 391
All The World Is Swaying, 182,
    183
All Through The Day, 403
All You Need Is A Girl, 247, 249,
    310
Allegheny Al, 367
All's Well With The World 312
Alone At Last (*Oh, I Say!*), 89, 90,
    91, 299
Alone At Last (*Very Good Eddie*),
    123
Alone With You, 333
Alpha Beta Pi, 338, 343

* And Her Mother Came Too, 228
And I Am All Alone, 134, 135,
    137, 138, 139, 266
And Love Was Born, 330
And Russia Is Her Name, 401
Angling By A Babbling Brook, 36,
    38, 39, 40
* Annie Laurie, 197
Another Little Girl, 110, 112
Any Girl, 182, 183
Any Moment Now, 397
Any Old Night, 111, 113
Anything Can Happen Any Day,
    310
Armful Of Trouble, 343
* At Our Tango Tea, 97
At That San Francisco Fair, 111
At The Ball, 223, 224
At The Casino, 25, 39
At The Fair, 287
At The Play, 208
At The Thé Dansant, 182

Babbling Babette, 237
Babes In The Woods, 117, 119,
    122, 137, 353
Baby Vampire, The, 133, 140, 141
Bachelor, The, 147
Back In My Shell, 387
Back To The Heather, 296, 299
Bagpipe Serenade, The, 47
* Balling The Jack, 98
Ballooning, 49
† Banks Of The Wye, 115

Be A Little Sunbeam, 148
Be Happy, Too, 289
* Be My Little Baby Bumble Bee, 157
* Beautiful, Beautiful Bed, 110, 111
Because I Am A Duke, 36, 38
Because You Love The Singer, 237
Before I Met You, 166, 169
* Begin The Beguine, 401
Bella Mia, 176
Best Sort Of Mother, Best Sort Of
      Child, 105
Betty's Advice, 62
Big Show, The, 182, 183
Big Spring Drive, The, 177, 179
Bill, 167, 204, 287, 289, 388
* Blue Bells Of Scotland, 197
Blue Bulgarian Band, The, 60
Blue Danube Blues, 216, 217, 218
Blue Eyes, 295, 299
Bluff, 36
* Blumenlied, 291
Boat Sails On Wednesday, A, 57
Bob White, 196
Bohemia, 70
Bojangles Of Harlem, 358, 360
Bongo On The Congo, 247, 248
* Bosphorus, 64, 66
Bought And Paid For, 92, 270,
      273
Bow Belles, 296, 298
Boy With A Drum, 376
Bread And Butter, 273, 274
Breeze Kissed Your Hair, The, 318
Bright Lights, 135, 136, 138
Bring 'Em Back, 200
Bubbles Of Bliss, 269
Buggy Riding, 200, 201
Bull Frog Patrol, The, 161, 179,
      189, 190
Bully Song, 289
Bumble Bee, The, 159, 189
Bungalow In Quogue, 155, 234
Business Of Our Own, A, 193
Butterflies Of Fashion, 183
* By The Beautiful Sea, 97
By The Blue Lagoon, 58
* By The Light Of The Silvery
      Moon, 280
Bygone Days, 72

Californ-i-ay, 396
Call Me Flo, 69
* Campbells Are Coming, The, 48
Can I Forget You, 367
Canajoharie, 200
Can't Help Lovin' Dat Man, 284,
      287, 288, 290
Can't Help Singing, 396
* Can't You Hear Me Callin',
      Caroline?, 97
Can't You See I Mean You?, 103,
      122, 130
Casino Music Hall, The, 130
Catamarang, 60, 210
Catskills, Hello, 195
Centennial, 404
Chaplin Walk, The, 110, 111
Charlie Is The Darling Of My
      Heart, 295, 297
Cheer Up, 289
Cheer Up! Girls, 50
Chick! Chick! Chick!, 201
* Chiu Chie, 294
Chopin Ad Lib, 222, 224
Church 'Round The Corner, The,
      206, 208, 210
Cinderella Girl, 272, 273
Cinderella Sue, 403
Cinderella's Ride, 272
* Cingalese Girls, 280, 281
City Chap, The, 269
Clementina, 343
Cleopatterer, 152, 154
C'mon Folks, 287
Coaching, 248
Coal Black Lady, 289
Come Along Pretty Girl, 60
Come Around On Our Veranda, 48
Come On Over Here, 73, 81, 85
Come Out Of The Kitchen, 135,
      138
Come Tiny Goldfish To Me, 61
* Comin' Thru The Rye, 48
Confidential Source, 67
* Congo Love Song, 195, 196
* Constant Lover, 115
Coo-oo, Coo-oo, 60
Correspondence School, The, 76
Cottage In Kent, A, 233, 234

Cotton Blossom, 286
† Courtship de Dance, 101
Cover Girl, 400
Cretonne, 178
Crickets Are Calling, The, 152,
    153, 154
Cross-Cross, 273
† Cupid At The Plaza, 110, 112
Cupid, The Winner, 201
* Cupid's Garden, 36, 38, 39
Curtsey, The, 296
* Cute Soldier Boy, 173, 174

Daisy, 138
Dance, Dance, Dance, 76
Dance Away The Night, 293
Dance Like A Fool, 352
Dance Through Life With Me,
    133, 140, 141
Dancers Of The Cafe Kaboul, 272
† Dancing Courtship, A, 159
Dancing Kangaroo, The, 36
Dancing M.D., A, 159
* Dancing The Devil Away, 280, 281
Dancing Time, 223, 224, 256, 257
* Dardanella, 218, 219, 220, 240,
    241, 242, 243
Days Gone By, 247
Dear Algerian Land, 272
Dear Little Peter Pan, 238
Dear Old Fashioned Prison Of
    Mine, 247, 248
Dearly Beloved, 393-94
De Goblin's Glide, 64, 65
Didn't You Believe?, 216, 218
* Dinah, 159
Ding Dong, It's Kissing Time, 200,
    201
Dining Out, 54
Do I Do Wrong?, 298, 342
Do It Now, 166
Dolls, The, 237, 238
Don't Ask Me Not To Sing, 320,
    339, 342
Don't Ever Leave Me, 307, 308, 309
Don't Tempt Me, 140, 141
Don't Turn My Picture To The
    Wall, 70, 85, 176

Don't You Want A Paper, Dearie?,
    48
Don't You Want To Take Me?,
    195, 197
* Down By The Erie, 195, 196
* Down Home Rag, The, 197
Downcast Eye, The, 41
Dream A Dream, 265, 266
Dream Of A Ladies Cloak Room
    Attendant, 352
Dreaming Of Allah, 272
Drift With Me, 60, 133, 139, 140
† Driga Serenade, 116
* Duel, The, 64
D'ye Love Me?, 264, 265, 266

Each Pearl A Thought, 89
Eastern Moon, 51
Easy Pickin's, 217, 218, 219
Edinboro Wriggle, The, 64, 65, 66
Edna May's Irish Song, 42
Egern On The Tegern See, 333,
    341
Eight Little Girls, 62
Elbow Room, 397
Enchanted Train, The, 218, 247,
    249
Eulalie, 55
Evening Hymn, 209
* Every Bee Has A Bud Of Its Own,
    182
Every Day, 146, 148
Every Day In Every Way, 227,
    228, 229
Every Girl, 216, 217
Every Girl I Meet, 60, 65
Every Girl In All America, 172,
    174
* Every Little Movement, 68
Every Little While (*Go To It*), 132
Every Little While (*Stolen
    Dreams*), 312
* Everybody's Doing It, 112

Fair Lady, 296, 297
Faith, Hope and Charity, 189, 190,
    224

Fan Me With A Movement Slow, 68, 70
Farandola, 387
Fashion Show, The, 119
Father And Mother. *See* Mother And Father
Finale Ultimo, 397
Fine Romance, A, 359, 360
First Day Of May, The, 144, 145
First Mate Martin, 306
First Rose Of Summer, The, 189, 190, 223, 224, 235
Flap-a-Doodle, 272
* Florrie The Flapper, 97
Flubby Dub, 145, 148, 150
Folks Who Live On The Hill, The, 367
Follow Handy Andy, 257
Follow Me Round, 67
* Follow On, 157, 159
† Foolishness, 102
For The Man I Love, 233
Fountain Of Youth, The, 269
Frantzi, 58
Fraulein Katrina, 53
Frieda, 53, 54
Frolic Of A Breeze, The, 44
Funny Little Something, 182, 183

Gaiety Chorus Girls, The, 347
Gallivantin' Around, 356
Gentlemen Unafraid, 372, 374
* Gilbert The Filbert, 97
Ginger Town, 190
Girl For Each Day In The Week, A, 183
Girl Is On Your Mind, A, 307, 309
Girlie, 173, 174
Girls Are Like A Rainbow, 195, 196
Girls In The Sea, 201
Gloria's Romance [themes for silent film], 128
Go, Little Boat, 160, 185
Go-Getter, The, 268
Golden Sprite, The, 272
Good King James, 295, 297
Good Morning, Dearie, 217

Good Night Boat, 195, 197
Good-By And Good Luck, 173
Good-bye, Everybody, 90
* Goodbye, My Lady Love, 287, 291
* Good-bye Broadway, 159
* Googy-oo, 36, 37, 38
Got My Eye On You, 35
Grab A Girl, 256
Grandma's Song, 367
Green River Glide, 218
Greenwich Village, 166, 167
Growing Men, The, 239
Gypsy Caravan, 257, 259

* Half Past Two, 69
Hand In Hand, 346, 348
* Handle To My Name, 35
Hands Up, 117
Happy Wedding Day, A, 189
Have A Heart (*Have A Heart*), 135, 137
Have A Heart (*Ziegfeld Follies*), 128, 129, 137
Have An Old Waltz With Me, 90
"Have You Forgotten Me?" Blues, 227, 229
Hay Ride, 50
Head Over Heels, 181, 182
Heart For Sale, A, 195, 196, 197
Heaven In My Arms, 382, 384
Heavenly Party, A, 370
Heaven's Gift To The Girls, 265
He Is The Type, 269
He Must Be Nice To Mother, 72
He Wore A Star, 367
He'll Be There, 40
* Hello, People, 55
Henry, 297
Her First Can Can, 35
Here Am I, 306, 307, 308, 309
Hey, Feller, 287, 289
Hh! Cha! Cha!, 318, 320, 321
High, Wide And Handsome, 367
Hippopotamus, 59
His Majesty's Dragoons, 295
Honeymoon Inn, 135, 137
Honeymoon Isle, 233
Honeymoon Land, 173, 174, 197

Honeymoon Lane, 80, 93
Honor System, The, 159
Hoop-la-la, Papa!, 70
Hoot Mon, 140, 141
Hot Dog, 229
Hot Spot, 339
How Do You Do, Katinka?, 228, 229
How Was I To Know, 139, 141
How Would I Know?, 373, 374, 376
How'd You Like To Spoon With Me?, 43, 50, 57
Howdy, How Do You Do?, 59
† Human Nature, 101
Hurry Now, 176
Hydrophobia Blues, 271

* I Ain't Agoin' To Weep No More, 19
I Am Daguerre, 200
I Am Human After All, 141
I Am So Eager, 330, 391
* I 'Ave A Motter, 85
I Believe In Signs, 190
I Believed All She Said, 177, 178, 179
I Can Trust Myself With A Lot Of Girls, 177
I Can't Forget Your Eyes, 89, 90, 91, 266, 273
I Can't Say That You're The Only Girl, 53
I Don't Want You To Be A Sister To Me, 62
I Dream Too Much, 352, 355
I Got Love, 355, 356
† I Have Been About A Bit, 101
I Have The Room Above Her, 356
I Just Couldn't Do Without You, 48
I Know And She Knows, 89, 90
I Love The Lassies, 195, 197
I Might Fall Back On You, 287, 289, 291
I Never Do A Thing Like That, 21
I Never Thought, 176, 179
I Saw The Roses And Remembered You, 236, 321

I Want My Little Gob, 189
I Want To Be The One To Show Her That, 72
I Want To Be There, 256, 258
I Want To Marry, 200
I Want To Sing In Opera, 67
I Want You To See My Girl, 59
I Was Lonely, 182, 183
I Will Knit A Suit Of Dreams, 173-74
I Wonder, 76, 78, 79
I Wonder Why, 133, 140, 141
I Won't Dance, 345, 347, 348, 351, 359
I Would Like To Play A Lover's Part, 289
I'd Like A Lighthouse, 195, 197
I'd Like To Have A Million In The Bank, 119
I'd Like To Meet Your Father, 50
I'd Love To Dance Through Life With You, 114
If, 173, 174
If I Find The Girl, 119, 122
If The Girl Wants You, 55
* If The Man In The Moon Was A Coon, 280
If We Were On Our Honeymoon (Railway Duet), 81, 85-86, 291
If You Are As Good As You Look, 269
If You Think It's Love You're Right, 256, 257, 258
If You Would Only Love Me, 73
If You're A Friend Of Mine, 293
I'll Be Hard To Handle, 337, 339, 342-43
I'll Be Waiting 'Neath Your Window, 69, 70
I'll Lead You A Merry Song And Dance, 257
I'll Share Them All With You, 312
I'm A Crazy Daffydill, 67
I'm A Prize, 233
I'm Alone, 330, 331, 333
I'm Coming Home, 330
I'm Dreaming, 308
I'm Going To Find A Girl, 153, 155

I'm Here, Little Girls, I'm Here, 135, 137
I'm Looking For An Irish Husband, 88
I'm Old Fashioned, 394
I'm So Busy, 135, 137
I'm The Echo (You're The Song That I Sing), 355, 356
I'm The Human Brush (That Paints The Crimson On Paree), 64, 66
I'm The Old Man In The Moon, 159, 161
I'm To Be Married To-day, 166
Important Man, The, 36, 38
In A Shady Bungalow, 25
In Araby With You, 271, 272, 273
In Arcady, 110, 112
In Dahomey, 287
In Love, 296, 299
In Love In Vain, 403
In Love With Love, 237, 239, 293
In Other Words, Seventeen, 380, 381, 382, 384
* In The Gloaming, 362
* In The Good Old Summer Time, 159
In The Heart Of The Dark, 382, 384
In The Valley Of Montbijou, 67
In Vodeodo, 296, 298
Indian Fox Trot, 173, 174
* Indian Love Call, 218
Indignation Meeting, 271
Is This Not A Lovely Spot?, 247, 249
Isn't It Great To Be Married?, 103, 119, 122, 130
It Can't Be Done, 133, 141
It Isn't Your Fault, 103
It Wasn't My Fault, 103, 139, 140-41
It Won't Mean A Thing, 265, 332
It's A Great Big Land, 155
It's A Hard, Hard World, 167
It's A Long, Long Day, 233
* It's A Long Way To Tipperary, 97
It's Always Been The Same Way, 60

It's Gayer Whistling As You Go, 373, 375
It's Getting Hotter In The North, 289
It's Greek To Me, 173
It's Immaterial To Me, 173
It's Not In The Cards, 358
It's The Nighttime, 208
I've A Little Favor, 48
I've A Million Reasons Why I Love You, 50
I've Been Waiting For You All The Time, 189, 190
I've Got A New Idea, 308
I've Got Money In The Bank, 88
I've Got To Dance, 123
I've Had My Share, 151, 154
I've Just Been Waiting For You, 114
I've Looked For Trouble, 273
I've Never Found A Girl Like You, 154
I've Played For You, 154
I've Taken Such A Fancy To You, 69
I've Told Every Little Star, 324, 328, 330, 332, 406

Jazz, 196
Joan Of Arc. *See* You Can't Keep A Good Girl Down
Jockey On The Carrousel, 355
* Jolly Good Fellow, 101, 102
Journey's End, 223, 224, 268, 269, 270
Joy Bells, 233, 267
Joy Of That Kiss, The, 77, 79
Jubilo, 189, 190
June Bells, 267
Just A Little Line, 189
Just Because You're You, 150, 260
Just Good Friends, 55
Just Let Me Look At You, 370
Just One Kiss, 178
Just Wait, 248
Just You Watch My Step, 152

Ka-lu-a, 217, 218, 219, 221, 223, 224, 240, 242, 243

Kan The Kaiser, 172
Katy Was a Business Girl, 50
Katy-did, 89, 90, 91, 229
Keep Going, 115
† Keep Moving, 112
Keep Smiling, 347
* Keep The Home Fires Burning, 129
Keep Your Rabbits Rabbi, We've
    Rabbits Of Our Own, 198-99
Kettle Song, The, 177, 178
* Kingdom Comin', 190
Kiss A Four Leaf Clover, 272, 273,
    274
* Kiss Me Again, 157, 158, 159
Koo-La-Loo, 144

Ladies, Have A Care, 182
Ladies Are Present, 249
Land O' Good Times, De, 372, 374
Land Of Let's Pretend, The, 57, 98
Land Where The Good Songs Go,
    The, 147, 159, 160
* Last Long Mile, The, 164, 173
* Last Rose Of Summer, The, 190,
    239
Last Time I Saw Paris, The, 385,
    401
Lazy But Free, 352
Le Sport American, 217, 218
Leader Of The Labour Party, The,
    45
Leaders Of The Modern Regime,
    272
Leave It To Jane, 152
Left All Alone Again Blues, 194,
    196, 197, 198
Lena, Lena, 60
Let Us Build A Little Nest, 71, 72,
    183
Let's Begin, 338, 339, 343
Let's Go, 172
Let's Make A Night Of It, 144
Let's Say Good Night Till It's
    Morning, 264, 266
L'Histoire De Madam De La Tour,
    382
Life On The Wicked Stage, 287,
    288, 291

Like The Nymphs Of Spring, 268
Little Angel Cake, 237
Little Backyard Band, 193
Little Billie, 155
Little Bit Of Ribbon, A, 144, 145,
    147
Little Bit Of Silk, A, 88
Little Church Around The Corner,
    The, 50
Little Eva, 50
Little Feet That Lightly Beat, 295,
    297
Little Golden Maid, 76, 79
Little Gypsy Lady, 239
* Little Love, A Little Kiss, A, 116
Little Love (But Not For Me), A,
    116, 122
Little Pep, A, 190
Little Red Riding Hood, 237, 239
Little Thing Like A Kiss, A, 86
Little Tune, Go Away, 177, 178
Little Zouave, 373
London, Dear Old London, 223
Lonely Feet, 346, 348, 350
* Lonely In Town, 101, 102
Lonesome Walls, 377
Long Ago (And Far Away), 398,
    399, 400
Long Live Our Free America, 404
* Long-Haired Mamma, 289
Look For The Silver Lining, 193,
    206, 207, 208, 209, 298
Look In Her Eyes, 86, 136
Look In His Eyes, 136
Look In The Book, 140, 141
Look Me Over Dearie, 66
Looking All Over For You, 223
* Looking For A Boy, 367
Lorelei, The, 206, 210
Love And The Moon, 230
Love Blossoms, 103
† Love Is King, 35
Love Is Like A Rubber Band
    (Hoop Song), 68
Love Is Like A Violin, 92, 128
Love Parade, The, 318
Lovely Lassie, 227
Lovely To Look At, 351
Love's Charming Art, 68

* Lucky, 280
Lullaby, 178, 181
Lulu, 140

Ma Angelina, 19
Ma Blossom, 21
* Ma Blushin' Rosie, 239
* Ma Butterfly, 19
Magic Melody, The, 110, 111, 112
Magic Train, The. *See* Enchanted Train, The
Magician Does His Stuff, The, 239
Magnolia In The Woods, 264
Mah-Jong, 233
Maid Of Montbijou, 67
Make Believe, 284, 286, 290, 319
Make Way For Tomorrow, 399
Man Around The House, A, 193
* Man I Love, The, 289, 401
* Man Who Wrote The "Merry Widow" Waltz, The, 51
Manicure Girl, The, 63
Marcella, 21
March Of The Toys, The, 44
* March Of The Toys [by Victor Herbert], 158, 159
† Marie-Louise, 69
Mark Twain (Portrait For Orchestra), 391, 392
Mary McGee, 50
* Matchmaker, 312
May Tells All, 381
Me, 182, 183
Me And My Boss, 293
Me And The Roll And You, 383
Meet Her With A Taximeter, 54
Meet Me At Twilight, 45, 46
Meet Me Down On Main Street, 223, 321
* Meet Me In St. Louis, 137
Melican Papa, 217
Melodies Of May, 330, 332
* Mendebras, 146
* Mermaid's Song, The, 240
Midnight Music, 398
Mighty Svengali Legree, The, 21
Military Maids, 36
Military Mannequin, The, 200

Mind The Paint, 73
* Minnie The Moocher, 362
Mis'ry's Comin' Aroun', 289, 291, 389
* Miss Phoebe, 19
* M-i-s-s-i-s-s-i-p-p-i, 195
Mr. And Mrs. Rorer, 247
Mr. Chamberlain, 44, 45
Mr. Gravvins—Mr. Gripps, 223, 224
Mister Man, 373, 375
Mitzi's Lullaby, 182, 183
† Mix-up Rag, The, 116
Mollie O'Donahue, 307, 310
* Molly Malone, 131
Molly O'Hallerhan, 42
* Molly O'Halloran, 42
Moments Of The Dance, 182
* Monte Carlo Moon, 64
Moo Cow, 140
Moon Love, 233, 235
Moon Of Love, 200, 201
Moon Song, 166, 168
More And More, 396
Mormon Life, A, 256, 257
Morning Glory, 227, 229, 270
* Mosquitos Frolic, The, 158
Mother And Father, 60
Motoring Along The Old Post Road, 176
My Angeline. *See* Ma Angelina
My Beautiful Circus Girl, 346
* My Beautiful Lady, 190
My Boy, 178
My Castle In The Air, 131, 132
My Celia, 41
My Heart I Cannot Give You, 67
* My Heart Stood Still, 321
* My Hero, 85
My Houseboat On The Harlem, 256
My Husband's First Wife, 306, 308
My Lady Of The Nile, 129
My Lady's Dress, 101, 103, 218
My Mindanao Chocolate Soldier, 102, 103
My Otaheitee Lady, 81
My Own Light Infantry, 177, 179
My Peaches And Cream, 77, 79

* My Wild Irish Rose, 239
  Mystic Hussars, The, 238, 239

  Napoleon, 135, 137
  National Dish, The, 239
  Naughty Boy, 306, 310
  Naughty Nobleman, 227
  Navy Foxtrot Man, The, 189
  Negro Peanut Vender's Street Cry, 356
  Nerves, 223
  Nervous Wrecks, 208
  Nesting Time, 144, 147, 148
  Never Gonna Dance, 360, 361
  Never Marry A Girl With Cold Feet!, 50, 63
  New Love Is Old, A, 318, 320
† New York Way, 35
  Niagara Falls, 217, 218
  Night Flies By, 330
  Night Was Made For Love, The, 236, 318, 320, 321
  No One Else But You, 294, 296, 298
  No One Knows, 269, 270
  Nobody Else But Me, 405
* Nobody Home Cake Walk, 111
* Nobody Wants Me, 276
  Nodding Roses, 117, 119, 122, 239, 240
  Non-Stop Dancing, 233, 235
  Not Here! Not Here!, 57
* Not Like Other Girls, 36
  Not Yet, 166, 168
  Not You, 178, 179
  Now That I Have Springtime, 346, 348
  Nursery Clock, The, 237
  Nursery Fanfare, 179
† Nurses Are We, 9

* O Promise Me, 85
  Ocean Of Love, An, 117
  Ode To A Passing Kidney Stone, 351
  Oh, Daddy, Please, 144
† Oh, Doctor, 70
  Oh, Lady! Lady!, 166
  Oh, You Beautiful Person, 190

  Oh Promise Me You'll Write To Him Today, 184, 190
  Oh You Beautiful Spring, 77, 79, 189
* Oklahoma!, 396
  Ol' Man River, 284, 285, 287, 288, 289, 290, 389, 400
  Old Bill Baker, 123
* Old Black Joe, 190
  Old Boy Neutral, 119, 122
* Old Clarinet, The, 89, 90, 91
  Old New York, 200
  Old Town, The, 201
  Old-Fashioned Wife, An, 144, 145, 147, 148
  On A Desert Island With You, 247
* On The Atchison, Topeka And The Santa Fe, 402
* On The Banks Of The Wabash, 195
  On The Beam, 394
  On The Sands At Wah-Ki-Ki, 116, 123
  On The Shore At Le Lei Wi, 119, 123
  On With The Dance, 206, 210
  Once In A Blue Moon, 238, 239, 280
  Once In A Million Moons, 396
* One Alone, 364
  One Moment Alone, 318
  One More Dance, 330, 333
  One Thing Different, 36, 37
  One, Two, Three, 176
  Oo-Oo, 60
  Oo-Oo-Oo, 77
  Ooo, Ooo, Lena!, 69
  Oriental Dreams, 223, 310
  Oriental Moon, 307, 310
  Our Last Dance, 372, 374
  Our Little Nest, 166, 167
  Our Lovely Rose, 238, 239, 240
  Our Song, 362
  Out Of The Blue, 306, 309
  Over The Hills, 190

  Package Of Seeds, A, 101, 103, 144, 145, 147

Pal Like You, A, 144, 147
Pale Venetian Moon, 227, 229
Palm Beach Girl, The, 160
* Parade Of The Wooden Soldiers, The, 229
Paris Is A Paridise For Coons, 64, 65, 90
Peach Girl, 227, 228
Peach Of A Life, A, 152
Peaches, 158, 160
Peaches And Cream. *See* My Peaches And Cream
† Pearl Of Broadway, 280
† Pearl Of Ceylon, 280, 281
Pergola Patrol, The, 223
Peter Pan (*Have A Heart*), 136, 138
† Peter Pan (*Ninety in the Shade*), 102, 103
† Pianologue, 115
Pick Yourself Up, 358, 360
Picture I Want To See, The, 159, 160, 167
Pie, 237, 239
Pill A Day, A, 269
Plain Rustic Ride ('Neath The Silv'ry Moon), 46
Play Us A Polka Dot, 306, 309
Poker Love, 48
Polka Dot, The, 247
Polly Believed In Preparedness, 138
Poor Pierrot, 318
Poor Prune, 154
Portrait Parade, The, 272
Praise The Day, 295
* Pretty Milliners, The, 64
Prince Do And Dare, 296, 298
Prisoner Of Love, A, 77
Put Me To The Test, 398, 400
* Put Me To The Test [by George Gershwin], 398

* Quadalquiver, 195
Quarrel And Part, 172

Raggedy Ann, 238, 239
Ragtime Restaurant, The, 77, 78

Railroad Song, 404
* Raindrops, 36
Raining, 42
Recipe, A, 48
Reckless, 352
Reckless Boy. *See* Sweetest Girl, Silly Boy, I Love You
Red, White And Blue, 57
† Regular Guy, A, 101
Remind Me, 387
Reminiscences, 138
* Rhapsody In Blue, 281
* Rich Man, Poor Man, 101, 102
Right Now, 50
Right Romance, The, 404
Rip Van Winkle And His Little Men, 196
Road That Lies Before, The, 135, 137
Rock-a-Bye Baby Dear. *See* Lullaby
Roll On, Rolling Road, 346, 348
Rolled Into One, 144, 147, 148
Romeo And Juliet, 296
Rosalie, 45, 92
Rose Of Delight, 271, 272
Rose Ruby, 218
Rose-Marie, 216
Roses Are Nodding, 248
Rub A Dub, 36, 38
Runaway Colts, 172

Sally, 206, 210
Samarkand, 135
Same Old Game, The, 119
* Same Old Moon, The, 280, 281
Same Sort Of Girl, 96, 97, 98, 105
* Sammy, 159
* Saskatchewan, 195, 196
Saturday Night, 131
Saturday 'Till Monday, 36, 38, 39, 40
Scenario For Orchestra, 388, 389
Schnitza Komisski, The, 206, 207, 210
* Schwanda, The Bag-Pipe Player, 360
Semiramis, 190
* Serenade, 79

† Sergeant Philip Of The Dancers, 68-69
* Sergeant Wix, 36, 37
Seven Days, 256
Shadow Of The Moon, 247, 249
She Didn't Say "Yes," 318, 320, 321
She's On Her Way, 272
She's Spanish, 196
Shimmy With Me, 223
* Shine On Harvest Moon, 280
Shine Out, All You Little Stars, 58
Shop, 135
Shorty George, The, 392, 394
Shower Of Rice, 172, 174
Shufflin' Sam, 247, 249
* Siboney, 362, 401
Sidonie, 90
Signorina Adelina, 178
Silenzio, 227
Simple Little Tune, 140, 141
Since The Days Of Grandmamma, 75, 76, 77, 78
Sing! Sing! You Tetrazzini!, 76, 79
Sing Song Girl, 216
Sing Trovatore, 64, 66
Singing A Song In Your Arms, 352
Sir Galahad, 153
Siren's Song, The, 153, 154, 179, 265
Sitting Pretty, 249
Skeleton Janitor, The, 238
Smoke, 173
Smoke Gets In Your Eyes, 146, 336, 339, 341, 342, 359, 387
Snip, Snip, Snip, 189
Social Game, The, 206
Society, 115, 141
* Society Farmerettes, The, 158
Some Day, 297, 298
Some Fine Day, 194
Some Little Girl, 169
Some One (*Miss Springtime*), 131
Some Party, 188, 190
Some Sort Of Somebody, 116, 119, 122
Somebody Wants To Go To Sleep, 346, 348
Someone (*Blue Eyes*), 298
† Something Like This, 70

Something's Got To Happen, 338, 339, 343
Song Is You, The, 331, 332, 333, 341, 391
Song Of The Sheriffs, 21
So's Your Old Man, 263, 265
† Spring Is Here (*Lucky*), 280, 281, 309
Spring Is Here (*Sweet Adeline*), 306, 308, 309
Ssh, You'll Waken Mr. Doyle, 92
Star Of Hitchy Koo, The, 200, 201
* Star-Spangled Banner, The, 73, 88
Steady Little Girlie, 132
Stepping Stones, 238
Stitching, Stitching, 177
Stolen Dreams, 312
Strolling, Or What Have You?, 264
Subway Express, The, 49
Sun About To Rise, The, 307, 308, 309
Sun Shines Brighter, The, 153, 154, 310
Sun Starts To Shine Again, The, 166, 169
Sunny, 263, 265, 266
Sunshine, 264, 266, 273
Sure Thing, 400
Susan, 36, 40, 123
* Susan Brown From A Country Town, 64
Susie, 272, 274
Susse Pariserin, Die, 94
Suzette And Her Pet, 58
Sweetest Girl, Silly Boy, I Love You, 54
Sweetest Sight That I Have Seen, 379
Sweetest Thing In Life, The, 260
Sweetie, 200
Swing Your Sweetheart 'Round The Fire, 397
* Sylvia, 97
Sympathetic Someone, 269, 270, 293

Ta, Ta, Little Girl, 68
Take A Chance, 184

Take A Step With Me, 92
Take Me For A Honeymoon Ride,
  307
Take The Eyes Of Mabel, 133
Te Deum, 291
Teacher, Teacher, 188, 189
* Teasing, 64
Teepee, 174
Telephone Girls, 193
Tell Me All Your Troubles, Cutie,
  160
* Tell Me, Pretty Maiden, 55
Tell Me Why The World, 141
That "Come Hither" Look, 130
* That Deviling Tune, 64
That Little Something, 274, 280,
  281, 282
That Lucky Fellow, 382, 384
That Lucky Lady, 382
That's A Thing That's Really
  Wanted, 55
That's All Right For McGilligan,
  66
That's The Life, 138
There Is A Happy Land (Tale Of
  Woe), 66
There Isn't One Girl, 247
There It Is Again, 152, 154
There'll Come A Day, 395
There's A Funny Old House, 346,
  347
There's A Hill Beyond A Hill, 330,
  333
There's A Joy That Steals Upon
  You, 346
There's A Resting Place For Every
  Girl, 68
There's Lots Of Room For You, 257
There's No Better Use For Time
  Than Kissing, 177, 178, 179
There's Something Rather Odd
  About Augustus, 54
These Orchids If You Please, 394
They Didn't Believe Me, 96, 97,
  98, 104, 113, 123, 137, 146,
  157, 266, 353
Things Have Changed From Then
  To Now, 21, 22
Things I Want, The, 367

Think Of Where You Might Be
  Instead Of Where You Are,
  178
Thirteen Collar, 117, 119, 123
This Little Girl, 206
Those "Come Hither" Eyes, 115
Those Days Are Gone Forever, 223
365 Days, 129, 132
* Throw Me A Rose, 132
Till Good Luck Comes My Way,
  287
Till The Clouds Roll By, 143, 144,
  145, 146, 147, 148
Times Square, 227
To The End Of The World
  Together, 29
To The Fair, 256
To Think He Remembered Me, 265
Today Is Spring, 182
Toddle, 216, 218
Tonsils, 265
Toodle Oo, 136, 137
Toot-Toot!, 172
Touch Of Your Hand, The, 338,
  339, 342
Toy Clog Dance, 159
* Treasure Hunt, The, 280
Treasure Island, 200, 201
Triangle, The, 102, 103
Trouble About The Drama, The,
  295
Try To Forget, 318, 321
Tulip Time In Sing Sing, 248
Turkey Trot, 66
'Twas Not So Long Ago, 306, 307,
  309
Twenty-five Years Ago, 183
* Two Big Eyes, 115
Two Heads Are Better Than One,
  115
Two Hearts Are Better Than One,
  179, 404
Two Little Bluebirds, 264, 265
Two Total Losses, 265

Under The Linden Tree, 46
Under The Sky, 265
Up With The Lark, 403

Vienna, 51
Vigilantes, The, 77
Virginia Hoe Down, 372
* Volunteers, 36
Vorderveele, 182

Wait Till Tomorrow, 152, 155
Waiting Around The Corner, 166, 169
Waiting For You, 36, 37, 39, 40
Walk, Walk, Walk, 77
Walking Home With Josie, 269, 270
Waltz In Swing Time, 358, 360
Waltz Me Up To The Altar, Walter, 79
Waltz Time Girl, The, 77, 79
Way Down East, 206
Way Down Town, 216, 217, 218
Way You Look Tonight, The, 360
We Belong Together, 331, 333
We Want To Laugh, 159
We Were So Young, 350
* Wearing Of The Green, The, 42-43
Wedding Bells Are Calling Me, 112, 119, 122
Wedding Bells Are Ringing, 218
Wedding In The Spring, 394
Wedding Knell, The, 264, 266
Weeping Willow Tree, 256, 258
Welcome To The Bride, 346
We'll Make A Bet, 200
We'll See, 140, 141
We'll Take Care Of You All (The Little Refugees), 98
Well This Is Jolly, 89
We're Crooks, 158, 160
We're Going To Be Pals, 147, 148
We're On Our Way, 119
What Can I Say, 297
What Good Are Words?, 346, 348
What I'm Longing To Say, 152, 154, 155
* What Kind Of Place Is This?, 64
What Kind Of Soldier Are You?, 372, 373, 374
What Would You Do For $50,000?, 138

What's Become Of Spring, 312
What's Good About Good-Night?, 370
What's In The Air, To-night?, 346
What's The Use?, 256
Wheatless Days, 167
When A New Star, 376
When I Discover My Man, 198
When I Fell In Love With You, 267, 269
When I Marry Mr. Pilbeam, 296, 297
When I Went To School, 239
When I've Got The Moon, 352
When Rogers Come To Town, 21
When Spring Is In The Air, 330, 333
When The Bo Tree Blossoms Again, 280, 281, 282
When The Lights Are Low, 129
When The Orchestra Is Playing Your Favorite Dance, 148, 154
When The Ships Come Home, 166, 167, 168
When Three Is Company (Cupid Song), 81, 86, 150, 260
When We Get Our Divorce, 264, 266
When You Hear That Humming, 373
When You Wake Up Dancing, 173, 174
* When You Wore A Tulip, 97
* When You're A Long, Long Way From Home, 97
When You're In Love, You'll Know, 132
Where Did The Bird Hear That?, 77, 79
Where Is The Girl For Me?, 101, 103, 190, 191
While Mary Sleeps, 346
Whip-Poor-Will, 192, 193, 206, 207, 208, 209
Whirlwind Trot, 138
Whistle When You're Lonely, 61
Whistling Boy, The, 362
Whistling Dan, 101, 103, 154
White Cavaliers, The, 239

Index

Who?, 190, 263, 264, 265, 266, 267, 405

Who Cares, 141, 218

Whoop-de-oodle-do!, 223

Who's Complaining, 400

Who's Zoo In Girl Land, 159

Whose Baby Are You?, 194, 197, 198, 265

Why? (*The City Chap*), 267

Why? (*Leave It to Jane*), 153

Why Can't It Happen To Me?, 138

Why Can't They Hand It To Me?, 148

Why Do I Love You?, 285, 287, 289, 290, 298, 321

Why Don't They Dance The Polka?, 98

Why Don't You Write To Me Blues. *See* "Have You Forgotten Me?" Blues

Why Was I Born?, 307, 308, 309

* Widows, 64

Wife Of Your Own, A, 89, 90

Wild Rose, 206, 207, 208, 210, 239

Will It All End In Smoke?, 85, 86

Will You Marry Me Tomorrow, Maria?, 367

Wine, Wine! (Champagne Song), 28

Wine, Women And Song, 190

Winter In Central Park, 307

With Type a-Ticking, 182

Without The Girl—Inside, 51

* Without Thinking Of You, 280

Woman's Heart, A, 89, 90

* Women, 298

Wonderful Dad, 237, 239

* Wonderful Days, 102

Won't You Buy A Little Canoe, 45

Won't You Have A Little Feather, 260

Won't You Kiss Me Once Before I Go?, 42

Won't You Let Me Carry Your Parcel?, 54

Wood Nymphs, The, 237

Words Are Not Needed, 145, 146, 147

Worries, 247

* Yama Yama Man, The, 157, 159

Year From Today, A, 247, 248, 249

Yesterdays, 338, 342, 378

Yo! Ho! When You're In The Chorus, 21

You Alone Would Do, 248

You And Your Kiss, 387

You Are Doing Very Well, 346, 348

You Are Love, 287, 288, 290

You Are There, 297

You Can't Keep A Good Girl Down, 206, 210

You Can't Make Love By Wireless, 233

* You Can't Play Every Instrument In The Band, 80

You Couldn't Be Cuter, 370

* You Don't Take A Sandwich To A Banquet, 110, 111

You Found Me And I Found You, 166, 168, 188

You Inspire A Mad Desire, 343

You Know And I Know, 104, 110, 111

You Must Come Over, 211

You Never Can Tell, 96, 98

You Never Knew About Me, 144, 145, 147

You Said Something, 134, 135, 137

You Tell 'Em, 192

You Want The Best Seats, We Have 'Em, 223

You Were Never Lovelier, 393

You Will—Won't You?, 272, 273

Your Dream (Is The Same As My Dream), 372, 374, 376, 387

You're Devastating, 298, 338, 342

You're Here And I'm Here, 93, 94, 98, 111, 134, 158

You're Just A Perfect Peach Beyond My Reach, 68

You're The Little Girl I've Looked For So Long, 161

You're The Only Girl He Loves, 72, 168

You've Got To Meet Sweet Marguerite, 312

Part II

Abbott (Bud) and Costello (Lou), 386
Abeles, Julian, 240, 241
Academy of Music (Baltimore), 193, 205
Ackerman, P. Dodd, 248
Adams, Franklin P., 199, 353
Ade, George, 151
Adelphi Theatre (Philadelphia), 74
Adolphus, Theodor, 373
Adonis, 34
Aiken, D. M., 145
Aldwych Theatre (London), 44
Alfred, Julian, 89, 102, 248
All After Sophie, 79
Alvin Theatre (New York), 329, 381
Amazons, The, 81
Amenities of Collecting, and Kindred Affections, 301
Americana, 276
Amselberg (or Anselberg), Isaac, 6; Rosa, 6
Anderson Galleries, 301, 303
Annie Oakley, 405
Ansell, John, 223, 234
Apollo Theatre (Atlantic City, N. J.), 97, 134, 151, 215, 305
Arcadians, The, 69
Arlen, Harold, 364
Arthur, Daniel V., 99, 104
Arthurs, George, 67
As Thousands Cheer, 341
ASCAP, 251, 387, 390, 406
Ascherberg, Hopwood and Crew, Ltd., 131

Ashley, Hammond, 363
Astaire, Adele, 226, 229
Astaire, Fred, 142, 226, 228, 229, 264, 348, 351, 356, 357, 358, 359, 360, 392, 393
Astor Theatre (New York), 73, 176, 366
Austin, Dr. Oliver, 3, 324-25

Babes and the Baron, The, 44
Baby Mine, 174
Baker, Evelyn, 42
Baker, Graham, 369
Balderston, Katherine C., 313
Ball, Ernest, 26-27
Ballard, Lucinda, 405
Ballkonigin, Die, 94
Band Wagon, The, 314, 315, 401
Baravalle, Victor, 195, 217, 228, 236, 269, 287, 319, 331, 339
Barnes, T. Roy, 310
Barrie, James M., 105, 261
Barrymore, Ethel, 353
Bartholomae, Philip, 116, 117, 123, 124
Bayes, Nora, 66
Beauty of Bath, The, 44-45, 120
Beauty Prize, The, 232-35, 267, 291
Beery, Wallace, 353
Beethoven, Ludwig van, 333
Begum, The, 15
Belasco, David, 220
Belasco Theatre (Washington, D.C.), 58

Bellamy, George Anne, 295
Belle of New York, The, 157
Bendell, Alfred, 89
Bendix, Max, 257, 258
Bennett, David, 111, 117, 257, 269, 273, 280
Bennett, Robert Russell, 4, 138, 211, 236, 248, 249, 264, 269, 273, 280, 284, 285, 298, 307, 318, 319, 327, 339, 347, 354, 357, 359, 366, 373, 383, 388
Bennington, Whitney, 37
Benrimo, 111, 133
Bentley, Irene. *See* Smith, Mrs. Harry B.
Bereny, Henry, 69
Berlin, Irving, 3, 23, 58, 156, 244-45, 260, 378, 387
Berman, Pandro, 350, 353, 356, 357, 358
Bernard, Barney, 65
Bernard, Felix, 241, 243
Bernard, Sam, 47, 58
Berry, Witt, 297
Biggers, Earl Derr, 385
Bijou Theatre (New York), 35 (older theatre), 199 (newer theatre)
Black, Johnny S., 241
Black Crook, The, 13
Blackbirds of 1928, 351
Blakely, James, 57
Blakeman, Daniel, 20, 21
Bledsoe, Jules, 325
Blossom, Henry, 108
Blow, Sidney, 89
Blue Bell in Paradise, 41
Blue Eyes, 259, 294-99, 313, 341
Blue Paradise, The, 157
Blumenthal, A. C., 326, 333, 335, 385
Bolm, Adolf, 156, 161
Bolton, Guy, 99-100, 103, 107-9, 117, 120, 121, 123, 124, 126, 127, 131, 132, 135, 144, 145, 148, 151, 152, 165, 167, 169, 170, 191, 203, 204, 205, 207, 212, 213, 220, 231, 244, 245, 250, 394, 404, 405

Bordoni, Irene, 115, 116
Borne, Hal, 358, 360
Bovill, C. H., 53, 55, 132
Bowers, Robert Hood, 160
Boykin, Edward, 371
Bradley's (Gaming House), 304
Brady, William A., 106, 107
Braham, Philip, 130
Braley, Berton, 164, 173
Breitenfeld, Emil, 165, 172, 173
Brewster's Millions, 191, 261
Brian, Donald, 67, 95, 98
Brice, Elizabeth, 157, 161
Brice, Fanny, 211
Brill, Leighton, 406
Broadway Theatre (New York), 51, 63
Brooke, Clifford, 257
Brown, Joe E., 310
Browne, Porter Emerson, 104
Brownies, The, 15
Bryan, Gertrude, 245
Bryan, Vincent, 51
Buck, Gene, 128, 150
Bunch and Judy, The, 220, 221, 225-30, 270
Burkan, Nathan, 220, 240, 241
Burke, Billie, 73, 81, 126, 230, 326
Burke, Marie, 299
Burnside, R. H., 49, 238, 269, 273
Burress, William, 71
Burton, David, 257
Bussell, Rev. W. Kemp, 62
Butt, Sir Alfred, 33, 34, 293, 299
Butterfly Ballet, 206
Byrne, Donn, 343

Cabaret Girl, The, 220, 221-25, 231, 235, 245, 257, 270, 310
Cahill, Marie, 68, 99-101, 103, 104, 196
Caine, Georgia, 43
Caldwell, Anne, 49, 126, 187, 188, 191, 193, 196, 197, 199, 206, 212, 220, 231, 238, 239, 240, 261, 270
Calthrop, G. E., 347
Camille, 324

Canary, The, 184, 187, 191
Can't Help Singing, 395-97
Captain Jinks of the Horse Marines, 204
Carle, Richard, 47-47, 69, 81, 99, 101, 103, 104, 386
Carminati, Tullio, 327, 331
Carnegie Hall (New York), 388
Caroline, 395
Carrington, Katharine, 327
Carroll, Harry, 211
Carson, Doris, 317, 320
Carter, Frank, 202-3
Caryll, Ivan, 15, 16, 45, 61, 62, 79, 108, 184, 190, 212
Casino Theatre (New York), 25, 47, 49, 51, 58, 88, 114, 165
Castle, Irene and Vernon, 107, 120, 161
Cat and the Fiddle, The, 236, 316-22, 324, 328, 341
Catch of the Season, The, 41-43, 44
Catlett, Walter, 206, 255, 257, 310
Cawthorn, Joseph, 80, 95, 184, 226, 227, 264, 265
Ceballos, Larry, 386
Centennial Summer (Kern musical), 401-4
Centennial Summer (novel), 401-2
Century Girl, The, 156, 158
Century Theatre (New York), 156, 158
Chaminade, Cécile, 190
Champagne and Orchids, 351, 352
Champagne Sec, 341
Chaplin, Saul, 387, 399
Charm School, The, 198, 199
Chauve Souris, 229
Chestnut St. Opera (Philadelphia), 48
Chocolate Soldier, The, 57
Chodorov, Edward, 369
Chopin, Frederic, 190
Christine, P. H., 103
Cinderella Sue, 403
City Chap, The, 267-70, 293
Claire, Ina, 95, 128, 220
Clark, Alexander, 59
Clarke, Harry, 184
Clayton, Jan, 405

Cleveland Symphony Orchestra, 388
Cobb, Henry Ives, Jr., 136
Cohan, George M., 47, 71, 98, 172, 197, 209, 230, 317, 387
Cohan Theatre (New York), 115, 181, 322
Cohan's Grand Opera House (Chicago), 71
Cohn, Harry, 392, 397
College Widow, The, 151
Collier, Constance, 352
Collier, William, 133
Collins, Harry, 167
Colonial Theatre (Boston), 199
Columbia Pictures, 392, 397
Colvan, Zeke, 373
Comelli, 234
Comstock, Ray, 49, 107-110, 116, 117, 119, 120, 121, 126, 127, 132, 148, 151, 152, 155, 161, 169, 185, 192, 193, 231, 244, 245, 246, 250
Conwell, O'Kane, 195
Cooper, Kathleen Ritter, 304, 342, 350, 361, 362, 368, 371, 378, 387, 389, 400
Copland, Aaron, 391
Country Girl, A, 30
Cousin Lucy, 114, 141, 179
Cover Girl, 397-400
Coward, Noel, 353
Coyne, Joseph, 95
Cribben, Joseph, 406
Criss Cross, 266, 270-74, 275, 322
Criterion Theatre (New York), 45, 49, 50, 54, 69
Criterion Theatre (New York— Loew's Filmhouse), 396
Cromwell, John, 355
Crook, John, 73, 105
Cugat, Xavier, 394
Cummings, Jack, 364

Dabney, Ford, 111
Dairymaids, The, 50, 51, 63
Dale, Alan, 37-38, 63, 78, 81-82, 88, 90, 145, 153, 178, 188, 228, 273, 286, 288

Daly, William, 189
Daly's Theatre (London), 57, 299
Daly's Theatre (New York), 43, 47, 59, 76
Dame de Chez Maxim's, La, 69
Damsel in Distress, 398
Dare, Danny, 307
Darewski, Herman, 105
Darling Twins, 219
Darnley, Herbert, 35, 36, 38
Daves, Delmer, 392
David, Worton, 67, 97, 111
Davies, Marion, 109, 144, 145, 157
Davis, Bessie McCoy, 67, 157
Day, Edith, 299
Day, Frederick, 62, 63, 65
De Angelis, Jefferson, 180
de Frece, Lauri, 56, 62, 120, 213
DeKoven, Reginald, 14, 43, 150, 184
De Packh, Maurice, 228, 273, 403
De Sylva, Buddy, 191, 193, 206, 209, 211, 260
De Sylva, Brown and Henderson, 239
De Wolfe, Elsie, 108, 119
Dear Sir, 72, 252-59, 260, 261, 271, 298, 299, 359
Debussy, Claude, 190
Delroy, Irene, 311
Des Graz, Charles Geoffrey, 313
Dickey, Paul, 115
Dickson, Dorothy, 144, 176, 178, 209, 212, 213, 214, 223, 225, 231
Dietz, Howard, 253-54, 257, 258
Dillingham, Charles, 61, 115, 156, 157, 158, 160, 161, 184, 187, 188, 193, 196, 198, 291, 220, 226, 227, 229, 230, 231, 235, 238, 240, 260, 261, 262, 267, 268, 269, 270, 277, 279, 282, 310, 318, 322-23
Dittenhofer, Judge, 8
Dixon, Adèle, 345, 347
Dolan, Robert Emmett, 383
Doll Girl, The, 81-86, 94, 150, 260, 291
Dollar Princess, The, 57, 58
Dolly Sisters, 192, 251

Donahue, Jack, 262, 264
Donnelly, Dorothy, 283
Dooley, Johnny, 227
Dooley, Ray, 211, 226, 227
Dougall, Bernard, 337
Dovey, Alice, 117
Dowling, Eddie, 230
Dragon, Carmen, 399
Dresser, Louise, 58, 59, 134, 177, 178
Dressler, Marie, 29
Dreyer, David, 358
Dreyfus, Louis, 3, 270
Dreyfus, Max, 26-27, 29, 39, 41, 45, 236, 270, 314, 315, 375, 390
Dreyfuss, Henry, 319
Drury Lane Theatre (London), 299, 344, 345, 347
DuBois, Henri, 72
Duchess of Dantzig, The, 30
Duchin, Eddie, 341
Duff-Gordon, Lady, 156, 161, 177
Duffy, James, 70
Dukedom Large Enough, 301
Duncan Sisters, 244-45, 251
Dunne, Irene, 269, 356, 366, 367, 369, 370, 393
Durbin, Deanna, 395, 396
Dvorak, Anton, 249

Eagle, Oscar, 192
Earl and the Girl, The, 30, 41, 43
Eaton, Mary, 210, 211, 278, 281
Echo, The, 61
Eddy, Nelson, 351
Edelman, Louis F., 392
Edens, Roger, 353
Ediss, Connie, 59
Edwardes, George, 14, 30, 31, 33, 34, 47, 94, 95, 153
Edwards, Julian, 26
Elliot, Williams, 143, 148, 165, 185
Ellis, Mary, 334
Ellis, Melville, 63, 89, 117, 119, 120
Eltinge, Julian, 34, 114
Empire Theatre (Syracuse, N. Y.), 71, 100

Endymion, 87
Engel, Carl, 113
Englander, Ludwig, 47
English Daisy, An, 27, 34, 40-41
Ephraim, Lee, 294
Erlanger, Abraham, 46, 104, 126, 127, 131, 135, 155, 283
Erlanger Theatre (Philadelphia), 271
Errol, Leon, 206, 207, 310
Eugene, Max C., 36, 38, 39
Europe, James Reese, 111
Evangeline, 34
Evans, Maurice, 401
Everard, George, 35-36, 38
Excuse Me, 164

Fad and Fancies, 104
Faibisy, 145
Fall, Leo, 57, 67, 81, 82, 90
Farkoa, Maurice, 115, 120
Farley, Terence, 10
Fascinating Flora, 49, 50
Fears, Peggy, 326, 327, 329, 333, 335, 385
Felix, Seymour, 399
Ferber, Edna, 3, 275, 276, 287, 288, 304, 390
Fessier, Michael, 392
Feydeau, George, 69
Fields, Dorothy, 3, 351, 353, 354, 357, 361, 367, 386, 395, 405, 406
Fields, Herbert, 3, 351, 367, 405
Fields, Lew, 27, 28, 40, 63, 160, 161, 351
Fields, W. C., 211
Finck, Herman, 33, 97, 115, 344
Finn, Elsie, 354
First National (film company), 310, 311, 312
First Nights and First Editions, 87
First Prize, The, 231
Fischer, Fred, 50, 219-20, 231, 240, 241, 242, 243
Flame Within, The, 352
Fledermaus, Die, 340
Fletcher, Bramwell, 311
Fliegende Hollander, Der, 240

Florodora, 55, 210
Fluffy Ruffles, 53, 54
Fonda, Henry, 354
For Love of Mike, 133
Ford, Hugh, 226
Ford Hour, The (radio program), 389
Forrest Theatre (Philadelphia), 171 (older theatre), 337 (second theatre)
Fortune Hunter, The, 261
Foster, Allan, 257
Foster, Lewis, R., 395
Fox, Dorothy, 403
Fox, Harry, 174, 192
Foy, Eddie, 43, 48
Foy Eddie, Jr., 317, 320
Francis, W. T., 42, 54
Franklin, Irene, 306, 307
Freeborn, Cassius, 200
Friedland, Anatol, 173, 174
Friml, Rudolf, 79, 103, 211, 218, 262, 361, 378
Frohman, Charles, 31, 32, 33, 34, 41, 42, 43, 44, 45, 47, 50, 53, 54, 61, 67, 68, 69, 80, 81, 83, 88, 92, 93, 94, 95, 104, 113-14, 315
Fully That, 120, 121
Fulton Theatre (New York), 246
Fun of the Fayre, 310

Gaiety Girl, A, 14
Gaiety Theatre (London), 13, 14, 30, 45, 48, 80, 102, 113, 129
Gaige, Crosby, 180
Gallagher, Richard "Skeet," 267, 270, 281
Gallagher and Shean, 224
Gallico, Paolo, 25
Game of Chess, 312
Garden Theatre (New York), 15
Garnett, Tay, 369
Garrick Theatre (Philadelphia), 225, 267, 278, 316, 317, 327
Gates and Morange, 125, 217, 307
Gay Divorce, 349
Gay Hussars, The, 58

Gelsey, Erwin, 359, 399
Gensler, Lewis, 175
Gentlemen Unafraid, 230, 370-76, 387
Gershwin, George, 122, 158, 175, 235, 260, 281, 289, 304, 361, 366, 368, 378, 384, 385, 398, 401, 404
Gershwin, Ira, 364, 378, 385, 397, 398
Gerstenberger, Emil, 388
Gest, Morris, 148, 151, 152, 155, 161, 165, 192, 193, 231, 244, 245, 246, 250
Gideon, Melville, 58
Gilbert, Jean, 72, 91
Gilbert and Sullivan, 13, 14, 45, 150, 246
Gillen, Charles P., 20, 22
Girl and the Miner, The, 74
Girl and the Wizard, The, 58
Girl from Kay's, The, 30, 47
Girl from Montmartre, The, 69, 70
Girl from the States, The, 58
Girl from Utah, The, 94-99, 104, 158
Girl of the Golden West, The, 75
Girl of the Overland Trail, 395
Girl of Today, A, 104, 111
Girls of Gottenberg, The, 53, 54
Girls Will Be Girls, 133, 134
Glaser, Lulu, 58
Glen, Helen, 235
Globe Theatre (New York), 61, 66, 81, 127, 128, 184, 211, 217, 227, 237, 271, 317, 318, 323
Gloria's Romance, 126, 127-28, 155, 259
Go To It, 132, 187
Goddard, Charles W., 115
Goetz, Ray, 51
Golden, John, 41, 69, 81, 92, 115
Golden Bells, 343
Golden Widow, The, 58-59
Goldsmith, Oliver, 302, 312
Good Morning, Dearie, 212, 215-21, 224, 262, 271, 278, 322
Goodman, Al, 319
Goodman, Philip, 251-55, 258, 259

Goodwin, J. Cheever, 40
Gordon, Kitty, 58, 65
Gordon, Max, 3, 314-17, 319, 322, 325, 335-38, 340, 341, 343, 371, 379, 380, 381, 384, 401
Gould, Frank, 55
Gow, James, 354
Gowns By Roberta (Kern musical), 337, 338
Gowns By Roberta (novel), 198, 334, 335, 337, 401
Grant, Charles N., 72
Granville, Bernard, 128
Grayson, Charles, 386
Great White Way, The, 51
Green, John, 365, 371, 383
Green, Morris, 251
Green, Richard, 371, 378
Green Grow the Lilacs, 392
Greenbank, Percy, 31, 95
Greene, Schuyler, 104, 111, 112, 115, 116, 137
Grey, Clifford, 103, 204
Grieg, Edvard, 321
Griffin, Norman, 222, 223, 224
Groody, Louise, 164, 173, 194, 196, 217
Grossmith, George, Jr., 45, 47, 53, 54, 57, 120, 129, 130, 212, 213, 214, 220, 222, 223, 224, 232, 235
Grossmith, Lawrence, 111, 120, 320
Guggenheim, Daniel, 8
Guggenheim (game), 364
Gwyther, Geoffrey, 223, 297

Haines, Herbert E., 42, 44
Hajos, Mizzi. *See* Mitzi
Hale, Binnie, 345
Hall, Bettina, 316, 319, 320
Hall, Owen, 31, 45
Hall, Thurston, 134, 402
Hamilton, Cosmo, 42
Hammerstein, Arthur, 276, 283, 304, 305, 325
Hammerstein, Dorothy, 344, 362, 368

Hammerstein, Oscar, II, 3, 230, 262, 265, 270, 275, 277, 282, 283, 284, 285, 287, 288, 289, 290, 293, 294, 299, 300, 304, 305, 306, 307, 308, 309, 313, 323, 324, 325, 326, 329, 331, 333, 334, 343, 344, 346, 347, 349, 351, 352, 356, 365, 366, 368, 370, 372, 373, 375, 376, 377, 378, 379, 381, 385, 386, 390, 391, 392, 394, 395, 396, 403, 405-407
Hammerstein, Reginald, 307
Hammerstein's Theatre (New York), 306
Hand, Judge Learned, 241-43
Harbach, Otto, 3, 68, 108, 230, 261, 262, 270, 277, 278, 279, 281, 311, 315-16, 319, 321, 334, 335-37, 341, 343, 370, 371, 373, 375, 376, 394
Harbach, William, 311
Harburg, E. Y., 395, 403
Hardwicke, Cedric, 299
Harker, Joseph and Phil, 223, 234, 297
Harkrider, John W., 287, 331
Harline, Leigh, 392
Harlow, Jean, 352, 353
Harmanus Bleecker Hall (Albany, N. Y.), 165
Harms, Alec, 27
Harms, T. B., Co., 25-27, 41, 43, 45, 55, 59, 67, 70, 158, 220, 228, 236, 289, 345, 358
Harms, Tom, 27, 45
Harris, F. Clifford, 42, 44, 69
Harris, Sam, 71, 244-45
Harrison, Lee, 65
Hartford Opera Players, 150
Hartman, Mr. and Mrs. Lee, 405
Harwood, H. M., 130
Harwood, John, 294
Haskell, Jack, 221
Havana, 55
Have a Heart, 127, 134-39, 140, 141, 142, 171
Hawley, Andros, 36
Hayfoot, Strawfoot, 376

Hayman, Alf, 43
Hayworth, Rita, 392, 393, 397, 398, 399
Hazzard, John (Jack) E., 119, 123, 195
Head Over Heels, 180-84, 186
Hedden, Irene, 21
Heidelberg University, 23
Heindl, Anton, 173
Helen of Troy, New York, 246
Hello, Broadway!, 197
Hen-Pecks, The, 63
Henson, Leslie, 130, 212, 213, 221, 225, 231
Herald Square Theatre (New York), 48
Herbert, Joseph W., 49, 58, 59, 77, 108
Herbert, Victor, 5, 16, 26, 28, 47, 54, 62, 79, 98, 99, 108, 150, 156, 157-61, 198, 206, 211, 230, 240, 241, 251
Here's Looking at You, 165
Heuberger, Richard, 68
Heyward, DuBose, 344, 377
Hicks, Seymour, 27, 33, 34, 41-42, 43, 44, 45
High Jinks, 103
High, Wide and Handsome, 362-65, 395
Hill, Ethel, 361
Hines, Elizabeth, 276, 277
Hirsch, Louis A., 10, 58, 69, 185, 378
Hirschfeld, Max, 111, 119, 145, 167
Hirschfeld, Dr. Samuel, 367
Hirst, George, 373
His Majesty's Theatre (London), 334
Hitchcock, Raymond, 199-201
Hitchy-Koo of 1920, 199-201
H.M.S. Pinafore, 13, 51
Hoare, Douglas, 89
Hobart, George V., 71, 72, 73, 183
Holde, Nick, 326, 385
Hollinshead, John, 13, 14
Holloway, Stanley, 225, 347
Holmes, Edward "Teddy," 179, 345
Holstein, Mark, 3, 313, 405
Hope, Bob, 336, 343

Hopkins, Arthur, 324
Hopper, Edna Wallace, 29, 48
Hopper, Edward, 401
Hoschna, Karl, 62
Houp-La, 150-51, 165, 180
Howard, Arthur Platt, 209
Howland, Jobyna, 59
Hoyt, Charles, 127
Hubbell, Raymond, 58
Huffman, J. C., 63, 88
Hughes, Rupert, 164
Hurst, Fannie, 377
Hyatt, John Kennett, 371
Hyman, Dr. Harold, 3, 406
Hyperion Theatre (New Haven,
    Connecticut), 35

I Dream Too Much, 355-56, 357
I Won't Dance, 356, 358
Idell, Albert E., 401
In Dahomey, 31
In Other Words, 379
In Town, 14
Interlude, 361
International Revue, 351
Irene, 205, 210, 215, 230
Irwin, Wallace, 54

Jackson, Felix, 395
Janis, Elsie, 115-16, 161
Jardon, Dorothy, 65
Jarnagin, Jerry, 307
Jazz Singer, The, 299
J.E.B. Holding Corporation, 162
John, Graham, 293, 294, 310
Johnson, Albert, 385
Jolson, Al, 64, 65, 344
Jones, A. L., 251
Jones, Sidney, 21, 59, 95
Jones, Stephen, 217, 228
Josephson, Max D., 180
Joy of Living, 369-70
Joy of Loving, The, 369
Just the Other Day, 305

Kahn, Otto, 260
Kailimai, Henry, 116

Kakeles, Bertha Amselberg [or
    Anselberg], 6, 185
Kakeles, Emanuel, 6
Kakeles, Emanuel Gerrit, 7
Kakeles, Fannie, *See* Kern, Fannie
    Kakeles
Kakeles, Henrietta, 6
Kakeles, Dr. Moses, 8
Kakeles, Dr. Sarah Welt, 9
Kakeles, Seligman, 6-9, 26, 185
Kalman, Emmerich, 57, 126, 131,
    132, 155
Kalmar, Bert, 278, 281
Kanin, Michael, 403
Karl and Sieglinde, 326
Kelly, Edith, 54, 55
Kelly, Gene, 398-99
Kemps, The, 165
Kennedy, Dr. Forster, 351
Kennerley, Mitchell, 301, 302
Kerker, Gustave, 15, 16, 49
Kern, Bertram, 17
Kern, Betty (Elisabeth Jane), 11f., 24,
    53, 54, 55, 56, 60, 72, 77, 94,
    113, 185, 300, 352, 364, 365,
    367, 371, 378, 387, 390, 394,
    402, 406
Kern, Charles, 10, 17
Kern, Edna (Mrs. Joseph), 282
Kern, Edwin, 10, 53
Kern, Eva Leale, 54, 56, 57, 60, 66,
    68, 80, 113, 120, 125, 139,
    162, 163, 164, 184, 185, 198,
    211, 212, 221, 282, 299, 300,
    324, 334, 335, 353, 354, 357,
    362, 363, 364, 365, 367, 368,
    405, 406
Kern, Fannie Kakeles, 8, 9-13, 17,
    52, 53
Kern, Henry, 9-13, 17, 23, 52, 53
Kern, Irving, 10, 17
Kern, Jerome David; ambitions as
    serious composer, 171; attacks
    jazz, 197, 249-50; birth, 10; and
    book auctions, 300; break-
    through, 99; death, 406-407;
    education, 11-13, 19, 22-23, 25;
    first full score, 74-79; first
    London trip, 31-34; funeral, 3-5;

marriage, 62; moves: to Bronx-
ville, 125; California, 362;
Newark, 17
Kern, Joseph, 10, 17, 53, 283
Kern, Milton, 10
King, Charles, 157, 161
King, Dennis, 325, 378
King of Cadonia, The, 59, 65, 210
Kings Theatre (Southsea), 294
Kingsway Theatre (London), 186
Kipling, Rudyard, 374
Kiss Waltz, The, 67
Kitty Grey, 55
Kiviette, 257, 339
Klaw, Marc, 46, 104, 131, 155
Kleine, George, 126
Klorer, John, 395
Knickerbocker Theatre (New York),
53, 57, 58, 61, 67, 80, 88, 92,
95, 101, 260
Knight, Percival, 58, 60
Knopf, Edwin and/or Mildred, 364,
405
Knox, Judge John C., 241
Kollo, Walter, 73, 85
Kostelanetz, André, 3, 354, 391
Krier, George, 59
Krueger Auditorium (Newark,
N. J.), 20
Kummer, Clare, 99, 103

La Belle Paree, 63-66, 140, 141
Lady, Be Good! (1941 film), 385
Lady In Red, The, 103, 191
Lady Madcap, 46
Lady Mary, 293
Lambert, Alexander, 25
Lampke, Mr. and Mrs. A. C., 163
Lamplighter, The (mini-operetta),
251
Lange, Gustave, 291
Lardner, Ring, 123
Laska, Edward, 43
Latham, Fred G., 189, 195, 228, 248
Laughing Husband, The, 93-94, 128,
270
Laurillard, Edward, 129, 212, 224
Laye, Evelyn, 294, 297, 313

Leale, Albert, 56
Leale, Elizabeth Jane, 56
Leale, Ethel, 56, 62
Leale, Eva. *See* Kern, Eva Leale
Leale, George Draper, 56, 60
Leave It to Jane, 103, 148, 151-55,
170, 250, 278
Lee, Bert, 97
Leffler and Bratton, 219
Lehar, Franz, 51, 79, 90
Lehman, Emanuel, 8
LeMaire, Charles, 248, 307
Leno, Dan, 35
Leonidoff, Leon, 361
Leslie, Fred, 234
Lester, Edwin, 208, 375, 391
Levy, Harold A., 182
Levy, Henri, 9
Lewis, Ada, 118, 195
Liberty Theatre (New York), 135,
194, 269
Lieber Augustin, 82, 137
Lillie, Beatrice, 187
Lindsay, Howard, 359
Lipton, Dan, 111
Little Cherub, The, 45, 54
Little Christopher (Columbus), 15-16
Little Miss Fix-It, 66, 67
Little Night Music, A, 402
Little Thing, The, 127, 203, 207,
210
Livingston, Billi, 373
London, Paris and Broadway, 213
Long, J. P., 111
Lonsdale, Frederick, 59
Look Who's Here, 74-76
Lopez, Vincent, 251
Los Angeles Youth Symphony, 388
Losee, Harry, 381, 383
Lotito, Louis A., 235, 323, 372
Loughry, Joseph, 53
Love Insurance, 385
Love o' Mike, 103, 133, 139-42, 143,
144, 149, 218
Love Song, 354
Lowell, Helen, 74, 366
Lucile. *See* Duff-Gordon, Lady
Lucky, 277-82, 309
Luders, Gustav, 26

Luescher, Mark, 198
Lusitania (ocean liner), 114, 130
Lyceum Publishing Co., 25, 26
Lyceum Theatre (Rochester, N. Y.),
    115
Lyric Theatre (Cincinnati, O.), 118
Lyric Theatre (New York), 44
Lyric Theatre (Philadelphia), 133

McCormack, Frank, 119
McCormack, John, 190, 235
MacDonald, Donald, 134
MacDonald, Jeanette, 335, 351
MacDonough, Glen, 58, 199
McGhie, John, 102, 153
McIntyre, Frank, 245, 251
McKenna, Kenneth, 373, 375
McNally, John J., 54
Mack, George E., 251
Madame Butterfly, 393
Madame Sherry, 62, 68
Madden, Edward, 58, 63, 65, 66
Madel von Montmartre, Das, 69
Maggs, Benjamin A., 313
Maid of Money, 192
Malone, J. A. E., 95, 212, 221
Mamba's Daughters, 377
Mamoulian, Rouben, 365, 366, 367
Man in the Sky, The, 312
Marbury, Elisabeth "Bessie," 107-10,
    116, 117, 119, 120, 121, 127,
    132, 133, 135, 142, 378, 379
Marion, George, 183
Mark, F. W., 105
Marks, Edward B., 24-25, 26
Marks, Robert, 173, 177
Marlowe, Harry, 61
Marriage Market, The, 88, 94
Marsh, Howard, 325, 327
Martin, Francis, 386
Martin, Mary, 3
Mary, 205, 215, 230
Mayhew, Stella, 64, 65
Mayo, Margaret, 174, 176
Meet Me In St. Louis, 402
Melodious Menu, The, 19
Men of the Sky, 312
Mercer, Johnny, 375, 403, 405

Mercer, Mabel, 239
Mermel, Regina, 313
Merrick, Leonard, 389
Merry Widow, The, 51, 55, 67
Messer Marco Polo, 343
Metaxa, Georges, 318, 319, 320
Metropolitan Opera (New York),
    260
MGM, 351, 352, 371, 405
Milk White Flag, A, 14, 127
Miller, Alice Duer, 198, 334, 337,
    353, 401
Miller, Betty Kern. *See* Kern, Betty
Miller, Charles, 359
Miller, Marilyn, 202-8, 210, 211,
    212, 222, 260, 262, 264,
    265, 266, 310, 313
Milton, Robert, 102, 167, 198, 231
"Mind-the-Paint" Girl, The, 73
Minnelli, Vincente, 378, 380, 383
Miron, J. C., 12
Miron, Joseph, 12
Miss Caprice, 82, 137
Miss Information, 115-16, 122, 123
Miss 1917, 156-61, 165, 185
Miss Springtime, 131-32, 137
Mr. Popple (of Ippleton), 109
Mr. Wix of Wickham, 35-40, 41, 63,
    88, 151, 155
Mitchell, Julian, 133, 191, 264
Mitzi, 65, 150-51, 180, 181, 182,
    183
Modern Eve, A, 114
Molinare, Nicanor, 394
Monckton, Lionel, 31, 61
Monkhouse, Gladys, 189
Moore, Colleen, 310
Moore, Grace, 200, 361-62
Morals of Marcus, The, 51
Morange, Edward A., 125
Morgan, Helen, 276, 283, 288, 289,
    304, 305, 308, 324
Morley, Christopher, 356
Morley, Victor, 43
Morros, Borris, 366
Morse, Theodore, 42
Motzan, Otto, 111
Mozart, Wolfgang Amadeus, 10
Murder at the Vanities, 341

Murphy, C. W., 111
Murphy, Lyle, 392
Music Box Revue, 245
Music Box Theatre, 380
Music in the Air, 324-33, 334, 335, 341, 353, 391
My Lady's Maid, 46
Myrtil, Odette, 320

Nancy Brown, 196
National Institute of Arts and Letters, 401
National Theatre (Washington, D.C.), 284
Naughty Marietta, 62
Neighborhood Book Shop, 303
Neil, Robert, 19-21
Neil and Tompson Cafe, 19
Never Gonna Dance, 358
New Amsterdam Theatre (New York), 55, 128, 131, 150, 155, 207, 210, 211, 262, 279, 310, 340
New Girl, A, 187, 188
New World Symphony, 249
New York College of Music, 25
Newark Yacht Club, 19-21, 303
Newman, Alfred, 273, 361
Newman, Mr. and Mrs. Nathan, 221
Newton, A. Edward, 301
Nicolai, George H., 211
Nicolai-Welch-DeMilt, 211
Night Boat, The, 193-98, 210, 262, 322
Ninety in the Shade, 99-105, 115, 121, 122, 154, 161, 191, 359
Nobody Home, 109-13, 124, 250
Norris, Kathleen, 353
North, Edmund, 354
Norworth, Jack, 66
Notoriety, 15
Novello, Ivor, 129-30, 228

Oberon, 240
Odds and Ends, 94
O'Dea, James, 49
O'Denishawn, Florence, 211

Of Thee I Sing, 322
Off the Earth, 15
Oh, Boy!, 103, 127, 139, 143-49, 151, 154, 155, 164, 165, 178, 186, 187, 211, 249, 250, 268, 278, 348
Oh, I Say!, 89-91, 266, 273, 299
Oh, Joy!, 186, 187
Oh, Lady! Lady!!, 56, 165-69, 170, 174, 184, 188, 250
Oh, My Dear!, 185, 192
Oh! Oh! Delphine, 75
Oklahoma!, 51, 392, 394, 396
Olivari, Carlos, 392
Oliver, Edna May, 145, 287
Olsen, George, 268, 270
O'Neill, Alice V., 248
One Night in the Tropics, 374, 385-87
Opera Ball, The, 68, 99
Orchid, The, 30, 48
O'Shea, Daniel, 354
Our Miss Gibbs, 61
Over Night, 116

Pagano, Ernest, 392
Palace Theatre (London), 33-34, 176, 273, 323, 345
Pan, Hermes, 355, 358, 359
Paramount Pictures, 362
Parsons' Theatre (Hartford, Connecticut), 151
Passing Show, The (London), 94
Passing Show, The (New York), 14
Pember, Clifford, 167
Pennington, Ann, 71, 128
Peter Pan, 261, 262
Pether, R. E., 42
Physioc, Joseph, 177
Piccadilly Theatre (London), 294, 299
Pierce, Austin, 25
Pinero, Arthur Wing, 73, 81
Pink Lady, The, 62, 190, 196
Pins and Needles, 379
Pioneer Days, 47
Playhouse (Wilmington, Del.), 164, 381

Poiret, Paul, 228
Polish Wedding, A, 71-72, 91, 93, 168, 183
Pollak, Walter and/or Elsie, 44, 324, 406
Pom-Pom, 126
Pondal Rios, Sixto, 392
Pons, Lily, 3, 353, 354, 355, 361
Porgy, 344
Porgy and Bess, 366
Porter, Cole, 3, 115, 384, 401, 404
Powell, W. C., 42
Preminger, Otto, 403
Prentice, Charles, 347
Previn, Charles, 385, 386
Prince Ananias, 14
Princess Theatre (New York), 105, 106ff., 188, 191, 192, 204, 209, 231, 244, 246, 247, 248, 257, 270, 291, 332, 352, 359, 378, 379
Puccini, Giacomo, 393
Puppenmaedel, Das, 83
Purcell, Gertrude, 386

Queen of the Movies, The, 94

Radio City Music Hall, 355, 359, 361, 369, 393, 399
Raft, George, 267
Rafter, Frank, 37
Raleigh, Cecil, 15
Randall, Carl, 128, 168
Randall, David, 301
Raphaelson, Samson, 369
Rasch, Albertina, 280, 319, 381, 383
Raset, Val, 392, 399
Rasimi, Madam B., 200
Read, Mary, 273
Reader, Ralph, 344
Reckless, 353
Red Mill, The, 47, 198
Red Petticoat, The, 76-79, 366
Reinheimer, Howard, 354, 356, 357, 391
Reisig, Theodore, 37
Reisman, Leo, 217

Reynolds, Herbert. *See* Rourke, M. E.
Reynolds, James, 257, 264, 273, 277, 278
Reynolds, Tom, 57, 68
Rice, Edward E., 15, 34, 35, 40, 156
Rich Mr. Hoggenheimer, The, 47-48
Ricketts, Tom, 37
Riggs, Lynn, 392
Ring, Blanche, 92
Ripley, Madame, 37
Ripples, 310
Riskin, Edward, 361
Riskin, Robert, 361
Ritz Revue, The, 251
Riviera, 357, 363, 385
Riviera Girl, The, 155, 235
RKO, 354, 356, 358, 367, 369
Rob Roy, 14
Roberta, 298, 338-43, 344, 345, 348, 349, 350-51, 358, 375, 401
Roberti, Lyda, 343
Robeson, Paul, 276, 277, 293, 299, 325, 356, 400
Robin, Leo, 402-3, 404
Robin Hood, 15
Robinson, Clark, 339
Rock-a-bye Baby, 115, 174-80, 181, 186, 212, 252
Rockefeller Center, 371
Rodgers, Richard, 3, 5, 239, 372, 390, 392, 405
Rodzinski, Artur, 388, 389
Rogers, E. W., 92
Rogers, Ginger, 350, 356, 357, 359, 360, 393
Romberg, Sigmund, 3, 361, 364, 379
Rose, Billy, 390
Rose, Edward, 164
Rose Briar, 230
Rosenbach, A. S. W., 301
Rosenfeld, Sidney, 99
Rosenkavalier, Der, 123, 240
Ross, Adrian, 31, 57, 59, 67, 95
Rosy Rapture, the Pride of the Beauty Chorus, 105
Rourke, M. E., 46, 48, 50, 51, 53, 55, 57, 60, 62, 65, 66, 70, 79, 83, 86, 88, 103, 112, 117, 122,

123, 127, 131, 137, 141, 150, 175, 236
Roxy Theatre (New York), 386, 403
Royce, Edward "Teddy," 45, 93, 136, 145, 153, 167, 177, 189, 207, 217, 220, 228, 240, 252
Ruben, José, 319
Rubens, Paul A., 31, 50, 94, 108, 109, 111, 113
Ruby, Harry, 278, 281, 282
Rumbold, Hugh, 42
Runaway Girl, A, 41
Russell, Kennedy, 296
Ryan, Frank, 395

Saddler, Frank, 77, 89, 111, 119, 136, 138, 140, 145, 153, 167, 200, 211
St. Louis Municipal Light Opera Company, 371
St. Mary's Parish Church (Walton-on-Thames), 62
Salinger, Conrad, 392, 403
Sally, 205-11, 212-14, 215, 222, 223, 224, 225, 231, 235, 254, 262, 265, 266, 271, 278, 292, 310, 322
Sally in [of] Our Alley, 205
Sally, Irene and Mary, 230
Sally of the Alley, 207
Salter, H. J., 395
Salzer, Gus, 95, 136, 207, 257, 258, 264, 280, 307
Sanderson, Julia, 51, 55, 67, 80, 95, 157, 184, 199, 353
Santley, Joseph, 188, 235
Saratoga Trunk, 390
Savage, Henry, 57, 126, 134, 135, 142, 150, 164, 171, 173, 174, 180
Savoy, Raymond, 373
Sawyer, Ivy, 188, 235, 281
Say When, 165
Schanzer, Rudolf, 69
School Girl, The, 30
Schubert, Franz, 45
Schumann, Robert, 240, 243
Schwab, Laurence, 372

Schwartz, Arthur, 327, 332, 383, 397, 398
Scola, Kathryn, 387
Scott, Allan, 359, 369
Scott, Temple, 303, 313
Segal, Vivienne, 157-59, 166, 335
Seiter, William A., 392
Seligman, James, 8
Selling, G. C. M., 58
Selwyn, Archie and/or Edgar, 106, 107, 175, 180, 252, 253, 255
Sentimental Library, A, 334
Sessler, Charles, 301, 303, 312, 313
Shattuck, Truly, 28
Shaw, Artie, 378, 391
Shaw, Oscar, 119, 153, 217, 255
Shaw, Steven Kern, 395
She's A Good Fellow, 186-91, 197, 224
Shilkret, Nathaniel, 359
Shipman, Helen, 187, 188
Shop Girl, The, 41
Short, Hassard, 264, 279, 280, 337, 380, 383
Show Boat, 16, 44, 86, 168, 177, 234, 259, 275-77, 278, 282-92 293, 294, 298, 299, 305, 312, 315, 319, 321, 322, 325, 333, 337, 342, 344, 356, 379, 385, 395, 405
Show Boat (Ferber novel), 275-76
Show Boat (Kern's yacht), 304, 305
Shubert Brothers, 43, 44, 46, 51, 58, 59, 63, 65, 67, 68, 73, 74, 79, 88, 106, 110, 132, 133, 142, 230, 377
Shubert Theatre (Detroit), 246
Shubert Theatre (New Haven), 175, 236, 271
Shubert Theatre (New York), 139
Silver Slipper, The, 40
Silvers, Phil, 399, 400
Simmons, B. J., and Co., 296
Simon, Robert, 141, 291
Simple Simon, 310
Sims, George R., 15
Siren, The, 67, 69
Sitting Pretty, 218, 245-51, 252, 309, 310, 342, 348, 355

Skinner, Frank, 386, 395
Slaughter, Walter, 27
Sleap, Frank, 225
Sloane, A. Baldwin, 58
Smetana, Bedrich, 361
Smith, Chris, 98
Smith, Edgar, 28, 41, 63
Smith, Gerrit, 7, 8
Smith, Harry B., 14, 47, 69, 70, 81,
    86-88, 90, 92, 93, 95, 99, 103,
    108, 111, 112, 114, 120, 122,
    132, 144, 185, 191, 300, 313,
    334, 356
Smith, Mrs. Harry B., 86-88, 150
Smith, Queenie, 247, 248, 249
Smith, Robert B., 69, 70
Smith, Sydney, 132
Smith, Winchell, 261
Sobel, Rabbi Ronald, 9f.
Solman, Alfred, 42
Sondheim, Stephen, 402
Song of Russia, 401
Sousa, John Philip, 28
Spencer, Herbert, 403
Spewack, Sam and Bella, 378
Spigelgass, Leonard, 385-87
Spring Chicken, The, 45, 47
Stamper, Dave, 66
State Fair, 402
Steiner, Max, 248, 355
Stepping Stones, 211, 235-40, 255,
    293, 322, 323
Stevens, George, 359
Stevenson, Douglas, 187, 188, 200
Stolen Dreams, 311-12
Stoloff, Maurice, 399
Stone, Dorothy, 235, 237, 238,
    270-73
Stone, Fred, 231, 235, 237, 238,
    270-73, 310
Straus, Oscar, 51, 57
Stravinsky, Igor, 353
Strike Me Pink, 328
Strike the Lyre, 133
Stroud, Gregory, 213
Stuart, Leslie, 55
Styne, Jule, 365
Sullivan, Arthur (Sir), 79. *See also*
    Gilbert and Sullivan

Sunny, 234, 262-67, 270, 273, 278,
    322, 345, 370
Sunshine Girl, The, 86
Sutherland, A. Edward, 386
Swan Hotel (Walton-on-Thames),
    56, 57
Swasey, William A., 106
Sweet Adeline, 249, 305-10, 315,
    322, 323, 325, 333, 350
Swing Time, 357-61
Sydney, Thomas, 132

Talbot, Howard, 31, 67
Tamara, 336-37
Tanner, James T., 94
Tarkington, Booth, 230, 401
Taylor, Charles H., 42, 81
Taylor, Deems, 3, 61
Tell Me More, 235
Templeton, Faye, 34
Teppe, Herman Patrick, 217
Terris, Norma, 283, 285, 293
Thanatopsis Literary and Inside
    Straight Club, 365
Thatcher, Heather, 213, 224, 225,
    232
Theatre Guild, The, 344
Their Wedding Night, 91
Theodore and Co., 103, 129-30
Thomas, Augustus, Jr., 132
Thomson, Virgil, 389, 391
Three Sisters, 249, 344-48, 350
Three Twins, 157, 261
Three's A Crowd, 314
Tiller, John, 264
Time Square Theatre, 253, 256
Titheridge, Dion, 228
Tobin, Genevieve, 72, 255, 257
Tompson, Rosewell Co., 19-22
Tonight's the Night, 113, 120, 121,
    235
Toot-Toot!, 164-65, 171-74, 184
Top Hat, 355
Topsy and Eva, 245
Tours, Frank E., 50, 63, 68, 140,
    177, 369
Towne, Gene, 369
Townsend, Leo, 395

Tree, Dolly, 223
Tremont Theatre (Boston), 181
Troxler, Gus, 20, 21
Truex, Ernest, 117
Truman, President Harry, 4
Twain, Mark, 391
20th Century Fox, 401, 402, 403
Twentieth Century Girl, The, 15
Tyler, George, 192
Tynan, Nicholas J., 20, 21

Uncle Tom's Cabin (Kern musical),
    19-23, 24, 304
Uncle Tom's Cabin (Stowe's novel
    and its dramatization), 19
Universal Pictures, 356, 357, 362,
    385, 387, 395
Urban, Joseph, 128, 156, 182, 207,
    277, 287, 288, 331

Valli, Valli, 71, 271
Van, Billy, 134
Van and Schenck, 211
Van Curler Opera House (Sche-
    nectady, N.Y.), 117, 143
Van Druten, John, 171, 389-90
Van Upp, Virginia, 399
Vanity Fair, 252-54
Venus, 1916, 45
Very Good Eddie, 103, 116-24, 127,
    130, 137, 176, 184, 187, 229,
    250, 308
Very Warm for May, 379-84
Vidor, Charles, 399
Voegtlin, Arthur, 63
von Doenhoff, Albert, 25
von Suppé, Franz, 309, 367

Wagner, J. H., 35-36, 38
Wagner, Richard, 240, 243, 353
Walker, Harry Leslie, 162
Wallis, Bertram, 297
Walton-on-Thames, Eng., 56-57, 62
Waltz Dream, A, 51
Warner Bros., 312, 313, 350
Warren, Harry, 364, 383, 404-5

Warshawsky, Curtis B. and Samuel J.,
    395
Wayburn, Ned, 156, 195, 200
Webb, Clifton, 263, 352
Weber, Carl Maria von, 240
Weber, Joe, 27, 28, 40
Weinberger, Jaromir, 360
Wells, Gabriel, 303
Werrenrath, Reinald, 326, 329
West, Clarence, 77
West, Paul, 46, 48, 49, 50, 60, 74,
    79, 260
When Claudia Smiles, 92
When Dreams Come True, 94
When You're In Love, 361-62
White, Al, Jr., 373
White Chrysanthemum, The, 48
Whiteman, Paul, 278, 281
Whiting, Jack, 311
Williams, Hattie, 45, 54, 69, 81
Wilson, William J., 63
Wimperis, Arthur, 97, 115
Winninger, Charles, 327
Winsome Widow, A, 69, 157
Winter Garden Theatre (London),
    212, 213, 214, 220, 224, 225,
    232, 234, 235
Winter Garden Theatre (New York),
    63, 230
Wise, Rabbi Stephen, 198
Witmark, Isidore, 27
Wittels, David G., 355
Wizard of Oz, The, 371
Wizard of the Nile, The, 16
Wodehouse, P. G., 44, 120, 121,
    126, 127, 131, 132, 135, 136,
    137, 144, 145, 146, 147, 148,
    151, 152, 155, 165, 167, 168,
    169, 170, 191, 203, 204, 206,
    207, 212, 220, 231, 234, 245,
    248, 250, 257, 287, 293
Wolff and Co., 17, 19, 23-24, 52, 53
Woman Haters, The, 73
Woodring, Harry H., 373
Woods, Al, 73
Woodward, Matthew, 67
Woolf, Benjamin Edward, 150-51
Woolf, Edgar Allan, 150, 164, 173,
    174, 175

Woollcott, Alexander, 273, 275, 335, 341, 353
Worcester Theatre (Worcester, Mass.), 192
Wordsworth, Bishop Christopher, 146
Work, Henry Clay, 190
Worster, Howett, 299
Worth, Cedric, 361
Wynn, Ed, 310

You Were Never Lovelier, 392-94
You'll Never Get Rich, 392
Youmans, Vincent, 218, 378
Young, Felix, 369
Young, Rida Johnson, 75, 77, 78

Zahn, Mabel, 303

Ziegfeld, Florenz, Jr., 61, 67, 69, 73, 128, 156, 160, 161, 187, 191, 201, 202-8, 211, 213, 214, 230, 260, 262, 268, 276, 277, 282, 283, 284, 285, 288, 289, 292, 304, 310, 313, 315, 318, 322, 325-26
Ziegfeld Follies of 1911, 67
Ziegfeld Follies of 1916, 123, 128-29, 137
Ziegfeld Follies of 1917, 150, 260
Ziegfeld Follies of 1919, 202-3
Ziegfeld Follies of 1921, 211
Ziegfeld Theatre (New York), 283, 286
Ziehrer, Carl, 68
Zip Goes a Million, 192-93, 207, 210, 261

1980